The Early Stained Glass of
Canterbury Cathedral

The Early Stained Glass of Canterbury Cathedral

CIRCA 1175–1220

Madeline Harrison
Caviness

Princeton University
Press

Copyright © 1977 by Princeton University Press

Published by Princeton University Press,
Princeton, New Jersey
IN THE UNITED KINGDOM: *Princeton University Press,*
Guildford, Surrey

All Rights Reserved

Publication of this book has been aided by
The Andrew W. Mellon Foundation

This book has been composed in Linotype Granjon

Printed in the United States of America
by Princeton University Press,
Princeton, New Jersey

Library of Congress Cataloging in Publication Data

Caviness, Madeline Harrison, 1938–
    The early stained glass of Canterbury Cathedral
circa 1175-1220.

    Bibliography: p.
    Includes index.
    1. Glass painting and staining, Romanesque—
England—Canterbury.   2. Glass painting and
staining, Gothic—England—Canterbury.
3. Glass painting and staining—England—Canterbury.   4. Canterbury Cathedral.   I. Title.
NK5344.C3C38   748.5′922′34   77-10419
ISBN 0-691-03927-5

TO THE MEMORY
OF MY MOTHER
Gwendoline Fownes Harrison

Contents

LIST OF PLATES

LIST OF TEXT FIGURES

LIST OF APPENDIX FIGURES

Acknowledgments

THE research and writing for this book were done with the help of grants from the Mellon Centre for Studies in British Art, London (formerly Mellon Foundation for British Art), Radcliffe College, the British Academy, and the Radcliffe Institute, where I was a Fellow from 1970 to 1972. The Fine Arts Department of Harvard University gave initial help with photographic expenses, and the Victoria and Albert Museum generously supplied color film for photographing the Canterbury glass.

My personal thanks are due to many people who gave their advice or technical assistance, and especially to those colleagues who discussed ideas with me; specific acknowledgments are made in the notes, but I take full responsibility for the ideas presented. I am indebted to: Mr. Michael Archer of the Victoria and Albert Museum; Dr. Larry Ayres of the University of California at Santa Barbara; Ms. Clara Bargellini Camara; Professor Jean Bony of the University of California at Berkeley; Dr. Robert Brill of the Corning Museum of Glass; Ms. Jonnie Cleveland M.F.A., who did the drawings for the text figures and appendix figures 1–5; Mr. Frederick Cole, F.M.G.P., glass restorer of Canterbury Cathedral; Professor Giles Constable of Harvard University; the Dean and Chapter of Canterbury Cathedral, especially the late Canon Herbert Waddams, and the Cathedral staff, who have moved, or tolerated, stepladders all over their building; Dr. Debby Dluhy of Boston College; Professor C. R. Dodwell of Manchester University; Mr. B. C. Doughty, Surveyor of Canterbury Cathedral, who generously supplied appendix figures 8–20; Mr. David DuBon of the Philadelphia Museum of Art; Mr. Colin Dudley of Christ Church College, Canterbury; Mr. George Easton, retired glazier to the Cathedral, who climbed the roofs and scaffolds with me when he was approaching the age of eighty; Mr. W. L. Entwistle, photographer of Canterbury; Dr. Peter Fergusson of Wellesley College; the Friends of Canterbury Cathedral; Professor Emerita Terci Frisch of Wellesley College; Dr. Dorothy Glass of the State University of New York at Buffalo; Dr. Rosalie Green of the Princeton Index of Christian Art; Dr. Jane Hayward of the Cloisters; the late Mr. John Hunt; Dr. Dorothy Gillerman of Brown University; Professor Louis Grodecki of the Sorbonne, who read the text and generously debated many points with me; Professor Peter Kidson of the Courtauld Institute of Art; Professor Ernst Kitzinger of Harvard University; Mr. Dennis King, F.M.G.P., glazier of Norwich; the Rev. Brother Lawrence (Christopher Christianson) of the Society of St. Francis; Dr. Meredith Lillich of Syracuse University; Dr. Janet Martin of Princeton University; Dr. Peter Newton of York University; Dr. Walter Oakeshott of Lincoln College, Oxford; Ms. Anne Oakley of the Chapter Library, Canterbury; Madame Françoise Perrot; Monsieur Léon Pressouyre; Dr. Virginia Raguin of Holy Cross College; Mr. Kunihide Sakai of Hitotsubashi University, who placed a copy of the *Miraculi Sancti Thomae* at my disposal while I was in Japan; Professor Willibald Sauerländer of Munich University; Professor Meyer Schapiro of Columbia University; Dr. Linda Seidel of Harvard University; Dr. Kenneth Severens of Oberlin College; Mr. F. W. Smith, Borough Librarian of Dewsbury; Dr. Mary Evelyn Stringer of Mississippi State College for Women at Columbus; Dr. Hanns Swarzenski of the Boston Museum of Fine Arts, who has generously shared his knowledge and love of English art; Dr. William Urry of St. Edmund Hall, Oxford; Mademoiselle J. Vinsot of Monuments Historiques, Paris; the late Professor Francis Wormald, whose encouragement steered me into art historical studies; and Professor George Zarnecki of the Courtauld Institute of Art.

In addition, I am grateful to the following institutions for answering queries or supplying photographs, or for allowing me to examine materials in their collections: Archaeologisch Instituut der Rijks-Universiteit, Utrecht; Bayerisches Nationalmuseum, Munich; Bibliothèque Municipale, Metz; Bibliothèque Nationale, Paris; Bibliothèque Royale, Brussels; Bodleian Library, Oxford; British Library, London; Burgerbibliothek, Bern; Conway Library of the Courtauld Institute, London; Corpus Christi College, Cambridge; Detroit Institute of Arts; Dumbarton Oaks Library, Washington, D.C.; Lambeth Palace Library, London; Pierpont Morgan Library, New York; Museo Arqueológico Nacional, Madrid; the Queen's Chapel of the Savoy, London; Trinity College, Cambridge; University Library, Cambridge; Virginia Museum of Fine Arts, Richmond; and the Warburg Institute, London.

Another debt I owe to my fellow women, both those who formed a scholarly community at the Radcliffe Institute, and those who took over my roles of housekeeper and mother at various times; my mother especially carried much of this burden, and was a constant source of encouragement and support. Ms. Judy Solar helped to revise parts of the text, and Ms. Louise Seidel has patiently typed and retyped the manuscript. The greatest single debt, however, is to my husband, who has spent his vacations photographing and measuring glass with me, and who has never waivered in his determination that I should continue my art historical studies.

Note on the Illustrations

PHOTOGRAPHIC CREDITS are acknowledged in the list of illustrations. I am also grateful for permission from the owners of the works of art. All photographs of Canterbury Cathedral are reproduced by kind permission of the Dean and Chapter. Others are reproduced by courtesy of the following: the Archbishop of Canterbury and the Trustees of Lambeth Palace Library, London; the Bayerisches Nationalmuseum, Munich; the Bibliothèque Nationale, Paris; the Bibliothèque Royale Albert Ier, Brussels; the Bodleian Library, Oxford; the British Library Board, London; the Burgerbibliothek, Bern; the Dean and Chapter of Winchester

Cathedral; the Fogg Art Museum, Cambridge, Mass.; the Master and Fellows of Corpus Christi College, Cambridge; the Master and Fellows of St. John's College, Cambridge; the Master and Fellows of Trinity College, Cambridge; the Musée Condé, Chantilly; the Pierpont Morgan Library, New York; the Syndics of the Cambridge University ·Library; the Victoria and Albert Museum, London; the Virginia Museum of Fine Arts, Richmond.

The Early Stained Glass of
Canterbury Cathedral

Introduction

Canterbury, *"that rock on which the main current of English art struck and parted asunder only to meet again on the other side."*

Francis Bond[1]

It would be hard to overestimate the importance of the early stained glass of Christ Church, Canterbury, in the history of English painting styles. Close contacts with the continent during the entire period of the rebuilding and decoration of the cathedral church resulted in a very early assimilation of the Gothic style, or even participation in its development, in painting as in architecture.[2] In spite of a somewhat unsatisfactory knowledge of the Canterbury windows and recent skepticism about their authenticity, they have inevitably been cited in many of the art historical studies that span this period.[3] In most cases the dates proposed by Rackham for the windows in his monograph of 1949 have subsequently been accepted, and they have been used to date other works.[4] And yet we are still without sufficient proof of the dates of the Canterbury glass, and it is not surprising that wide differences of opinion are possible.[5] Nonetheless,

NOTE on citations: Any work that is cited only once is cited in full in the footnotes, and not listed in the bibliography. Works cited more than once are listed in the bibliography, and cited by author and date in the notes.

[1] Francis Bond, *English Cathedrals*, London, 1912, p. 29.

[2] For the architecture see Jean Bony, 1949; "Origines des piles gothiques anglaises à fûts en délit," *Gedenkschrift Ernst Gall*, ed. Margarete Kuhn & Louis Grodecki, Munich, 1965, pp. 95–99 and 115; Bony, 1957–1958, p. 48.

[3] For example, Emile Mâle in André Michel, *Histoire générale de l'art* II Part 1, Paris, 1907, p. 375; Saunders, 1932, pp. 100–102, 236–38; Walter Oakeshott, *The Sequence of English Medieval Art*, London, 1950, p. 47; Beer, 1952, p. 49; Boase, 1953, pp. 291–93; Rickert, 1965, pp. 109–10, 113; Brieger, 1957, pp. 94–95; and van der Boom, 1960, pp. 118–21.

[4] Rackham, 1949, pp. 15–17. The date of ca. 1220 given by Professor Grodecki to the ambulatory windows of Sens Cathedral probably reflects the same date given to the Trinity Chapel windows of Canterbury (Grodecki in *Vitrail*, p. 139 and fig. 101).

[5] For a lengthy dispute over the dating of Adam and related choir clerestory figures, see: Heaton, 1907, pp. 172–76; Rackham, 1928; Evetts, 1941, p. 98; Herbert Read, review of Rackham, 1949, in *Burlington Magazine* 92

great advances have been made since Gostling compared the glass to the Bayeux tapestry,[6] or Westlake proposed an earlier date for the Trinity Chapel and corona glass than for the clerestory figures of the choir.[7]

Little is known of the early history of the windows of Christ Church. Unlike the famous windows of St.-Denis Abbey Church, which were discussed in some detail by Abbot Suger at the time of their creation,[8] those at Canterbury, Chartres, Bourges, Laon—indeed almost all of the early Gothic monuments—passed uncommented by their contemporaries. No doubt this was in part because these brilliant walls of glass were not as novel to an audience already familiar with large colored windows; the glazing of the earlier Canterbury choir, built by Lanfranc and Conrad in the early part of the twelfth century and destroyed in the fire of 1174, had been the subject of high praise by William of Malmesbury, but the new glazing in the reconstructed east end was neglected by Gervase, whose enthusiasm was captured by the latest Gothic style of architecture and sculpture.[9] In the course of this study it will emerge, however, that the glazing was carried out with considerable tenacity, and must have been a passionate concern of its patrons, the Benedictine monks of Christ Church, of whom Gervase was one. The sheer quantity of glass was tremendous: three tiers of windows throughout the choir and eastern transepts, two tiers in the Trinity Chapel, and one in the corona, a total of 104 arched or lancet windows and two oculi (plan). This was, of course, far exceeded at Chartres in the rebuilding following the

fire of 1194, when 173 windows were glazed in the first four decades of the thirteenth century; but the Canterbury glazing program must have been one of the most ambitious to have been attempted at the time of its inception, about 1175–1180. In its organization as much as in its extent, the Canterbury glazing was remarkable. The encyclopedic program is comparable to the mosaic decoration of Monreale Cathedral, or to the illustrations of the great twelfth-century Bibles.

There is little to suggest now that the glass was repaired during the Middle Ages, but from a fourteenth-century record of the subjects in twelve typological biblical windows, it seems possible that the order of some of these had been interfered with, since extraneous subjects are interpolated.[10] The subject matter may not have been very well understood at this time; the roll was evidently placed in the choir as a guide to the windows, which proves the difficulty experienced in reading inscriptions then two hundred years old. In view of this difficulty of access to the art of an earlier time, it is not surprising that in later years the glass was sacrificed to other needs. In the fifteenth century the lower third of each of two windows of the Trinity Chapel was blocked by the chapel of Edward the Confessor, and the first of the twelve windows with biblical subjects, obscured by the fifteenth-century Lady Chapel, was filled by 1657; no glass has survived from either of these locations.[11]

The sixteenth-century antiquarians whose accounts of windows often provide valuable records of lost glass were seldom interested in religious

(1950), 55 (cf. Grodecki, pp. 294–97, and Rackham, p. 357 of the same volume); Grodecki and Rackham, *Burlington Magazine* 93 (1951), 94–95; van der Boom, 1960, p. 120.

[6] Gostling, 1774, p. 215; a judgment repeated by [John Burnby], *An Historical Description of the Metropolitical Church of Christ, Canterbury*, 2nd ed., Canterbury, 1783, p. 37, and many other local writers.

[7] Westlake, I, 1881, 70.

[8] Sugerus, *Liber de Rebus in Administratione sua Gestis, cap.* XXXIV, see *Abbot Suger, on the Abbey Church of St.-Denis and Its Treasures*, ed. E. Panofsky, Princeton, 1946, pp. 72–77 and 192–201.

[9] William of Malmesbury, 1870, p. 234; Gervase, *Tractatus*, ed. Stubbs, I, 1879, pp. 19–29. The aesthetic attitudes

of Gervase have been discussed by: Carl Schnaase, *Geschichte der bildenden Kunst im Mittelalter* III, 2nd ed., Düsseldorf, 1872, 179–85; Paul Frankl, *The Gothic: Literary Sources and Interpretations through Eight Centuries*, Princeton, 1960, pp. 24–35; Walter Oakeshott, *Classical Inspiration in Medieval Art*, London, 1959, pp. 81–82.

[10] Canterbury, Cathedral Library, MS C246, ed. James, 1901; for these confusions, *ibid.*, p. 3.

[11] Eveleigh C. Woodruff and William Danks, *Memorials of the Cathedral and Priory of Christ in Canterbury*, London, 1912, p. 420, stated that the choir aisle window was filled in 1663, but the painting by Johnson shows it already blocked in 1657 (see n. 13 below).

subjects or inscriptions of early date; the notes in British Library, Harleian MS 1366, made in Canterbury in 1599, are those of a student of heraldry who passed over the early glass, recording only coats of arms and monuments. The first evidence of a revival of interest in the earlier glass is in William Somner's *Antiquities of Canterbury* of 1640, in which he praised, but unfortunately only briefly described, the windows of the eastern part of the cathedral.[12] Two years later much of the glass was broken by the Parliamentarians, and the details of their triumphs, printed in *Cathedrall Newes from Canterbury*, are in some cases the only record we possess of the contents of the windows.[13] Repairs carried out after 1660 probably only added to the disorder of the glass.[14] In the eighteenth century the first systematic antiquarian description was printed, that of Gostling in 1744.[15] At the end of the century, however, the glass was once more moved about; in 1799 the remaining clerestory figures were rearranged in two fifteenth-century windows in the southwest transept and the west end of the nave, their present location.[16] These changes were noted in the second edition of Hasted's survey of Kent in 1800, and this author also referred to the fragmentary panels still surviving in the north choir aisle "triforium" windows, the first time they had found a place in the descriptions.[17]

During the hundred years between Hasted's first edition and 1897, when Williams anonymously published the first monograph on the Canterbury windows, a great amount of research had con-

tributed to an understanding of them. Gervase's chronicle of the rebuilding in 1175–1184 had been edited,[18] as had the twelfth-century texts which recorded the miracles at the tomb of Becket, and which are the basis for the scenes in the Trinity Chapel glass.[19] The fourteenth-century record of the choir window inscriptions had already been printed by Somner in 1640, but it had now been made available in a more recent book by Winston.[20]

On a less esoteric level were numerous scrutinies of the glass itself; with a revival of interest in Gothic architecture came a better understanding of the monumental arts associated with it. If the decay of the stonework at Canterbury was partially responsible for the loss of glass, the repair of the stonework was the occasion of the first major restoration of the glass. In 1819 George Austin Sr. began work on the cathedral restoration; the most urgent task was the reconstruction of the oculus in the southeast transept, which was caving in. Work was extended from there to include most of the fabric, including some restoration to the glass.[21] The revival of a Gothic aesthetic occasioned detailed studies of the existing medieval glass, and from this period come five important series of drawings and tracings of the Canterbury glass.[22] In the absence of photographs, these served for study purposes and as illustrations to Williams's book and others.[23] With a similar activity continuing elsewhere, it became possible for the first time to make comparisons with continental glass, and to attempt to see the Canterbury productions as a part

[12] Somner, 1640, pp. 174–75, 385–96.

[13] Culmer, ca. 1643. A painting by Thomas Johnson, dated 1657 and showing the destruction in progress in the choir, has been published by Derek Ingram Hill, "The Iconoclasts in Canterbury Cathedral," *C.C.C.* 1974, pp. 20–22, illus. facing p. 17.

[14] Evelyn, III, 1955, 395.

[15] Gostling, 1774, pp. 214–18. Subsequent editions were more complete and accurate, as the 2nd, 1777, pp. 311–27.

[16] Williams, 1897, p. 3. That extensive work was done on the windows in the period 1780–1800 has been confirmed by Anne Oakley, who was kind enough to search the accounts.

[17] Hasted, XI, 1800, 377–82.

[18] Gervase, ed. Stubbs, 1879 and English translation by Willis, 1845.

[19] Robertson ed., I, 1875, and II, 1876 (see also William of Canterbury and Benedict of Peterborough).

[20] Somner, 1640, pp. 385–96; Winston, I, 1847, 353–64.

[21] Austin's obituary, 1849, pp. 659–60.

[22] Victoria and Albert Museum, London, Department of Prints: Joyce, 1841; O. Hudson, watercolor drawings made from tracings, dated 1848; Clayton and Bell, 1895. Tracings made by the Canterbury glazier, Samuel Caldwell, Sr., are in the Williams Coll., and a few by his predecessor, George Austin, Jr., are in the cathedral library.

[23] Williams, 1897, used Caldwell's tracings; Gilbert, 1842, Pls. I and II used Joyce's drawings, as did Loftie, 1876, facing pp. 1, 8, 10. Lewis Day, *Windows: A Book about Stained and Painted Glass*, London, 1909, used Hudson's drawings for figs. 250 and 292.

of broader developments. Based on working drawings by designers who had a very acute perception of ornamental features, these studies, however, tended to present a much more satisfactory analysis of ornament than of figural style. Within a few years of each other were published the volumes that are still the only basic reference works for this aspect of stained glass, the volumes on Bourges and related glass by Cahier and Martin, and the works by Winston and Westlake for English glass.[24]

The preoccupations of the present century have been more varied. The continuing antiquarian tradition gave rise to several more catalogues, but these paid more attention than before to subject matter and textual sources, and to a problem that had grown unheeded out of the nineteenth-century restorations, that of the authenticity of the glass. Williams had used the texts of the miracles of Becket for identification of the Trinity Chapel scenes. Another important study of textual sources was made by James, who re-edited the fourteenth-century record of the choir subjects, and proved that the inscriptions in these windows were partially shared with Peterborough Abbey.[25] In his catalogue of 1925, Mason was able to use both of these textual studies, and made some new identifications in the Trinity Chapel.[26] He also indicated the problem of restoration in the glass. A series of popular, but succinct and accurate, handbooks to the glass has been printed since; the most recent, by Ingram Hill, appeared in the 1960s.[27]

In the same catalogue tradition is the fuller publication by Rackham. Conceived ten years before the inception of the European *Corpus Vitrearum Medii Aevi*, this book was intended as a complete illustrated account of the glass.[28] It is not a true catalogue, however, since certain types of information (such as measurements of panels and discussion of restoration) are not systematically included. Concessions were made to the general reader, and also to a broader framework of study than that of a mere catalogue. Almost for the first time a chronology of glazing was argued from style, and the questions of French influence and the "Authorship and Production of the Canterbury Windows" were reviewed, but dating was still based entirely on archaeological evidence.

Rackham's book can be seen as the summation of nineteenth-century achievements; the only major area to which he attached little importance, although it had been broached by his predecessors, was ornament. In this century, ironically, when great advances have been made in the study of manuscripts by close attention to decoration,[29] the topic has been sadly neglected in stained glass. When the Canterbury glass was photographed about 1926 by Noel Heaton for the Victoria and Albert Museum, almost no ornament was included. A full consideration of ornament may be indicated as one of the great lacunae in Canterbury studies.

A second lacuna has impeded study. This is the lack of records of the extensive restorations to which the glass has been subjected. The replacements occasionally noticed by Williams, Mason, and Rackham are but a few of the total number, although the work of restoration was going on as they prepared their texts. This problem was very aptly outlined by Oakeshott in his review of Rackham's book.[30] It is not, of course, one that is specific to Canterbury, although the work of one restorer there has tended to accentuate it.[31] Most unfortunately, Caldwell, Jr. was able to convince

[24] Cahier and Martin, 1841; Winston, 1847; Westlake, 1881–1894.

[25] James, 1901.

[26] Mason, 1925, pp. 29–43.

[27] J.M.C. Crum, *Cathedral Church of Christ, Canterbury—Notes on the Old Glass*, Plymouth, 1930. Derek Ingram Hill, *The Stained Glass of Canterbury Cathedral*, Canterbury [1962].

[28] Rackham, 1949.

[29] For instance, Ellen J. Beer, *Beiträge zur oberrheinischen Buchmalerei in der ersten Hälfte des 14. Jahr-*

hunderts unter besonderer Berücksichtigung der Initialornamentik, Basel, 1959; and L.M.J. Delaissé's pioneer work on Flemish manuscripts, *La Miniature flamande, le mécénat de Philippe le Bon* (Catalogue of the exhibition in Brussels, Amsterdam, and Paris), 1959, pp. 15ff.

[30] Oakeshott, 1951, pp. 86–89.

[31] Hans Wentzel, "Die Farbenfenster des 13. Jahrhunderts in der Stiftskirche zu Bücken an der Weser," *Niederdeutsche Beiträge zur Kunstgeschichte* 1 (1961), 62–66, fig. 55. One of the aims of the *Corpus Vitrearum Medii Aevi* is to provide detailed records of restoration.

Rackham of the authenticity of quantities of glass that had no place in the original glazing of the cathedral.[32] Rackham was later able to indicate only in the most circumspect manner that these panels were not worthy of serious attention.[33] It has remained until now for anyone to attempt a systematic evaluation of the glass, although Rackham and Caldwell, Jr. drew up a list of restorations in 1951, working from photographs.[34] A more complete examination carried out in the summers of 1967 and 1971 allows us far more certain stylistic judgments than were possible to Rackham.

In the twenty years since Rackham's book appeared, a large corpus of literature on related topics has been produced. It is time this was assimilated into Canterbury glass studies, in much the same way as Williams drew on the nineteenth-century edition of the miracles of Becket and Westlake's comparative studies of the glass. Historians have investigated the financial records of the monastery[35] and the records of tradesmen renting land in the town.[36] Dodwell has taken up the survey made by James of the library holdings, and ex-

tended it into a thorough study of the productions of the Canterbury scriptoria up to 1200.[37] Detailed studies of other works of art have also opened up further possibilities of comparison. Oakeshott's work on the *Artists of the Winchester Bible*, which contains a succinct characterization of the several different hands that he surmised worked on that manuscript in the years following 1160 or so, has been followed by another study by Larry Ayres.[38] Florens Deuchler has published a detailed study of the Ingeborg Psalter.[39] Willibald Sauerländer has made outstanding contributions to our knowledge of early Gothic sculpture in northern France.[40] The "Year 1200" exhibition and symposium at the Metropolitan Museum of Art, New York, in 1970 drew attention to the art of this period.[41] There have been several important studies of continental glass with affinities to Canterbury, such as Deuchler's doctoral dissertation on the east windows of Laon Cathedral,[42] Beer's monograph on the rose windows of Lausanne,[43] and the *Corpus* of Notre-Dame, Paris.[44] The chronology of the glazing of Chartres Cathedral is still controversial,[45] but Gro-

[32] The "Miscellaneous Early Glass" described by Rackham, 1949, pp. 112–14, fig. 21, included four Evangelist symbols and several prophets from Petham, as proved by C. R. Councer, "The Ancient Glass from Petham Church now in Canterbury Cathedral," *Archaeologia Cantiana* 65 (1952), 167–70. Other panels are either modern or made up of scraps: the Virgin and Child "restored to" the east window of the Crypt in 1939, Rackham, 1949, pp. 65–67, Pl. VII; nine medallions placed by Samuel Caldwell, Jr. in the south choir aisle triforium windows in 1920 (said by Mr. Easton to be of recent facture), Rackham, 1949, pp. 50–51, 72–73, figs. 22, 23, 24, 26, 27a; two roundels in Window s:V of the Trinity Chapel, Rackham, 1949, p. 103; much of the glass in Window n:VII, Rackham, 1949, pp. 83–85.

[33] Rackham, 1957, pp. 36, 38, 45, 48, 63, 69. However, in all cases Rackham continued to overestimate the amount of thirteenth-century glass reused by Caldwell.

[34] Bernard Rackham and Samuel Caldwell, Jr., typescript, Department of Ceramics, Victoria and Albert Museum, cf. Caviness, 1967.

[35] Most recently, Barnes and Powell, eds., 1960. Earlier studies were largely untapped by Rackham: C. E. Woodruff, 1932, pp. 13–32, and 1936, pp. 38–80; Smith, 1940, pp. 353–69, and 1943.

[36] Urry, 1967. Unfortunately rentals have survived only for lands held by Christ Church.

[37] James, 1903; cf. Dodwell, 1954.

[38] Oakeshott, 1945; cf. Ayres, 1970.

[39] Deuchler, 1967.

[40] Willibald Sauerländer, "Die Marienkrönungsportale von Senlis und Mantes," *Wallraf-Richartz Jahrbuch* 20 (1958), 115–62; "Die kunstgeschichtliche Stellung der Westportale von Notre-Dame in Paris," *Marburger Jahrbuch für Kunstwissenschaft* 17 (1959), 1–56; "Sens and York: An Inquiry into the Sculpture from St. Mary's Abbey in the Yorkshire Museum," *Journal of the British Archaeological Association*, 3rd ser. 20 (1959), 53–69; and 1966, 1970.

[41] *The Year 1200* I and III.

[42] Florens Deuchler, "Die Chorfenster der Kathedrale in Laon, ein iconographischer und stilgeschichtlicher Beitrag zur Kenntnis nordfranzösischer Glasmalereien des 13. Jahrhunderts," Ph.D. dissertation, Bonn, 1956. Many of the conclusions from this study were published by Deuchler, 1967.

[43] Beer, 1952.

[44] *Corpus, France* I.

[45] Delaporte and Houvet, I, 1926: these dates have generally been accepted, as by Grodecki in *Vitrail*, p. 124; cf. Frankl, 1963, p. 321, and Grodecki, "Chronique: Vitrail," *Bulletin Monumental* 121 (1964), pp. 99–103, and Jan van der Meulen, "Histoire de la construction de la cathédrale Notre-Dame de Chartres après 1194," *Bulletin de la Société Archéologique d'Eure-et-Loir* 23 (1965), 81–126.

decki has been able to isolate one significant master from among the many painters and localize his development in northeast France.[46] Also fundamental for method was the same author's article in which he traced atelier connections from Poitiers to Bourges and Chartres, demonstrating the ability of traveling artisans to cut across local stylistic groupings.[47] At the same time, Grodecki has been conscious of the close ties that might have existed between glass painters and artists in other media, a topic to which Wentzel has also given attention.[48]

The framework within which one now views the Canterbury windows has thus been immeasurably extended. The aims of the present study are both broader and more detailed than could have been outlined in 1949. It is now desirable, as suggested by Oakeshott,[49] to recognize differences of style within a single group of windows, indicating the presence of different artistic personalities. Only after such a detailed analysis as this can the processes of change in style become apparent.

The period 1175–1220 embraces a phase of English art history which is still insufficiently understood.[50] Little is known of centers of manuscript production after the disintegration of the great monastic scriptoria, so in that field, with the possible exception of Oakeshott's and Ayre's studies of the Winchester Bible, no one has yet attempted to study closely a group of artists working in the same location in England during this period of experimentation and stylistic change.[51] A great number of important manuscripts are without a secured provenance.[52] Recent scholarship has localized two books, long thought to be French or English, in the north of France, but the concept

of a Channel School still has some usefulness.[53] The surviving Canterbury windows and the Winchester Bible are, however, unique monuments from the period, affording the possibility of a study of transitional styles not to be found elsewhere.

THIS book has grown out of my doctoral dissertation on the Gothic Trinity Chapel windows.[54] In the past seven years some of my views have been modified by new observation, others seem to be confirmed. The only glass which has not by now been thoroughly examined for restorations is in the north oculus, but for this good nineteenth-century tracings survive.[55] It is now possible to select only the best-preserved panels for illustration, and to discuss both the iconography and the style with a full knowledge of the extent to which they have been tampered with.

The form of this book has been modified by the projected publication of the *Corpus Vitrearum* for Canterbury. In order to facilitate cross-referencing between the two works, I refer to the windows by the numbers given under the *Corpus* system; for those wishing to refer back to Rackham, a concordance with his window numbers is given in the Appendix. The *Corpus* will contain all catalogue information, such as measurements, complete restoration charts, and discussion of condition; new photographs are being taken to reproduce the existing state of the glass. In the present study I have preferred to use the 1926 photographs, when available, partly because the glass was then clean and in better condition than now (its rapid deterioration, noticed from the scaffolds during my examinations, has been cause for some alarm, and con-

---

[46] Grodecki, 1965, pp. 171–94.

[47] Grodecki, 1948, pp. 87–110.

[48] Grodecki, 1955, p. 615; and *Sainte-Chapelle*, Paris, 1961, p. 100; Hans Wentzel, "Glasmaler und maler im Mittelalter," *Zeitschrift für Kunstwissenschaft* 3 (1949), 53–62.

[49] Oakeshott, 1951, p. 88.

[50] For a broad survey, Homburger, 1958.

[51] Cf. Swarzenski, 1943, on Weingarten.

[52] For example, the Munich Psalter (Munich, Staatsbibliothek, MS Clm 835); Cambridge, Trinity College, MS

B.11.4; London, British Library, Arundel MS 157 and Royal MS I.D.X; Imola, Bibliotheca Communale, MS 100, and British Library, Harl. MS 5102. See Rickert, 1965, pp. 98–100.

[53] The Manerius Bible (Paris, Bibliothèque Sainte-Geneviève, MSS 8–10), and the Ingeborg Psalter (Chantilly, Musée Condé, MS 1695); see Rickert, 1965, p. 90 n. 1, and p. 94.

[54] Caviness, 1970.

[55] Among Caldwell's drawings in the cathedral library; they appear to be Austin's tracings.

servation is imperative).[56] Many of the judgments and reconstructions given in this book depend on the materials that will be fully published in the *Corpus*; the aim of the present study is to introduce a greater amount of personal interpretation, and especially a greater amount of comparative material than is admissible in the *Corpus* format. I have thought it reasonable to combine in a montage panels that once belonged together (fig. 127), or even to mount the original head on its body (figs. 215, 217). If the Fogg medallion had been loaned to the Metropolitan Museum in 1970, it might there have been matched with the ornament from the Victoria and Albert Museum; but the glass being too fragile to travel, tracings had to be used to confirm the fit of both panels in the Trinity Chapel, Window n:VI; the result is figures 115 and 116. It is only by matching the "right" ornament to the scattered figure panels that one can apprehend the distinctive qualities of different designers and painters. It has taken me ten years to grasp the physical complexities of the Canterbury glass, its development in space as it was originally planned, and, by contrast, the present confusion. As I walk through the cathedral church now I see a vision of its windows, if not as they appeared to Henry III in 1220, at least as they appeared to Gostling in 1774. It is this vision I hope to convey to my readers.

Style is given the lengthiest consideration in this book, perhaps partly because of a modern bias towards this aspect of art history, but also because it has been only slightly treated by other authors. I have to acknowledge a post-Renaissance need to deal with styles as manifestations of individual beings; whether all the masters recognized here will stand the test of time, and whether other lesser per-

sonalities will have to be acknowledged, are perhaps of less importance than the recognition of the outstanding qualities of a glass painter such as the Methuselah Master. With his early style as the basis of the Canterbury glazing, it becomes possible to trace the evolution of succesive generations, and to weigh the extent of external influences.

It would be surprising if one could write on Canterbury without most of one's ideas being anticipated in some form by previous authors. One of the outstanding of these is Clement Heaton, who in 1907 claimed a place for the Canterbury glass between that of St.-Denis and the windows of Chartres and Sens. In 1939 Arnold referred almost casually to the impact of the Interdict of 1207-1213 on the Trinity Chapel glazing, an idea which was more laboriously worked out by Sulkis in an unpublished master's thesis,[57] and independently by myself a few years later.[58] Certain ideas seem to be "in the air" at a given time. Within the space of a few months Grodecki, Hayward, and myself arrived at the same conclusions as to the twelfth-century date of glass from Troyes. More astonishing is the parallel direction taken by Ayres's work and my own, which was not due to any collaboration, nor even to the fact that we were both students of Professor Kitzinger. At the time of writing I had not read the typescript of Ayres's recently completed study of the Morgan Master, because it seemed wiser that our conclusions remain independent. It is hoped that the rather "early" dates offered here for both the earliest and the latest of the Canterbury glass may be accepted on the basis of the evidence derived from style, content, and historical probability. It is a happy accident that the thirteenth-century date hitherto accepted for the so-called "Master of the Gothic

---

[56] A. R. Dufty, "Through a Stained Glass Less Darkly," *The Times* (London), September 23, 1972; Caviness, "Saving Canterbury's Medieval Glass," *Country Life* (September 28, 1972), pp. 739–40; the international colloquium of the *Corpus Vitrearum Medii Aevi* convened in Canterbury in September 1972 to inspect some of the glass and discuss methods of conservation; see E. Bacher, "Das VIII. Colloquium des Corpus Vitrearum Medii Aevi in York und Canterbury, 25. September-1. Oktober 1972,"

Österreichische Zeitschrift für Kunst und Denkmalpflege 27 (1973), pp. 76–77; P.A.T. Burman, "Corpus Vitrearum Medii Aevi," *The British Society of Master Glass-Painters Journal* 15 (1972–1973), 27–33; subsequently, Joseph Robinson, "Conservation and the Ancient Stained Glass," *C.C.C.* 1974, pp. 23–24.

[57] Sulkis, 1964.

[58] Caviness, 1970, pp. 184–86.

Majesty" of the Winchester Bible and for the Sigena paintings is being challenged by Ayres.[59]

The investigation of the subject matter was begun chiefly to prove the unity of the program, and thence to focus upon the traits that might indicate who laid the master plan for the windows, and when. If the individual painter tends nowadays to be given all the credit for artistic productions, we should recall that in the Middle Ages the prime creator was the patron; the man who "made" a work might be the one who had it made by a craftsman.[60] It is, therefore, important to know who was chiefly responsible for the choice of subjects, especially in a program as complex and as tightly organized as that of the Canterbury glazing. In searching for a date for the execution of the Canterbury windows, I have investigated also their moment of inception, as a *terminus a quo*. At the same time, one has to be prepared to accept breaks in the continuity of execution, the possibility that designs of an early date may be executed by an artist of the next generation working in a radically different style; and glass, unlike manuscript illumination or wall painting, does not reveal this secret except to a prepared eye, since no underdrawing is preserved.

Artistic creation is better understood if one considers the demands of subject matter. This is especially true of medieval art, when the artist generally worked from some sort of model, and creative copying has to be taken into account.[61] Valuable insight into this process has been given by Kitzinger, who separated the pictorial design source or "motif book" from the "iconographical guide."[62] I have attempted to make this distinction, discussing iconographical sources in the chapters on subject matter, and motifs, or what one might call aids to drawing, in the chapter on style; but there is necessarily some overlapping, as when an iconographical model is also imitated in some aspects of style; a summary of these various sources shows

another dimension of this historical insight, since it documents major exchanges and influences in the period more precisely than does style alone.

The chapters on subject matter could no doubt have been extended to formidable length. It remains, for instance, to investigate all the sources of the ideas and verses for the extended series of typological subjects, but it is hoped that the new reconstructions of each window will stimulate more work. An expert analysis of the epigraphy, from the very large number of intact inscriptions that survive in the glass of all periods, also remains to be done. Its interest for me would be to see whether it confirmed my chronology and approximate datings.

My working method was to undertake the historical investigation only after the sections on style and iconography had been completed, in order to avoid the temptation to accept certain dates for the windows *a priori*. For the reader's benefit this order has been reversed in the present volume, since historical events are a natural prelude to the sequence of styles.

An important question related to patronage is how the glazing was financed, and when. Rackham made little use of the detailed accounts that have been preserved for Christ Church, but he rather arbitrarily connected a year of unusually high expenditure (1213–1214) with glazing expenses.[63] Other studies have made the financial system much clearer. The absence of any reference to glazing, either in payments to artists or purchase of materials, makes it possible to indicate, by analogy with other monuments, a limited number of ways in which the windows could be financed. Such a study does not produce a precise date for the glazing, but knowledge of the socioeconomic conditions in which much early Gothic art was produced is not irrelevant for the art historian.

Underlying financial uncertainties and difficulties was the turbulence of ecclesiastical and political

[59] Oakeshott, 1945, pp. 7, 16; Pächt, 1961, p. 175.

[60] Swarzenski, 1967, p. 18.

[61] Hanns Swarzenski, "The Role of Copies in the Formation of the Styles of the Eleventh Century," in *Romanesque and Gothic Art: Studies in Western Art (Acts of the*

XX International Congress of the History of Art) 1, ed. M. Meiss, Princeton, 1963, pp. 7–10.

[62] Kitzinger, "Norman Sicily," 1966, pp. 139–40.

[63] Rackham, 1949, p. 16.

events in the period during which the east end of Canterbury Cathedral was being rebuilt. Our own distinctions between history and art history were not observed by the historical writers of the time; Gervase describes the rebuilding as the most important feature of the years 1174–1184, then abruptly turns to a chronicle of the events leading to bitter disputes with the new Archbishop Baldwin. To him, no doubt, this was not an interpolation, but a continuation of his record of the significant events affecting the lives of the monks of Christ Church. These other aspects of the history of Christ Church are just as relevant to the creation of the windows as considerations of development and change in style; they are also complementary in that the presence of continental contacts, suggested by a study of style, can be proved from a close scrutiny of events during the period of disturbances from Becket's exile to the exile of Archbishop Stephen Langton and all the inmates of the house during the Interdict of 1207–1213. It was precisely during these difficult times that links with the continent were strengthened in art as in politics. Had calm prevailed, Canterbury might have been materially richer but more isolationist; it is not just the result of geographical location that York and Durham were provincial centers, in contrast to Canterbury.

This was a period when many of the great monastic centers became intellectual backwaters, overshadowed by the secular schools at Paris, Oxford, Chartres, and Laon. An intense intellectual life continued at Canterbury at least to the turn of the century; if the era of the great monastic theologians was over (and even Latin was in a decline, as is proved by the inscriptions in the later glass), there was a strong generation of politicians whose letters are eloquent and sometimes brilliant.[64] The artistic vitality of Canterbury at the turn of the century exceeded that of its peers—Sarum, Westminster, St. Albans, Winchester, Worcester, Peterborough. Ironically, perhaps, after the great achievements of Canterbury in the new Gothic architectural and painting style, it was for the other centers to evolve a specifically English Gothic idiom, as exemplified by the architecture of Salisbury Cathedral or the manuscripts associated with a "Sarum Illuminator."[65]

IN THIS introduction I have attempted to outline the existing legacy of Canterbury studies, and to indicate some of the lacunae that might now be filled. With the change in style from late Romanesque to Gothic as a central problem, the aim of this study is to bring together as much material as possible to bear on the production of the windows. An analysis of styles by comparison with other Canterbury works and with those from other regions indicates a phase of eclecticism and experimentation. This will be demonstrated not only in figure compositions but also in ornament, an aspect of the windows that has already been noted as somewhat neglected since the nineteenth century. The relation of the subject matter to already existing works will also be discussed, and a date proposed for the intellectual inception of the glazing program. Speculation as to the date of execution of this program would not be valid without reference to the account rolls and chronicles of Christ Church, and this implies a survey of the socioeconomic conditions prevailing during the period of glazing. Finally, it will be possible to draw some conclusions as to the date of execution of the windows. The datings so far proposed have relied rather too heavily on isolated archaeological observations. When I began to look closely at the ornament in the Trinity Chapel windows, I became aware that the date given by Rackham, about 1220, implies that at least some of the ornament was extremely archaic. This sort of conclusion is a difficult one to accept for Canterbury, in view of its cosmopolitan contacts, particularly when one finds that it shares an identical repertory of ornamental designs with the Sens windows.

A true idea of the development of English glass painting in the thirteenth century will not be pos-

[64] Stubbs, ed., 1865.

[65] For architecture, Bony, 1949, p. 13; Brieger, 1957, p. 3; for west country manuscripts of about 1240–1260, see Hollaender, 1942–44, pp. 230–62; D. H. Turner, "The Evesham Psalter," *Journal of the Warburg and Courtauld Institutes* 27 (1964), 32–37.

sible until better documentation exists for Salisbury and Lincoln; my conclusion that both are later in inception than Canterbury may be modified by later researchers. A chapter in preparation on the Lincoln glass by Morgan will advance our knowledge of that monument;[66] the last serious treatment was published in 1946.[67] No study can be definitive, and it is hoped at least that the con-

clusions reached here have a broader base, and a higher degree of probability, than those of previous works. It is also my hope that this book, together with the *Corpus*, will restore confidence in one of the best preserved-collections of glass painting of the period 1175–1220, so that it may once more take its place as a great monument of English medieval art.

[66] Peter Kidson and Nigel Morgan, monograph on Lincoln Cathedral (forthcoming).

[67] Lafond, 1946.

I. Method of Study:
Problems of Restoration and the
Authenticity of Medieval Glass

"Who would ever think that the primary task of the historian of glass painting is one of textual criticism?"

Jean Lafond[1]

DURING the past two decades it has become increasingly apparent that one of the chief impediments to the study of medieval stained glass is uncertainty about its authenticity; such doubts are especially disturbing to the historian of style. Oakeshott greeted Rackham's book with the question, "To what extent has the restoration gone?"[2] In 1951, unfortunately too late in many instances to profit from study of the glass while it was still down after the war, the plan for an international *Corpus Vitrearum Medii Aevi* was formed, and it is hoped that eventually all surviving medieval glass will be studied, with special attention given to authenticity. Since no such documentation existed for Canterbury, the essential groundwork of my own study has been the laborious authentication of individual panels, and of each piece of glass within the figured panels. In 1967 and 1971 scaffolding was erected on the exterior of the building to give access to the windows, since it is the outer surface that most easily reveals the age of a piece of glass.[3] In this examination I was helped by George Easton, the retired foreman of the cathedral glassworks, who had worked there since the first decade of this century. Even with his expert knowledge and very good memory for the glass he had handled, this inspection alone might be insuf-

[1] Lafond, 1946, p. 122.
[2] Oakeshott, 1951, p. 88.
[3] For initial training in these methods of detection, I am grateful to Louis Grodecki, and the late Jean Lafond and Marcel Aubert, who in 1960–1961 permitted me to observe their examination of the glass from the abbey church of St.-Ouen of Rouen, then in the course of restoration. The results of this examination have since been published in the *Corpus, France* IV–2/1.

ficient to solve all questions of restoration. Fortunately, the results could in many cases be checked against prerestoration tracings or drawings, and compared with earlier accounts of the glass. Particularly valuable are the mid-nineteenth century drawings that predate George Austin, Jr.'s work of restoration. The correspondence was satisfactory enough to indicate the high degree of accuracy of Mr. Easton's judgments, so that they may be accepted in the case of the ancestors of Christ from the clerestory and other panels for which no early records are available. In the absence of any early records, however, it was seldom possible to say whether a piece was a copy of the original or a free restoration.

The restoration of stained glass is more treacherous than that of any other of the medieval arts except mosaics, owing to peculiarities of the technique.[4] If a piece of glass in an otherwise well-preserved panel is missing, the gap can be filled in one of four ways.[5] The modern painter can select a piece of new glass to match as well as possible and leave it unpainted; or paint such a piece to conform with the style of the original glass; or he can select from a box of fragments a medieval piece (contemporary with the original or not) which is the right color, and insert it as a stopgap, ignoring any paint it may have on it; fourthly, he may take such an old piece, wipe it clean with acid, and repaint it to conform with the style and design of the original. Normally the first three can be detected fairly easily, even from a photograph, and, in fact, the first method has the sole advantage of extreme ease of detection. In case of doubt, a new piece can usually be identified by a close examination of the edge and the outer surface, even if these have been tampered with. In the fourth instance one has to rely on stylistic judgment almost entirely.

A more important problem for the art historian than a decision as to whether a given piece of glass is original or not is to assess the degree of authen-

ticity retained in restoration. For instance, if almost all the glass in a panel is new but it is known that the restorer worked from original leading, then the outlines of the composition are original. Such a panel is an authentic outline drawing, and probably retains its original iconography. This of course may apply to the whole or to a small part of a panel only. More important, it was common in the nineteenth century to take out an original piece if it was badly shattered or severely pitted, or if it was a fragment that had remained in the leads when the rest of the piece fell out. Thus in some instances the glass painter had an original, or part of it, from which to copy the trace-lines and with which to match the new glass. In this way new glass may give a better indication of the original than an old piece interpolated from elsewhere. Text figure 1 illustrates some of these possibilities. Drawing 1 shows the (conjectural) original appearance of the Sower in north choir aisle n:XV, 17; 2a shows the figure as recorded in Williams's tracing before 1897,[6] the head being missing and the glass in the garments much broken and mended by additional leads; 3a shows the actual restoration by Caldwell, Sr., who replaced two pieces of missing drapery by extraneous fragments and painted a head according to his own design on new glass; 2b represents a hypothetical alternative to 2a, the original head badly cracked; 3b is a restoration, using new glass, with the features copied from the broken original; 2c is another alternative, with part of the original head missing; 3c shows a restoration using new glass and partially copied from the original. In the restoration charts, 3a, b, and c look the same, as they do on examination of the glass itself. For a knowledge of the actual degree of authenticity retained in restoration, a prerestoration drawing is needed. This illustration exposes the limitations of the method used by Easton and myself where no other records exist, and also the limitations of restoration charts. Error will be on the side of overdiscrimination, however,

[4] For mosaics, see Kitzinger, 1960, p. 118.
[5] Some methods were described in detail by Jean Verrier in *Vitrail*, pp. 85–87.

[6] Williams Collection, no. 17.

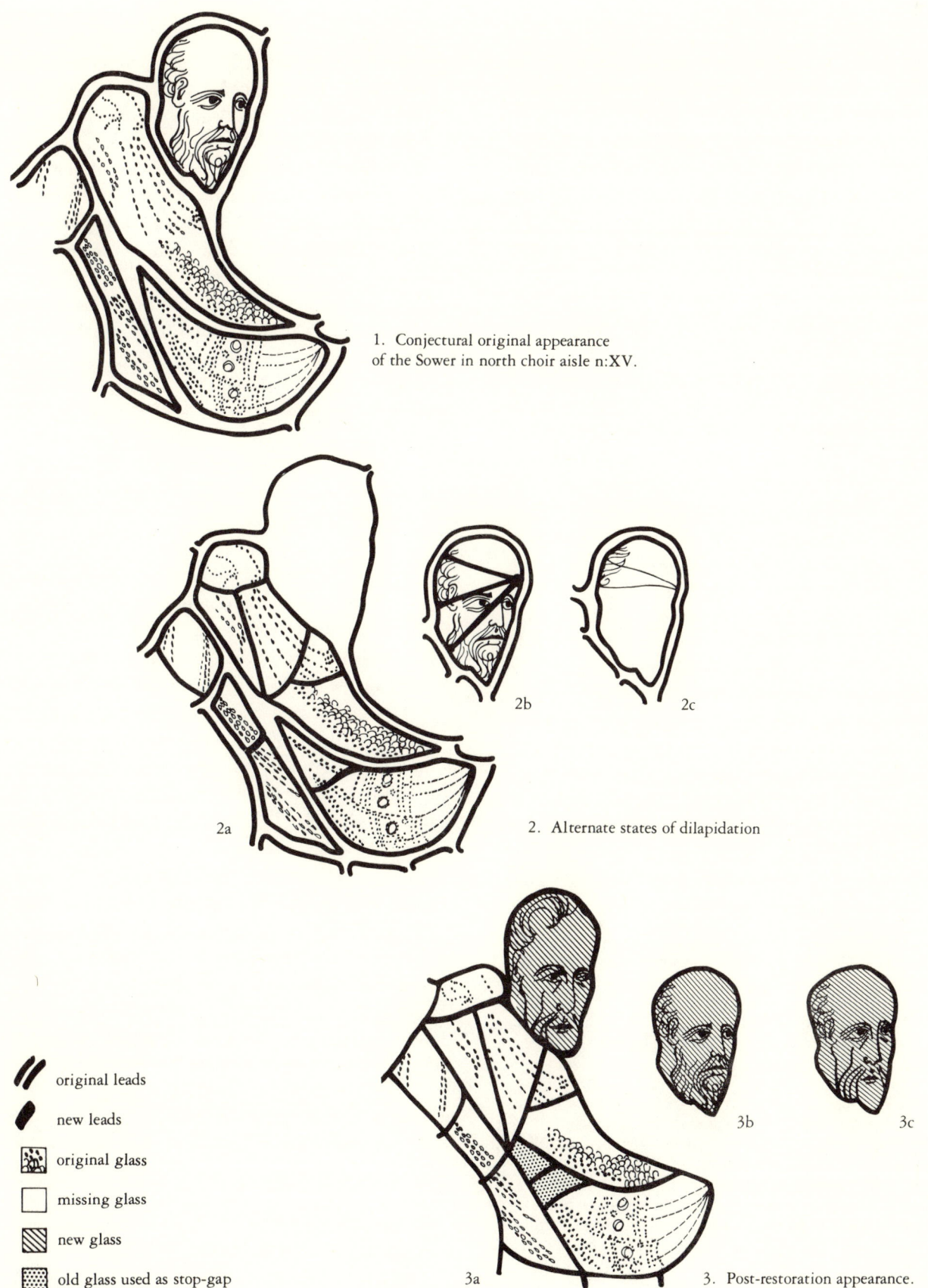

1. Conjectural original appearance
of the Sower in north choir aisle n:XV.

2b   2c

2a   2. Alternate states of dilapidation

original leads

new leads

original glass

missing glass

new glass

old glass used as stop-gap

3b   3c

3a   3. Post-restoration appearance.

Text fig. 1. Courses of dilapidation and repair in glass.

in contrast to the previous indiscriminate acceptance of almost all the existing Canterbury glass as
authentic.

Methods of restoration have changed considerably over the years. These changes, in both attitudes
and materials, can be traced at Canterbury in some
detail, at least in the period after the mid-nineteenth
century. Comparatively little is known of earlier
methods because early restorations have been largely obliterated in the course of subsequent ones.
There are indications that work done on the glass
in the seventeenth and eighteenth centuries was
very careless. Gaps were filled haphazardly with
old glass from elsewhere in the cathedral, whole
panels being interpolated from other windows and
cut down to fit if necessary. Evelyn said that the
windows were repaired after the breakages of
1644, but this probably involved the shifting of
panels to fill gaps. It is generally assumed that there
was a further drastic reordering in the eighteenth
century. Some panels may even have been turned
inside out so that the paint was exposed to weathering; the Fogg medallion showed signs of weathering on both sides prior to cleaning in 1970. Up to
the middle of the nineteenth century there had been
virtually no releading, and losses were probably
as great from glass simply falling out as from icon-
oclastic destruction. Even after 1900 much of the
glass was still in its original leads, and at the beginning of the First World War Caldwell and
Easton found the sills of the north choir aisle
"triforium" thickly covered with glass fragments,
many of which they fitted back in subsequent restoration.[7]

From the first half of the nineteenth century until a decade ago the restoration of the Canterbury

glass was entrusted to four successive generations
of the same family, and the evolution of techniques
can be closely followed. In 1819 George Austin, Sr.
began to direct repairs to the cathedral. Although
the architectural structure was his major concern,
he apparently also restored the glass. In the obituary on his death in 1848, it was said that he painted
in the Gothic style, and that "the imitation is so
curiously correct that many artists when asked to
point out the new glass have failed to fix on the
right lights." This was found to be all the more
remarkable, since he had "no previous knowledge
of the art of glass painting."[8] However, none of his
work is now in evidence, and the testimony given
in the obituary is more interesting for its bearing
on Austin's son, George Austin, Jr., whose work is
to be seen everywhere in the cathedral, and who
trained with his father.

Austin, Sr. was an older man than Viollet-le-
Duc, who did not become active in the Commission des Monuments Historiques until the 1840s,[9]
and whose important article on stained glass was
not published until 1868.[10] Austin was thus a pioneer in the revival of Gothic arts, and it is not
surprising that he was self-taught in glass painting;
the craft had almost died out in the seventeenth and
eighteenth centuries, and where it was still known
it had little in common with medieval practice. It
was only in the later part of Austin, Sr.'s lifetime that an intense interest in medieval glass was
aroused; in the 1840s the Reverend J. G. Joyce
made his series of drawings of Canterbury glass
for the glass painter Thomas Willement, and the
Reverend O. Hudson did several watercolor tracings that supplement drawings by the Austins.[11]

---

[7] Unfortunately, almost no original leads now remain;
a few are preserved in the Cathedral Library.

[8] Austin's obituary, 1849, pp. 659–60.

[9] Johnson, 1965, p. 26.

[10] E. Viollet-le-Duc, "Vitrail," *Dictionnaire raisonné de
l'architecture française* IX, Paris, 1868, 373–462.

[11] Joyce's Album of 1841 is in the Victoria and Albert
Museum, London, Department of Prints, 93.H.29. The
freehand drawings are about one-third the original size,
and the leading is not accurately represented. O. Hudson's
watercolor tracings are mounted in single sheets, Victoria
and Albert Museum, Department of Prints, nos. 415.1–17;

his tracing of the Virgin from the Jesse Window as reproduced by Day, 1913, fig. 16, and by Rackham, 1949, Pl.
Bb, facing p. 13. Some small watercolors of glass are in
the Austin Album, Cathedral Library, Add. MS 1. Austin,
Jr.'s tracing of Josiah from the Jesse Window is also in
the cathedral library. In 1963 other tracings were depos-
ited there, after Caldwell, Jr.'s death. Austin's tracings of
other corona panels had been used subsequently, and
marks ("N"), indicating new glass, were added then, according to Easton. The date and authorship of other
tracings are uncertain; even those of north choir aisle subjects backed by newspapers dated 1854 are suspect, as Eas-

Making such records of early glass was a fashionable hobby, especially among the clergy.[12] This sort of work continued throughout the nineteenth century, as in the album of drawings made at Canterbury for the glass painters Clayton and Bell sometime between 1871 and 1895,[13] and those made, probably with the aid of the restorer, Caldwell, Sr., to illustrate Miss Williams's book of 1897.[14] These drawings, done by or for glass painters, had an aesthetic as well as a practical function; just as the Neo-Classic painters of the eighteenth century had made drawings of Italian High Renaissance sculpture, so the Gothic Revival artists made studies of medieval works. The drawings were not done with the intention of providing accurate archaeological records, but if used with caution, they are often useful indicators of the condition of a panel at that time.

The drawings of the 1840s preceded by a few years the systematic restorations to the glass carried out by George Austin, Jr. After 1848 the two sons of Austin, Sr. divided his duties; Harry succeeded as surveyor to the cathedral, and George the younger was in business as a glass painter until his retirement in 1862.[15] George Austin, Jr. was a young man during the decade in which the revival of glass painting gained impetus in England and France. For him, as for none of the later restorers, it was natural to recreate the "Gothic style," but the "Gothic" that inspired his generation was the phase we now call late Romanesque or proto-Gothic. Especially admired were the classicizing features of the glass paintings of the north choir aisle, as stated by Gilbert in 1842, who quoted Joyce, the artist of the drawings in his illustration.[16] It was primarily this early Canterbury style that was imitated by Austin, Jr. His work in the east window of the corona deceived Westlake only thirty years later; Westlake, one of the most savant historians of glass painting of his time, selected Austin's *Crucifixion* for illustration and high praise as an original thirteenth-century work.[17] Such confusion was more to be expected when Austin copied an original, as in the case of the Jesse Tree figures.

There are few records preserved of the manner in which George Austin, Jr.'s restorations were carried out. In 1854 "a particular description of what has been done by Mr. George Austin to the old windows in the Church" was shown at a Chapter meeting, and it was agreed to ask him to keep this record in a book;[18] no such account has survived, although Mason referred to Austin's "notes" in 1925.[19] It is apparent from the Chapter Minutes that Austin had a monopoly of the cathedral glazing, although he was not in the permanent employ of the Chapter. He obtained a contract to glaze the whole of the fourteenth-century nave, on the grounds that the iconographic scheme and color balance would be destroyed if other painters were allowed to work in the same area.[20] He seems to have had far too much freedom to remove old glass and to introduce copies in its stead. It was thus that two figures from a Jesse Window recorded in the east window of the corona in the 1840s were re-

---

ton says Caldwell had a cupboard full of such old newspapers. Furthermore, Austin did not restore the choir aisle glass, and would have been unlikely to make working tracings. The only Trinity Chapel subject, of n:III, 25, seems to have been traced after Austin's restoration.

[12] Compare, from the same period, the volumes by C. A. Buckler (London, British Library, Buckler Bequest xvi and xvii, Add. MSS 37138 and 37139), and by Charles Winston, a lawyer who dabbled in glass painting (British Library, Add. MS 35211). Neither of these men worked at Canterbury.

[13] The Clayton and Bell *Album of Water-colours* ii, is dated 1895; Victoria and Albert Museum, Department of Prints, 94.J.34. Permission to make these drawings was granted at St. Catherine's Chapter, 1871 (Canterbury, Cathedral Library, Chapter Minutes, 1854–1884, p. 287).

[14] Williams Coll. In almost every instance there is a tracing on wax paper and a finished ink drawing for reproduction. The tracings were in some cases made before restoration (north choir aisle and "triforia" glass), but have occasionally been used by Caldwell, Sr. to sketch in missing heads, etc., and a number of these details have been copied in the ink drawings, so that the plates in Williams's book are not accurate records of the glass prior to Caldwell's restoration.

[15] Caldwell, 1951, p. 22.

[16] Gilbert, 1842, p. 19.

[17] Westlake, i, 1881, p. 102, Pls. LX, LXI; the Crucifixion was of Austin's own design, though the Virgin was copied from n:IV, 15. Another panel illustrated (Pl. LXII, a) is a copy by Austin in Trinity Chapel n:III, 22 of n:IV, 10.

[18] Chapter Minutes, 1854–1884, p. 7.

[19] Mason, 1925, p. 10.

[20] Chapter Minutes, 1854–1884, pp. 28–29.

moved in 1854, and Austin's copies of them, still extant in the adjacent corona window and in the southeast transept, were made about that time.[21] Although these particular panels remained in the shop until 1906, there was a market for old glass before then. An extract from a letter by Joyce to Willement, which forms the preface to the album of 1841, contains an interesting passage about the possibility of obtaining some old glass: "The great strictness enforced of late by ecclesiastical compulsion (not before it was necessary) renders it, I fear, almost a hopeless case; there is just a possibility that I may succeed through young Mr. Austin, as in his Father's private Store Room and Closets many bits doubtless are lying about, and this is the only channel through which it is at all possible."[22] Williams says some of the clerestory figures had been sold as early as 1799, but were brought back in the 1860s.[23]

The ethics of restoration in the nineteenth century were not our own. It was extremely common for glass painters to substitute new glass, faithfully copied from the original, and to throw out the darkened and decayed pieces, just as present-day stone masons discard moldings that have rotted. Only modern cleaning techniques allow such glass to be restored to translucence.[24] In cases where the original has been preserved and can be compared with the copy at Canterbury, it can be seen that George Austin made academic and idealized copies, but they nonetheless give a fairly accurate idea of the character of the original—compare, for instance, the head of Semei by Austin, as it appeared in the photograph of 1926 (fig. 85), and the origi-

nal in the Victoria and Albert Museum (fig. 86).[25] Whatever his proficiency in recreating the "Gothic" style, however, Austin was handicapped by the glass then available for use in restoration. The purples, blues, and greens, especially, were too brilliant and hard in tone to harmonize with twelfth- or thirteenth-century glass. Aesthetically, therefore, he may have felt it preferable to renew a whole panel than to mix old and new glass; the two original Jesse figures would have appeared somber in the windows glazed by Austin with a complete tree. That these panels were not sold until fifty years later, by Austin's great-nephew, suggests that Austin did not remove them from the cathedral because of an immediate possibility of sale.

Rackham has drawn together the records of Austin's restorations contained in the cathedral library. In 1853 and 1854, some work was done on the lower row of genealogical figures in the west window. The east window of the corona was repaired in 1854. The three windows on the north side of the Trinity Chapel (n:II, III, IV) were probably the next to receive attention, Window n:II in 1855.[26] These still retain much of Austin's glass. In the Trinity Chapel no attempt was made to invent scenes to fill gaps, as the texts of the miracles were not yet widely known, so Austin made copies of existing panels, with some modification of colors.[27]

Austin seldom tampered with the surface of the glass he used in restoration. There are only a few instances, chiefly in white glass, where he has applied a "flux," or false patina, to the outer surface to tone down the piece. This is hard and white, and unlike genuine patina on the old glass at Can-

---

[21] Caviness, 1975, p. 374. The window in the transept chapel was "highly approved" by the Chapter in 1854 (Chapter Minutes, p. 7). In the adjacent chapel window, glazed in 1852, are copies of two panels now in the Virginia Museum of Fine Arts, Richmond, which, like the Jesse panels, had been sold to Nelson in 1906; see Caviness, 1973, p. 54.

[22] Joyce, 1841, pp. 2–3.

[23] Williams, 1897, p. 3.

[24] For example, the well-known case of the Winchester College Chapel glass, which was replaced by Betton and Evans. Some of the original glass has now been cleaned by Dennis King; see John H. Harvey and Dennis King, "Winchester College Stained Glass," *Archaeologia* 103 (1971), 153–58.

[25] The head was replaced by Austin in 1855; see Rackham, 1949, p. 27, and Oakeshott, 1951, p. 87. Austin's head has since been replaced by Caldwell, Jr. The original, Victoria and Albert Museum, C. 854-1920, was first recognized by Baker and Lammer, 1960, Pl. 1, p. 60. The provenance has since been confirmed; *The Year 1200* 1, no. 225, pp. 221–22.

[26] Rackham, 1949, pp. 26–27.

[27] This was the most frequent way of "composing" used by the Caldwells, as well as by Austin. It has given the false impression that the same cartoon was reused in the Middle Ages [Rackham, 1949, p. 13, who cited Trinity Chapel n:V(3), and n:IV(8)]; both are modern adaptations from s:II(10).

terbury, it cannot easily be scraped or flaked off. It is unlikely to have been applied with an intent to deceive on close inspection.

The next two generations must have been very conscious of the unpleasant tonality of Austin's glass, much of which they replaced. Late in the nineteenth century there was a reaction against the practice of replacing old glass with new, and a sentimental mystique began to surround the qualities of old glass. It was realized that imperfections in its facture, and even subsequent pitting, added to its luminosity and to the subtle variations of tone and light intensity. In 1876 Fowler read a paper to the British Archaeological Association in which he criticized the antiqued glass produced in the Gothic revival, and applauded an "awakening sensibility to the beauty of ancient glass." In 1910 he was quoted by Noel Heaton, who went so far as to say "the weathering of old glass is one of its chief glories." That Heaton could also quote Winston, from the mid-nineteenth century, that weathering is "like a perfecting by God of the work of man," shows that this new aesthetic approach had its beginnings in the picturesque, as defined by writers such as Prosper Merimée, though Romanticism was now tempered by scientific inquiry.[28] It was a broad movement, which encompassed the "discovery" of Tang pottery, and of patinated bronzes in the west.

Austin's nephew, Samuel Caldwell, Sr., who was in charge of restorations from 1862 to 1908, was as much a part of this movement as Austin had been of the Gothic revival. Under his direction, fragments abandoned by Austin were sorted and boxed by color for reuse. He developed in his shop methods of cleaning, repainting, and refiring old glass. He claimed to have used chiefly medieval glass in his restorations.[29] Where this was the case the results are much further removed from the original than are Austin's replacements, and the panels often have a kaleidoscopic appearance. Even the leading lines cannot be accepted as medieval outline drawing.[30] The use of old fragments without recutting or repainting was not satisfactory except at some distance from the eye, such as in the outer figures of the oculus in the northeast transept, which were provided by Caldwell, Jr. It was often found preferable to clean an old piece with acid and repaint it. This method was used chiefly from around 1890 to about 1914 by Caldwell, Sr. and his son, in the windows on the south side of the Trinity Chapel (s:II, VI, and VII).[31]

It was easier, however, to apply "flux" and acid to a new piece of glass, since refiring an old piece was hazardous and required extraordinary technical skill.[32] This explains the methods used by Samuel Caldwell, Jr. After 1908 he continued to draw on the boxes of old fragments but increasingly he used new glass treated so as to appear old, at first applying a false patina and eventually also employing acid to bleach the colors and to give the effect of pitting. He replaced much of his great-uncle's and father's work in restoring the windows a second or even a third time, during the two world wars. Thus today a piece of drapery may be a copy of a copy of a lost original. Ironically, with all the technical means at his disposal to make the glass look old, Caldwell could not paint, as his great-uncle had been able to do, in a convincingly Gothic style. His work was misleading chiefly because he enjoyed telling antiquarian experts that his glass was in fact old. Frequently he said that the original piece had been found in Austin's boxes of frag-

---

[28] Noel Heaton, "The Foundation of Stained Glass Work," *Journal of the Royal Society of Arts* 58 (1910), 455, 459. Heaton was reporting some of the first chemical analyses of ancient glass, to be followed by Léon Appert, *Note sur les verres des vitraux anciens*, Paris, 1924.

[29] For example, Williams, 1897, p. 29, said Trinity Chapel n:V was completed in 1894, using old fragments. In fact, much of this glass was new.

[30] For example, Trinity Chapel n:V(1) and s:II(3–8).

[31] For example, in Trinity Chapel s:VI, the horse in panel 1 and the drapery in 7, restored in 1906. Glass that

has been cleaned and refired appears to have been resurfaced in the kiln, and it has not developed a patina, as has the glass that was less thoroughly cleaned. It has a very bright outer surface, but is less smooth than modern glass.

[32] A wood-fired kiln, which required very careful control, was used throughout this period. Many experiments were tried, including the fusion of two broken edges from a piece of glass in the north choir aisle "triforium"; the join was still intact in 1967.

ments and replaced. This was occasionally true, but usually the pieces supplied were new.[33]

Caldwell, Jr. had trained with his father from 1878, and in the early years it is not possible to tell their work apart. The difference that emerged later, as outlined above, was not so much stylistic as technical. The son was in charge of all restorations to the glass from 1908 to his retirement in 1952.[34] During this long period the cathedral glass was taken out for two wars. All, except for a few panels leaded by Austin, were releaded at some time by Easton. The chronology of Caldwell, Jr.'s work can be given from Mason's book up to 1925, from the *Annual Reports* since 1927, and from his own "Memories of a Craftsman." Easton was also extremely helpful on occasion in remembering dates of restoration, since he joined Caldwell in the glassworks in 1906. In 1892, according to Caldwell himself, work was begun on the south windows of the Trinity Chapel and continued sporadically until 1909.[35] These had not been touched by Austin, but panels had earlier been moved to other locations in the cathedral. After the First World War much glass must have been kept in the shop for restoration, among it the very decayed panels from the north choir aisle "triforium." About 1920 Window n:V of the Trinity Chapel, already restored by Caldwell, Sr., had two panels added; about the same time, Window s:II was completed with panels moved down from the south "triforium," and Window s:VI was filled, some panels being brought from s:II. Canon Mason directed these restorations, and contributed much to an understanding of the subject matter. The restoration of panels to locations in Windows n:V, s:II, and s:VI, as already to s:VII, was archaeologically correct.

The greater part of seven windows in the Trinity Chapel was now filled with original glass.

A few panels were then placed in Window n:VII, which had perhaps retained its border. The first was a figure of an archbishop partly composed of old glass that had been used as a ground between medallions in the "triforium." By 1954 the window was completely filled with colored glass, but except for one semicircle (n:VII, 15), it was all made up by Caldwell, Jr. with a sparing use of old glass. The same is true of two medallions in Window s:IV, placed there in the 1920s.[36]

The late 1940s saw the cleaning, releading, and restoration of the Trinity Chapel windows previously restored by Austin (n:II, III, IV). The east window of the corona must have been restored about the same time. The two original Jesse Tree figures now in Window n:III of the corona were returned to the cathedral by the executors of Philip Nelson only in 1953, at which time they were releaded by Easton. Apart from this, little restoration work has been done in the upper church since Caldwell's retirement.[37] It is Caldwell, Jr., through his longevity and the event of two world wars, who stands out as the Canterbury restorer who handled all of the early glass, some of it twice. He had a reputation as an honest and talented craftsman, and trust was placed in him almost to the end of his life. In Rackham's book four of the color plates of glass supposedly of the early period in fact show figure panels made up by Caldwell.[38]

Because Caldwell's work has been so misleading, it is worth recording some of his methods in detail. The techniques were more sophisticated than those outlined by Knowles early in Caldwell's career.[39] He took endless trouble over each piece of

---

[33] The skirt of Abraham's tunic in the Sacrifice of Isaac (corona east, 3) was replaced by Austin, and appeared unbroken in Nelson, 1913, Pl. VI, but the old fragments were subsequently found and put back; see Caviness, 1967, p. 177. On the other hand, in Trinity Chapel n:III(4), a very disordered panel, Caldwell placed a head on the left that he claimed was the original, but that on examination proved to be of Austin's facture. See Bernard Rackham, "Old Glass Reinstated," *C.C.C.* 42 (1947), pp. 20–23, and 1949, Pl. XII.

[34] He died, aged 101 (according to Mr. Easton and Dr. Urry), in August 1963.

[35] Caldwell, 1951, p. 22.

[36] Rackham, 1957, p. 48; Caviness, 1967, pp. 5–6, 113–16.

[37] The examination with scaffolding in 1967 and 1971 was the first detailed inspection since the Second World War. Dilapidation was found, and a program of conservation is now in hand.

[38] Rackham, 1949, Pls. VII, XI, XIII, and frontispiece.

[39] J. A. Knowles, "Forgeries of Ancient Stained Glass: Methods of Their Production and Detection," *Journal of the Royal Society of Arts* 72 (1923), 38–56.

glass, particularly in his later work on the north side of the Trinity Chapel. Modern glass was carefully selected, of the right thickness and as near as possible to the right color.[40] The edge, generally cut with a diamond, according to modern practice, was often grozed down and roughened afterwards to approximate a medieval grozed edge.[41] The blues were frequently treated with acid all over both surfaces to lighten the color, leaving a roughened inner surface that feels only slightly less sharp than that of a genuinely decayed piece. Acid was then allowed to work on random spots on one surface to give the effect of pitting. In the early years the acid pitting on the outer surface was not further abraded, but a flux of putty powder and ground glass was fired on, giving a hard white "patina." However, the pits made by acid have a slightly rounded lip and do not feel as sharp as genuine weathering. This "fault" is readily noticeable in the windows of the north choir aisle "triforium," which were restored between the wars. The next step perfected by Caldwell was to abrade the whole surface with emery paper after pitting with acid, leaving a narrow raised strip around the edges as if it had been protected by the leads; the lip of the pits was sharpened in the process. A flux applied thinly over this made the forgery very hard to detect. One of the incomparable Canterbury forgeries is the head of the woman on the left in Trinity Chapel n:IV(15), an instance in which the style of painting is convincing because the tracelines were copied from another head, though even these were partially removed to give the appearance of being effaced (fig. 159).

Without Easton to explain these methods and to remember the pieces treated in this way, detection would have been very difficult. Being forewarned, however, I was able to notice occasional discrepancies that might betray this sort of work elsewhere. For instance, a natural patina seldom spreads evenly over a piece of glass, but tends to develop more

quickly in the center and lower part, which are less protected from rain by the leads. The false patina does not regard variations of environment and tends to cover the surface evenly, and to the same extent in the upper as in the lower part of the window. Generally the flux was also harder. Again, the whiteness of a flux is rather monotonous. Most old glass develops a colored patina, yellowish in the case of the blues and some yellows, rust-colored on the reds, pinkish on pinks and whites. This was very apparent in the ornament of the windows examined, which had not been thoroughly cleaned in the last restoration. Even from a distance, panels made up by Caldwell, Jr. to simulate old glass, such as those in Window s:VI of the Trinity Chapel, appear too white on the outer surface to the critical eye.[42]

To summarize the restoration methods used at Canterbury during the century between 1850 and 1950, the work of Austin, up to 1862, is often the most accurate archaeologically; wherever possible he seems to have copied a damaged original. His work is also the easiest to detect, the nineteenth-century glass generally having an unpleasantly hot tone. The surface has not been greatly tampered with, though he sometimes used a crude flux on the outside. Distinctions between Austin's glass and well-preserved medieval glass are only occasionally difficult to make. Some of the medieval blues (especially in the north choir aisle and corona windows), acid greens, and pinks are very hard, and the outer surfaces are still intact; conversely, some of Austin's glass has begun to pit on the outside. The distinction between Austin's pieces and old glass is more easily made from inside on the basis of tonality and style. His colors are very brilliant compared with the old. Austin's figure painting is strong, a pleasing approximation of a late Romanesque style, though of course not free from Gothic revival traits.

The work of Samuel Caldwell, Sr. (cathedral

---

[40] In these years Easton was several times sent to London to select glass, generally at Heatley's.

[41] Some pieces still in the shop in 1967 were almost perfect forgeries; with the edge only partially visible under leading, detection would be impossible.

[42] In his restoration of the glass at Nackington in 1935, Caldwell let the new glass lie out under rusting iron to develop a brownish patina.

glass painter, 1862–1906) and his son (1906–1952) overlapped during the years 1878 to 1906. Both used old fragments in restoration, at first untouched, later recut or even cleaned and repainted. Their painting styles were weak, uncertain, loosely organized, in contrast with the authority and rhythm of Austin's draftsmanship. To some extent their draperies approximate the driest or the freest of the Trinity Chapel styles (in Windows n:V and s:II respectively) but the faces are seldom convincing (e.g., fig. 100). An amusing insight into the workings of the shop is provided by Easton's testimony that Caldwell, Jr.'s sister, who was the creator of the children's character Rupert Bear, was occasionally called in to help with a difficult face. These restorations would probably not have been so long accepted as original if it were not for the reuse of old glass and eventually elaborate faking techniques, and Caldwell's own testimony to their authenticity.

The implications for the art historian of these restoration techniques are not only archaeological. Stylistic observations have been hampered by the very confusing material that has been accepted until now as original. Austin's restorations are not very troublesome and have a higher degree of authenticity than much that has been done since. Caldwell, Jr.'s work is ubiquitous in the cathedral, and has tended to lead to interpretations that are false—the chief of which is that the Trinity Chapel ambulatory windows are the work of a single designer. There are, for instance, no authentic instances of the reuse of the same cartoon in these windows; instances cited by Rackham are in every case Caldwell's adaptations from an existing composition. The appearance in every window of facial types and draperies favored by Caldwell

gives a deceptive impression of homogeneity. This has been increased by the reuse of extraneous glass, so that in a given window the style is not as homogeneous as it should be. Furthermore, Caldwell was more eclectic than the previous restorers; albums of photographs of glass in other cathedrals, such as Chartres or Rouen,[43] were available to him and probably influenced his style as much as did Canterbury painting. He seems to have added a "Chartrain" element to the Canterbury glass, for instance, in the heavily draped Madonna in the east window of the crypt.[44]

A second type of confusion has arisen from the availability of the texts on which the miracle series was based. These were edited in 1875–1876, and their relevance to the glass was recognized by Williams in 1897. Mason, Urry, and Rackham have made further identifications with the help of these texts. The Caldwells may also have used them, however, for designing or reconstructing scenes.[45] Other scholarship to which the younger Caldwell had access were the chemical analyses of medieval glass made by Noel Heaton. Easton told me that on occasion "flux" (false patina) and "frit" (the vitreous enamel used for the trace-lines) were obtained from Heaton, the inference being that a medieval formula was used. Even with chemical analysis, therefore, it might be impossible to detect which pieces retain only original paint and which have been repainted.

Once this confusing restoration has been recognized, it becomes possible to define the original styles and suggest a division by ateliers. Comparisons with manuscripts and stained glass from other centers can also be made with greater sureness. But first a brief consideration of the historical context is in order.

[43] Delaporte and Houvet, 1926, for Chartres, and Ritter, 1926, for Rouen.

[44] Rackham, 1949, Pl. VII.

[45] Mason, 1925, p. 29, found an identification for the scenes in Trinity Chapel n:V(2 and 3); and Rackham, 1949, (p. 85) added panel 1 to the series, although it had been made up by Caldwell, Sr. in 1894; one wonders if Caldwell had already read the same text. Similarly, two

medallions in Window n:VII(10 and 14) were identified by William Urry, "The Thirteenth Century Miracle Glass: An Identification," *C.C.C.* 31 (October 1938), 13–14. They have little old glass in them, and may have been created around the inscriptions and a few fragments, perhaps with the help of the text. There may be some degree of accuracy in the reconstruction.

II. The Historical Background and the Problem of Dating

"Cantet igitur novum domino canticum felix Cantuariensis ecclesia . . ."

Pope Honorius III[1]

IN THE late twelfth century, and into the thirteenth, Christ Church, Canterbury, was still of paramount importance, not only as the first church of England but also as one of the richest and most powerful of the Benedictine houses.[2] It has even been said, as by the contemporary writer Gerald of Wales, that the monks were given to luxurious living.[3] At the same time, Christ Church was conspicuous in the ecclesiastical history of England as the site of the bitterest quarrels between the monks, the secular clergy, and the king, from the time of Archbishop Thomas Becket and Henry II to that of Archbishop Stephen Langton and King John. During these disputes, the riches and power of the monks were gradually dissipated. The friars took over the religious instruction of the people.[4] Archbishop Baldwin, who was one of the last monks to hold that office, was a Cistercian not a Benedictine, and his tenure only served to make greater the distinction between the convent and the archbishopric; by the middle of the thirteenth century even their archives had been separated.[5] The quarrels were very costly; the monks borrowed large sums of money early in the thirteenth century, and these debts were not settled until 1285–1287.[6] Nonetheless, this is the

[1] "Therefore let the fortunate church of Canterbury sing unto the Lord a new song." Letter to Langton of January 26, 1219, quoted by Foreville, 1958, p. 163.

[2] By the end of the twelfth century the monks owned between a third and a half of the domestic property of Canterbury, but more lucrative were high rents from London properties; Urry, 1967, pp. 23, 35–36.

[3] Poole, 1955, p. 228.

[4] Stubbs, 1865, pp. cxix–cxx.

[5] F.R.H. du Boulay, "The Archbishops as Territorial Magnates," *Medieval Records of the Archbishops of Canterbury; A Course of Public Lectures Delivered in Lambeth Palace Library*, London, 1962, pp. 54–55.

[6] Smith, 1943, pp. 17–18, 26. As much as 20 percent interest was paid on loans from Italian merchants.

era of the splendid rebuilding and decoration of the eastern part of the church; it is clear that in the case of Christ Church external difficulties and financial stress were not an insurmountable obstacle to the completion of an extremely ambitious building program.[7]

Rather than attempting here an analysis of all the crosscurrents that may have affected the glazing program, my main purpose in this chapter is to survey the contemporary records and events that might give some indication of the date of the glass. This is necessary in part because in the past some over-hasty conclusions have been reached. A brief outline of the history of Christ Church in the period from the fire of 1174 to the translation of the relics of St. Thomas to the Trinity Chapel in 1220 may remind the reader of the order of events.

In 1174, the year of the fire, Richard, prior of Dover, was elected archbishop of Canterbury. Although it was during his archiepiscopacy that the rebuilding progressed rapidly, he was apparently not a man of strong character, and the onus of the work must have been carried largely by the brethren.[8] Among the monks were many men of letters who still earned Canterbury a name as a center of learning, and one of their closest acquaintances was John of Salisbury, who lived among them up to 1177;[9] Gervase, the chronicler, has given us the most important document of local history of the period, and Nigel of Whiteacre was widely known for his satirical verse.[10] Benedict, who was prior from 1175 until 1177 and then became abbot of Peterborough, was a prolific writer, a great promoter of the cult of St. Thomas, and had probably been much interested in the new building at Canterbury. At Peterborough he directed the rebuilding of the nave up to his death in 1193, and founded there a chapel of St. Thomas. Bale and Dart supposed that Benedict had a degree from Oxford, but he was described by his medieval biographer as only sufficiently learned;[11] we shall see that his interpretation of the miracles of Becket that he had collected was quite conventional.

Archbishop Richard's tenure was peaceful and prosperous. The building continued smoothly after the departure of Benedict until the architect, William of Sens, fell from the scaffold in the summer of 1178.[12] Even this did not prevent the completion of the choir by Easter, 1180, under the new architect, William the Englishman. The building was not entirely finished when Baldwin succeeded Archbishop Richard in 1184, but from this time the chronicle of Gervase centers on the disputes with the Cistercian archbishop rather than on the building.[13]

Baldwin wished to found a college of canons and a chapel, to be dedicated to Sts. Stephen and Thomas, at Hackington near Canterbury, a project that had been envisaged by Sts. Anselm and Thomas. The monks objected because they feared the new church would compete with the first church of England. They appealed to Rome, and the case went through many vicissitudes between 1184 and 1190, when Baldwin died on crusade.[14]

[7] On financing building projects of the twelfth century, see Boase, 1953, pp. 268–71.

[8] Richard was blamed by his contemporaries "for the failure of the church to profit by the martyrdom of Becket" (Poole, 1955, p. 221).

[9] Webb, 1932, pp. 16, 122.

[10] Haskins, 1927, p. 51, saw Canterbury in the time of Becket as "the best example of a vigorous cathedral community." For Nigel, formerly known as Wireker, see Stubbs, 1865, p. lxxxv; Polycarp Leyser, *Historia Poetarum et Poematum Medii Aevi*, Magdeburg, 1721, pp. 751–58; and F.J.E. Raby, *A History of Christian Latin Poetry*, Oxford, 1927, p. 337, with bibliography; more recently, J. H. Mozley, "Nigel Wireker or Wetekre," *Modern Language Review* 27 (1932), 314–17; Nigel de Longchamps, *Speculum Stultorum*, ed. J. H. Mozley and Robert R. Raymo, Berkeley and Los Angeles, 1960, p. 1; Urry, 1967, pp. 59, 153–54.

[11] The few known facts about Benedict's life have been collected in Robertson, II, 1876, xix, and in the *Dictionary of National Biography*, I, Oxford, 1921–1922, 213–14. The chief source is the chronicle of Swafham; see Roberti Swaphami "Historia Coenobii Burgensis," ed. Sparke, 1723, pp. 97–103. For his work at Peterborough, see Boase, 1953, pp. 265–66; J. Dart, *The History and Antiquities of the Cathedral Church of Canterbury*, London, 1726, p. 183.

[12] Gervase, ed. Stubbs, 1879, p. 20.

[13] *Ibid.*, pp. 29ff.

[14] David Knowles, *The Monastic Order in England . . . 942–1216*, Cambridge, 1940, pp. 319–22, and Dodwell, 1954, pp. 112–13. The dispute was followed in detail by Stubbs, 1865, pp. xxxviii–lxxxiv; see also C. R. Cheney, *Hubert Walter*, London, 1967, pp. 135ff.

The Popes Lucius III and Gregory VIII supported Baldwin, as did the English bishops (all but Hugh of Lincoln) and the Cistercians; Urban III was able temporarily to turn events in the favor of the monks, so that by the time of Gregory VIII the proposed site had been moved to Lambeth.[15] At the height of the quarrel, the monks were virtually imprisoned in their convent for over a year (1188–1189), and they suspended services in the cathedral church.[16] The dispute continued under Baldwin's successor, Hubert Walter (1193–1205); he had already supported Baldwin, as bishop of Salisbury, and his election was unpopular with the Christ Church monks.[17] He continued to try to build at Lambeth, but when permission was finally given for only a small foundation, by Pope Innocent III in 1201, he capitulated with good grace and became known as one of the great benefactors of Christ Church.[18] The peace was again broken, however, by disputes with King John over the election of Stephen Langton to the archiepiscopacy, and in 1207 all the loyal and able-bodied monks left Christ Church to find refuge with their old ally, the Benedictine house of St.-Bertin at St.-Omer.[19] They returned only in 1213, with the dispute settled in favor of Langton.[20] During the years of exile, and into 1214, England was under an interdict. Christ Church suffered considerable financial loss in spite of restitutions made after the return.[21]

In subsequent years, the history of Christ Church was dominated by the archbishops rather than the brethren. Stephen Langton, trained in Paris, was already famous as a theologian, and his interest in canon law brought him to the front in the negotiations for Magna Carta.[22] Though an international figure, his interests did not take him away from Canterbury entirely. It was he who finally realized the monks' dream of translating the relics of Thomas Becket to a gold shrine in the upper church. Elias of Dereham, a member of his brother's household who had previously served Hubert Walter, and Walter of Colchester from St. Albans are credited with supervising the work on the shrine.[23] Langton himself delivered a long address on the translation.[24] The monks probably played a very inconspicuous part; it is to Matthew Paris of St. Albans that we owe the most detailed account of the translation.[25]

The historical and archaeological evidence that has to be considered in suggesting dates for the windows is drawn from contemporary chronicles, letters, and financial records, and from the windows themselves. This evidence has later to be weighed with that of iconography and style. First, however, the building dates for the various parts

[15] Stubbs, 1865, p. lxxx; on pp. xliii–xlvi Stubbs listed the major alliances in the quarrel.

[16] *Ibid.*, pp. lx–lxi, cxl.

[17] *Ibid.*, pp. lxxxv–xciii. For his election at Salisbury in 1189, see Poole, 1955, p. 221.

[18] Gervase, ed. Stubbs, 1880, pp. 410–14.

[19] The prior of Christ Church and the abbot of St.-Bertin agreed to make a pact of mutual aid, ca. 1200; Historical Manuscripts Commission, *Fifth Report*, London, 1876, p. 449, B390. For the exile see Gervase, ed. Stubbs, 1880, pp. lxiii–lxiv and 99–100; August Potthast, *Regesta Pontificum Romanorum* I, London and Paris, 1874, 271, no. 3177; Martène and Durand, 1717, cols. 688–89 (John of Ypres). Seventy monks, with associates bringing the number to a hundred, were received at St.-Bertin; sixteen stayed more than a year.

[20] Langton had been consecrated archbishop by the pope in 1207, but King John would not accept his election; after the king's acquiescence, Langton returned to England in 1213 to release him from excommunication; Poole, 1955, pp. 445–61.

[21] Barnes and Powell, 1960, pp. 53–55.

[22] Powicke, 1929, pp. 23–128. Langton is perhaps best known for having divided the Bible into standard chapters and verses, and for standardizing the order of the books.

[23] Matthaei Parisiensis, 1866, p. 242. By 1220 Elias was a canon of Salisbury, as described by Matthew. According to Powicke, 1929, pp. 136–37, Elias was allowed to return from exile about 1217, but a record of repayment to him in 1216 of a loan to Christ Church seems to indicate he was already in Canterbury that year (C. E. Woodruff, 1932, p. 17).

[24] "Tractatus de translatione," ed. Giles, 1845, II, 269–97.

[25] Matthaei Parisiensis, 1866, pp. 241–42. Another account of Matthew Paris, composed for his life of Stephen Langton, was printed from British Library, MS Cotton Nero D. I by Felix Liebermann, *Ungedrückte Anglo-Normannische Geschichtsquellen*, Strasbourg, 1879, pp. 328–29. The version that probably came from Canterbury omits mention of Elias of Dereham and Walter of Colchester; Robertson, IV, 1879, 426–28. Several accounts are given in translation by Mason, 1920, pp. 70–83.

of the reconstructed east end may be given from Gervase's account; each must be a *terminus post quem* for the glazing of that part (text figs. 2a and b).

The remodeling of the choir was begun in September 1175, and the two sexpartite and one quadripartite bays of the choir were vaulted in 1176–1177.[26] There are three tiers of windows in this part of the building; three lower windows in the north and south aisles were not altered in the remodeling.[27] A program of typological subjects was begun in the westernmost window on the north side, to be continued through the transepts, and presumably to be completed in the south choir aisle. The first of these windows on the north has been blocked; of the rest, a good part of the glass in the second and third (n:XV and n:XIV) is *in situ*. Vertically above each of the choir aisle windows is a smaller trilobed opening, at triforium level, though not in a true triforium (St & Nt:IX–XI, text fig. 2c); this was a device for increasing the height of the choir. The original subjects of these windows are in some doubt, but in all probability scenes from the lives of the two Canterbury archbishops, Sts. Dunstan and Alphage, are at least in part *in situ* on the north side. These may originally have been divided between north and south. The *terminus post quem* for these two lower series would be the time of vaulting the aisles, 1175–1176.[28] The third level of glazing is the clerestory, surely glazed after the vaulting of the choir in 1176–1177. Five pointed lancets on either side were glazed with ancestors of Christ, beginning on the north in the westernmost window with the creation of Adam and Adam digging, and apparently finishing opposite on the south side with the Virgin and Christ (N:XXV–XXI, S:XXI–XXV); no figures from the south side of the choir are preserved, and only a few borders are *in situ* on the north side. The surviving figures from the north side have been removed to the perpendicular windows of the nave and westerly transepts.

The eastern transepts, crossing, and presbytery

were constructed in 1177–1178, but the vaulting operation was interrupted by the fall of William of Sens from the scaffold. The last double bay of the vault, over the high altar, was completed in 1179 by English William;[29] this would be the *terminus post quem* for the glazing of the four clerestory windows in this bay, but the lower windows and those further west could have been installed after 1178. The three-story lighting scheme is maintained in this part of the building (text fig. 2c). There are twelve lower windows, six on the north and six on the south (n & s:VIII–XIII). The typological program was extended into the transepts, and most probably into the presbytery aisles as well, but was interrupted in the four transept chapels by lives of saints, only fragments of which survive *in situ*, in St. Martin's Chapel (n:X). Once more, there is no glass extant from the south side. Some panels from the north transept (n:XI & XIII) are now in the lower parts of the two windows in the north choir aisle. Windows in the triforia of the transepts and above the aisle windows flanking the presbytery retain no original figures, and there is no record of their subjects (Nt & St:II–VIII). In the clerestory, the ancestry of Christ was continued in the north transept and into the presbytery, and ran back on the south side (N & S:XI–XX, text fig. 2a). A number of these figures are preserved, but few are *in situ*; most, like their companions from the choir, were removed to the perpendicular windows.

The Trinity Chapel ambulatory windows were not ready for glazing until 1182, and the clerestory and corona were only completed in 1184.[30] This part of the building has only two registers of windows. In some of the twelve windows of the ambulatory are extensive remains of a series dealing with the miracles of St. Thomas (text fig. 2d), while the lower corona windows have a Jesse Tree and a typological Redemption window (Corona I, n & s:II–VII). The clerestory of the Trinity Chapel had figures of the ancestors of Christ (N & S:III–X), but this series was interrupted in three windows of the apse (Trinity Chapel I, N & S:II);

---

[26] Gervase, ed. Stubbs, 1879, pp. 19–20.
[27] Willis, 1845, p. 78, fig. 21, considered that these windows were enlarged but there is no evidence for this.

[28] Gervase, ed. Stubbs, 1879, p. 19.
[29] *Ibid.*, pp. 20–21.
[30] *Ibid.*, pp. 28–29.

these may have contained narrative subjects. Some of the figures of ancestors are preserved, but they, too, are now in the great perpendicular windows.

From this brief survey it will be seen that some glass survives from windows included in each of the three basic building campaigns, which terminated in 1177, 1179, and 1184. The stonework, at least, can be closely dated. Crucial to this study is the existence of the original iron armatures in almost every window. They are fixed into very decayed wooden frames, of uncertain age, which could have been installed at any time after the completion of the stonework.[31]

Previous opinions on the date of the glass have relied on the date of the building, on the one hand, and on representations of the shrine of 1220 in two windows of the Trinity Chapel, on the other. Loftie, writing in 1876, dated the north choir aisle glass about 1185, that is, close to the completion of the building; but he noticed the representations of the shrine, and dated the Trinity Chapel glass after 1220.[32] Rackham modified this theory, preferring to date the clerestory glass of the choir about 1178, when scaffolding used in the construction would have been in place.[33] Nelson, Saunders, Rackham, and Beer dated the Trinity Chapel glass about 1220–1230, as did I in a previous paper, on the basis of style and the scenes with the shrine.[34] Westlake had suggested 1220–1240,[35] but a much-neglected article by Clement Heaton proposed a date-span of 1175 to 1206 for all the glazing.[36] Most writers have placed the choir aisle glass between the clerestory and the Trinity Chapel in their chronologies,[37] but Rackham was the only one to suggest a firm date on the basis of financial records; he linked heavy expenditures in 1213–1214 with the choir aisle glazing, though preferring on stylistic grounds to date it about 1200.[38] A more

interesting hypothesis is that of Arnold, who suggested that in 1180 all the clerestory windows west of the temporary screen that closed off the choir were already glazed, and implied that the north choir aisle glass was also completed then. The Trinity Chapel glass he placed later, suggesting that its execution was interrupted by the exile of 1207–1213, and that Windows n:III and n:IV dated from at least as late as 1220. The Sts. Dunstan and Alphage series he thought to date from a previous structure, thus before 1174.[39] An interruption during the exile was also postulated by Sulkis.[40]

In spite of the very full account of the rebuilding by Gervase, and the amount of material conserved in financial records, there is no extant contemporary mention of the Canterbury windows. Indirect evidence has therefore been carefully sifted. The dating hinges in part on the question of whether a Gothic building was considered complete before it was glazed. It was customary at one time to date glass according to the date of the construction of the building. Grodecki has pointed out that there are documented exceptions to this rule; where funds were lacking for immediate glazing, the windows might be boarded up, as at Angers. Grodecki disputed Rackham's theory that the scaffolding used in construction was also used for the glazing of the clerestory.[41] The argument is not a strong one; in the Middle Ages the cost of labor in erecting and dismantling scaffolding would not have been great, and the materials could be used again. Furthermore, Easton told me all the Canterbury clerestory glass was taken out for the last war from ladders, the gallery being wide enough to stand a ladder on, and it presumably could have been put in place the same way. On the other hand, in at least one case where caution was applied in dating glass, it has been possible subsequently to prove that the

---

[31] There is little evidence of repairs to these irons until after the world wars, when some were damaged. According to Easton, a chemical analysis was made to find an explanation for their lack of corrosion, and a high zinc content was found.

[32] Loftie, 1876, pp. 12, 10.

[33] Rackham, 1949, pp. 15–16; in 1928, p. 33, he dated the clerestory glass 1174–1200.

[34] Nelson, 1913, p. 109; Saunders, 1932, pp. 100–102;

Rackham, 1949, p. 17 (1210–1230); Beer, 1952, p. 49; Caviness, 1965, p. 195.

[35] Westlake, I, 1881, 110.

[36] Heaton, 1907, pp. 173–75.

[37] Evetts, 1941, p. 118; Saunders, 1932, pp. 100–102.

[38] Rackham, 1949, p. 16.

[39] Arnold and Saint, 1939, pp. 57–60, 63–64, 70–76.

[40] Sulkis, 1964, pp. 110–16.

[41] Grodecki, 1951, p. 94, citing Poitiers, Chartres, and Angers.

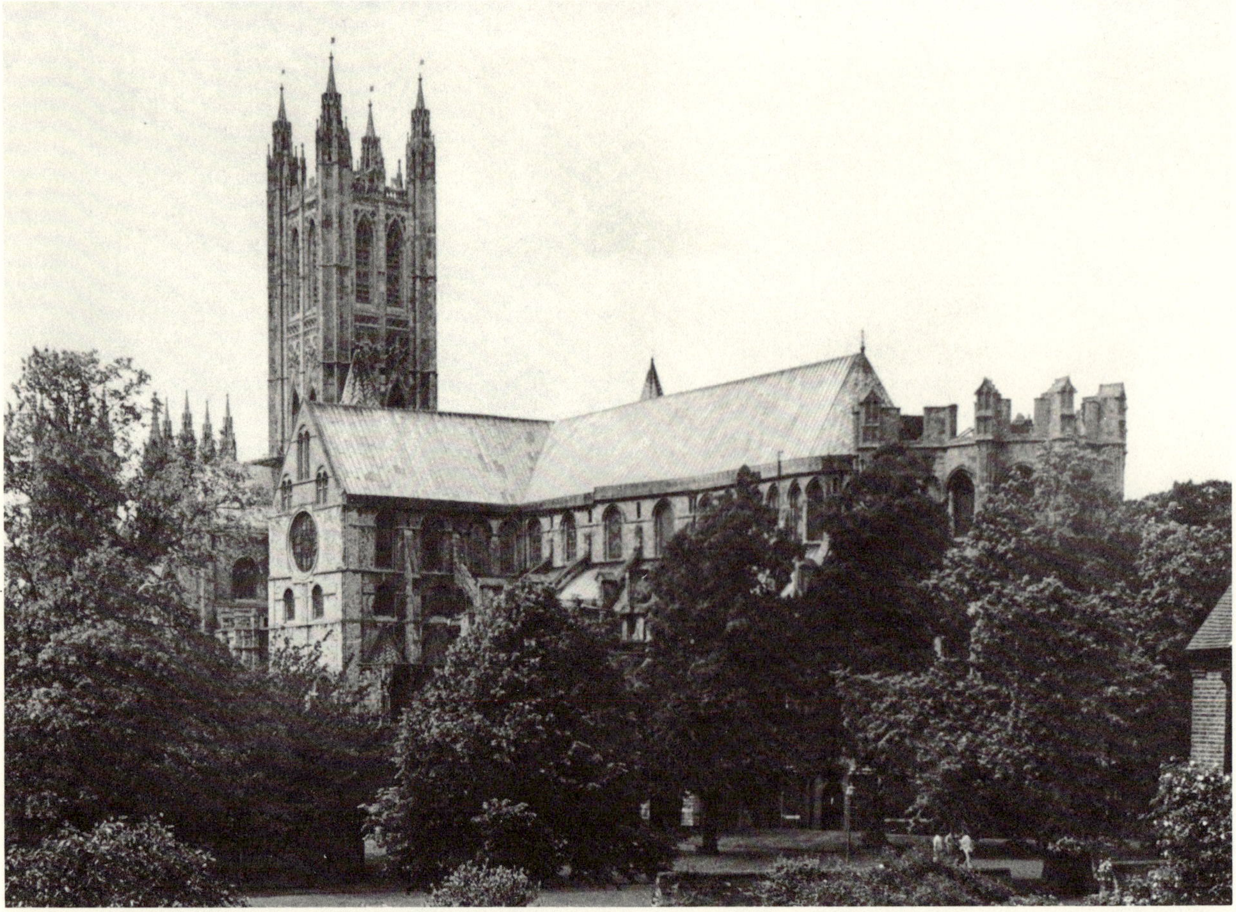

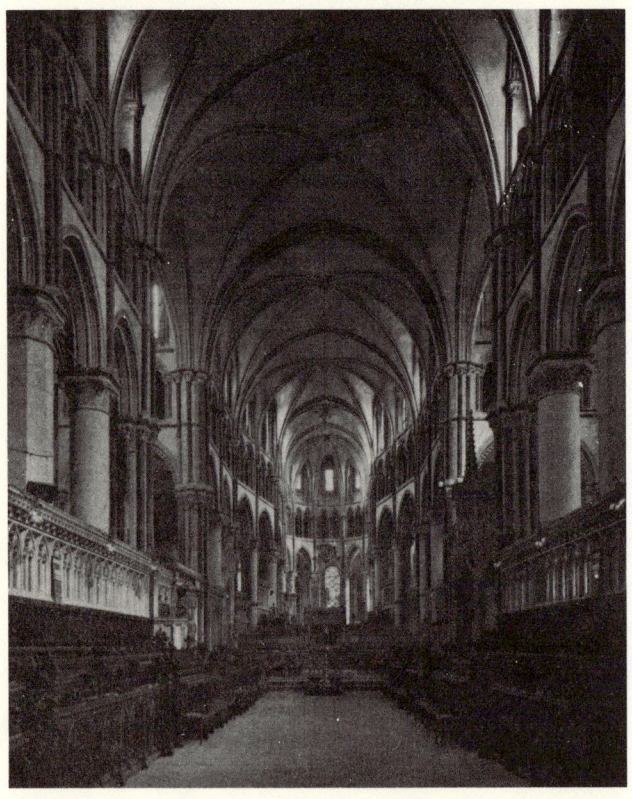

Text fig. 2a. Canterbury Cathedral from the southeast

b. Interior view from the choir to the Trinity Chapel

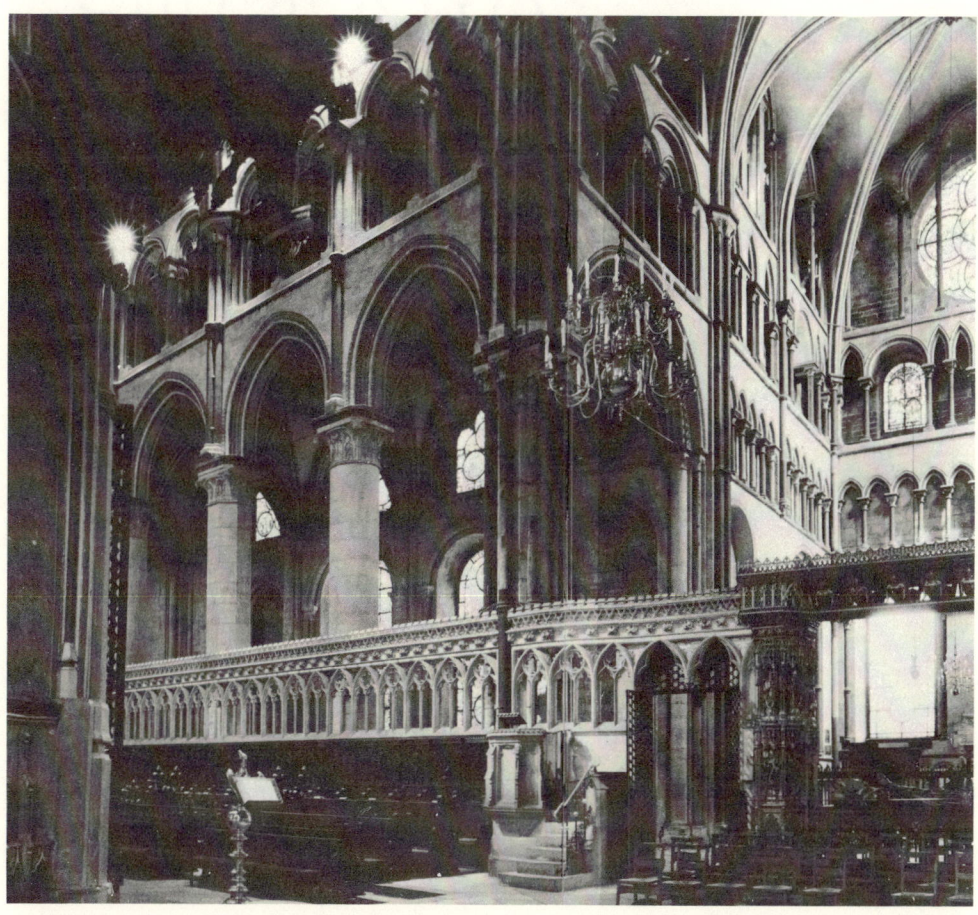

c. Interior view of the north side of the choir and northeast transept

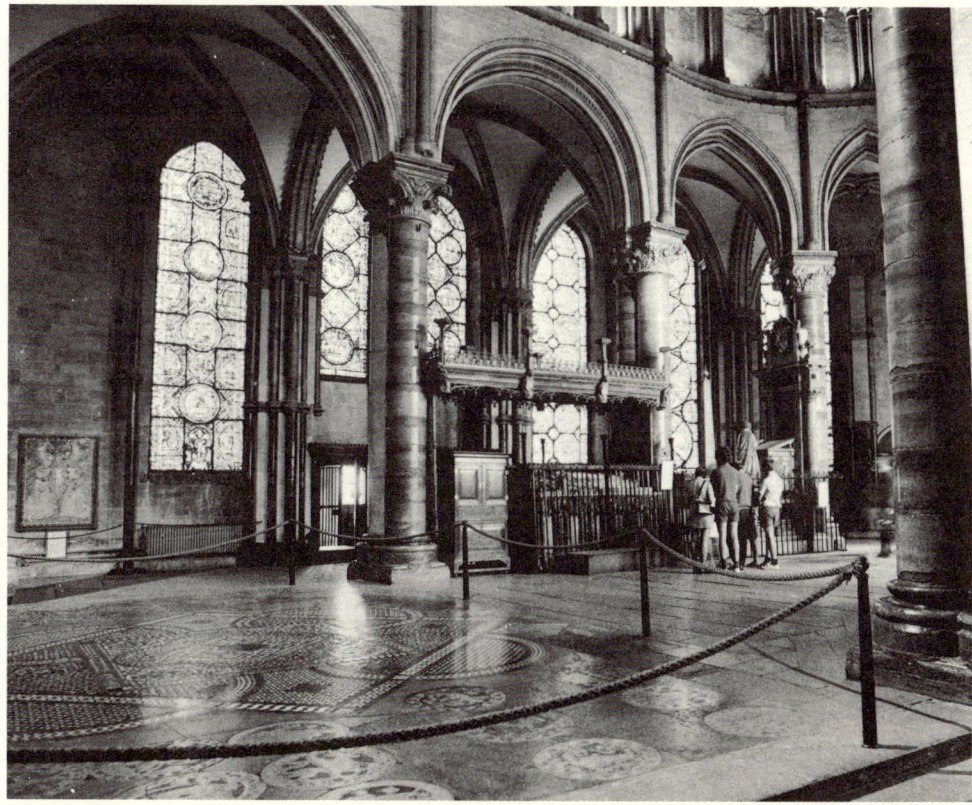

d. Interior view of the north side of the Trinity Chapel

glazing was complete before the consecration of the building; the glass of the Sainte-Chapelle of Paris was thus firmly dated to the years immediately preceding 1248 by documents discovered by Dyer-Spencer.[42]

Gervase's text is extremely disappointing when it comes to the glass; he was far more alert to the newness of the architectural and sculptural styles,[43] but this may be because the earlier building was also sumptuously glazed. He does, however, say that in 1180, when the monks entered the choir at Easter, William the Englishman had placed a wooden partition across the east end, between the next to last piers so far constructed, and in it were three glass windows (plan 19).[44] These were presumably mentioned because glass in a temporary structure would be a rather unusual luxury; but the possibility cannot be dismissed that they were stained glass windows that could be moved to the permanent building when it was completed. Gervase stressed the haste with which the choir was finished for the entry at Easter, and one cannot be certain that it was completely glazed. Four points are in favor of its having been so. First, the position of the 1180 screen coincided exactly with a change in the ironwork of the clerestory windows, from a primitive straight-bar type uniformly used to the west, to more highly evolved curved-bar designs to the east, in Windows N:X–S:X. This must indicate a break in the glazing program. Second, it will be seen that the essential plan for the subjects in the windows probably dates from 1177–1179, suggesting that the windows *could* have been glazed as the building progressed. Third, it would seem strange to provide glass for the temporary structure unless the permanent windows were

glazed, especially since in the new Gothic style an unprecedented area of the wall was opened up into windows to provide space for colored glass; the aspect of the interior would be very dreary if these windows were boarded up (text fig. 2d). For an occasion of such importance to the monks as the re-entry into the choir, the convent would wish the new church to look its best.[45] Fourth, there is no evidence yet of financial duress; this point will be given more detailed consideration later. Against these arguments in favor of the glazing of the choir by Easter 1180, is the fact that Gervase described the building as scarcely ready.[46]

Gervase's account of the building breaks off at the election of Archbishop Baldwin in 1184. Although he mentions the lead roofing of the crossing tower "and other parts," it appears that the corona was never fully complete on the outside in the middle ages.[47] As we have seen, Baldwin's tenure was a very uneasy one, and it was this that preoccupied Gervase. There is, however, another indication of less propitious circumstances for the completion of the building; for the year 1183, Gervase noted that nothing was done on account of lack of funds.[48]

The investigation now turns in two directions, first to the letters written by the monks during the dispute over the college of canons, and second to the available financial records and a discussion of the financing of the building and glazing.

From the letters of Christ Church in the period 1187–1199, which have been edited by Stubbs, it is evident that the monks had two major concerns about their church. One was that the archbishop would remove the relics of St. Thomas to the new foundation dedicated to him, and the other was

[42] Jeannette Dyer-Spencer, "Les Vitraux de la Sainte-Chapelle de Paris," *Bulletin Monumental* 95 (1932), 337.

[43] Gervase, ed. Stubbs, 1879, p. 27.

[44] *Ibid.*, p. 22: "Paries quoque ligneus ad secludendas tempestates ex parte orientis per transversum inter pilarios penultimos positus est, tres vitreas continens fenestras." I am indebted to Dr. Kenneth Severens for confirmation of the position of this screen.

[45] Gervase, ed. Stubbs, 1879, p. 23; he described the re-entry into the choir at Easter as if the monks were following Christ (in the Eucharist) into Galilee. Their ex-

clusion after the fire he likened to the expulsion of Adam from Eden (p. 24).

[46] *Ibid.*, p. 22: "Chorum itaque, cum summo labore et festinatione nimia utcunque vix tamen praeparatum. . . ."

[47] Cathedral Library, Chapter Minutes, 1854–1884, pp. 85, 98, and 111–12; entries under the years 1858, 1859, and 1860 concerning the selection of plans to *complete* "Becket's Crown"; Scott and Willis as well as Austin and Burgess were consulted. Somner, 1640, pp. 171–72, supposed the unfinished state of the corona to have been the result of late medieval alterations.

[48] Gervase, ed. Stubbs, 1879, p. 29.

that this building enterprise would prevent them from "perfecting" their own church.[49]

It is evident that the translation of St. Thomas to the upper church was planned all along,[50] but the monks were perhaps awaiting a suitable occasion; before Easter 1180, Prior Alan incurred the displeasure of the other monks by moving the relics of Sts. Dunstan and Alphage in secret to their traditional places on either side of the main altar.[51] In 1180 and 1181 preparations were made for the translation of St. Thomas, "who alone of the saints was still waiting for his chapel to be finished."[52] In 1185 Prior Alan asked the king's permission for the translation.[53] It was no doubt with this translation in mind that the Trinity Chapel had been so much prolonged beyond the previous structure in the rebuilding. In commenting on the shape of the Trinity Chapel, Gervase mentioned that a passageway was left around the east end for processions.[54] As in the case of many churches constructed around the relics of a saint, the passageway may also have been intended for pilgrims.[55] Had the translation taken place as planned, it would have been one of the earliest of such moment in the English church, preceding those of St. Felix, St. Ethelred, and St. Ethelbert at Ramsey, St. Guthlac at Croyland, St. Edmund at Bury St. Edmunds, St. John at Beverley, and St. Oswin at Tynemouth, all of which were completed in the 1190s.[56] As it turned out, even St. Wulfstan was translated to a shrine in the new building at Worcester two years before Thomas Becket was so honored.[57] The monks may well have been concerned that with all the delay their prize would be snatched away to become the glory of a more modern building. They must have expressed such fears to Urban III, for in 1187 he inquired whether Baldwin had any intention of translating the body of the martyr to the new church.[58] About that time, one of the monks had a vision in which Baldwin appeared and said he intended to destroy the new work (the cathedral church), which suggests something of the distrust the monks had for their archbishop.[59] In 1193, under Pope Celestine III, Hubert Walter offered conditions to the monks for his foundation at Lambeth, among which was a pledge not to allow the translation of St. Thomas to any church other than their own.[60] They refused the terms, however, and the dispute continued until the chapel at Lambeth was demolished by order of Pope Innocent III in 1199, and rebuilt on a smaller scale.[61]

Another difficulty between the monks and the archbishops was the responsibility for the fabric of the cathedral and the allotment of funds to this end. Lanfranc's program of reform included the separation of the estates of the monks from those of the archbishop,[62] but Anselm, Thomas, and Richard gave up the altar offerings to the monks. In 1185 Baldwin took the offerings, which were his by right, much to the annoyance of the brethren.[63] In 1186 he founded a fraternity to raise funds for building at Hackington, and in the same year he promised a quarter of the offerings of Christ Church to the monks and another quarter to the fabric of the cathedral, keeping only one quarter for his own use. The building may already have been insecurely financed, but the monks proceeded now to send numerous envoys to Rome, which caused them to go deeply into debt.[64] Meanwhile,

[49] More important political issues were stated by Stubbs, 1865, pp. xxxvii–xxxviii.

[50] It was recommended by Pope Alexander III at the time of the canonization, 1173; Robertson VII, 1885, 546.

[51] Gervase, ed. Stubbs, 1879, p. 23; the overt issue was that all the monks had not been convened for the occasion, but it may be they had hoped for a more public ceremony.

[52] Ibid., p. 26.

[53] Foreville, 1958, p. 5, quoted in Robertson, VII, 1885, 581–82.

[54] Gervase, ed. Stubbs, 1879, p. 28.

[55] André Grabar, Martyrium: Recherches sur le culte des reliques et l'art chrétien antique I, Paris, 1946, 467ff.

[56] Brieger, 1957, pp. 6–7.

[57] Boase, 1953, pp. 269, 290.

[58] Stubbs, 1865, p. liv. The inquiry was made of Peter of Blois and William of St. Faith, and the former replied that there was no such intention.

[59] Ibid., pp. xl–xli.

[60] Ibid., p. xcv.

[61] Ibid., pp. ciii–civ.

[62] Ibid., pp. xxix–xxx.

[63] Ibid., pp. xxxviii–xxxix.

[64] For the practice of borrowing in the monasteries, see Boase, 1953, pp. 268–71. By the death of Hubert Walter in 1205 the convent was in debt £653.16.0 (Smith, 1943, p. 18). The earliest accounts, of 1198, show a high de-

there is little evidence that the pilgrims to the tomb brought in significant revenue after hospitality extended to them had been offset.[65] Nonetheless, in 1199 the convent undertook the completion and perfecting of the cathedral church, at the same time conceding to Hubert Walter the disputed offerings.[66] The glazing of the new building must have been envisaged as an important part of this "perfecting."

The question inevitably arises as to how the monks proposed to finance the work. At no time is the foundation of a fraternity recorded, although this was a common practice in the twelfth century.[67] Not until 1219 did Stephen Langton again obtain papal permission to turn over a quarter of the offerings to the renovation of the eastern part of the building, from the time of the translation until it was finished.[68] Indulgences granted to all who attended the translation would only obliquely have affected the financing of this renovation.[69]

The Christ Church accounts are fairly complete for the years 1198–1337, but although they provide much of interest for the historian, they are not detailed enough to show spending on the fabric.[70] In fact, such major expenditures tend to be elusive because the regular incomes allotted to the sacrist for the fabric generally cover only running repairs and minor building projects. An allocation was made by the treasurer in 1221 for the *nova opera*, but after that we lose sight of this money.[71] In 1236 a separate account was kept for the building of the cloister.[72]

Another reason for the absence of accounts may be individual benefactions of works of art; the obit of a Christ Church monk, Richard the Crusader, who had been in exile with the others, credits him with the building of the cloister, and it may be assumed that the acount of 1236 was opened after his death.[73] The martyrology published by Stubbs, however, reveals no donors of glass, although it notes that Archbishop Ralph of Rheims left his glossed Old and New Testaments in 1194 or 1195, and Louis VII of France, who died in 1180, was remembered for his annual gifts made *in perpetuum* to the conventual church.[74] Hubert Walter's benefactions were listed by Gervase, and again there is no mention of glass.[75]

There remains the evidence of the windows themselves. From the analysis of the textual sources in Chapter Eight, it seems that the final program of glazing of the Trinity Chapel was decided, or could have been decided, as early as 1179, after the completion of Benedict's Book IV; *tituli* for use in the glass may have been written then, possibly by Benedict himself. The selection of subjects appears arbitrary from a theological point of view, however, and it is more likely to be accounted for by historical chance. The emphasis put on this most recent book of the miracles, indeed, makes it probable that the program was planned in detail soon after the text was written; by 1220 it would be irrelevant whether events of 1174–1179 or of 1171–1174 were portrayed. Furthermore, the most recent recipients of the saint's mercy would be the most

gree of organization, but loans are put on the credit side (Smith, 1940, p. 354).

[65] C. E. Woodruff, 1932, p. 19. Urry, 1967, p. 36, found that local rents brought more income than offerings at the shrine in many years.

[66] Stubbs, 1865, p. 499, letter 534.

[67] The fraternity for Hackington has already been noted. Rose Graham, "An Appeal of about 1175 for the Building Fund of St. Paul's Cathedral Church," *Journal of the British Archaeological Association* 3rd ser. 10 (1945–1947), 75, claimed St. Paul's as the earliest example of a fraternity in England, but found many examples in France going back to the eleventh century. Among later fraternities were Winchester, 1202; Lincoln, 1205; and Worcester, 1224.

[68] Foreville, 1958, pp. 7, 165.

[69] *Ibid.*, pp. 37ff., 165–66.

[70] See Smith, 1940 and 1943, and C. E. Woodruff, 1932 and 1936. The accounts preserved are synopses of the detailed originals, made for audit. For the sacrist's rolls for the period 1341/42–1474/75, see C. E. Woodruff, 1936; there are a few entries before 1341 in the *Assisa Scaccarii*, including an allowance in 1255 for glaziers; C. E. Woodruff, 1936, pp. 44-45. From 1436 to 1443 and 1471 to ca. 1520, the treasurer's building accounts were separate; Smith, 1943, p. 222.

[71] Smith, 1943, p. 21 and n. 1.

[72] Woodruff, 1936, p. 44.

[73] *Ibid.*, p. 45.

[74] Stubbs, 1865, pp. 557–61, printed extracts from a martyrology of Christ Church. Neither Dr. Urry nor I have been able to trace the manuscript edited by Stubbs.

[75] Gervase, ed. Stubbs, 1880, pp. 413–14.

readily available if an appeal was made for funds for the glazing. Individual contributions sufficient to provide the donor's own story in glass would explain another imbalance in the choice of subjects. Appendix figure 6 records the age of the beneficiary, when it is known. Eight or nine of the total forty-one or forty-two recipients of mercy represented in the glass were children, two more were young people. This is not in itself surprising, but in fact the proportion of child cures described in the texts is less. Children who were cured in the 1170s between the ages of one and ten would have been between twenty and forty in 1200, and it is not unreasonable to suppose that about that time they may have contributed to the glazing. Of the rest, six or seven were monks, nuns, or monastic servants whose houses might have made a contribution. Two others were servants of wealthy men, one of whom had come to the shrine to give thanks.[76] Individual contributions of this sort have parallels at Bourges and Chartres, where many windows are "signed" in the lower corners by representations of the donors.[77] Against this hypothesis is the fact that in only one surviving instance is a name recorded in the Trinity Chapel glass; however, the lowest panels in every window have been destroyed.

The second aspect of the contents of the Trinity Chapel windows, which has frequently been commented upon by other writers, is the representation of the shrine. This appears twice authentically and once in a nineteenth-century restoration. In one scene St. Thomas emerges from the shrine to appear to a sleeping monk; the inscription has gone except for some fragments and the word *feretro*, "shrine" (fig. 164). The scene has usually been in-

terpreted as the vision of either Benedict or William in which they were encouraged to write down the miracles occurring at the tomb. If this interpretation is correct, the shrine is a conscious anachronism on the part of both the artist and the writer of the verse, because the visions occurred before 1173.[78] One might wonder whether some unrecorded vision is represented, perhaps encouraging the construction of the shrine. The other representation is very ordinary: a woman kneels in thanksgiving before it.[79] The inscription is gone. What is curious about these representations is that they are not only broadly similar to each other but also seem to bear some resemblance to the original shrine. As a consequence, it has been supposed that the glass cannot be dated much before 1220, and may be later. In view of the importance of this conclusion, it is worth re-examining the evidence.

The issue has been somewhat confused by an unlabeled marginal sketch made by R. Scarlet in 1599, which was reproduced by Rackham.[80] If this drawing is indeed of the shrine, which was demolished in 1538, it clearly cannot have been made at firsthand.[81] Furthermore, it differs from the only other extant drawing of the shrine; in fact, it looks remarkably like the tomb of Hubert Walter, which is still to be seen on the south side of the Trinity Chapel.[82] The other drawing, now partially destroyed by fire, is in the British Library, Cotton MS Tib. E.VIII, f.269, and is probably a poor copy of an earlier sketch. It shows a large stone base with five arched apertures in the side and three in the end, surmounted by a plain rectangular eaved structure with three prominent finials on the apex of the roof.[83] Perhaps this shows the cover, rather than the more ornate shrine;[84] below is a description

---

[76] Richard Sunieve, a stable boy, was accompanied by his master and mistress in his pilgrimage of thanksgiving to the tomb, as represented in Window n:II(9).

[77] These are generally trade guilds or wealthy individuals; see Delaporte and Houvet, 1926, pp. 6–7.

[78] Window n:III(1). Both accounts are given at the beginning of the texts.

[79] Window s:VII(22). Panel 21 is a modern adaptation of the same scene.

[80] Rackham, 1949, Pl. Bd. See *ibid.*, pp. 21–22, for this manuscript, British Library, Harl. MS 1366.

[81] For the date of the destruction, see J. Wickham Legg and W. H. St. John Hope, *Inventories of Christ Church,*

Canterbury, with Historical and Topographical Introductions and Illustrative Documents, Westminster, 1902, p. 169 and n. 2.

[82] The tomb of Hubert Walter has seven semiattached pilasters and six trefoil arches on the front, instead of six and five as in the drawing. However, the slanted cover has alternate circles and diamonds in relief, with portrait heads, as in the drawing. There is no record of figures other than angels on the shrine.

[83] This drawing has been reproduced many times, e.g., Stanley, 1904, facing p. 222; and Gough Nichols, 1875, facing p. 188.

[84] Comparison with a contemporary drawing of the

which was transcribed before the fire by Stowe and Dugdale. Gough Nichols, with the help of their free transcriptions, reconstructed the original as follows: "All above the stone worke was first of wood, jewells of gold set with stone . . . wrought upon with gold wier. Then agayn with jewells of gold as broch[es, images of angels, and rings] 10 or 12 together, cramped with gold into the ground of gold. The s[poils of which filled two] chests, such as 6 or 8 men could but convay out of the church. At [one side was a stone, with] an angell of gold poyntyng thereunto, offred there by a kinge of France: [which King Henry put] into a ring, and woar it on his thomb."[85] In the glass (fig. 164), the shrine rests on a stone base with arches and columns, which has a more authentic appearance than the base in the Cotton drawing. The sides and top in the glass are decorated with various geometric and vegetal designs, but there is no sign either of a gold angel or of jewels. The chief point of correspondence is the finials: the center one shown in the drawing is known to have been added in 1314, the other two presumably being original.[86] On balance, the resemblance seems close enough for one to suppose that the design of the shrine, if not the shrine itself, was available to the glass painter as a model.

The question then arises, how early was the shrine designed? In 1205 Hubert Walter is recorded as taking up residence at Canterbury to supervise old and new building work, which was interrupted by his death later that year.[87] He was buried on the south side of the Trinity Chapel, under Window s:IV, no doubt in anticipation of the position of the shrine, but whether his tomb was completed by the exile of 1207 is not certain (plan). The shrine was not mentioned until 1216, when a

gold chalice was sold "for the shrine"; its designer, Elias of Dereham, was then in Canterbury, but can only recently have returned from exile.[88] It is possible, however, that Elias had designed the shrine before the exile; he was an associate of Hubert Walter, executor of his will, and custodian of the archbishopric between 1205 and 1207.[89]

In summary, the representations of the shrine appear to me very meager proof of the date of the glass, especially if one has to assume that the windows postdated the translation of 1220.

This historical survey does not serve to indicate any precise dates for the glazing of the building, other than a *terminus post quem* for each part. It has been argued that the choir and eastern transepts may have been glazed when the choir was put into use in 1180, but this will have to be tested by a study of the style and iconography of the windows. Glazing to the east of the wooden partition may have been a very protracted affair; the lack of funds for building in 1183, indicated in Gervase's entry for that year, may have made the quarrels with Baldwin all the more acrimonious. Work would have been halted again in 1188–89, when the monks were imprisoned in their convent, owing to the difficulty of getting materials. It is clear from the terms of agreement with Hubert Walter that work on the cathedral was not finished by 1199. Possibly in those years of peace, from 1199 to 1207, an intensive effort was made to make the building ready for the translation. It is extremely unlikely that this work continued during the exile, when none but the old and infirm were left at Christ Church. The prior of Dover handed over the offerings made during the exile after the monks' return in 1213,[90] but King John never

---

shrine of Edward the Confessor in Westminster was suggested by J. G. O'Neilly and L. E. Tanner, "The Shrine of St. Edward the Confessor," *Archaeologia* 100 (1966), 150–54, Pl. LVIIa and b, fig. 15. I am grateful to Dr. Urry for this reference.

[85] Gough Nichols, 1875, p. 190.

[86] Mason, 1920, p. 111. He did not think that the drawing and the representation in the window could not be reconciled (pp. 107–13).

[87] *Ibid.*, p. 412, and Walter F. Hook, *Lives of the Archbishops of Canterbury*, II, London, 1862, 653.

[88] C. E. Woodruff, 1932, p. 17 and n. 1; Dr. Urry has pointed out to me that the meaning of "vendito ad feretrum" is not clear; it may be to raise funds for the shrine (as Woodruff), or, more probably, an interdepartmental sale for use at the shrine.

[89] Charles R. Young, *Hubert Walter, Lord of Canterbury and Lord of England*, Durham (N.C.), 1968, pp. 61–62, 166.

[90] Barnes and Powell, 1960, p. 38, n. 7.

made other losses good to them, and his handling of their case does not suggest that he allowed any work to continue on the fabric. The translation may again have been delayed to enable the Trinity Chapel to be made ready, but there were other factors, too; Louis of France was campaigning in England in 1216–1217, and Archbishop Langton was away from 1216 till 1218.[91] Finally, after so many delays, it was decided to plan the translation for the fiftieth anniversary year of the martyrdom, on the day of the burial of Henry II, 7 July 1220.[92] This raises again the problem of the appearance of the Trinity Chapel in that year.

If Easter 1180 was an important event for the monks, it had little significance outside Canterbury. The occasion of 7 July 1220 was, however, an important event in the history of the Roman Church; it was regarded as a jubilee, a time of general remission of sins, which was almost without precedent.[93] In England, for the first time in more than fifty years, there was accord between the king, the archbishop, the convent of Christ Church, and the pope. The young King Henry III was present, as were the papal legate, the archbishop of Rheims, and many other illustrious persons.[94] For the occasion—or to commemorate it—the vaults of the Trinity Chapel were painted with representations of saints and English kings, including Henry III, dated in the fourth year of his reign, 1220.[95] Even if attention was centered on the rich gold shrine, it is scarcely credible that this great event took place in a building that was not yet glazed. From 1199 to 1219 or so there had been, in times of peace, a recurrent preoccupation with the completion, "perfecting," and renovation of the cathedral church.

[91] Poole, 1955, pp. 483–86; Powicke, 1929, pp. 128, 134.
[92] As recalled by Langton in his "Tractatus de Translatione Beati Thomae" (ed. Giles, 1845, p. 292). Other reasons are suggested in three sermons written for the feast of the translation, J. A. Giles, ed., *Anecdota Bedae, Lanfranci et Aliorum* (Caxton Society, no. 7), London, 1851, pp. 295–96. July 7 was the date of the return of the monks from exile, and the birth of St. Thomas.
[93] Foreville, 1958, pp. 8, 10–11, 29–32.
[94] *Ibid.*, pp. 8–9.
[95] Caviness, 1974, p. 69.

III. Method of Study: Style and Ornament

"The painters . . . on glass . . . employed intricate patterns, in order to mingle hues beautifully with each other, and make one perfect melody of them all."

John Ruskin[1]

ALL THE internal evidence points to a single atelier operating at Canterbury over an extended period of time. The personnel within this shop changed, and with them the style of the windows, but it is clear that the latest work is directly related to the earliest in a way that suggests the younger painters received much of their training in Canterbury, and were heirs to the model books accumulated by their masters. Within the shop a number of teams seem to have been employed; their work can be distinguished on the basis of composition, ornament, and figure style. A single master was probably responsible for the overall design of a window, just as one artist might design the combination of ornament and figures in an historiated initial or a piece of metalwork; in each there is an interaction between geometric forms, figure compositions, and vegetal ornament.[2] There is abundant evidence at Canterbury that each window was carefully designed as a unit, to achieve harmony of colors, consistent tonality, and compositional balance. Some of the teams, especially in the early period, seem to have consisted essentially of one master, presumably with a number of technical assistants for cutting glass, mixing paint, firing, and leading, and possibly with some painters to help with repetitive elements of ornament; at other times, perhaps when the work was hurried, there were more assistants engaged in executing designs by one master. The continuity of the atelier is attested by the painters who appear first as assistants, and later take over the design and execution of other windows. The unity of the atelier can be

[1] *Lectures on Art Delivered before the University of Oxford in Hilary Term, 1870*, New York, 1874, ¶180.
[2] For the design of manuscript initials, see R. Branner, "The Manerius Signatures," *Art Bulletin* 50 (1968), 183.

argued from the exchange of ideas that seems to have occurred between different teams, and from the presence of a master plan controlling not only the subject matter but also basic elements of design in all parts of the building.[3]

In spite of the unity of the Canterbury productions, and the logic of their development, it is necessary to view them in the broader context of French styles. The work of certain teams or individual designers is very closely connected with developments on the continent. In the absence of any securely dated collections of glass in the period, these comparisons may help to establish a relative chronology. To remind the reader of the nature of the collections to which I most frequently refer, a brief note is given on each.

Comparative material

TROYES, CATHEDRAL OF ST.-PIERRE
(AUBE)

The glass from this cathedral church falls into two basic groups: twelfth-century panels that have been removed and are in scattered collections make up one group, and thirteenth-century glass *in situ* in the eastern parts of the cathedral, the other. The twelfth-century panels have most recently been published by Grodecki.[4] Close examination of several has revealed that they were releaded in the thirteenth century, and some repairs were made then; it is most probable that they came from the earlier building, which was damaged by fire in 1188.[5] Grodecki has indicated that there were at least four windows: a Public Life of Christ, Temptation(s) of Christ, Life and Miracles of St. Nicholas, and Death of the Virgin. The panels are now housed in the Victoria and Albert Museum in London, the Cluny Museum in Paris, the treasury of Troyes Cathedral, the Pitcairn Collection in Pennsylvania, the Martin and Brummer Collections in New York, the Wellesley College Art Museum, and a private collection in Canada. They are all of very small dimensions, and painted in a dis-

tinctive style that is close to manuscript illuminations, particularly to one hand of the Capucines Bible.[6]

The glass presently in the cathedral windows postdates the rebuilding, which began in 1205–1206; the lower chapels date from this campaign, whereas the triforium and clerestory of the choir may belong to the second quarter of the century.[7] The lower windows are thus the only ones that have any interest for Canterbury; most have been dated by Lafond to about 1215–1220.[8] In the axial chapel, dedicated to the Virgin, are two windows with the Life of the Virgin, and two with the Public Life of Christ. A fifth has a typological Infancy cycle, and Lafond has suggested that a Tree of Jesse, now in a chapel on the north side, may have been originally in the sixth window of the Lady Chapel. Lafond has compared these windows in style to the glass of Soissons Cathedral, and one panel at Orbais. The figures are calm and classicizing, with draperies in the *muldenfaltenstil*. The order of panels follows the French norm, from the bottom up, except in the case of the typological window, and one with the Public Life of Christ.

---

[3] Little is known of actual workshop organization in the early Middle Ages before the existence of guilds. Grodecki has concluded that the three ateliers who worked for the Sainte-Chapelle were under an "overseer"; *Corpus, France* I, p. 92. See *Corpus, France* IV–2/1, p. 43 for evidence from the fourteenth century.

[4] Grodecki, 1973.

[5] The documents relating to the fire have been assessed most recently by J. Roserot de Melin, *Bibliographie commentée des sources d'une histoire de la cathédrale de Troyes*, II, Paris, 1970, p. 14. My suggestion of an earlier date for the Troyes glass (1970, n. 223 and p. 190) has

since been confirmed by the evidence for an early restoration that I detected in a panel in Wellesley College Art Museum, and in the Victoria and Albert Museum panels; see M. H. Caviness, "'De Convenientia et Cohaerentia Antiqui et Novi Operis': Medieval Conservation, Restoration, Pastiche and Forgery," in Peter Bloch *et al.*, eds., *Intuition und Kunstwissenschaft: Festschrift für Hanns Swarzenski*, Berlin, 1973, pp. 207–208.

[6] Paris, Bibliothèque Nationale, MS. lat. 16743–46; first investigated by Grodecki, 1963, pp. 137–39.

[7] Grodecki, 1973, p. 201.

[8] Lafond, 1955, p. 31.

Other styles are found in the lateral chapels on the north and south, adjacent to the Lady Chapel; on the north are two windows with the Miracles and Martyrdom of St. Andrew, and on the south two windows with a Life of St. Peter. With the exception of the Martyrdom of St. Andrew window, which is in a rather advanced style and may date from 1235–1240, the others have been grouped by Lafond as developing from the style of the late twelfth-century fragments preserved in Notre-Dame, Paris.

YORK MINSTER

As in the case of Troyes Cathedral, remnants of twelfth-century glass seem to have been preserved during subsequent medieval rebuilding. These early panels may have been in the choir, which was rebuilt by Archbishop Roger of Pont-l'Evêque (1154–1181), but of which only the crypt survives. To the Jesse Tree panel and Daniel in the Lions' Den, noticed by Boase, now in the north nave aisle and the north transept,[9] may be added several panels that were incorporated into the glazing of the chapter house and the clerestory of the nave.[10] These are as yet unpublished, and a study by Peter Newton is awaited. Examination has been possible in the restoration shop; their ultimate destination is undecided. The panels are large and most are square. Subjects include an Emmaus cycle, and scenes from Lives of St. Nicholas and St. Benedict. There are a number of rich border panels.[11]

RHEIMS, ABBEY CHURCH OF ST.-REMI (MARNE)

Abbot Peter of Celles (1162–1181) is known to have remodeled much of the church.[12] Large seated figures in the clerestory of the nave and in the trib-une and clerestory of the choir have been divided by Grodecki into two series; the older figures, which are slightly smaller, may have been made for the small openings of the nave clerestory, in which twelve are still positioned.[13] The other remnants consist of three seated bishops and St. Andrew, now in the tribune. Associated with this early series are six standing figures of kings, also in the tribune, whom Grodecki has identified as Joseph, Eliakim, Jeroboam, Isaac, Abiud, and Matthan or Methuselah; these presumably are from a genealogy of Christ that insisted on royalty. On the basis of the history of the building and the style of these figures, a date of mid-twelfth century has been suggested.

A Crucifixion and Annunciation in the apse of the tribune may be in their place of origin, but they are heavily restored, and much altered. In the nineteenth century the Crucifixion had a white ground, and beneath it were formerly Ecclesia riding a composite animal comprising the Evangelist symbols, and Synagogue. Only the bodies of Christ, Mary, and John are old. The style is not the same as that of the clerestory figures, but Grodecki has placed all in the same campaign, about 1185–1200; this date depends on the new findings of Paillard-Prache, who has concluded that the upper stories of the choir were not completed under Peter of Celles.[14]

In the clerestory of the choir forty of an original sixty-six seated figures have survived, in the triplets on the north and south; the glass from the apse was destroyed in the First World War. There are two figures in each light, the scale adjusted to the triplets. In the first three triplets from the west on the south side, eight of the upper figures are probably well preserved, and eight of the lower ones appear to be partly old; on the north side the greater part of twenty-four figures in the first four bays

---

[9] Boase, 1953, p. 237.

[10] These were noticed by F. Harrison, *The Painted Glass of York*, London, 1927, pp. 9, 36–38, who ascribed to them a thirteenth-century date.

[11] Westlake, I, 1881, Pls. XI, XII. *The Year 1200* I, nos. 222–24.

[12] Three letters from Peter of Celles, dating from 1179/80, speak of the reconstruction of the choir and the ren-

ovation of the nave and portal. See Victor Mortet and Paul Deschamps, *Recueil de textes relatifs à l'histoire de l'architecture*, II, Paris, 1929, 139–40.

[13] Grodecki, 1975, pp. 73–76.

[14] Thesis defended April 15, 1975, at the University of Paris–Sorbonne (Lettres et Civilisations); I am indebted to Louis Grodecki for this information.

may be ancient.[15] In each case an archbishop is placed below an apostle, evangelist, or prophet. The order of the figures has been interfered with, and many of the inscriptions are modern; no weight can therefore be attached to the fact that William of the White Hands does not appear among the archbishops; the glazing may well have been under way during his episcopacy (1175–1202).[16] The head of Abiud is now in the Metropolitan Museum of Art, New York.[17]

The rich ornament of both the tribune and clerestory has been heavily restored; the famous *grisailles* in the tribune may be based in part on old panels.[18] An examination of the clerestory glass revealed a fair quantity of old borders, some panels even in medieval leading, but in all probability these have changed places in the various restorations. The greatest care has been taken to refer only to original designs.

ORBAIS, ABBEY CHURCH OF ST.-PIERRE (MARNE)

The date of beginning the new building, from the east, has been given by Frankl and others as about 1200.[19] It was evidently a protracted affair; the lower chapels, with small round-headed lights, appear considerably older than the clerestory, which has triplets in the transepts and adjacent bay to the east, but the Chartrain doublet and rose in the apse. The building seems never to have been completed beyond the transept.

Surviving glass falls into three groups. Most frequently referred to is the east window of the axial chapel, with a typological Crucifixion; this has

been dated by Grodecki about 1210–1215 and by Deuchler about 1210.[20] The upper two-thirds of the window is intact.

Lafond and Grodecki have drawn attention to another Crucifixion, with Ecclesia and Synagogue, now over the porch in the south transept.[21] The style is close to that of Soissons, the date probably about 1220.

Fragments in the clerestory are unpublished, but seem to have included bishops as well as the Virgin and Christ, two figures in each light.[22] They are not in the style of the later Crucifixion, and further study will be necessary for dating.

SOISSONS CATHEDRAL (AISNE)

The choir of the Gothic cathedral was put into use in 1212, according to an inscription. The central window was glazed by Philippe Auguste before 1224; only parts of the original glazing of the upper windows of the choir remain, including one fragment of the Jesse Tree and a Creation cycle.[23] The Virgin from the Jesse was destroyed in the Berlin museums during the Second World War, but another panel is in the Pitcairn Collection in Pennsylvania. From the lower chapel windows, panels with a Life of Sts. Nicaise and Eutropia are now in the Louvre and in the Isabella Stewart Gardner Museum in Boston; others treating Sts. Crispin and Crispinian, and Blaise, are in the Marmottan Museum in Paris.[24] All are in a very refined and distinctive style, with *muldenfaltenstil* drapery, which Grodecki has associated with Laon and St.-Quentin.

---

[15] My own examinations, made from the exterior passage in 1971 and 1973, have shown that several of the figures previously accepted as ancient are entirely modern (cf. Grodecki, 1975, p. 66, where he referred to forty-eight figures). It remains to reveal the extent of restoration in the forty that are essentially ancient.

[16] Cf. W. M. Hinckle, "The Clerestory Windows in the Apse and Choir of Saint-Remi, Reims," *The Portal of the Saints of Reims Cathedral*, New York, 1965, Appendix G, n.p.

[17] *The Year 1200* I, no. 202.

[18] Grodecki, 1975, p. 70. A related panel is in the Cloisters collection; see "Stained Glass Windows," *The Metropolitan Museum of Art Bulletin* 30 (1971), n.p.

[19] Paul Frankl, *Gothic Architecture*, Harmondsworth and Baltimore, 1962, p. 86. The date, which seems to be concluded from the presence of Chartrain features, might be moved back for the construction of the chapels.

[20] *Vitrail*, p. 117; Deuchler, 1967, p. 157.

[21] Lafond, 1955, p. 36; *Vitrail*, p. 18.

[22] The Virgin and Child and Christ are seated, but the other fragments may not belong to the same program.

[23] *Vitrail*, p. 123.

[24] Louis Grodecki, "Les Vitraux soissonnais du Louvre, du Musée Marmottan et des collections américaines," *La Revue des Arts* 10 (1960), 163–78.

Now included in the choir windows on the north side are four seated figures which may have come from St.-Yved of Braisne; identified by inscriptions as Cainan, Amminadab, Salathiel, and Jeconiah, they evidently belonged to a genealogy of Christ.[25] More attenuated than the Jesse figures, their style associates them with a Canterbury clerestory window of ca. 1190. Related figures are in the Walters Art Gallery in Baltimore and the City Art Museum of St. Louis.

ST.-QUENTIN, COLLEGIATE CHURCH
(AISNE)

The rebuilding of the chapels was begun about 1212. In 1220 a chantry was founded in one of the south chapels, and in 1229 relics were translated.[26] The surviving glass of thirteenth-century date forms two groups, the later of which—in the choir clerestory—does not concern us.[27] In the axial chapel of Our Lady are seven narrow lancets, the center three of which retain much glass of about 1225 or later. On the left is a typological early Life of Christ, which reads from the top. It is matched on the right by a window with identical armature in which the Life of the Virgin is represented, reading upwards. The center window has an armature that describes fan shapes, in which twelve upper panels are ancient; some certainly belong to a Life of St. Stephen, but the order has been altered and the lower six panels are modern. I was fortunate to be able to examine these windows from exterior scaffolding in 1973.

SENS, CATHEDRAL OF ST.-ETIENNE
(YONNE)

The ambulatory wall is thought to have been begun about 1140. There was a consecration in 1163. Accepted opinion that an axial chapel of horseshoe plan was part of the twelfth-century building has been questioned by Severens; the present structure dates from ca. 1240.[28] The glass is essentially of two periods, but panels have been mixed in the axial chapel during some restoration. Important original remains are in the ambulatory and in the clerestory of the choir. The upper levels were clearly not completed in their present form until well into the thirteenth century, and this later glazing does not concern us.

The principal early glass is *in situ* in the four windows of the north ambulatory. From the east the subjects, which read variously up or down, are the Parable of the Good Samaritan, the Parable of the Prodigal Son, the Life of St. Eustace, and the later Life of Thomas Becket.[29] The glass has generally been dated after a fire in 1184, which may have damaged the cathedral fabric. Recently assigned dates are in the thirteenth century: Grodecki puts the group before 1225; Sulkis envisages a period of glazing from about 1209 to about 1220.[30] The windows appear moderately well preserved, with the exception of the lower third of the St. Eustace window. The glass was in medieval leads until quite recent times, which may account for the few breakages.[31]

The glass at present in the axial chapel is chiefly later, but the date of 1230 or so assigned by Grodecki to the Lives of Sts. Peter and Paul and Savinian is too early for the present structure. Miscellaneous fragments have been added in restoration, including two well-preserved scenes from the St. Eustace window.[32]

CHARTRES, CATHEDRAL OF NOTRE-DAME
(EURE-ET-LOIR)

This collection is so well known that only a few comments are necessary; as an ensemble it is one of the best preserved of Gothic glazing programs.

[25] I am grateful to Mademoiselle Jeanne Vinsot for this information. The removal of glass from St.-Yved is mentioned by Fleury, 1882, pp. 123–24.

[26] P. Héliot, "Chronologie de la basilique de Saint-Quentin," *Bulletin monumental* 117 (1959), 10, 27–32.

[27] *Vitrail*, p. 123; the other group is described by Grodecki, 1965, and Fleury, 1882, pp. 125–32.

[28] Kenneth W. Severens, "The Early Campaign at Sens, 1140–1145," *Journal of the Society of Architectural Historians* 29 (1970), pp. 98ff.

[29] The clearest description is still that of Lucien Bégule, *La Cathédrale de Sens*, Paris, 1929, pp. 43–74.

[30] *Vitrail*, p. 139; Sulkis, 1964, p. 116.

[31] Jean Lafond, *Le Vitrail*, Paris, 1966, p. 106, n. 24.

[32] Madame Françoise Perrot was kind enough to point this out to me.

Points of comparison with Canterbury have been found only in the nave windows of the aisles and clerestory, including the west rose, and one window in the north transept adjacent to the nave. The best description is still that of Delaporte, and the photographs taken by Houvet have only just been replaced by Fiévet for the Monuments Historiques.[33]

The nave includes, on the south side from the west, windows with the stories of John the Evangelist, Mary Magdalen, the Good Samaritan, the Dormition of the Virgin, and the Miracles of the Virgin. On the north are the stories of the Flood, St. Lubin, St. Eustace, Joseph, St. Nicholas, and the Redemption, with the Parable of the Prodigal Son in the transept. Of these, Grodecki has grouped together the Flood, and the Lives of Sts. Lubin and Nicholas, and associated them with the Master of the Redemption Window at Bourges.[34] The St. Eustace window he has attributed to the master of the two lateral windows in St.-Quentin.[35]

The west rose has a Last Judgment; its style is close to that of the Joseph Master in the nave. The clerestory on the south side has standing figures of saints and apostles, while on the north a similar disposition is varied in five of the fourteen lancets by seated figures, from two to six in a window, including three prophets. A fifth lancet has Abraham preparing to sacrifice Isaac.

The most frequently accepted date for the glazing of the nave aisle windows is 1200–1210/15; the transepts and choir would be later.[36] This chronology has, however, been questioned in recent times.[37]

The part played by composition and ornament in the Canterbury windows

---

THE Canterbury windows are some of the most richly ornate to have been preserved as a series. In spite of considerable individual variation, they maintain a consistent decorative level, so that even those that are relatively lacking in color have a rich brilliance. The light is broken up by small patterns, much as silver may be enlivened with repoussé, or gold leaf by punched tooling.[38]

The composition of a window is controlled by the iron armature; ornament includes the border, the areas between the figure compositions, and the edging lines of medallions. Ornament between the figure subjects generally fills concave-shaped "negative" areas, whereas the figures are in convex, expanding shapes. A strict division between ornament and figure compositions is not always apparent, however, as in Window n:IV of the Trinity Chapel ambulatory, in which all the blue grounds have delicate tendrils picked out from a grey wash, and aediculae are so schematized as to resemble decorative frames rather than buildings (Col. Pl. III and fig. 159).

In tracing atelier traditions, ornament is often more useful than figure compositions and style. Ornamental motifs tend to be very long-lived; their execution is less idiosyncratic than is that of the figures, but at the same time they are less responsive to a "model." Links that can be proved by the use of similar ornament may also have a bearing on the transmission of styles. But here a *caveat* is necessary, because patterns may equally be passed from one shop to another without significant stylistic exchange.[39] Some of the border designs in use in the thirteenth century are derived from motifs already current in the middle of the twelfth, and it is the changed style of execution rather than the similarity of motif that is significant. Not only motifs, therefore, but also their style of execution and the total decorative effect of the windows deserve to be considered, in conjunction

---

[33] Delaporte and Houvet, 1926, pp. 160–95, 381–411.

[34] *Vitrail*, p. 139 and 1948.

[35] Grodecki, 1965.

[36] *Vitrail*, p. 124.

[37] Frankl, 1963; Jan van der Meulen, "Histoire de la construction de la cathédrale Notre-Dame de Chartres après 1194," *Bulletin de la Société archéologique d'Eure et Loir* 23 (1965), 81–126.

[38] Johnson, 1965, p. 65, Pl. 10. Mojmir Frinta, "Punchmarks in the Ingeborg Psalter," *The Year 1200* III, 1975.

[39] Read, 1926, p. 38.

with the style of the figure compositions, for the bearing they have on authorship, and on links with other glass or with works in other media. Some general remarks about contemporary trends will be useful first, since there are few recent publications that deal satisfactorily with ornament.

The first stage in planning a window was to determine the pattern of the armature. The stone masons either left the windows void or boarded them up temporarily. Before the glass could be assembled panel by panel, a wooden frame was recessed into the stonework, and the ends of iron bars were riveted to it.[40] Broad trends in the design of armatures in the hundred years from about 1150 to 1250 are easy to define, but they do not provide a means of close dating, or even a chronology except in the work of one shop. Ironwork, like other aspects of style, is a more sure indication of the aesthetic of an individual designer than of the date of a window.[41]

At the beginning of this period armatures were generally rectilinear, usually containing square and inscribed circular compositions in alternation. In clerestory windows it was customary to paint large figures that the viewer could discern from a distance; at Augsburg before 1150,[42] and later in St.-Remi of Rheims, and in the choir and eastern transepts of Canterbury Cathedral, such large figures are cut across by a minimal number of straight bars, which are purely supporting elements without decorative value. In lower windows the panels are smaller. Their size was determined by the number of scenes required by the subject matter rather than by structural factors. The decorative potential of ironwork was fully realized when large typological or narrative windows became popular, for which complex geometric structures were designed. By 1200 the armature had begun to assume considerable aesthetic interest, which can be linked historically with an increasing knowl-

edge of Euclidian geometry.[43] Regardless of this development, however, straight bars were still *de rigueur* for some subjects, such as the Tree of Jesse. Furthermore, at Angers between 1155 and 1180 a system combining straight bars and complex geometric figures panels was used, as also at Poitiers in some windows of about 1215.[44] This compositional method developed together with the curved-bar armature, and both are seen in the thirteenth-century windows of Chartres and Bourges. The same shapes may be provided for the figure subjects by either method, as can be demonstrated in two Chartres windows (text fig. 3). In Window

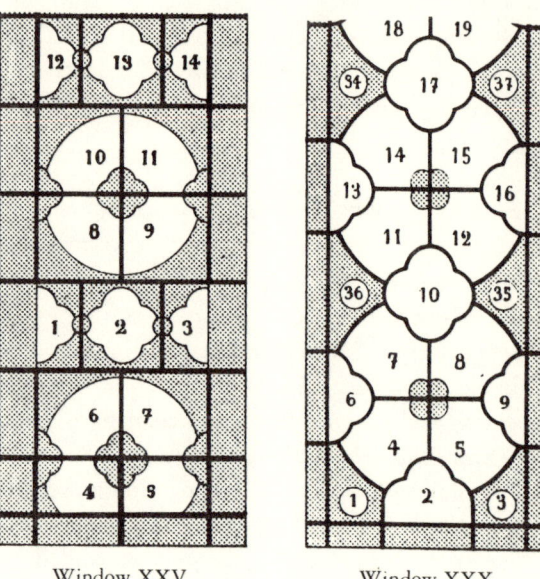

Window XXV   Window XXX

Text fig. 3. Armatures of Chartres windows
(after Delaporte and Houvet)

XXX the irons provide firm accents, which reinforce the decorative bands defining pictorial subjects. Their intersections form a closely knit geometry. In Window XXV the figure panels are largely defined by decorative bands alone. Though the variety afforded by the curved bar gives a far more

---

[40] At Canterbury the wooden frames as well as the irons are said to be the originals. Since the irons do not slot into the stonework in this period, the building date is not necessarily that of the window design.

[41] Cf. Frankl, 1963, pp. 302–303, and criticism by Louis Grodecki, "Chronique," *Bulletin monumental* 122 (1964), 99–103.

[42] See Grodecki in *Vitrail*, p. 96; and Wentzel, 1954, pp. 15–16, Pls. 1 & 1–6 (dated ca. 1130–1140).

[43] Haskins, 1927, pp. 286–87, 311.

[44] For Angers, see *Vitrail*, fig. 72, and Hayward and Grodecki, 1966, p. 13, numerous illustrations. For Poitiers, see Grodecki, 1948, Pl. 18g–l, and comments pp. 90-93.

lavish appearance than does the easily constructed straight bar, curved bars virtually disappear after about 1250, probably in part for reasons of economy.

During the same period, 1150–1250, the ornament becomes progressively less rich in design and coloring. Wide borders, rosettes, and luxuriant vegetal motifs fill large areas of the windows of St.-Denis, Angers, and St.-Remi of Rheims, painted before the turn of the century. The iconographic repertory was then comparatively restricted and, in spite of the relatively small windows of early Gothic buildings, all the available space was not used for figure compositions. In the thirteenth century, increasingly less space and effort were given to ornament. Borders became narrower, and were rather dryly and mechanically executed. The areas between figured panels were filled with geometric patterns, often in red, white, and blue glass with a minimum of painting (misleadingly called "mosaic" grounds since the nineteenth century),[45] instead of vegetal scrolls (rinceaux) and rosettes. The Sainte-Chapelle of Paris, glazed about 1243–1248, and much of the thirteenth-century glass of Chartres represent the later trend. Elaborate ornament came back in grisaille windows in the second half of the century, and soon after 1300 stereotyped acanthus foliage was replaced by vigorous natural forms.

The development of ornament in Gothic windows, as also to some extent the development of a "Gothic" figure style, was influenced by stained glass techniques;[46] as windows grew larger and more numerous in the new cathedrals, it became necessary to develop more rapid techniques of glazing. Ornament such as that in Window n:XIV of the north choir aisle at Canterbury must have been extremely time-consuming to execute; the glass was painted on both sides to give full body

to the vine leaves in the border (fig. 2). Interlaced stems here and in Window n:XV meant the cutting and leading of many small pieces, an arduous and skilled job; a single element in the repeating border design of Window n:XV contains twenty-seven pieces of seventeen different shapes (fig. 1). Such designs were therefore progressively modified by simplification and to some extent, at least within a group of related windows, this provides a basis for chronology. Modifications of this sort occur in the corona and Trinity Chapel glass, as also at Sens and Chartres. The most economical designs used areas of color no larger than the normal size of a "muff," in the thirteenth century perhaps about five by eight or nine inches. To avoid leadlines that crossed the ground and thus were not part of the design, motifs had to be spaced at intervals of a few inches, as if from horror vacui. Motifs that overlapped were therefore discarded in favor of motifs that spread over the surface as space-filling elements. This development is quite clear from a comparison of the borders in Window n:XIV of the north choir aisle and Window s:II of the Trinity Chapel ambulatory at Canterbury (figs. 2, 174). In Window s:II, however, organic motifs are not only spread out and flattened into a single plane, but there is also a degree of distortion or abstraction; plant growth is in two or more directions, responding to the available space rather than to natural law. At the same time, plant species are no longer recognizable. The economy of this border is remarkable; thirteen pieces per unit of design have been cut from five patterns. The border of the east window of the corona is comparable, with twenty-four pieces per unit cut from six patterns. It is not surprising that a design so economical and pleasing had considerable success, being used also at Bourges, Chartres, Troyes, and Auxerre.[47]

---

[45] Winston, I, 1847, 33, used "mosaic." "Diaper mosaic" or "geometrical diaper," as used by Lafond, 1946, p. 150, are more accurate, since the glass is usually painted.

[46] Grodecki, 1955, p. 619.

[47] For the Joseph Window in Bourges Cathedral, see Cahier and Martin, 1841, Mosaiques C; comparison with Canterbury was made by Westlake, I, 1881, Pl. LXIIIA and b. At Chartres this type of border was used in the

Death of the Virgin Window in the south nave aisle, and in a clerestory window on the north side (Delaporte and Houvet, 1926, Window VII, Pl. XXII and Col. Pl. III; and Window CLXII, Pl. CCLXVII). Another variant is in the window with Miracles of St. Andrew in Troyes Cathedral; the relation to Canterbury was noticed by Lafond, 1955, p. 31. For the example at Auxerre, I am indebted to Virginia Raguin.

Other coincidences indicate a shared repertory of forms with Chartres and Bourges, in windows which must be approximately contemporary with the Trinity Chapel glazing, though few of them go beyond superficial resemblances.[48] Some broad distinctions from these two monuments can be made. Canterbury used curved-bar armatures in lower windows of this period, to the exclusion of the other type. On the other hand, the simple quatrefoil found at Chartres and Bourges[49] does not appear in the early or middle groups of windows at Canterbury, except inscribed in a circle in the choir aisle "triforium." Tiers of roundels, such as those in Windows n:IV and s:II of the Trinity Chapel, were not used at Chartres, though they were at Bourges and Laon.[50] Although this has the appearance of a very simple "early" form, it cannot support an earlier dating than Chartres, since it is used in the Sainte-Chapelle as late as 1243–1248.[51]

Grodecki has recognized a conservative character in the glass of several monuments in the region to the northeast of Paris, including Canterbury.[52] Chartres, as he has indicated, provides a meeting of several regional styles.[53] The St.-Eustace Window has wide, rich borders, *rinceaux* with fleshy acanthus, and intricately painted edging lines around the scenes, which link it with the northeasterly group. The Prodigal Son Window has affinities with Laon.[54] The Joseph Window, on the north side of the nave next to the St.-Eustace Window, has to be associated with Sens, and is also closest of all the Chartrain windows to the most

easterly of the Trinity Chapel windows at Canterbury.[55] Included in the same general "Channel school" group with Canterbury are Rheims, St.-Quentin, Troyes, Orbais, Châlons-sur-Marne, Laon, and Soissons, as well as Sens. Peculiar to most glass in this regional group is lavish ornament, especially in fleshy acanthus; *rinceaux* are preferred to "mosaic" grounds. Red, which is sparingly used in the figures, is concentrated in the grounds of borders and *rinceaux*, making these ornamental areas extraordinarily brilliant. Beaded edging lines to both borders and medallions add a scintillating effect; the cumulative impact of the finely executed detail of the ornament is to create a highly wrought surface resembling jeweled or enameled inlay. The affinity with metalwork is to be expected in a region bordering on the Meuse.

The glass of these several monuments provides examples that are well distributed throughout the period, from about 1150 at Châlons to perhaps as late as 1220 at Soissons.[56] In both ornament and figure style, however, there are individual variations that preclude any theory of linear development and point to the existence of subgroups. Thus *grisaille*, which is highly developed in the tribune of St.-Remi of Rheims and in some of the windows at Soissons, is not prominent at Canterbury.[57] In borders at St.-Remi and Soissons palmettes are most often placed sideways, whereas at Sens and Canterbury borders are generally conceived as a continuous plant growth up the sides of the window, sometimes with strapwork providing a kind of trellis, sometimes supported on their own white

[48] Westlake, I, 1881, p. 108, compared the composition of Trinity Chapel n:III with the Joseph Window at Chartres; he may have meant the St. Nicholas Window, LX, or the St. Thomas the Apostle Window, XLVI (see Delaporte and Houvet, 1926, pp. 391–94, Pls. CLVIII–CLXI and pp. 357–63, Pls. CXXXVI–CXXXIX). Cf. also the armature of the Relics of St. Stephen Window in Bourges, *Vitrail*, fig. 105.

[49] For examples in the south nave aisle of Chartres, see Delaporte and Houvet, 1926, Window IV, pp. 160–64, Pls. X–XIII; Window VI, pp. 168–70, Pls. XVII–XXI; Window VII, pp. 171–76, Pls. XXII–XXV. For Bourges, see *Vitrail*, Pl. VI.

[50] For the Passion Window in Bourges, see Grodecki, 1948, Pl. 18b; for Laon, the lateral windows in the east end of the choir, dated about 1200–1205, see Deuchler, 1967, pp. 150, 157, and 264, figs. 210, 240–44.

[51] *Corpus, France* I, Baie D, plan facing p. 74.

[52] Grodecki, 1965, p. 178.

[53] *Ibid.*, pp. 171–72.

[54] *Ibid.*, p. 178 n. 28.

[55] Delaporte and Houvet, 1926, Window LXI, Pls. CLXII–CLXVI. Frankl, 1963, p. 316, has already attributed the Joseph Window to the painter of the Prodigal Son Window in Sens.

[56] Grodecki, *Vitrail*, pp. 107–108, 117–24.

[57] For St.-Remi and Soissons, see Cahier and Martin, 1841, Mosaiques F. For the impact of St.-Remi, Meredith Lillich, "The Band Window: A Theory of Origin and Development," *Gesta* 9 (1970), 28. One *grisaille* panel, of unknown provenance, is now in the crypt at Canterbury; see B. Rackham in *C.C.C.* 33 (1939), 28–29, illus. facing p. 34.

interlaced stems. Exceptions at Canterbury are restricted to one group of windows, and where the
Soissons–St.-Remi type occurs, it may be under the
influence of one or other of those monuments.
However, as with the *grisaille*, Canterbury rejected a type of border common at St.-Remi, consisting of nearly abstract geometric designs. There
is a basic distinction here. All the St.-Remi border
designs, heterogeneous though they appear at first
sight, could be derived from late twelfth-century
metalwork,[58] whereas the Canterbury foliage,
whether climbing or "sideways" shoots, shares a
vocabulary in common with some mid-century
manuscript borders. Canterbury could not have derived its vigorous plant growth from St.-Remi. But
if Canterbury did not adopt the full repertory of
ornament used at St.-Remi, it is equally true that
St.-Remi did not develop armature design; all the
extant windows have straight bars, those in the
clerestory being strictly comparable to the more
westerly of the Canterbury windows. At St.-Quen-
tin, Laon, Orbais, and Sens are armatures comparable to the more evolved types used elsewhere at
Canterbury.

Canterbury alone of the monuments of this regional group spans the full development from
Romanesque to Gothic, and provides an opportunity to trace, step by step, the changes in composition and ornament, as well as in figure style, that
took place in the period. The ornament progresses
in a far more linear way than the figure styles: in
the figures there are experiments that are multi-
directional and that do not lend themselves to
chronological ordering, whereas ornamental features such as the *rinceaux* establish in the clearest
possible way the continuity of development from
a late Romanesque classicizing trend to its complete reversal in Gothic (figs. 179–184). For the
sake of clarity, and chiefly in response to the figure styles, the glass has been divided into three
periods, early, middle, and late. The extent to
which there is overlapping and shading off between these periods should be stressed. The most
complete break in the development occurs near the
end of the glazing, about midpoint in the Trinity
Chapel, but if the ambulatory windows of Sens are
inserted here, they bridge this gap with astonishing
completeness.

General stylistic background

THE manuscripts produced in Canterbury in the
latter half of the twelfth century are very few;
after the Eadwine Psalter and the Dover Bible of
mid-century, there is only one richly illustrated
book preserved from Christ Church—the third
copy of the Utrecht Psalter.[59] On the basis of this
evidence Dodwell has referred to a "decline in artistic activites." This has been attributed to two factors, the preoccupation of the monastic community
with ecclesiastical and political disputes in the pe-

riod after 1180, and the general phenomenon of
intellectual decline in the monasteries.[60] Yet much
of the glass must have been painted between 1180
and about 1220. The fact that glass painting was
then the chief artistic activity of Christ Church may
account for the decline in manuscript production.
That decline was at first only quantitative; there is
no falling off in quality until the thirteenth-century Psalter.[61]

The glass of Canterbury cannot be understood in

[58] For examples see: Fritz Witte, *Tausand Jahre deutscher Kunst am Rhein*, I, Berlin, 1932, Pls. 51 (Shrine of St. Aetherius, ca. 1170), 57 (Shrine of Innocent and Mauritius, ca. 1185); 64, 67 (Three Kings Shrine), and 60 (Shrine of St. Albinus, 1186).

[59] Paris, Bibliothèque Nationale, MS Lat. 8846; the illustrations are reproduced in *Psautier*. See also Dodwell, 1954, pp. 98–100, who dated it in the period 1170–1200 on the basis of script and illustrations. The most recent discussion is by Adelheid Heimann, *The Year 1200* I, no.

257, pp. 257–59, with bibliography, and *The Year 1200* III, 1975, pp. 313–38.

[60] Dodwell, 1954, pp. 112–13.

[61] Paris, Bibliothèque Nationale, MS Lat. 770; dated on the basis of the calendar about 1220 by Francis A. Gasquet and Edmund Bishop, *The Bosworth Psalter*, London, 1908, pp. 68–69. A description of the miniatures is in V. Leroquais, *Les Psautiers manuscrits latins des biblio-
thèques publiques de la France*, II, Paris, 1940–1941, pp. 52–54.

relation only to the differences of style between the Dover Bible, the Great Canterbury Psalter, and the Little Canterbury Psalter. In the early windows there is also an intimate relationship to the Winchester Bible styles, which widens the base of comparison. More importantly, as suggested in the Introduction, the glass has always been at the center of the Anglo-French debate. The glazing was carried on, at least in part, in the crucial period between Abbot Suger's glass at St.-Denis and the rebuilding of Chartres Cathedral after the fire of 1194;[62] this is the great period of Châlons-sur-Marne, St.-Remi of Rheims, and the earliest glass of Notre-Dame of Paris.

The immediate background of the first styles in the glass cannot be completely explored; there is no glass of earlier or related style preserved in the south of England. The earlier choir of Christ Church, built under Anselm and Priors Ernulf and Conrad, and consecrated in 1130, was renowned for the brilliancy of its windows, according to William of Malmesbury;[63] some of these same windows appeared small and dark to Gervase fifty years later.[64] Whether there was any mid-century glazing which might have been influenced by St.-Denis cannot be proved, but iconographic influences that appear in York in glass painted during the archiepiscopacy of Roger of Pont-l'Evêque (1154–1181) might have filtered through Canterbury in the 1140s and 1150s, when Roger was there as one of Theobald's clerks.[65] Yet the glass of York, which may at present be dated around 1170–1180, scarcely appears as a precursor of the Canterbury glass of a decade later. There is far greater emphasis on linear organization of drapery folds than at Canterbury, and little back-painting to give depth. The York glass, though damaged, is of very high quality; but it stands in relation to Canterbury as a separate branch or peak. One has to look at other

media for the origins of the Canterbury styles. Even so, the training of at least one master remains just as obscure as that of his contemporary, Nicholas of Verdun; it is impossible to derive the style of a singular genius from his general milieu.

Recognition can be given to a number of distinctive hands working at Canterbury, yet the final decision as to how many personal styles there are is a difficult one; personal style was a less conscious, and therefore a less consistent, feature in medieval art than in the art of the Renaissance or the present. Furthermore, style, though a legitimate dimension of medieval art, has to be treated with caution in making chronological judgments, because it interacts in a very complex way with other factors, such as subject matter. It is sometimes preferable to speak of a difference of mode, rather than a difference of style; modes that are distinct from each other may be contemporary, or may even be present in the work of the same painter. Models played a very important role, not only in determining the iconography of a scene but also, in varying degrees, in influencing style.[66] The biblical subjects in the Canterbury windows, in the north choir aisle and corona, surely had models that go back well into the twelfth century, and some long before, whereas the hagiographical scenes in the Trinity Chapel must have been of more recent origin; there cannot have been an iconographical guide prior to the completion of the texts in 1179. The two modes, biblical and historical or hagiographical, tended to coincide with two stylistic poles around 1200, the one looking back to Romanesque, the other already Gothic in sentiment. It was in the invention of scenes from recent history that the artist had greatest freedom to develop a new style. Works of this type may sometimes appear precocious,[67] and they also tend to be international in style; recensions of saints' lives can

---

[62] As suggested by Henri Gérente as early as 1846, quoted by Rackham, 1949, p. 20.

[63] William of Malmesbury, 1870, p. 138. This often-quoted passage may be translated: "Nothing comparable was to be seen in England, either for the brilliancy of the glass windows, the splendor of the marble pavement, or the ceiling with colored pictures." See also Boase, 1953, p. 32.

[64] Ed. Stubbs, 1879, p. 12, "Super quos [pilarios] murus solidus parvulis et obscuris distinctus erat fenestris," which

may be translated, "Above which piers the solid wall was interrupted by very small dark windows." One of these windows is preserved, walled into the present triforium roof at the extreme northwest end of the choir.

[65] Boase, 1953, p. 234. See also Knowles, 1951, pp. 12–14.

[66] Kitzinger, "Norman Sicily," 1966, pp. 130ff.

[67] For example, the earliest preserved recension of the *Topographia Hibernica* of Gerald of Wales, London, British Library, MS Royal 13.B.viii, from St. Augustine's, Canterbury, which must date soon after 1188; see Boase,

be supposed to have been very quickly disseminated, since hagiographical collections were rapidly increasing in popularity.[68] One may even wonder if there were not itinerant artists who specialized in designing hagiographical subjects; at a later time, at least, one can cite Matthew Paris's atelier, specializing in secular and hagiographical narrative cycles, and W. de Brailes, in biblical subjects.[69] The style groupings of the early part of the thirteenth century coincide to some extent with these divisions; among Psalters and Bibles there are homogeneous groups that have little relevance to the place of ownership of the books. Similarly, there are stronger connections between the Life of Cuthbert, which was in all probability made at Durham, and the Canterbury, Sens, and Chartres hagiographical windows, than exist between the Trinity Chapel glass and the two extant Christ Church Psalters or a Canterbury Bible of 1224–1253.[70]

There has been no detailed study of the styles of the Canterbury windows; although the various groups of windows have frequently been referred to in general publications, the relationships of one painter to another, or of the Canterbury artists to those working elsewhere, have not been defined.[71] The comparative chronology proposed by Rackham is largely confirmed in this study, with some slight refinements.[72] The development of style is very clear if a subject from one of the typological windows of the northeast transept is compared with one from the more easterly of the Trinity Chapel ambulatory windows (figs. 89, 92). In the ornament certain motifs were repeated or imitated until they became rather dry and impoverished; the process is not unlike the gradual "decline" of

sculpture in the Early Christian period. It would be mistaken, however, to characterize the later masters at Canterbury as mere imitators.[73] The process of flattening and stretching forms may be, as Grodecki has suggested, a response to the specific needs of the glazier.[74] By insisting only on essentials, the artist is able to evoke far more, as comparison between the Sower from the transept and Wiliam of Kellett Returning to Work in the Trinity Chapel shows. The early master built up his landscape setting very painstakingly, with sweeping hills, rocks, pasture and ploughed land, and a tree; overlapping of these elements implies spatial recession. In a panel of similar size the Trinity Chapel painter presents, with great clarity, a man striding out of the city to work in the forest. There are no distant hills, the groundline is kept low. A single tree, which stands for a forest, and the city walls are spread out as space-fillers on either side. Full representation is eschewed by the Gothic glass painter. More important than the loss of classicism is a new positive stylistic force—rapid, shorthand, expressive, and eminently suited to hagiography.

The clerestory figures can legitimately be used to establish a chronology of style; all illustrate the same theme, the genealogy of Christ, so there is no necessity for the artists to introduce new modes. More than half the figures survive, and although losses are great from the south side, especially from the choir, there are enough to corroborate the west to east chronology, which is apparent in figures from the north. Three well-defined stylistic phases are represented. The first, in figures from the choir, corresponds with a "dynamic" late Romanesque phase;[75] these figures are massive, powerful, and

---

1953, p. 197, Pl. 31e, and Gransden, 1972, pp. 48–49, figs. 2 & 3.

[68] Wormald, 1952–1953, pp. 249, 261–62.

[69] For lists of attributed works see Rickert, 1965, pp. 104–105, 108–10, and Brieger, 1957, pp. 86–91 and 136–54.

[70] Paris, Bibliothèque Nationale, MSS Lat. 8846 and Lat. 770. The latter is datable before 1220; see Wormald, 1939, I, p. 64. I am grateful to Dr. Plummer of the Pierpont Morgan Library for bringing this manuscript to my attention. The third manuscript is the Bible of Robert de Bello, abbot of St. Augustine's (1224–1253), London, British Library, Burney MS 3, which has been discussed and illustrated by Brieger, 1957, pp. 81–82, Pl. 21a and c,

and by Rickert, 1965, p. 103, Pl. 100. Its relation to the Christ Church glazing was discussed by Rackham, 1950, p. 357, and by Grodecki, 1951, p. 94.

[71] Such a study was called for by Oakeshott, 1951, p. 88.

[72] Rackham, 1949, pp. 15–17.

[73] Caviness, 1965, pp. 194, 196.

[74] Grodecki, 1955, p. 619.

[75] A "dynamic" or "baroque" style in Byzantine art of the second half of the twelfth century, with Western parallels, has been discussed by Kitzinger, "Norman Sicily," 1966, p. 137, and "Byzantine Contribution," 1966, pp. 40–41.

restless or even agitated (figs. 6, 8, 9, 12, 13). The second phase reaches its peak in figures from the north side of the Trinity Chapel, above the pilgrim steps; Amminadàb and Nahshon are calm, quietly outlined, and have a higher degree of classical poise but less physical power (figs. 151, 152). This is a "proto-Gothic" classicizing style, corresponding to the brief transitional phase which has come to be associated, too rigidly, with the "year 1200."[76] Figures from the easternmost Trinity Chapel clerestory windows are again active and restless, yet they differ in all other respects from the "dynamic" group; pose and gesture are elegant, draperies fall in ornamental passages that prevent an apprehension of the body or limbs underlying them (figs. 216, 217). These figures are truly Gothic, in the same way that the illustrations of Matthew Paris's *Chronicles* of the middle of the thirteenth century are Gothic.[77]

When the three phases are as clearly differenti-

ated as this, it seems that each style did not grow out of the previous one, but actually ran counter to it. A modern bias might give rise to the assumption that they were the creation of three successive and rebellious generations of artists. This is not borne out by close study; at least one of the painters changed his style, from the "dynamic" figures of prophets in the north oculus to the classicizing King and Virgin of the Jesse Tree in the corona (figs. 129–31, 133, 134). There is a certain arbitrariness, therefore, in assigning such a painter to the middle rather than to the early period.

In the following chapters approximate periods for the activity of several artists are suggested by dated comparisons; more precise dating becomes possible when this chronology is correlated with the historical and iconographical evidence presented in other chapters. For the reader's convenience these dates are assimilated into the chart in Appendix figure 7.

[76] Defined by, among others, Grodecki, 1955, p. 620, and 1963, pp. 140–41. See also Sauerländer, 1971, pp. 506–507.

[77] London, British Library, Royal MS 14 C.vii; see Brieger, 1957, pp. 136–38, Pl. 42a.

IV. The Transitional Windows:
The Early and Middle Periods

"I cannot see . . . that one can explore a chain of mountains by jumping from one peak to another."

L. M. J. Delaissé[1]

THE ATTEMPT to trace the chronological development of the Canterbury glass paintings through a scrutiny of the visual material—composition, ornament, and style—has led to the emergence of some remarkable individual artist. Among the greatest is the first to appear on the scene, whom I name the Methuselah Master.[2] Others are distinctly lesser artistic personalities; it is as though the shop expanded and numerous painters merged their styles during part of the middle period. Each of these amorphous styles seems, however, to have contributed to the process of change between Romanesque and Gothic.

The early period: the Methuselah Master

THE windows of the choir at clerestory and lower levels have several distinctive features. The armatures of the north choir aisle windows are of early types; the second (n:XV) consists of a grid of straight bars (Appendix fig. 1). The glass *in situ* shows that square panels were alternated with inscribed circles, as in the central west window of Chartres Cathedral of the mid-twelfth century.[3] The third (n:XIV), with circles in the center flanked by inscribed semicircles, had a precursor

[1] L.M.J. Delaissé, "Millard Meiss, *French Painting in the Time of Jean de Berry*, Part I" (review), *Art Bulletin* 52 (1970), 209.

[2] Previously identified as the "Master of the North Choir Aisle Windows" (Caviness, 1965, pp. 194ff.) and as the "Classical Master" (Caviness, 1970, pp. 80–81). A part of this section was presented at the Ninth Conference on Medieval Studies sponsored by the Medieval Institute, Western Michigan University, Kalamazoo, in May 1974, in a paper entitled "The Methuselah Master of Canterbury and the Twelfth Century Renaissance."

[3] Delaporte and Houvet, 1926, Pls. IV, v.

in St.-Denis.[4] This composition, and the use of knots in the ornament to link adjacent circles, is much like a page in a late twelfth-century manuscript, Paris, Bibliothèque Nationale, MS Lat. 11534, f.6v, a Bible once associated with Canterbury, but more probably from the north of France.[5] Little can be said of the aisle windows on the south side, as only the armatures (and a record of the subjects) remain, but from the fact that Window s:XV, facing n:XV, is paired with it in armature design, it seems probable that the designer was the same (Appendix fig. 1). Its neighbors are perhaps less primitive in appearance, but even Window s:XVI may be seen as an early experiment with the quadrilobe (Appendix fig. 1). This window is divided into three units, each of which is built up from a square in the center, a more sophisticated articulation than the grid. Yet the lobes of the quatrefoils are not controlled by the compass, as they came to be in the middle period. Window s:XIV has intersecting circles and cannot be distinguished from the middle group in the transepts.

The painted ornament from the north side of the choir is extremely vigorous and imposing. The clerestory borders are as great as ten to fourteen inches wide, whereas in the Trinity Chapel they are in the range of five and a half to eight inches. Even small palmettes, such as fill the corners outside the medallions of choir aisle Window n:XV, are strong and rich, and do not have the cramped appearance of some of the Trinity Chapel ornament (figs. 27, 197). The two borders in situ in the choir aisle are highly individual, though both are of the climbing kind. That of the second window is unique in retaining a slightly archaic beading on the central stem (fig. 1); this feature is

closely comparable to the border of the St.-Benedict Window of St.-Denis, which probably dates from 1144.[6] Elaborate strap-work and persistent beading, as in others of the St.-Denis borders, was reiterated at York sometime between the glazing of St.-Denis and Canterbury.[7] The Canterbury Master, however, preferred to develop naturalistic foliage and interweaving; with the crisp and stylized palmettes and acanthus of this north choir aisle border are interspersed serrated trefoil leaves on slender stems, which spring above delicately drawn leaf scars and bend across the main branch. Both blue and red are used in the ground—as in many of the Canterbury borders—but the foliage is unusually rich in color; the palette, with delicate shades of near-white, pale pink, acid green, and pale blue, with accents of hot yellow, is identical to that of the figure scenes.

Even the trefoil leaves of this border scarcely prepare us for the vine trellis in Window n:XIV (fig. 2). Set off against red and blue grounds, a single white stem winds from one side to the other behind a yellow support, while at regular intervals leaves with bunches of grapes grow across in front of it. In spite of the whitish coloring of the leaves and the variously yellow, green, or blue hue of the grapes, the effect is extraordinarily naturalistic, chiefly because of the depth of modeling which is built up on both sides of the glass. This border represents a trend quite contrary to the standard legacy of St.-Denis.[8] The great delicacy of the Canterbury border recalls the observation of plant life recorded in the herbals, as for instance in an early twelfth-century manuscript in Oxford, Bodleian Library, MS 130.[9] On the other hand, the vine trellis brings to mind sculpted examples from late

---

[4] Grodecki, 1961a, fig. 4.

[5] *Corpus Switzerland* I, 51–52, ascribed to Canterbury. There is a close relationship to the Manerius Bible (Paris, Bibliothèque Sainte-Geneviève, MSS 8–10) in some of the illustrations; both are probably continental productions; see *The Year 1200* I, no. 246, 247–48. The coincidence with window designs was noticed by A. van der Boom, "Het eerste internationale Congres voor glasschilderkunst gehouden te Bern," *Koninklijke nederlandse Oudheidkundige Bond, Bulletin*, 6th ser. VI (1953), 106, n. 12.

[6] Grodecki, 1976, pp. 127–28, type C, fig. 204.

[7] *The Year 1200* I, nos. 222, 223, 218–20; and Westlake, I, 1881, Pl. XIh, XII, XIIIm, XXIII (York); cf. Grodecki,

1976, pp. 126–31, types B, F, J, H, figs. 194, 195, 205, 206, 207 (St.-Denis). Westlake's claim (I, 1881, 42) that the York borders are purely English or Norman in character has been rightly challenged by Lafond, 1946, p. 152.

[8] One border design, in the griffin windows of the ambulatory, has a stiff vine with small green and purple leaves. Made in the nineteenth century, it was based on a drawing by Percier; see Grodecki, 1976, p. 123, Pl. XV, fig. 187.

[9] R. T. Gunther, *The Herbal of Apuleius Barbarus from the Early Twelfth Century Manuscript Formerly in the Abbey of Bury St. Edmunds* (Roxburghe Club), 1925; and see Gransden, 1972, p. 51, figs. 9–10.

antiquity.[10] Naturalistic vines reappear in late twelfth-century sculpture at Rheims, Sens, and Canterbury, and in the enamel plaques of the Klosterneuburg ambo of 1181.[11] Of all the surviving Canterbury ornament, this border preeminently bears the stamp of the twelfth-century renascence.

In the same window of the north choir aisle are other developed leaf forms. The ornament *in situ* maintains the high standard of the border, without introducing recognizable species (fig. 179). Where the medallions nearly touch, the white edging is twisted into an elaborate knot. In the central space is a rosette of leaves in the full range of colors used in the neighboring border. From the rosette spring two pairs of intertwined *rinceaux* with slender white acanthus foliage and blue leafy clusters resembling oak; the ground is red.

The clerestory borders are somewhat bolder in design and coloring than the lower ones, and tend to use a more hackneyed repertory of acanthus and palmette, although in at least one example surviving in the choir the execution is extremely painstaking. Another very fine border, which is unfortunately misplaced in the crypt east window, deserves attention; its large dimensions may indicate an origin in the clerestory, and the vigorous execution suggests a westerly rather than an easterly position (fig. 3).[12] It departs, however, from the normal type of continuous growth up the sides of the window. Elaborate palmettes, with long curled leaves resembling plumes, in white, yellow, and mid-blue, grow sideways on a red ground between rosettes of yellow, white, green, and pink leaves on a blue ground. The rosettes are encircled in white, and framed by a wreathlike growth of leaves. The whole appears as a crisp and distilled version of one of the rich Anglo-Saxon manuscript borders of the Winchester School, such as the "Benedictional" of Archbishop Robert.[13] Comparable to the Canterbury border is that of the St. Eustace Window in Chartres Cathedral, the work of a master from the northeast of France; this too has the echo of "Winchester" ornament in the lozenges that are interspersed with the trellis (fig. 4).[14] Very similar are the palmettes with long white, yellow, and blue leaves on a red ground in a border in the clerestory of St.-Remi of Rheims, which, however, lacks the rosettes of the Canterbury border (fig. 5).[15] In view of the aridity of the York ornament in the decades preceding the Canterbury glass, borders of this kind at Canterbury and on the continent may have an aspect of revival, which is paralleled in manuscripts. The motif of continuous growth developed from the center along a trellis is also found in the early books.[16] The introduction in the English manuscripts of an entirely different repertory of designs has been ascribed to the Alexis Master of the St. Albans Psalter before 1123,[17] but there is a revival in the mid-century manuscripts

[10] For instance at the Temple of Hadrian at Cyzicus (A.D. 123–39); see Bernard Ashmole, "Cyriac of Ancona and the Temple of Hadrian at Cyzicus," *Journal of the Warburg and Courtauld Institutes* 19 (1956), figs. 39b–e.

[11] Reused pieces over the cloister doorway of Rheims Cathedral include a wide border of inhabited vine; Sauerländer, 1970, Pl. 56, p. 48, dated it about 1180. At Sens an inhabited vine is on one side of the trumeau of the central west portal, illustrated in Richard Hamann-McLean, "Zur baugeschichte der Kathedrale von Reims," *Gedenkschrift Ernst Gall*, ed. M. Kühn and L. Grodecki, Berlin, 1965, fig. 135. In Canterbury the easternmost roof-boss in the choir, which must date from 1177, has curled vine leaves and grapes; see Cave, 1935, Pl. VIII, 4, p. 43. For the Klosterneuburg ambo plaques, see Rüdiger Becksmann, "Das Jesse-Fenster aus dem spätromanischen Chor des Freiburger Münsters; ein Beitrag zur Kunst um 1200," *Zeitschrift des deutschen Vereins für Kunstwissenschaft* 23 (1969), fig. 25.

[12] Cf. Rackham, 1949, p. 67 and J. Hayward in *The*

Year 1200 I, no. 227, 223–24, who accepted Samuel Caldwell's assertion that it belonged to the crypt east window. The two topmost panels, which curve to fit the frame, are entirely modern.

[13] Rouen, *Bibliothèque Publique*, MS Y 7, a pontifical; see Rickert, 1965, Pl. 29B, pp. 38, 223.

[14] Grodecki, 1965, p. 178, derived this border type from earlier examples in glass, as in Poitiers, ca. 1160–1170, but the latter has a prominent Romanesque interlace.

[15] In the center lancet of the third bay from the west on the north side; one panel is preserved in medieval leads, and five other panels are largely ancient. The photograph, unfortunately, is of a modern panel. Before restoration this design was in the third lancet; I am grateful to Mlle Vinsot for this information.

[16] As in the tenth-century New Minster "Memorial," British Library, MS Cotton Vesp. A.viii, illus. Rickert, 1965, Pl. 25.

[17] See Pächt, Dodwell, and Wormald, 1960, pp. 97–99.

of plant forms to frame the pictures.[18] Swarzenski has discussed the influence of Anglo-Saxon ornament in twelfth-century manuscripts on the continent;[19] trellis work is generally accepted as of English origin, though it had spread to the continent by 1200.[20]

The figure painting *in situ* in the north choir aisle and the paintings removed from the clerestory above show the same qualities as the ornament, and support an attribution on a single great master, named for the most imposing of his perfectly preserved figures, Methuselah. His work has certain "early" features, combined with a new naturalism and an awareness of the antique as well as the Anglo-Saxon tradition.[21] Classicizing qualities were recognized as long ago as 1842, when Sir John Gilbert referred to the "Grecian beauty and strength" of the Magi's horses, which he likened to the Elgin marbles.[22] The sensitivity to individual forms that is so apparent in the vine border pervades this master's treatment of the human figure. On the other hand, the breadth of his style is such that for a long time I was unwilling to attribute to one hand the upper and the lower windows; the upper figures have a far more dynamic aspect than the lower, which are serenely classicizing.

Included in the *oeuvre* of the Methuselah Master are Adam digging from Window N:XXV,[23] Jared and Enoch from Window N:XXII,[24] and Methuselah and Lamech from Window N:XXI,[25] that is, all the figures surviving from the choir clerestory (figs. 6, 8, 9, 12, 13). To them has to be added the figure of Noah from Window N:XX, in the northeast transept, although the window design has been modified by the introduction of canopies over the figures, and the paired figure of Shem has to be attributed to another hand (figs. 66, 67);[26] it seems that a design by the Methuselah Master for Noah was taken over by an artist who worked in a

very different idiom, just as in the Winchester Bible Oakeshott noticed that drawings by the Master of the Leaping Figures were painted by the Morgan Master.[27] The Methuselah Master's work broke off in the lower windows at the same point. Window n:XIII has a simple armature consisting of full and half-circles; the surviving medallions, however, justify an attribution to another designer.

The six ancestors of Christ attributed to the Methuselah Master are characterized by angular poses and by extraordinary vigor and restlessness. All but Enoch have one arm detached from the body, the hand placed on the hip, the silhouette pierced through inside the elbow in a sculptural way. All the knees and feet are widely spaced, on different levels, the broad shoulders are twisted into the picture plane, the heads turned into three-quarter view. The calmest figures are Methuselah and Jared, from adjacent positions; the former adopts the classical philosopher's pose, his chin resting on his hand. He presents a powerful and brooding aspect. The monumentality of the figure, and the suggestion of sheer weight and bulk, are astonishing at any time within the period of glazing. None of the figures in this group holds an attribute; instead their hands are employed in tense gestures. Contributing to their powerful monumentality is the absence of canopies and the severe restriction of colors. On a blue ground the basic colors are green, white, and yellow, with pink as a flesh color. Silvery blue and brilliant red are used very sparingly. The paint is handled with extraordinary freedom and sureness, both in modeling washes on the outer surface and rapidly modulated stabbing or sweeping lines inside. Such broad handling indicates that the Master was well aware of the effect his works must have even when placed sixty feet above eye level. The treatment is essentially painterly; though working without col-

[18] For example in the Bury Bible, illus. Boase, 1953, Pl. 54a.

[19] Swarzenski, 1943, pp. 8, 53.

[20] See *The Year 1200* I, p. 292.

[21] The kinds of models he used are discussed in Chapter Six.

[22] Gilbert, 1842, pp. 20–21.

[23] Now in the great west window, L4; Rackham, 1949, p. 31.

[24] Now in the south window of the southwest transept, Q4 and Q8; Rackham, 1949, p. 32.

[25] Now in the southwest transept window, Q5 and Q1; Rackham, 1949, pp. 32–33.

[26] Now in the southwest transept window, Q2, and clerestory N:XIII; Rackham, p. 33.

[27] Oakeshott, 1945, pp. 7–8, 13–15, Pls. XXIX, XL.

or on his brush, the painter's interest is in the broad handling of form and the breaking up of color and mass; in these large-scale works he shows little interest in the aesthetic potential of line, little of that quality one might call graphic sensibility.

The monumental style of the Methuselah Master is not easily recognizable in the small-scale historiated panels of the lower windows; yet the earliest style in the surviving glass of the north choir aisle is, I believe, an extension of his versatile creative abilities to another mode, even if close analysis suggests that in the execution he was aided by other painters. Evetts has noticed resemblances in facial types between the upper and the lower windows in this part of the building.[28] One might cite Adam and Herod (in the Magi before Herod); both have the same solemn, even melancholy expression, the moustache seeming to draw the corners of the mouth down (figs. 6, 27). In both the hair on the head is fanned out into wavy strands, but is more tightly organized in the beard. The pensive mood and pose of Herod are not too distant from Methuselah. Although the painting of draperies tends to be more detailed in the lower windows, at least in one figure, that of Balaam in the top of Window n:XV, the draperies have a swirling, vibrant quality achieved by powerful brushwork (fig. 19). Above the waist the downward sweep of the tunic is abruptly caught by the belt, and dramatically broken by a series of short, tapered strokes alternated with blobs extending into hooks, which resemble the pad and claw of a cat's paw; the same technique is used in Enoch (fig. 9).

The north choir aisle windows differ from the clerestory in several ways. The figures are more serene, more classicizing in spirit, than the patriarchs. They are also more varied, in physical type, pose, colors, and especially in brushwork. Only Balaam gives some indication of the Master's ability to compensate for distance from the eye; in lower panels he used a full repertory of more miniaturesque effects. And as the severe restriction of color in the clerestory is very powerful at a distance, so in the lower windows the Master employed a more subtle palette. The north choir aisle

glass is some of the most brilliant in the cathedral, in spite of the northerly situation and the shadows cast by neighboring buildings. It is dominated by the limpid blue grounds to the figure panels, but the cool blues are "balanced" by warm yellows and reds; these colors are used nonrealistically, as in the yellow horse of one of the Magi, or the red lining of the clouds in the same panel. Red also plays a large part in the decorative elements of the window, but it is avoided in the draperies. These are predominantly green, purple, or yellow, with occasional white or pale blue. Very fine nuances of tone are recognizable in the purples, varying from near-white, as in the flesh tones, to deep murrey or brownish pink. Blues also vary, both paler and deeper shades being available to distinguish draperies from the mid-blue ground. Greens are carefully selected from a bluish mid-green and a yellowish acid green; both are used in different bands in the waters of the Red Sea (fig. 30).

The Methuselah Master is a great colorist, able to create effects of extraordinary richness even with the few colors available to the stained-glass artist in the twelfth century. He is also a very accomplished painter, capable of an astonishing variety of linear and painterly effects, in which he exploits both surfaces of the glass. As a designer he achieves clarity and serenity in a symbolic mode as consistently as monumentality and restlessness in a more dramatic one. Naturalism is pursued in the easeful and unified articulation of the human form, in the varieties of physical types and of drapery textures, but violent motion or emotion is eschewed. His awareness of the physical world was obviously acute, and in the choir aisle windows there is a wealth of minute observation, as in the carefully rendered skin color and profiles of the Queen of Sheba's African attendants (fig. 44); but detail is strictly subordinated to essential organization. Rhythmic spacing and grouping of figures give a floating or even static quality to the action; the compositions express a state of being, at once classicizing and in harmony with the exegetical mode; Old and New Testament events are distilled into motionless equivalents of each other.

[28] Evetts, 1941, p. 118.

The question "What happened next?" is never posed, as it must be in a narrative mode.

In his compositional organization the Methuselah Master relied heavily on Romanesque conventions. The unbroken blue ground around distinct groups or figures forms one or more vertical caesurae, which have great dramatic impact, as in the Destruction of Sodom in n:XV, where it isolates Lot's wife from the fleeing figures and from the burning city (Col. Pl. 1). Massed groups, like the Gentiles led by Christ (fig. 37), take on a collective quality and tend to be isolated from the main figures, who function autonomously within their own space, occasionally touching but seldom overlapping others. Similarly, the elements of a composition rarely extend beyond the inner edging line, though they touch it. Except in the remarkable composition of the Magi riding (fig. 23), in which the leader's horse disappears through a gateway, and the pursuing Balaam who reaches towards the same star (fig. 19), there is no indication of an extension of action or space beyond the picture frame. Architecture is used, like the ground, to emphasize groupings; the isolation of Pharaoh is dramatized by the aedicule set over his throne, which is also the pretext for the fiery red ground behind him (fig. 30). Very similar grouping and spacing of figures and the articulation of action by architectural frames have been noticed in the St. Albans Psalter;[29] The convention may have been introduced into England, at Bury St. Edmunds, by the Alexis Master before 1123. There is some possibility, therefore, that the Methuselah Master took this aspect of his art from a model which also served painters in Peterborough, perhaps about 1170; the question of his reliance on this East Anglian cycle is considered in Chapter Six. Comparison with a scene from the Albani Psalter, however, will show how significant is the change from this Romanesque style of a previous generation. Whereas there is little individuality in the figures that make up a crowd in the Psalter, the Methu-selah Master, though still restricted in his repertory of poses, has concentrated all his extraordinary prowess on the distinctive qualities of face and dress of each person; he has also imbued them with a psychological awareness of each other, a possibility of intercommunication, as between Joseph and his brothers (fig. 48). At the same time it becomes possible for the viewer to empathize—say, with the dignified figure of Moses who looks back in care of his flock, and with the women and children who follow (fig. 30). The most compelling image of metamorphosis before Bernini's *Daphne* is surely the delicate figure of Lot's wife, motionless, slender and white, still a woman yet imminently a pillar of salt. It will be no surprise to have to admit a Byzantine model for this scene, from which some of the humanistic qualities must derive (figs. 51, 53, 54).

One of the remarkable distinctions of the Methuselah Master is his combination in these lower windows of linear and painterly sensibilities. In spite of individual variations between one figure and another, a similar construction can be perceived. Faces, bodies, and limbs are organized into a system of open circles and ellipses. This structuring of forms by a tight linear web has a parallel in the work of a great draftsman, the Master of the Apocrypha Drawings of the Winchester Bible.[30] His seated figure of King Antiochus shows his use of finely modulated curving lines, often grouped in twos or threes; they sweep upward in an open ellipse over the torso, and pull the mantle into curving pleats over the arm, much as they do in the Methusaleh Master's Pharaoh (figs. 30, 31). The figures, too, of the Apocrypha Master have a poised elegance, not, however, always fitting to the subject; the executioner of I Maccabees 1 has the tiptoeing *gehende-stand* and turned head which is a favorite pose of the Methuselah Master, as in Christ and the foremost Gentile (figs. 37, 38). Such a pose has a long history and is a convention of the English twelfth-century artist.[31]

---

29 Pächt, Dodwell, and Wormald, 1960, pp. 107–108, 119–20.

30 Oakeshott, 1945, pp. 8–10.

31 Cf. the Bayeux Tapestry of the end of the eleventh century; Frank Stanton, ed., *The Bayeux Tapestry: A Comprehensive Survey*, 2nd ed., London, 1965, Pl. 29; and a tenth-century manuscript from St. Gall, Stiftsbibliothek, MS 64, illus. H. Woodruff, 1929, fig. 29.

Linear patterning, executed on the inner surface of the glass, is supplemented by broad modeling washes frequently applied on the outer surface. This is true of the pleats of Pharaoh's mantle, and many of the heads. There are also subtle variations in draperies within the same panel; the broad, rather stark handling of Pharaoh's mantle over the shoulder, and the comparable stiffness of the skirt of his robe, contrast with a passage of crumpled material in his lap in which washes are used rather than line. In the foreground of the same panel the woman's robe is modeled with an intricate pattern of slashes, each heavy sweep of the brush tapered rapidly and modified by one or two fine parallel strokes to create an effect of half-tones. Moses' robes are given more painterly treatment; the positioning of lines is tentative, the blacks are not as positive, and they are attenuated by numerous fine strokes. Variety is a constant factor; there are no examples in the Master's work of easily copied schemata, though these begin to appear in his assistants' work.

In his capacity for individual variation and in his painterly qualities the Methuselah Master draws near the "Winchester" Master of the Morgan Leaf. For instance, the strongly suggested plasticity of the figure of the Prophet of 1 Kings 13, with thigh-clinging draperies represented by soft, tentative strokes, is paralleled in the painting of Abraham in the initial to Psalm 102 in the Winchester Bible (figs. 55, 56). Even the facial type of the man on the extreme right in the Canterbury panel could derive from a model similar to the Morgan Master's head of Abraham; they share an organization of the hair into rows of curls, a close beard revealing the shape of the chin, an aquiline nose, and high cheekbones. The glass painting is more brittle and linear in this figure, possibly due to an assistant's hand. In the same panel the head of

King Jeroboam, though it differs in the flattening of the far side of the face and in the crisp, scalloped edge of the short beard, is very close in type to the King Antiochus of the Apocrypha Master of the Winchester Bible (fig. 31). This multiple relationship to the artists of the Winchester Bible has to be extended also to the Master of the Leaping Figures: the closest parallels for the poses of some of the clerestory figures are in his drawings; Noah might be compared to Elisha in pose and latent energy (figs. 66, 68). Yet in the Canterbury glass there is no vestige of the damp-fold drapery system so rigorously adhered to by the Master of the Leaping Figures, even though it is present in the Lambeth Bible from St. Augustine's[32] and the wall painting of St. Paul at Malta in St. Anselm's Chapel.[33] The Methuselah Master's use of the leaping figure is fleeting. The ponderous figures of Jared and Methuselah find parallels in the initial to Baruch by the Morgan Master (figs. 8, 12, 14). The king is seated in the philosopher's pose, his elbow resting on one drawn-up knee; the prophet gestures in the manner of Jared. In the manuscript, as in the glass, the bulk of the figures is emphasized by mantles that sweep around in depth, clarifying major articulations. The large-scale figures are rather more broadly handled, with less minutiae of folds and loops, but they are remarkably close in spirit. The most salient general distinction to be made is between the elegance of the Morgan Master and the greater directness of the Methuselah Master.

Winchester connections appear again in at least one of the clerestory figures of the eastern transepts, of the middle period. Joanna is remarkably similar to a drawing for the initials to Psalm 110 (figs. 82, 84). Oakeshott attributed these to the "Master of the Gothic Majesty," but more recently Ayres has seen this work as a mature development

[32] London, Lambeth Palace, MSS 3 and 4, Dodwell, 1954, pp. 81–84, 123, Pls. 31a, 48a, 49b, 50a and c, 51a, 52a, 53a, 59a, 60a; and C. R. Dodwell, *The Great Lambeth Bible*, London and New York, 1959.

[33] Tristram, 1944, Pls. 23–24, Suppl. Pl. 1, who (p. 23) dated it between about 1153 and 1175 on archaeological evidence and about 1160 on style. Dodwell, 1954, p. 50, compared it with the Dover Bible, which he dated 1140–

1160. See also Grabar and Nordenfalk, 1958, pp. 115, 117; André Grabar dated the work "around the close of the twelfth century," by comparison with the Winchester Bible and the Great Canterbury Psalter in Paris. Demus and Hirmer, 1970, pp. 121, 124, 509, compared it with the Bury Bible. Byzantine influences were discussed and illustrated by Kitzinger, "Byzantine Contribution," 1966, p. 38, figs. 8 and 9.

of the Morgan Master's style, a postulate which seems entirely acceptable.[34] There are earlier affinities with the "Gothic" master; the head of Adam bears a close similarity to the head of the Lord in the initial to Isaiah.[35]

What remains perplexing is the totally parallel development of styles at Canterbury, where designs by the Methuselah Master seem to carry over archaisms comparable to those of the Master of the Leaping Figures and the Master of the Apocrypha Drawings; yet in its execution his *oeuvre* rivals the paintings of the Morgan Master. Furthermore, a development in the Morgan Master's style is even reflected in the next stage of the Canterbury clerestory glazing. A connection with the Morgan Master is suggested with some reluctance, since it seems that already far too many important works have been associated with, if not actually attributed to him, and while each of them may reflect some aspect of a very varied style, they would not independently have been grouped together. On the one hand, there are the Sigena frescoes, which are thought to be a monumental work of the Master himself; in them there is a heightening of the dynamic mood, which has suggested to Demus renewed contacts with Byzantine art.[36] On the other hand, there is the Westminster Psalter and contemporary St. Albans productions, which reflect a calmer mood. Dodwell's view that the Sigena paintings were influenced by the Great Canterbury Psalter, Lat. 8846, which was known to have been in Spain in the Middle Ages, has been countered by Pächt, who viewed the paintings as works of a Winchester artist, and supposed that the artist of the Psalter must also have been Winchester-trained.[37] These questions are not easily resolved.

Swarzenski has suggested to me that the Sigena paintings are part of a wider stylistic trend in Spain, the miniatures of the Huesca Missal also offer significant points of comparison with the Great Canterbury Psalter and the Sigena paintings.[38] Yet is is hard to avoid the conclusion that this style is largely English in origin. Whether it belongs to Winchester or Canterbury is perhaps a question one should not ask in a period when local styles were rapidly disappearing. Neither the Methuselah Master nor the artist of the Great Canterbury Psalter seem to have derived their styles from the Dover Bible or the St. Paul fresco; equally, the style of the Morgan Master does not grow out of the Psalter of Henry of Blois, or even out of the work of his older collaborators on the Bible itself. In the same way, it might be said that the younger master of the Milan candlestick, whose classicizing style has been so hard to place in time and space, is not close to the rigid formulations of the older master.[39]

The serene style of the Methuselah Master is also found in a series of relief sculptures that seem to have been part of the choir enclosure hastily erected before Easter 1180.[40] Busts of Old Testament patriarchs are framed in quatrefoils; their round heads, with neatly incised hair and beards, and the similarly incised planes of drapery correspond well with Pharaoh or the group of Herod and the Magi in the north choir aisle windows (figs. 27, 30, 33). It is hard to avoid the conclusion that they are contemporary. About the same time, perhaps, the vaults of the nave of St. Gabriel's Chapel in the crypt were painted with scenes and busts framed in *rinceaux*; these must postdate the fire of 1174.[41] The preserved underdrawing of the busts and the

---

[34] First proposed in his Harvard doctoral thesis, 1970, and published in Ayres, 1974, pp. 209, 219. I am especially indebted to him for the loan of a copy of the thesis, and for a frank exchange of ideas during the period this book was in preparation.

[35] Oakeshott, 1945, Pl. XXXVII.

[36] Demus and Hirmer, 1970, p. 511.

[37] Dodwell, 1954, p. 99. Pächt, 1961, p. 171, n. 37.

[38] Jesús Domínguez Bordona, *Miniatura* (*Ars Hispaniae* 18) Madrid [1958], pp. 76–77, fig. 85, who also noticed the resemblance to Sigena.

[39] O. Homburger, *Der Trivulzio-Kandelaber; Ein Mei-*

sterwerk frühgotischer Plastik [Zurich], 1949, pp. 10–11, Pls. 12, 13.

[40] Prior to 1971 only two pieces were known; see Arthur Gardner, *English Medieval Sculpture*, Cambridge, 1951, p. 84, fig. 145, and George Zarnecki, *Later English Romanesque Sculpture, 1140–1210*, London, 1953, p. 46, fig. 111. Several more pieces have been found in the cloister. I am grateful to Professor Zarnecki for information and photographs, and especially for communicating his new idea that they are from the choir enclosure.

[41] Tristram, 1944, p. 104, Pls. 20–22, Suppl. Pl. 2c.

character of the *rinceaux* are similar to the Jesse page of the Great Psalter in Paris, but the greater use of curving line places them closer in style to the Methuselah Master.

One of the central issues in any discussion of the early Canterbury glass must be the role it played in the development of glass painting between St.-Denis and Chartres.[42] Neither the architecture nor the glass of Chartres Cathedral after the fire of 1194 derive in a straight line from St.-Denis of fifty years earlier, nor can all that happened between be ascribed to the Ile-de-France. It may be debatable whether the region to the east of Paris, as far as Burgundy in the south, the Meuse in the east, and extending across the Channel into southern England, provided a strong polarity to Parisian art, or whether it rather carried the mainstream of development towards a Gothic style.[43] However, already in some of the glass of St.-Denis Grodecki has recognized a "Mosan" hand, which is prophetic of the style that dominates the glass of this easterly region through the later part of the century. Affinities were found between this Signum Tau panel in St.-Denis and the work of a painter responsible for the glass panels of about 1175 that were later incorporated into the thirteenth-century building of Troyes Cathedral.[44] More surprising, perhaps, is a certain similarity between the *Tau* panel and Joseph and his Brethren at Canterbury (figs. 48, 49). The grouping and isolating of figures are the same, with the ground forming two caesurae. Motifs have been carried over, such as the positioning of the arms of the central figure, the fall of his mantle in a vertical plane all but hiding the wide, high belt that grips his torso; in the standing figures to the right in each instance draperies are pulled into stiff pleats behind the legs and a cas-

cade of V-folds between them, and are drawn in tightly under the knees. But these appear as archaic conventions in the work of an assistant of the Methuselah Master. Markedly different from St.-Denis is the Master's introduction of architectures and spatial settings, his insistence on individuality in the figures, and on plasticity and ease, and his use of a changed proportion of head to body. The panels from Troyes illustrate a divergent trend, only in a few aspects parallel to the development we see in the early Canterbury glass.[45] In spite of a more classicizing proportion, and greater ease in the figures, the facial types and draperies have little individual variation. The artist's work has an exquisite quality reminiscent of niello metalwork; its effect relies almost entirely on fine modulation of line, and there is no back-painting. His style is also seen in manuscripts of the region, and no doubt it was important in the formation of a "proto-Gothic" style in the northeast of France, as Grodecki has suggested.[46] One could not, however, derive the Methuselah Master's style from Troyes. Nor was he influenced by the books illuminated in a less exquisite variant of the Troyes style, which may have been brought from Pontigny by Thomas Becket and Herbert of Bosham.[47]

It is important to distinguish between the classicism of the Methuselah Master, which was very short-lived, and that of the continental productions, which seems to rise slowly from the idealization of the Troyes Master to the equally strong idealization of the Ingeborg Psalter or the Antique Master at Rheims; much stronger in the Methuselah Master are the ingredients of humanism and naturalism, resulting in a particularization of figures and events, which is to some extent incompatible with idealization.[48] Much stronger also is his

[42] Rackham, 1949, pp. 18–20; Heaton, 1907.

[43] As postulated by Homburger, 1958, pp. 31–35.

[44] Grodecki, 1963, p. 137, n. 38; at that time he dated the Troyes glass ca. 1200, and questioned whether a date later than 1145 should be given to the *Signum Tau* panel. He now accepts it as part of the glazing program of Suger (Grodecki, 1976, p. 105). The panel appears to Grodecki to be heavily restored, but the drapery system was not altered in restoration (p. 104, figs. 138, 140–42).

[45] Illus. Grodecki, 1963, figs. 1, 3, 5, 6, 7; *Medieval Art,*

nos. 179–82; *Metropolitan Museum of Art Bulletin* 30 (1971–1972), in color, n.p.

[46] Grodecki, 1963, pp. 140–41.

[47] George Zarnecki, "The Transition from Romanesque to Gothic in English Sculpture," in *Romanesque and Gothic Art; Studies in Western Art (Acts of the Twentieth International Congress of the History of Art),* Princeton, 1963, fig. 10; *The Year 1200* I, no. 240, 241–42, with bibliography.

[48] Ayres, 1969, pp. 45–47, has similarly distinguished the

evident fondness for marble columns, altars, and pagan statuary *all'antica*, all of which suggest that his aesthetic could have been formed by the intellectual climate of England in the time of John of Salisbury and Henry of Blois—the one of Canterbury, the other of Winchester.[49] In fact, an anecdote told of Henry by John has, in its attitude to the Romans, an echo in the scene of Christ leading the Gentiles (fig. 37): when Henry was mocked for bringing home to Winchester a boatload of pagan statuary, he is reported to have explained that he "wished to remove the heathen gods from Rome before the contemporary Romans made them once more the objects of their veneration and cult; which they would be likely to do because spiritually the Romans in their innate and deep-rooted avarice always adored idols."[50] In the glass panel, the Gentiles look longingly back to their idol; the statue itself, though painted on blue glass and with an overly large head and demonic horns, is portrayed as a *contrapposto* nude. The limbs and torso have a suppleness and unity scarcely seen in the art of the west since antiquity, even in the

many such statues which appear in Carolingian and Romanesque art (e.g., fig. 42);[51] comparison with the stiff figure in the mid-century Lambeth Bible from St. Augustine's, Canterbury, shows how different is the attitude of the Methuselah Master to his subject (figs. 37, 39). In all probability the Methuselah Master had before him, or had somewhere seen, examples of antique sculpture, perhaps a small bronze such as the second- or third-century Jupiter that was excavated in the Low Countries in the nineteenth century (fig. 40).[52]

The classicism of the Methuselah Master was not practiced in the same degree by his immediate followers. One of the assistants, who may be called the V-fold painter, showed a tendency to schematize drapery into heavy V's with little sensitivity to form. Such passages, as in the skirt of the Queen of Sheba, both recall the *Signum Tau* panel of St.-Denis and provide a direct link with the later Gothic styles of Canterbury (fig. 44, cf. figs. 49, 92). It is the lesser artist who transmits such traditional motifs.

The middle period

WITH the exception of the oculi in the transepts, there is no change in armature design at clerestory level until Windows N:X and S:X, which are the first in the Trinity Chapel; they were also the first beyond the point where a temporary wooden partition closed off the choir and presbytery in 1180. Up to this point all the clerestory lancets conform

to the straight-bar composition used in the choir by the Methuselah Master; each has three horizontal bars, spaced at thirty-inch intervals, in addition to bars in parallel with the window frame to define the borders (Appendix fig. 5). The seated figures from the transepts and presbytery, however, are given canopies.

---

naturalistic trend of English miniaturists of the 1190s from continental work.

[49] Henry of Blois, a cousin of Henry II, was Bishop of Winchester from 1129 to 1171; see Knowles, 1951, pp. 34–37, 157. John of Salisbury entered the service of Archbishop Theobald in 1153/54 and was intermittently in Canterbury until 1177, when he became Bishop of Chartres, where he died in 1180; see Webb, 1932, pp. 15–124, also pp. 140, 169 for his Canterbury connections.

[50] Quoted by Hans Liebeschütz, *Mediaeval Humanism in the Life and Writings of John of Salisbury*, London, 1950 (repr. 1968), p. 59 from the *Historia Pontificalis* cap. 40, ed. R. Poole, p. 82.

[51] For example, Stettiner, 1895–1905, Pl. 43, fig. 2;

Pl. 160; Pl. 173, fig. 6; Pl. 183, fig. 2. Several such figures are in the Eadwine Psalter, Cambridge, Trinity College, MS R 17 1, ff. 126, 141, 146, 152, 172, 169. Cf. also the late eleventh-century wall paintings in Civate (Demus and Hirmer, 1970, p. 72) and the blue idols in an eleventh-century Byzantine manuscript, Smyrna MS B. 8 (Strzygowski, 1899, Pl. IV).

[52] David Gordon Mitten and Suzannah F. Doeringer, *Master Bronzes from the Classical World*, Greenwich, Conn., 1967, p. 274; A. N. Zadoks-Josephus Jitta, W.J.T. Peters, and W. A. Van Es, *Roman Bronze Statuettes from the Netherlands* II, Groningen, 1969, no. 30, pp. 70ff. I am indebted to Dr. Isings of the Provincial Oudheidkundig Museum for the last reference.

A clear division is much harder to make at the lower levels, particularly because almost no glass from the south side has survived except in the Trinity Chapel; only broad distinctions can be made on the basis of the armatures alone. Two qualities distinguish the ironwork of the lower windows of the transepts and presbytery, the corona, and the westernmost group in the Trinity Chapel, as well as all the windows at triforium level in the choir, transepts, and presbytery, and the oculi. These are the persistence of simple grid armatures (Appendix figs. 1, 2),[53] and the use of a number of highly individual and experimental compositons, a very few of which have continental parallels. In this entire section of the building there are only three instances of armatures paired facing each other, but these are sufficient to indicate a master plan. The eastern transepts are dominated by the identically designed oculi, and fragments of ornament *in situ* in the south rose match those in the north.[54] Windows n:X and s:X, in the outerlying chapels of the transepts, are a matching pair, but there is no point in the building from which they can be seen at one time. At triforium level in the choir the second windows from the west are a pair, as are n:XV and s:XV immediately below them.

There are a number of experiments with circles of different sizes, sometimes intersecting or placed within each other. Window s:XIV on the south side of the choir belongs with this group, as do s:XI and s:XII in the end of the south transept,[55] n:X and s:X in the chapels (Appendix fig. 1), and several of the "triforium" windows. Window n:XIII, in the north transept, has circles linked by a combination of arcs and straight bars, much like the system of the "triforium." Windows n:XII and n:IX, in the north transept also, experiment with squares linked by rectilinear or rhomboid forms. The canted square is introduced in Window s:VIII, on the south side of the presbytery, the east window of the corona, and again in Trinity Chapel n:V and s:V, and partially in n:VI (Appendix figs. 1, 2). In the two former it is used in conjunction with quatrefoils built up from central squares, a structure that appears also in the oculi. The centers of the part-circles forming the lobes are not consistently placed on the centers of the sides of the square except in the corona.

The ruling factor in the typological windows—which include the east window of the corona—was the need to provide groups of two, four, or six types around a central antitype. This suggested to the designers that interest should concentrate on the central panels, whether squares, canted squares, or circles, and that subsidiary panels should form petal or star compositions around these. The result is a clear articulation into three or more units, a distinct advance from the overall grid of the choir aisles (n:XV and s:XV). The windows of the transept chapels and Trinity Chapel ambulatory did not have to meet this need, and they are narrower; these compositions of the middle group allow for a continuous sequence of narrative subjects, but in the latest narrative windows the star is used. A distinction was not consistently made in earlier monuments;[56] whereas the composite quatrefoil was used in a typological window at Châlons-sur-Marne, at St.-Denis during the preceding decade it was probably given to the strictly narrative Early Life of Christ.[57] Later, in the Redemption Window at Chartres, there is a return to the grid, with lobes forming quatrefoils inscribed in ornament (Appendix fig. 21). One of the few continental experiments that strictly parallels the Canterbury group is the typological east window of the Benedictine abbey church of Orbais, not far from Rheims, which may date from after 1200 (Appendix figs. 3, 13).

The experimental nature of the compositions in

[53] In windows s:IX, s:XIII of the typological series, n:II and III, s:II and III of the corona, and also in the windows at triforium level in the eastern transepts.

[54] The outer border, next to the stonework, is ancient but for two panels in the bottom of the window.

[55] The original ironwork was taken out after World War II for glazing by Bossanyi; it has been preserved in the tribune, and a reconstruction was possible on paper. Westlake, 1, 1881, Pl. LVIII & l, published slightly inaccurate drawings of these.

[56] Grodecki, 1948, pp. 90–91, has indicated the appearance of the star composition in the twelfth century in Angers, Poitiers, and Châlons.

[57] Grodecki, 1961b, fig. 13.

this group is confirmed by the figure styles and ornament. There is no dominant "transitional" master. Several distinctive and divergent hands can be recognized, making it impossible to establish an internal chronology on the basis of style. Considerable overlapping of hands, though, suggests that all the artists were part of the same operation. Some worked only to the west of the 1180 screen, while their fellows continued to contribute to the glazing of the corona and Trinity Chapel; they will be studied in this order.

THE JOANNA MASTER AND THE FIGURES FROM THE CLERESTORY OF THE EASTERN TRANSEPTS AND PRESBYTERY

This group has in common the use of canopies over the figures, and a marked loss of plastic and organic qualities in both ornament and figures, compared with the work of the Methuselah Master. These traits justify an attribution to a single designer, named the Joanna Master, although several disparate hands took part in the execution. Including Noah from Window N:XX, designed by the Methuselah Master, eighteen out of the original thirty-six figures from this part of the building have survived, or exactly half. In addition, seven borders are probably *in situ*.[58] From the north side are Noah and Shem from Window N:XX (figs. 66, 67),[59] Peleg and Reu from N:XVI (fig. 76),[60] Terah and Abraham from N:XIV (figs. 77, 78),[61] Isaac from N:XIII, Judah and Phares from N:XII (fig. 80),[62] Hezron and Ram from N:XI.[63] From the south side are Neri from Window S:XII (fig. 70),[64] Zorobabel and Rhesa from S:XIII,[65] Joanna and Juda from S:XIV (fig. 82),[66] Joseph and Semei from S:XV (fig. 85).[67] Two figures, at present in N.XIV, are the creation of Caldwell, Jr., incorporating a small amount of ancient glass.[68]

The legacy of the earlier Master is apparent in some of the ornament. Borders are predominantly of the climbing variety and the white stems are marked by leaf scars below the shoots. A pair in the north transept have blue and red grounds and intricately interlaced stems; one of the motifs can be traced at least as far back as the Bury Bible (figs. 71, 72).[69] The foliage, however, tends to be rather flat, consisting chiefly of palmettes. In two windows of the south transept clusters of very delicate trefoil leaves are introduced, but these, too, are flat (fig. 75). Colors, in accordance with the figure panels, tend to be restricted to green, white, and pink, and in four cases the ground is entirely blue.[70]

Of this group all but Neri are characterized by quieter poses than those from the choir; the arms are confined within a single outline, and the whole figure is swathed in great sweeps of drapery, which tend to unify it and to restrict movement. Even Neri is a more compact and calm version, in reverse, of Noah (figs. 66, 70). The heads, though varied from profile to full face, are more quietly inclined. Only the feet, still placed on different levels or in different planes, express some of the restlessness of the choir group. The figures have less

---

[58] In Windows N:XX, N:XIV, N:XIII, N:XII, and S:XII, S:XIII, S:XIV.

[59] Now in the southwest transept window, Q2, and clerestory N:XIII; Rackham, 1949, p. 33.

[60] Southwest transept window, Q6 and Q7; Rackham, 1949, p. 34.

[61] Southwest transept window, Q3 and M1; Rackham, 1949, p. 35.

[62] Isaac has been returned to Window N:XIII; Judah and Phares are in clerestory S:XIV; Rackham, 1949, pp. 35–36.

[63] West window L1 and L7; Rackham, 1949, p. 36.

[64] Neri is now in Window S:XIII, but the top panel has been heightened to fit this window. Since Cosam is in a quatrefoil that would fit Window S:X, in which he was seen by Gostling, but not S:XI, it may be necessary to

shift the locations given to all these figures by Austin and Rackham one to the east; Rackham, p. 42.

[65] Zorobabel is in the southwest transept window, M8; Rhesa is in Window S:XIII; Rackham, 1949, p. 42. The lower panel of Rhesa is almost entirely modern.

[66] In the southwest transept window, H1 and H8; Rackham, 1949, pp. 42–43.

[67] West window, L5 and L3; Rackham, 1949, p. 43.

[68] Rackham, 1949, p. 46, G and H. The inscriptions are entirely modern. The only significant old glass is in both the heads, which belong to Peleg and Zorobabel.

[69] The motif was a common one, of long duration; for the Bury Bible, see n. 18 above. Stems with interlaced shoots are also in the Winchester Bible, Vol. 1, f.5, Genesis initial.

[70] Windows N:XII, S:XIII and S:XIV; also N:XXI, in the choir.

individual identity; most hold a large furled scroll in one hand and none is engaged in a specific activity or event, as are Adam digging and Enoch carried up to heaven. Pink and white or green and white predominate in the draperies of most figures, enlivened by yellow and silvery blue in a few, with some red in canopies, edgings, and thrones.

There is a distinct loss of monumentality in all but a few figures, arising partly from the addition of fussy architectural features and a consequent reduction in size of the ancestors of Christ. The figures, too, are elongate, with slight physiques and small heads. A serene pose is achieved at the expense of plasticity, as though an idealizing classicism had been substituted for the more naturalistic classicism of the Methuselah Master. Some of the figures demand comparison with the roughly contemporary clerestory series in St.-Remi of Rheims. Canterbury glass-painting had perhaps entered a phase parallel with the art of the continent, but the *rapprochement* was not as yet complete. The colors are similar, with the same use of yellow and pale blue in juxtaposition, or more normally of green or pink with white. Yet placed side by side, the Terah of Canterbury has a stiffness of articulation and a linear tension not present in the Hosea from Rheims; he lacks the ease, breadth, and ponderation of the French counterpart (figs. 77, 83). Even Joanna, so consciously brought into a frontal, broad-shouldered pose, drops one foot and turns his knee out (fig. 82). Any effect of plasticity is negated by the edges of drapery which curve across the picture plane. Significantly the same trend is observable in the late work of the Morgan Master of the Winchester Bible, which used to be attributed to a "Master of the Gothic Majesty." It has already been noticed that one of his unfinished drawings in the initials to Psalm 110 in fact comes very close to the drapery system of Joanna (figs. 82, 84). What is perhaps surprising is that the wide platform of the knees in the drawing, and the generally broader proportion, are much closer to the Methuselah Master's figure of Herod, for example, than is Joanna (fig. 27).

To some extent the Joanna Master's style may develop from the Methuselah Master, whose ca-pacity to create serene figures is certainly demonstrated in the typological windows. The variable execution, however, seldom approaches the painterly qualities of work attributed to the Methuselah Master. Bold linear brushwork in a figure such as Reu does not have the fluidity and freedom of Lamech, whom it most resembles (figs. 76, 13); it is constrained to follow a more unified surface pattern, instead of describing the rounded forms of the underlying figure, and the folds are hardened. One of the most powerfully drawn figures is Abraham, companion to Terah, yet very different. He is represented in depth, his head turned over his shoulder, his feet crossed at the ankle, his foreshortened left thigh emphasized by catenary folds. Of the middle period he is the only one preserved that approaches Jared in ease and sheer physical presence, yet even so he is in proportions much taller and slighter (figs. 78, 8).

In other figures there is some evidence of hurried execution. The painting of Semei is cursory in the extreme, consisting almost entirely of insensitive strokes brusquely applied on the inner surface (figs. 85, 86). Elsewhere the execution is more painstaking but lacks boldness; soft effects achieved by numerous fine lines and washes, as in Shem, are lost from the distance of floor level (fig. 67). The work of such a painter presages the miniaturesque effects of some of the much smaller figures of the Trinity Chapel clerestory, in which monumentality is abandoned entirely.

Shem and Phares (figs. 67, 80), from opposite sides of the north transept, may both be attributed to the Fogg Medallion Master in execution; his style will be treated more fully below, since he also worked in the Trinity Chapel. Phares evidently much resembles Terah (fig. 77) in pose and drapery system, as if both were based on the same design, but Phares is even narrower, more elongate and fragile, and less compact. His face is inexpressive and bland. Terah provides a link with the work of the Master of the Public Life of Christ who designed and executed Window n:XIII of the typological series, likewise in the north transept; the manner in which his arm is caught in a loop of his mantle is repeated in the left-hand disciple in the Calling of Nathanael (figs. 77, 88).

THE MASTER OF THE PUBLIC LIFE OF CHRIST

Six panels from the Fourth Window of the typological series are preserved in Window n:XIV of the north choir aisle, though unfortunately divested of all original ornament but the edging lines.[71] It is conjectured that eight rosettes framed in concave diamonds, now in the south window of the south west transept, belonged to Window n:XIII. They would fit between the full and half-circles in the armature (Appendix fig. 11).[72] This composition is slightly more sophisticated than that of Window n:XIV in that it avoids irons cutting through the center of ornamental bosses, and adheres strictly to the actual form of the figure compositions. The rosettes are extremely fine, consisting of densely packed radiating foliage with several highly differentiated leaf types. In the center are fleshy palmettes, with the tips turned over, then pairs of fronds with small leaves like oak, and finally very delicate leaf sprays reserved in a thin coat of *grisaille* on blue glass. They much resemble the rosettes in Window n:XIV in general character. Their attribution to Window n:XIII is confirmed by the equally painstakingly drawn fig leaves in the Calling of Nathanael (fig. 88).

The artist's style is classicizing, but of a more pictorial and generalized kind than the Methuselah Master's. The spatial relationships of figures and objects are explored, but he is less interested in the depiction of individuals. The compositions lack the clarity of the Methuselah Master's work. Symmetry and a central axis are avoided, so that a kind of excitement flows evenly across the scenes. Figures are scattered across the panels, their heads more or less evenly spaced; they are organized into a series of overlapping planes in depth, as in the Miracle at Cana, where the servants and water jars are in front of the table, the wedding guests behind it, or in the Miraculous Draught of Fishes,

where the two boats overlap (fig. 87). In the Calling of Nathanael two events are shown as continuous narrative, a mode not employed in the choir aisle; Phillip speaking to Nathanael is in the right foreground, while Nathanael appears again to the left with Christ (fig. 88). Events are clarified by labels, and by scrolls with spoken words, devices which were less often necessary in the Methuselah Master's paintings, and which add to the crowding of the compositions. These panels must have made great demands on the glass cutters and lead glaziers.

The figures, few of whom are clearly seen as individuals, are small and little differentiated one from another. The few heads surviving seem to indicate that one flesh tint was used throughout. Draperies are uniformly and softly treated, with occasional sharper folds (as in the standing figure of Nathanael, fig. 88). Mantles tend to hide the articulation but emphasize the plasticity of figures, by a series of twists around them; in this respect an affinity with Terah from the clerestory has already been noticed. Detail is particularized where the narrative demands it, as in the leaves of the fig trees or the disciples' net full of fish (figs. 88, 87). Here the three-dimensional potential of the white glass is fully exploited, almost as if it were sculptural relief; the net and the heads of the fish breaking through it are painted on the inner surface, the tails and other fish are more dimly seen, painted on the outer surface. The freely undulating white waves demonstrate the artist's pictorial sense, in contrast with the decorative green and white scale pattern formed by the waves in Noah's Ark by the Methuselah Master (figs. 87, 143).

White plays a large part in the color scheme, being used for such extensive areas as waves, sails, and the tablecloth as well as draperies. Red is scarce, green and pink common. The Calling of Nathanael has an exquisite palette of yellow, mid-green, acid green, white, and a little soft pink on a limpid blue ground. These color combinations are less common in the work of the Methuselah Master than in the clerestory of the transepts. The

[71] Rackham, 1949, pp. 63–65.

[72] Cf. Mason, 1925, p. 14.

change in design sources which can be documented after the third window (n:XIV) may account in part for this artist's style; his ability to integrate the figures into a single action, his interest in spatial depth and in the substantial appearance of such a figure as the standing Nathanael, demonstrate his strongly classicizing bent. In this sense his style is only a modification of that of the Methuselah Master, with a shift in emphasis from the symbolic to the narrative character of events, and a consequent reliance on inscriptions to explain relationships.

THE MASTER OF THE PARABLE OF THE SOWER

This artist might stand alongside the Methuselah Master as a distinctive early hand; he is drawn into the middle group by his collaboration, in the north oculus, with an artist who also worked in the corona and Trinity Chapel, the Jesse Master. In design types and color the ornament of the oculi conforms with the ornament in other windows by the Jesse Master, and will therefore be discussed among his *oeuvre*. Nine figure compositions from the sixth window of the typological series have survived in the north choir aisle.[73] All are attributed to the same artist; they illustrate the Parables of the Sower and the Three Measures of Meal. In all probability the armature of Window n:XI, which is situated in the northeast transept immediately below the oculus, was designed by the master, but no ornament from this window has yet been recognized. With him also is associated a panel, now in the Virginia Museum of Fine Arts, showing a disputation scene, perhaps a subject from a Life of St. Stephen once in that saint's chapel in the same transept (Window n:IX, Appendix fig. 1).[74]

The armature of the St. Stephen Window is very conservative, essentially like that of north choir aisle n:XIV, but too narrow to accommodate semicircles flanking the central circles; these areas must have been filled with ornament. The composition of Window n:XI is far more interesting (Appendix fig. 1). Although the bars are straight, the lengths are broken up so that panels of various sizes are formed; the border is interrupted by four figure panels above and below and at the sides, so that a large cross is suggested. Comparable features appear in the Crucifixion Window in the tribune of St.-Remi[75] and in the Redemption Window at Orbais, which is dominated by a Crucifixion. As at Orbais, circles are inscribed in alternation with rectangles in the center of the window (Appendix fig. 3). However, part-circles are also inscribed in alternate flanking panels by the Master of the Parable of the Sower. The whole composition is a manneristic syncopation of the regular grid with alternating squares and circles previously used in the choir aisle, and it offers the possibility of emphasizing certain scenes above others.

The palette of the Master of the Parable of the Sower is heightened by considerable amounts of red, not only as an edging but also in draperies, which, combined with much of the hot yellow used also by the Methuselah Master, makes his panels exceedingly brilliant (Col. Pl. II). A variety of greens and three blues are still in use, but there is perhaps less subtle variation in the pinks. Collaborating with other artists, in the oculus and the hagiographical series, he used more pink, green, and white, but the red frames to his figures of Moses and Synagogue are the hottest accents in the oculus.

The compositions have a monumental clarity; figures are frequently isolated in their own compartment of an arcade, as Moses and Synagogue and the three personifications of Virtuous States (figs. 105, 103), or they are aligned in the same plane, as Ecclesia with the three sons of Noah or the Three Righteous Men (fig. 100). The compact grouping of figures that was a feature of the Methuselah Master's style is used only rarely,

[73] Rackham, 1949, pp. 58–61, 65.
[74] Caviness, 1973, pp. 7–13. An engraving by Le Keux in Britton, 1836, Pl. v, shows two colored medallions in the top of this window.

[75] Illus. Jacques Dupont and Cesare Gnudi, *Gothic Painting*, Geneva, 1954, p. 32. This window is heavily restored, but I believe the essentials of composition are original.

as, for instance, in the Pharisees Turning Away from Christ (fig. 94), or in two groups of Jews and Gentiles from the top of Window n:XI. The background of these figures is reduced to a minimum—an arcade, a bench, or a low ground-line with grass and flowers; the Pharisees have no synagogue and altar which might have compared with the pagan idol and temple in the scene of Christ Leading the Gentiles (fig. 37). Scrolls are preferred to labels introduced into the ground, though both are used (Col. Pl. II, figs. 95, 97, 100). The scrolls are decorative space-fillers where other accoutrements are so reduced. In three of the preserved panels, however, the Master of the Parable of the Sower does introduce complex spatial settings. One is in the scene of Julian and Maurice, where a recession is strongly suggested by the footrest, and by the column set behind their bowl of coins (fig. 97). Most remarkable of his compositions are the two Sowers, one in a circular, the other in a rectilinear frame. Both stride energetically across a varied landscape, with ploughland, grassy hillocks, and trees. One is built up from a standard groundline by a series of sweeping curves; the other is more emphatic in the delineation of foreground, middle ground, and distance (figs. 89, 95). Double curves in the trees, hills, plants, and even in the sweep of birds' wings, echo the arched backs of the Sowers, which are characteristic of the Master's design.

His figures frequently adopt the striding pose used by the Methuselah Master, but, as in Synagogue, it is modified by the arch of the back, with hips thrust forward, and a more even distribution of the weight (fig. 105, cf. fig. 37). Often the position of the back foot is "corrected" from the pointed toe, which causes the Methuselah Master's figures to float, to a profile that carries weight on the ball of the foot, as in Virginity, Moses, and Temperance (figs. 103, 105, 107). The figures are taller in proportion to their heads and tend to be lean and narrow-shouldered. Draperies have stiffly

pleated edges and strong vertical pull; only where action is portrayed do the skirt and mantle billow out behind, as in the Sower on Stony Ground (fig. 89). Mantles tend to be treated as a kind of long scarf, enveloping the shoulders. The skirts, which fall rather straight over the weight-bearing leg, are drawn tightly over the free leg, the folds encircling thigh and calf muscles in the manner of damp-fold drapery. The vertical fall tends also to be interrupted by a band of ornament in the skirt. In spite of the modeling washes that are applied, especially in the heads, the work of the Master of the Parable of the Sower is predominantly linear; there are few soft passages.

Many of the heads have been replaced; among those preserved are some finely differentiated types. One—as in the Sower on Good Ground and among Thorns—has a high forehead framed by receding hair, protruding cheekbones, and a wispy beard (fig. 95). His brows are furrowed, his eyebrows slant down. It is a facial type that at once recalls St. Paul as represented in the mosaics of the Palatina in Palermo.[76] Another type is the young man with slightly disordered curls (fig. 103); the angels, seen in profile above the Three Righteous Men, may be the clue to the origin of this hair style. A more ordered version is used for angels in the Sicilian mosaics,[77] and this is very faithfully reflected in the work of the Methuselah Master (figs. 51, 53).

It seems, indeed, that the Methuselah Master and the Master of the Parable of the Sower shared a "motif book" of Byzantine subjects. The Prophet in the Sacrifice of Jeroboam and Christ from whom the Pharisees turn away are adaptations of a very common type of figure, one that appeared in the West in the *Hortus Deliciarum*, the German flabellum in the British Library, Add. MS 42497, the Freiburg model-book page, the Ingeborg Psalter,[78] as well as the Great Canterbury Psalter (figs. 55, 94, 57). The presence of Byzantine models in Canterbury is felt in the Dover Bible of 1140–1160;[79]

---

[76] Illus. Dodwell, 1954, Pl. 64b.

[77] As the angels with Abraham in the Palatina; illus. *ibid.*, Pl. 48b.

[78] Deuchler, 1967, figs. 24, 219, 227, 230.

[79] Dodwell, 1954, pp. 84–87, Pls. 51c and d, 54a–d, 56a–c, 57a–d, 61b and d, 62a and b, 63a–c, 64a and b; Kitzinger, "Norman Sicily," 1966, p. 137, pointed out the anachronism of comparing the Bible with the Monreale

the later figures in the glass are calmer, contrary to the development of style in the east, which is reflected in the Monreale mosaics of the 1180s. The Byzantine models used by the early masters may therefore belong to the era of the Martorana and Palatina.[80]

The dominant formative influence on the style of the Master of the Parable of the Sower is not, however, Byzantine. Like the Methuselah Master, he has taken over some of the conventions of English work of the 1170s. In his Moses and Synagogue and in the Three Sons of Noah, the heavier proportions of the figures and the damp-fold drapery system, with an S-curve describing the front of the thigh, the kneecap and the back of the calf, and a cascade of V-folds between the thighs, recall similar features in the Circumcision of Isaac, a detail of the Kennet ciborium on loan to the Victoria and Albert Museum (figs. 105, 100, 101). Also similar are the stiffly lifted ends of the mantles, the ornamental bands across the skirts, and the facial type and hair of the patriarchs.[81] In a more animated scene on the ciborium, that of David rescuing the lamb from the bear, the tunic sweeps back from the thigh much as it does in the Sower on Stony Ground.[82]

The closest contemporary style is in the Great Canterbury Psalter in Paris. The palette of these paintings is hot and brilliant, with much orange, vermilion, and brownish-purple, offset by soft green and two tones of bright blue. In spite of the gold grounds and the fuller palette available to the miniaturist, his color approaches that of the Master of the Parable of the Sower in intensity; and if the glass-painter was perhaps influenced by the manuscript in his use of reds, it may be questioned whether the miniaturists had not intensified their colors in response to the glass. The figures in the Psalter are elongate, mannered, and rather stiff; their shoulders tend to be narrow, enveloped in

their mantles, but their thighs are strongly outlined, tensed in repose and in action. Draperies are harshly folded and few figures have the grace of those of the Master of the Parable of the Sower. Only rarely can a specific comparison be suggested, as between the archer on f.21 and the Temperance of the north oculus (fig. 107),[83] or the swordsman on f.15v and Prudence (figs. 108, 106), or Melchizadek and Abraham on f.1v and the Sons of Noah (figs. 102, 100). Apart from the extensive use of landscape settings in the Canterbury Psalter, which derive from the Utrecht Psalter, and which resemble the settings for the Sower, there is a shared repertory of specific motifs. Three kinds of tree appear, one corresponding to the writhing growth with clumps of ornamental foliage of the Sower on Stony Ground (fig. 89), another with a few stiff but more or less naturalistic leaves, as in Balaam by the Methuselah Master (fig. 19), the third rather like a mushroom with a single clump of undifferentiated foliage, as in the Sower on Good Ground and among Thorns (fig. 95). Scrolls and schematized architecture with columns punctuating the action are also part of the compositional repertory. From these comparisons with the Great Canterbury Psalter in Paris it seems that the Master of the Parable of the Sower must have worked in the same period, about 1175–1200.

THE LIVES OF STS. DUNSTAN AND ALPHAGE

The Master of the Parable of the Sower may have played some part in the design and execution of these hagiographical subjects. The surviving fragmentary panels are now in three windows of the north choir aisle at triforium level, immediately over Windows n:XVI (blocked), XV, and XIV of the typological series (Plan, text fig. 2c). The ornament is almost certainly *in situ* in these win-

mosaics of twenty years or more later, but accepted that the style could be traced back to the Palatina.

[80] The Martorana mosaics have been dated between 1143 and 1151; Demus, 1949, p. 82. Ernst Kitzinger, "The Mosaics of the Cappella Palatina in Palermo: An Essay on the Choice and Arrangement of Subjects," *Art Bulletin* 31 (1949), 287, dated the mosaics in the drum of the

Palatina to 1143, the rest of the decoration except in the apse to the late 1140s to 1150s.

[81] Moses' head is a restoration by Austin, but probably a good copy of the original.

[82] Illus. Swarzenski, 1967, fig. 450.

[83] For f.21 see *Psautier*, Pl. XXI.

dows; it is of a type associated with the Fogg Medallion Master (fig. 109). That the figure panels are in their approximate intended positions is also certain; one quatrefoil in the St. Dunstan series has been cut down to fit the circular irons in Window Nt:X, but intact it would have fitted the existing irons in St:XI. The predominantly cold tones of the figured panels, with white, very pale blue, green, and pale pink on a limpid blue ground, and a sparing use of red stand out dramatically from the brilliant ornament, with its red ground and splashes of yellow. Stylistic comparisons are hampered by the extent of restoration and the scarcity of prerestoration accounts.[84] Two panels only are moderately well preserved, the Siege of Canterbury by the Danes (fig. 113) and St. Alphage Taken Aboard a Danish Ship, both in the easternmost window, Nt:IX. Some others are authentic outline drawings. There is also the question of mode; these are the only hagiographical subjects, other than the St. Stephen panel and a single fragmentary scene of St. Martin, that survive outside the Trinity Chapel at Canterbury. Most of the compositions have none of the distilled clarity that characterizes the work of both the early Masters, but to some extent this is offset by their large size and restricted colors. The scenes are extremely complicated, better suited to line drawing than to glass because of the intricacy of cutting and leading. They may reflect quite closely an ancient pictorial tradition, as suggested by the Viking prow on the Danish boat.[85] Like many pages of the Great Canterbury Psalter, the scenes are divided into zones in order to give some sort of clarity to diversified action; so God and the angels are in a heavenly zone, separated from the sleeping figure of St. Dunstan (fig. 109), or heaven and hell are defined by arcs. Architectural settings appear in oblique perspective, some of them asserting conti-

nuity of space beyond the frame, as in St. Dunstan's vision (fig. 109); such structures frequently occur in the Utrecht Psalter recensions. The scene of the siege of Canterbury seems to be based on a model in common with one of the prefatory pages now in the Pierpont Morgan Library (figs. 113, 114); the page is possibly from Canterbury, perhaps even from another Utrecht Psalter copy of the first half of the twelfth century.[86] The number of figures in the glass panel is much reduced, and they are more symmetrically distributed, but the same leaping position is favored. Interestingly, the composition in the glass is closer to this early picture than to the equivalent scene in the Great Canterbury Psalter.[87]

Two hands may have worked on these hagiographical series. One is archaic, the other belongs to the middle period. The archaic hand is apparent in two well-preserved fragments, the angel from the scene of the miracle at Glastonbury and St. Dunstan at Calne (figs. 110, 111). The thigh of each is firmly outlined, and the skirt below the knee is pulled into a series of crisp pleats that emphatically turn round the shins. The pose of St. Dunstan is close to that of a small portrait of Archbishop Baldwin in a Christ Church manuscript, which may date between 1184 and 1190 (Cambridge, Corpus Christi College, MS 200, fig. 112), yet by comparison St. Dunstan is stiff. It would be logical to place this figure between the two author portraits so aptly compared by Dodwell, the other being from a Smaragdus of ca. 1150–1180;[88] here the interlocking catenary folds of the chasuble are similar to the glass, and comparable attention is given to the hems of the garments. Some of the graphic conventions of the glass painter are close to those of the Apocrypha Master of the Winchester Bible (fig. 31). There are also parallels in the most archaic work of the Methu-

[84] Drawings made by the elder Caldwell and used in illustration of Miss Williams's book are preserved in the Emily Williams Collection in the cathedral library. Williams, 1897, Pls. 6–8. Other nineteenth-century drawings are in the Clayton and Bell Album in the Print Room of the Victoria and Albert Museum; neither series is complete. Williams's account of the subjects (pp. 15–17) is the earliest.

[85] Cf. Noah's Ark in the eleventh-century "Caedmon" manuscript, Oxford, Bodleian Library, MS Junius 11, p. 66, illus. Rickert, 1967, Pl. 44.

[86] James, 1936–1937; Dodwell, 1954, p. 100; Heimann in *The Year 1200* I, 259.

[87] F.2v, *Psautier*, Pl. IV (upper right).

[88] London, British Library, MS Royal 10 A xiii, f.2v; Dodwell, 1954, Pl. 68a.

selah Master, and back-painting is comparable. Yet in outline these stiff, elongate beings lack the power of the Methuselah Master's figures.

The other painter is recognized in a few figures. Brittle, unstructured lines appear in the drapery and chainmail, and the faces are insipid. Figures are thin and weightless, quite lacking in the contained energy characteristic of both the Methuselah Master and the Master of the Parable of the Sower. Part of a circular medallion now in Ireland contains a few related fragments.[89] The painter's typical qualities are recognized again in a medallion in America, from which I name him the Fogg Medallion Master. It is important to observe that he seems to have begun his career in collaboration with one of the earliest looking hands in the glass, one that stylistically could date from ca. 1175–1185.

THE FOGG MEDALLION MASTER

As we have seen, this artist collaborated in the Sts. Dunstan and Alphage series, and executed figures for the clerestory of the northeast transept, notably Shem and Phares (figs. 67, 80). He is responsible for the well-preserved panel in the Fogg Museum in Cambridge, Mass., which can now be said with certainty to come from Window n:VI in the north ambulatory of the Trinity Chapel, and to represent a scene in the Life of Thomas Becket (Col. Pl. IV & fig. 115).[90] A panel of ornament from the same window has been identified in the Victoria and Albert Museum (fig. 116),[91] and other fragments are in the "triforium" windows on the south side of the choir. The glass in situ in Window n:V is in the same style (fig. 120), and one isolated fragment has been inserted in a figure panel in Window n:III.[92]

The compositions of these windows are remarkable for the rather arbitrary use of circles and canted squares or parts of both in the armatures; the forms intersect, which is a new principle, but the geometries are not yet tightly knit (Ap-

pendix fig. 2). In the ornament, which is given much importance, a very idiosyncratic kind of rinceau appears, generally on a red ground. The stem winds in a large spiral, ending with a composite flower-like palmette in the center, the "petals" of which extend widely to intertwine with the outer circles of the spiral. This fantastic vegetal form differs markedly from the more natural-looking leafy sprigs of north choir aisle Window n:XIV (figs. 116, 179).

Recognition of this type of rinceau leads to a more precise limitation of the group of windows associated with the same designer. It may be inferred that he provided the essential elements of design for a group of windows distributed on either side of the partition of 1180 and spanning the three vertical levels of glazing. To the west of the Trinity Chapel are ten small windows with a trefoil head, at triforium level but opened in the aisle walls on the north and south sides of the choir and presbytery (Plan, Nt:II, etc.). Two of the three on the north side of the choir have much of their ornament in situ; there has been patching with miscellaneous fragments on the south side. The borders present a variety of types of design, predominantly sideways-growing palmettes, but with one more abstract experiment; one border panel is relentlessly composed with a compass, a series of circles being subdivided each into four fan-shaped leaves (fig. 121). It much resembles a border in the choir clerestory of St.-Remi of Rheims.[93] Another, in Window Nt:IX, has a simple series of palmettes, without a trellis, growing from the center bottom and up the sides of the window, in traditional manner. A pair to this border is in clerestory N:XII. This window originally had the figures of Phares and Judah that are easily attributable to the Fogg Medallion Master. There is little appreciable change in the character of his ornament on the north side of the Trinity Chapel. Beaded central veins, however, are used only in the "triforium" above examples of this same "ar-

[89] The Year 1200 I, no. 226, 222–23.
[90] Caviness, 1965.
[91] The Year 1200 I, no. 228, 224–25.
[92] Caviness, 1967, p. 51; Rackham, 1949, Pl. XII (lower

scene). The insertion could have been made by Austin.

[93] In the center lancet of the first bay from the west on the north side. Examination has shown that ten upper panels are largely ancient.

chaic" trait in the choir. In The Trinity Chapel, Window n:VII has a border of the sideways-palmette variety.[94] Elaborate palmettes spring from a quatrefoil leaf and the leaves are very delicately painted, curling and fleshy; these features are also found in a fragment of *rinceaux* now in clerestory N:VII which unfortunately is of uncertain provenance (fig. 122). In Trinity Chapel Window n:V, the border is in keeping with the richness and vigor of the *rinceaux*, with the same insistence on depth; pink and yellow leaves overlap in front of and behind the droplet-shaped white stems. The forms are only slightly more flaccid than those of the border to the first clerestory window (N: XXV), which it much resembles in type.

Whether any of the windows on the south side of the Trinity Chapel were actually executed under the Fogg Medallion Master's supervision remains open to question; the armature of Window S:V in the ambulatory is paired with N:V facing it, but no glass is *in situ*. There is no evidence in the surviving glass to indicate that he worked on any of the ambulatory windows further east, or that he provided glass for the Trinity Chapel clerestory. His activity is thus restricted to the early and middle periods, which is in keeping with the transitional character of his work.

The brilliance of the Victoria and Albert Museum panel, with its red ground, would set off very well the cool, clear colors of the Fogg medallion (Col. Pl. IV); pale blue, which had been used in the clerestory of the choir and transepts, is now daringly employed in two tones against the deeper blue ground; other colors are soft green, pale yellow, and pink. Red appears in the aedicula and edging, and also in the dalmatic of the archbishop. In these panels the Master is a delicate colorist. His figure style is otherwise astonishingly negative, as free from Romanesque as from Gothic stylization. The figures in position in Window n:V of the Trinity Chapel look large and stiff compared with those in the windows to the east; the contrast is quite apparent in Window n:III, where two fig-

ures by the Fogg Medallion Master have been inserted in restoration. Their scale is not unlike that of the hagiographical series in the "triforium," in which the master had been a minor painter.

In the Trinity Chapel panels full use is not made of the circles or canted squares; they are pared down by rectilinear architectural frames, within which the figures are tightly confined (fig. 120). There are affinities in composition with the work of the Master of the Parable of the Sower, in the way figures are bracketed under arcades and in the use of scrolls as space-fillers. The figures themselves, however, are entirely different; they are poised, weightless and motionless, with impassive faces; the only action is in their hands, which reach out to make sharp, stabbing gestures (fig. 115). Shem shows a similar modification of outline as compared with Joanna (figs. 67, 82). In the draperies the paint appears to be laid on with a thin brush in uncertain, brittle lines without modeling washes, and there is little back-painting.

Stylistically, the Trinity Chapel windows attributed to the Fogg Medallion Master form a transition between the earlier hagiographical scenes relating to Sts. Dunstan and Alphage, in which the action is rather lost in pictorial complexity, and the other miracle windows, which are highly charged with drama and stripped of unnecessary detail (figs. 109, 197). This is the moment of calm, the gathering of forces before a definitive mode is found. Such an innocuous style, much more than the inimitable style of the Methuselah Master, was capable of forming the basis of a new departure. The Fogg Medallion Master rejected the richness and variety of the Methuselah Master's work in favor of more generalized representation. He made some lasting formulations. Throughout the rest of the series of miracles the use of an arcaded aedicula to impose order and clarity was never abandoned, a restricted number of facial types was settled upon, and figures tend to be insubstantial. The tomb of Thomas Becket, which first appears in Window n:V of the Trinity Chapel, is faithfully reproduced

---

[94] Two lengths of this border are in the Virginia Museum of Arts, Richmond; Caviness, 1973, figs. 1, 2, and cover. Close examination from the fire escape in 1974

revealed that only one panel in the Trinity Chapel is intact.

in the rest of the series. It takes the form of a rectilinear sarcophagus with two elliptical holes cut in the marble side (figs. 120, 159).[95]

Neither the ornament nor the figure style gives very precise clues as to the origins of the Fogg Medallion Master or the time span of his work, but considered together they indicate an earlier date than I had previously supposed.[96] The type of *rinceaux* associated with him has parallels in manuscripts, wall paintings, and metalwork, and occurs commonly on the continent as well as in England in the twelfth century. Goldschmidt has attributed its appearance on the continent to English influence,[97] but a Norman origin was proposed by Wormald, who signaled its presence in the Christ Church Passionale, British Library, Harley MS 624, of the first half of the twelfth century.[98] Such scrolls were also part of the decorative repertory of the manuscripts given to Christ Church by Thomas Becket on his return from France; they may have been made in the north of France about 1160–1170.[99] In these the "flowers" are elaborate and have long tentacle-like petals that intertwine with the stems, much as they do in the glass (figs. 109, 122). They lack the leaf scars, which, however, are as strong in the glass as in the earlier manuscripts. One piece of ornament, unfortunately not *in situ* in the south choir aisle "triforium," looks remarkably early (fig. 123); it compares quite well with an initial in a Christ Church book dated by Dodwell 1110–1140, Cambridge, Trinity College, MS B. 2. 36.[100] In both the "calyx" is circular, and "petals" turn over in hard shell-like forms; cross-hatching is used on the far side of

the petal. This particular form does not appear elsewhere in the glass. It has often been observed that fleshy, organic *rinceaux* were modified in the thirteenth century, becoming more spindly and less plastic, with the omission of such traits as the rings on the bark below a shoot.[101] Twelfth-century examples bear this out; in vault paintings in the nave at Ely, round, fleshy stems are used to frame medallions with figure subjects.[102] St. Gabriel's Chapel in the crypt of Canterbury Cathedral has similar vegetal forms, framing the remnants of figures, which have some of the new naturalism of the Morgan and Methuselah Masters. *Rinceaux* of similar character are also found in metalwork, as in the English ciboria of about 1170 (fig. 101).[103] These comparisons would allow a very early dating for the "triforium" ornament, of 1175–1180. The form is long-lived, however. Strong, vegetal scrolls also occur in the Cuthbert Life in the British Library, which is generally dated about 1200; the "blossoms" are pronged acanthus, only slightly less rich than the vegetation of the Tree of Jesse page in the Great Canterbury Psalter in Paris.[104] An even later occurrence of *rinceaux* that much resemble the Victoria and Albert Museum panel is in an initial in a Christ Church Register, which can be dated between 1213 and 1216 or 1218 (figs. 116, 125).[105] The central leaf has a beaded stem, but there are no leaf scars or intertwining of leaves and stems. This trend towards flat stems and dry leafage is confirmed in the Little Canterbury Psalter in Paris, which has to be dated before 1220 (fig. 126). The maximum date span of the ornament associated with the Fogg Medallion Master seems

---

[95] The tomb in the Burial of Thomas Becket in Sens has the same shape. The marbled sides are most often pink, rarely blue or yellow.

[96] Caviness, 1965, pp. 195–96.

[97] Adolf Goldschmidt, "English Influence on Medieval Art of the Continent," *Medieval Studies in Memory of A. Kingsley Porter*, ed. R. W. Koehler, II, Cambridge, Mass., 1939, 715.

[98] Wormald, 1943, p. 34, Pl. xivb.

[99] Dodwell, 1954, pp. 106–109, Pls. 65a and c.

[100] *Ibid.*, p. 121, Pl. 26a.

[101] Tristram, 1944, pp. 55, 70. For a more detailed discussion see Plummer, pp. 44–45.

[102] Tristram, 1944, Pl. 83 and Suppl. Pl. 5a; dated (p. 55) in the second half of the twelfth century.

[103] Swarzenski, 1967, figs. 448–50 (Kennet ciborium on loan to the Victoria and Albert Museum). See also *The Year 1200* I, nos. 171, 172, pp. 164–66 (Malmesbury ciborium in the Pierpont Morgan Library and Warwick ciborium in the Victoria and Albert Museum), and comments by Sauerländer, 1971, p. 515.

[104] London, British Library, Add. MS 39945 (Yates Thompson MS 26). Dated in the period 1189–1212 by Boase, 1953, pp. 287–88, cf. Pächt, 1962, p. 20 (late twelfth century). Initials with scrollwork are on ff. 2v and 7v.

[105] Cathedral Library, Register K. Rental Y, f.23. I am grateful to Dr. Urry for pointing this out to me. The dating is his, from paleographical evidence and that provided by names in the rental (Urry, 1967, p. 18).

to be 1175 to about 1200; by 1220 his vigorous *rinceaux* would be extremely archaic, a feature inconsistent with their high quality.

Although the *rinceaux* used by the Master do not presuppose any other than an English origin, they do provide a link with one French monument; in Châlons-sur-Marne such spirals with flower-like palmettes are used as a wide border (fig. 124). The earliest glass of Châlons, however, has rather meager ornament, and Grodecki has commented upon its enrichment towards the end of the twelfth century.[106] This does not suggest that Châlons is the source for Canterbury. Sideways-growing palmettes are also found in borders at Châlons, as they are in St.-Remi, Soissons Cathedral, and St.-Quentin,[107] but so are they in York well before the turn of the century.[108] It is chiefly the geometric precision of one "triforium" border, already referred to above, that suggests some contact with the northern French centers, principally, perhaps, with St.-Remi. Similarity in composition between Windows n:V and VI of the Trinity Chapel and two windows in the Lady Chapel at St.-Quentin is more likely to indicate Canterbury influence in the thirteenth century, as suggested by the iconography (Appendix figs. 2, 3); Grodecki has tentatively concluded that these windows are as late as 1220.[109]

The "neutral" figure style of the Fogg Medallion Master, at once archaic and advanced, is very hard to place in time, but its relatives are English. There is a certain general similarity with the Guthlac Roll, in the use of aediculae, the static poses of the figures and reliance on gestures to convey drama, the impassive sameness of the faces, and the tall, thin figure types.[110] The drawing of the drapery is, however, quite different, though it has not aided

in reaching an agreement as to the date of the roll.[111] For the Fogg Medallion Master one of the closest comparisons that can be made is with the Worksop Bestiary in New York, which is dated before 1187.[112] Figures are heavily outlined but details of facial features and drapery folds are generally rather freely and sketchily treated. The lack of structure and of any sense of underlying form in the tunic of the reclining man illustrated here compares very well with the tunic of the right-hand figure in the Fogg medallion (figs. 117, 115). In the same book is another painting, also of a reclining figure, in which still sketchy but more insistent hooked folds are used; this drapery system is more highly developed by the older artist of the Ingeborg Psalter, who probably painted in the north of France in the 1190s.[113] The rather flatter and more elongate figures by his younger assistant are paralleled by the clerestory figures attributed to the Fogg Medallion Master; Phares adopts a pose very similar to that of Herod in the Massacre of the Innocents in the Psalter, with torso, shoulders, and arm flattened into the plane of the picture, and the stomach and legs disproportionate and distorted (figs. 80, 81). Both artists reject much of the classicism of their older contemporaries. The comparison with the Worksop Bestiary tends to confirm that the activities of both the Ingeborg Psalter artist and the Fogg Medallion Master belong to the last decade or two of the twelfth century. This may be further confirmed by comparison with an unfinished painting in the Winchester Bible by the Morgan Master, in which the paint much resembles the washes and tracelines of heads by the Fogg Medallion Master (figs. 119, 118). He seems to have outlived both the Methuselah Master and the Master of the Parable of the Sower.

---

[106] *Vitrail*, pp. 107–108. The *rinceaux* border was admired by L. Magne, *L'Oeuvre des peintres verriers français . . .* , Paris, 1885, p. xii, fig. 6.

[107] For Châlons, Westlake, I, 1881, Pl. xvia; and Ferdinand de Lasteyrie, *Histoire de la peinture sur verre*, II, Paris, 1856, Pl. xxii. For St.-Remi, Westlake, I, 1881, Pl. xxxiv D; it has not been possible to verify whether this border, to the Crucifixion in the tribune, is old, but it resembles an original panel in the clerestory. For Soissons, see Cahier and Martin, 1841, Mosaiques F, 4 and 8. For St.-Quentin, Grodecki, 1965, fig. 117, and Westlake, I, 1881, Pl. xv.

[108] Westlake, I, 1881, Pl. xxiii.

[109] Grodecki, 1965, p. 188.

[110] Warner, 1928. One scene is illus. Read, 1926, fig. 3a.

[111] The date proposed by Warner, 1928, p. 18, of ca. 1196, which coincides with a translation of the relics, was regarded as too early by Homburger, 1958, p. 40, and Boase, 1953, p. 288.

[112] *The Year 1200* I, no. 259, 260–61, with bibliography.

[113] Pierpont Morgan Library, MS 81, f.60v, cf. Deuchler, 1967, fig. 28. The same observation was made independently by Ayres, 1974, p. 221.

So also did another far more accomplished painter who had collaborated in the north oculus.

THE JESSE TREE MASTER[114]

In spite of an important development of style, the figures of major prophets in the north oculus (figs. 129–131), the ancestors Boaz and Salmon (fig. 127) from the clerestory over the central steps to the Trinity Chapel (Window N:IX), and the two surviving panels from a Tree of Jesse in the corona (figs. 133, 134) may be attributed to the same hand. This is corroborated by the use of similar ornamental motifs in all three windows. Work by the Master of the Parable of the Sower in the north oculus allows an early date for this window. The other two windows were situated to the east of the partition of 1180, and the building dates give a *terminus post quem* of 1184 for the corona glass, which is the most advanced in style.

The compositions and ornament *in situ* in the oculi of the easterly transept gables are identical. The geometric ironwork is of great interest (Appendix fig. 2). The center is encircled by an iron; within it a canted square and inside that a square are developed by a process of continuous halving, or joining the midpoints of the sides of the first figure; this process has been studied by Dudley.[115] On the sides of the canted square are four semicircles. The outer ring of the composition is less obviously organized; four contiguous part-circles describe petaloid forms, with trefoils between them.[116] The double outlines of the petals in the irons recall the composition of Window s:XII, situated below the south oculus (Appendix fig. 1).

The concept of grouping varied shapes in fours around a central element is very old,[117] Baltrušaitis compared the oculus to a page in a tenth-century Gospel Lectionary from Cambrai.[118] Similar constructions were used in eleventh-century ivories, such as an example in the Metropolitan Museum, New York.[119] The early constructions, however, are usually quite irregular. Grodecki has noticed an almost contemporaneous appearance, in the mid-twelfth century, of close-knit geometries in glass and metalwork, as in the Stavelot Altar and the Châlons-sur-Marne glass;[120] even more elaborate was the destroyed retable from Stavelot.[121] Examples from the Meuse and Cologne are numerous;[122] very similar to the oculus is a piece of metalwork in the Hermitage.[123] Once more we find Canterbury in tune with developments in this region of the continent, which reflect the twelfth-century recovery of Euclidean geometry. The entirely geometric *opus Alexandrinum* mosaic, which was laid at the top of the steps from the main altar and in front of the position of Becket's shrine in the Trinity Chapel, is further evidence of this preoccupation with the ruler and compasses (text fig. 2d); it has been compared with the north oculus by Dudley.[124] Although it has never been closely dated, a complete change in the flooring of the eastern part of the Trinity Chapel has suggested new contacts with the continent, and I am inclined to attribute these to the period after the Interdict;[125] a date between 1180 and 1207 would then be most probable for the *opus Alexandrinum*.

Clerestory Window N:IX, on the north side of the Trinity Chapel, is the first to abandon completely the use of horizontal bars that are consis-

[114] Caviness, 1975.
[115] Dudley, 1969, fig. 3e–l, pp. 26–27.
[116] *Ibid.*, fig. 7.
[117] Numerous examples from the antique period on were discussed and illustrated by Ellen J. Beer, "Nouvelles Réflexions sur l'image du monde dans la cathédrale de Lausanne," *Revue de l'Art* 10 (1970), 57–62.
[118] Jurgis Baltrušaitis, *Réveils et prodiges; le gothique fantastique*, Paris [1960], p. 41, fig. 27.
[119] R. H. Randall, "An 11th Century Ivory Pectoral Cross," *Journal of the Warburg and Courtauld Institutes* 25 (1962), 159–71, fig. 2.
[120] L. Grodecki, "A propos des Vitraux de Châlons-sur-Marne: deux points d'iconographie mosane," *L'Art mosan*, ed. Pierre Francastel, Paris, 1953, pp. 163ff.

[121] A drawing was reproduced in O. von Falke and H. Frauberger, *Deutsche Schmelzarbeiten des Mittelalters*, Frankfort, 1904, Pl. 70.
[122] Hanns Swarzenski, "The Song of the Three Worthies," *Bulletin of the Boston Museum of Fine Arts* 56 (1958), 47.
[123] No. 265 in the Basilevsky collection, illus. Rosalie Green, *Essays in Honor of E. Panofsky* (de Artibus Opuscula 40, 1961), Pl. 55, fig. 8.
[124] Dudley, 1969, figs. 7 and 8.
[125] N. E. Toke, "The Opus Alexandrinum and Sculpted Stone Roundels in the Retro-Choir of Canterbury Cathedral," *Archaeologia Cantiana* 42 (1930), 194–98; cf. Caviness, 1974, p. 69.

tently found to the west of the partition; the "transitional" nature of Window N:X will be considered later. In the central axis of the window Boaz and Salmon (fig. 127) were set in large circles with a small circle between them for ornament. The border of the window is not defined by irons, and it is interrupted by wide edging bands encircling the irons that enclose figures; a similar use of ornamental edgings outside the irons occurs in the north choir aisle "triforium" windows, and in Window n:VI of the Trinity Chapel, attributed to the Fogg Medallion Master (figs. 109, 115, 116). Although the composition is simple and conservative, the use of curved irons at clerestory level is radically new.

The ornamental motif favored by the Jesse Tree Master consists of flat serrated leaves arranged in radiating patterns of fours. This is used in the borders of the outer and inner circles of the oculi; the outer circle has pairs of white stems, but the inner one has only interlocking leaves, as does the edging around the figure panels in clerestory N:IX (figs. 127, 128). In spite of the great distance of these panels from the viewer, the interstices between the main leaves are also painted with smaller and more delicate quatrefoils. This dense patterning is omitted from bands dividing the figures of the Jesse Tree from one another, although they were closer to the viewer (figs. 133, 134); this is one of the indications of a later date. The straight-bar armature of the Jesse Window has to be regarded as standard for that subject, and so not indicative of an early date.

The leaf motif is an old one; it occurred commonly in eleventh-century manuscripts and ivories, and a variant was used in the St. Albans Psalter.[126] It is also found in enamel plaques of the Klosterneuburg Ambo,[127] and in one lancet of the clerestory of St.-Remi.[128] Its appeal in this later period may have been its geometric precision, since it was possible to draw the leaves with a compass, as was evidently done in the oculus and the Jesse Window, and at St.-Remi. The Jesse Tree Master

is not alone in using the motif at Canterbury; broader, heavier leaves arranged in radiating patterns make up two borders in the clerestory of the southeast transept, but in these the leaves are drawn freehand.[129] The Methuselah Master also used half the motif—leaves in V's—as a delicate monochrome edging to panels in the north choir aisle (fig. 27).

The palette of the Jesse Tree Master, especially in the oculus and clerestory window, tends to a predominance of white, pink, and green,[130] a restriction that has been noticed in much of the work of the Joanna Master and his assistants in the clerestory of the transepts. Red is added to the clerestory panels, in small roundels on the blue ground. The Jesse panels are richer and more brilliant, chiefly by the addition of greater amounts of yellow in the blossoms, and red in the ornamental bands between the figures and the orb of Josiah;[131] limpid blue appears only in the Virgin's orb, where it is outlined in yellow against the more somber, slightly greenish-blue ground. The robes of both figures are green and purple, of somewhat different shades, thus avoiding the large amounts of white that are used in the prophets of the oculus and in the ancestors of Christ.

Two of the Jesse Tree Master's early figures (figs. 129, 131), in the oculus, adopt the energized "leaping" pose of Noah (fig. 66), yet they are more compact and have greater organic unity, in spite of the contorted position. They are more heavily draped; the mantles twisted over the shoulder and across the stomach assert the plasticity and unity of the figures. Broad sweeps of drapery are set off against more planar, decorative passages, such as the skirts of Jeremiah and Daniel or the mantle of Ezechiel (figs. 129, 130, 131). Crisp, pleated edges are only fleetingly visible; usually they are looped under and serve to emphasize curvatures, contributing to the softer appearance of these figures compared with the Methuselah Master's work in the choir clerestory (figs. 8, 9, 12). Such thick, looped edges are a common feature of English and continental works from the 1170s on; the glass from

---

[126] Pächt, Dodwell, and Wormald, 1960, pp. 98, 103, Pl. 131b–d.
[127] Röhrig, 1955, figs. 13, 16, 38, 40, 43.
[128] The center lancet in the first bay on the south side.

[129] Clerestory Windows S:XII and S:XIII; in Window N:XXII a single motif appears in the center at the bottom.
[130] Rackham, 1949, Pl. IV (color).
[131] Rackham, 1957, Pl. 4 (color).

Troyes and related manuscripts may be cited,[132] and the kings in niello on the St. Oswald reliquary in Hildesheim.[133] The same feature appears in the Ingeborg Psalter group of the late twelfth to early thirteenth century.[134]

A tract on the angels included in an English Bestiary (Cambridge University Library, MS Kk. 4.25) has an illustration of Tobias in which the pose and strong graphic techniques are very close to the early work of the Jesse Tree Master (fig. 132).[135] The draftsman, perhaps working in St. Albans around 1200,[136] demonstrates the affinity between glass painting and the graphic arts, one that becomes even clearer with the advent of prints in the fifteenth century. Both the Jesse Tree Master and the artist of the manuscript are concerned with the linear organization of mass. Thick, certain strokes outline the figures and indicate the unwieldiness of heavy mantles, while finer, more closely spaced lines suggest the lighter fabrics of the tunic, as in Ezechiel (fig. 130). Passages of complicated drapery folds detach themselves from the figures to fall in the picture plane, as between the thighs of Tobias, Jeremiah, and Daniel (figs. 132, 129, 131). The greater elegance of some passages in the drawings, however, suggests that they are later.

The two clerestory figures, which may be identified as Boaz and Salmon from Window N:IX display similar drapery passages. Because of the large scale, lead-lines are now ingeniously used to outline curving folds. The poses, slightly more relaxed, are sprawling, as if to fill the circles of the ironwork; the provenance is proved by the way in which the hands and feet have either been cut off or altered to accommodate the figures to their present oval frames; curving lead-lines below Salmon's hem and above his left arm, which fall on the same circle, originally echoed the circular edging line (fig. 127).

In spite of an actual reduction in size, Salmon has qualities of monumentality that are closer to the work of the Methuselah Master than to some of the immediately preceding figures of the transept clerestories, in which miniaturesque effects were noticed. The contained power of this figure is also reminiscent of the early work of Nicholas of Verdun in the Klosterneuburg ambo of 1181; such a figure as Jacob in the scene of benediction is, however, more classicizing in proportion and organic unity.[137] On the other hand, both artists evince a parallel interest in surface textures of drapery, with a bold use of dark accents. A loss of breadth and power can be detected in the four Apostles set in paired semicircles in a nave clerestory window of Chartres (CLXVIII); this is most noticeable in a figure which in pose resembles Salmon. Gesture is more elegant, the figure is more compact but more attenuated, imprisoned in softly curving draperies. Stylistically, Salmon belongs between the Klosterneuburg ambo and Chartres, where the glazing of the nave may date from the first decade of the thirteenth century.

The Jesse Tree in the corona is the Master's last work. His hand is recognizable in the handling of draperies, especially in the characteristic folds between the thighs (figs. 133, 134). The most striking change is in the calm frontal pose of the figures, to some extent demanded by tradition. The symmetrical pose of the figures, with both hands grasping the tree, the way in which they function as columnar statues in relation to the trunk, and the disposition of the large ornamental blossoms, follow very closely the tradition of St.-Denis and Chartres, which had already been reflected in the York glass of ca. 1170.[138] The composition appears quite archaic beside the French windows and manuscript pages of the late twelfth to early thirteenth century, as in the Ingeborg Psalter and related

[132] Grodecki, 1963, Pls. XLVII, XLVIII.

[133] Swarzenski, 1967, fig. 484.

[134] For example, London, British Library, Add. MS 15452; Deuchler, 1967, Pls. LI, LII and passim; The Year 1200 I, no. 251, 252.

[135] A Catalogue of the Manuscripts Preserved in the Library of the University of Cambridge, edited for the Syndics of the University Press, III, Cambridge, 1858, no. 2040, 670–73.

[136] The drawings have been considered close to Matthew Paris in style. They have frequently been dated early in the thirteenth century; Swarzenski, 1967, fig. 545, p. 84; Rickert, 1965, p. 108; Brieger, 1957, pp. 149–50, Pl. 50; D. H. Turner, The Year 1200 II, Pls. 188–89.

[137] Röhrig, 1955, Pl. 38.

[138] Caviness, 1975, pp. 375–376, figs. 6 and 7.

Bible in the British Library, Add. MS 15452, or the Psalter of Blanche of Castile, Paris, Bibliothèque de l'Arsenal, MS 1186.[139] In the thirteenth-century windows of Troyes, Soissons, and St.-Germain-lès-Corbeil, as in the manuscripts, more fluid but meager *rinceaux* replace the great blossoms, and the design is more unified.[140] Of this group only the earliest example, the Ingeborg Psalter, has figures that are clearly structured, with well-defined volumes underlying the drapery.

Very close relations observable between the style of the Jesse Tree Master and the sculpture and glass of Sens Cathedral will have to be considered more fully in connection with other painters. Elsewhere I have drawn attention to the similarity that exists between the seated figures of the Liberal Arts of the central portal of Sens, generally dated in the 1190s or close to 1200, and the Jesse Tree figures.[141] In both series the knees form a broad platform from which the torso is built up, the rotund stomach clearly outlined, and the upper part of the body squared off by the firm line of the belt. This structural precision is only partially masked by mantles that weave around the figures. Some of the sculpted figures, however, adopt more restless poses comparable to that of Salmon.[142] The origins of this classicizing style at Sens remain obscure; it does not seem to grow logically out of the earlier portal of St. John, and Sauerländer has suggested the resolution of this problem may be bound up with the sources for the glass of the ambulatory.[143]

The painting of Christ in Majesty at the summit of the Becket Window at Sens seems directly related to the designs for the Canterbury Jesse Tree, and may even be a replica of the lost Christ from the corona (figs. 135, 137). Seated, like the Virgin, on an orb edged with gold, the figure has the clar-

ity of structure and quiet outline typical of the Jesse designs. His symmetrically extended arms mimic the Jesse Tree figures, the wide sleeves of his purple robe falling in evenly looped folds, as in the Virgin. As with the two surviving Canterbury figures, his mantle is green. Red is used in the orb, as in Josiah's, and the flanking angels in green and hot yellow take on the decorative brilliance of the blossoms of the tree. Comparison with the Christ in Majesty from the summit of the Prodigal Son Window in Chartres suggests that the style of Sens represents an earlier phase (fig. 195). The Chartres figure is more "Gothic," with articulation of the human form masked by enveloping, decoratively arranged draperies.

Earlier continental parallels for the Jesse Tree figures exist at St.-Remi of Rheims, as comparison of the Virgin with Hosea indicates (figs. 133, 83).[144] The classicizing style of St.-Remi, if it belongs to the 1180s, is rather an isolated phenomenon in France. The very assured style of the clerestory figures, in which there is none of the constant experimentation found at Canterbury, is quite obscure in its origins. Far more certain is the presence in England of a "new style" by 1195;[145] the Great Seal, of which the matrix was made for Richard I in London in that year, was put into use in 1198, when it was attached to documents sent to Canterbury.[146] The figure of Josiah is so close to the representation of Richard on the seal that this could conceivably have been the model that inspired the Jesse Tree Master (figs. 134, 136). Whether there was in some sense a "court style," formed as Gauthier has suggested by "le goût Plantagenêt," or whether it was rather the product of the great Benedictine houses—St.-Remi, Christ Church, Westminster—is not easily resolved on the basis of surviving material.[147] At about the

---

[139] For the first two, Deuchler, 1967, figs. 18, 170; for the Arsenal Psalter, Caviness, 1975, fig. 5.

[140] For Troyes, Lafond, 1955, pp. 32, 42–43; illus. West-lake I, 1881, Pl. xlvb; for Soissons, *Vitrail*, fig. 92, p. 123; for St.-Germain, Musée du Louvre, *L'Europe gothique*, Paris, 1968, no. 195, p. 117, fig. 62.

[141] Caviness, 1975, p. 379, fig. 18.

[142] Sauerländer, 1966, figs. 69, 52.

[143] Sauerländer, 1970, p. 49.

[144] Caviness, 1975, p. 379.

[145] Boase, 1953, p. 275; Saxl, 1954, pp. 20–21; Ayres, 1969, pp. 50–54.

[146] W. de Gray Birch, *British Museum: Catalogue of Seals in the Department of Manuscripts*, I, London, 1887, nos. 87–90, 14; Poole, 1955, p. 373, n. 6; Lionel Landon, *The Itinerary of Richard I* (Pipe Roll Society LI N.S. 13) London, 1935, pp. 178, 183.

[147] M. M. Gauthier, "Le Gout plantagenêt," *Stil und*

same time, the Westminster Psalter paintings show a variant of this serene, classicizing style,[148] and at Canterbury the way was prepared by the Methuselah Master.

A date soon after 1198, which seems most probable for the Jesse Window, would allow the possibility that the Master's earlier style evolved over the previous ten to twenty years; he may have begun work on the oculus before 1180, which would explain his collaboration with the more archaic Master of the Parable of the Sower.

THE MASTER OF THE REDEMPTION WINDOW AND HIS ASSISTANTS

Many features of the east window of the corona follow the postulates of more westerly windows in the early and middle groups, but, as already observed in the work of the Joanna Master and Jesse Master, there is also evidence of a *rapprochement* with continental works. The composition takes up one of the earlier experiments with the composite quatrefoil; as in Window s:VIII on the south side of the presbytery, the ordinary and canted square are used in alternation in the central axis (Appendix figs. 1, 2). Whereas, however, the ordinary squares have semicircles on the sides, the canted squares are flanked by four small circular compositions delineated by white stems in the intermediate panels of ornament, without the use of encircling irons; a parallel is in the St. Eustace Window in Chartres (Appendix fig. 3).[149] At Chartres, also, the composite quatrefoil is the main component of a Redemption Window similar to the Canterbury one, but as in a much earlier example of the compositional type at St.-Denis, the ironwork is rectilinear with semicircles inscribed.[150] The more varied Canterbury solution is one exceptionally well suited to the meaning of the window,

since it provides groupings of four types around each antitype, while giving greater importance to three of the five central scenes, the Crucifixion, Resurrection, and Pentecost (Appendix fig. 20). In view of the versatility in armature design documented throughout the typological windows at Canterbury, it is not necessary to suppose that the corona east window depends directly on the Chartrain compositions.

In color the east window resembles others of the middle group. Limpid blue is sparingly used in the ornament; the blues are otherwise slightly greenish and heavily patinated. Red forms the background to the *rinceaux*, while the figures are less brilliant, with much white, purple, and green in the draperies. The palette differs from that of the Fogg Medallion Master only in the absence of very pale blues in the figures, but this is compensated by an equally delicate shade of green in the landscapes. The *rinceaux* are of a type quite different from his composite blossoms; both the ornament and the figure compositions show a direct dependence on the Methuselah Master.

The *rinceaux* present only a slight modification of the naturalistic leafy bunches of north choir aisle Window n:XIV (figs. 179, 182). The small leaves are still delicate and fleshy, but they are less highly differentiated; leaves and stems spread out with no intertwining and less overlapping, as if they had been carefully separated and pressed between the pages of a book. This trend to simplification, and eventually to hardening and impoverishment, will be followed more closely in the context of the glass of Sens and the easternmost windows of the Trinity Chapel. It corresponds with developments in the sculpted capitals and bosses of the choir and Trinity Chapel. In the choir capitals palmettes are introduced but they are stiff and highly stylized. There was, as Newman has remarked, a gradual

---

überlieferung in der Kunst des Abendlandes I (*Akten des 21. Internationalen Kongresses für Kunstgeschichte in Bonn, 1964*) Berlin, 1967, 142.

[148] London, British Library, Royal MS 2 A xxii, generally associated with the St. Albans scriptorium. See E. G. Millar, *English Illuminated Manuscripts from the Xth to the XIIIth Centuries*, London, 1926, Pls. 62–63, pp. 90–91; Boase, 1953, pp. 284–87, Pl. 85b; Rickert, 1965,

pp. 92–93; Turner, *The Year 1200* II, 135–36, figs. 177–79; Grodecki, 1963, p. 131.

[149] Grodecki, 1965, pp. 172ff.

[150] For St.-Denis, see Grodecki, 1961b, fig. 13. The Chartres window is on the north side of the nave, Window LIX, Delaporte and Houvet, 1926, pp. 383–91, Pls. CLIV–CLVII.

loosening of the vegetal forms in the capitals as the building progressed east;[151] the last two pairs in the Trinity Chapel have delicate and vital leafy scrolls, with numerous leaves somewhat resembling oak arranged rather freely so that they overlap (fig. 180). They are very nearly identical to the *rinceaux* of the choir and the corona east window. The capitals must be dated about 1182; in view of the gradual and consistent development from the choir capitals, sculpting long *après la pose* is highly unlikely.[152] The only feature that seems archaic by comparison with the corona glass is the beaded stem, which does not appear in the glass after north choir aisle Window n:XV and some of the "triforium" ornament. On the other hand, a date for the glass close to 1184, when the corona was nearing completion, seems rather early in view of the economical border and certain aspects of the figure style.

As with the *rinceaux*, some of the figure compositions from the third typological window were taken over and modified in the corona east window. These modifications document a trend away from the distilled clarity of the Methuselah Master and towards a more agitated and dramatic representation of events. The Ascent of Enoch, like the Calling of Nathanael by the Master of the Public life of Christ, is represented in two episodes as continuous narrative. Some of the types are balanced against each other in pairs, as for instance the Ascent of Enoch with the Ascent of Elijah, the Consecration of Aaron and His Sons with Moses and Jethro, and Moses Striking the Rock with the *Signum Tau* (fig. 137), but the visual similarity of types to antitypes is not great and many of the scenes have a direct narrative import that belies the anagogical inscriptions. The "disappearing Christ" bears only a conceptual resemblance to Enoch or Elijah.

Extension of space beyond the picture frame, so evident in the Ascension, is carried even further in the summit of the window, where the flames of Pentecost descend from the Godhead represented in the panel above (fig. 137). In Noah's Ark, which was perhaps based on the same scene by the Methuselah Master in the north choir aisle, a significant modification is seen in the way forms break out of the edging at the top in one of the few undisturbed areas of this heavily restored panel (figs. 143, 144).

Another scene taken over from the choir aisle is Moses and Jethro; it is freely copied, without the use of the same cartoon (figs. 137, 139). The change of style is slight but significant. There is less area of ground, resulting in more crowding and less clarity. The tightly constrained figure of Jethro from the earlier window is animated by a swinging mantle, which also serves as a space filler. There is a reduction in plasticity, especially in the handling of the drapery over the thigh. The different appearance of the corona designs cannot therefore be imputed entirely to different models. Loss of clarity in composition and in individual articulation is also clear from a comparison of Christ among the Doctors with the similarly composed scene of Pentecost.

The figures in the corona east window are animated but also stereotyped. Frequently they assume a pose of half-kneeling or leaping, the legs in the same position in both (figs. 137, 201). Hemlines are agitated and mantles swirl up in a variety of floating drapery patterns. All these basic elements of design suggest that a single master planned the whole window. In some cases the Methuselah Master provided him with a point of departure, but his work also reflects the pictorial richness of the Master of the Public Life of Christ and the movement suggested by the Master of the Parable of the Sower. His innovations are in the adoption of a very limited repertory of poses and a compression of pictorial space. The rocky hill from which Moses strikes water, for instance, rises vertically in the plane of the window, instead of receding in layers to a distant skyline as in the Sower (figs. 204, 89).

---

[151] John Newman, *North East and East Kent* (*The Buildings of England*, ed. N. Pevsner), Harmondsworth, 1969, pp. 174–75, figs. 27 and 28; cf. Cave, 1935, p. 46, who saw the naturalistic foliage of the Trinity Chapel bosses as a sudden importation, perhaps by English William.

[152] The early date is supported by comparison with a boss in the Madeleine at Vézelay, dated by Sauerländer (1966, Pl. 4, pp. 16–17) about 1180–1190.

Analysis of the painting styles is hampered by the very large number of restored heads in this window. The draperies are characterized by mannerisms that suggest the execution was divided between at least two painters. One may be called the Crumpled Silk Painter, for his painstaking representation of bulky naturalistic folds. These are generally, as in the Pentecost, swept aside, so that they do not altogether mask the articulation of the limbs, yet the eye dwells on the rich draperies rather than on the human forms (fig. 137). This interest in the complex behavior of materials is part of a broader stylistic phenomenon, as already observed in the Jesse Master's work. The Pentecost figures, with their quick rhythms of crumpled drapery, compare well with a group of Apostles in the Ingeborg Psalter by the older master.[153] There is one trait, however, which is oddly stylized. In the Ascent of Enoch the ends of his mantle are swept up into a tight shell-like motif, a static and horizontal form that is common in English art of the twelfth century; it occurs with regularity in the Dover Bible and occasionally in the Great Canterbury Psalter in Paris.[154]

The other hand I identify as the Fitz-Eisulf Master, whose mature work is in the Trinity Chapel. His style is generally much less archaic than that of the Crumpled Silk Painter, although some aspects derive from the Master of the Parable of the Sower. In the Sundial of Hezekiah, and in the skirt of Moses Striking the Rock, drapery folds are large and heavy, the material frozen into writhing pleats. A relation to the Sower on Stony Ground is evident, but the swirling motion has been arrested (figs. 89, 137). These hard pleats appeared already in the Life of St. Martin in the northeast transept chapel dedicated to the Saint, judging from the sole surviving fragment;[155] this increases the probability that the younger painter was a direct follower of the Master of the Parable of the Sower, who provided two or three windows in the same transept. Comparison of the Moses in the oculus with Moses Striking the Rock demonstrates

a loss of vigor in the pupil's figures (figs. 105, 204). On the other hand, he developed shorthand schemata for draperies that were reiterated in the easternmost windows of the Trinity Chapel, and that there became a salient feature of the new Gothic style. Figures in profile wear deeply bloused tunics masking the belt almost entirely; these are described by regular loops radiating from a point just behind the shoulder, which tend to flatten the torso, arm, and shoulder (figs. 205, 206). The legs are delineated by means of V-folds and the knees are clearly indicated, often appearing bony and prominent. The brushwork is at times very broad and sweeping, lacking the finesse of the Crumpled Silk Painter. In this, it breaks away from the miniaturesque effects that had been exploited by other painters of the middle group.

THE PETRONELLA MASTER

This artist is the most miniaturesque of all the Canterbury glass painters, and also the most French-looking. He provided Window n:IV in the Trinity Chapel, much of n:III, and the figures of Amminadab and Nahshon for clerestory N:X, which is over the steps to the Trinity Chapel, immediately to the east of the 1180 partition (plan). All are on the north side, but the ironwork in Trinity Chapel s:III and IV matches n:III and IV, which face them, and there is a strong probability that these were glazed by the same team.[156] The master is named for the scenes dealing with the cure of Petronella, an epileptic nun (Col. Pl. III).

It is problematic whether he should be included in the middle period, or attached to the late phase; many aspects of his work are conservative, however, and it is only the design and some of the ornament in Window n:III that suggest he may have collaborated with the Fitz-Eisulf Master. The armature design for clerestory N:X is a tentative and very slight departure from the straight-bar type that prevailed to the west; the horizontals are still firmly drawn across the figures, and only the

---

[153] Deuchler, 1967, fig. 34.
[154] Boase, 1953, Pls. 56c, 57a; *Psautier*, Pls. xviii, xx,
[155] Rackham, 1949, Pl. 31b (skirt of St. Martin's tunic).

[156] None of the glass now in Window s:IV is *in situ*; Caviness, 1967, p. 113.

vertical bars, which before would have marked off the border, are bowed out into a series of undulations, so that the elbows and knees of the figures in each case are comfortably framed in part of an ellipse (figs. 151, 152). This is the only "transitional" armature in the Trinity Chapel clerestory; the others provide pairs of clearly described geometric shapes with a marked reduction in scale of the figures. Chronologically this tentative step should come before the fully evolved new type that appeared in the next window, N:IX; this was painted by the Jesse Tree Master, and has been placed as early as the 1180s to 1190s on stylistic grounds. The Petronella Master may have been active then, too, although he worked in quite a different idiom.

No ornament from the clerestory window has been identified, but the Trinity Chapel windows are quite complete in this respect. Window n:IV is very conservative in composition, consisting of two tiers of roundels inscribed in irons that are predominantly vertical and horizontal, but that circle small ornamental bosses between the figure subjects. The border is of the sideways-growing variety favored by the Fogg Medallion Master, but the plant forms are richer and more varied than his; it somewhat resembles the border now in the crypt, which I conjecture came from the choir clerestory (figs. 3, 172), but closer parallels are on the continent, especially examples formerly at Soissons. Other examples can be cited in St.-Quentin, Châlons-sur-Marne, and St.-Remi of Rheims, although the latter—in the clerestory—is much drier.[157] The border is the most brilliantly colored element in window n:IV, with sharp accents of green and yellow against the red and blue ground areas. The ornamental bosses are delicate in coloring and drawing, with fragile heads of pink and green foliage on a soft blue ground centered on a pale blue quatrefoil; this plant type had already appeared in the border of clerestory Window S:XIV, and it is used again in the *rinceaux* of

Window n:III in the Trinity Chapel. Bosses in Lincoln Cathedral are remarkably similar in design, though with fewer leaves.[158]

In spite of the harsh coloring and bold design of the border, and the use of red edging bands round the figure compositions, the predominant aspect of Window n:IV is subtle, delicate, and highly wrought. The master characteristically modified the blue grounds to his figures, in the clerestory by the addition of red roundels, in the lower window by a thin grey wash in which tendrils are picked out. Against this soft blue the delicate shades of the draperies are better seen—pale pinks, mid- or acid green, white, some cool yellow, and little red. Petronella wears a pale green tunic over a long bluish-white robe; these subtle colors are barely seen from a distance (Col. Pl. III).

The Petronella Master had a tendency to decorate every surface, not only the grounds; he added marble graining to the tomb of Becket and the throne of Nahshon, a lozenge pattern to the tomb top and to the throne of Amminadab, and palmette ornament to architraves. The clerestory figures have robes decorated with bands of blue, yellow, or green, which, far from emphasizing the three-dimensionality of the figures, as they did in the Methuselah Master's work, appear as elegant surface decoration (figs. 151, 152, 8).

The architectural settings likewise have no spatial existence; they are reduced to exquisitely ordered, symmetrical aediculae, generally no more than an arch and lintel over four slender columns, with the inscription frequently placed in the cornice (fig. 159); in the outdoor scene with Petronella the inscription alone forms an arch between two doorways (Col. Pl. III). The way in which the aediculae function within the circular medallions brings to mind early Byzantine metalwork, notably the Missorium of Emperor Theodosius of A.D. 388 or the sixth-century Cyprus treasure.[159] The even spacing of columns recalls canon tables; the use of structures resembling canon tables to frame

[157] One ancient panel is preserved in the first lancet of the first bay from the west, on the south side.
[158] Day, 1913, fig. 10, cf. fig. 14.
[159] For the Missorium in the Madrid Real Academia de

la Historia, see Volbach, 1961, p. 24, Pl. 53. For the Cyprus treasure, divided between the Metropolitan Museum, New York, and Nicosia, see *ibid.*, p. 41.

scenes seems to occur in South Italian manuscripts early in the thirteenth century.[160] A more probable derivation for the Canterbury aediculae is St. Augustine's Gospels, a sixth-century Roman book preserved in Cambridge, Corpus Christi College, MS 286, in which the portrait of St. Luke and scenes from his gospel are framed by four columns with lintel and arch; an inscription is placed in the cornice and there is much embellishment of the architecture with ornament and marbling (fig. 161);[161] the book was in the library of St. Augustine's during the Middle Ages, and the restrained quality of its decoration may have had great appeal to the glass painters during the *antiquisant* phase of their art;[162] the flat, ornamental quality of this aedicula was readily adopted by the Gothic artist in preference to the sturdy three-dimensional structures that the Methuselah Master culled from the Utrecht Psalter tradition.

The aediculae are a backdrop to dramas enacted in a shallow space, which is generally closed off by the tomb in the right foreground. Slender figures seem to dance across this stage, the direction of movement tending to converge on the center. They are represented in a great variety of postures; expressive gestures and swirling draperies add to the drama, and a variety of facial types and expressions is suggested. There is a marked contrast between these tiny, lithe figures and the more stiff, impassive and large figures by the Fogg Medallion Master in the neighboring window to the west (figs. 159, 120).

The figures in Window n:IV are very delicately painted, with little use of back-painting except in the broadest shading of draperies. These are light and clinging, with varied and subtle modeling and a minuteness in the strokes similar to some passages by the Methuselah Master (fig. 55). The group of nuns around Petronella have skirts in which the material is caught up into tiny rucks

over the knees, and hangs in finely looped folds behind the thighs (Col. Pl. III). The figures, already slender in outline, appear extremely fragile and even gaunt from the light handling of paint. There is no reduction of folds to a bold, linear design, as in the work of the Fitz-Eisulf Master. The clerestory figures are equally exquisite and refined, soft draperies clinging to their narrow shoulders and gaunt limbs; quite remarkable is the way in which Nahshon's mantle settles into tiny rucks around his neck (fig. 152). The figures are quietly outlined, with none of the contained power of the choir figures or the uncouthness of the transept designs. The whole aspect is one of elegance and composure.

Recognition of these figures as perfectly preserved examples of this very distinctive Master's work has great importance for an understanding of Canterbury's relation to the continent in this period.[163] They are the only figures preserved from the clerestory that suggest a complete *rapprochement* with the St.-Remi choir clerestory figures. They confirm my earlier conclusion that the author of Window n:IV was a French artist, or one such as the architect, English William, who was profoundly influenced by developments in the region of northeast France.[164]

The affinities between the St.-Remi figures and Nahshon and Amminadab are manifold (figs. 83, 154, 151, 152). They have the same serene aspect, with a degree of ponderation. They adopt similar poses, with their feet firmly planted on the same level and the hands grasping a scroll or the folds of their garments. The draperies fall softly in catenary folds and elegant loops, and are ornamented with many-colored trimmings. The rather more slender proportions of the Petronella Master's figures may also reflect a similar tendency in the Crucifixion, and it is tempting to claim that the Petronella Master must have seen the glazing of

[160] For example, a Sicilian medical manuscript, illus. Theodore Meyer-Steineg and Karl Sudhoff, *Geschichte der Medizin im Uberblick mit Abbildungen*, Jena, 1921, fig. 95.

[161] Wormald, 1954, Pl. II.

[162] The importance of models of this period was stressed by Kitzinger, 1966a, p. 41.

[163] No photographs of them seem to have existed before 1971. Perhaps their authenticity had been in doubt, as the exterior surface of the glass is relatively little pitted or patinated.

[164] Caviness, 1970, p. 100.

St.-Remi as it was nearing its completion. Why he modified the armature design from this prototype is not yet explained, but it could have been an afterthought.

Lafond has already suggested a Parisian derivation for the diapered blue ground in Window n:IV of the Trinity Chapel ambulatory.[165] This decorative technique was used at Le Champ about 1160, Troyes about 1170, Notre-Dame of Paris about 1180, Lincoln about 1200, and Strasbourg about 1200 and later.[166] The technique was also known at Bourges.[167] Examples in Denmark and in the church of the Pantocrator in Istanbul may be imputed to German influences,[168] and Grodecki's claim that it is essentially a Rhenish, Mosan, and English feature remains valid.[169] Comparable designs appear also in some northern French manuscripts.[170]

Comparison with the Parisian glass—late twelfth-century panels with scenes from the life of St. Matthew that have been incorporated at some time into the south rose window of Notre-Dame—demonstrates other affinities with the Petronella Master (fig. 156, Col. Pl. III). In the Notre-Dame panels, curved inscriptions are used above the figures and in one instance this curved band functions as an arch on which is supported a superstructure of turrets and roofs.[171] Supporting

columns are in all cases lacking, however, and the sense of surface design is not as developed as at Canterbury. In spite of a more robust canon of proportion in the Parisian figures, comparison may be made with the Petronella Master in the sensitive handling of draperies, resulting in the proliferation of minute folds and loops, as behind the thighs, and a subtle use of half-tones. On the other hand, this sensitivity is not prevalent in the northeast of France, whereas Ayres has pointed out that it was present in some English work early in the 1190s; the Crucifixion miniature in the Bodleian Library, MS Tanner 169, published by him, provides certain affinities with the Notre-Dame glass.[172]

Even closer than the Notre-Dame fragments are the two windows with a life of St. Peter in the Lady Chapel of Troyes Cathedral, which have been described in the previous chapter. The medallions have triple edgings of red, white bead, and blue with a schematized cufic motif. Gestures are dramatically silhouetted between groups of figures, and architectural setting is reduced to a minimum. The figures are more attenuated than the earlier ones from Notre-Dame, and minutely painted draperies tend to flatten the limbs; skirts are blown back to create an effect of movement, and mantles cling round the shoulders. The colors of the dra-

[165] Lafond, 1946, p. 153. For the technique see Jean Lafond, *Trois Etudes sur la technique du vitrail*, Rouen, 1943, p. 25; Jean-Jacques Gruber, in *Vitrail*, p. 65, who cited the twelfth-century treatise of Theophilus; Frodl-Kraft, 1970, pp. 39–40. The scrollwork of these grounds is in reserve against a grey wash, which lends a deeper tone to the blue; in painting, the whole piece of glass was covered with *grisaille*, the design being then drawn with a blunt instrument before the paint was fired. The same technique was used in most of the Canterbury inscriptions.

[166] Le Champ (Isère), *Vitrail*, Pl. XI. I am grateful to Mrs. Ernest Brummer of New York for allowing me to see the Troyes pieces in her late husband's collection, the most important of which were exhibited in New York in 1968 (*Medieval Art*, no. 182, illus.). Another Brummer piece with diaper ground is in the Wellesley College Art Museum, no. 1949.19. For Notre-Dame see *Corpus, France* I, Pl. 9, G17. For Strasbourg, see Ahnne and Beyer, 1960, Pls. 1 and 2, dated after 1190 and between 1235 and 1240 respectively (p. 16). Other Rhenish examples are in Wentzel, 1954, Pls. 18, 22, 25, 36. For Lincoln see Lafond, 1946, Pl. XXII, pp. 153–54 and n. 89.

[167] Cahier and Martin, 1841, Pl. XVIE-G, illustrated

three panels with donors, but they were already "dispersés."

[168] *Corpus, Scandinavia* I, pp. 164, 170, Pls. I, 31, 32, IV, 39; pp. 302–303, Pl. 13g. The Pantocrator fragments were first published by A.H.S. Megaw, "Notes on Recent Work of the Byzantine Institute in Istanbul," *Dumbarton Oaks Papers* 17 (1963), 333–71, who dated them ca. 1130. Cf. Jean Lafond, "Découverte de vitraux historiés du moyen âge à Constantinople," *Cahiers archéologiques* 18 (1968), 231–38 (1204–1261), and Frodl-Kraft, 1970, pp. 27–28.

[169] Review of Megaw, *Bulletin Monumental* 123 (1965), 84.

[170] As a background to lettering or in a framing band; e.g., Paris, Bibliothèque Nationale, MS Lat. 11535, ff.74, 144, 166v, and the Bible of St. André-au-Bois, Boulogne, Bibliothèque Municipale, MS 2, illus. Rosy Schilling, "The Decretum Gratiani formerly in the C. W. Dyson Perrins Collection," *Journal of the British Archaeological Assoc.* 3rd series 26 (1963), Pl. 1.

[171] Illus. *Vitrail*, fig. 76.

[172] Ayres, 1969, fig. 5a, pp. 47–48.

peries are two tones of green, with white, hot yellow, or very pale blue; less often a brownish-purple is used. Red is employed sparingly in architectural settings and details of costume. But for the hotter tone of the yellow, this is the palette of the Petronella Master, and the details of figure drawing are also extremely close to his work (figs. 155, 159).

Unfortunately the provenance of a panel of glass that might have direct bearing on the training of the Petronella Master cannot be established; this is the tiny figure of Synagogue, now in a private collection in America, which came there with the alleged provenance of St.-Remi (fig. 157).[173] Despite Grodecki's claim that it is English,[174] I can find no place for it on the English side of the Channel—except at Canterbury, and there it does not fit any of the armatures. The ornament, rather meager and dry, is close to that of the east window of Orbais Abbey Church, near Rheims. The figure is only slightly less sensitive in handling than Petronella, and the use of green and cool yellow in the draperies, of a red edging band round the figure, and of a pale blue edging with palmette design around the missing larger panels, would be in keeping with the Master's work.

Once more the sculpture of Sens is relevant to the discussion. Whereas the robust figures of the Jesse Tree Master draw close to the Liberal Arts of the central portal at Sens, the expressive style of the Petronella Master has affinities with the archivolt reliefs of the slightly earlier portal of St. John, which Sauerländer dates between 1184 and 1200 (figs. 162, 163).[175] In the scenes illustrated, the coverlet clings and swirls over the reclining figures, clearly outlining their legs and the edge of the bed, without any monumental simplification. Paradoxically, the glass in the ambulatory at Sens is more harshly painted than either Window n:IV or n:III at Canterbury. On the other hand, Window n:III,

in its composition, border design, and some of the figure painting, seems to betray the influence of the Fitz-Eisulf Master, although the designing and delicate coloring must be attributed to the Petronella Master. The mature work of the Fitz-Eisulf Master is so closely connected with the Sens glazing that a fuller discussion of Window n:III will be in order later.

The relation of the Petronella Master to manuscript painting on both sides of the Channel is equally ambivalent. The author portrait in a Bestiary in Cambridge, University Library, MS Ii.4.26, seems a mannered variant of his elegant style, with an extreme sensitivity to complex drapery folds and resulting fragility and elongation of form; it has been dated late in the twelfth century.[176] The portrait is framed by slender columns, and has an exuberance of sculpted decoration in the capitals and lectern that are readily paralleled in Window n:III of the Trinity Chapel (fig. 164). The proliferation of folds in the lower hem of the garment suggests a date later than the Petronella Master. This tendency is also present in the prefatory pages to a Psalter of Augustinian use, Cambridge Trinity College, MS B.11.4, in which the translation of Becket occurs in the calendar, thus dating it after 1220.[177] Tall, wiry figures are partially enveloped in fluttering draperies, and their tense movements are very close in feeling to the twisting figures in Window n:III (figs. 167, 168). In English manuscripts this rather exaggerated figure style was prolonged to an extreme phase in the middle of the thirteenth century, as in the books associated with Salisbury, such as the Chichester Missal.[178] The Petronella Master's figures are quite free of the extravagance and nervousness even of the Psalter in Cambridge. In view of the precocious trend of the Tanner manuscript of 1192–93 and the relationship to French works of the 1180s to 1190s, a

---

[173] Formerly with Demotte in New York, see *Catalogue of an Exhibition of Stained Glass,* New York, [1928], no. 6. I am grateful to David DuBon of the Philadelphia Museum of Art for helping me locate this panel. It was later exhibited in New York, *Medieval Art,* no. 190, with a suggested provenance of Sens.

[174] Verbal communication, 1970.

[175] Sauerländer, 1970, pp. 99–102.

[176] Boase, 1953, pp. 287–88, 295, Pl. 53b.

[177] M. R. James, *The Western Manuscripts in the Library of Trinity College,* Cambridge, 1 (1900), pp. 331–37; Brieger, 1957, pp. 92–94, Pl. 23b; Rickert, 1965, pp. 98–99.

[178] Manchester, John Rylands Library, MS Lat. R. 24. See Hollaender, 1942–1944, pp. 232–38, Pls. i–v; Rickert, 1965, pp. 106–107, Pl. 108.

date well before 1220 must be proposed for his work.

Mannerisms are also present in the "Psalter of Blanche of Castile," traditionally dated 1200–1223;[179] the heads are rather large, the bodies emaciated, and there is a tendency in some drapery passages for the underlying form to disintegrate. The clinging draperies in the Visitation, with tiny loops behind the thigh and trailing hems, and the stiffly uplifted ends of the mantles, are close to those of the nuns in the scene with Petronella, but the formula has become hardened (fig. 158, Col. Pl. III). The style of the Petronella Master, who was most probably French in training, could be developed in different directions and thus form the basis of the diverging French court and English styles of about 1220. Closest to his style is a Bible in two volumes, Paris, Bibliothèque Nationale, MS Lat. 11535–34, now attributed to Champagne or the Ile-de-France, but once associated with Canterbury.[180] The drawing and coloring of the miniatures is delicate, the figures are elongate and at times sensitive. The palette of this miniaturist differs from the glass painter in the use of orange and buff, but his subtle combinations of greens with yellow and pale blues and pinks are identical to those of the Petronella Master. The illustrations are closely related in iconography to those in the Manerius Bible, Paris, Bibliothèque Sainte-Geneviève, MS 8–10, which was written in France by a Canterbury scribe. Neither book can be closely dated, but they must be ca. 1200.

Both the internal chronology of glazing and the dated comparisons would allow that the clerestory figures were designed in the two decades after 1180. The first design may have been modified by the addition of a curved armature under the impact of the Jesse Master's design for the neighboring window, which has been dated in the 1180s to 1190s. In the 1190s one might expect the full impact of St.-Remi to be felt in the figures; the Petronella Master was evidently aware of the latest developments there. The conservative nature of Window n:IV in the Trinity Chapel would allow a date in the same period; the exile of 1207 may be accepted as the *terminus ante quem*, as for the work of the Jesse Master. Reasons for placing the later work of the Petronella Master—in Window n:III and another clerestory window—after the exile will be considered in the following chapter.

---

[179] Paris, Bibliothèque de l'Arsenal, MS 1186; for the date, Henry Martin, *Les Joyaux de l'Arsenal I: Psautier de Saint Louis et de Blanche de Castille*, Paris, [1909], p. 11.

[180] *The Year 1200* I, no. 246, 247–48, with bibliography. The association with Canterbury was made by Ellen Beer, *Corpus, Switzerland*, I, 51–52, figs. 17, 18.

V. The Gothic Windows:
Sens, Canterbury, and Chartres

IN SPITE OF the historical fact of the exile of the Christ Church community in 1207–1213, there is no evidence for a complete break in the glazing of the eastern part of the church; the Master whose style dominates the rest of the surviving Trinity Chapel ambulatory windows (n and s:II, and s:VI and VII) had already participated in the glazing of the east window of the corona. He is named for the series of scenes in Window n:II relating events in the household of Jordan Fitz-Eisulf (fig. 197). There is confirmation in Window s:VII that he was a pupil of the Master of the Parable of the Sower, and thus within the Canterbury tradition. It cannot be said, then, that French glaziers were recruited during the exile and that they brought the Gothic style to Canterbury. On the other hand, the easternmost windows on the north and south sides (n and s:II) show significant changes in composition, especially in the role of ornament, and a complete mastery of the new style.

These windows have much in common with those of the French Gothic cathedrals—Bourges, Rouen, Chartres—in the intensity of colors, combining somber and brilliant effects. They also achieve unity of design by the principle of subdivision, as compared to the additive designs of an earlier phase; and ornament is subordinated to the historiated scenes. Both ornament and figure scenes are reduced to essentials, the ornament frequently

---

[1] Paraphrased by R. L. Poole, *Studies in Chronology and History*, Oxford, 1934, p. 297. The reference to Carmentis is from Ovid's *Fasti*, i, 493. "And, although the same city did not give us birth, nevertheless one who calls to mind the native country of the brave, which is indivisible so far as we are concerned and which Carmentis mentions, does not doubt that we have the same native country." I am indebted to Professor Janet Martin of Princeton for the translation.

sacrificed in naturalistic quality in order to fill the ground and to harmonize in color. In the same way naturalistic detail is suppressed in the scenes in favor of a more generalized representation; figures, draperies, and landscape are abstractly treated and kept in the plane of the window. The result is an extremely effective dramatic mode, in which movement and gesture are silhouetted against the blue grounds, but in which everything is subordinated ultimately to the unity of the Gothic building. The viewer's experience in the Trinity Chapel is a radically different one from that in the choir aisle; there the limpid colors are in harmony with a mood of rational clarity, which is present in the

Methuselah Master's exploration of the physical world and in the exegesis of the Bible; here the dim lighting heightens the awareness of the brilliance of chromatic effects, but at the same time analytic visual experience is replaced by a series of vivid impressions.[2] It is almost impossible to stand still and analyze the Trinity Chapel windows in detail, so strong is the total impact of vibrant color and movement apprehended in shifting, diagonal views. For many of the pilgrims, as they moved past the shrine, their mystical experience must have been intensified by the colors and forms in the windows, even if these impressions were not consciously received.

The Canterbury–Sens Designer: composition and ornament[3]

A DIRECT line of development can be traced from early typological windows of Canterbury, and the corona east window of the middle group, to the four choir ambulatory windows of Sens Cathedral, and back to the easternmost windows of the Trinity Chapel ambulatory.[4] In the same tradition is the Joseph Window in the nave of Chartres Cathedral.[5] The chronology is inescapable in the face of the visual evidence, and stands quite apart from historical probability. Exchange with Sens was very likely to have occurred at any time during the entire period 1160–1220, and it remains hypothetical whether the Sens windows were provided by members of the Canterbury atelier when they were in exile, or composed from patterns carried between the two centers.

Correspondences in ornamental motifs between Sens and Canterbury were noted and illustrated by Westlake in 1881; he also made loose connections

with Chartres, and concluded that the windows of both Sens and Canterbury stemmed from Chartres.[6] Heaton derived the Sens windows from Canterbury.[7] Frankl attributed the Joseph Window in Chartres to a Sens designer.[8] Arnold referred loosely to a deterioration in some of the Trinity Chapel windows, which he supposed were painted after the exile, and he seemed to be referring to Windows n:III and n:IV.[9] In an unpublished master's thesis Sulkis has reached conclusions similar to my own, although we differ on many points of detail, among them the inclusion of the Chartres window in this group. Her thesis was not well received in France,[10] but more assiduous attention to composition, ornament, and iconography, as well as figure style, must give it a firmer base.

There is a progressive tendency at Canterbury to somber color effects; the most dramatic change is in the intensity of the blues. The north choir aisle

[2] Johnson, 1965, pp. 15–16.

[3] Much of the material in this and the third section of this chapter, was presented at the Eighth Conference on Medieval Studies sponsored by the Medieval Institute of Western Michigan University, Kalamazoo, in April-May 1973, in a paper entitled "Sens and Canterbury: 1175–1220."

[4] For the Sens glass see: Lucien Bégule, *La Cathédrale de Sens*, Lyon, 1929, pp. 43–54; Grodecki in *Vitrail*, pp.

123, 139; Sulkis, 1964. Dates given vary from soon after 1184 to 1225.

[5] Delaporte and Houvert, 1926, Window LXI, pp. 395–98, Pls. CLXII–CLXVI, colored Pls. XIV–XVI.

[6] Westlake, I, 1881, pp. 110–13, Pl. LXIII.

[7] Heaton, 1907, p. 173.

[8] Frankl, 1963, p. 316.

[9] Arnold and Saint, 1939, pp. 70, 75.

[10] Grodecki, *Bulletin Monumental* 125 (1967), p. 107.

windows at lower and "triforium" level, and the surviving panels from the choir clerestory, are dominated by a limpid blue, which on close exterior examination proves to be exceptionally well preserved. When one passes into the Trinity Chapel, it is as if a cloud suddenly covered the sun; the blue grounds are somber, greenish in hue, and turn out to be heavily patinated, no doubt due to different facture (Col. Pls. I, II; cf. III, IV). The same difference is, of course, observable at Chartres, between the mid-twelfth–century west windows and the thirteenth-century glazing of the new building. Window n:V of the Trinity Chapel ambulatory and the east window of the corona have some of the limpid blues, but now used sparingly in the *rinceaux*, whereas the blues that predominate are denser. It was perhaps to enliven these heavier blues that the Petronella Master used a diaper design in Window n:IV in the Trinity Chapel, and introduced red roundels into the grounds of the panels from Window N:X of the clerestory. Further east in the Trinity Chapel there is a reduction in the number of shades uesd; pinks tend to a monotonous murrey tone, white is common, and so is mustard yellow. Red, still strongly present in the grounds of the *rinceaux* of the "triforium" windows of the choir, as in the corona east window and Window n:V of the Trinity Chapel, is less emphatic in the more easterly of the Trinity Chapel ambulatory windows; there is, however, individual variation, and Window n:III appears green and red, between the predominantly soft blue with pink, white, and green of Window n:IV, and the more intense blue with deep pink, white, and hot yellow of Window n:II.

At Sens an identical range of tonal variation is apparent in the ambulatory as in the corona and easterly group of Trinity Chapel windows. This impression is strengthened by comparison with Chartres, where typically red rather than yellow is the dominant hot accent. At Chartres two windows

of the nave stand out from the rest for their bluish appearance; the St. Eustace Window, for which Grodecki has demonstrated an origin in the northeast of France,[11] and its neighbor, the Joseph Window (Appendix fig. 3, LXI, LXII). The former is cool and delicate in hue, with pink, white, green, and some pale yellow floating against soft blue, and warm reds in the ornament; to this palette the Joseph Master added hot yellow. These are the colors, too, of the west rose and some clerestory lights on the north side of the nave.[12]

These observations are sufficiently reinforced by a study of the composition and ornament to justify an attribution to a single atelier that worked successively at Sens, Canterbury, and Chartres; relatively minor changes in the design or execution of the ornament in this group of windows indicate the chronology of work. The windows that are most intimately associated with Sens are the corona east window and Trinity Chapel ambulatory n:II and III, s:II and III, all of which are attributed, in whole or in part, to the Fitz-Eisulf Master. His personal style, however, appears only fleetingly at Sens. On the other hand, the figures in the Joseph Window at Chartres might be the work of the painter who executed the Prodigal Son Window at Sens. "Atelier" should be defined here in the broadest sense, as artisans who shared the same pattern books.

Among the many experiments in composition made at Canterbury in the typological windows, two on the south side arrived at a formula whereby the entire "picture surface" of the window (that is, the area within the borders) was divided into square units; in these cases circles or quatrefoils were inscribed in the squares (Appendix fig. 1, s:XII and s:XVI). This principle was taken up and used consistently in the related Sens–Canterbury–Chartres group, in which the classic star pattern was developed.

In Trinity Chapel Windows n and s:III circles

[11] Grodecki, 1965, pp. 178–80.

[12] The doublets and their small roses in the clerestory do not always form homogeneous groups of three; it is as if the execution of the lights was assigned to different ateliers to speed up the glazing of a bay. The cool palette of the Joseph Master is observable in lights CLXVIII,

CLXX, CLXXII, and CLXXIII–CLXXV; his personal style is less in evidence; see Delaporte and Houvet, 1926, pp. 514–18, Pls. CCLXX, CCLXXI, CCLXXIV, CCLXXIII. The west rose was attributed to the Joseph Master by Grodecki, in *Vitrail*, p. 129, and by Frankl, 1963, p. 316.

form the basic unit of design, divided diagonally into four quarters; the glass *in situ* on the north side shows that each quadrant had a petal-shaped figure panel inscribed. There is a fundamental difference from the tiers of medallions used by the same Master in Window n:IV, but a similarity to the typological windows mentioned above (Appendix figs. 1, 2). The border design, which is very similar to others of the Sens–Canterbury group, and the use of a geometric diaper ground outside the circles, must be due to new influences.

These new influences in the work of the Petronella Master in Window n:III extend to the figure style as well. Occasionally more robust figure types are introduced; in one panel the leading lame woman has substantial calf muscles, which are defined under her long skirt by hairpin-looped drapery folds; the contrast with her emaciated companion is marked (fig. 171). In another panel a horseman rides out of a three-dimensionally conceived city; his rounded stomach, and especially the stiff pleats of his tunic and flaring mantle, bring him close to the tradition of the Master of the Parable of the Sower and of the Fitz-Eisulf Master, the roots of which were in English art of the 1170s to 1180s; comparison with a similar figure in the Worksop Bestiary serves to underline the delicacy of touch of the Petronella Master (figs. 169, 170). That the influences to which the Petronella Master was subject in Window n:III are not entirely due to his Canterbury colleague can be affirmed by examination of the early work of the Fitz-Eisulf Master.

Not all of the windows attributed to the Fitz-Eisulf Master are advanced in composition; Window s:VI on the south side is very conservative, its neighbor, s:VII, is idiosyncratic and quite in keeping with the experiments of the middle period (Appendix fig. 1). The composition, consisting of interlocking fan shapes, is repeated in the east window at St.-Quentin, where other windows have been noticed for their similarity to Windows n and s:V in the westerly part of the Trinity Chapel (Appendix fig. 2). The border of Window s:VII is of the same type as that of Window n:XV in

the north choir aisle, but the crossing of stems is masked by a leaf, there are no leaf scars or beading, and growth is not consistently in one direction (figs. 173, 1). So too the *rinceaux* in this window show organic disintegration. The figure panels have the same mélange of conventional motif and rapid execution. The palette is dull except in the use of red in the draperies; the blue grounds are very dark, and there is much deep pink, green, and white in the figures. Some of the figure groups and drapery treatment are close to the Master of the Parable of the Sower in style, but with the loss of physical strength already noticed in the corona east window (figs. 89, 93). These figures have a new kind of vigor, however, arrived at by exaggerated postures and bold shorthand treatment of drapery. A panel in Window s:VI shows some of the more meticulous drawing of the Master's early phase (fig. 187). On the other hand, the dry, flaccid vegetal motifs of this window indicate a later date.

It may be suggested that Windows n:IV–VII and s:VI–VII of the Trinity Chapel were largely complete before the exile of 1207, as must have been the corona windows. The impoverished ornament of the first two windows on the south side is explicable if these windows were hastily abandoned in an incomplete state in 1207, and fully completed only after the return in 1213. It may have been at this time that a representation of the shrine, instead of the tomb, was included in one scene.

The definitive step in the geometric articulation of window compositions was made at Sens. Probably the Canterbury experiments, in the oculi, the floor mosaic, and Windows s:XII and XVI with typological subjects, were of some importance, but it has already been suggested that these are related to the continental metalwork tradition. Continuous halving was also used later in the rose window of Lausanne, but in the Chartrain context the Joseph Window is almost unique for its overt use of such structuring. This seems to be another instance of "resistance to Chartres" present in an autonomous local school that extended from Canterbury to Lausanne.[13] Each of the designs at Sens

---

[13] Bony, 1957–1958, pp. 47–49.

is developed from a square unit. In one of the most evolved compositions, that of the typological Good Samaritan Window, a canted square is defined in the center of each unit by joining the midpoints of the figure three times in succession. Part-circles inscribed within the corners of the basic square unit are centered on the sides of the first canted square formed by halving (Appendix fig. 4); the relationships are thus largely hidden. The result is a more compact grouping of panels related in subject matter than was provided by the lozenge with four separate circles in the corona east window (Appendix fig. 2). The Prodigal Son Window at Sens uses the square unit in quite a different way; the armature provides only a regular grid of squares, but within them each figure composition is outlined by a canted square fused with four semicircles, which are centered on the midpoints of the sides (Appendix fig. 4). The two hagiographical windows, with the lives of Sts. Eustace and Thomas Becket, however, return to the star composition, although it was better suited to typological windows. The St. Eustace Window has three canted squares in the center, which are found by continuous halving, exactly as in the Good Samaritan Window. Within the basic square unit is inscribed a circle, in ornament, and circles or semicircles of the same radius describe four petaloid panels that emanate in a star pattern from the sides of the canted square; the centers of these arcs fall on the midpoints of the sides of the basic square (Appendix fig. 4). The design is ingenious, and must have been created for this window; the circles echo the round head of the light, and their intersections provide two and a half complete circles, whether one reads from the top down or from the bottom up. The Becket Window again used the hidden basic square with a canted square inscribed in ornament between the midpoints. Part-circles are centered on the sides of the canted square, and a full circle of the same radius is the center of the design (Appendix fig. 4; fig. 186).

The design of the St. Eustace Window at Sens is, to my knowledge, very nearly unique—its only counterpart is in Window n:II of the Trinity Chapel (Appendix figs. 2, 3).[14] The Sens armature seems to have been designed for the Romanesque stonework; two and a half units of the design fit exactly. There is strict control by ruler and compasses—petals form contrapuntal circles that read from the bottom up, or from the top down. The Canterbury example proves on analysis to be only an adaptation of the visual pattern, not the geometric structure, to a taller Gothic lancet; the petals do not form larger circles, nor are they described by true arcs, and the square in the center is not developed by successively joining the midpoints of a series of square figures, as the canted squares are formed at Sens. This seems to suggest the primacy of Sens in respect to the latest Canterbury glazing. The modifications at Canterbury allow greater space for scenes, which now fill the hatchet-shaped areas between the petals as well, but this is at the expense of ornament. Meager *rinceaux* between the circles are on a blue ground, as are some in the Becket Window at Sens, and contribute to the bluish tonality of the window.

Window s:II of the Trinity Chapel derives in a similar way from the Becket Window at Sens; at Canterbury the composition is heightened to four very nearly complete square units, each with a lozenge inscribed in the ornament. Only the central circular figure panels are missing, their positions being occupied by small ornamental bosses, while greater importance is given to the full circles centered on the midpoints of the sides of the canted squares (Appendix fig. 4, fig. 185). The articulation of tiers of roundels into basic units of four by means of ornament is very subtle, and it is in marked contrast to the archaic additive composition of Window n:IV by the Petronella Master.

The canted square was used at Canterbury in windows of the middle period, but not as part of a tightly organized geometric system; in Windows n:V and VI, and s:V of the Trinity Chapel, all of which may have been the work of the Fogg Medallion Master, canted squares intersect arbitrarily with circular forms (Appendix fig. 2). Perhaps related to these experiments is the tomb of Archbishop Hubert Walter, who died in 1205, which is

[14] A comparison implied by Westlake, I, 1881, p. 110; the Sens armature is illus. Pl. LVIIIO.

situated under Window s:IV in the ambulatory.[15] On the slanted Purbeck lid are canted squares linked by circles. These are developed from the basic square slabs from which the piece is composed, with a much tighter control than is apparent in the windows of the middle group (Appendix fig. 2). Whether it is a precursor to the Sens developments, or whether execution of the tomb was deferred until after the exile cannot at present be determined.[16]

The composition of the Joseph Window at Chartres is another variation on the basic square with continuous halving, much like Window s:II in the Trinity Chapel, but with a different distribution of irons (Appendix fig. 4).[17] The central rosette is outlined in iron, as is the large canted square, and semicircles on the sides of the canted square have ornamental edging bands. By subdividing the canted square into four, the designer has compressed eight scenes into his unit of design. The density of figure compositions and cramping of ornament are comparable to Window n:II of the Trinity Chapel, and suggest a date later than Sens.

The Sens atelier evidently contributed to developments at Canterbury, but equally it derived much from the Canterbury tradition. The Thomas Becket Window and the typological Good Samaritan Window most probably depend on common models or lost Canterbury prototypes for their subjects. This dependence is also demonstrated in the ornament.

Sens borrowed a repertory of ornamental motifs from Canterbury, specifically from the work of the Methuselah Master, the Master of the Redemption Window, and the Petronella Master. Among these borrowings may have been the "cufic" edgings to panels.[18] Pairs of flat, serrated leaves put to similar use in the Prodigal Son Window recall a motif

in north choir aisle Window n:XV and in the Jesse Window (figs. 27, 133).[19] Among the *rinceaux* at Sens appears an almost exact duplicate of those of the corona east window; within the circles of the St. Eustace Window are white stems on a red ground, with green, yellow, blue, and white leafy shoots (figs. 181, 182). The color distribution and the leaf types correspond exactly with the corona ornament; it will be remembered that these *rinceaux* were closely related to similar features in the north choir aisle and the Trinity Chapel capitals (figs. 179, 180). *Rinceaux* in the Becket Window at Sens, on the other hand, are less fleshy. Some are based on the delicate leafy heads used in the bosses of Window n:IV of the Trinity Chapel, and they correspond almost exactly with the *rinceaux* of Window n:III, although the colors are different (figs. 164, 166). The Canterbury origin is again proved by the earlier use of this plant type in a border of the transept clerestory (fig. 75). In the central spaces of the Becket Window, however, are more commonplace acanthus scrolls with no organic unity; this type is carried back to Canterbury in Window s:II (figs. 183, 184).

It has never been noticed before that of the four Sens border designs, three have almost exact replicas at Canterbury. One of the richest is in the Good Samaritan Window; it belongs to the climbing type, and has paired interlocked stems which much resemble the border of clerestory N:XIV (figs. 73, 71). In the clerestory border a pair of secondary shoots woven through the interlaced stems make this the focus of the design. At Sens the interlace is simplified and a central palmette given greater prominence; growth is less organic, the leaf scars being less strongly drawn, and the "calyx" of the palmette is inverted. Variants of this simplified motif occur at Rouen, in the nave clere-

---

[15] W. H. St. John Hope, "On the Tomb of an Archbishop Recently Opened in the Cathedral Church of Canterbury," *Vetusta Monumenta* VII.1 (1893), 1–2.

[16] Professor Zarnecki informed me by letter that in his view the sculptures cannot be dated with certainty before 1207.

[17] Also illus. Westlake, I, 1881, Pl. LVIIIp in the context of the Canterbury armatures.

[18] Caviness, 1965, p. 196. Such motifs could have been copied from Middle Eastern silks coming to Canterbury;

see Gertrude Robinson and H. Urquhart, "Seal Bags in the Treasury of the Cathedral Church at Canterbury," *Archaeologia* 84 (1935), 185–87, Pl. L, 1; S.D.T. Spittle, "Cufic Lettering and Christian Art," *Archaeological Journal* 111 (1954), pp. 148, 151.

[19] The possibility that Sens borrowed from manuscripts cannot be excluded; see, for instance, the eleventh-century Flemish Gospels, Brussels, Bibliothèque Royale, MS 18383, f.11v.

story of Chartres, at Angers, and elsewhere. In the examples at Chartres and Angers the design is more loosely organized and the painting is very brittle, indicative of a later date.[20] A similarly desiccated version appeared in Salisbury well after 1220.[21] The Sens design is in fact very nearly a replica of an an original Canterbury design, which was copied by Austin in his Jesse Window in the corona in 1861 (figs. 73, 74). Since he also included replicas of the surviving figures from the original Jesse Tree, it is tempting to think the original of the border had the same provenance.[22] The motif is repeated at Sens, with the same colors, but with a slight simplification of the palmette.

Two others of the Sens borders have identical counterparts at Canterbury; rubbings made in Canterbury and held against the windows in Sens proved to fit very closely. One duplicated design is in Window n:II of the Trinity Chapel and the Thomas Becket Window in Sens (figs. 175, 176).[23] The other is in the St. Eustace Window at Sens, and an unfortunately misplaced fragment now in the south choir aisle "triforium" (figs. 178, 177).[24] The equally crisp painting of the leaves in these borders, as well as the repetition of design and colors, would make them virtually interchangeable; it is not possible to suggest a chronology.

The chronology may be argued from comparison with other Canterbury windows. The narrow, economical borders of Windows n:II and III, which are comparable in motif, are in marked contrast to the rich, colorful border of Window n:IV; this abrupt change in neighboring windows, within the *oeuvre* of the Petronella Master, might logically be the result of an interruption in the work and new influences from Sens. The use of geometric diaper ground outside the circles in Window n:III has a counterpart in the St. Eustace Window in Sens, and its appearance at Canterbury may also be ascribed to continental influences. On the other hand, very meager rosettes in the Joseph Window at Chartres seem to be based on the bosses in Window n:IV, and could have come out of a Canterbury motif book (fig. 198).

The chronology and approximate dates suggested here are supported by the ornament of contemporary manuscripts. Two dragons that are incongruously perched on an aedicula in Window n:III may have been taken from a book, an origin in keeping with the miniaturesque style of the Petronella Master; they are unique in glass of this period. Dragons with foliate tails are common in the initials of Christ Church books of the first half of the twelfth century, though Dodwell has shown that they go back to pre-Conquest art.[25] An example such as the one illustrated, from a Josephus, might explain how the glass painter came to misplace the beading of the vertebra (figs. 164, 165); others in the same book have more abundant foliage growing at intervals from the tail.[26]

---

[20] For Rouen, see Cahier and Martin, 1841, Mosaiques N 9; for Chartres, see Delaporte and Houvet, 1926, Window LXXII, Pl. CLXXXVI; for Angers, Thomas Becket Window of about 1225–1235, see Hayward and Grodecki, 1966, p. 38, illus.; see also Victoria and Albert Museum, Department of Ceramics, 5460–1858, a French panel, illus. Rackham, 1936, Pl. 2A (associated with Sens by Jane Hayward in *Medieval Art*, no. 190).

[21] Westlake, I, 1881, Pl. LXIXb (Jesse Window on the south side of the nave). The Short Chronicle of Matthew Paris ascribes the completion of the glazing to the episcopacy of Robert Bingham, 1228–1246 (quoted by Otto Lehmann-Brockhaus, *Lateinische Schriftquellen zur Kunst in England*, II, Munich, 1956, 498, no. 4107).

[22] Mr. Easton agrees that no part of this border is old, but that it appears to have been copied from a lost original. The two Jesse figures were returned to the cathedral in 1953; see Caviness, 1975, p. 374.

[23] Westlake, I, 1881, 110, Pl. LXIIIe and i; probably it is

due to his vague labeling of the figures that Williams (1897, p. 35) assumed the example in Sens to be in the St. Eustace Window. See also Arnold and Saint, 1939, p. 91. Color reproductions are in Marcel Aubert, *Vitraux des cathédrales de France, XIIe et XIIIe siècles*, Paris, 1951, Pl. VII (Becket border) and Baker and Lammer, 1960, Pl. VI, center.

[24] I am grateful to Frederick Cole for making a rubbing and color notes of the Canterbury border for me. The Sens border is in Westlake, I, 1881, Pl. LXIIIf.

[25] Dodwell, 1954, p. 23, figs. 14d and e. It may not be purely fortuitous that aediculae and furniture in Anglo-Saxon manuscripts were sometimes invaded by flora and fauna, for example, the mid-eleventh–century Gospels in Monte Cassino Library, MS BB 437, 439; see Rickert, 1965, Pl. 45. The treatment of the lectern and the foliage over the arch compare with that in Window n:III, panel 4; Rackham, 1949, Pl. XII.

[26] Dodwell, 1954, figs. 25a and b.

The sculptors borrowed this motif for roof-bosses in the choir aisles prior to 1180,[27] and by 1200 they were the commonplace of book illumination;[28] they appear in France also, as in the north French Bible, Bibliothèque Nationale, MS Lat. 11534, f.53. It is clear from the Bible of Robert de Bello, British Library, Burney MS 3, that the dragon had by then lost its vigor and become no more than a lithe bird-like creature entwined in spiral foliage;[29] Robert was abbot of St. Augustine's, Canterbury, from 1224 to 1243, but the glass dragons are much closer to those in the Josephus of a hundred years earlier. A date after 1220 seems highly improbable for the glass.

Rinceaux in manuscripts tend to confirm a date in the first two decades of the thirteenth century for the Sens and Canterbury group of windows. A very spindly variation on the oak-leaf type of cluster, which had appeared in the choir aisle and corona, frames an initial in Cambridge, Trinity College, MS B.11.4, a Psalter with an Augustinian calendar later than 1220. More stylized *rinceaux* with small trefoil leaves and no leaf clusters or leaf scars appear in one of the Peterborough Psalters associated with Robert de Lindseye, Abbot 1212–1224;[30] these are comparable to the work in Window s:II of the Trinity Chapel. Scrolls with sparse leafage occur throughout the Bible of Robert de

Bello, and the Morgan Lothian Bible, a St. Albans book of the first quarter of the thirteenth century.[31] The "late" appearance of the *rinceaux* in the Little Canterbury Psalter in Paris of before 1220 has already been noticed; in the same book is a rosette much akin to those in Window s:VI of the Trinity Chapel.

At Chartres *rinceaux* rarely predominate in a window; they are more often used in conjunction with geometric diaper;[32] exceptions are the St. Eustace and Joseph Windows. In the latter (fig. 196) they are very cramped, and comparable to the banal palmettes of Window s:II or clerestory N:V (fig. 183). The Prodigal Son Window, near these nave windows but in the north transept, should perhaps be placed in the same regional group, originating in the northeast of France.[33] "Cufic" and beaded edging lines are in the Canterbury–Sens tradition, and the groundwork consists entirely of palmettes and *rinceaux*. The palette, with much red, is not different from that general at Chartres, but it could stem from Laon. The figures, however, are less serene and classicizing than those of Laon or Soissons; their wiry physiques, with striding, twisting motion and swinging garments, may owe much to the Sens–Canterbury tradition (fig. 195).

The Sens painters

THE styles of the four windows in the north choir ambulatory of Sens Cathedral are intimately related to all phases of the Canterbury styles. The two modes, biblical and hagiographical, are so clearly distinguished at Sens that Sulkis supposed the Thomas Becket Window might be a decade later than the biblical windows;[34] the St. Eustace

Window, which she did not include in her study, is even more "advanced" looking. Archaism in the typological Good Samaritan Window might be explained by the use of an early iconographical guide —of Canterbury origin—but the Parable of the Prodigal Son, which is treated at Sens in a sequence of twelve narrative scenes, without types,

[27] Illus. Cave, 1935, Pl. IX 3 and 4, p. 45; he identified one boss as having ducks with truncated bills, but they appear to be winged dragons with foliate tails.

[28] For example, in the Cuthbert Life of about 1200, London, British Library, Add. MS 39943, f.7v.

[29] Rickert, 1965, Pl. 100.

[30] Cambridge, Fitzwilliam Museum, MS 12, f.159, Brieger, 1957, Pl. 26b.

[31] New York, Pierpont Morgan Library, MS 791; illus. Rickert, 1965, Pl. 94. Plummer (p. 5) dated it ca. 1208, but it may be later.

[32] Grodecki, 1965, p. 178.

[33] Grodecki, in *Vitrail* (p. 129) associated it with Laon. See Delaporte and Houvet, 1926, Window LVIII, pp. 381–83, Pls. CL–CLIII.

[34] Sulkis, 1964, p. 116.

was not included in the Canterbury cycle. In both these biblical windows each subject is presented with the distilled clarity that was seen in the Methuselah Master's work. Figures are grouped or isolated against a limpid blue ground. They are generally static or slow-moving, and quietly outlined. There is almost always a clear central accent. Some of the repertory of individual figures is shared with the Methuselah Master's atelier, but these are common in the period; for instance, the servant on the right in figure 188 seems to derive from the more graceful "skating" pose used frequently by the Methuselah Master, as in the Gentile looking back at the pagan idol (fig. 37). The familiar pose of the Prophet of 1 Kings 13 is repeated in Christ before Pilate in the Good Samaritan Window (figs. 55, 58). Such a comparison serves to underline the substantial appearance of the Methuselah Master's figures, and the slighter treatment they are given at Sens. The Queen of Sheba was painted by an assistant, the V-fold Painter, whose insistent drapery folds whittled away the lower legs (fig. 44); this tendency, which belongs to the middle phase at Canterbury, is seen quite clearly at Sens in such figures as the harlots with the Prodigal Son (fig. 45). These compositions in the Sens glass are clarified to the point of appearing stark and denuded; such isolation of three or four figures in a row was practiced at times by the Master of the Parable of the Sower (fig. 100), but like him also the artist of the Prodigal son Window was not afraid of setting one figure in an extensive landscape if the subject demanded it, as in the scene of the Son as a swineherd. Yet there is an aridity in this landscape, to be found in the Redemption Window of the middle phase of Canterbury but not in the earlier scenes with the Sower. So, too, the swirling mantles that are used occasionally in the windows at Sens as space-fillers and to activate the figures, are as stiff as those of the Redemption Master (figs. 137, 138, 188). Moses in the scene with the golden calf in the Good Samaritan Window (fig. 207) could be taken from the same motif book as Enoch by the Crumpled Silk Painter (fig. 137).

Echoes of the corona east window are as frequent as those of the north choir aisle windows.

In color, as in style, the four Sens windows divide into two pairs. The biblical windows have lucid blue grounds, the blues in the hagiographical windows are more somber. Red is used in large quantities in the Prodigal Son Window, as a surround to the figure compositions, but in the draperies pink and white predominate, with some mid-green and splashes of hot yellow. Except in the brilliance of the unbroken reds, it is a typical palette of the Canterbury middle period, as in the corona east window, the Public Life of Christ, or the Jesse Master's work. The Good Samaritan Window, with less red and more green and yellow, is very close indeed to the coloring of the Calling of Nathanael from the Public Life of Christ, but the refinement of tints is reminiscent of the Methuselah Master's work; there is a full range of pinks, from near-white to deep purple, yellowish green appears in two hues, as well as a mid-green. A very pale blue is also used, as in the hill behind the wounded traveller, where it stands out clearly from the mid-blue ground.

The hagiographical windows, situated to the west, are darker and bluer; the grounds to the figures are greenish, and more blue is used in the ornament than in either of the other windows. The St. Eustace Window is cold in tone, with much white in figures and ornament, some pink and green, and touches of red or pale yellow. The effect is much like that of Window n:IV in the Trinity Chapel at Canterbury. The Becket Window is more brilliant, by the addition of mustard yellow, and more subtle in the use of varied greens and pinks; its counterpart is Window n:II of the Trinity Chapel.

The hagiographical windows share a common repertory of simplified and symmetrical aediculae, consisting essentially of an architrave with slender, evenly spaced columns, and hangings (figs. 186, 200). These appeared at Canterbury in the panels ascribed to the Parable of the Sower, Fogg Medallion, and Redemption Masters, and are a constant feature of the later Trinity Chapel designs. The Sens compositions are crowded, but restrained; the figures are generally static, upright, and often grouped in massed verticals. The Becket medallions are composed in the manner of the Fogg Medallion Master, the figures contained within a squared-off architectural unit, and confronting one another with stabbing gestures across a brief caesura (figs. 186, 115). Draperies are generally, though not always, quietly outlined, and the figures are slender and insubstantial. Compared with the comely harlots in the Prodigal Son Window, a group of women and children demonstrate a lack of plasticity in the harsh relentless lines of their drapery (figs. 203, 45); these women and children should be compared with the work of the Fitz-Eisulf Master as it appears in the corona. Other traits in both of the Sens hagiographical windows suggest a very close link with the corona east window painters; the kneeling figure of St. Eustace's wife is comparable to Elisha at Canterbury in the bloused tunic and the system of V-folds which fall from the thigh and at the same time delineate the knee and calf (figs. 200, 137). The messenger kneeling before Thomas Becket has drapery comparable to that of Enoch even in the uplifted shell-fold of the skirt of his tunic, and in both figures the thigh appears rounded and shortened by the bunching of "crumpled silk" folds at the back (figs. 202, 137). Elsewhere the mantle of St. Eustace fans out in pleats that are almost as harsh as those in the Sundial of Hezekiah (figs. 137, 138). The heads in this panel reproduce the same types that are preserved in Moses with Jethro.

What, then, is the precise nature of the relationship of the Sens styles to the Canterbury glass? In the biblical windows the coincidences are eclectic; they consist mainly in borrowed motifs from the Canterbury windows of the early and middle periods. They could be explained by the use of a motif book in conjunction with the iconographical guide for the Good Samaritan Window, which is almost certainly of Canterbury origin. This interpretation makes allowance for the great difference in style between the two Sens windows, and it avoids the postulate that Canterbury is the sole

source of the Sens biblical styles; it remains to investigate more fully the other elements. A certain refinement and metallic precision brings the Sens painters closer to the Mosan tradition and to the idealized classicism of the continent. So, too, the denuded compositions may be a legacy of north French and Mosan metalwork or the Châlons-sur-Marne glass.[35] Whether the robust, classicizing figures of the harlots derive entirely from the Methuselah Master's designs, or whether they depend also on the sculptures of the central west portal depends ultimately on the chronology accepted; the date of 1190–1200 generally given to these portal sculptures is earlier than that recently ascribed to the ambulatory glass. On the other hand, there is the possibility that the Methuselah Master's work was known in Sens before 1190, and might therefore have influenced the sculptors in a general way. More specific are resemblances between some of the sculpted figures, especially the Virgins (fig. 104), and the isolated standing figures of the Master of the Parable of the Sower (fig. 103). Both are attenuated, elegant in proportion and stance, with heavy draperies either clinging to the limbs or falling rather stiffly to frame the sinuous outlines of the body. The mysterious origins of this classicizing style in the central portal may then lie outside France, in the Canterbury glass paintings of about 1180. The Jesse Master, whose late work has been dated about 1200, provides a double link with the Sens glass and sculpture. Conversely, the Petronella Master's style may have owed something to the previous stylistic phase in the sculpture, of the St. John portal of the 1180s to 1190s.

The best explanation available at the present time seems to be that a single "Canterbury–Sens Designer" was responsible for the composition and ornament of all four windows at Sens; reusing ornamental motifs from Canterbury, he consolidated the design formula that he had used in the corona east window to create unified "star" compositions. The execution of the biblical windows may have been given to local artists. The Becket Window was probably based on designs by the Fogg Medal-

---

[35] Cf. also Berlin, Kupferstichkabinett, MS 78 A 6; Swarzenski, 1967, p. 58, fig. 259, from Liège, ca. 1160; Dr.

Rosalie Green brought this to my attention.

lion Master, previously used at Canterbury, but the execution of this and the St. Eustace Window is most closely related to the corona east window. The painters occasionally added floating draperies to the Becket designs, just as they had to Jethro in the corona, to animate the figures. Rapid brushwork, staccato gestures, and the subordination of individual figures to the action result in a successful hagiographical mode, one which, however, had already been applied in the typological scenes of the east window of the corona. At Sens there was perhaps an awareness that this style was most suitable for hagiography, whereas a more archaic and classicizing one would lend dignity to biblical events. At Chartres the new style permeated biblical narrative in the Joseph and Prodigal Son Windows.

The development of the style of the Fitz-Eisulf Master at Canterbury

THE career of this painter has been traced from the corona east window and windows s:VI and VII of the Trinity Chapel ambulatory to Sens. The next phase of his style is seen in the easternmost windows of the Trinity Chapel. It belongs to the late stage of Canterbury glazing, to which a date after 1220 has frequently been given.[36]

Beyond the first bay of the Trinity Chapel the composition of the clerestory and ambulatory windows was controlled by an overseer who saw that the armature designs were in most cases paired facing each other. Though not coinciding exactly with this new plan, the surviving Becket miracle scenes in Windows n:II–IV and s:II–VII of the ambulatory are also homogeneous in design, and the execution of all but Windows n:III and IV is dominated by a single painter, the Fitz-Eisulf Master, whose eponymous work is in Window n:II (fig. 197). It may be the overseer who insisted on a canonical representation of the tomb as a rectilinear marble sarcophagus with two elliptical holes cut in the side, as it had appeared in Window n:V. In other matters the Petronella Master and the Fitz-Eisulf Master departed from the tenets of the Fogg Medallion Master. Inscriptions are confined to the hexameters on strips above or below the figures and not supplemented by philacteries with speech (figs. 159, 167, 197). Architectures tend to be flat, symmetrical, and unrealistic, although this trend is less marked even in the mature work of the Fitz-Eisulf Master than in the Petronella Master's windows (figs. 205, 208, 159). The figures are small, wiry, and active, and more scenes are crowded into each window than in Window n:V. An excited mood pervades all of these windows; narrative and meaning are communicated without the use of labels, and even the inscriptions provided are somewhat redundant. Apart from these general similarities, however, it is as if the Petronella Master and the Fitz-Eisulf Master began at different poles in Windows n:IV and s:VII; their styles grew together, with mutual exchanges, in Windows n:II and III and s:II. The impact of Sens during the years of exile may have something to do with this, but the debt is less clear in the figure painting than in the composition and ornament.

Window s:VII is but a slight departure from the work of the Master of the Parable of the Sower. Even the palette, which is dominated by the new heavy blues, includes much red in the draperies, such as was used by this Master; the pink, white, and green are otherwise typical of the middle period. Figures are often paired or grouped together so that several heads are painted on the same piece of glass; the workmen setting out to look for William of Gloucester are composed as a group much like the Gentiles following Christ (figs. 93, 37); they are taller, however, more like the attenuated figures of the Master of the Parable of the Sower. Indeed, the arched back and swirling mantle and tunic of one figure are very like the Sower on Stony Ground, but in the execution there is a loss

[36] Rackham, 1949, pp. 81–82. This dating is on the basis of two representations of the shrine of St. Thomas.

of vigor and plasticity (figs. 93, 89). This panel is unique in Window s:VII for the use of swirling mantles; elsewhere the drapery is calmly outlined, even where a spinning motion is indicated (figs. 189, 190). The figure in the doorway in s:VII is not unlike the representations of Noah's sons or the three virtuous states (figs. 194, 100, 103). His facial type, with high forehead and cheekbones and close beard, resembles the Byzantine type for St. Paul, which was used for the Sower on Good Ground (fig. 95). The same grave expression, with an archaic furrow shaped like a teardrop between the brows, appears in Window s:VI (fig. 187). One pair of figures, the physicians examining Elias of Reading, has an instructive counterpart in the scene of the Presentation of Samuel in the Temple by the assistant of the Methuselah Master, the V-fold Painter; the facial types and the insistence on V-folds are similar, yet the later painting is more mannered and elegant, the figures flatter and more vertical (figs. 190, 60). In the composition as a whole, breadth and clarity have given way to tension and compression. There is an almost total rejection of the classicism of the early masters, in spite of a comparable humanism.

In Windows n:II and III and s:II the stronger hues of the Sens hagiographical windows are adopted; the most frequent hot accent is mustard yellow. Acid yellow-green, little used at Canterbury since the early phase except by the Petronella Master, reappears as a tint distinct from the more usual mid-green. As noted above, each window has distinct tinctorial qualities, but there is a new sharpness. The compositions and figure painting show a marked advance beyond even the St. Eustace Window at Sens. Spatial settings are minimized, as they had been in the Petronella Master's work in Window n:IV. Many of the scenes, like his, have a strict rhythm of movement that tends to hold the action within the pictorial field in spite of overlapping the frames. The figures are articulated more often as individuals and less as crowds than in the work of the early Canterbury Masters

or Window s:VII. As at Sens, there is little tendency to specific description of individuals or textures; facial types are quite standardized within broad categories, and the same flesh tint is used for all. The greatest change is from the stern, inexpressive figures of Sens to more vital attitudes and facial expressions that aid in the storytelling at Canterbury. Archaisms such as the uplifted shell motif in draperies are not found after a few occurrences at Sens. There is less tendency for draperies to reveal substantial form other than bony knees and rotund stomachs; they are boldly and clearly painted, with some use of exterior washes, and follow schemata such as the looped-fold system, regardless of the sex or age of the subject. The brushwork is increasingly strong and rapid (figs. 92, 206).

In the masterly sequence of mad Matilda in Window n:II, the maniac's violent contortions gradually subside before the tomb; no flight of demons is needed to illustrate her cure (figs. 209–211). Although the artist probably had recourse to early models—the sequence is remarkably like that of Luxuria dancing and then reviled from Anglo-Saxon recensions of the *Psychomachia*[37]—what is new is the application of this intensely expressive mode to specific secular persons. On the whole, revivals of themes from the more remote past are not as important in this Master's work as is his dependence on the designs of his predecessors at Canterbury and Sens. A common pose shows the weight shifted forward on to one slightly bent leg, the other foot pointed and turned out, the body thrust into frontal view and the shoulders into the plane of the picture surface (figs. 93, 199, 209). Essentially this is the Romanesque "skating" pose also used by the Methuselah Master, but a loosening of outline by the addition of swirling draperies, a slackening of joints, and especially a *déhanchement* have transformed it into one of Gothic elegance. The pose is adjusted to the action of the figures, varying from a *gehende stand* to an extended movement, and seldom retains the floating,

[37] Illus. F. Wormald, *English Drawings of the Tenth and Eleventh Centuries*, London, 1952, figs. 6a and b (British Library, Add. MS 24199, f.18 and Cambridge, Corpus Christi College, MS 23, f.24). See also Stettiner, 1905, Pl. 54, figs. 4, 10, 16; Pl. 59, figs. 1, 9; Pl. 60, fig. 16; the third manuscript of this group in British Library, MS Cleo. C viii.

poised quality of the figures in the north choir aisle (fig. 37).

The cumulative experience of the Canterbury–Sens atelier was probably collected in model or motif books.[38] Thus the difficult three-quarter back view of the blind woman in Window n:II(2), which is more fussy and exquisite in the painting of draperies than most of the Fitz-Eisulf Master's work, seems to be copied from the same model as Moses in the scene of the Golden Calf

in the Good Samaritan Window at Sens (figs. 208, 207). We have seen that Moses in turn was related to Enoch in the corona east window. Ultimately one thinks of an early model for the figure, such as the Utrecht Psalter, but the treatment in the Trinity Chapel is far more successful than that of similar figures in the late twelfth-century copy, MS Lat. 8846; there is a strong probability that the figure had been filtered through the advanced classicism of the Methuselah Master.

The Joseph Window in Chartres

THE Joseph Window in Chartres, which has been attributed to the Canterbury–Sens Designer, has to be discussed in relation to this phase of the Canterbury glazing, although it has been responsibly dated in the first decade of the century.

The Chartres window demonstrates the parting of the ways. There can be no doubt that the designs and color scheme link it with the Fitz-Eisulf Master of Window n:II, yet many of the figures are robust and classicizing, as if tempered by the style of the Prodigal Son painter from Sens. A few of the numerous traits that point to the Fitz-Eisulf Master will be enumerated first.

Several of the aediculae are of the extremely simplified kind used in the Sens hagiographical windows and at Canterbury, consisting of a roof or arches supported on slender columns. Landscapes are generally reduced to the groundline and a few bulbous trees; hills, where they appear, are arid, as in the corona east window and at Sens. Figures turn towards each other, singly or in groups, and gesture dramatically across the intervening space; frequent use is made of the twisting figure, moving one way and turning his head the other. Both Window n:II and the Joseph Window have scenes that are centered in the window and others that are symmetrically paired to the sides. In both windows, scenes are designed with a central axis, which tends to act as a focus for the movement. Thus Joseph is lowered into the pit by two groups of his brothers

evenly distributed on either side, and Potiphar's wife and Joseph are seated on either side of a central column (figs. 198, 196). So too the figures confront each other in pairs in Trinity Chapel n:II, 2 (figs. 197, 208). The lateral scenes are planned with a view to overall symmetry, which is slightly more advanced in the Joseph Window; here twisting figures are used to link paired panels, as in the two representations of the jailer who first leads Joseph away and then throws him into prison (fig. 196).

Some of the individual figures are unquestionably creations of the same artist; sensitive drapery folds and clear articulation, combined with a gentle expressiveness, are marked in Jordan Fitz-Eisulf and his wife as they are in Joseph and Potiphar's wife (figs. 196, 197h). One of the boys stoning frogs is from the same model as the jailer throwing Joseph into prison (figs. 199, 196). These, however, are among the most plastically rendered figures of the Fitz-Eisulf Master in the Trinity Chapel, and among the more attenuated in the Joseph Window.

Commonly the figures in the Joseph Window are stockier and more robust than the Fitz-Eisulf Master's; they have impassive, idealized features, and avoid the more extravagant attitudes of some of those at Canterbury. In these qualities they are close to the Prodigal Son Window at Sens; Joseph before Potiphar is much like the three figures in the scene of the return of the Prodigal in facial

---

[38] Kitzinger, 1966b, pp. 139–41. Arnold supposed the glass painters at Sens and Canterbury kept drawings on

parchment; Arnold and Saint, 1939, p. 89.

type, proportions, the strong outlining of his thigh, and even in the rather fussy uplifted end of his mantle (figs. 196, 188). The brushwork in general is more deliberate and less fluid than the late work of the Fitz-Eisulf Master. Other motifs suggest a close relationship to the Prodigal Son painter; among them are the trefoil arches that frame Joseph and Potiphar's wife.

The aspect of idealized classicism present in the Joseph Window is shared with other windows of the nave; its neighbor, the St. Eustace Window, also by an artist from the region north and east of Paris, represents another branch. It is rather calmer and more uniform in proportion of figures and in drapery, close to glass at Laon and Soissons and in the same tradition as the younger master of the Ingeborg Psalter.[39] Much less common in the Chartrain styles is the frenetic activity of the figures and the immediacy of the narrative events in the Joseph Window. The hagiographical mode, so successful in the St. Eustace Window at Sens and in the Becket miracle series has been transposed into biblical narrative. The influence of the Fitz-Eisulf Master is the most likely explanation for this rejection of the slow-moving clarity of the Prodigal Son Window at Sens.

Grodecki has attributed the west rose of Chartres to the Joseph Master, an attribution that is justified from its color and figure style. He has viewed the stronger, looser brushwork appearing in these large figures as a possible result of Parisian influence in the later work of the Master.[40] Other possibilities should be borne in mind; one is an adjustment to painting at clerestory level, such as the Methuselah and Jesse Masters had already made at Canterbury. The other is the parallel development that occurred

at about the same time at Canterbury, in the late work of the Fitz-Eisulf Master.

The history of Chartrain glass painting remains to be written, and to this point judgments as to the chronology of glazing and identity of artists are tentative. One of the complexities of Chartres is that there was surely a productive interaction between the artists who worked alongside each other, which eventually resulted in the formation of a more or less prevalent Chartrain style. In the nave windows various regional styles are reflected, which reinforces the argument that they were the first to be glazed. The Joseph Master may now be said with some certainty to have come from Sens, as the St. Eustace Master came from the region of St.-Quentin. The Prodigal Son Window has traits of ornament and figure painting that also suggest a northern artist. The palette is more like the eastern windows of Laon Cathedral than the Canterbury–Sens group, and a close connection with Sens is unlikely in view of the almost complete lack of coincidence with the Prodigal Son compositions there. The Prodigal Son Window serves to underline the importance of the Petronella Master's style; conventions of dramatic representation that were still fresh in Window n:III of the Trinity Chapel ambulatory have become stiff and mannered, and there is a contrived clarity in the compositions (figs. 167, 195). On the other hand, the Christ in Majesty from the summit of the window is strictly comparable to the latest of the Trinity Chapel clerestory figures, Hezekiah and Josiah from Window N:V, notably in his jointless arms, elegant swathes of drapery, and undulating hems (figs. 195, 216). By this period there was most probably an exchange of ideas with the Chartres painters.

The dates of the Trinity Chapel ambulatory windows

Two Christ Church productions can be firmly dated in or before 1220, and thus have considerable bearing on the date of the Trinity Chapel windows.

These are the Little Canterbury Psalter in Paris and the Trinity Chapel vault paintings, which were sketched before their destruction in the nine-

[39] Deuchler, 1967, p. 121, figs. 25, 26, 30, 31, 32, 35, 36, 37, 38.

[40] *Vitrail*, p. 129 (cf. the Last Judgment rose of Notre-Dame).

teenth century. Both are far more advanced in style than even the latest work of the Fitz-Eisulf Master.

The Psalter, Paris, Bibliothèque Nationale, MS Lat. 770, can be dated before 1220 by the absence in the calendar of the feast of the translation of Becket's relics on 7 July.[41] In spite of being rather poorly drawn, the illustrations in this book betray mannerisms rooted in the style of the Trinity Chapel glass; the impact of the Christ Church windows is also apparent in that the very unusual subject of Julian and Maurice, the rich men of the Parable of the Sower, is copied (figs. 97, 98). Elsewhere, flared tunics, outlined in much the same fashion as in the later glass, are flattened by a straight white line that emphasizes the horizontal hem and allows no fine and sensitive pleating of the sort so conspicuous in the glass of all periods (fig. 192). The folds are delineated in a dry manner over a thick colored wash; their distribution is uncertain and has little reference to underlying forms. Figures are distorted in violent action, their hands exaggeratedly large. Occasional more sensitive passages, especially in the figure of Christ in the Flagellation (fig. 192), or the seminude river gods of the Beatus page (fig. 126), are a distant echo of the Methuselah Master; the torso of Christ is constructed much like that of Adam (fig. 6), and the grace and unity of this figure contrast with the caricatured flagellants. A second manuscript of Canterbury provenance is the Bible of Robert de Bello (London, British Library, Burney MS 3), which can be dated approximately in the period 1224–1253. It has been cited by Rackham and van der Boom as an example of the influence of the early Christ Church glass on local manuscript painting.[42] In view of the short figures with overly large heads, the occasionally agitated hemlines picked out in white, and the loss of all classical, easeful pose, it seems impossible to reverse this

chronology, even in respect of the latest Canterbury glazing. A date for the Bible in the region of 1225–1230 would accord well with the Little Canterbury Psalter. The Trinity Chapel ambulatory glass should be placed significantly earlier.

It has been overlooked until recently that the vaults of the Trinity Chapel were, until the middle of the nineteenth century, decorated with paintings.[43] Before these disappeared completely, sketches were made by the elder Austin. The style they suggest is comparable to the drawing by Brother William preserved in the St. Albans scriptorium, which can be dated before ca. 1232.[44] The figures are thickset, with a heavy outline. The draperies fall vertically or are caught up over the arm, and the hems are delineated by serpentine lines (fig. 193). The paintings are dated by inscription in the year of the translation, and it is highly probable that the windows of the Chapel had been completed sometime before. The internal evidence has suggested that Windows n:IV–VII were glazed before 1207, and s:IV–VII partially finished. Windows n:II and III and s:II could have been completed in 1213–1216, and the finishing touches put to s:VI and VII; plans were already underway for the shrine in 1216, so that its representation in two instances in these windows, in anticipation of the translation, is quite plausible. Colored paving tiles were probably laid on the eastern part of the Trinity Chapel floor in the same period; they are closely related to *dalles* at St.-Bertin of St.-Omer, which was the first home of the monks in exile.[45] The vault paintings commemorate the translation ceremony, recording the presence of Henry III, and must have been done in 1220. They were perhaps the last stage in "perfecting" the building, the decoration of which had absorbed much of the energies and financial resources of the community since the 1170s.

---

[41] See above, Chapter Three, n.61.

[42] Rackham, 1949, p. 12; van der Boom, 1960, p. 120.

[43] Caviness, 1974.

[44] London, British Library, MS Cotton Nero C I, f.156, a miscellaneous collection containing additions to the

Chronica Majora; Brieger, 1957, p. 161, Pl. 55a, and A. G. Little, ed., *Franciscan History and Legend in English Medieval Art*, Manchester, 1937, p. 37, Pl. 1. Brother William died about 1232.

[45] See Chapter Four, n.125.

The chronology of the Trinity Chapel clerestory glazing

LESS easily resolved is the question of whether the Trinity Chapel clerestory was completely glazed by July 1220. Some of the surviving figures and ornament are perplexing, because of a mélange of archaic and advanced traits. Possibly, as in the lower windows, these are indicative of a break in the work and its hasty completion. In few cases are attributions to the major painters of the lower windows possible. Exceptions are the figures of Nahshon and Amminadab already attributed to the Petronella Master, and Salmon and Boaz attributed to the Jesse Master, which are from adjacent windows on the north side at the entrance to the Chapel; they fit into the *oeuvre* of these masters of the 1180s to 1190s, and the exile would be a firm *terminus ante quem*. The decision to change to the new armature design was made at this time, perhaps after the Petronella Master had done his drawings (App. fig. 5). No precedent for the new design has survived on the continent; following St.-Remi there are several series of seated clerestory figures, placed two in each window, but none are in curved armatures. At Strasbourg are figures of ca. 1200. Extant examples *in situ* at Orbais may be as late as 1230. At Soissons are four figures of ancestors of Christ in the choir clerestory. Related figures are scattered in American collections.[46] Only at Chartres, on the north side of the nave, are seated figures framed in ellipses and quatrefoils, but the armatures are not curved (fig. 212).[47] The added height of these lancets allows three units of design, with ornamental bosses between and grounds of *rinceaux* or geometric diaper. The color and ornament of these windows are closely related to the Sens–Canterbury group. On the south side, and in the eastern part of the building the predominant mode of clerestory glazing is with single standing figures—as also at Bourges and the cathedral of Rheims. More rarely at Chartres there are series of three scenes set in *rinceaux* or geometric diaper, but always with straight-bar armatures.[48] The few examples at Chartres of seated figures in the clerestory should be seen as the last flowering of a tradition that came from the northeast. There are many arguments to support the primacy of Canterbury, at least in inception.

Nineteen figures are preserved from the Trinity Chapel clerestory; the series from the north side is complete for Windows N:V–N:X, and there is one figure from Window N:IV.[49] Their condition is poor, however; even where most of the glass is ancient, the panels have been cut down or altered to fit the great perpendicular windows in which they are now set, and some of the figures have been distorted in early releading. The quality of original painting is remarkably uneven, and several artists seem to have executed this part of the series, as if the work were hurried. There is a certain consistency in the designs after the first bay where, as we have seen, two distinctive masters worked alongside each other on the north side, the Petronella Master and the Jesse Master. While modifying the armature designs of their windows, they kept the figures large; circles used by the Jesse Master in Window N:IX allow the figures to expand much more than do the quatrefoils and ellipses to the east (App. fig. 15). These two masters set certain canons for the rest of the series; roundels were afterwards used sporadically in the blue grounds, and following the Jesse Master's designs,

[46] In the Walters Art Gallery, Baltimore, and the City Art Museum, St. Louis; cf. also *The Year 1200* I, no. 202, pp. 195–96.

[47] Delaporte and Houvet, 1926, Window CLXV, Pl. CCLXVIII, Window CLXXIII, Pl. CCLXXIII; cf. the mannered geometries of Window CXXII, Pl. CCXXX, which is in the apse.

[48] *Ibid.,* Windows CLII and CLIII, Pls. CCLXII and CCLXIII over the Prodigal Son Window in the transept.

[49] The figures are: Amminadab and Nahshon from N:X, now in the west window, L6 and L2; Salmon and Boaz

from N:IX, certainly the figures now in the southwest transept window, M2 and M7; Obed and Jesse from N:VIII, now west window, I2 and I6; David and Nathan from N:VII, now southwest transept window, H4 and H5; Rehoboam and Abijah from N:VI, now west window, I3 and I5; Hezekiah and Josiah from N:V, now southwest transept window, M3 and M6; Jeconiah from N:IV, now west window, I1. A figure identified by Mason and Rackham as Salathiel, now west window I7, is almost entirely modern. Cf. Rackham, 1949, pp. 36–39.

most others employed leads in the grounds in parallel with the geometric figure of the armature (figs. 127, 151, 152, 213–216). This feature links them with a tradition known in Châlons-sur-Marne in the latter half of the twelfth century.[50] It is not used in the comparable clerestory panels at Chartres. The consistent features, and the pairing of armature designs across the Trinity Chapel after the first bay, indicate a single overseer, and the individual figures are sufficiently related in pose and scale to bear this out. The situation is analogous to that in the clerestory of the transepts.

The ancestors of Christ return to restless poses that, on a miniature scale, mimic the dynamic figures of the Methuselah Master or the Jesse Master. Several are seated with their knees turned sideways, or with one leg drawn up into a leaping posture. They gesture widely, with arms akimbo or hands thrust out to the sides. There is a return to distinctive attributes, other than the scrolls that all carry. Architectural features are abandoned, and settings are of the simplest kind, with benches or arcs and no footstools. The effect is flat and decorative. The new compositions give greater space to ornament than previously. The colors tend to be somber, deep blues, greens, and purples, enlivened chiefly by white. The palette is less delicate than that of the Petronella Master.

One of the earliest-looking figures is Cosam, from Window S:X on the south side of the first bay (fig. 218).[51] In spite of distortions of the shoulders and arms to fill a quatrefoil, there is an attempt to render draperies plastically, especially over the knees and thigh, and to give them texture. The tiny rucks and folds recall the work of the Petro-

nella Master, or of the Crumpled Silk Painter in the corona east window. This fine, miniaturesque handling belongs to the period before the exile. The head, with its tight sculptural curls, is almost classical in appearance, markedly different from Hezekiah (fig. 216). The dryly painted zigzag border of this window may be of later date, completed, like the ornament of the first bay in the ambulatory, after the exile.

On the north side, small figures of Obed and Jesse in quatrefoils from Window N:VIII could be by the Petronella Master; Obed, particularly, has a facial type similar to Amminadab, and delicate drapery folds quite typical of the Petronella Master's work (fig. 153). As in Window n:III in the ambulatory, he had accommodated himself to new principles of design, and this window too may postdate the exile.

Surprisingly, the next four figures on the north side, David and Nathan from N:VII, Rehoboam and Abijah from N:VI, have some pronounced archaisms. Draperies are organized into patterns of firm, crisp lines; distinctly Romanesque is the torso of Rehoboam with its high belt and flat mantle, which invites comparison with the central figure in the *Signum Tau* panel from St.-Denis (figs. 214, 49). Equally archaic is his companion, Abijah, whose thighs are outlined in damp-fold drapery and ornamented with semicircles that recall Anglo-Saxon drawings or German metalwork.[52] The original head of this figure, identified by Oakeshott, has since disappeared; it is strong and linear, confirming the metallic impression (fig. 215).[53] The bold style of the inscriptions could indicate an early date, or an extreme archaism. Restorations

---

[50] Grodecki, *Vitrail*, p. 108, fig. 78, Pl. XII; cf. also the glass of Normée, *ibid.*, fig. 37.

[51] Gostling's record that this figure was in Window S:X has to be accepted; the quatrefoil exactly fits the ironwork of that window, and the figure is evidently designed for a quatrefoil. Rackham, following Austin, assigned Cosam to Window S:XI (p. 41).

[52] As in a few figures in the Aelfric Pentateuch from St. Augustine's, London, British Library, Cotton MS Claudius B.IV, e.g. f.38v, and the figure of Matthew on the portable altar of Eilbertus from the Guelph Treasure, now in the Berlin Museum; see Swarzenski, 1967, fig. 241, dated in the second third of the twelfth century. Rehoboam

has been compared by Heimann to a figure in the Great Canterbury Psalter (*The Year 1200*, III, 323, figs. 22, 23).

[53] Oakeshott, 1951, recognized the original head in Rackham, 1949, Pl. 50a. He remarked on its general resemblance to the early twelfth-century wall paintings in Canterbury, that is, in the apse of St. Gabriel's Chapel; cf. Tristram, 1944, frontispiece and Pls. 1, 11, 12, 14, 15, 19, and Suppl. Pls. 2a and b, and Rickert, 1967, Pl. 77. The paintings have deteriorated severely since the Courtauld photographs were taken early in the 1950s: see Eve Baker, "St. Gabriel's Chapel, Canterbury Cathedral," *C.C.C.* 64 (1969), pp. 4–7.

and releading may prevent any solution to the mystery of these figures; their production after 1213 seems almost incredible, but there are other examples of archaism in English art,[54] and the explanation may lie in the use of an early model. Similarly harsh lines in David and Nathan suggest the same painter, but here traits such as the looped end of Nathan's mantle and the use of hairpin folds betray the late date. Nathan, quietly outlined and rigidly frontal, might be a provincial repetition of a figure such as Daniel from the Chartres nave clerestory (figs. 213, 212). Chartrain connections, with Canterbury probably now the receiver, have been suggested for Hezekiah and Josiah from Window N:V. The poorly preserved figure of Jeconiah, from the next window to the east, is attributed to the Fitz-Eisulf Master, on the basis of the painterly treatment of his mantle as it fans out over the bench ends; the attribution confirms a date after 1213 for these easterly windows, as does the character of the *rinceaux* surrounding Hezekiah and Jeconiah (figs. 216, 217). Insistent hairpin folds in the draperies of Jeconiah, and of two very small figures that may be from Window N:III, are a hardening of the *muldenfaltenstil*, which was used with greater effect at Chartres.[55]

In the three windows of the apse there is a radical change in ornament, which may also be attributed to continental influences; the grounds are of bold geometric designs in red, blue, and white. In Window N:II is an unpainted diagonal lattice, in Window S:II an unpainted scale pattern. The borders are identical, with leaves arranged in fours in the manner of the Jesse Master, but poor in execution. The axial window is given a slightly richer treatment, with white flowers in the latticework ground, and a border of the climbing variety with delicate foliage of the type used by the Petronella Master. The borders confirm the continuity of the Canterbury atelier in spite of new influences. Enigmatically, the only panel which must, from its large dimensions, come from the axial window, and which appropriately represents the Last Judgment, is in a style close to that of the corona east window;[56] especially notable are the draperies, which curve softly over the shoulders of the figures (figs. 137, 146). The early date proposed for this group may be defended by comparison with one of the stray panels in the south rose of Notre-Dame, in which draperies and gestures, as well as color scheme, are almost identical to the Last Judgment (fig. 147). Lafond dated this panel in the last quarter of the twelfth century, but he suspected later overpainting; in view of the Canterbury panel, the paint may be considered original, but the hand is different from that of the rest of the St. Matthew series (cf. fig. 156).[57] The Last Judgment is another example of the close affinity between the Canterbury painters and French work in the period before 1207; most probably the axial window was planned, and work begun on the figure panels, before the exile, as it was also at the lower level. Panels painted at that time may have been set hastily into grounds of the new time-saving variety at the time of the 1220 translation. If a date before 1210–1215 is accepted for the glazing of the nave of Chartres, there is little difficulty in assigning to all of the Trinity Chapel windows a date before July 1220.

---

[54] See, for instance, the prefatory pages of the unglossed Psalter of Robert de Lindesey, London, Society of Antiquaries, MS 59A, Brieger, 1957, p. 82 and Pl. 24b, and also the pages by W. de Brailes in Baltimore, Walters Art Gallery, MS 500 (*ibid.*, p. 89, Pl. 28), for which Swarzenski suggested that an early model was used.

[55] For example, in the clerestory of the south transept, Delaporte and Houvet, 1926, Pl. cc (Ezechiel).

[56] Caviness, 1973, p. 13.

[57] *Corpus, France* I, 56, 61. Lafond was unable to make a close examination of the glass in the roses.

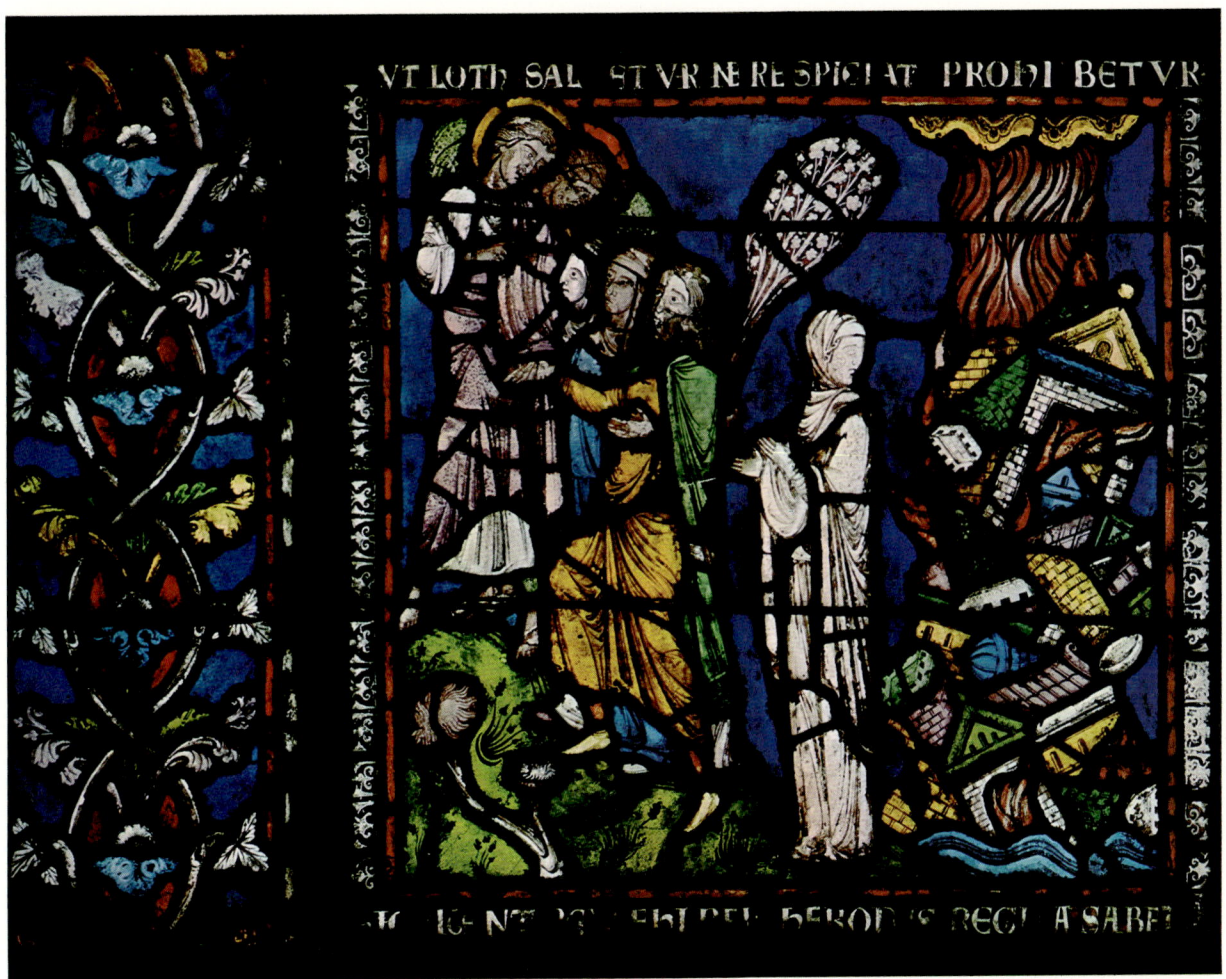

I. North choir aisle n:XV (10). Destruction of Sodom

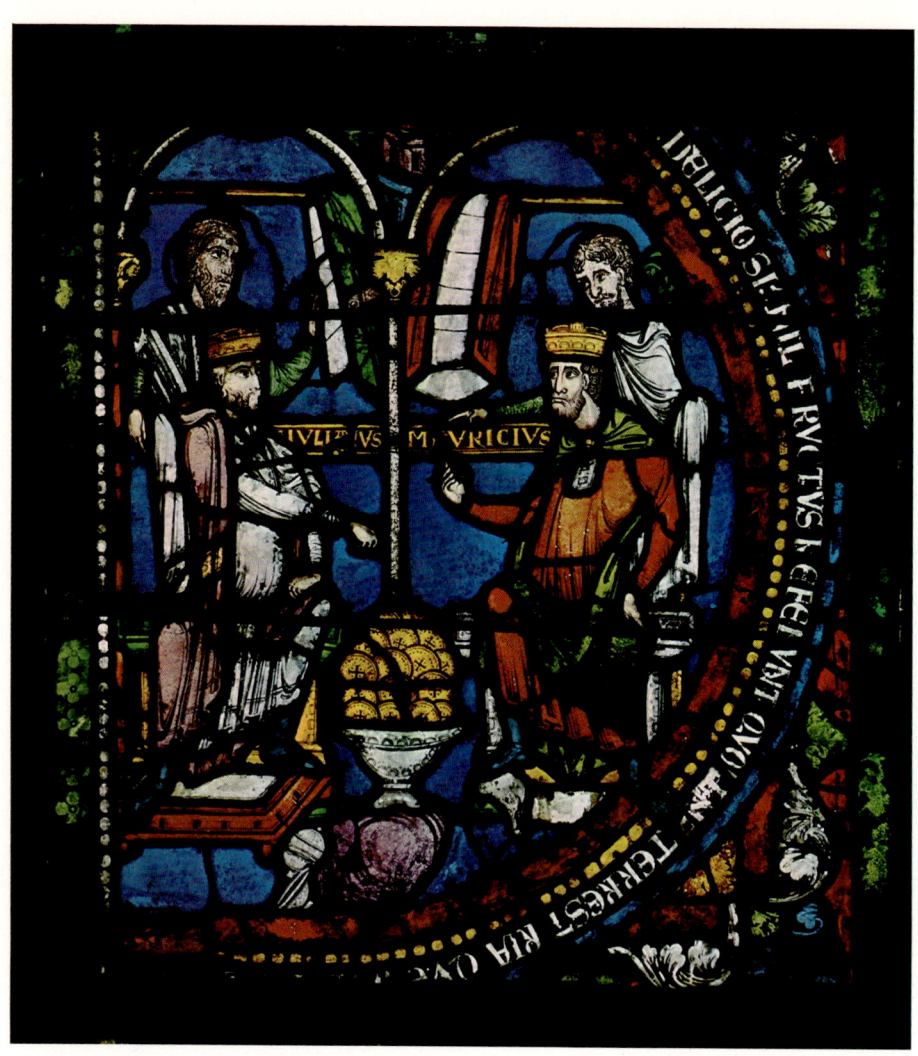

II. Julian the Apostate and Maurice Tiberius
   (the thorny ground) from the sixth
   typological window

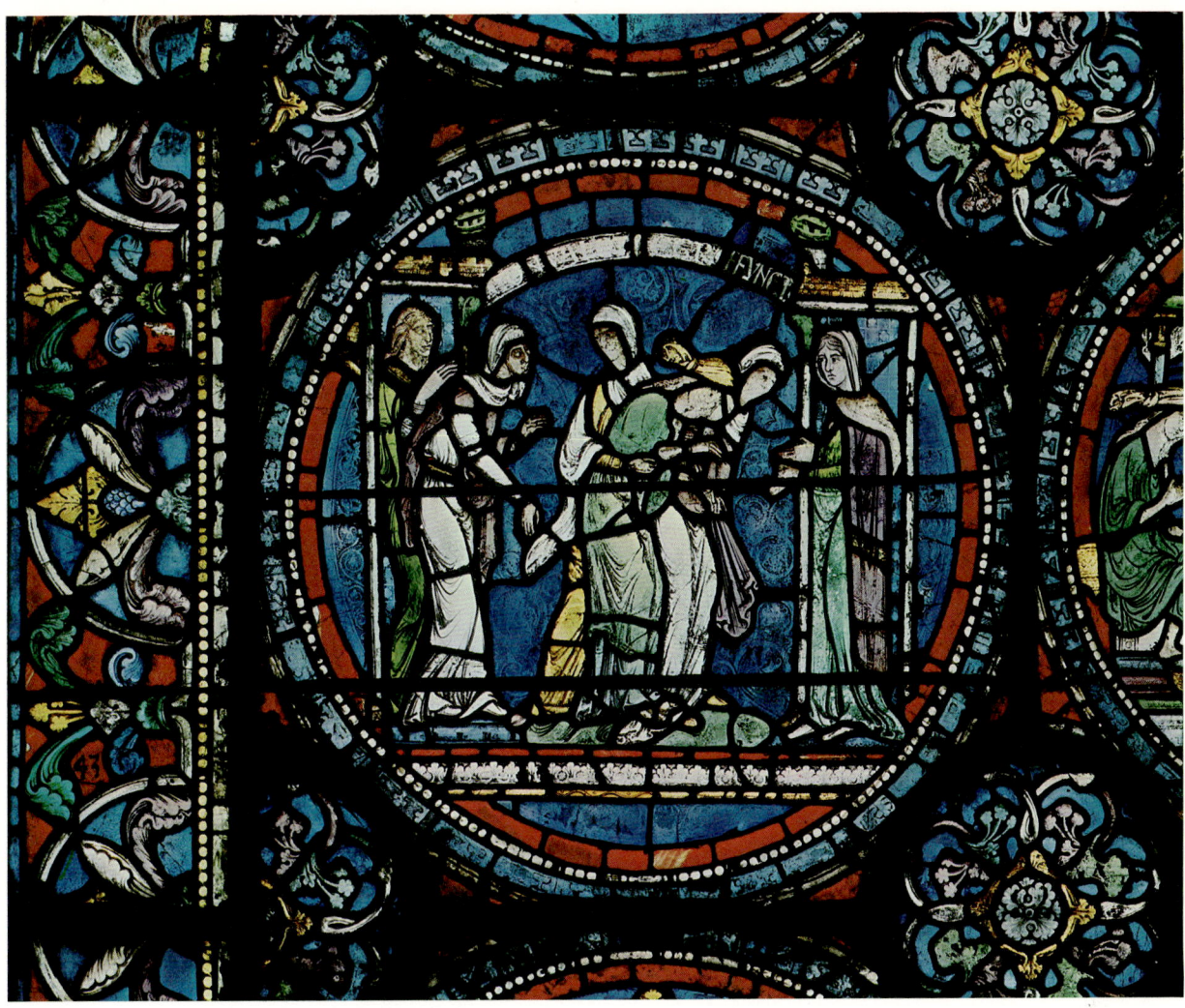

III. Trinity Chapel n:IV (3). Petronella with epilepsy

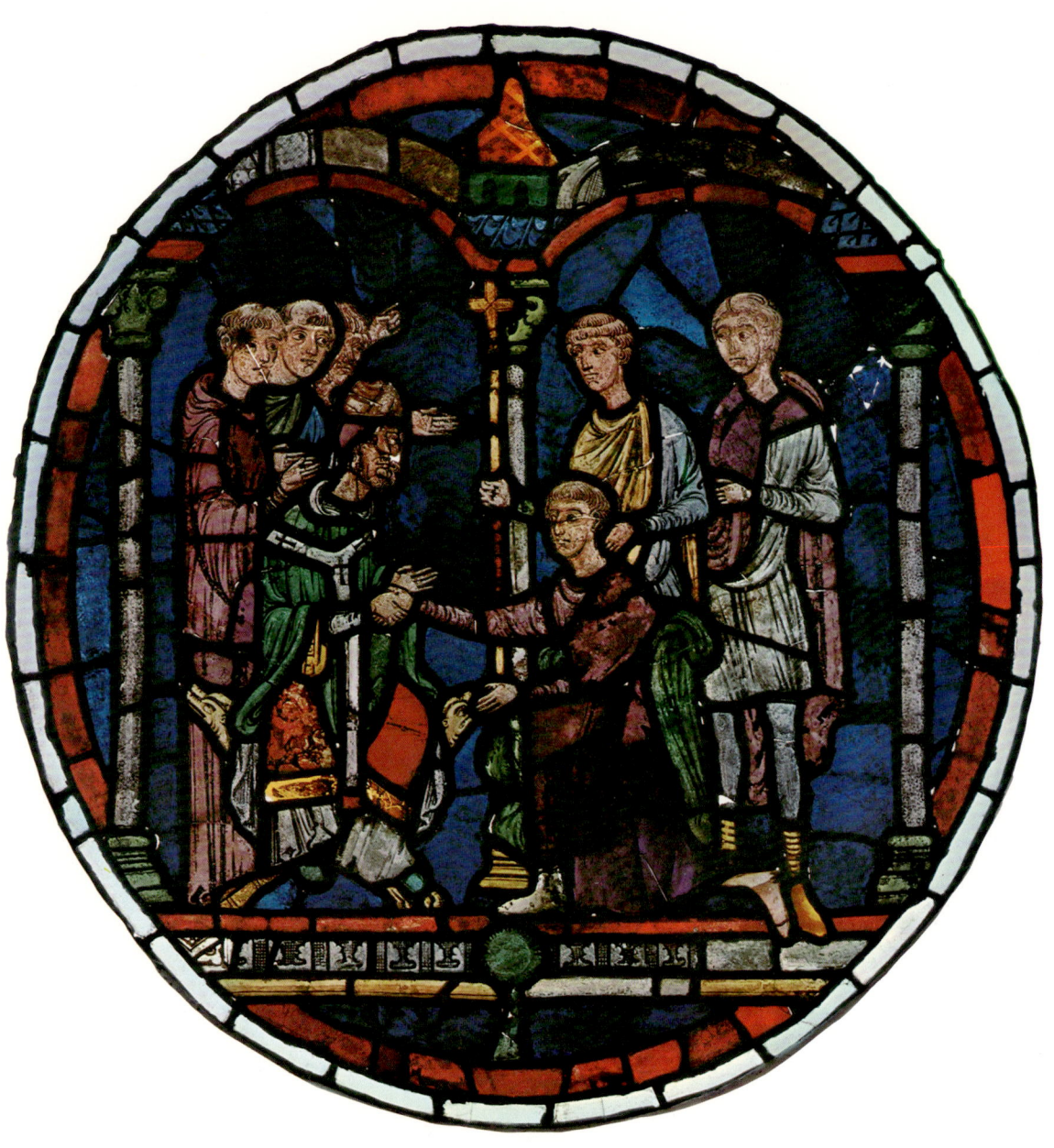

IV. Fogg Museum, Medallion from the life of Becket,
    formerly Trinity Chapel n:VI

VI. The Iconographic Program

"Ars hinc pictoris variavit nube coloris,
Et foris expressit quod clausum litera gessit."[1]

IN INVESTIGATING the iconography of the windows I have kept certain limited aims in view. The principal ones are to see the choice of subjects in relation to broader trends in the history of thought, and ultimately to observe the interaction of artistic creativity with different kinds of subject matter. Textual and pictorial sources have been sought insofar as they have important bearing on our understanding of the working methods of the artists and their patrons; they are especially useful in indicating the extent to which extraneous influences may have operated at Canterbury.

Less than half the early glass of Christ Church is extant, but with the help of texts it is possible to reconstruct with remarkable completeness the whole program of glazing. This is due in part to the fact that the windows were divided into three extensive cycles, and even without any concrete evidence for the contents of an individual window, in the form of glass or early description, there is the possibility of reasonable conjecture. Rackham has already emphasized the unity of planning at Canterbury in contrast to the apparently arbitrary selection of subjects at Chartres.[2] Donors, whether individuals or groups, apparently chose the subject matter of the Chartres windows, and the result is a compendium similar to the *vitae sanctorum* then current; as one might expect from this manner of glazing, the windows reflect popular themes rather than the theology of the schools of Paris or Chartres. Many of the lives of saints in the Chartres windows depend on the liturgical manuscripts once

[1] "The artist's glowing colours here unfold/The hidden meaning wrapped in texts of old." Translation by Canon Wilson, "On Some Twelfth Century Paintings on the Vaulted Roof in the Chapter House of Worcester Cathedral," *Associated Architectural Societies' Reports and Papers* 32 (1913), pp. 133–34.

[2] Rackham, 1949, p. 2.

preserved there, which would have been familiar to clergy and educated laity alike.[3] Collections of lives were also available for private reading, though the most famous, that of Jacobus of Voragine, was not compiled until later in the thirteenth century.[4]

In the French secular cathedrals sculptural programs generally afford a grandiose treatment of Christian themes, ranging from the Creation to recent church history or the Second Coming.[5] Elaborate programs in glass were devised in the same period, and in the twelfth-century west facade of Chartres the two are interconnected. At Canterbury, where there is no important figural sculpture, the glazing program expressed many of the ideas that might have been as conspicuously contained in a sculpted portal; no portal of this monastic church would have been accessible to both laity and brethren, whereas the windows were seen by all. Many of the essential differences between the glazing program of Chartres and that of Canterbury arise from the fact that Canterbury was a monastic foundation.

The monasteries were, by 1180, comparatively conservative centers of learning. They had assimilated into their libraries the biblical glosses of the twelfth century, together with some scientific and even classical works, which were the discoveries of the twelfth-century renascence. During the second half of the twelfth century word and image were extremely close, and this relationship was preserved into the thirteenth century in the monastic context. It was the concrete image that dominated the mode of thought of such men as Nigel of White-acre, Gervase, Benedict, and William of Canterbury, rather than the abstract idea, which was to fascinate the schoolmen. In the era of St.-Denis and after, inscriptions as much as pictures are a part of art; even such small objects as the Bury St. Ed-

mund's cross, now in the Metropolitan Museum of Art, are heavily inscribed, as are the English and Mosan enamels.[6] Among German examples of this kind of art is the Gumbertus Bible, which dates from before 1195; scenes on each illuminated page are woven together by verses (fig. 140).[7] The Canterbury subjects are not only labeled, but most are also elaborately commented upon in verse inscriptions, so that the image is always controlled and glossed by a text. The treatment is bookish and esoteric; the typological windows were less a poor man's Bible than an elaborate display of twelfth-century theology, which could only be fully understood by the literate.

Bookish, too, is the ordering of subjects within each window at Canterbury, from top to bottom and from left to right (Appendix figs. 8–19). This implies a certain habit of mind rather than the existence of models in codex form; it runs counter to the tradition of St.-Denis, and to the order of all the narrative windows of Chartres, Sens, Bourges, Laon, and the Sainte-Chapelle, which read upwards. With the life of Christ or of a saint this had the advantage of leading upwards to a final scene of reception into heaven, an expedient device used at Canterbury in the east window of the corona, the last in the typological life of Christ. The only other exception at Canterbury is the Tree of Jesse, but the disposition is normal in books as well as windows, and it may be argued that a genealogy can be read either way.

There are few monuments of Western art for which such a tightly organized program can be reconstructed, and it is tempting to compare the Canterbury glass with Byzantine mosaic decoration of the middle period.[8] Such programs may not, however, have been rare in the interiors of the abbey churches; parts of the Canterbury program

---

[3] Delaporte and Houvet, 1926, pp. 11–12 and 14.

[4] *Golden Legend*, pp. vi–vii.

[5] Adolf Katzenellenbogen, "Iconographic Novelties and Transformations in the Sculpture of French Church Façades, ca. 1160–1190," in *Romanesque and Gothic Art; Studies in Western Art* (*Acts of the Twentieth International Congress of the History of Art*), Princeton, 1963, pp. 108–18.

[6] For the Bury cross see most recently *The Year 1200* I, no. 60, pp. 52–56, with bibliography.

[7] Erlangen, Universitätsbibliothek, MS 121; see G. Swarzenski, *Die Salzburger Malerei von den ersten Anfängen bis zur Blütezeit des romanischen Stils*, Leipzig, 1908–1913, pp. 129–42, 163–64, figs. 118–24, 126–28, 131–36, 148–51.

[8] For the "classical system" of Byzantine mosaic decoration, see Otto Demus, *Byzantine Mosaic Decoration*, Boston, 1955, pp. 14–29.

certainly had parallels in paintings, now lost or partially destroyed, such as those of Worcester Chapter House, the Peterborough choir stalls, or the chapel of the Holy Sepulchre at Winchester, all of probable twelfth-century date.[9] The English paintings in the chapter house at Sigena survived intact until recent times; they comprised cycles of Old and New Testament subjects, and a genealogy of Christ.[10] The text of *Pictor in Carmine* was composed in England, probably about 1200 by Adam of Dore, a Cistercian; it provided a choice of typological verses and subjects for the decoration of churches.[11] The painted roof of St. Michael's in Hildesheim is evidence of continental monastic preoccupation with elaborate and extended iconographic schemes, as is the Klosterneuburg ambo of 1181.[12] Canterbury also has some parallels among glazing programs of the period 1180–1220, and its distinction perhaps lies more in its comparatively complete documentation and survival than in its uniqueness. There is evidence in the triforium and clerestory windows of the abbey church of St.-Remi of Rheims of careful organization; only fragments of the program have survived, but Grodecki has called it "un véritable résumé de l'histoire sacrée et de l'histoire de l'église de Reims." The inception of this program, in the nave, is now placed by Grodecki about 1150, well before that of

Canterbury, but the choir glazing may be later than the earliest Canterbury glass.[13] Slightly later than Canterbury, Lincoln Cathedral was provided with a series of types and antitypes as well as hagiographical subjects and a Last Judgment.[14] Even among French secular cathedrals there is the exception of Bourges, which in the first four decades of the thirteenth century was supplied with an ordered program.[15]

Mâle discovered certain normative rules about thirteenth-century iconography that are useful for a survey of trends; he established, for instance, that the south side of a building was often reserved for New Testament subjects, being flooded with light, whereas the north was usually reserved for Old Testament figures.[16] The east windows were given greatest importance, generally containing Christological subjects, such as the Crucifixion or Redemption, and the west occasionally had a Last Judgment, perhaps by the etymological association of *occidere* and *occidens*.[17] But there is no doubt that exceptions were common, and that decorative programs were highly idiosyncratic and carefully adjusted to the specific structure and function of the building. This is certainly true of Canterbury, where it may be said that only the component parts have antecedents; the way in which they are ordered is unique.

The subjects of the windows

As DESCRIBED in Chapter Two, the program was contained only in the choir, eastern transepts, presbytery, Trinity Chapel, and corona, that is, in the new eastern part of the cathedral church

rebuilt after the fire of 1174 (plan). This was primarily for the use of the monks of Christ Church, to whom it was of immense personal importance; when the chronicler Gervase wrote of

[9] A twelfth- or thirteenth-century record of the Worcester inscriptions, contained in Worcester Chapter Library, MS F.81, was edited by M. R. James, "On Two Series of Paintings Formerly at Worcester Priory," *Proceedings of the Cambridge Antiquarian Society* 10 (1900–1901), 99–110. For a translation see note 1 above. A connection with Peterborough was suggested by Lady Trenchard Cox, 1959, pp. 169–70. For Winchester see Tristram, 1944, p. 42, and (after cleaning) Demus and Hirmer, 1970, pp. 509–11, Pl. 123 and fig. 41.

[10] Pächt, 1961, pp. 166–69.

[11] James, 1951, p. 144.

[12] For Hildesheim see Sommer, 1966. Descriptions of the Klosterneuburg ambo are in C. Drexler and Thomas Strommer, *Der Verduner Altar im Stifte Klosterneuburg*, Vienna, 1913, and Röhrig, 1955.

[13] *Vitrail*, p. 108; Grodecki, 1975, pp. 76–77.

[14] Lafond, 1946, pp. 147–49.

[15] Cahier and Martin, 1841; Amedée Boinet, *La Cathédrale de Bourges*, Paris (1925), pp. 117–22; Grodecki in *Vitrail*, p. 139.

[16] Mâle, 1958, p. 5ff.

[17] *Ibid.*, p. 6.

the entry into the new choir at Easter 1180, he explained the monks' jubilation by likening their expulsion from that part of the church to the expulsion from Eden.[18] Small wonder that the windows are essentially esoteric, and that popular hagiographical subjects, which may have been a concession to the pilgrim traffic, were carefully integrated with biblical and ecclesiastical history.

A single, unifying theme spanning the choir and Trinity Chapel is provided by the figures from the genealogy of Christ that were represented, two in each window of the clerestory, beginning on the north side next to the western transept with the creation of Adam and Adam digging, and presumably ending in the opposite window with the Virgin and Christ; the series thus began with Adam on the side of darkness and ended with Christ on the side of light, although many Old Testament figures were also represented on the south side. There are forty-nine clerestory windows, the plain lancets interrupted in the ends of the eastern transepts by *oculi*; only in the inner part of the north one do figures remain *in situ*. These are Moses and Synagogue (fig. 105), surrounded by four Virtues and four Prophets; Austin's reconstruction with Christ and Ecclesia and the four Evangelists on the south side is a reasonable conjecture, though no early record has survived of the contents of this window. The genealogical figures were also interrupted in the eastern end of the building, where the three windows of the apse have irons describing three medallions in each, suggesting that they were designed for narrative subjects. Austin assumed, apparently from fragments he found, that these were Christological; this has been partly confirmed by the rediscovery of a panel with the Last Judgment from the axial window, now in the Virginia Museum of Arts (fig. 146).[19] Less reliable is his suggestion that scenes from the lives of Moses and John the Baptist were in the

next windows on each side (plan, N:III, S:III); each has two lozenges in the ironwork, and in one of them Gostling saw genealogical figures in the 1770s.[20] It seems that as many as forty-four windows may have had ancestors of Christ, giving a total of eighty-eight figures including God the Father and Christ.

In the fourteenth century, twelve lower windows of the eastern part of the church were still filled with types and antitypes.[21] Of these only parts of four survive, all the panels being placed in two windows in the north choir aisle. *In situ* are the upper panels of the second and third windows of the medieval lists; the first was blocked in the later Middle Ages, and the rest of the lower windows of the choir, eastern transepts, and presbytery retain only the schemes of their original ironwork.[22] The exact location of the twelve windows has been established by a close study of the ironwork and the medieval texts, and although the sequence is generally logical there are some interruptions towards the end of the series (Appendix figs. 1, 8–19). There was a total of eighteen windows in this part of the building, which left six to be filled with other subjects. The first six typological windows were in continuous sequence, from the north side of the choir through to the end of the northeast transept. They were interrupted by the transept chapels, and the seventh and eighth were situated on either side of the presbytery. The ninth and tenth were in the end of the southeast transept, the eleventh and twelfth in the south aisle of the choir. There is evidence that the windows of the four transept chapels were glazed with the lives of the saints over whose altars they were positioned. The contents of Windows s:XIII and s:XVI (Appendix fig. 1) cannot be surmised.

The series does not, however, seem quite complete as recorded in the fourteenth century; the New Testament subjects extend from the Annun-

[18] Gervase, ed. Stubbs, 1879, p. 24; conversely, Origen interpreted Eden as an allegory of the future Church (quoted by Mâle, 1958, p. 136).

[19] Caviness, 1973, pp. 11–13.

[20] Gostling, 1777, p. 327, window 23 (N:III); cf. Williams, 1897, p. 2.

[21] James, 1901, edited the inscriptions from a fourteenth-century roll in the cathedral library, MS C 246.

[22] The original irons from windows s:XI and s:XII are stored in the cathedral, see Chapter Three, n. 97. The irons in S:XV, s:X, s:IX, and n:XIII are new, but, with the possible exception of s:IX, there is no reason to suppose they do not correspond in design to the originals. In the case of n:XIII figure panels and ornament now scattered elsewhere would fit the present armature.

ciation to the Resurrection, each with two or more types from the Old Testament, but James postulated that a thirteenth window was at least planned, with the Ascension, Pentecost, and Christ in Majesty.[23] These subjects are in fact extant, separated physically from the choir series by the Trinity Chapel, but given the most prominent position in the east window of the corona. The relation of this to the choir windows was not recorded in the medieval texts, either because it was forgotten in the later Middle Ages or because the roll, at least, may have been hung in the choir.

The corona also contained a Tree of Jesse, probably in the window on the north side adjacent to the east one, of which two original figures survive.[24] In the later Sainte-Chapelle the Jesse Tree was similarly situated in relation to the Passion.[25] The contents of the other three windows of the corona are conjectural, but in all probability they were Christological, perhaps partially reiterating, as do the east window and the Jesse Tree, themes already appearing in other parts of the cathedral. The Redemption of the east window was completed by the Last Judgment in the clerestory of the apse, which as seen from the choir or presbytery would appear directly above it (text fig. 2b). Thus the easternmost windows provided a summing up of the essential program of the upper church, and this program was very closely knit in its spatial development.

The subjects of the "triforium" windows of the choir, transepts, and presbytery are also uncertain; the ironwork of the ten windows in the choir and presbytery suggests that they contained narrative subjects, three in each window, and it is certain that scenes from the Lives of Sts. Dunstan and Alphage now on the north side of the choir are partially *in situ* (text fig. 2c). They were thus loosely associated with the altars of these saints, which had been to the north and south of the high

altar since the time of Conrad, and which were replaced in the same positions in 1180 (plan).[26] Other hagiographical cycles were certainly associated with side altars; in the chapel of St. Martin in the northeast corner of the north transept is one fragmentary panel from the life of this saint, and the fourteenth-century record of the theological subjects of the choir windows includes, erroneously, some scenes from the life of St. Gregory, whose chapel was in the southeast transept.[27] By far the most extended cycle, however, is that of the miracles of St. Thomas. Subjects survive *in situ* in seven of the twelve windows of the Trinity Chapel ambulatory.[28] That the cycle began with the life of St. Thomas is certain, but at least ten of the windows showed posthumous miracles, many of them worked at the tomb, which was in the crypt from 1170 until 1220. There were originally at least 180 scenes in these ten windows. Two surviving scenes depict a shrine such as that in the Trinity Chapel itself, to which the relics were translated in 1220 (fig. 164).[29]

The St. Thomas cycle is, in a sense, an interpolation in the biblical cycle of the choir and corona. On the other hand, it is closely linked to the thematic whole. Just as the patriarchs and kings of the clerestory were the spiritual ancestors of Christ, so the canonized churchmen whose lives were represented—Gregory, Stephen, Martin, Dunstan, Alphage, and Thomas Becket—were the spiritual descendants of Christ. Each of the three divisions of scripture mentioned by Vincent of Beauvais was thus included.[30] Old and New Testament histories are closely interwoven, and also represented are scenes of recent Church history. The miracles of Becket, the Church's latest martyr, were very nearly contemporary. Conceptually and visually the miracles of Christ, whose works were continued through his saints, were powerfully invoked.

[23] James, 1901, p. 42.

[24] Caviness, 1975, p. 373–74.

[25] *Corpus, France* I, 81–82.

[26] Gervase, ed. Stubbs, 1879, pp. 13, 22–23. A schematic plan of Conrad's choir is in Southern, 1963, p. 265; a more accurate reconstruction has been prepared by Colin Dudley.

[27] James, 1901, pp. 26, 35, and 42.

[28] Windows n:II, III, IV, V, s:VI and VII. The top two panels in Window s:II may also be *in situ*, but they are very poorly preserved; see Caviness, 1967, pp. 98, 101–102.

[29] Window n:III(1), and Window s:VII(22); panel 21 in the same window is a restoration, based on the design of 22; *ibid.*, pp. 162–63.

[30] Mâle, 1958, p. 133.

The planning and execution of the program

THE pages that follow will contain frequent references to the contributions to the glazing made by Benedict, abbot of Peterborough from 1177 to 1193, and formerly prior of Christ Church. For the reader's convenience, their implications will be summarized here for the bearing they have upon the planning of the program. The detailed evidence will be presented later, in connection with each part of the program.

The verses and a pictorial guide used in the first three typological windows, in the choir, may have come from Peterborough. They could have been sent back to Canterbury soon after Benedict's arrival in Peterborough, which was in the year that the choir was vaulted,[31] though it is equally possible Benedict carried them to Peterborough with him from Canterbury. A series of *tituli* for the miracles of St. Thomas, including a large number of subjects from Benedict's book of 1179, may have been composed by or for Benedict, who also had access to the early books of William's text; these compositions must postdate 1179. As we have seen in Chapter Two if the subjects were selected by about 1200, a number of the people who featured in the miracles of the 1179s as children and youths might still have been living, and able to contribute money for the glazing.

There is evidence that the program was modified as the building progressed; the typological windows may have been intended to end on the south side of the choir, but instead the Redemption Window was placed in the east end of the corona. This window was hurriedly composed, duplicating several subjects from earlier in the series. The subjects of the Trinity Chapel clerestory may have had to be expanded after William the Englishman took over the work in 1179; he prolonged the Trinity Chapel beyond its former extent, and very probably beyond that intended by William of Sens.[32] A change in plan is evident from the capitals of the wall arcade embedded in the "pilgrim steps," indicating that the raised ambulatory was not intended from the beginning. Eight clerestory windows in the apse seem to have had subjects other than the genealogy of St. Luke, and some of these may also be afterthoughts in the program as it was envisaged in 1177. The twelve windows of the Trinity Chapel ambulatory were planned only after the change of architect, which happened in the same year Benedict composed his last book of miracles.

Conceptually, then, the program may go back to about 1180. It will emerge as essentially conservative and monastic. The only clear coincidence is with another English abbey. The texts for the lives of the Canterbury saints, Dunstan, Alphage, and Thomas, were products of Christ Church. The models, unless some were sent from Peterborough, and apart from a few recent importations from Sicilian art before Monreale, were in the Canterbury libraries. The only clear dependence on French tradition is in the Jesse Window of the corona, but it was not new to England. Conversely, some of the typological windows seem to have been imitated elsewhere—at St.-Quentin, Sens, Lincoln, and even, perhaps, in modified form at Chartres. In the content of the windows there is no trace of influence from Stephen Langton, archbishop from 1207–1228, who had been trained in the new schools at Paris. If the program selected by the monks about 1180, with the help of their former prior, was not completed until Langton's archiepiscopacy, this proves only the extraordinary tenacity of the brothers, which was also manifest in the forty years of planning and waiting for the translation of the relics of their martyr. The Becket series is evidence that Christ Church was a major participant in the struggle for an art form with greater popular appeal than that possessed by the esoteric scriptural commentaries already provided in the choir; this glazing was the last effort to compete with the new cathedrals. Had the program not taken so long to complete, it could be cited as the forerunner of Bourges, Chartres, and Rouen.

[31] Gervase, ed. Stubbs, 1879, p. 20.

[32] Professor Bony, in conversation in 1969, agreed that there is architectural evidence for a change in plan.

VII. Biblical Subjects

". . . especially in cathedral and parish churches, where public stations take place, I think it an excusable concession that [our contemporaries] should enjoy at least that class of pictures which, as being the books of the laity, can suggest divine things to the unlearned, and stir up the learned to the love of the scriptures."

Pictor in Carmine,
tr. M. R. James.[1]

BIBLICAL subjects are represented in two of the great cycles, the one in the clerestory, the other in the lower windows of the western part of the twelfth-century building. Both are typological, dealing with Old Testament subjects only insofar as they were seen to relate to the New. There are no purely narrative programs, either of the Gospel story or of Old Testament history. The intent seems less to provide "books of the laity" than to "stir up the learned."

The ancestors of Christ

FIGURES from the genealogical series are among the most famous representations of English Romanesque art. Although they have been removed from the clerestory and placed in random order in the south window of the southwest transept and in the great west window of the nave, it is possible to attempt a reconstruction of the original order from the notes published by Gostling in 1777, and from measurements of the glass and ironwork.[2] Lacunae already present in the eighteenth century can be filled from two biblical genealogies, contained in Luke 3:23–38, and Matthew 1:1–17. The list given by Luke goes back to Adam; there are seventy-six figures including Christ, or seventy-seven if God the Father is counted as the creator of Adam. Matthew lists only forty-one figures, from Abraham to Christ, and diverges sharply from Luke's list after King David. The generations are counted as fourteen from the Creation to David, fourteen from David to the exile in Babylon, and fourteen from that time to Christ; in fact the last section has thirteen only, but Jeconiah may have been

---

[1] James, 1951, p. 141.
[2] Gostling, 1777, pp. 326–27; the numbering of windows on the plan was corrected in this edition.

counted twice to give equal divisions and to avoid thirteen. We have seen that the Canterbury clerestory figures may have numbered eighty-eight, including God the Father and Christ. It is evident from Gostling's notes that the sequence was that of Luke's complete genealogy except for an interpolation in at least three windows on the north side of the Trinity Chapel—N:VI (20), N:V (21), N:IV (22)—in which Rehoboam, Abijah, Josiah, Hezekiah, and Jeconiah were taken from Matthew. Austin noticed that if the list from Luke were resumed in Window S:IV (28), where it had been broken off in Window N:VII (19)—after five narrative windows in the apse—and if the Virgin were included as well as Joseph, there would be enough figures to fill the remaining windows of the clerestory.[3] There are some difficulties with this assumption. Figures seen by Gostling in Windows S:IX(33) and S:XII–XV(36–39) have to be moved into S:X(34) and S:XIII–XVI(37–40); Neri is indeed in Window S:XIII(37) now, and Rackham assumed he might be *in situ*, but a study of the restoration and comparison of measurements indicate that he was at one time certainly in S:XII(36), as Gostling saw him.[4] The figure Rackham identified as Cosam, from the fragmentary inscription "co . . . ," is in a quatrefoil that fits Window S:X (34), but not the straight-bar armature of Window S:XI(35), which is the position Austin and Rackham would assign to this figure (Appendix fig. 5, fig. 218).[5] Furthermore, a figure of Joseph, clearly identified by inscription, was seen by Gostling in Window N:III(23), and the size and lead lines of the existing panel show that it was made for either Window N:III(23) or S:III(27). The companion figure has "ac . . . ," perhaps for Achim of Matthew's list; these are not, then, the Jonan and Joseph that should have been in Window S:VI (30), according to Rackham and Austin.[6] It appears, rather, that there were only three narrative

windows in the apse, and furthermore that the whole program may not have been as rationally executed as has been supposed. It is even possible that Austin suppressed part of the evidence, in the form of the figure of Cosam, which was taken out of the cathedral in the nineteenth century.[7] It is not improbable that some mistakes were made in executing the figures, because of the long delay in glazing the east end.

The clerestory figures are recognizable chiefly by their name bands. A number, however, are also given attributes or characteristic postures. As already noticed in the chapters on style, there are three distinct groups. Three of the figures by the Methuselah Master adopt postures from narrative cycles—Adam, Enoch, and Noah; the Joanna Master, working in the transepts and presbytery, conferred no characteristic postures or attributes; in the Trinity Chapel several figures hold attributes. Although the program has conceptual unity, the sources may have varied. The conceptual base will be explored first.

There are significant differences between the Canterbury series of genealogical figures and other extant representations. One common way of representing the ancestors of Christ in the twelfth and thirteenth centuries was the Tree of Jesse, in which only a few of the kings of Judea, from Jesse to the Virgin and Christ, were shown. Another common form was the "gallery of kings," such as were sculpted on portals.[8] In both types of "genealogy," kingship is emphasized, and the Virgin rather than Joseph is the royal parent. Katzenellenbogen, following a suggestion made by Kitzinger, has indicated that these crowned figures are to be interpreted as honoring the kings of France, although they are represented in the guise of Old Testament figures.[9] In the nave windows of St.-Remi in Rheims, Grodecki has identified a series of crowned ancestors from Matthew's genealogy, among whom

---

[3] Quoted by Williams, 1897, pp. 2, 4.

[4] Rackham, 1949, p. 42; cf. Gostling, 1777, p. 327. The order of figures had been disturbed by Gostling's time; in the northeast transept figures from windows N:XVIII(8) and N:XVI(10) were in N:XV(11) and N:XIV(12), those from N:XIV(12) in N:XIII(13).

[5] Rackham, 1949, p. 41.

[6] *Ibid.*, pp. 40, 45–46.

[7] Rackham, 1928, pp. 33–34.

[8] Mâle, 1958, pp. 167–73, discussed examples at Paris, Amiens, Chartres, and Rheims.

[9] Katzenellenbogen, 1959, pp. 27–30.

is Isaac; this liberal bestowing of crowns suggests a wish to stress kingship in the genealogy.[10] In the extended genealogies of Matthew and Luke, however, patriarchs are as numerous as kings, and descent is traced through Joseph, making some difficulties for the commentators.[11] By including all the figures mentioned by Luke, which extend back long before the royal line of David, the Canterbury theologians avoided emphasis on kingship and placed it rather on the patriarchs, priests, and prophets. This would be especially true if the kings from Matthew were not envisaged in the first plan. Such emphasis of the church over royalty would be expected in a monastic house whose recently canonized archbishop suffered martyrdom under Henry II. There may also have been some influence from John of Salisbury's theories of kingship. He saw patriarchs and priests as enlightened rulers of Israel; kings were only given "in the anger of God" because the Israelites had "showed themselves not content to have God for their King."[12]

The Canterbury series is not, however, to be taken in a purely historical sense. With the revived interest in the historical interpretation of the Bible in the latter part of the twelfth century, at least one genealogy was composed from a reading of the Old Testament, but it differs greatly from those given by Luke or Matthew and includes sixty-six figures. This is the *compendium historiae in genealogia Christi* of Peter of Poitiers. It was probably composed after 1167, and recensions were commonly found in institutions of learning.[13] The

"tree" was laid out in descending order, after the manner of Arab genealogies that had already been adapted in Spain for the genealogy of Christ according to Matthew. Neither the earlier nor the more recent historical tables of descent had a very strong pictorial tradition, although there were some Spanish copies with occasional busts of the figures beside their names.[14]

Perhaps the tradition of portrait busts in illustration of the genealogy comes from such tables. It was evidently current in the art of the West and also of Byzantium by the twelfth century: at Hildesheim, forty-two of the patriarchs and minor figures from Luke were included in this form, alongside the Tree of Jesse. In the Great Canterbury Psalter in Paris the Tree of Jesse takes the form of six portrait busts, in ascending order from Jesse to Christ, between busts of apostles and prophets.[15] Other examples in Western manuscripts from the late twelfth to early thirteenth century were found by Swarzenski; they include the English Imola Psalter.[16] At Sigena, in frescoes of English origin, was a series of portrait busts based on Luke and Matthew, numbering seventy in all. The church of the Nativity at Bethlehem has a series of such busts dating from 1169; they are also included in the Monreale program, from which Demus supposed this to be the characteristic Byzantine mode of representing the ancestry of Christ,[17] a theory that has to be modified. Because of the researches of Mâle, Ligtenberg, and Watson on the Tree of Jesse, this form has too readily been accepted as the normal Western way of representing the de-

---

[10] Grodecki, 1975, p. 70.

[11] *Glossa Ordinaria, P. L.*, cxiv, cols. 69–70; the author explained that although Christ was not born of the seed of Joseph, it was not customary in scripture to trace a genealogy through the female line, and in any case Joseph and Mary were of the same tribe.

[12] Quoted by John Dickinson, "The Medieval Conception of Kingship as Developed in the *Polycraticus* of John of Salisbury," *Speculum* 1 (1926), 310–11.

[13] See H. Vollmer, *Deutsche Bibelauszüge des Mittelalters zum Stammbaum Christi* (Akademische Verlagsgesellschaft Athenaion) Potsdam, 1931, pp. 127–88 (Latin text from Hamburg, Staats- und Universitätsbibliothek, MS theol. 2029, ff.1–18v); Philip Samuel More, *The Works of Peter of Poitiers*, Washington, D.C., 1936, pp. 97–117.

A thirteenth-century English recension, Cambridge (Mass.), Houghton Library, MS Typ. 216H is omitted from his list; see Harvard College Library, *Illuminated and Calligraphic Manuscripts*, Cambridge, Mass., 1955, no. 25.

[14] Watson, 1934, pp. 37–46; Wilhelm Neuss, *Die Apokalypse des Heiligen Johannes in der Altspanischen und Altchristlichen Bibel-illustration*, Münster in Westfalen, 1931, pp. 119–25, Pls. x–xvi; Neuss, *Die Katalanische Bibel-illustration um die Wende des ersten Jahrtausends und die altspanische Buchmalerei*, Bonn and Leipzig, 1922, Pl. 18, figs. 55–56.

[15] *Psautier*, Pl. 8.

[16] Swarzenski, 1936, p. 101, n.2.

[17] Demus, 1949, pp. 314–15.

scent of Christ,[18] but portrait medallions seem to have been as common. An early example in the West is in an eleventh-century manuscript in Prague, the Vyšehrad Gospels, in which four pages are filled with busts in circles or diamonds, representing the ancestors of Matthew's genealogy and placed before his gospel.[19]

There was, besides, a Byzantine tradition for representing ancestors as standing figures.[20] In the two domes of the inner narthex of the Kariye Djami in Istanbul is a series of sixty-six ancestors, executed in mosaics in 1320–1321. The possiblity cannot be ruled out that there was an earlier Eastern model for these, since the textual source for the names taken, with additions, from Luke and Matthew goes back to the mid-eleventh century.[21]

Characteristic of the West around 1200 seem to be a variety of experiments with renderings of the theme. Hildesheim, Sigena, and Canterbury are each different manifestations of this. The *Hortus Deliciarum* of Herade of Landsberg includes two highly original forms, one a descending table with portrait medallions, which are suspended on a fishing rod and line held by God the Father, the other a schematic ascending tree.[22] The Virgin and Christ are at the top of this tree, and below them forty heads, fourteen of them crowned; these portraits can therefore be identified with the figures in Matthew's genealogy. This "Tree of Abraham" shows more than the royal line. There are other examples of supplemented Jesse Trees, in parallel with Hildesheim and the *Hortus Deliciarum*. In the hall of the abbey of Moissac are vault paintings of about 1200 in which seated, uncrowned figures with scrolls are represented alongside a central Tree of Jesse, as well as six portrait medallions of

prophets.[23] The tradition of representing ancestors, other than the kings of a Jesse Tree, as seated figures seems, however, to come from England.

Two series of seated ancestors in manuscripts are associated with the portrait of St. Matthew at the beginning of his gospel. One is in the tenth-to-eleventh-century Gospels, probably from St.-Bertin, but with strong Anglo-Saxon influence, in the Boulogne Public Library (MS 11, f.11); the other is a mid-twelfth–century Winchcombe book in Dublin (Trinity College, MS 53, f.7v). Both have been discussed by Heimann.[24] In the Boulogne manuscript four figures—a king and Abraham, Isaac and Jacob—are represented seated on the same pages as the evangelist portrait, while opposite are twenty-four busts in rows under arcades; two sections of the genealogy of Matthew are thus represented. In the Winchcombe manuscript are twenty-eight ancestors under arches. Most are drawn only from the waist up, but some in the bottom row are clearly seated. A German example, in a manuscript of about 1260 from Mainz, belongs perhaps to a different tradition; twelve couples are represented seated.[25]

The Canterbury series differs from earlier examples in following Luke rather than Matthew for most of its length, and is thus one of the most extended series known. After the appearance at St.-Denis in 1144 of the "classic" Tree of Jesse formula, there were experimental variants around 1200 and into the thirteenth century, either elaborations on the Jesse Tree—as at Hildesheim, Moissac, and in the *Hortus*—or quite different types of pictorial representation. Although Matthew's genealogy was most frequently used, Luke was followed at Hildesheim, and partially at Canterbury

[18] Mâle, 1953, pp. 168–75; R. Ligtenberg, "De Genealogie van Christus in de beeldende Kunst der Middeleeuwen, voornamelijk van het Westen," *Oudheidkundig Jaarboek, Bulletin van den nederl. Oudheidkundigen* 9 (1929), pp. 1–54; Watson, 1934.

[19] Prague, University Library, MS XIV A 13; see Heimann, 1965, p. 88, with bibliography, and Gertrud Schiller, *Ikonographie der Christlichen Kunst*, I, Gütersloh, 1966, 25, fig. 20.

[20] Heimann, 1965, p. 88.

[21] Paul A. Underwood, *The Kariye Djami*, New York, 1966, I, 15, 49–54.

[22] Watson, 1934, pp. 134–37.

[23] Paul Deschamps and Marc Thibout, *La Peinture murale en France au début de l'époque gothique, de Philippe Auguste à la fin du règne de Charles V (1180–1380)*, Paris [1963], Pl. XLI, p. 97.

[24] Heimann, 1965, pp. 87–89, Pls. 13 and 14c and d; for the Boulogne Gospels see also Hanns Swarzenski, "The Anhalt Morgan Gospels," *Art Bulletin* 31 (1949), pp. 78–80.

[25] Aschaffenburg, Schlossbibliothek, MS 13, f.18; Swarzenski, 1936, no. 17, p. 101, fig. 222.

and Sigena. The latter series of seventy portrait busts is the only one extant to rival Canterbury in completeness. That all these examples are monastic productions strengthens the view that the prime interest of the Canterbury figures was their spiritual relation to Christ, rather than their royal nature. St.-Denis is thus an exception among the monastic houses in preferring the Tree of Jesse, and the obvious reason is its strong royal ties.

For an interpretation of the ancestors one has to turn to the commentaries on the Old Testament as well as to passages on Luke or Matthew. The *Glossa Ordinaria*, a work of the school of Laon of the first half of the twelfth century, interprets most of the major figures who occur in the genealogy of Matthew as precursors of Christ in the spiritual sense.[26] So also Origen had seen Adam as a prefiguration of Christ when he left the Garden of Eden and put on the animal skins that symbolized mortality.[27] The Canterbury representation of Adam digging is thus a conscious allusion to his Christlike nature, and not a mere convention taken over from narrative cycles (fig. 6). The same is true of the representation of Enoch, whose ascent prefigured the Ascension (fig. 9). The *Glossa* also gives etymological reasons for accepting ancestors as partaking of the nature of Christ; thus "Christ is Phares, that is the divider, who separated the sheep from the goats. And he is Esrom, that is the arrow or wound, which penetrated the hearts of his listeners;" so also "Aram is interpreted as the *chosen one* or the *most high*" as prophesied by Hosea and in the Psalms.[28] The gloss on the relevant passages in Luke is less full, but Methuselah, Enoch, and Seth are mentioned as Christ-figures.[29] The same themes are elaborated in the commentary on Genesis 4–5; even the sinful Lamech is interpreted as signifying humiliation, a

vital stage between man's descent to earth and his finding of spiritual strength and repose.[30] The exegesis is here tropological, or moral, whereas in the case of Enoch it is allegorical. These interpretations were evidently of more significance for the informed viewer of the Canterbury windows than the historical nature of the figures represented. Although the generations from Adam to Christ represent the history of the world from the Fall to the Redemption, they more importantly demonstrate the spiritual unity of the Old and New Testaments, the continuity from the epoch before grace to that under grace. Conversely, the gnostic Marcion, who wished to sever the links between the Old and New Testaments, cut the genealogy out of his edition of Luke.[31] The bond between the Testaments is also the theme of the "twelve" typological windows of the choir and presbytery, which therefore reinforce the message of the upper windows.

The *Glossa* was probably known in Canterbury by 1175 or 1180. Among the books owned by Herbert of Bosham were a glossed Pentateuch and Gospels, and other books with the *Maior Glossatura* of Peter the Lombard were given to Christ Church by him.[32] Benedict, Prior of Christ Church and, after 1177, Abbot of Peterborough, left to the latter house a glossed Bible in fifteen volumes.[33] But there is evidence that the Canterbury clerestory figures may have been influenced by an earlier commentary upon the Old Testament that formed the preface to an illustrated Pentateuch. This is Aelfric's treatise "On the Old and New Testament" and his paraphrase in Anglo-Saxon of the Pentateuch and Joshua. Extant eleventh-century copies of the text seem to come from Canterbury. The illustrated copy, British Library, MS Cotton Claudius B.IV, is a St. Augustine's book; the treatise is

---

[26] *Glossa Ordinaria, P. L.*, cxiv, cols. 65–70; the gloss used to be included, as by Migne, in the *oeuvre* of the Carolingian scholar Walafrid Strabo; Glunz, 1933, pp. 213–17, pointed out its dependence on Anselm of Laon and John the Scot, and concluded it was a production of a follower, perhaps Peter the Lombard in the first half of the twelfth century.

[27] Quoted by Mâle, 1958, p. 137, from Migne, *Patrol. grec.* xi, col. 101.

[28] *Glossa Ordinaria* on Matthew, *P. L.*, cxiv, col. 66.

[29] *Ibid.*, col. 25.

[30] *Ibid.*, col. 103.

[31] F. F. B[ruce], *The New Bible Dictionary*, ed. J. D. Douglas, Grand Rapids, (rev. ed.) 1965, p. 459.

[32] Oxford, Bodleian Library, MS Auct. E inf. 7 and Cambridge, Trinity College, MS B.5.5; for these and others see Dodwell, 1954, pp. 105–107; Glunz, 1933, p. 214, n. 4.

[33] Glunz, 1933, p. 229.

missing and the preface to Genesis is incomplete; the other copy, British Library, MS Laud. Misc. 509, has the treatise and full preface, but no pictures. It is a reasonable conjecture that this may have been a Christ Church book.[34] The treatise will be considered first for its bearing on the content of the windows.

Aelfric, like the authors of the *Glossa*, saw the principal Old Testament figures as precursors of Christ. His exegesis is embodied in the following passage, in the seventeenth-century translation of William de L'Isle:

> We will speake hereof in order now briefly (because we haue often thereof written more at large) that thou maiest consider also the meaning of it. That *Adam* who on the sixt day was by God made, betokeneth our Sauiour Christ, who (in the sixth age) came into the world and renewed vs according to his Image. *Eva*, whom God tooke & made out of *Adams* side, betokeneth Gods Church, which sprung since out of Christs side. The slaughter of *Abel* most truly signifies our Sauiours death, whom the [Iewes], euill brethren like *Cain*, slew. *Seth* Adams Son, and his third also, is, raising of seed, & he signifies vndoubtedly Christ who rose from death on *the* third day. The seuenth man from *Adam* was called *Enoh*, he did according to *the* good liking of God, & God him tooke vp body & all, out of this life, & he liueth yet, as doth *the* famous Prophet *Elias,* so also taken to *that* other life, and both shall come against Antichrist, to confute his falsehood by *the* power of God. Yet by *that* fiend they shall be slaine, and rise againe, as all men doe. *Noe* who kept in the Arke while the generall floud drowned all the world but eight persons, is interpreted *requies*, that is *rest* in English; and he betokened Christ, who came forth vnto vs to redeeme vs from the stormy billowes of this world vnto rest and happiness *with* him. And so forth to *the* end, euery holy father by word or work plainely giues testimony to our Sauiour and his comming.[35]

Other types of Christ are Isaac, Joshua, David, and Solomon.

The illustrations to Aelfric's Pentateuch are remarkably dull. There are, to be sure, a few inter-

esting narrative scenes and cycles, but the predominant mode of illustration consists in showing each Old Testament figure seated with his wife and children standing behind him, in the left-hand frame, and then carried away to his burial in the right-hand frame (fig. 11). Effectively this is a series of seated ancestors of Christ, from Adam to Jacob, with other figures up to Joshua. Supplementary narrative scenes are given for only a few ancestors: Adam, Enoch, Noah, then Abraham, Isaac, and Jacob. A painter could use this set of pictures as an iconographical guide for the early figures in a genealogy; these were lacking in illustrations to Matthew's gospel, and no comparable illustrations to Luke's fuller genealogy have been found. The artist would have a choice of representational mode for the figures with narrative cycles, but others would simply be taken over as seated figures, isolated from their families. This is precisely the kind of choice the Methuselah Master made in designing the figures from Adam to Noah; Adam is digging, as he is in Aelfric (figs. 6, 7); Enoch is pulled up to heaven by the hand of God, as he is in Aelfric (figs. 9, 11); and Noah speaks with God, as he does in Aelfric (figs. 66, 69). Jared, Methuselah, and Lamech are seated in restless poses, with a variety of gestures (figs. 8, 12, 13). The resemblances, however, are frequently of a general kind, more conceptual than visual. One may assume borrowing of motifs from other sources also, and these will be investigated below. There is still a strong case for supposing that the St. Augustine's Aelfric is the actual iconographical guide used, perhaps a little before 1180, for the clerestory windows.

It cannot be proved that the Cotton Aelfric was lent to Christ Church in this period, but it is not impossible. Some time had passed since the quarrels over the profession of obedience of the abbots of St. Augustine's to the archbishops,[36] and by 1175 relations were good enough to warrant bring-

---

[34] S. J. Crawford, *The Old English Version of the Heptateuch, Aelfric's Treatise on the Old and New Testament and His Preface to Genesis*, London, 1922, pp. 2-3, 440-41.

[35] *Ibid.*, pp. 22-24; the whole treatise is printed on pp. 15-55.

[36] *New Palaeographical Society*, Pl. 61; in the Christ Church professions of obedience, British Library, MS Cotton Cleo. E.I, Silvester was entered in 1157 when forced to comply.

ing Roger from Christ Church to be abbot of St. Augustine's, where he remained in office until 1213. He brought with him relics of Thomas Becket, and there was some exchange of lands. It is certain that someone towards the end of the twelfth century made heavy use of the book; commentaries in English and Latin were added at that time, in a poor hand that unfortunately cannot be localized with certainty. The English is in the southeastern dialect.[37] The Latin, taken from Flavius Josephus, pseudo-Methodius, Jerome, Bede, and someone called Norman, is much preoccupied with genealogies, occasionally counting the generations from Luke (for example, f.9v). It is tempting to connect these scribblings with the moment of inception of the glazing program.

Adam digging was commonly included in narrative cycles. The stooped figure from clerestory N:XXV(1) is not so much like his counterpart in the Aelfric manuscript, as the Adam of the preceding scene, who however, is almost hidden behind a tree instead of standing beside it. This is the figure clad in an animal skin, whereas the Aelfric digger wears a cloth tunic (figs. 6, 7). The scene in the "Caedmon" manuscript, Oxford, Bodleian Library, MS Junius 11, p. 13, is no closer, except that the vigorous tree resembles the one by the Methuselah Master. If, as James has suggested, this is the *Genesis Anglice depicta* of Eastry's list, it was in Christ Church in the Middle Ages and could have been a supplementary model.[38] The originality of the Canterbury figure lies in its isolation from a narrative context, and the exclusion of Eve, so that the spade becomes an at-

tribute. The Adam among the Six Ages of the World in the north choir aisle, who is seated with a pick or hoe as an attribute, belongs to a different iconographic tradition.

Distinguishing features of Adam digging are his dress and his implement. The spade, as Henderson has remarked, is in the Anglo-Saxon tradition, although it also occurred in wall paintings at Tavant and perhaps at St.-Savin, under Anglo-Saxon influence.[39] It is the implement in the clerestory window, the Genesis cycle in the Great Canterbury Psalter in Paris,[40] the Psalter pages by W. de Brailes formerly in the Chester Beatty collection,[41] and the Bible of Robert de Bello, abbot of St. Augustine's, Canterbury, from 1224 to 1253.[42] It also appears in glass of about 1175 at Normée.[43] A mattock or pick is the implement used in the Palermito Cappella Palatina mosaics of about 1160, the Monreale mosaics,[44] and the Sigena paintings.[45] These three representations are closely similar in pose, with Adam clad in a hair tunic, as he is also in the Canterbury Psalter. A different tradition is reflected in two thirteenth-century French works, in which Adam has a plain loincloth and spade; these are the Good Samaritan Window in the nave of Chartres Cathedral,[46] and the mid-century Bible picture book in the Pierpont Morgan Library.[47] Apart from the contiguous occurrences of the hair loincloth and the spade in the Aelfric manuscript, and their combination in the glass, both features are found in the tiny figure of Adam in the Bible of Robert de Bello, which must be considerably later than the window. Together they form a distinctive Canterbury tradition, and the dependence

[37] *Palaeographical Society*, II, Pls. 71–72; Neil Ker, *Catalogue of Manuscripts Containing Anglo-Saxon*, Oxford, 1957, no. 142, pp. 178–79. I am indebted to Dr. Urry for studying this hand; in his view it could belong to either house. To him also I owe the information about Abbot Roger. See also Hasted, 12, 1801, 191–93; *William Thorne's Chronicle of St. Augustine's Abbey Canterbury*, tr. A. H. Davis, Oxford, 1934, p. 100; and Knowles, Brooke, and London, 1972, p. 36.

[38] James, 1903, p. 51, no. 304, and pp. xxv–xxvi.

[39] Henderson, 1963, p. 24.

[40] Bibliothèque Nationale, MS Lat. 8846, f.1; *Psautier*, Pl. I.

[41] Now Cambridge, Fitzwilliam Museum, MS 330; Sir Sydney Cockerell, *The Work of W. de Brailes, an English*

Illuminator of the Thirteenth Century, Cambridge (Roxburghe Club), 1930, Pl. 2 and Rickert, 1965, Pl. 102.

[42] London, British Library, Burney MS 3, f.5v, reproduced by Rickert, 1965, Pl. 100, and by Rackham, 1949, Pl. 8e.

[43] *Vitrail*, fig. 37.

[44] Kitzinger, 1960, fig. 21, Pl. 17, and p. 50.

[45] Pächt, 1961, fig. 9. This scene is unusual in including the angel instructing Adam, from an apocryphal source.

[46] Delaporte and Houvet, 1926, Pl. xx.

[47] MS 638, f.2; facsimiles by Sir Sydney Cockerell, *A Book of Old Testament Illustrations of the Middle of the Thirteenth Century*, Cambridge, 1927, and newly edited with a preface by J. Plummer, *Old Testament Miniatures*, New York (1969).

of the glass on the Aelfric manuscript is thus confirmed.

A survey of representations of Enoch carried up to heaven is also decisive, in spite of divergences between the clerestory figure and the Enoch of the Aelfric manuscript (figs. 9, 11). The scene in the Bodleian "Caedmon" is quite different, with Enoch in the center.[48] The English Psalter in Munich belongs to the same group.[49] Henderson has supposed that the figure at St.-Savin stems from the Aelfric tradition;[50] as at Canterbury the ladder has been eliminated, and there is room only for clouds and the hand of God (figs. 9, 10). A certain power has been added to the Methuselah Master's figure by the twist of his body; the little figure in the Aelfric is a helpless child by comparison. More original is the scene of Enoch led away by God that was executed in enamels for the Klosterneuburg ambo by Nicholas of Verdun;[51] the date of 1181 is closely contemporary with the Methuselah Master's creation. In the typological window in the corona another type of representation was chosen. Of these three, only the clerestory figure derives from the Aelfric manuscript.

Noah has undergone the same transformation as Enoch; he is powerful, energetic and no longer subservient (figs. 66, 69). Like Enoch he is scarcely seated, although a bench is provided. Other figures by the Methuselah Master show the same free reference to the iconographical guide; Methuselah bears some relation to Cainan (figs. 12, 15), who also draws up one knee and rests his head on his hand, but the clerestory figure is closer to the type of the classical philosopher in spirit and perhaps also in pose. By a different artist is Jacob with Joseph; the forcefulness of Jacob, as well as the

moldings of his throne and the way his heels are placed together, may be recalled in the clerestory figure of Jared, who, however, also bears some resemblance to his counterpart in the Aelfric manuscript, even in his double-pronged beard (figs. 8, 11).

The Cotton Aelfric provides a considerable repertory of seated poses; they were eclectically drawn upon by the Methuselah Master, whose creations reflect their predominantly restless mood. Other images were in his mind's eye, too; Lamech can be compared with a little drawing in an early twelfth-century astronomical manuscript of unknown provenance, Oxford, Bodleian Library, MS Bodl. 614 (figs. 13, 18).[52] It is characteristic of his monumental figures for the upper windows that he took such a pose, already extravagant, and twisted the shoulders into violent action. The English lineage of these figures is paralleled on the continent, in the line that Swarzenski has traced from the Rheims manuscripts to the evangelist portraits in the St.-Amand Gospel books and the figures by Nicholas of Verdun on the shrines in Tournai and Cologne.[53] So too, the evangelist portraits in the Dover Bible of mid-century are precursors of the Methuselah Master's patriarchs.[54]

The Joanna Master, if he looked at the Aelfric manuscript at all, selected seated rather than "narrative" figures, and preferred the occasional calmer, more frontal poses.[55] His motif book must have included others of this kind; there may be some influence from the static, frontal and symmetrical figures frequently used to denote majesty in an earlier period, as on book covers or on royal seals.[56] Other examples of this mode discussed in the preceding chapter are strictly contemporary. It is

---

[48] Pächt, 1962, pp. 6–8, fig. 1.

[49] Staatsbibliothek, Clm 835, f.9v; photograph in the Princeton Index of Christian Art.

[50] Henderson, 1963, pp. 16–17.

[51] Röhrig, 1955, fig. 41.

[52] F. Saxl, "Illuminated Science Manuscripts in England," Lectures, 1, London, 1957, 108–109.

[53] Swarzenski, 1967, p. 35. More recently, "The Style of Nicholas of Verdun: Saint-Amand and Reims," Gatherings in Honor of Dorothy E. Miner, ed. Ursula E. McCracken, Lilian M. C. Randall, Richard H. Randall, Jr., Baltimore, 1974, pp. 111–14.

[54] Cambridge, Corpus Christi, MS 4; illus. Dodwell, 1954, Pl. 34.

[55] For example, Lamech on f.12.

[56] For example, the mid-eleventh–century Elder of the Apocalypse on the cover of a St.-Bertin manuscript, London, British Library, Add. MS 37768, illustrated in Goldschmidt, 1926, no. 38, and in Swarzenski, 1967, fig. 154; also a Christ in Majesty in the Victoria and Albert Museum, ibid., fig. 138, p. 48. For seals, see Saxl, 1954, Pls. I, II, vid.

tempting to suggest the Canterbury figures may reflect a Sicilian motif book, based on the Cappella Palatina mosaics of the 1140s to 1150s. The Apostles of the Pentecost, represented in the transept, are calmly outlined and have a clarity and plasticity of structure that the artist could not have found in early English models. Terah, with his wrist caught in his mantle, and his clearly outlined stomach and knees, could be freely adapted from the portrait of St. James (figs. 77, 79). Like the Canterbury figures, all the Apostles have furled scrolls.

The Aelfric manuscript would have no application for the later figures in the genealogy. Several from the Trinity Chapel hold attributes. Hezekiah has a sundial and Josiah has the "book of the law" represented as an open scroll (fig. 216); similar representations have been recognized by Heimann in the mid-twelfth–century Winchcombe book, where they form part of the abbreviated series from Matthew's genealogy.[57] It is surprising in the Canterbury context that the inscription on Josiah's scroll is in mock Hebrew, in spite of the fact that Herbert of Bosham had been proficient in Hebrew, and Hebrew studies continued to spread in England in the thirteenth century.[58] Hezekiah is also represented in the corona east window, in a narrative scene with the sundial, which may have suggested his attribute for the clerestory. King David has a crown, which had

already become customary in portraits in the Tree of Jesse, as at St.-Denis and Chartres in the mid-twelfth century. The figure that must be Jeconiah has a closed book and a bowl of coins (fig. 217). Both attributes are suspect in that the glass may be of late medieval facture; if copied from the original they could be construed as objects from the Temple of Solomon surrendered to Nebuchadnezzar (4 Kings 24:12–13). Most other figures are without distinguishing features apart from inscriptions; Abijah and Rehoboam, who have attributes in the Winchcombe initial, have none at Canterbury (figs. 214, 215). In contrast to the manuscript, in which twenty-two of twenty-eight figures have attributes, most of which Heimann took to have been bestowed *ad hoc*, the Canterbury series shows little inventiveness in spite of its rarity.[59] Only one other surviving figure has an attribute; he is Nathan from Luke's genealogy, who carries the scepter that he had saved for Solomon (fig. 213). The bestowing of attributes is not consistent enough, even in the latest figures to be executed, to presuppose an iconographical guide. Each painter seems to have had considerable latitude, as noted in the preceding chapter. The use of attributes was part of a trend that by 1220 was very general; the Old Testament figures of the central north portal of Chartres, for instance, hold attributes that carry far deeper meaning than the few at Canterbury.[60]

The typological windows: the cycle

TWELVE windows in the upper church were evidently famous in the Middle Ages; the verse inscriptions from them were copied several times, and survive in three manuscripts of the thirteenth, fourteenth, and fifteenth centuries. The best known is the fourteenth-century roll, MS C.246 in the cathedral library at Canterbury, which was edited

by James.[61] According to James the earlier manuscript, Cambridge, Corpus Christi, MS 400, may be the one from which the roll was copied; in a few readings it appears more correct.[62] A third version may be substantially more accurate, both in including a few verses left out of the roll, and in reflecting the layout of the windows by writing

[57] Heimann, 1965, pp. 90–92.
[58] Beryl Smalley, *The Study of the Bible in the Middle Ages*, 2nd ed., Oxford, 1952, pp. 338–55, 365–66.
[59] Heimann, 1965, p. 91.
[60] Katzenellenbogen, 1959, pp. 62–65, figs. 50, 51.

[61] James, 1901.
[62] M. R. James, *A Descriptive Catalogue of the Manuscripts in the Library of Corpus Christi College, Cambridge*, II/1, Cambridge, 1911, p. 266.

the titles and verses in three columns, the anti-types in the center. It seems to have been written by William Glastynbury, monk of Christ Church, and is now MS 256 in Corpus Christi, Oxford; it has been edited by Woodruff.[63] Although it does not altogether clarify some confusion about the contents of the eighth, ninth, and tenth windows, this manuscript is extremely useful for the subjects indicated in the ninth window, with the Parable of the Good Samaritan, and I have relied on it for my reconstruction (Appendix fig. 16).

Although it was never included in the cycle as recorded in the medieval manuscripts, the east window of the corona has to be considered in relation to the "twelve" typological windows of the choir, transepts, and presbytery, from which it is separated by the flight of steps from presbytery level and by the Trinity Chapel ambulatory. Like the Jesse Tree on its north flank, it is in part the summation of a more extensive program to the west. Possibly two or three of the five New Testament scenes it contains—the Crucifixion, Entombment, Resurrection, Ascension, and Pentecost—were planned for the last window in the south choir aisle (s:XVI), which no groups of subjects given in the medieval records will fit satisfactorily (Appendix figs. 8–20). At the time the decision was made to extend the Trinity Chapel and add the corona, the plan for the windows would have been altered, to give the Redemption the most prominent position in the east end. The Crucifixion, Entombment, and Resurrection had already been represented, with some of their types, in the twelfth window (Appendix fig. 19), but the Ascension, Pentecost, and Last Judgment were needed to complete the cycle. As we have seen, the last was placed in the axial window of the clerestory, di-rectly above the corona east window as seen from the choir.

There is evidence, which will be considered more fully below, that the thirteen typological windows at Canterbury were composed *ad hoc* from a variety of sources. Eleven have groups of three subjects, an antitype and two types, but there is no systematic selection of events *ante legem* and *sub lege*; a few types are even chosen from more recent history. The first three windows of the series used the same subjects and inscriptions as the Peterborough choir stall paintings, which may have been begun a decade or so earlier (1155–1175),[64] but contrary to James's expectation the Peterborough cycle does not coincide with the windows at the end of the series;[65] the source for these has not been found, although there are coincidences of subject matter with other cycles, especially with *Pictor in Carmine*.[66] The most original part of the cycle deals with the ministry of Christ; three whole windows were given to his parables (Appendix figs. 13, 15, 16). The Good Samaritan Window had four types to each of three antitypes. This number equals that in the corona east window. There are signs that the east window was hurriedly composed, using elements from preceding windows in the series; at least two compositions and one inscription were repeated.

The history of typological programs has been outlined several times and need not be given fully here.[67] There has been some dispute as to whether Mosan and Rhenish or French works were more important in creating a twelfth-century tradition, and Mâle's theory of the primacy of St.-Denis has been modified by Künstle and Grodecki.[68] It seems quite unnecessary to impute all the later English cycles to the influence of Suger's windows, as Mâle

[63] C. E. Woodruff, 1925. I am indebted to William Urry for this reference, and for his critique of the edition.

[64] During the abbacy of William of Waterville; for the dates see Hugonis Candidi, *Historia Coenobi Burgensis*, ed. Sparke, 1723, p. 94.

[65] James, 1901, p. 10.

[66] James, 1951, pp. 149–50.

[67] Henrik Cornell, *Biblia Pauperum*, Stockholm, 1925, pp. 120–44; Fritz Goldkuhle, *Mittelalterliche Wand-malerei in St. Maria Lyskirchen* (Bonner Beiträge zur Kunstwissenschaft 3), Düsseldorf, 1954, pp. 69–76. P. Bloch, "Typologische Kunst," *Miscellanea Mediaevalia* 6 (1969), 127–42, and "Typologie," *Lexikon der Christlichen Ikonographie*, IV, Rome, Freiburg, Basle, 1972, cols. 395–404.

[68] Karl Künstle, *Ikonographie der Christlichen Kunst*, I, Freiburg im Breisgau, 1928, 82–90; Grodecki, 1961a, p. 41.

and Saunders were inclined to do.[69] The vogue for this kind of subject matter was of longer duration in England and the Rhineland than in France. None of the French windows after St.-Denis makes use of such elaborate verses; long inscriptions are replaced entirely by labels in the single windows of Sens, St.-Quentin, Chartres, Bourges, Lyon, Rouen, Le Mans, and Tours. There are no extended cycles of typological windows from the thirteenth century in France.

As a mode of thought, and even as an art form, typology goes back to very early times; St. Paul makes frequent reference to Old Testament events in relation to the New, as do the early Church Fathers.[70] Prudentius gave inscriptions to be placed under Biblical scenes for "two-fold nourishment," a few of which allude to Old Testament prefigurations.[71] The existence of typological paintings in England as far back as the seventh century is attested by Bede, who described paintings brought to Monkwearmouth from the continent.[72] Descriptions are preserved of Carolingian decorations at Ingelheim and St. Gall, but contrary to some claims, these were not typological cycles.[73] The eleventh-century Byzantine Gospels in the Bibliothèque Nationale (MS grec. 74) has the brazen serpent with the cross to illustrate the illusion made in John 3:13.[74] But continuity of these pictorial traditions cannot be proved. In the second half of the twelfth century, typology burgeoned under the impact of cur-

rent allegorical, tropological, and anagogical exegesis. The commentaries of Peter the Lombard and the School of Laon were readily available, in England as on the continent. Like genealogies, typology was "in the air," and it received a variety of elaborate treatments. The principal sources for the program of the Klosterneuburg Ambo of 1181 have recently been found in liturgical texts.[75] The Canterbury cycle is one of several of the latter part of the twelfth century in England; others are the Kennet, Malmesbury, and Warwick ciboria, the Worcester Chapter House paintings, and possibly the Peterborough choir stall paintings.[76] *Pictor in Carmine* shows the diversity of subjects available for selection. Windows at Lincoln were later in inception than Canterbury. The most developed cycles are those of the end of the twelfth century; they went out of vogue under the impact of the new scholasticism, and came back only later in the thirteenth century with the creation of the *Biblia Pauperum* proper. Quite possibly the fourteenth-century record of inscriptions reflects currently renewed interest in the themes of the windows. The earlier productions, however, were highly esoteric and essentially a specialty of the monasteries.

The thirteen windows at Canterbury constitute the longest cycle of the period of which we have record. It differed from Peterborough and *Pictor* in including Parables. There are, effectively, three groups of windows. In the choir are the first three,

[69] Mâle, 1953, pp. 164–65; Saunders, 1932, p. 129.

[70] For early textual sources see J. Daniélou, *Sacramentum Futuri: Etude sur les origines de la typologie biblique*, Paris, 1950.

[71] Prudentius, *Dittochaeon*, ed. H. J. Thomson, II, Cambridge, Mass., 1953, 346–71, especially p. 353.

[72] Beda Venerabilis, *History of the Abbots of Weremouth and Jarrow*, ed. J. A. Giles, *Complete Works, in the Original Latin, [with] a New English Translation of the Historical Works* . . . III, London, 1843, 375–76; see also Peter Hunter Blair, *An Introduction to Anglo-Saxon England*, Cambridge, 1956, pp. 154–55.

[73] Roger Hinks, *Carolingian Art*, London, 1935, p. 100; K. J. Conant, *Carolingian and Romanesque Architecture*, Harmondsworth and Baltimore, 2nd ed., 1966, p. 24; cf. Julius Schlosser, *Schriftquellen zur Geschichte der karolingischen Kunst*, Vienna, 1892, pp. 321–23, 326–32.

[74] Omont, 1908, Pl. 148; so also Jonah Cast Up is a type of the Resurrection in illustration of Matthew 12: 39–41

(1, Pl. 41). A similarly isolated type was that of Samson and the Gates of Gaza, for the Resurrection in the eleventh-century picture cycle in Mainz Cathedral; see E. Steinmann, *Die Tituli und die kirchliche Wandmalerei im Abendlande vom V. bis zum XI. Jahrhundert*, Leipzig, 1892, pp. 115–16.

[75] Helmut Buschhausen, "The Theological Sources of the Klosterneuburg Altarpiece," *The Year 1200* III, 1975, pp. 122–31.

[76] Swarzenski, 1967, figs. 448–50 and 453, pp. 76–77, with bibliography (Kennet and Malmesbury ciboria); *The Year 1200* I, nos. 171 and 172, 164–66; and Sauerländer, 1971, pp. 514–15 (Malmesbury and Warwick ciboria). For the Worcester program see Chapter Six, n. 9; copies in the form of misericords were studied by Lady Trenchard Cox, 1959, who also noticed a connection with the thirteenth-century leaves bound in Eton College, MS 177 (p. 168), and postulated a pictorial dependence on Peterborough (pp. 169–70).

which deal with the early life of Christ up to the temptations. The ministry began in the northeast transept with the Calling of Nathanael. Six windows were given to teaching and miracles, and the series of twelve closed with three windows treating the Passion; had these been placed on the south side of the choir, as perhaps originally intended, the distribution would be quite symmetrical. The decision to extend the program into the presbytery and to add a thirteenth window, with the Passion and Redemption, in the corona, threw off the symmetry of the program.

In the selection of subjects several themes are favored. This underlying unity also extends to the corona window, indicating that it was composed in the spirit of the rest of the program. Dominant ideas are the authority of the Church and condemnation of the Jews for rejecting Christ; in the ministry cycle eschatological teachings are emphasized over moral teachings or miracles. The Church and the priesthood are treated in several of the types chosen from the era after Christ; they include Gregory Ordaining Readers as a type of Christ Reading in the Synagogue, and the Doctors of the Church as a type of the Sermon on the Mount, both in the fourth window. Christ is the first priest and the Church Fathers are his spiritual followers. He was represented as priest and king in the sixth window.[77] In the seventh, kings obey Peter and Paul, and in the tenth, the Emperor Constantine is dissuaded from slaughtering children; the Church's authority over temporal rulers is demonstrated. Sacraments were represented in the form of Paul Baptizing (fourth window), Christ Baptizing (seventh window), Peter and Paul Giving Absolution (eighth window), and the Consecration of Aaron's Sons (evoking ordination, in the corona). Stephen and Paul are stoned as types of the Debtor Beaten by his Fellow Servants in the

eighth window, and elsewhere Peter and Paul fulfill their priesthood in preaching. In the corona Pentecost is prominent, with Peter or John seated in the center (fig. 137);[78] the Virgin is not included. Alongside it are scenes of the High Priest Entering the Holy of Holies and Jethro Advising Moses on the delegation of authority. This stress on the authority of the Church is to be expected in a monastic foundation that was continually appealing to the pope against the king, and that had had an archbishop martyred for his stand against the crown. From the more recent era, Theophilus, the clerk, represents penitence (tenth window), and monks wash the feet of the poor as a type of the Child among the Disciples (seventh window). The ecclesiastical nature of the selection is apparent when it is realized the only other types not taken from the Old Testament deal with the Last Judgment, except one scene with Mary of Egypt and one with lion cubs (Appendix figs. 17, 19).

The Spies with the Grapes of Eshcol are represented in the corona as a type of the Crucifixion, no doubt in reference to the wine of the Eucharist. The verse inscription, however, refers to the spy who turns away from the grapes as the Israelite who does not recognize Christ, the one who follows as the gentile who adores him. This theme is represented over and over again in the cycle. From the sixth window are the two scenes of the Jews Turning from Christ and the Gentiles Following, formerly appendaged to Christ Teaching the Apostles, and below were the Pharisees Tempting Christ and the Pharisees Turning Away from Christ as a commentary on the Parable of the Sower. So too the Pharisees leave Peter in the fourth and eighth windows. In contrast with these scenes are Paul and the Gentile Church (fourth window), Christ Leading the Gentiles (second window), the Gentile Church Coming to Christ,

---

[77] There may be anti-Jewish overtones here as well. The *Glossa Ordinaria* has an extract from Bede's commentary on Mark: "by killing they (the Jews) could not stop him from being their king, for he is indeed at once king and priest"; quoted by Sabrina Longland, "Pilate Answered: What I Have Written I Have Written," *Metropolitan Museum of Art Bulletin* 26 (1968), p. 427, from the *Glossa Ordinaria, P. L.,* cxiv, col. 238.

[78] Peter was commonly in the center in the latter part of the twelfth century; see Meyer Schapiro, *The Parma Ildefonsus: A Romanesque Illuminated Manuscript from Cluny and Related Works* [New York], 1964, pp. 43–44. The head in the glass is ancient, but may not be *in situ*; it is that of a young man. A mitred head to the left is surely a stopgap.

and Peter and Paul Preaching to the Jews and Gentiles (fifth window). In the seventh window is the Gentile Church with Jesus, and there is even a scene of Jews punished in the eighth window. The vehemence is surprising on the part of a religious house that was on good terms with its local Jewish community, who actually built a synagogue on land rented from Christ Church,[79] though it is in line with sentiments expressed in the Bury St. Edmunds cross in the second half of the twelfth century.[80] It is significant that in the Canterbury program condemnation of the Jews is closely related to praise of the gentiles; this can be explained by the changed attitude to the Roman world brought about by the twelfth-century renascence. As already suggested, the treatment of gentiles has much in common with the ideas of John of Salisbury.

The third important theme is eschatological. Salvation and damnation are the subjects of the Parables of the Sower, the Three Measures of Meal, the Net and the Harvest (sixth window), the Debtor or Unmerciful Servant, the Great Supper and the Marriage Feast (eighth window), and the Good Shepherd (seventh window); the Good Samaritan story is interpreted as an allegory of the Fall and Redemption. But the selection of parables is not altogether explained by a preference for this theme. The Prodigal Son, Dives and Lazarus, and the Wise and Foolish Virgins, all absent from the records of the twelve windows, were equally to be interpreted in this sense, and they were more commonly represented, at least in the thirteenth century.[81] The Good Shepherd, on the other hand, was very rarely illustrated after the Early Christian period. The author of the Canterbury program may have had some pictorial sources at hand; the parables are seldom illustrated outside Byzantine or Ottonian manuscripts, but there may have been early models in Canterbury. The fragment of the sixth-century Gospels from St. Augustine's includes the Parable of the Fig-Tree among scenes illustrating Luke's gospel.[82] The four mid-twelfth-century leaves in London and New York, which are perhaps related to the less complete prefatory cycle to the Great Canterbury Psalter in Paris, illustrate the Parables of the Debtor, Laborers in the Vineyard, Dives and Lazarus, and the Wise and Foolish Virgins.[83] The Bury St. Edmunds New Testament drawings include the Parables of the Wicked Husbandmen, the Good Samaritan, and the Marriage Feast.[84] These two complementary manuscript cycles indicate the popularity of the parables in twelfth-century England, and the Christ Church windows may be viewed in this context.

The commentaries on the parables, supplied by the types, either differ from or go beyond the interpretations given in the *Glossa Ordinaria*; closest is the explanation of the Good Samaritan, but the allegory of the Fall and the Old Law is not completed by the Redemption.[85] Fuller treatment is given in a homily of Bede and by Hugh of St. Victor in his *Allegoriae in Novum Testamentum*, but the former does not treat the other parables, whereas Hugh of St. Victor's moral interpretation of the Three Measures of Meal is slightly different from that in the sixth window, and for the Parable of the Sower he added nothing to the gospel explanation.[86] So far no single textual source has come to light that might have been the basis of the program, whereas some of the themes can be accounted for separately. In all probability the program was put together in Canterbury about 1180 by someone with a degree of training in exegesis. Continental prototypes do not seem to have played a significant part.

The Canterbury typological cycle differs from that at St.-Denis in several fundamental ways; as already mentioned, the order of the subjects in the windows is reversed. Furthermore, there is no evi-

[79] Urry, 1967, p. 120. Jews were among the townspeople who passed food in to the monks when they were confined by Archbishop Baldwin in 1188–1189; see Stubbs, 1865, p. lxi.

[80] *The Year 1200* I, no. 60, 56, with bibliography.

[81] *Mâle*, 1958, p. 197.

[82] Wormald, 1954, Pl. IX.

[83] James, 1936–1937, pp. 9–10, Pls. V and VI.

[84] Cambridge, Pembroke College, MS 120; see Parker, 1969, p. 295, Pls. XXXII, XXXIV, XXXV.

[85] *P. L.*, CXIV, cols. 131, 133–34, 146, 286–82.

[86] J. A. Giles, ed., *The Complete Works of Venerable Bede*, V, London, 1843, 91–96; *P. L.*, CLXXV, cols. 792, 794; see also cols. 814–15 for the Good Samaritan.

dence of inscriptions treating New Testament subjects as antitypes in the St.-Denis windows; the subjects recorded by Suger and partially preserved are glossed Old Testament events. Grodecki has suggested, on the basis of one surviving panel, that the Crucifixion was represented with types, but without inscriptions.[87] The full circular form of this *Signum Tau* panel, however, was paired with one other medallion, which is not in accordance with later practice. The images at St.-Denis are highly ideated, at times almost diagrammatic—as, for instance, the Ark of the Covenant.[88] In contrast, the surviving Canterbury scenes are predominantly allegorical, and consequently operate on a more direct visual level; types for the same event look alike, and may also resemble the New Testament scene as well. With the juxtaposition of scenes so similar, the elements of each composition become visual equivalents of one another, and virtually interchangeable. The two types of the Magi with the star are Moses leading the Israelites and Christ leading the Gentiles (figs. 30, 37). In stance and gesture Moses is clearly a type of Christ, the Jewish Israelites of the Christian gentiles. Moses' rod becomes Christ's cross, the Red Sea becomes the baptismal font, the pillar of fire becomes a church. Pharaoh, placed to the right under a canopy, is like the demonic idol in position and colors; all are parallels explicitly mentioned in a sermon for Quadragessima by Honorius of Autun.[89] Visual repetitions and echoes are reinforced by repetitions and rhymes in the verses:

Exit ab erumpna populus *duc*ente columpna
Stella Magos *dux*it: *Lux* Christus utrisque re*lux*it.
Stella Magos *dux*it: et eos ab Herode re*dux*it;
sic Sathanam gentes fugiunt: Te Christe sequentes.

The program as a whole seems to reflect visual conceptualization of a kind quite removed from Suger's ideas. Nor is it present in the Klosterneuburg ambo, where the exegesis is controlled by historical divisions. How far it is a part of the Methuselah Master's creation may be ascertained from a study of the design sources.

The typological windows: design sources and related series

GUNTON published his observation that there are coincidences between the Peterborough and Canterbury verses in 1686.[90] In 1897 and 1901 James was able to compare the inscriptions from the first part of the series in more detail, and found that twenty-one correspond exactly. He supposed either that there was a common textual source or that Benedict of Peterborough sent copies of the inscriptions in newly completed choir stall paintings back to his old house, Christ Church, shortly after 1177.[91] Since the full publication of the only complete copy of the Peterborough paintings, in the early fourteenth-century Psalter from Peterborough in the Bibliothèque Royale in Brussels, it has been possible to ascertain that only the Canterbury verses in the first to third windows coincided with Peterborough, that is, those already noticed by James.[92] The question of the relation between the Peterborough and Canterbury series has recently been reconsidered by Sandler.[93] Contrary to Sandler, it is my view that coincidences between the compositions in the Psalter and in the extant Canterbury panels lead to the conclusion that the Canterbury and Peterborough pictures, as well as the inscriptions, are directly related to each other.[94] Sandler has also challenged the early date of the

[87] Grodecki, 1976, p. 105. For a fuller consideration of the relation of Old Testament to New Testament subjects, see Konrad Hoffmann, "Sugers 'Anagogisches Fenster' in St. Denis," *Wallraf-Richartz-Jahrbuch* 30 (1968), 57–59, 76–78.

[88] Grodecki, 1961a, fig. 7; 1976, figs. 128–29.

[89] *Opera Liturgica: Gemma Animae, P.L.,* clxxii, col. 742.

[90] Quoted by James, 1897, pp. 179–80.

[91] James, 1897, p. 185; and 1901, p. 10.

[92] MS 9961–62; see van der Gheyn, 1906, pp. 6–11.

[93] Lucy Freeman Sandler, "Peterborough Abbey and the Peterborough Psalter in Brussels," *Journal of the British Archaeological Association,* 3rd ser. 33 (1970), 36–49.

[94] *Ibid.,* p. 39.

Peterborough choir stall paintings, which makes a digression necessary to review her evidence.[95]

It is clear from the historical sources that William of Waterville laid out a choir between 1155 and 1175. This is slightly earlier than the Canterbury choir enclosure of "marble" (1180), and may well have been, as Sandler envisaged, a "temporary" affair; it is, however, hard to visualize it in any other form than an enclosure, perhaps of wood, marking off the choir. Before 1194 this choir was extended into the nave by Benedict, formerly prior of Christ Church, who placed a *pulpitum* or choir screen across the nave. New choir stalls were provided by Walter of Bury St. Edmund's (1233-1245), of which Sandler has convincingly demonstrated that parts survive. It is still an open question whether the paintings which, according to her equally convincing reconstruction, were on the backs of these choir stalls in the seventeenth century were in fact painted as late as the 1230s to 1240s. Against this is the rarity of long typological cycles and verses composed in the thirteenth century, and the latency between the Canterbury windows and the Peterborough cycle. Other possibilities remain open: one is that William of Waterville began a series of typological paintings on the panels of his choir enclosure, and that this program was extended by Benedict after 1177; the hypothesis has the advantage of explaining why the program had to be eked out in the middle, by the addition of extra types for extra seats across the *pulpitum*, and why it diverged from Canterbury at this point. Another possibility is that Benedict himself was responsible for the whole program at Peterborough, and used a model book from Canterbury for the first part. In either case these twelfth-century paintings could have been incorporated into the thirteenth-century choir stalls, which were perhaps provided to meet the current fashion for higher choir enclosures, or to extend the choir further.

From the visual evidence it is hard to avoid the conclusion that most of the scenes in the Canterbury glass and in the Peterborough Psalter derive from common models. Since comparisons have to be made with the fourteenth-century manuscript copy, direct dependence can only be indicated when the Canterbury glass painter and the miniaturist both followed the earlier version; in other cases it is speculation whether one or both neglected the model. If the Methuselah Master had a model book—of Peterborough origin according to James's hypothesis—he used it, like the Aelfric recension, rather freely and in conjunction with other material. The question of whether he had a Canterbury model book, which Benedict took to Peterborough, cannot be resolved; if he had, the same model book could have been given to the Psalter miniaturists to copy, and if its pages were disordered this might account for the confusions in the Psalter.[96]

From the first window (n:XVI), the westernmost in the north choir aisle, neither glass nor armature survive, and my reconstruction is conjectural (Appendix fig. 8). Twelve subjects were included, all of which are also represented in the Peterborough Psalter (ff. 10-10v). Four of the six types at Canterbury had the same verse inscriptions, and the two prophets had abbreviated versions of the same inscriptions.

In the second window (n:XV) the first fourteen out of twenty-one subjects have survived *in situ*. The verses used throughout the window coincide with Peterborough (ff. 11-13 of the Psalter) with significant variation only in the case of the prophecy of Balaam. Eleven of the fourteen surviving scenes may be regarded as compositionally dependent on a common model. At the top of the window are the two types of the Magi journeying, Balaam on his ass and the prophet Isaiah (Appendix fig. 9). Comparison with the same types on f. 11 of the Psalter shows that the figures are essentially similar in depiction (figs. 19-22); they are shown in the same sense, Balaam moving to the right on his ass, Isaiah standing to the left of a city gate. Relatively minor adjustments are in the inclusion of a tree behind Balaam, to fill the empty space in the asymmetrical glass panel, and the accommodation of the inscription on the frame of Isaiah's pan-

[95] *Ibid.*, pp. 40-42.

[96] *Ibid.*, pp. 42-44.

el so that his hand is freed to point at the star in the adjacent scene with the Magi; in the same way Balaam's gesture in the glass is concentrated on the star ahead of him, whereas in the Psalter he holds his whip jauntily over his shoulder. These scenes already provide a *caveat* against trying to reconstruct the appearance of the lost model; in the Psalter, where the scenes are arranged four on a page, the relationship between type and antitype is neglected, the scenes are laterally compressed into a narrow format, and Gothic architectural frames have been added. On the other hand, the Methuselah Master has made alterations of a kind one would expect in glass painting, accommodating his figures to oddly shaped panels and adding details as fillers.

The death of Herod, with the deaths of Saul and of Doeg as types, was omitted at Canterbury. The weight of evidence here is slightly in favor of Peterborough being the older cycle, from which a selection was made in the windows. These subjects would not fit in the second window, and it may have been considered inappropriate to place the death of Herod in the top of the third. The third window (n:XIV) resumed the New Testament story with Christ among the Doctors, which is preserved in the summit. The first seven scenes corresponded in subjects and inscriptions to the Peterborough cycle, but the iconographical guide was then abandoned; the sequence dealing with the temptations of Christ was contracted into two scenes in the third window, and in the fourth window (n:XIII) the extensive ministry cycle began. Two of the four scenes *in situ* in the third window are close to their counterparts in the Peterborough Psalter, bringing the total for the two windows to thirteen out of eighteen corresponding scenes (figs. 19–22, 27, 28, 30, 34, 37, 41, 44, 46, 48, 50, 55, 59–61, 63, 64). These will be briefly listed, with a note as to whether the compositions have been reversed in copying; such reversals have often been noticed, but

no practical explanation has been forthcoming.[97] Perhaps at some stage tracings were made on thin parchment and turned face down for transferral.

	Canterbury N. Choir Aisle	Brussels B. R. MS 9961–62	
Balaam	Window II (1)	f. 11	
Isaiah	Window II (3)	f. 11	
Exodus	Window II (4)	f. 11	reversed
Magi with Herod	Window II (5)	f. 11v	
Christ and Gentiles	Window II (6)	f. 11v	
Solomon and Sheba	Window II (7)	f. 11v	
Joseph and Brethren	Window II (9)	f. 11v	
Dream of Magi	Window II (11)	f. 12[98]	
Jeroboam's Sacrifice	Window II (12)	f. 12	reversed
Presentation of Samuel	Window II (13)	f. 12v	reversed
Presentation of Christ	Window II (14)	f. 12v	
Moses and Jethro	Window III (2)	f. 24	
Daniel with Elders	Window III (3)	f. 24[99]	

The resemblance is sometimes only in one or two principal figures—Joseph, Moses, Jethro, etc.—but it is astonishing how faithfully stance and gesture have been preserved, even in such figures as Christ leading the gentiles and Moses leading the Israelites, where the Romanesque *gehende stand* is commuted into a Gothic *déhanchement* (figs. 37, 41). Sometimes the miniaturist has misunderstood his model; for instance, he has transformed the attendants of the Queen of Sheba, who are drawn on a small scale in the glass, into children (figs. 44, 46).

---

[97] Madeline Harrison, "A Life of St. Edward the Confessor in Early Fourteenth Century Stained Glass at Fécamp, in Normandy," *Journal of the Warburg and Courtauld Institutes* 26 (1963), 31, 33, Pls. 10a and b, 12c and d. K. J. Galbraith, "The Iconography of the Biblical Scenes at Malmesbury Abbey," *Journal of the*

British Archaeological Association 28 (1965), p. 40.
[98] Rackham, 1949, fig. 16f; cf. van der Gheyn, 1906, Pl. x.
[99] Rackham, 1949, fig. 19c; cf. van der Gheyn, 1906, Pl. xiv.

Some significant divergences between the two sets of pictures may be noticed; certain motifs in the glass can be traced to other models, but whether or not they also reflect the iconographical guide cannot be proved. On the whole, the miniaturist may be supposed the more automatic copyist, since he has neglected the order and sense of the pictures; the Methuselah Master, given the opportunity to elucidate meanings in his monumental art form, has perhaps improved the overall symmetry of each group of scenes. The Presentation of Christ (fig. 63), being placed in the center of the window, is a symmetrical composition, whereas in the Psalter it repeats the asymmetry of the Presentation of Samuel (figs. 64, 60). A discrepancy in the figure on the left may be due to restoration of the glass; in the miniature it is Joseph who carries a basket of doves and a candle, in the glass the nimbed head is that of a young man, like an angel, but this may be a stopgap. He is balanced on the right in the glass by another figure with a nimb and candle, presumably Anna.[100] Joseph is generally included in the Presentation scene, frequently accompanied by a female attendant, as in the Benedictional of St. Ethelwold,[101] and the Great Canterbury Psalter in Paris;[102] in the latter she holds doves and a taper. Occasionally Joseph is left out, and only the attendant shown, as in the St. Albans Psalter.[103] In the Infancy Window at the west end of Chartres, dating from the mid-twelfth century, a symmetrical scene with Mary and Simeon on either side of Christ and the altar is separated from a medallion with three female attendants, the leader holding doves, the followers, candles in reference to Candlemas or the feast of the Purification.[104] Canterbury may follow an early model in that the symmetrical arrangement was common from the ninth century on.[105]

As observed by Ayres, the Presentation of Samuel on the Morgan Leaf resembles both the scene in the Stavelot Bible of the late eleventh century and the Canterbury glass painting;[106] corn and wine brought by Elkanah could be understood as prophetic of the Eucharist, and oxen make up a trinity of offerings. In the Morgan Leaf and the glass there are three baskets of corn and three oxen. The Brussels Psalter differs in placing the baskets on the altar, and in having only two oxen (fig. 61). At Canterbury the ark of the covenant, containing Aaron's rod, the tablets of the law, and the pot of manna, is placed on the altar (fig. 60); it much resembles the ark carried out of Sinai in one of the prefatory scenes to the Great Canterbury Psalter in Paris.[107] There are other differences between the Peterborough Psalter and Canterbury; the miniaturist has crowded the figures before the altar, giving Hannah the wine jar, which should be carried by an attendant, and placing a redundant male figure beyond. A man with a cap and book is behind Eli, but does not appear in the glass.

Scenes such as these could be taken over from narrative biblical cycles and adapted to their typological function. Others are nonhistorical and had to be composed in the typological context. One such scene shows Christ leading the gentiles away from pagan gods (figs. 37, 41). The Peterborough Psalter has preserved its essential elements—the church, the figure of Christ posed much as he is in the glass, with a scroll, the demon over the heads of the gentiles—but there is no dramatic tension, no details *all'antica*, and no allure of the antique. The scene as it appears in the glass could be adapted from a *Psychomachia* illustration of Faith and the Cult of the Gods; recensions of this very popular illustrated work were in all the great medieval libraries. A tenth-century manuscript in Bern (Burgerbibliothek, MS 264), provides some of the classicizing elements, such as the two altars and the idol on a column (fig. 42);[108] by transposing these

---

[100] The head is a replacement, but the long robe indicates a female figure.

[101] Illus. Pächt, Dodwell, and Wormald, 1960, Pl. 125c.

[102] F.4v, *Psautier*, Pl. 5.

[103] Pächt, Dodwell, and Wormald, 1960, Pl. 20a.

[104] Delaporte and Houvet, 1926, Pl. IV; Mâle, 1953, fig. 105.

[105] For the origins of Candlemas and the symmetrical type of Presentation see Dorothy Shorr, "The Iconographic Development of the Presentation in the Temple," *Art Bulletin* 28 (1946), pp. 18–20.

[106] Ayres, 1970, p. 173.

[107] F.2v, *Psautier*, Pl. 4.

[108] Stettiner, 1895, pp. 70–130; H. Woodruff, 1929, pp.

elements into the scene of Christ and the gentiles, Christ is equated with Faith, the gentiles with the Cult of the Gods. Outmoded personifications are revitalized as literal beings in accordance with current humanistic trends. The demon also is an ancient motif; in at least one Anglo-Saxon recension of the *Psychomachia* the Cult of the Gods takes demonic form, but this picture showing Faith in violent struggle with her opponent is less like the scene in the glass than is the continental version.[109] Another pictorial source for the demon may have supplemented the typological guide; it is in the Cotton Aelfric (fig. 43). The men of Sodom are under the sway of the devil; their twisting movements, close grouping, and certain details of dress, much resemble the gentiles portrayed by the Methuselah Master.

Other elements that have been added or changed by the Canterbury Master demonstrate the strength of his style. Several figures are calmer and more classicizing in pose than their counterparts in the Peterborough Psalter, as, for instance, Solomon (figs. 44, 46), Pharoah (figs. 30, 34), and Herod (figs. 27, 28). The latter, with crossed legs and angular gestures in the Peterborough Psalter, is mirrored in the Great Canterbury Psalter, and it may be suggested that this image derives from the iconographical guide (figs. 28, 29); the Methuselah Master departed from his model, preferring a philosopher's pose. So, too, he altered the banal scene of the Magi riding, as represented in the two Psalters, to a more interesting composition with the leading horseman disappearing through a doorway (fig. 23). This motif crops up in the St. Albans Psalter and has been traced by Pächt to a Carolingian prototype.[110] The Methuselah Master's disappearing figure, however, is in fuller view, and he turns back over his shoulder to look at the star; he

is comparable to the leader in the scene in the "Psalter of Henry of Blois," a Winchester book of the 1150s, except that in this scene the door frame is omitted (fig. 24). If the Canterbury Master trained in this circle, as I have suggested, he would have known the Winchester book or its prototype.

For the Adoration of the Magi the Gothic Psalter has a common form of composition, with the Madonna and Child seated to the right and turning to face the Magi. In the "Psalter of Henry of Blois" and the glass the Madonna is represented frontally, under a baldachin (figs. 24, 25). The Methuselah Master's composition, however, is entirely symmetrical and includes three shepherds on the right.[111] The prototype could be ancient; on a Palestinian ampulla in Monza, dating from the sixth century, the shepherds approach from the right, the Magi from the left of a Theotokos image (fig. 26).[112] The theme was taken up in sculpted tympana, probably because of its symmetry, and occurred in the twelfth century in Vézelay.[113] What is more interesting is the juxtaposition in the fourth century of the Adoration of the Magi, with a king and three attendants each side of a frontally enthroned Madonna and Child, and Joseph and his Brothers; the two scenes, with other symmetrical images of majesty, are on the sides of a silver reliquary casket in San Nazaro Maggiore, Milan.[114]

Except in the figure of Moses, the scene of Exodus in the glass and the Gothic Psalter do not much resemble each other (figs. 30, 34). The Methuselah Master has given Pharaoh a more majestic air, enthroned with his scepter and arms-bearer under a baldachin, and he has included children with the Israelites. The image of Pharaoh seems to be taken from the Aelfric manuscript, where it is similarly labeled above (fig. 32). The motif of women and children occurs several times in the Utrecht and

---

43-44; Hanns Swarzenski, *Vorgotische Miniaturen: Die ersten Jahrhunderte deutcher Malerei*, 2nd ed., Königstein im Taurus and Leipzig, 1931, p. 93.

[109] For example, Stettiner, 1905, Pl. 183, fig. 2 (Brussels, Bibliothèque Royale, MS 9968–72, f.78b).

[110] Pächt, Dodwell, and Wormald, 1960, p. 55, Pl. 105c.

[111] The panel is heavily restored, but the lead-lines essentially follow the originals, and the group of shepherds is ancient.

[112] A. Grabar, *Les Ampoules de Terre Sainte*, Paris, 1958, Monza no. 3, obverse, pp. 20–21, 53–54; no. 1, Pl. II, has the Annunciation to the Shepherds on the right.

[113] Mâle, 1953, fig. 50; Katzenellenbogen, 1959, pp. 7–9, fig. 11. Symmetrical Adorations, but without shepherds, are also at Bourges and Paris; Mâle, 1953, fig. 54. Sauerländer, 1970, Pl. 40.

[114] Volbach, 1961, Pls. 110, 112, 113.

Eadwine Psalters; the grouping closest to the depiction of the Israelites in the glass is an illustration to Psalm 76 (77) in Utrecht, but the women here tail behind the men and flocks, and the attitude of Moses is very different (fig. 35). The Methuselah Master probably drew on several sources; the attitude of Moses is found in the Capucins Bible, where women with children follow him closely; Ayres has demonstrated that *moduli* connected with this book were known in England by 1183.[115] None of these models provides the Master with the classicism of his draperies and physiognomies; the realistic proportions of the children, the sculptural qualities of the draperies, and especially the veil of the woman in profile, seem to reflect much more directly a work of antiquity such as the Ara Pacis reliefs (fig. 36).

The model for the Destruction of Sodom was Byzantine or Sicilian. The Peterborough Psalter has an avenging angel over the city, the city gates still stand, and there are no angels with Lot and his daughters; this type of representation is found also in a prefatory scene to another English Psalter, Cambridge, Trinity College, MS B 11.4, f.10. In the Aelfric manuscript the episode is treated more fully, with three separate scenes showing the destruction of the city and its inhabitants, Lot's wife paralyzed and his daughters taking refuge in another town, and Lot leading his daughters into the hills.[116] These scenes are compressed in a work by W. de Brailes in the thirteenth century, a prefatory page in the Walters Gallery in Baltimore.[117] The closest extant parallels for the Canterbury scene are in Sicilian mosaics, in the Old Testament cycles of the Cappella Palatina and Monreale. The Palatina scene of about 1160, crowded into a spandrel and lacking the Methuselah Master's hilly landscape, includes the essential iconographic elements, such as the two angels, the isolated figure of Lot's wife, and the flames from the burning city rising in a column into the sky (figs. 53, 51). It is easy to imagine a common model, much like the little scene in the eleventh-century Byzantine Gospels, Paris, Bibliothèque Nationale, MS grec. 74, p. 147, in which the stance of Lot's wife is close to the glass (fig. 54). In the Monreale scene, which was not executed until the 1180s, Lot has a more energetic stride than the Methuselah Master's figure, there are no angels, and other details differ.[118] It seems that something like the earlier model available to the Methuselah Master was also known to the miniaturist who illustrated a Psalter with a French commentary, perhaps from the diocese of Tournai, now in the Pierpont Morgan Library (MS 338). At the opening to Psalm 49 two scenes show Sodom burning and the flight of Lot, with the angels; his wife holds her hands in a familiar gesture (fig. 52). Two goats have crept in from somewhere, and the hilly landscape has gone; otherwise the scenes have much in common. The Morgan Psalter has been assigned by Liebman and Deuchler to the same atelier as the Ingeborg Psalter, and dated about 1190–1195.[119]

Perhaps also of Byzantine origin is the representation of Noah's Ark in the third window (fig. 143), in the north choir aisle, where it served as a type of the Baptism of Christ. In the Peterborough Psalter the ark is of a common type, with a boat-like hull. At Canterbury there is no hull. Lafond supposed that the Lincoln glass painter used the same model, more faithfully including the hull.[120] But the Canterbury ark is not cut off by the frame, as it is in a lost panel of about 1205 from Poitiers.[121] It seems that on occasion the ark was represented

[115] Paris, Bibliothèque Nationale, MS Lat. 16743, f.36, reproduced, Grodecki, 1963, fig. 12; Ayres, 1969, pp. 45–46. Women with children are also in the Smyrna Octateuch, Smyrna, Evangelical School, MS A–1, f.78v; see Strzygowski, 1899, Pls. xxxviii, xxxix.

[116] British Library, MS Cotton Cl. B.iv, ff.32v–33. George Henderson, "Late Antique Influences in Some English Mediaeval Illustrations of Genesis: The Caedmon, Aelfric and Egerton Manuscripts," *Journal of the Warburg and Courtauld Institutes* 25 (1962), pp. 1965–96, postulated the existence of an early Greek source for much of the Aelfric iconography, but this hypothesis has been countered by C. R. Dodwell, "L'Originalité iconographique de plusiers illustrations anglo-saxones de l'Ancien Testament," *Cahiers de civilisation médiévale* 14 (1971), pp. 319–28.

[117] MS 500; illus. Brieger, 1957, Pl. 28b.

[118] Demus, 1949, p. 249, Pl. 104B.

[119] Deuchler, 1967, pp. 168ff., with bibliography.

[120] Lafond, 1946, p. 127.

[121] *Vitrail*, fig. 85.

as a basilican structure rising straight from the water. At Canterbury both the aisle and the upper nave walls have pilasters, and Noah emerges from a casement in the roof; two sides of the building are visible and the aisle incongruously continues round the second face. This could be a misinterpretation of a drawing of an ancient building, such as one in a tenth-century *Psychomachia* fragment in the Vatican, which is labeled "templum Domini."[122] The ark was, indeed, seen as a type of the Church by Augustine, Tertullian, Beatus of Liebana, and also by Gregory of Nazianzus.[123] The ninth-century illustrated recension of Gregory's Homilies, Bibliothèque Nationale, MS grec. 510, has on f.360 a three-storied ark with double aisles on two sides, which rises straight from the water (fig. 145).[124] Its context is the peace of the Church, contrasted on the same page with dissent in the Church, which is illustrated by the Tower of Babel. The image is drawn from another sermon of Gregory's in the same collection, in which he said of his father during the Arian heresy, "like the great Noe, the father of this second world, he caused this church to be called a second Jerusalem and a second ark bourne above the waters."[125] This is the only illustration I have found in context, but the literary image was surely commonly understood. The Vienna Genesis predates MS grec. 510, though it, too, is probably of Eastern origin.[126] The ark there is like a three-tiered ziggurat. Two-dimensional structures, generally of two stories, are in the Millstatt Genesis,[127] the San Marco mosaics, the reliefs by Guglielmo at Modena,[128] and a late

thirteenth-century Hebrew Bible in the British Library, Add. MS 11639, f.521. All may have had early models of Eastern origin.

In using the ecclesiastical ark in preference to the more usual boat-ark, the Methuselah Master has expanded the meaning of his scene, as a type of Baptism or entry into the Church.[129] The same composition was used by the Master of the Redemption Window as a type of the Resurrection; it is close to scenes of the Pentecost and the ordination of Aaron's sons, which treat the foundation of the Church. The model shared with Peterborough may have been modified by knowledge of the texts.[130]

It may also have been sporadically used later in the Canterbury series, even though the inscriptions were different. In the Redemption Window, Moses Receiving the Tablets of the Law is similar to the Peterborough scene in which Moses is instructed not to let the people approach Mount Sinai (figs. 137, 141); the composition is reversed, but the elements and the pose of Moses are the same. The motif of the lamb and chalice in the *Signum Tau* scene is also repeated in the Psalter.[131] Other scenes that occur in both—the Entombment and Jonah Cast Up—do not resemble each other. In this and other windows of the series there are many subjects not represented at Peterborough. A few of the rarer and more interesting of these will be investigated.

The fourth window dealt with the Public Life of Christ, from the Calling of Nathanael to the cure of a leper after the Sermon on the Mount.

[122] MS Cod. reg. 596, f.26b, Stettiner, 1905, Pl. 13.

[123] *Sancti Augustini Opera, P. L.* xxxv, cols. 1434–35, xxxvii, col. 1358; xli, cols. 472, 476; xliii, col. 397. *Tertulliani Opera Omnia, P. L.* i, cols. 696, 1209. For the commentary on the Apocalypse by Beatus, see *Beati in Apocalipsin Libri Duodecim*, ed. Henry A. Sanders [Rome], 1930, pp. 66–67, 156–57.

[124] Omont, 1929, Pl. li.

[125] *Funeral Orations by Saint Gregory Nazianzen and Saint Ambrose*, tr. Leo P. McCauley, John J. Sullivan, Martin R. P. McGuire, and Roy J. Deferrari, New York, 1953, p. 132.

[126] Emmy Wellesz, *The Vienna Genesis*, New York, 1960, pp. 13–14, Pl. i. I am grateful to Clara Bargellini Camara for pointing out this example to me.

[127] Klagenfurt, Kärnten Collection, MS 6/19, f.21; see

Hermann Menhardt, "Die Bilder der Millstätter Genesis und ihre Verwandten," *Kärntner Museumsschriften*, iii (1954), 300–301, fig. 6. Mary Evelyn Stringer was kind enough to indicate this example.

[128] A. K. Porter, *Lombard Architecture*, iv, New Haven, 1917, Pl. 145, fig. 3.

[129] The association was made by Augustine, *In Joannis Evangelium*, tractatus vi, 1, 19, *P. L.* xxxv, col. 1434–35, and by Tertullian, *Liber de Baptismo, P. L.* i, col. 1209.

[130] Even Nazianzus could have been known, since excerpts were in the Christ Church library by the fourteenth century; see James, 1903, p. 16, no. 25 and p. 18, no. 38. John of Salisbury probably knew the Latin translations by Henricus Aristippus, according to Webb, 1932, pp. 160–61.

[131] F.56v, illus. van der Gheyn, 1906, Pl. xxv.

Six scenes are preserved, in Window n:XIV.[132] The types for the Marriage at Cana are the Six Ages of the World and the Six Ages of Man, which are related to the six waterpots used for the miracle, mentioned in John 2:6. The six pots had been included in the foreground of earlier representations, including a group of eleventh-century ivories.[133] The twelfth-century page in the British Library, Add. MS 37472, and the prefatory cycle to the Great Canterbury Psalter in Paris have three scenes in illustration of the miracle.[134] The glass painter has perhaps combined two of these scenes —the guests seated, and two servants with the waterpots.

The types are rather more unusual, although there is textual authority for them in St. Augustine.[135] Both series of Ages have attributes. Heimann has noticed a parallel between the Winchcombe Gospels and the Canterbury Ages of the World, in that Abraham carries a flame in both,[136] though at Canterbury he also has a sword. It is notable that the figures, although seated, are not otherwise represented as they were in the clerestory windows; Adam now has a long tunic and a hoe or pick, Noah carries a two-storied ark of the kind already discussed. Even those who had attributes in the genealogical series are differently represented here; David has a harp as well as a crown, and Jeconiah a crown and scepter instead of a book and a bowl of coins. The Six Ages of Man are standing, holding genre objects that could have been invented for the scene; no parallel has been found elsewhere.[137] The boy has a ball and curved stick, the youth a scepter, the young man a sword,

the grown man a purse and bread, the old man a pair of crutches. Labels are provided for both series, as if it were feared the attributes alone would not serve to identify the figures.

The Miraculous Draught of Fishes had as types Paul with the Gentile Church and Peter Preaching to the Jews, but only the second of these is preserved. Type and antitype are not sufficiently close visually to be understood without the inscriptions; the relationships are more conceptual than visual, more symbolic than allegorical. The compositions could have been taken over from Bible illustration; scenes of teaching were especially common—Paul, Peter, and even Moses were represented instructing the people in initials at the beginning of their books.[138]

The Calling of Nathanael, which was first in the window, has lost its types; they were Adam and Eve with Fig Leaves and the People under the Law. The link with the New Testament scene is through the fig tree under which Christ saw Nathanael, according to John 1:48. This is consequently carefully represented and labeled in the glass (fig. 88). The scene is very unusual in showing the events in continuous narrative; on the right Philip takes Nathanael by the arm, and on the left Christ, with Peter and Andrew standing behind him, addresses Nathanael. One of the fullest cycles of the calling of the disciples is in the Paris Homilies of Gregory of Nazianzus, Bibliothèque Nationale, MS grec. 510, but except in the use of continuous narrative and the recognizable fig tree, there is little in common between the two scenes with Nathanael.[139] It is conjecture whether

[132] Rackham, 1949, pp. 63–65.

[133] Goldschmidt, 1926, no. 312, Pl. LXXIX, p. 60; O. von Falke, Robert Schmidt, and G. Swarzenski, *Der Welfenschatz*, Frankfurt am Main, 1930, no. 43, Pl. 6.

[134] James, 1936–1937, Pl. IV. *Psautier*, Pl. 6.

[135] *P. L.* XLII, col. 892, cited by Heimann, 1965, p. 93, n. 19.

[136] *Ibid.*

[137] Six Ages of Man are represented in sculptures of 1196 on the Baptistry at Parma, by Antelami, but they have no attributes; Wilhelm Molsdorf, *Christliche Symbolik der mittelalterlichen Kunst*, 2nd ed., Leipzig, 1926, pp. 246–47; the series described, *ibid.*, pp. 247–48, in the Great Canterbury Psalter in Paris belongs to the decoration added in the fourteenth century.

[138] An early example, at the beginning of Paul's Epistle to the Romans, is in the tenth-century manuscript in St. Gall, Stiftsbibliothek, MS 64; illus. H. Woodruff, 1929, fig. 29. Moses is represented teaching in British Library, Add. MS 15452, illus. *The Year 1200* I, 252. Peter, holding the keys and the word of the Lord, is shown at the opening to his first Epistle in the Winchester Bible, II, f.430v; Ayres, 1970, p. 148.

[139] Omont, 1929, Pl. XXX (f.87v). The disposition of figures at Canterbury is the same as in the Echternach Gospels, except that Nathanael is not represented a second time in the Ottonian work; see Peter Metz, *The Golden Gospels of Echternach*, London, 1957, Pl. 49.

the model for the Master of the Public Life of Christ at Canterbury was Byzantine, or whether it might have belonged to the English tradition of continuous narrative; in either case it is quite surprising to find this mode in Canterbury towards the end of the twelfth century, when it had, as Pächt has remarked, been generally superseded,[140] and an early model must have played some part.

It is less probable that an earlier model existed in Canterbury for the Parable of the Sower in the sixth window. This parable was rarely illustrated in the West before the fourteenth century, but a single scene showing the Sower with the birds, the stony ground, the thorns, and the healthy wheat was in the *Hortus Deliciarum*. It seems to be modeled quite closely on illustrations to the Gospels in Byzantine manuscripts.[141] The Canterbury artist departed from this tradition in dividing the story into two scenes, the birds and the stony ground in one, the thorns and good ground in the other. The first Sower holds the seed in his mantle in much the same way as the figure in the *Hortus* (figs. 89, 91), but this is a common motif, found also in Labors of the Months.[142] An early prototype is in the Utrecht Psalter and its first copy, British Library, MS Harl. 603, in an illustration to Psalm 36(37) (fig. 90). The other Sower in the glass, who carries a basket and turns to look back over his shoulder, illustrates the same psalm in the Eadwine Psalter and its last copy, the Great Canterbury Psalter in Paris,[143] which is closer to the glass (figs. 95, 96). These *moduli* rule out the necessity for the Master of the Parable of the Sower to have found an illustration of the parable itself as his model.

It is even less likely that he followed an iconographical guide that included types. The rather stark compositions of the Pharisees Turning Away

from Christ and the Three Righteous Men require no specific models (fig. 94). On the other hand, the representation of the Emperors Julian the Apostate and Maurice Tiberius as men in whom the word is choked by "the deceiptfulness of riches" has a pictorial complexity suggesting derivation from a model; but the only picture that can partially be related to this is in the ninth-century Gregory of Nazianzus in Paris, Bibliothèque Nationale, MS grec. 510 (figs. 97, 99). In illustration of the homily "against Julian," the manuscript has a cycle of pictures of his life, which Weitzmann has demonstrated could have been taken from an illustrated history.[144]

The inappropriateness of the Byzantine texts, however, and the uniqueness of the Gregory illustration, make it an improbable model for the Canterbury glass painter. In the glass the Emperor Julian is mirrored by another, entitled MAURICIUS. The inscription, now damaged, reads: ISTI SPINOSI LOCUPLETES DELICIOSI. NIL FRUCTUS REFERUNT QUONIAM TERRESTRIA QUERUNT,[145] which has been translated by Rackham: "These thorny ones are the rich and luxurious; they bear nought of fruit since they seek earthly things."[146] Gold coins heaped in a vessel between them emphasize their wealth.

The Emperor Julian plays a prominent role in the lives of Sts. John and Paul, who were martyred for refusing to offer incense to a pagan statue. According to the account in the Hyde Breviary and the version later incorporated into the Golden Legend, Julian the Apostate boasted that he had been a cleric and could have risen high in the Church, hence his connection with the choking of the word.[147] The evidence from the burned Breviary in Canterbury, however, is that these lessons were not read at Christ Church on 26 June, as greater

---

[140] Pächt, 1962, pp. 20–21.

[141] For example, Paris, Bibliothèque Nationale, MS grec. 74, f.70, illus. Omont, 1908. Also Florence, Laurentiana, MS Plut. VI, 23, f.25v; photograph in the Princeton Index of Christian Art.

[142] J. C. Webster, *The Labors of the Months*, Princeton, 1938, p. 129, Pl. X, no. 22; and p. 171, Pl. LVIII, no. 92, of eleventh to twelfth-century date. See also the Ingeborg Psalter, f.8, Deuchler, 1967, fig. 10, and reliefs of Notre-Dame, Paris, Mâle, 1958, fig. 40.

[143] For the Eadwine Psalter, Cambridge, Trinity College,

MS R.17.1, see M. R. James, *The Canterbury Psalter*, London, 1935, f.62b.

[144] K. Weitzmann, "Illustrations for the Chronicles of Sozomenos, Theodoret, and Malalas," *Byzantion* 16 (1942–1943), 100–108.

[145] James, 1901, p. 18.

[146] Rackham, 1949, p. 59.

[147] Tolhurst, 1937, f.273. I am very grateful to Mr. C. Hohler for solving this mystery. See also *Golden Legend*, pp. 327–30.

importance was attached to the feast of St. Salvius.[148]

Another version of the Julian story was certainly known in Canterbury, according to which the emperor insulted the archbishop of Caesarea, St. Basil, and threatened to destroy the town; St. Basil prayed to the Virgin and she sent St. Mercurius to kill Julian. Some time in the eleventh or twelfth century this story was culled from the Life of St. Basil attributed to Amphilochius, and appeared in English collections of the miracles of the Virgin,[149] including those of William of Malmesbury and Nigel of Whiteacre.[150] Nigel's verses were presumably written at Canterbury, about 1175 or later. In these and another late twelfth-century version, the miracle is grouped with three others at the beginning, as examples of the power of the Virgin over the four elements; Julian is interpreted as earth, for no better reason than that man is earth.[151]

The presence of Maurice Tiberius, Christian Emperor of the East in the time of Gregory the Great, in this scene remains puzzling. He was held in high esteem in the East, and even in the West by Isidore of Seville.[152] Maurice was, however, opposed by Gregory on many issues, among them his high taxation and his ordinance forbidding soldiers from entering the monasteries. Gregory's letters about the ordinance likened him to Julian the Apostate: "Julian handed down that ordinance first —so they say who have revived the old laws—and

we all know how much he was the adversary of God." In his letter to Maurice he was more circumspect. The *Registrum Gregorii* exists in many medieval copies, and was known in Canterbury in the eighth century.[153] Perhaps also known would be the words of Gregory's biographer, John the Deacon, who said that Maurice was "most avaricious and rapacious," and even the "adversary of God."[154] The letters, however, are the only text to link the two emperors.

The images of the two emperors can also be understood in the context of virtue and vice; the opposing type shows Daniel, Job, and Noah as the "good ground," crowned by angels. As Katzenellenbogen has shown, Old Testament figures were occasionally selected to illustrate virtues; an eleventh-century manuscript from Moissac, on the other hand, shows Exultatio (self-aggrandizement) as an unnamed king enthroned with his arms-bearer.[155] In the typological context it was no doubt thought necessary to find historical figures to represent vice, balancing the virtuous Old Testament figures opposite. The choice is significant; instead of Old Testament kings corrupted by riches and wordly things, they are "Roman" emperors, such as might have been named by John of Salisbury; John, who probably knew the lives of Sts. John and Paul as well as Nigel's text, and who may have known Gregory of Nazianzus' recently translated works, referred very frequently to Julian's unholy

---

[148] Wormald, 1939, p. 66.

[149] Henry L. D. Ward, *Catalogue of Romances in the Department of Manuscripts in the British Museum*, II, London, 1893, 591–92. See also Adolf Mussafia, "Studien zu den mittelalterlichen Marienlegenden," Kaiserliche Akademie der Wissenschaften in Wien, *Sitzungsberichte* (Phil. Hist. Classe) 115 (1888), pp. 17–21.

[150] J. H. Mozley, "The Unprinted Poems of Nigel Wireker," *Speculum* 7 (1932), pp. 404–15. Nigel's verses are in a manuscript that may be autograph, British Library, MS Cotton Vesp. D.xix, ff.5–24v. William of Malmesbury's prose work is preserved in Salisbury, Chapter Library, MS 97.

[151] British Library, Cotton Cleo. MS C.x, see Ward, Catalogue of Romances, II, 600–603. The miracle *de apostata Juliano interfecto* was printed by Karl Neuhaus, *Die Lateinischen Vorlagen zu den alt-französischen Adgar'schen Marien-Legenden*, Aschersleben [1886–1887], pp. 23–25.

[152] Isidore, *Chronicon, P. L.*, LXXXIII, col. 1055; cf.

Julian, who is recorded as reintroducing pagan cults and persecuting Christians, col. 1049.

[153] "Quam legem primum, sicuti dicunt qui leges veteres noverunt, Julianus protulit, de quo scimus omnes, quantum Deo adversus fuit," *Gregorii I Papae Registrum Epistolarum*, I, part I, 1887 (Monumenta Germaniae Historica, Epistolarum, I), letter III, 64, p. 225; the letter to Maurice is no. III, 61, pp. 219–22: "Inquire I beseech you what Emperor is it who made a similar law and see whether it becomes you to imitate him," quoted in translation by Sir Henry Howorth, *Saint Gregory the Great*, London, 1912, pp. 113–14. The letters were known to Bede who saw them in Canterbury; *Registrum Epistolarum*, II, 1899, p. vii.

[154] *S. Gregorii Papae Vita, P. L.*, LXXV, cols. 160, 162, 166.

[155] Adolf Katzenellenbogen, *Allegories of the Virtues and Vices in Mediaeval Art*, London, 1939, pp. 11, 57, fig. 11.

behavior and death in his *Policraticus*.[156] Whatever the literary precedent, however, the reign of Henry II had brought home to the brethren of Christ Church the evils of kingship, and it is consistent with the rest of the program to portray kings in the role of the "thorny ones."[157]

That this image of avaricious kings was a potent one is evident from the scene's reappearance in the Little Canterbury Psalter in Paris, which is dated before 1220, but which is clearly later than the window with the Sower (fig. 98). Before Psalm 97 (98) are shown two unnamed kings seated on either side of a bowl of coins; dependence on the composition in the glass is quite apparent, although the arms-bearers and aediculae have been omitted, and the illustration serves to document the influence of the glass on later works. To the right of it is a second scene, with one of the kings entombed and mourned by his queen. This is perhaps a sequel to the violent death of Julian, so often referred to not only by Gregory of Nazianzus but also by John of Salisbury and in the miracle *De Apostata Juliano interfecto*.[158]

Several of the Canterbury typological windows have relatives in windows elsewhere. If the first three windows demonstrate the existence of a pictorial guide that was shared with Peterborough, one can expect to find such guides for others of the series. One must also ask, where a relationship with other windows is established, whether these were based on the Canterbury windows, or were the source for them. The first window, from which only the subjects and inscriptions are known, was close to the Peterborough cycle, but it also has a counterpart, in the subjects and order of the scenes, in the collegiate church of St.-Quentin in the northeast of France. The ninth window corresponded quite closely in subjects and order of scenes to the Good Samaritan Window in Sens. At Lincoln is a fragment of the very rare scene of David bearing himself on his hands, which was also in the eleventh window. The Redemption Window in the corona, the thirteenth of the series, is part of a larger group, the most similar of which is at Chartres. Since the order of scenes is inverted for the first time at Canterbury, and follows from bottom to top in the continental tradition, I have previously accepted the possibility of a French prototype.[159] The preservation of twenty-one of the twenty-five scenes *in situ* makes the resolution of this question possible.

The French typological Redemption windows have been studied by Cahier and Martin[160] and Mâle.[161] All are dated in the thirteenth century, and none is part of a larger typological cycle. In spite of some resemblances between them, they do not seem to depend on a single prototype. The New Testament scenes at Bourges, Tours, and Le Mans are the Carrying of the Cross, the Crucifixion, and the Resurrection; and the scenes are disposed from bottom to top in the window, with a variable number of types around each antitype. At Rouen Old and New Testament scenes are placed in alternate registers; this and the date of about 1225 make it an unlikely candidate as a prototype of Canterbury. The glass of Le Mans and Tours is also later, about 1240.[162] Bourges is dated between 1200 and 1214 or 1218, and the Redemption Window in the nave of Chartres may belong to the first decade of the century.[163] The east window in the abbey church of Orbais, near Rheims, also dates from about 1210. These three, then, may be contemporary with the corona glazing at Canterbury. It has only a slight resemblance to Orbais,

---

[156] *Ioannis Saresberiensis Episcopi Carnotensis, Policratici . . . libri VIII*, ed. C.C.J. Webb, Oxford, 1929, II, 23, 176, 214, 379, 381–84, 386, 392–93.

[157] For the impact of the reign of the Norman king Roger II of Sicily, who was said to be renewing the ancient Roman Empire, see Helene Wieruszowski, "Roger II of Sicily, Rex Tyrannus in Twelfth-Century Political Thought," *Speculum* 38 (1963), 46–78.

[158] Gregorius Nazianzenus, *Omnia Quae Extant Opera*, ed. D.A.B. Caillau, Paris, I, 1842, Oratio IV para. CXXIII, pp. 175–76.

[159] Caviness, 1970, pp. 143–44, 147, 185.

[160] Cahier and Martin, 1841, Etudes I A, IV A and B, pp. 1–132.

[161] Mâle, 1958, pp. 142–53.

[162] *Vitrail*, pp. 155–56; Louis Grodecki, "Les Vitraux de la cathédrale du Mans," *Congrès Archéologique de France* 119 (1961), 80.

[163] *Vitrail*, pp. 124, 129.

in that the Crucifixion with types is placed in the axial window of an eastern chapel. Among the types are the *Signum Tau*, divided into three panels comprising the Tau painted on the lintel, the sacrifice of the Paschal lamb, and the sign painted on the foreheads of the Jews. The Grapes of Eshcol and the Sacrifice of Isaac also appear as types, as they do in Canterbury. Nine of the twenty-one panels are missing, but it appears that all were types centering on the single New Testament scene of Crucifixion. The Chartres window, placed in the nave, has a New Testament cycle of four main scenes, including the Entombment, and additional scenes of the Crowning with Thorns, Flagellation, and Christ in Majesty. Contrary to the corona window, and other French examples, the order is from the top down; in this it seems to follow the earlier Canterbury windows, and there is some overlapping of subjects with the twelfth window of the series (Appendix figs. 19, 21). The compositional arrangement, with composite quatrefoils to give groupings of five, had already been used at Canterbury in the oculi, and in the eighth window of the typological series (s:VIII, Appendix fig. 15). Coincidences of subject with the corona window amount to only six of the twenty-five scenes; the only counterparts that resemble each other compositionally are the Grapes of Eshcol, but the Chartres panel is modern (Appendix figs. 20, 21).[164] Nor can one suppose common models to have been used at Bourges and Canterbury for the few scenes that appear in both windows.

Several aspects of the corona east window suggest that it was composed *ad hoc*. If inverting the order of scenes was inspired by continental examples, the window was nonetheless imbued with a conservative English monastic taste for inscriptions, and we have seen the interpretation of the theme is specific to its situation. It is Christ's ministry as continued by his Church, and not his second coming, which is the dominant theme of the east window. Suffering and compassion, which are augmented in the Chartres window by additional scenes, are deemphasized at Canterbury; the En-

tombment is small, the Carrying of the Cross, Flagellation, and Crowning with Thorns are not represented. Where models have been found for individual scenes, most do not indicate recent continental origins. Borrowings from the Peterborough iconographical guide have already been mentioned, as have the duplication of Noah's Ark and Moses and Jethro, which had been composed by the Methuselah Master for the third window (figs. 143, 144, 137, 139). There may be other such borrowings from earlier windows of the series; in the twelfth window were the Crucifixion, Entombment, and Resurrection as antitypes, with Moses Marking the Lintel, Samson in Gaza, Jonah Swallowed by the Whale, and Jonah Cast Up, as types. Moses and the Burning Bush, used here as a rather unusual type of the Resurrection, had assumed its more common place as a type of the Annunciation in the first window; Moses receiving the Law had been included in the fourth window. Altogether twelve of the twenty-five subjects in the corona window had already been included earlier in the cycle, but only two can be proved to be compositional duplicates and only one (Samson in Gaza) has the same inscription. The number of repetitions suggests that there was no great inventiveness in composing the corona window, and supports the hypothesis that it was an afterthought.

Apart from coincidences with the Peterborough paintings and earlier windows in the cycle, there are connections with other earlier works. Several confirm links that have already become apparent. The Sacrifice of Isaac has the unusual feature of the faggots laid on the sacrificial altar in the form of a cross; the mosaics of the Cappella Palatina in Palermo provide the only other example known to me (figs. 148, 150), although Isaac carrying the faggots in the form of a cross is common. As in the mosaic, the angel, with fluttering draperies, appears from the left. There is also some similarity in the agitated drapery of Abraham, and it is probable that his shoulders and head, restored by Aus-

[164] Delaporte and Houvet, 1926, Window LIX, panel 8, pp. 384–85, Pl. CLVI.

tin, originally twisted back to look at the angel. Isaac is in the same contorted posture in both, although he is more upright in the mosaic. The chief difference is in the position of the ram in the thicket, on the right in the mosaic. A model very close to the Palatina mosaic seems to be reflected at Canterbury, and as with the Destruction of Sodom it is also reflected in the Morgan Psalter, MS 338, but not in Monreale.[165] The scene in the Psalter is at the beginning of Psalm 50, f.200v (fig. 149). The ram in the thicket is on the left, and the scene differs from Canterbury chiefly in that the crossed faggots are on the ground, and the fluttering draperies are missing.

The four types for the Ascension of Christ are all suggested in *Pictor in Carmine*;[166] they show the ascension of Elijah and of Enoch, the high priest entering the Holy of Holies, and the miraculous prolongation of Hezekiah's life (fig. 137). Hezekiah lies in bed, his face turned away from Isaiah, who stands behind the bed pointing at a semicircular sundial with twelve divisions. A small sun appears under an arch above. According to the inscription in the corona window, the sun returning ten degrees is the type of Christ, which makes the sundial an indispensable part of the scene. As Heimann has shown, the sundial is the attribute of Hezekiah not only in the Winchcombe Gospels and the Canterbury clerestory window (fig. 216), but also appears held by God above a crouched figure of Hezekiah in the Bury St. Edmunds Psalter in the Vatican, MS Reg.Lat.12, f.68v, of the second quarter of the eleventh century.[167] The Canterbury scene may be a fusion of the Byzantine tradition, which shows the king in bed, with the Western preference for a sundial.[168] The same elements are combined in a scene in the twelfth-century German Gumbertus Bible in Erlangen, in which the bed is closer to the Byzantine kind (fig. 140). The

scene, apart from its application to the Old Testament narrative in 4 Kings 20 and Isaiah 38, was used also for Psalm 60 in the Bury Psalter and the Utrecht copy, British Library, MS Harl. 603, and appears in a twelfth-century German Josephus, Berlin, Preussische Staatsbibliothek, MS Lat. F.226, f.88; the latter has four medallions with God and the sun, Isaiah and the king, the latter reclining in bed, but there is no sundial. Much later it appears as a type of the Resurrection of Christ in the Bible Moralisée in Oxford, Bodleian Library, MS 270b, f.183v, with a great "sundial" turned by water.[169]

The two types of the Ascension resemble each other visually; each has two figures, a landscape in the lower right and the ascendant patriarch moving towards clouds in the upper right. The disposition is normal for the Ascent of Elijah, and somewhat resembles the scene in the Dover Bible, for which Dodwell has postulated a Byzantine model.[170] The flames surrounding the chariot in the manuscript have been turned into clouds under it in the glass. This omits a charioteer grasping Elijah by the hand, and shows only Elijah in the chariot and Elisha reaching for his billowing mantle. The posture of Elisha is echoed in the Ascent of Enoch, whose arm is grasped by the hand of God emerging from a cloud. There is some resemblance in this scene to the one in the Aelfric manuscript that served for the Methuselah Master's model in the clerestory window, but this model does not explain the presence of a second figure of Enoch, clearly labeled, and crouched on the ground to the right (figs. 137, 11). This is a unique example of continuous narrative in the corona window; it can be explained not by dependence on a fuller cycle, but by an adaptation from an Early Christian composition for the Ascension of Christ. The fifth-century von Reider ivory plaque in Munich shows two figures huddled on the ground to the right,

---

[165] For Monreale see Kitzinger, 1960, Pl. 36, fig. 32; there are strong resemblances in pose and drapery systems, but the faggots are missing.

[166] James, 1951, p. 163.

[167] Adelheid Heimann, "Three Illustrations from the Bury St. Edmunds Psalter and Their Prototypes: Notes on the Iconography of Some Anglo-Saxon Drawings,"

Journal of the Warburg and Courtauld Institutes 29 (1966), 55–56.

[168] Hugo Buchthal, *The Miniatures of the Paris Psalter*, London, 1938, pp. 43–45, Pl. XIV.

[169] A. de Laborde, *La Bible moralisée illustrée conservée à Oxford, Paris, et Londres*, Paris, I, 1911, Pl. 183; cf. *ibid.*, II, 1912, Pl. 344.

[170] Dodwell, 1954, pp. 84–85, Pl. 54.

and in many details the scene corresponds with the Ascent of Enoch at Canterbury (fig. 142).[171] The striding position of Christ ascending was still current, though rare, in the twelfth century; an ivory of about 1160 in the Victoria and Albert Museum is perhaps English, but it lacks the crouched figures.[172] In the typological context it is surprising that the Ascent of Enoch does not follow the same formula as that of Christ, although it did so in the "Caedmon" manuscript in the Bodleian,[173] the symmetrical compositon was however, more suited to the center of the window, whereas the other formula made a better counterpart to the Ascent of Elijah. That such models could be adapted to different subject matter has also been demonstrated by Buchthal from the resemblance between the Munich ivory and several Byzantine examples of Moses Receiving the Tables of the Law, in which Moses strides up the mountain much as Christ in the Ascension.[174] A model of this kind, including a crowd of standing spectators as in the Paris Psalter, was evidently used for the Peterborough and corona scenes of Moses Receiving the Law; its resemblance to the Ascent of Enoch is thus fortuitous (fig. 137).

I have suggested that the corona window was composed in the spirit of the rest of the cycle, but as an afterthought. Some scenes even duplicated versions that may have been painted prior to 1180. Others confirm what is already known from Dodwell's study of the manuscripts, that there was a rich store of early models also available, some of them Byzantine.[175] The only recent importation seems to be from Sicily. There are no echoes of Bourges or Chartres to suggest dependence on these French Redemption Windows. On the contrary, it may be questioned whether the east window of Canterbury Cathedral, which was the culmination of one of the most extended typological cycles of its time, did not have some impact on the continent. The appearance at Chartres, next to a win-

dow by the Canterbury–Sens designer, of a popularized version suggests that it did.

Two other continental windows are related in some way to the Canterbury program. One is in the axial chapel of the collegiate church of St.-Quentin, north of Laon. The east window is flanked by a pair of thirteenth-century windows; the one on the left has New Testament subjects from the Annunciation to the Flight into Egypt flanked by types and the order, from top to bottom, is the reverse of that in its pair on the right, which shows the glorification of the Virgin without types. Grodecki was unable to explain this reversal.[176] The typological window in fact contains subjects that had been represented in the first two windows at Canterbury, and that therefore also occurred at Peterborough. There are some apparent deviations only in the lower part of the St.-Quentin window; the Sacrifice of Cain and Abel has been represented instead of Melchizedek and Abraham; David anointed by Samuel, which would be a very unusual type of the Presentation in the Temple, is almost certainly a Presentation of Samuel, since it shows the offerings of wine and cattle. The Fall of the Idols in Egypt is a very surprising subject for number 17, as it should be a type of the Flight. The subjects are listed below, with corresponding scenes in the north choir aisle windows and the Peterborough Psalter in Brussels; the numbers for the St.-Quentin Window are in Appendix fig. 3.[177]

Unfortunately, the equivalent Canterbury panels for nos. 3–8, 15 and 18 are not extant, so direct comparisons are possible only in a few instances. The St.-Quentin Adoration, far from looking like the composition by the Methuselah Master, much resembles its counterpart in the Gothic Psalter; in such a common scene however, the resemblance may be fortuitous. Of five other subjects preserved at Canterbury, St.-Quentin, and in the Psalter, three resemble one another in iconographic

---

[171] Arthur Haseloff, *Pre-Romanesque Sculpture in Italy*, New York [1931?], pp. 16–17, Pl. 19.

[172] *The Year 1200* I, no. 58, pp. 50–51; cf. Sauerländer, 1971, p. 512.

[173] Pächt, 1962, pp. 6–8, fig. 1.

[174] Buchthal, *The Miniatures of the Paris Psalter*, p. 35, figs. 10, 65, 68, 69, 73.

[175] Dodwell, 1954, pp. 81ff., especially p. 91.

[176] Grodecki, 1965, p. 182.

[177] Taken from *ibid.*, pp. 180–81.

	St.-Quentin	Canterbury	Psalter
1–2	Adoring Angels	—	—
3	Annunciation	n:XVI (2)	f.10
4	Gideon's Fleece	n:XVI (3)	f.10
5	Moses and the Burning Bush	n:XVI (1)	f.10
6	Nativity	n:XVI (8)	f.10v
7	Nebuchadnezzar's Dream	n:XVI (7)	f.10v
8	Aaron's Rod	n:XVI (9)	f.10v
9	Adoration of Kings	n:XV (8)	f.12
10	Balaam on his Ass	n:XV (1)	f.11
11	Solomon and Sheba	n:XV (7)	f.11v
12	Presentation in the Temple	n:XV (14)	f.12v
13	Sacrifice of Cain and Abel	cf. n:XV (15) Melchizedek and Abraham	f.12v
14	David annointed by Samuel? (Here identified as the Presentation of Samuel)	cf. n:XV (13) Samuel presented	f.12v
15	Massacre of Innocents	n:XV (20)	f.13
16	Isaiah	n:XV (3)	f.11
17	Fallen idols	cf. n:XV (16) David and Saul n:XV (18) Elijah flees from Jezebel	f.12v f.13
18	Flight into Egypt	n:XV (17)	f.13
19–20	Donors	—	—

elements and composition; in each case St.-Quentin is closer to Canterbury than to the Psalter. Paired for comparison are the Presentation of Christ in the Temple, Solomon and the Queen of Sheba, and the Presentation of Samuel.

The antitypes at St.-Quentin are in full lozenges; this shape accommodates the whole composition of the Presentation of Christ as seen at Canterbury (figs. 65, 63). Under a baldachin in the center is the altar, drawn in three-quarter view; the Virgin holds the Child over it in a seated position to be received by Simeon. On the left is Joseph with two doves (but without the candle that he holds at

Canterbury) and on the right is Anna with a candle. The chief difference is in the covered hands of Simeon, in which St.-Quentin agrees with the Peterborough Psalter; this was normal in Byzantine representations, and occurs also in the Ingeborg Psalter.

The types at St.-Quentin are compressed into quarter-circles; the composition of Solomon and the Queen of Sheba is reversed because of its position in the window, but many essential elements of the Canterbury scene are retained (figs. 47, 44). The seated king has a scepter and footstool, while the queen stands before him; the offering of gold at St.-Quentin is not in the Canterbury glass or the Psalter. Room is scarcely found in the St.-Quentin glass for an attendant close behind the queen and for the heads of two camels. By the same process the Presentation of Samuel is cut down at St.-Quentin, but essential elements are retained (figs. 60, 62). The priest is behind the altar on the left and receives Samuel with both outstretched hands. Samuel walks to the altar, and is followed by his mother and father with offerings of three cattle and a wine flask. Only the top of the female attendant's head shows at St.-Quentin, the wine is carried instead by Elkanah, and the parents have changed places; but the figure of Hannah is remarkably like that of the Canterbury attendant, even when allowance is made for the restoration of the drapery over the latter's arm.

These three scenes suggest that the St.-Quentin window was composed with the help of a pictorial guide from Canterbury, but the other two, Isaiah and Balaam, depart from their prototype. The more advanced composition of the St.-Quentin window—compared with the simple grid of Window n:XV at Canterbury—has been related to Trinity Chapel n:V; the axial window, with scenes relating to St. Stephen, has an armature of the same design as Trinity Chapel s:VII (Appendix figs. 2, 3). St.-Quentin is in the region encompassed by St.-Bertin and Pontigny, in which the Christ Church monks and their archbishop are known to have spent their exile of 1207–1213. Trinity Chapel Windows n:V and s:VII were among the last to be glazed before the exile, and the inference is that the brethren were able to make available sketches of all the windows so far completed. Héliot's date of ca. 1212–1230 for the building at St.-Quentin accords with this hypothesis.[178]

The ideas contained in the St.-Quentin window were not new in France, and the iconographical guide was thus easily assimilated. Mâle has previously connected the window with the sculptural programs of Laon and Amiens that deal with the Annunciation; several types occur in both places, and, as he noticed, all could have been taken from the *Speculum Ecclesiae* of Honorius of Autun.[179] But the Laon portal does not provide the full typological cycle up to the Flight into Egypt. The Peterborough–Canterbury cycle seems to have been followed at St.-Quentin, but evidently it was thought unnecessary to include the lengthy explanatory inscriptions, which by 1220 would have seemed quite old fashioned and redundant.

The other continental window closely related to a lost Canterbury prototype is in Sens, where we have already seen that direct connections existed in the glazing. Of the four extant windows in the ambulatory of Sens only the typological window of the Good Samaritan reads from the top down. Each of three major scenes from the parable is surrounded by four types, grouped according to era; thus scenes *ante legem* surround the Traveller Falling among Thieves,[180] the Priest and the Levite Passing By is the antitype for scenes *sub lege*, and the Samaritan Taking the Traveller to the Inn is paralleled in the Passion of Christ, which opened the era *sub gracia*. As in the case of the St.-Quentin window, texts would have been at hand to provide—or confirm—this interpretation. As Mâle has pointed out, it is common to the *Glossa Ordinaria*, Hugh of St. Victor, and Honorius of Autun.[181] Illustrations in the *Hortus Deliciarum* were glossed by the *Speculum Ecclesiae*, but there is no indication that the commentary was illustrated.[182] On the other hand, comparison between the sub-

jects from the ninth window in the Canterbury cycle and the extant Sens window shows how far they coincided.

Before a comparison can be made with the Sens window, some difficulties in reconstructing the Canterbury window have to be discussed. There is great discrepancy between the fourteenth-century roll and the notes by William Glastynbury as to the subjects in this window; a later hand even labels it the tenth, but probably this confusion arose from omission of the title for the eighth. M. R. James based his reconstruction on the titles given in the roll, except that he tentatively added two types to the sequence *ante legem*, which seemed to him indicated in the verses although no titles were given;[183] he thus arrived at a window with six types grouped around each of three antitypes, or twenty-one subjects in all. However, the verses in both manuscripts only supply four couplets for each group, with an extra line describing the first and second antitypes. This suggests, rather, four types for each scene of the parable, an arrangement confirmed by William Glastynbury at least for the lower two-thirds of the window.[184] It appears that he omitted one title and one line of verse in the upper part, and James's conjecture that the verse indicates a scene of the Conviction has been accepted. I have generally, however, preferred William's arrangement, with four types to each antitype (Appendix fig. 16). This reconstruction is much closer to the Sens window, which also has groups of four types, than the one proposed by James, which incorporates extra titles given in the roll. The three may be compared, see page 136.

In each group, three of the types at Canterbury correspond with three of the four at Sens.[185] There is something curiously systematic about this selection; was there, perhaps, a common model that provided three types in each group, and that was independently augmented at Sens and at Canterbury? Or was there a guide that provided at least

---

[178] See Chapter Three.

[179] Mâle, 1958, pp. 148–53.

[180] The Traveller among Thieves at Sens is heavily restored.

[181] Mâle, 1958, pp. 197–98.

[182] I am grateful to Dr. Rosalie Green for discussing this point with me.

[183] James, 1901, p. 33.

[184] F.187v, C. E. Woodruff, 1925, pp. 148–49.

[185] Cf. Arnold and Saint, 1939, p. 88, where it is said that the correspondence is exact.

Canterbury, Ninth Window		
James, after roll	*Wm.* Glastynbury	Sens
—	—	1 Holy Jerusalem
1 The Traveller among Thieves	†(1 line verse)	2 (restored)
2 Creation of Adam (1 line)	†(2 lines)	cf.3 God showing Adam & Eve the tree
3 Creation of Eve (1 line)		
4 The Fall— they eat fruit (2 lines)	†(1 line)	4
[5 Conviction]	[†](2 lines)	5
6 Expulsion	†(2 lines)	6
[7 Beginning of Toil]	—	—
8 The Priest and the Levite pass by	†(1 line)	7
9 Moses, Aaron and Pharaoh	†(2 lines)	9
10 Tau written on lintel	—	—
11 Exodus	†(2 lines)	cf.8 The Burning Bush
12 Law given	—	—
13 Golden Calf	†(2 lines)	10
14 Brazen Serpent	†(2 lines)	11
15 The Samaritan takes him to the inn	†(no verse)	12
16 The Betrayal	†(2 lines)	—
—	Christ before Pilate (1 line)	13
17 The Scourging (no verse)	—	14
18 The Crucifixion	†(2 lines)	15
19 The Entombment (no verse)	—	—
20 The Resurrection (no verse)	—	—
21 The Angel and the Women	†(2 lines)	16

† indicates the presence of the title in the manuscript.

five types from which a selection was made? The question is complicated by the existence of another window in Bourges, which also reads from the top down.[186] Like the Sens window, it begins with the Holy City, and altogether seven of the types from Sens are repeated; however, the Creation of Adam and the Creation of Eve, which are not at Sens but which were probably in one scene at Canterbury, are included as separate episodes. A few of the Sens and Bourges scenes are alike,[187] but for most of these an earlier prototype can be found that is closer to Sens.

No single pictorial model can be found for the Sens window. Examination of each cycle in turn indicates that it was put together from separate sources, and that types were not adapted so as to resemble each other or their antitype visually. First, the three essential scenes to illustrate the parable were chosen; to these were added scenes from a Genesis cycle, others from a Moses cycle, and finally those from the Passion.[188]

The four scenes that recount the parable of the Good Samaritan bear some resemblance to prefatory drawings in an early twelfth-century New Testament from Bury St. Edmunds, Cambridge, Pembroke College, MS 120, f.2. However, Parker has indicated the probable dependence of these on an Ottonian model, because of their close relationship to the cycle in the Golden Gospels of Henry III in Madrid.[189] The Sens cycle shows a similar adaptation from such a model by contracting the passing by of the Priest and the Levite into one moment in time. A similarly contracted cycle ap-

[186] Cahier and Martin, 1841, Pl. VI, pp. 191–219; Mâle, 1958, p. 199. Examples in Chartres and Rouen do not have the types grouped around antitypes.

[187] Alike are: God Showing Adam and Eve the Tree, Adam and Eve Eating the Apple (reversed), The Priest and Levite Pass By, The Traveller Led to the Inn, and the Flagellation.

[188] There is a marked similarity between some of the scenes from the Moses and Passion cycles at Sens and prefatory paintings in the Ingeborg Psalter, viz. the Burning Bush and the Golden Calf, and Christ before Pilate and the Scourging; Deuchler, 1967, figs. 16, 17, 29, 30.

[189] Madrid, Escorial Real Biblioteca, Vit. 17, f.109v; Parker, 1969, p. 281, Pls. XXXIV, XLVIIa.

peared in the now lost Gospel Book of Henry the Lion, of ca. 1175. *A priori* judgment cannot be made as to whether Sens depended on an English model from Canterbury or on continental traditions. Arnold claimed the primacy of Canterbury chiefly on the ground that the Sens window has been isolated from a series.[190] The inscriptions have been discarded, as they were at St.-Quentin, which might argue for a later date, but there is at present no iconographical evidence to prove this chronology.

There is one more striking parallel with a lost Canterbury typological window. In 1946 Lafond suggested that several of the fragmentary panels preserved in Lincoln Cathedral should be regarded as part of a typological sequence, and he was able to suggest a reconstruction for the Last Supper with two types, David Bearing Himself on His Hands and the Fall of Manna (Appendix fig. 18b).[191] The reconstruction, based on measurements and careful observation as well as a broad knowledge of window compositions, is entirely convincing. Quite independently, in working out the disposition of the lost Canterbury subjects in the existing armatures, I found that the same three subjects belonged in an identical composition in the eleventh window (Appendix fig. 18a). Although the subject of David Bearing Himself on His Hands in the manner of an acrobat has been traced by Heimann to the first half of the twelfth century,[192] it must have been quite rare to warrant a lengthy explanation by the author of *Pictor in Carmine*. And although *Pictor* names both David and the Fall of Manna among other types of the Last Supper,[193] the precise coincidence of window composition at Canterbury and Lincoln can only be explained by direct contacts.

Where the same subject is preserved at Canterbury and at Lincoln, on the other hand, correspondences in style are not close. A medallion with Adam digging and Eve spinning, now in the north rose, compares with the great figure of Adam only in the hair loincloth and spade, which we have seen are "Canterbury" features; the rather meager, delicate figures appear later in date. So too, Christ among the Doctors, also now in the north rose at Lincoln, is a simplified version of the scene compared with the panel in north choir aisle n:XIV; there is no aedicula, and no inscription. Noah's Ark, now in the south choir aisle at Lincoln, occupies a full circle, whereas the Canterbury representations are both semicircles. As already remarked, the ark at Lincoln has a boatlike hull, as has that in the Peterborough Psalter, but Canterbury followed a different tradition. The Crossing of the Red Sea served as a companion type to the Baptism of Christ at Lincoln as at Canterbury, but again with a discrepancy in shape between the circle preserved at Lincoln and the lost semicircle from Canterbury. There are no fragments at Lincoln to suggest that the typological series there had extensive inscriptions; probably they had only labels, as at Sens. Corresponding ornamental motifs show that the examples at Lincoln are slightly simplified, and a later date is also suggested by stylistic comparison and by the absence of inscriptions. The inception of the Canterbury program about 1177–1178 was certainly before that of the glazing of Lincoln Cathedral, where building was begun only in 1192.[194] It seems that one of the sources for the Lincoln program was Canterbury. A typological Passion window may have been a replica of the eleventh window in the Canterbury series; the three subjects at Lincoln were probably in the top of a lancet, where they were least likely to be destroyed, and that is the position they occupied at Canterbury also. Lincoln was otherwise richer in the range of purely narrative subjects than Canterbury; several popular saints' lives were included, and Lafond has remarked that they seem to have begun in the bottom of each window. This, as well as many other

[190] Arnold and Saint, 1939, pp. 88–89.

[191] Lafond, 1946, pp. 126–27, 130–31.

[192] Heimann, 1965, pp. 103–104.

[193] James, 1951, pp. 148, 160.

[194] Nikolaus Pevsner, *The Choir of Lincoln Cathedral: An Interpretation*, London, 1963, pp. 3–5. Lafond, 1946, p. 150, placed the glass ca. 1200–1220.

factors, suggests continental influence, perhaps predominantly Chartrain. It would be surprising if influence from Chartres did not supersede that of Canterbury in the second decade of the thirteenth century.[195]

THIS SURVEY of the intellectual trends reflected in the choice of biblical subjects, and of some of the specific sources for them, leads to a number of important conclusions. One is that, while reflecting twelfth-century trends in exegesis and pictorial typology on the continent, the Canterbury program could have been composed in Canterbury itself about 1175–1180. There are some specific anglicisms, in the ordering of subjects in the windows, and in the coincidence of subjects with other English programs, which preclude strong or specific continental influences. In overall tenor the program seems to reflect the intellects of men who were in Canterbury in the seventies. For specific design sources the artists drew heavily on early manuscripts in the Canterbury libraries, although to some extent they also borrowed motifs from Byzantine sources, most probably from Sicilian art before the execution of the Monreale mosaics in the eighties. In all probability, then, these ambitious programs were planned as the building progressed, beginning about 1175. There is evidence to suggest that the Canterbury windows, particularly the typological cycle, which was evidently famous in the Middle Ages, had some influence on the Gothic glazing of cathedrals on both sides of the Channel.

---

[195] Lafond, 1946, pp. 146–47 has suggested that the Thomas mentioned in an inscription may be the Comte de Perche, who died in Lincoln in 1217, and for whom a memorial window was given in Chartres.

VIII. Hagiographical Subjects

"Aula di claris radiat speciosa metallis
In qua plus fidei lux pretiosa micat
Martyribus medicis populo spes certa salutis
Venit et ex sacro crevit honore locus."

Apse mosaic,
Santa Maria Maggiore[1]

THE BIBLICAL programs in the Canterbury windows are grandiose in conception and lie beyond the grasp, both intellectual and physical, of the ordinary viewer; their ramifications in space and their layers of meaning require long study (text fig. 2c). Such contemplation, as experienced by Abbot Suger, would be more leisurely for the monks, who saw the windows for hours daily from their choir, than for the pilgrims.[2] These typological biblical subjects predominate in the program of the choir and eastern transepts, but even here a few more directly narrative lives of the saints are thinly interspersed.

As the viewer passed behind the high altar and mounted the pilgrim steps to the Trinity Chapel, his experience was of a quite different kind. As remarked earlier, the intense colors of the glass, though more somber, draw closer and create a total ambience of colored light (text fig. 2d). Reasoned contemplation gives way to devotion before the many dramatic images of miracles of healing at the tomb of St. Thomas, "the best physician of virtuous sick people."[3] In the fifty years after his death the cult of the saint grew prodigiously, his fame based as much on the posthumous miracles

[1] "The house of God shines with the brilliancy of the purest metals, and the light of the faith glows there more preciously, the physician martyrs have assumed the salvation of the people, and a sacred honor has been attached to this place." Translated by Edgar Waterman Anthony, *A History of Mosaics*, New York, 1968, p. 81. The apse mosaics of Santa Maria Maggiore in Rome date from the thirteenth century.

[2] For the often-quoted passage from *De Administratione*, Chapter 33, ". . . worthy meditation has induced me to reflect, transferring that which is material to that which is immaterial," see Teresa G. Frisch, *Gothic Art 1140–c.1450: Sources and Documents*, Englewood Cliffs, 1971, p. 9.

[3] A pilgrim's ampulla preserved in Canterbury, Guildhall Museum, is inscribed: OPTIMUS EGRORUM MEDICUS FIT THOMA BONORUM; quoted by Borenius, 1932, p. 45.

as on his living actions.[4] Within a decade the new enlarged upper chapel had been planned, with its roomy ambulatory, to accommodate his relics in a shrine and the crowds who would visit them. To those who had known Becket, or who had visited his miracle-working tomb in the crypt, the setting for the shrine must have been dramatic indeed. The twelve typological windows so ponderously laid out in the western part of the building were now complimented by a phalanx of twelve great windows, which shed their jeweled light on the shrine, and which recounted in over two hundred scenes the life and miracles of the "Lamb of Canterbury."

The methods of this chapter are necessarily rather different from those of the last. Hagiographical subject matter is more limited than biblical, in the sense that a saint may be of predominantly local importance, and also—depending when he lived—representation of his life will not have the great antiquity of tradition that hangs so heavily on biblical subjects. Then again, no pictorial sources have been found for the treatment of the saints whose lives are represented at Canterbury; speculation as to the nature of models, if any existed, must rely on stylistic rather than iconographic judgments. It is possible, however, to view the subjects in relation both to the framework of the rest of the program, and to prevailing attitudes that would have governed their choice.

The cycles: changes in emphasis

THE hagiographical windows incorporated earlier into the scheme of glazing are poorly preserved, but they do provide some basis of comparison with the Becket cycle. The most extensive remains are scenes from the lives of the Canterbury Archbishops Dunstan and Alphage, now in the three windows at triforium level on the north side of the choir. The junior Caldwell and Rackham supposed that they were originally in the lower windows of the presbytery near their altars (n:VIII and s:VIII, plan),[5] but we have used these windows for the reconstruction of the typological cycle, and the large medallions and one quatrefoil of the hagiographical series would not fit the ironwork. Clearly they were intended for the "triforia" from the beginning, where they would be readily visible from the saints' altars. The only existing armature which could have accommodated the quatrefoil with St. Dunstan is in this "triforium" on the south side.

The single narrow lancet in each of the four transept chapels probably had short lives of saints; one fragmentary panel remains in St. Martin's Chapel on the north side (n:X).[6] A panel from the Nelson-Hunt collection now in the Virginia Museum of Fine Arts may represent an early episode in the Life of St. Stephen, whose chapel was also in the north transept; a saint is shown in disputation with Jews.[7] An engraving published in 1836 shows two panels of figured glass in the top of each of these windows.[8] No doubt the preserved scene of St. Martin dividing his cloak, which occurred before his entry into the church, was one of the earliest in the sequence. The order of scenes, then, must have been from the top down, in the Canterbury tradition. On the south side were the chapels of St. John the Evangelist and St. Gregory the Great (with windows s:IX, s:X, see plan). The scribe of the fourteenth-century roll added five subjects from a Life of St. Gregory to the twelfth window, no doubt by mistake; the four pairs of leonine hexameters recorded indicate that the Gregory window too was heavily inscribed.[9]

To some extent hagiographical and biblical windows were also interwoven in the eastern extension; the twelve Becket windows were capped by the

---

[4] For reflections in literature and art see Walberg, 1929, and Borenius, 1932.

[5] Rackham, 1949, pp. 68–69.

[6] Rackham, 1949, pp. 111–12, fig. 31b.

[7] Caviness, 1973, p. 7.

[8] Britton, 1836, Pl. v.

[9] James, 1901, p. 26.

Redemption in the east window of the corona. About 1643 Richard Culmer claimed that an image of St. Augustine was broken in a window to the east of the shrine of Becket;[10] it may have been with christological scenes in the corona.

With the exception of the Evangelist, if his life was included, all the saints represented in the glass were churchmen with strong Canterbury connections; they spanned the history of the Church from the time of the mission of St. Augustine, who was sent by Gregory the Great, through the era of monastic reforms under Dunstan, the persecutions by the Danes under Alphage, and finally the very recent events of the martyrdom and miracles of Becket. A few scenes from saints' lives had been included in the typological cycle, and no doubt the full lives of canonized churchmen were also to be read in the context of events before and under grace. As in most hagiographical cycles, there are visual references to the life of Christ; these will be considered in more detail later.

Textual sources for the lives would have been readily available. The Lives of Sts. Dunstan and Alphage, as well as the prose accounts of the miracles of Becket, were all written at Christ Church. Alphage and Dunstan had been treated by Osbern, Dunstan again by Eadmer; lives of Thomas were written by John of Salisbury, Herbert of Bosham, and the monks Benedict and William. The non-English saints, on the other hand, were widely venerated and a variety of texts might have been available. It is notable that the appearance of Christ to Gregory while he washes the hands of the poor was included in the glass but was not recounted in the English lives by the Whitby monk and Bede;

the source was probably liturgical, as the episode was included in the life read on Gregory's feast day at Hyde, although there is some doubt that the lesson was read at Christ Church.[11] Such a source, however, would not have been illustrated, and whether pictorial models would have been available to the glass painters is a question less easily resolved. Related to it is the origin of the verses used as *tituli*, and their connection with the prose sources.

At Canterbury the Life of St. Gregory and the Miracles of St. Thomas were supplied with lengthy inscriptions, and there is some slight evidence that such was the case also with the Sts. Dunstan and Alphage series.[12] In the attention given to inscriptions, the Canterbury hagiographical cycles differ from those surviving in Notre-Dame, Paris, and in Sens, Chartres, and Bourges, to name only a few of the contemporary cycles in glass. The hagiographical verses may well have been composed by members of Christ Church.

Although the occurrence of *tituli* is rare in thirteenth-century pictorial lives, the practice of combining pictures with verses was an old one, as was the inclusion of scenes from the lives of the saints in church decoration.[13] Such *tituli*, and presumably the illustrations that accompanied them, were often connected with the translation of relics. Thus, verses on the Life of St. Wulfstan were probably composed for his translation in 1218, and they were used in slightly modified form in the windows in the cloister at Worcester.[14] *Tituli* and illustrations might be drawn from more than one textual source. In the case of the Guthlac roll in the British Library (MS Harl. Y.6) at least one scene is not

---

[10] Culmer, c.1643, p. 311. I am grateful to Dr. Urry for this reference.

[11] Tolhurst, ed., 1937, f.227, lesson xi. The burned Breviary, Canterbury Cathedral Library, MS Add. 6, has been transcribed by Dr. C. S. Phillips. The office for St. Gregory began on f.20; lessons ix–xii of Hyde, however, are not extant. The vision was later included in the *Golden Legend*, p. 182.

[12] Eastry's list of Christ Church books included a *Passio Sancti Elphegi, versifice*; James, 1903, p. 49, no. 281. Somner, 1640, pp. 241, 243, 262, 256, 265, refers to tables hung in the church, but all seem to be connected with tombs. In 1665 Pepys saw some calligraphy by Richard

Hoare, "the story of the several Archbishops of Canterbury, engrossed in vellum, to hang up in Canterbury Cathedral in tables, in lieu of the old ones, which are almost worn out" (Evelyn, 1955–1959, II, p. 559, n.2); perhaps these were transcripts of inscriptions in the glass, like the fourteenth-century roll, but they may have been for the archbishops' tombs. I am grateful to Dr. Urry for help on this question.

[13] Wormald, 1952–1953, pp. 253–54. In conversation in 1967 he was, however, quite skeptical about illustrations in glass evolving independently of illustrated texts in the later Middle Ages.

[14] *Ibid.*, pp. 252–53.

drawn from the Life by Felix. This series also may have been designed in connection with the translation, which took place in 1198, possibly for plaques on the shrine itself.[15]

Also pertinent to the composition of the windows was the tradition of *libelli*, or sumptuously illustrated manuscripts with the life and miracles of a particular saint, which Wormald conjectured were kept in the treasury rather than the library.[16] He has cited a number of English examples from the twelfth century and the turn of the thirteenth—such as the two Cuthbert Lives, Oxford, University College, MS 165, and British Library, Add. MS 39943.[17] *Libelli* devoted to one of the Canterbury saints would have been an ideal model for the glass painters, yet there is no evidence that such existed.[18] Around 1200, indeed, the time of the glazing, *libelli* were going out of fashion.[19] But if the windows at Chartres have the character of a compilation of *vitae sanctorum*, the Trinity Chapel at Canterbury resembles a *libellus*; and of these windows as of the *libelli* it may be said that "they were manifestations of the pride and grandeur of the monastic houses between the beginning of the Cluniac reforms and the coming of the friars."[20]

The attitude manifested in the selection of scenes to illustrate the lives of the Anglo-Saxon archbishops is profoundly different from that in the selection of miracles of St. Thomas. The latter are more humanistic, representing the saint in the role of martyr physician, while the former stress the supernatural. These differing attitudes can be documented in the English hagiographical tradition. As early as about 720, when the Venerable

Bede wrote his *Life of St. Cuthbert*, and later his *Ecclesiastical History*, he was able to take as his model the *Dialogues* of Gregory the Great.[21] He preferred to record miracles of healing rather than the perhaps more popular magical events that were rooted in Celtic superstition. Disease was a manifestation of the devil, and in combating it the saints imitated Christ.[22] Bede's *Life* was based on earlier texts and traditions, but events were selected with an eye to papal authority.[23] In his *Ecclesiastical History* he quoted a letter from Gregory to Augustine in which the pope warned: "you may rejoice because the souls of the English are by outward miracles drawn to inward grace; but [it is necessary] that you fear, lest amidst the wonders that are wrought, the weak mind may be puffed up by its own presumption."[24] As we shall see, this advice was not always heeded, but the Becket miracle series is very close to the spirit of Gregory and Bede.

The literalness of the depictions of disease and injury in the Trinity Chapel reflect a much later development. Some time in the twelfth century the recording of miracles became almost a legal exercise; many of the compilations of that era were made with the canonization of a local saintly personage in mind. Thus, Thomas Becket commissioned a work on Anselm of Canterbury, but ironically it was eclipsed by his own martyrdom and sainthood.[25] The process of canonization became more and more rigorous after the end of the century. By 1219, when Stephen Langton, archbishop of Canterbury and one of the new generation of schoolmen, was named head of a commission

---

[15] *Ibid.*, pp. 262–63.

[16] Wormald, 1952–1953, p. 256.

[17] See Mary Evelyn Stringer, "The Twelfth-Century Illustrations of the Life of Saint Cuthbert," Ph.D. dissertation, Harvard University, 1973.

[18] Alleged representations of the miracles of Becket in fourteenth-century glass in York Chapter House (Borenius, 1932, p. 44) provide no close parallels to the Trinity Chapel compositions, and may represent the tomb of some other saint. The Life of Becket, on the other hand, was illustrated in late twelfth or early thirteenth-century wall paintings in Sta. Maria de Tarrasa, Spain, and Brunswick Cathedral, Germany; see Boase, 1953, p. 204; Borenius, 1932, pp. 48–54; E. W. Anthony, *Romanesque Frescoes*, Princeton, 1951, p. 174, figs. 423, 424; J. Gerhardt, "Die

spätromanischen Wandmalereien im Dome zu Braunschweig," *Niedersächsisches Jahrbuch für Landesgeschichte* 11 (1934), 1–60.

[19] Wormald, 1952–1953, p. 261.

[20] *Ibid.*, p. 262.

[21] C. Grant Loomis, "The Miracle Traditions of the Venerable Bede," *Speculum* 21 (1946), 405.

[22] *Ibid.*, p. 411.

[23] *Ibid.*, pp. 416–18.

[24] *Bede's Ecclesiastical History of the English Nation*, tr. J. Stevens, London and New York, 1910, p. 54.

[25] Southern, 1963, pp. 337–39; Becket presented an account of Anselm's life and miracles to Pope Alexander III at the Council of Tours in May 1163, with a request for canonization.

to inquire into the miracles of St. Hugh of Lincoln, the task required a very exacting examination of the evidence.[26] Miracles were no longer vaguely set down from hearsay, as they had been at an earlier time. The names of the subjects of miraculous cures, sometimes their age, their place of dwelling, their ailment, and the manner in which the story was collected were all recorded. This was done in two texts compiled at Canterbury in 1173 and 1172–1174, which describe the miracles of St. Thomas. That of William dates from 1173, the year of the canonization, which was "in response to popular demand."[27] Many lives of the saint, variously historical and hagiographical, were also written about the same time.[28] Both Benedict and William added a book to their texts to bring them up to date, William in 1178–1179 and Benedict in or after 1179. It is possible that this was done in the hope of completing the translation in the near future, since the building was nearing completion. However, the event was again postponed until 1220, the fiftieth anniversary of the martyrdom.

Verisimilitude must have served not only to impress on the reader the sanctity of Thomas, but also to emphasize that the Canterbury texts were the most authentic. In the period before the translation, Benedict's account of the miracles was read to pilgrims in the chapter house, an extension of the usual monastic custom of liturgical readings and of readings to the brethren at meals.[29] The Christ church readings seem to have had a precedent on the pilgrim routes; it has been demonstrated that the *chanson de geste* owed much to the recitation of lives of the saints.[30] One of the early *libelli*, a collection of materials relating to St. James of Compostela, was most probably recited in this way.[31] Extended hagiographical compilations almost always emanated from the place that housed the relics of a saint, generally a monastery, which gave them the stamp of authenticity. Thus Eadmer, in rewriting Osbern's life of St. Dunstan, wished to produce an accurate and official life.[32] Copies of such official accounts might be presented to royalty or to a sister house, serving perhaps to suppress distorted versions based on mere hearsay. Again in the case of Christ Church, gifts of the *Miraculi Sancti Thomae* were made to Henry II, and overseas to the monastery of Igny.[33] Copies were also available in the library; one was signed out to Edward II and never returned.[34] Since the library copies were probably very plain, it cannot be claimed that they disseminated an iconographic tradition.[35] It is probable, however, that those who

---

[26] C. H. Lawrence, *St. Edmund of Abingdon: A Study in Hagiography and History*, Oxford, 1960, pp. 10–12. Under Innocent III, witnesses to the miracles had to appear in person, as in the applications for Gilbert of Sempringham in 1201 and for Wulfstan of Worcester in 1203.

[27] The canonization took place on February 21, 1173 (see Poole, 1955, p. 214). According to Walberg, 1929, p. 73, William, a monk of Christ Church, compiled his first five books in 1172–1174/75 (from internal evidence); Benedict, also of Christ Church, wrote his first three books in 1171–1173 (*ibid*., p. 61). In 1178–1179, William added his Book VI, and in 1179 Benedict wrote his Book V (Walberg, pp. 57, 72–73, and Benedict, ed. Robertson, 1876, p. xxiii, n. 1); Books VI and VII of Benedict were added later by another author (see Benedict, ed. Robertson, 1876, p. xxvi).

[28] The *Vita Sancti Thomae*, by "the annonymous of Lambeth" was composed in 1172–1173 (Walberg, 1929, p. 60). Four other authors had completed lives by 1198–1199: William of Canterbury and three of Becket's colleagues, John of Salisbury, Alan of Tewkesbury, and Herbert of Bosham. These four were used in the Quadrilogus compiled by E(lias) of Evesham in the last year

of the reign of Richard I (see Robertson, IV, 1879, xix–xx).

[29] Walberg, 1929, pp. 59–60.

[30] Joseph Bédier, *Les Légendes épiques: Recherches sur la formation des Chansons de Geste*, 3rd ed. III, Paris, 1929, 101ff.

[31] *Ibid*., pp. 75–76; the *Liber Jacobus* was compiled between 1173 and 1179. Its contents, listed *ibid*., pp. 76–78, make it a typical *libellus* as defined by Wormald, 1952–1953, pp. 249–50.

[32] Stubbs, 1874, p. xxxiii.

[33] Robertson, I, 1875, pp. xxvii–xxviii. From William's text, pp. 137–38, it is clear that his book of miracles was presented to the king and that he himself went to London on that occasion. The gift to Igny was sent by Odo, abbot of Battle, who had been prior of Christ Church to 1175. This must be the Cistercian abbey at Igny, between the Vesle and the Marne; see M. A. Dimier, "The Cistercian Abbey of Vauclair: Historical Summary," *Gesta* 5 (1966), 47, n. 1.

[34] James, 1903, p. xlvi. The entry, no. 29 in the "De defectibus librorum" of 1337 (Register L in the Chapter Library), is printed *ibid*., p. 148.

[35] The extant recensions are plain and unillustrated. Six of Benedict's texts are known: 1) London, Lambeth

saw the windows accepted them in much the same spirit as the written "eyewitness" accounts.

The concern with miracles of healing did not extend long into the thirteenth century. Wolpers has shown that hagiographical writing changed rapidly under the impact of the new scholasticism and of the friars; spiritual qualities were emphasized above miraculous events, and the great tradition from Bede to Eadmer, which had been prolonged by such minor authors as William and Benedict, died out.[36] With their emphasis on miracles of healing, with their *tituli* based, as we shall see, on two texts, with their creation intimately connected both with the translation of the relics they surrounded and with the influx of pilgrims, the St. Thomas windows represent the culmination of twelfth-century hagiography. Like the readings in the chapter house—which they may have superseded—they were designed to popularize the saint, and no doubt to encourage further miracles.[37] The Celtic element that continued, in spite of Bede, in the lives of the Anglo-Saxon saints, was

finally entirely suppressed. Represented are the diseases and failings of ordinary people. Stressed are the necessity of faith, the avoidance of futile medical treatments, and the offering at the shrine of the thanks, gifts, and ex-votos that were due to the saint. These lessons, and not the christological nature of the saint, are emphasized in the *tituli*; references to the public life of Christ are purely visual. The prose texts laid somewhat more emphasis on moral and spiritual interpretations. In one passage Benedict stressed the spiritual benefits of the miracles, pointing out that each person who came to beg for a cure at the tomb had to repent of his sins and resolve to lead a better life.[38] William held that the saint's miracles raising people from the dead confirmed the doctrine of resurrection, and elsewhere commented that the doctrine of transubstantiation was thought by some to be confirmed by miraculous changes in the blood of St. Thomas.[39] There are very few miracles in which supernatural beings figure, and none has survived in the glass except in Window n:V.

The lives of Sts. Dunstan and Alphage

THE scenes from the Lives of Sts. Dunstan and Alphage are somewhat archaic, being distinctly less humanistic. The saints were of great political importance to Canterbury, as predecessors of St.

Thomas. Their enemies were the pagan Danes, the king, rebellious churchmen, and the devil. The miracles represented were in the Celtic magical tradition, and demonstrated the potency of the

Palace Library, MS 135, ff.26–117v, probably a Christ Church book, twelfth-thirteenth century (M. R. James, "The Manuscripts in the Library at Lambeth Palace," *Cambridge Antiquarian Society* 30 [1900], 214–15); 2) Cambridge, Trinity College, MS B.14.37, from St. Augustine's, twelfth-thirteenth century (M. R. James, *The Western Manuscripts in the Library of Trinity College, Cambridge*, Cambridge, 1900, I, 436); 3) Paris, Bibliothèque Nationale, MS cod. sig. no. 5320, thirteenth century (formerly Count Bethun, MS Regius C.4187, Hagiographi Bollandiani, *Catalogus Codicum Hagiographicorum Latinorum Antiquiorum Saeculo XVI qui Asservantur in Bibliotheca Nationali Parisiensi*, II, Brussels, 1890, 197); 4) Brussels, Bibliothèque Royale, MS 3190, thirteenth century (cod. sig. no. 7959–61, J. van den Gheyn, *Catalogue des manuscrits de la Bibliothèque Royale de Belgique*, v, Brussels, 1905, 165–66); 5) Formerly Cheltenham, Phillipps Collection, from the Cistercian house of Aulne, thirteenth century (*Catalogus Librorum Manuscriptorum in Bibliotheca Thomae Phillipps, Bart.*, 1837,

no. 1842/732); 6) See no. 2 below. Of William's text there are only the two manuscripts known to Robertson: 1) Winchester College Library, a gift of William of Wykeham, late thirteenth century (Robertson, I, 1875, xxx–xxxi); 2) Montpellier Bibliothèque de l'Ecole de Medicine, MS 2, late twelfth century from Clairvaux (Robertson, IV, 1879, pp. xxiv–xxvi). Besides Books I–VI of William, this also contains Books I–IV of Benedict, and the Life of Becket by John of Salisbury.

[36] Theodor Wolpers, *Die englische Heiligenlegende des Mittelalters*, Tübingen, 1964, pp. 157–61. See also Southern, 1953, p. 255.

[37] Walberg, 1929, pp. 59–60, quoted William Fitz-Stephen, who died in 1191 (from Robertson, III, 1877, 151, xvi). It is not known how long the custom of public readings was continued.

[38] Benedict, ed. Robertson, 1876, Book III, ch. 11, p. 126.

[39] William, ed. Robertson, 1875, Book IV, chs. 45 and 49, pp. 355–56 and 360.

saints against their enemies. The selection seems to have been politically motivated and leaves the observer in no doubt where the right lay, in spite of the fact that the inscriptions have been lost. These scenes would not, however, have carried the popular appeal of the Thomas series.

Southern has demonstrated the importance to the inmates of Canterbury of their saints' relics. He quoted Gervase, who apologized for his description of the pre-Conquest church: "It was not my plan to describe the disposition of stones: but I do so here because I cannot fully explain the arrangement of the bodies of the saints in different parts of the church, unless, with the help of Eadmer who saw these things, I first describe the places where they lay." In the choir consecrated in 1130, Dunstan and Alphage were given pride of place; their effigies were placed on either side of Christ in Glory over the high altar.[40] During the time of Anselm, feasts added in their honor made them the equals of Gregory. Some new impetus to the cult of St. Dunstan may have been given later by a dispute with Glastonbury as to the true location of his relics.[41] After the rebuilding of the choir in 1174–1180, it was natural in a conservative monastic church to honor these early saints in the glass that was the glory of the new building; in 1180 the relics once more assumed their traditional place on either side of the high altar, as had most probably been planned from the beginning.[42]

The present series from the Lives comprises only four authentic scenes of St. Dunstan and three of St. Alphage (figs. 109, 113). All follow Osbern's accounts. In the case of St. Alphage, this was the official Life.[43] St. Dunstan, as we have seen, had had other biographers in the twelfth century.[44] Osbern's Life of about 1080–1090 and the corrected version by Eadmer of some twenty to thirty years later are, for our purposes, identical;[45] all the scenes represented in the glass are recorded in both texts. Osbern and Eadmer were both precentors of Christ Church, so either work would have been acceptable as the official account, though Eadmer's seems never to have equalled Osbern's in popularity.[46] It is clear, however, that some of the scenes could not have been taken from the Lives of St. Dunstan composed before Osbern's.[47] If any conclusions can be drawn from the four scenes preserved, one would agree with Stubbs that "Dunstan is the prophet of the evil days, the intercessor for better days to come, the great monastic reformer."[48] Three scenes are rather ordinary, including a much restored ordination, and two supernatural occurrences, Dunstan transported by angels into a closed chapel at Glastonbury, and his vision on Ascension Day (fig. 110).[49] The other two are relevant to later Church history. Dunstan was persecuted by King Eadwy during his life but when he saw him suffering in hell he was moved to pray for his release; the scene shows the saint at the gate of hell, like

---

[40] Southern, 1963, pp. 262, 265.

[41] *Ibid.*, pp. 266–67, 282.

[42] Gervase, ed. Stubbs, 1879, p. 22. Gervase points out (p. 24) that the other holy archbishops were all placed "as they were formerly."

[43] The "Vita S. Elphegi Archiepiscopi Cantuariensis, authore (*sic*) Osberno," was printed in [Henry Wharton], *Anglia Sacra, sive Collectio Historiarum Antiquitus Scriptarum de Archiepiscopis et Episcopis Angliae*, II, London, 1691, 122–42.

[44] The extant Lives were edited by Stubbs, 1874, that is, those of Osbern, Eadmer, and William of Malmesbury. The latter wrote, after 1120, for Glastonbury Abbey. There has been some confusion about these texts; Mason, 1925, p. 46, mentioned a Life by Osbert, but this is a mistake perpetuated by Jean Mabillon, *Acta Sanctorum Ordinis S. Benedicti in Saeculorum Classes Distributa*, Venice, 1733–1840, VII, 691–95, who followed Surius (Stubbs, 1874, p. xxxiv); the text given in the *Acta Sanctorum* is actually that of Eadmer.

[45] For the date of Osbern, see Stubbs, 1874, p. xxxi; and Eleanor S. Duckett, *St. Dunstan of Canterbury*, London, 1956, p. 234. Eadmer wrote in Anselm's lifetime, probably before 1109 (Stubbs, 1874, p. xxxiv).

[46] Stubbs found many thirteenth-century recensions of Osbern's Life, but only two complete manuscripts of Eadmer's (Stubbs, 1874, pp. xxxii, xxxiv).

[47] Stubbs, 1874, p. lxv; among Osbern's additions to the story were the release of King Eadwy from hell and the miracle at Calne, both of which are represented in the glass (north choir aisle "triforium," nt:XI [I,1] and nt:X [II,3], see Caviness, 1967, pp. 207, 214). See Osbern, pp. 104–105 and 113–14, of Stubbs's edition, and Eadmer, in Stubbs, 1874, pp. 196 and 213.

[48] Stubbs, 1874, p. lxiii.

[49] These are among the earliest and latest manifestations of his sanctity (Osbern in Stubbs, 1874, pp. 76 and 120–21, and Eadmer, *ibid.*, pp. 167 and 217).

Christ visiting Limbo to release the souls.[50] This forceful image of the power of an archbishop over his kingly tormentor would be appreciated by the advocates of Thomas Becket under Henry II or of Stephen Langton in the reign of King John. The other scene relates to Dunstan's struggle against the clergy in the course of his monastic reforms;[51] his enemies in the Scottish Church who met to complain to him at Calne were miraculously destroyed by a collapse of the floor (fig. 111),[52] an episode that responds to the monks' dislike of secular churchmen. The choice of subjects seems to bear the imprint of the same vindictiveness and tenacity to be found in the monks' letters during the disputes with Baldwin and his successor, Hubert Walter.[53]

The three surviving scenes with St. Alphage are scant evidence of selection; all show violent events at the end of his life—the siege of Canterbury by the Danes, their massacre of the monks and townspeople, and Alphage taken on board their ship as a prisoner.[54] The scenes are reminiscent of Old Testament history, and we have seen that one, at least, may have been modeled on the leaf in New York (figs. 113, 114).[55] But the dignity of Alphage in his humiliation is reminiscent of the Passion of Christ, and the final scene of the stoning must have resembled the martyrdom of Stephen. There is reference also to events to come; the saint menaced by armed knights brings to mind the more recent martyrdom of Becket, and the murderers of Becket would conversely be equated with the pagan Danes. One senses the same awareness of continuity with the past that spurred Anselm, Becket, Langton, and finally Edmund Rich to go into exile, as Dunstan had been the first to do.[56]

The Becket windows

The different emphasis in this series may be imputed in part to the relatively late compilation of the texts, and to the fact that such recent events were being treated. My purpose here is to explore in more detail the relation of the scenes to the prose texts, with special attention to the ideas behind the choice and ordering of the miracles for the windows, and also to return to the question of interpretation.

It seems that from the time of the first pilgrim to St. Thomas's tomb in the crypt, within a year of his death, some sort of record was kept by the custodians of the tomb of the miracles that either occurred there or of which they heard from pilgrims or by letter.[57] Benedict and William compiled prose accounts of these miracles in 1172–1174; their works are remarkably similar in motivation and contents, but there is seldom a textual dependence of one on the other, even where they recount the same events; and each includes some miracles that the other omits. The accounts have an extraordinary verisimilitude, but a comparison between two versions of the same story sometimes shows that what might appear as verbatim recording of speech is actually freely invented by the compiler.[58] We have seen that the attention to detail, especially

[50] Illus. Rackham, 1949, fig. 27b.

[51] In one scene he expels the secular canons, while reinstating the monks, now north choir aisle "triforium" nt:XI (I,3). This illustrates Osbern, in Stubbs, 1874, p. 113, or Eadmer, *ibid.*, p. 211, but the degree of recent restoration and lack of earlier documentation for the panel make it entirely suspect.

[52] North choir aisle "triforium," nt:X (II,3); Osbern, in Stubbs, 1874, pp. 113–14, and Eadmer, *ibid.*, p. 213. Considerable restorations by Caldwell, Jr. to the right half of the panel do not alter this identification.

[53] For the letters for the period 1187–1199 see Stubbs, 1865.

[54] North choir aisle "triforium," nt:IX (III,1, 3, and 2) respectively.

[55] Pierpont Morgan Library, MS 724, cf. Paris, Bibliothèque Nationale, MS Lat. 8846, f.76 (*Psautier*, fig. 52).

[56] Becket was intensely interested in Anselm, Langton in Becket, and Edmond Rich in Becket and Langton. Langton made gifts to the abbey of St.-Bertin to offset the hospitality given to Becket as well as to his own monks (Martène and Durand, 1717, col. 1813).

[57] Benedict, 1876, pp. xxiv, 35, 37.

[58] Cf., for instance, the two versions of the story of Eilward of Westoning, Benedict, ed. Robertson, 1876, Book IV, ch. 2, pp. 173–82, and William, ed. Robertson, 1875, Book II, ch. 3, pp. 156–58.

in recording names, ages, locations, and the manner in which the story reached Canterbury, is very close to that of the hearings that became part of the process of canonization around 1200, but the compilations were continued after St. Thomas's canonization in 1173. The accounts were extended by both writers in 1178–1179, at which time each added a book to the existing three or four of his text. William was still a monk at Christ Church and probably had some office at the tomb, but Benedict, who had been prior from 1175, had departed for Peterborough in 1177, where he was abbot. Book IV of his *Miraculi Sancti Thomae* must have been composed away from Canterbury, and at about the same time that he may have had some connection with the inscriptions and an iconographical guide used in the typological windows; it is tempting to think that the addition to his account of the miracles may also have been connected with the glazing program.

Appendix figure 1 is a table of the textual sources of each of the surviving series; "B." represents Benedict's text, "W." William's, and the references are to the book and chapter in which the miracle is recorded. Where both authors recorded the same miracle, the version followed in the glass is put first, the other in brackets after. If it is not possible to say which text is closer to the glass, both references are given as alternatives. It is seen that, at least in the random panels surviving, Benedict's text is used more frequently than William's: fifteen miracles are from Benedict (three of them told differently by William), seven are from William (two of them also told by Benedict), two or three are told by both; sixteen or seventeen of the total forty-one or forty-two are unidentified, but this is either because they represent such common diseases as lameness or leprosy, or because they are isolated scenes such as thanksgiving at the tomb,

and not specific enough for exact identification. There is none that could positively not be identified from the existing texts.

Why Benedict's account is preferred is not immediately clear; it was William's that was presented to Henry II. On the other hand, Benedict's was read in the chapter house.[59] There is another curious imbalance in the selection; eight of the fifteen miracles from Benedict's work are taken from Book IV, which was added in or after 1179, when he was at Peterborough. None, however, can be proved to have been taken from William's Book VI, which was added in 1178–1179. Benedict had five books copied at Peterborough some time after 1177. If these were William's, as Robertson and Walberg supposed, by about 1179 Benedict had access to precisely those books from both works from which subjects were selected for the glass.[60] At about the same time, he may either have sent verses to Canterbury for use in the choir windows, or brought verses from Canterbury for use in the choir stalls at Peterborough. It is tempting to think that he may have composed the series of verses for the Trinity Chapel windows. His facility with verse composition is proved by his authorship of the rhymed office of St. Thomas, known as the *Studens Livor*.[61] There are, however, other candidates for authorship of the *tituli*. Nigel of Whiteacre was a contemporary of Benedict's at Christ Church. In the later period Stephen Langton also composed verses.[62] About the time of the translation the lay poet Henry of Avranches was commissioned by the prior to write verses on the miracles of Becket; he labored on them for a week, but destroyed his efforts, and about 1221 complained to Langton that he had received no payment.[63] His Life of Becket and account of the translation, also in verse, are extant.[64] From a comparison of the work attributed to these various poets it may be possible

[59] William, ed. Robertson, 1875, pp. xxvii–xxviii, xxx, 137–38.

[60] Walberg, 1929, p. 73, from Benedict, ed. Robertson, 1876, p. xxiii.

[61] See R. W. Hunt, "Notes on the Distinctiones Monasticae et Morales," *Liber Floridus: Mittellateinische Studien* (Paul Lehman Festschrift), ed. Bernhard Bischoff and Suso Brechter, St. Ottilien, 1950, pp. 359–60.

[62] William Morris, ed., *Laudes Beatae Mariae Virginis*, Hammersmith, 1896. See also M. Dulong, "Etienne Langton versificateur," *Mélanges Mandonnet*, Paris, 1930, II, 183–90.

[63] Josiah Cox Russell and John Paul Hieronimus, *The Shorter Latin Poems of Master Henry of Avranches Relating to England*, Cambridge, Mass., 1935, pp. 88–93.

[64] *Ibid.*, pp. 64–78.

for others to resolve the question of the date and authorship of the *tituli*.

The subjects in the glass represent a unique mingling of the two prose texts, such as is known in none of the extant recensions. No other series of illustrations of the miracles of Thomas is known, which would indicate that the Canterbury windows are part of a tradition stemming from *tituli* based on both texts.[65] The organization of the subjects in the windows is curious. Clearly it is not chronological although one of the earliest miracles, that of William, a priest of London, occurs in Window n:V. The accounts themselves were not, however, chronologically ordered, as their authors noted. William seems to have grouped miracles loosely according to type for didactic purposes. Thus in Book IV, he collected together several miracles to show that St. Thomas was able to raise people from the dead, in order to strengthen belief in the resurrection. Similarly in the glass, Window s:V has subjects of which all, or all but one, involve people raised from the dead. Reference to the resurrection is not made in the inscriptions, but the parallel would be obvious to a medieval audience. In each of the other windows, cures of ailments, including madness, are mingled with rescue from natural calamity, prevention of miscarriage of justice in the secular courts, release from torment by demons, and one case of raising from the dead. The identifiable subjects in Window n:V are based on Benedict's Book I, in Window n:IV there is a preponderance of subjects from his Book II, and all the episodes in Window n:II are from his Book IV, but in other windows the order of the texts is not clear. The stories are variously told in two scenes or more; there are as many as nine in the case of the Plague in the House of Jordan Fitz-Eisulf in Window n:II. The number of scenes is not always

proportionate to the length of the original text. The grouping of panels coincides with the designs of ironwork, and the two must have been reciprocally planned. Thus in Window n:IV subjects are paired, in Window n:II they are in threes, sixes, or nines, the latter representing a full unit of the ironwork. As in the typological windows, the order is from top to bottom and from left to right. The narrative is made clear in most cases by a consistent use of the same color of garments and the same facial type in the several representations of an individual. Each moment in time is separated into a distinct scene, even if changes in the positions of the figures are minimal, as in the case of Window n:IV(15,16) (fig. 159). In this case the verses are rather repetitive and do not indicate a sequence of events. In another case, however, where a couplet suggested two distinct scenes, the verse was divided into two [Window n:IV(13, 14)]; the alternative would have been to provide a single scene with two actions, but there are no examples of continuous narrative in the miracle windows such as were rarely found in the typological windows. This more modern approach to the narrative mode is explicable by the fact that no precise models could have existed prior to 1179; there are not enough examples of split couplets to suppose that an early cycle of illustrated *tituli* with continuous narrative scenes existed as a model for the glass.[66]

It seems that the miracle windows, unlike the typological series, could be read as distinct units, in any order. Only the westernmost two windows on the north side should have been read together, since they contained a Life of Thomas Becket. They were thus prefixed to the miracles in the same way that one of the lives of Becket was often prefixed to the text of the miracles.[67] The prime

[65] The late Professor Wormald suggested to me that a mixed selection from both works might have had a place in the liturgy of Christ Church, but the evidence from the Burned Breviary and another fragmentary Breviary in the Cathedral Library, MS Add. 3, of fourteenth-century date, is negative; f.19v has the feast of the translation, 7 July, but there are no readings from the miracles.

[66] In the rest of the glass only the inscriptions in n:IV (3 and 4), might have belonged together, but they are

not sufficiently complete for one to be certain of this; Rackham, 1949, p. 88.

[67] Benedict, ed. Robertson, 1876, pp. xxi–xxii. Benedict wrote a "Passio," which is largely lost. William wrote a Life, which is found complete in the Winchester manuscript, prefacing his account of the miracles (William, ed. Robertson, 1875, pp. xxvi–xxvii). In the Montpellier manuscript of William's account, John of Salisbury's Life was given (Robertson, IV, 1879, xxv). In manuscripts the life

meaning of the miracle series was evidently narrative, and there seems to be little theological significance in the choice of stories or their grouping. Certain didactic themes, however, are emphasized. One is the rendering of dues to the saint, taught by scenes of thanksgiving and offering at the tomb, and of calamities that befell those who vowed pilgrimage but did not go.[68] These are lessons made clear in the texts, too.[69] As we have noted, another theme is the healing power of the saint, who was referred to at least once as *medicus*.[70] In one series in Window n:III scenes of the futile administration of medication and of the efficacious use of the blood of St. Thomas are juxtaposed, so that the acts become typological (fig. 162).[71] The persuasiveness of such imagery must be understood in an historical context when the task of healing was passing from the monasteries to the universities.[72]

There are, however, deeper meanings. The use of the blood of a saint, mixed with water and administered as a potion, was unique to Canterbury. Benedict said of the first use of blood: "I do not believe any previous case existed in which God allowed this prerogative; thus alone in the whole world the blood of the Lamb of Bethlehem and the blood of the Lamb of Canterbury were chosen

to be imbibed."[73] The cult of the blood of Thomas began very early; John of Salisbury carried two phials with him to Chartres in 1176, Benedict of Peterborough took some to his new abbey in 1177, and Reginald Fitzjocelin, bishop of Bath, gave some to Queen Margaret of Sicily between 1174 and 1183.[74] The first miracle in which it was used was that of the priest William of London, represented in Window n:V, which occurred on January 5, 1171.[75] Many inscriptions stress the use of blood. It would not be possible for a Christian audience to think of this without reference to Christ's blood, and the relationship was emphasized in Benedict's text: "Just as the blood of Christ brings eternal life to the soul which has been called back from the finality of death, so also the blood of the martyr gives back temporal life to the body divested of its soul."[76] If one looks at representations of the blood and water given at the tomb, the visual overtone is clearly that of the sacrament (figs. 159, 208). Two monks stand behind the tomb, on which are candles. The laity approach, fall on their knees, and are offered the cup to drink from.[77] That this was allowed to them, whereas the blood of Christ in the Eucharist was forbidden, would be significant. Saints' tombs had, of course, served

did not always precede the miracles of a saint; the *libellus* of St. Edmund in the Pierpont Morgan Library (MS 736) gives the martyrdom, miracles, and life in that order.

[68] Scenes of thanksgiving at the tomb are very frequent, with offerings of money, candles, or ex-voto coils of wire, crutches, and so on. Stories of calamity are those of Jordan Fitz-Eisulf, Window n:II(25–33), and William of Kellett, s:II(9–12).

[69] Benedict, ed. Robertson, 1876, Book IV, ch. 64, pp. 229–34; William, ed. Robertson, 1875, Book III, ch. 15, p. 274, who concluded his story of William of Kellett, "it is better, then, not to take an oath, than to take one and not keep it."

[70] Window s:II(16) has the end of an inscription: . . . MEDICE PRECES ET MUNERA ("to the physician prayers and gifts").

[71] Window n:III(20 and 19), from the story of Hugh of Jervaulx. Rackham, 1949, p. 95, followed Mason in identifying one scene as the administration of Extreme Unction, but the "abbot" is clearly one of the laity, presumably a physician (see Caviness, 1967, pp. 62, 63).

[72] C. H. Talbot, *Medicine in Medieval England*, London, 1967, pp. 50–51, has documented the series of ordi-

nances, between 1131 and 1215, that restricted the clergy in medical practice.

[73] Benedict, ed. Robertson, 1876, Book I, ch. 12, p. 43.

[74] A niello reliquary in the Metropolitan Museum in New York was once thought to have been made for John of Salisbury; see Joseph Breck, *Bulletin of the Metropolitan Museum of Art* 13 (1918), 220–24, also Borenius, 1932, pp. 78–79 and Pl. XXIX 1 and 2, and Swarzenski, 1943, p. 50, fig. 71. Cf. *The Year 1200* I, no. 85, 78–79. A second reliquary, commemorating Reginald of Bath's gift, is also in the Metropolitan Museum (acq. no. 63.160); see Thomas P. F. Hoving, "A Newly Discovered Reliquary of St. Thomas Becket," *Gesta* 4 (1965), 28–29. It is doubtful that the piece is of English workmanship; Dr. Swarzenski believes it to be south Italian. For Benedict, see Stanley, 1904, p. 192, who quoted Robert of Swaffham, ed. Sparke, 1723, p. 101.

[75] Benedict, ed. Robertson, 1876, Book I, ch. 12, p. 42.

[76] *Ibid.*, Book IV, ch. 65, p. 234.

[77] Cf. Christ offering bread and wine to the Apostles on the sixth-century paten from Riha; Marvin C. Ross, *Catalogue of the Byzantine and Early Mediaeval Antiquities in the Dumbarton Oaks Collection*, I, Washington, D.C., 1962, pp. 12–15, Pl. XI.

as altars through the twelfth century, and some ancient sarcophagi are still in use as both tombs and altars.[78] The act of drinking blood at an "altar" of this kind would take on some of the significance of the sacrament. St. Thomas, in giving his blood for the cure of those who followed him, partook of the nature of Christ and was his spiritual descendant.

There are other visual overtones, possibly arising from the authority of scriptural illustration and the fact that it provided a repertory for the artist wishing to create a new scene. However, borrowings from scriptural scenes become metaphorical. Two cures effected by touching strongly resemble the laying on of hands that occurs in the miracles of Christ; they might be compared with a scene in the Christological cycle of the Great Canterbury Psalter, Paris, Bibliothèque Nationale, MS Lat. 8846.[79] St. Thomas emerging from his shrine to appear to the sleeping author, cross in hand, appears as Christ rising from his tomb (fig. 164). William of Gloucester buried by a fall of earth and later dug out is like Joseph in the pit, a type of Christ's Burial and Resurrection (fig. 191). So also, in the same window, is the child buried in a collapsed house and miraculously dug out unharmed.[80] Christ is thus not only the type of St. Thomas the healer, but also of the suffering people.[81] These most recent manifestations of his nature are aptly placed between the cycle of his life and death and the windows of the eastern end with his Ascension and Second Coming.

The Trinity Chapel ambulatory windows, set low in the wall, were closest physically to the people as they circled the shrine (text fig. 2d). They were also the most immediate in their realistic portrayal of the unfortunate and the diseased. In almost all cases the names of the individuals have been suppresesd in the inscription, so that they became universal portrayals of lepers, cripples, and other afflicted people.[82] The artists showed their skills in depicting such an agitated figure as the madwoman in Window n:II; no issue of demons was needed to demonstrate her cure (figs. 209–211).[83] Almost nowhere are labels necessary, as were used in the north choir aisle.[84] The sorrowing parents of William Fitz-Eisulf are readily identified, as are the distraught parents of Rodbertulus (fig. 197). As we have seen, the painters of some of the Trinity Chapel windows are closely related to those working on the north choir aisle windows, yet their style is transformed, infused with new energy and realism. The events depicted are not as highly charged with symbolism as were those of the typological windows. This direct narrative mode could equally be applied to biblical stories, as it was at Chartres in the Joseph Window (fig. 196). In the second or third decade of the thirteenth century, English Bible illustrations were also infused with a new realism involving a greater repertory of scenes.[85] The Canterbury glass demonstrates how rapidly this transformation could take place, with a change of subject matter and of purpose. The creation of a series of illustrations for events of such recent history gave the artists an opportunity to work without reference to a long tradition or a revered model, and without a complex iconographical apparatus.

---

[78] As for instance in Saint-Sauveur, Aix-en-Provence; see E. LeBlant, *Les Sarcophages chrétiens de la Gaule*, Paris, 1886, pp. 43–44, Pl. LI, 2.

[79] Window n:IV, panel 2, and Window s:VI, panel 13.

[80] Window s:VII, panels 13–20, and 3–6; Joseph dug out of the pit is represented in the east window of the corona and that panel is an exact replica of s:VII(20). Little glass in it is old, however, except the inscription, and it is not known whether Austin restored the original or merely copied from the scene in Window s:VII.

[81] As in Matthew 25:35–40; this passage was illustrated literally in a mid-fourteenth–century window in the narthex of Strasbourg Cathedral (Ahnne and Beyer, 1960, pp. 12, 18 and Pl. 14) but earlier illustrations are rare.

For the early concept of *Christus medicus*, see Ernst H. Kantorowicz, "The Baptism of the Apostles," *Dumbarton Oaks Papers* 9–10 (1956), pp. 239–40, who cites Origen.

[82] The only surviving inscription in which a name figures is that in Window n:V, panel 9, with the name of William, priest of London.

[83] Cf. scenes in the Monreale mosaics and in the Winchester Bible, Kitzinger, 1966b, figs. 108, 109.

[84] Only in Window n:V, panel 9, are there labels "Sanguis" and "Aqua," referring to the mixing of the two as a potion.

[85] Plummer, 1953, pp. 46–47, with reference to the Morgan Lothian Bible.

IX. Conclusions

"Senlis, Laon or Sens . . . will only be understood if regarded in a large network of possible interrelations which may reach as far as Monreale, Canterbury, Liège, and elsewhere. And here serious work has barely begun, and the great problems seem all unresolved."

Willibald Sauerländer[1]

IN THE foregoing chapters we have seen that, in spite of the nineteenth and twentieth-century restorations, the painted glass of Canterbury Cathedral provides invaluable material for a study of painting styles. It has been possible to trace the ramifications of these styles over two or three generations, in the work of the artists who executed a program of glazing according to a single master plan laid out about 1175–1180 for the whole projected building. The hypothesis has been argued that the execution of this plan was essentially complete by the time the relics of Thomas Becket were translated to the Trinity Chapel in July 1220. The chronology of glazing proposed here is more compact and slightly earlier for the later glass than that of Rackham twenty-five years ago.

More radical, perhaps, will appear my acceptance of his early date for the choir clerestory glass, and my claim that the lower windows of the choir are almost equally early. A date before 1180 places the Methuselah Master's mature style slightly ahead of Nicholas of Verdun's commission for the Klosterneuburg Ambo, and the Morgan Master's work on the Winchester Bible. The origins of his style lie not, as I once thought, in the region that produced the Troyes glass and related manuscripts, but probably for the most part in England itself. The logical background for the formation of such a strong classicizing style was in the south of England after about mid-century; it was in England that scholarship in the classical "humanities" was most highly developed, notably by John of Salisbury, who spent several years in Rome and was later in Canterbury; the admiration of pagan antique sculpture seems to have been a particular failing of the English, who variously described the

[1] Willibald Sauerländer, "Sculpture on Early Gothic Churches: The State of Research and Open Questions," *Gesta* 9 (1970), 42.

statues of classical gods, visited them longingly, or even carried them home.[2] The aesthetic attitudes that were prevalent in the 1160s and 1170s explain the ready assimilation of a variety of *antiquisant* models in the work of the Methuselah Master.

Since investigation of the variety and richness of these models has been divided between two chapters, it is of interest here to notice how consistent they are in kind, and how strongly they indicate a preference for the antique. Both design sources and iconographical borrowings lead to works of antique flavor—the fourth-century reliquary in Milan, the sixth-century ampullae in Monza, a Prudentius manuscript, the Utrecht Psalter, and the Cotton Aelfric, and most recently the Palatina mosaics. In almost every case, however, the Master has infused his model with a higher degree of humanism, and his interpretation is often closer to works of genuine antiquity than was the supposed model or its genre; this is very clear in the case of the Exodus scene, ostensibly modeled on the Utrecht Psalter, and yet closer in style to the Ara Pacis (figs. 30, 35, 36). The survey of these models is also of interest for the works neglected. The Master showed no interest in the manuscripts of the immediately preceding generation, the Dover and Lambeth Bibles and the Eadwine Psalter, rich though they are in iconographic material. It is also notable that there is no trace of influence from the Monreale cycle. It is a curious turnabout that, whereas the Dover Bible artists of about 1160 preferred the newest dynamic style from Sicily, which Kitzinger has traced to the latest mosaics of the Palatina, the Methuselah Master—though perhaps contemporary with the Monreale artists—preferred the serener mode of the early Palatina.[3] That the impact of Monreale was so immediately felt in the Winchester Bible after 1180 is further argument for dating the choir win-

dows before 1180. What is more, the use of Sicilian marbles in the columns of the Trinity Chapel in the 1180s demonstrates that contact with Sicily was still close during the period of the Monreale decoration, and Mediterranean ties might have been strengthened under the Beneventan prior, Master Alan.[4]

I have suggested that the classicism of the Methuselah Master has nothing to do with that of the Antique Master of Rheims; the one now emerges as a genuine manifestation of the twelfth-century renascence, the other is more general and idealized, and warrants the term "proto-Gothic." The two phases can be compared approximately with the somewhat eclectic Early Renaissance assimilation of classical quotation, combined with a realism of parts, and the High Renaissance recreation of the antique without obvious reference to specific models, though this is not to claim that the medieval renascences were comparable in scale.

Our understanding of the proto-Renaissance of the twelfth century has been advanced by many scholars since the formulations of Panofsky in 1960. It is no longer necessary to envisage such a latency in the north of Europe between the revival in the humanities, which was accomplished about mid-century, and the development of an "intrinsic" classicism in the visual arts until the thirteenth-century (*sic*) sculpture of "Laon, Senlis, Chartres and Paris"—albeit "with Nicholas of Verdun in the van of the development."[5] Not only have the accepted dates for the sculptures of Laon and Senlis been moved back into the twelfth century through the perceptions of Sauerländer,[6] but also fundamental questions about the genesis and development of "proto-Gothic" art in the north of France, which were raised by Grodecki in 1961, have been pursued in a variety of media.[7] Of foremost importance was Deuchler's publication

---

[2] Erwin Panofsky, *Renaissance and Renascences in Western Art*, Stockholm [1960], pp. 68–69, 71–73. Part of the "Pagan Antiquities" of Master Gregory has been edited in translation by Caecilia Davis-Weyer, *Early Medieval Art 300–1150: Sources and Documents*, Englewood Cliffs, 1971, pp. 159–62.

[3] Kitzinger, 1966b, p. 137.

[4] For the use of Sicilian marble, Kenneth W. Severens, "William of Sens and the Double Columns at Sens and

Canterbury," *Journal of the Warburg and Courtauld Institutes* 30 (1970), 313. For Master Alan, prior of Christ Church 1179–1186, formerly a canon of Benevento, see Knowles, Brooke, and London, 1972, p. 34.

[5] Panofsky, *Renaissance and Renascences*, p. 62.

[6] Most recently in *Gesta* 9 (1970), 42, 43, with bibliography.

[7] Grodecki, 1963; see also his earlier discussion of "Gothic" style in painting, 1955, pp. 611, 619.

of the Ingeborg Psalter, as well as his organization in 1970 of the "Year 1200" exhibition and symposium.[8] Yet there is still much to be done in this enigmatic field, and any conclusions drawn at the present time must be tentative. The burden of evidence, however, suggests that the Methuselah Master and the Morgan Master may take their places quite naturally alongside Nicholas of Verdun as part of a nascent revival of the antique, which may be directly related to almost contemporary developments in the humanities.[9] The literary revival was the only cultural force, in the north, which could have transformed the succesive stylizations of the Romanesque into a more profound classicism; the first attempt to render figures more plastically and organically was aborted in the stylization of the "damp-fold" drapery system, even perhaps in the circle of Henry of Blois,[10] but both in Winchester and in Canterbury we see this replaced, by the late 1170s and 1180s, by a far more advanced and confident classicism. The latency between "proto-humanism" and this first stage of genuine classical revival in the visual arts is therefore narrowed to about twenty-five years, which still gives the famed scholars a generation's lead over the anonymous artists whom they—or other patrons—trained to an appreciation of the antique. The real dichotomy lies in the fact that this classicizing style had a limited appeal; it was an expression of a short-lived humanism that gave way abruptly to scholasticism on the one hand and a more popular spirituality on the other.[11] The end of the revival in letters is often associated with the death of John of Salisbury in 1180; more final perhaps is the countercurrent, expressed at Paris in 1210 by a decree prohibiting the reading or study of Aristotle's books on natural science.[12] Around 1200 art had once more to find a new mode, in keeping with the religious trends of the time.

It is in the period following the work of the Methuselah Master—that is, perhaps, after 1180—that Canterbury enters a truly transitional "middle phase," one that is chaotic and eclectic, and in which there are signs of intensified contacts with the continent. The assimilation of a new style, if it is imported, requires first a certain affinity with it—one might cite the impact of the Impressionists in Japan, which was possible because the Impressionists in turn had been influenced by Japanese art. During the middle period at Canterbury the styles of the early masters were neutralized; while contacts seem to have been maintained with the "late" Winchester hands and perhaps with the Palatina mosaics, there enters a new elegance that is close to contemporary French works. One painter (the Petronella Master) may even have been trained in France, but the style that he brought was not Gothic, nor was it radically different from a trend current in English art. By this time—perhaps approaching 1200 and extending into the thirteenth century—there was more clearly a single artistic province, which included Canterbury as a northern outpost, and which extended through much of northeastern France. The mainstream of development in this region may have been an idealized classicizing style, as in the Ingeborg Psalter, the Laon windows, and the windows of Soissons and St.-Quentin, which had an impact on Chartres. But other strands must be recognized; one that is radically opposed to this "proto-Gothic" style may have grown out of the eclecticism of the middle phase at Canterbury, and was carried to Sens and Chartres, only to rebound in a pronouncedly Gothic phase in the last windows to be glazed at Canterbury, in the eastern part of the Trinity Chapel ambulatory. The possible reasons for the ultimate triumph of this style at Canterbury will be dis-

[8] Deuchler, 1967; *The Year 1200* 1, especially pp. xxxiv–xxxv, by Konrad Hoffmann. See also the critique by Sauerländer, 1971, pp. 506–507.

[9] Otto Demus, "Nicholas of Verdun," *Encyclopedia of World Art* 10, London, 1965, cols. 634–40; Ayres, 1974, pp. 212–16, 221–23.

[10] As in the so-called Psalter of Henry of Blois; most recently, Francis Wormald, *The Winchester Psalter: British Museum Cotton MS Nero C IV*, London, 1972.

[11] The esoteric nature of the use of classical sources by John of Salisbury and his circle has been stressed by Janet Martin, "Uses of Tradition: Gellius, Petronius, and John of Salisbury," *Imitation and Adaptation: The Classical Tradition in the Middle Ages*, ed. Dennis M. Kratz, Columbus (Ohio), in press.

[12] Southern, 1953, p. 220, n.1.

cussed after I have tabulated the dating proposed here with that of related monuments.

In the first three decades or so of this century early dates were accepted only with great caution, and there has been a tendency to put such works as the Ingeborg Psalter, the Guthlac Roll, the British Library Cuthbert Life, and the Sigena frescoes in the thirteenth rather than the twelfth century. This, in fact, left one with a few surprisingly precocious works firmly dated in the twelfth century, such as the Klosterneuburg Ambo and the Worksop Bestiary. The following table of chronology gives *termini a quo* and *ante quem* from archaeological evidence, where this is available, and suggests a hypothetical chronology and dating based in part on the arguments of this book.[13]

	terminus a quo	date proposed here	*terminus ante quem*
Canterbury painting, St. Paul	1130	c.1160	1175
Troyes glass	—	1170–80	?1188
Klosterneuburg Ambo	1181	1181	1181
Worksop Bestiary	—	c.1185	1187
Rheims, St.-Rémi choir glass	c.1180	1180–90	—
Canterbury choir clerestory	1178	1178–80	?1180
Canterbury n. choir aisle and oculi	1178/79	1179–80	?1180
Canterbury Psalter, Lat. 8846	—	1175–90	—
Canterbury choir "triforium"	1178	c.1180	?1180
Canterbury clerestory of transepts	1179	c.1180–90	?1207
Winchester Bible, Masters of the Morgan Leaf and of the "Gothic Majesty"	1180	1180–90	?1186[14]

	terminus a quo	date proposed here	*terminus ante quem*
Sens St. John portal	1184	c.1185–90	—
Sens central portal	1184	c.1190–1200	—
Ingeborg Psalter	1193	c.1193–1210	1195/1213[15]
Canterbury corona	1184	1195–1207	1207/1220
Canterbury Trinity Chapel n:IV–n:VII	1184	1185–1207	1207/1220
Canterbury clerestory N:X and N:IX	1184	1185–1207	1207/1220
Cuthbert Life Y T MS 26	—	1190–1210	—
Orbais east window	c.1200	1200–10	—
Sens ambulatory windows	1184	1207–13	—
Psalter of Blanche of Castille	1200	1210–20	1225
St.-Quentin Lady Chapel windows	c.1215–20	c.1225	—
Chartres Prodigal Son window	1194	1210–20	—
Lincoln north rose and typological cycle	1192	c.1200–20	—
Canterbury Trinity Chapel n:II & III, s:II–VII, & clerestory	1184	1213–15/20	1220
Canterbury Psalter Lat. 770	1173	1215–20	1220
Canterbury Trinity Chapel vault paintings	1220	1220	1220

Listed in the chronology are a few English works which, though not produced at Canterbury, belong to the same general development as the Canterbury

[13] Full references for the archaeological evidence cited here have generally been given elsewhere, and may be found through the indices.

[14] Ayres, 1970, p. 322; 1974, p. 212.

[15] Deuchler, 1967, p. 148, cf. Reiner Haussherr, "Florens Deuchler: Der Ingeborgpsalter" (review), *Zeitschrift für Kunstgeschichte* 32 (1969), 54.

glass. Foremost in importance are the works in a "Winchester" style, the Great Bible and, one might add, the Sigena frescoes, which are closely allied to the "Canterbury" styles of the Methuselah Master and the Great Psalter in Paris[16] These works of biblical subject matter were followed by new essays in the hagiographical mode.

The Becket windows, the Cuthbert Life, and the lives of the saints at Sens were produced in a period when the great monastic scriptoria were rapidly changing and styles were becoming common property. The cult of saints tended still to center on the monasteries where their relics were kept, but the idiom of hagiographical writing and illustration was an international one. Canterbury was not alone among the English centers in participating in the development of this idiom. The realism that was a feature of the classicizing styles of southern England and northern France around 1175–1200 became more poignant in illustrations to the lives of saints. At the same time, perhaps partially under the duress of the exploding demand for hagiographical illustrations, the painstakingly modeled figures of the classicizing style were transformed into the dynamic, shorthand representations of the Gothic. Greater attention was given to action and emotion and less to ponderation and easeful balance of form. In the north choir aisle panels the style of painting is well suited to the content; many of the scenes based on biblical history are represented as concepts rather than events, eternally equated with each other intellectually and visually by their exegetical juxtapositions. The individual figures are poised, as if suspended. In the Trinity Chapel the action of the narrative is more fully told, and the symbolic element, though present, is reduced. The painter's repertory acquired a variety of easily recognizable poses and facial types. If in the twelfth century it was the biblical commentaries that provided the artists with their richest subject matter, in the thirteenth century it was the lives of the saints. Even stripped of their learned verses, the replicas of Canterbury windows in the secular churches of Sens, Lincoln, and St.-Quentin must still have seemed esoteric and lifeless to the laity. It was hagiographical cycles that filled the *lacuna* left by the schoolmen, whose dialectic was not material to inspire the visual arts. Thus, even in the period when the new universities had supplanted the monasteries as intellectual centers, the monasteries for a time retained their artistic supremacy. They were eventually superseded, first by the secular cathedrals and then by the court centers of Paris and London, which played the leading role in the further development of the High Gothic style.

---

[16] For the Winchester connections of Sigena, see Walter Oakeshott, *Sigena: Romanesque Paintings in Spain and the Winchester Bible Artists*, London, 1972; and Ayres, 1974, pp. 219ff., esp. n.95. The question of dating remains unresolved; one hopes that it can be determined independently of the dating of the Winchester Bible.

Appendix: Figures

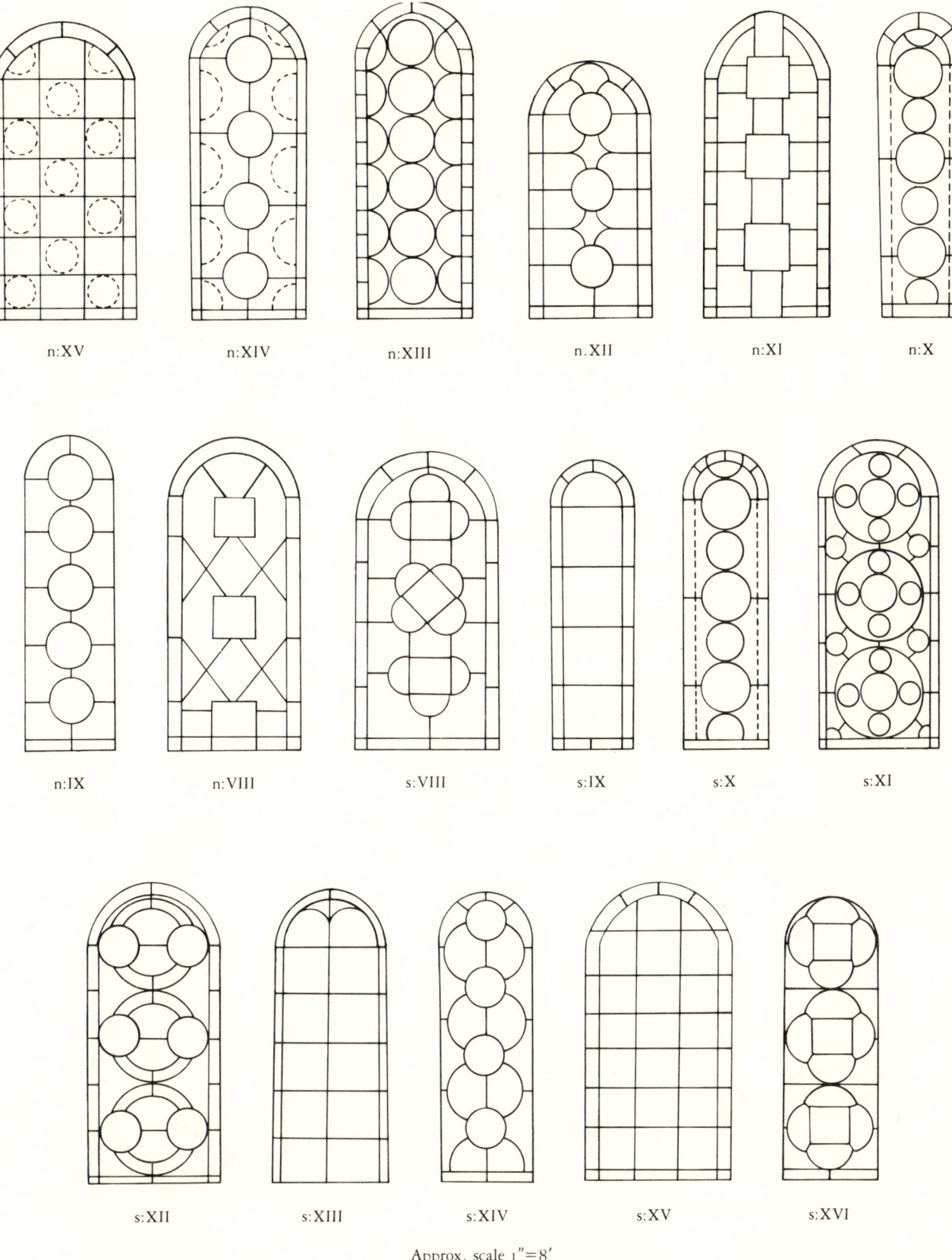

n:XV n:XIV n:XIII n.XII n:XI n:X

n:IX n:VIII s:VIII s:IX s:X s:XI

s:XII s:XIII s:XIV s:XV s:XVI

Approx. scale 1″=8′

Appendix fig. 1. Compositions of Canterbury windows: Choir, transepts and presbytery.

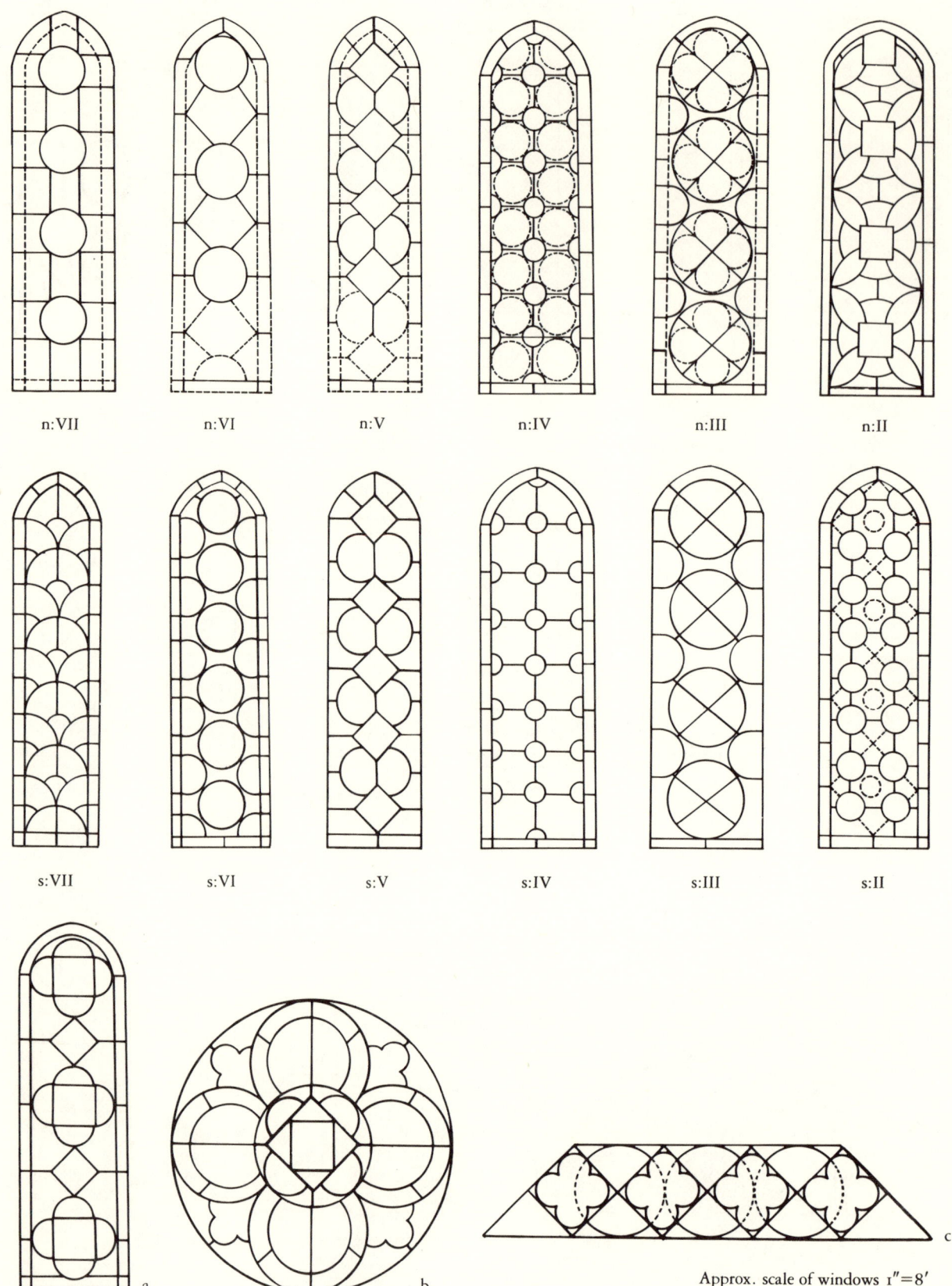

n:VII n:VI n:V n:IV n:III n:II

s:VII s:VI s:V s:IV s:III s:II

a b c

Approx. scale of windows 1″=8′

Appendix fig. 2. Compositions of Trinity Chapel ambulatory windows (top),
east window of the corona (a), oculi (b), and tomb of Hubert Walter (c).

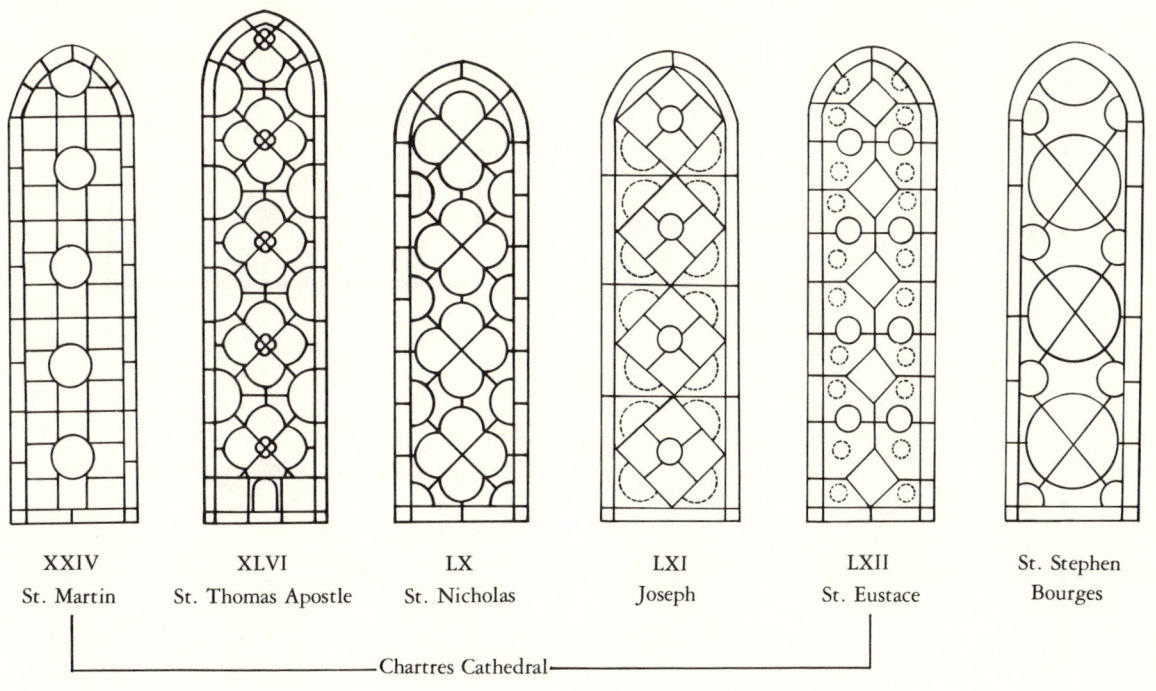

XXIV
St. Martin

XLVI
St. Thomas Apostle

LX
St. Nicholas

LXI
Joseph

LXII
St. Eustace

St. Stephen
Bourges

Chartres Cathedral

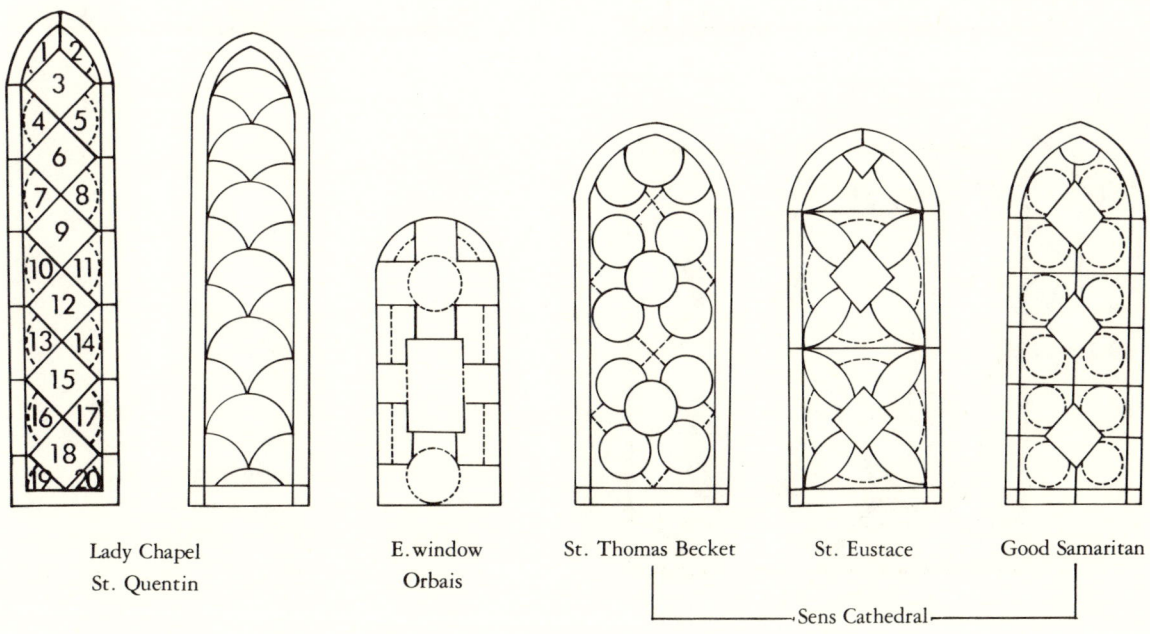

Lady Chapel
St. Quentin

E. window
Orbais

St. Thomas Becket

St. Eustace

Good Samaritan

Sens Cathedral

Appendix fig. 3. Compositions of related French windows.

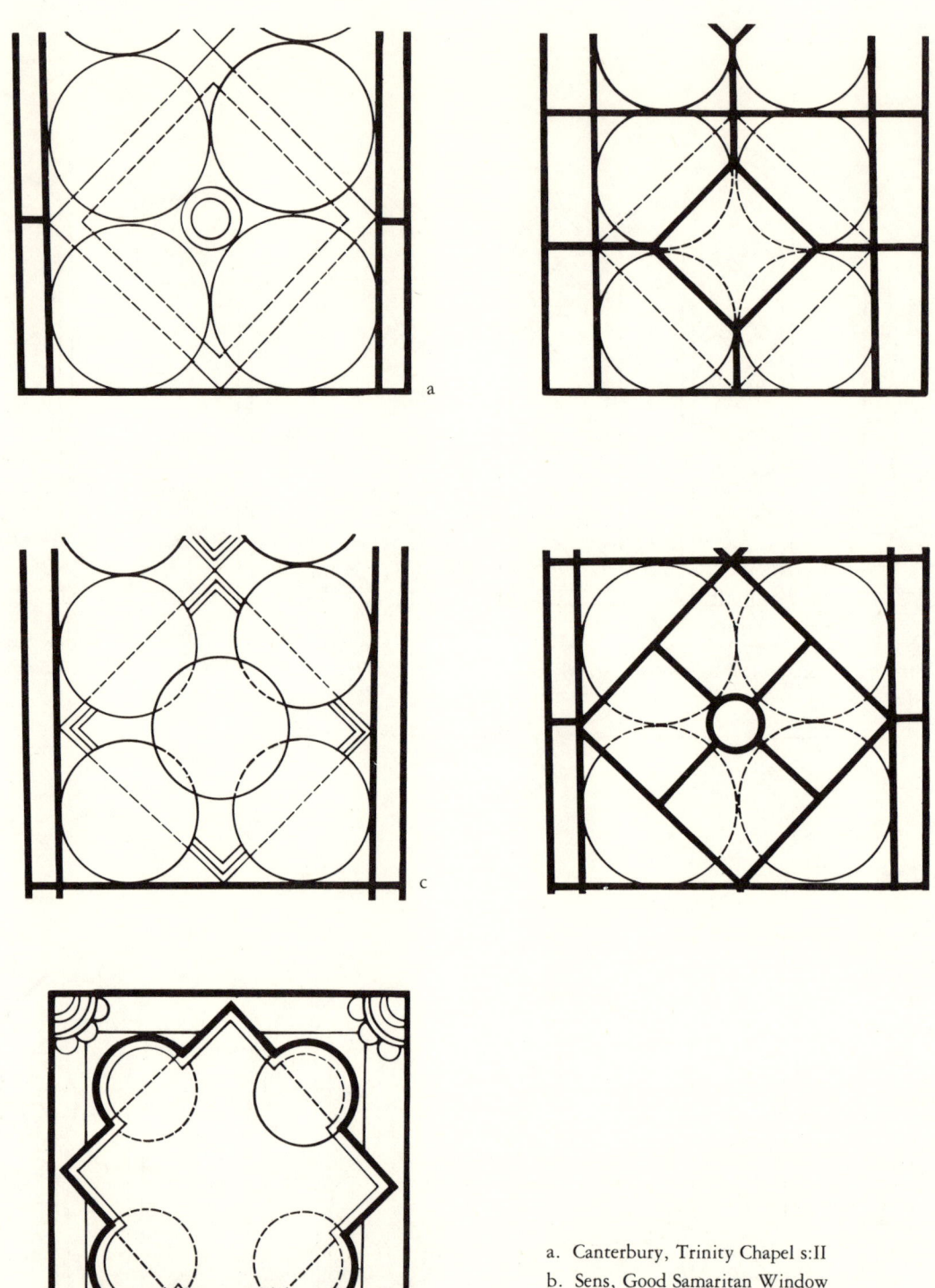

a. Canterbury, Trinity Chapel s:II
b. Sens, Good Samaritan Window
c. Sens, Thomas Becket Window
d. Chartres, Joseph Window (LXI)
e. Sens, Prodigal Son Window, single panel

Appendix fig. 4. Compositions of windows by the Canterbury-Sens Designer.

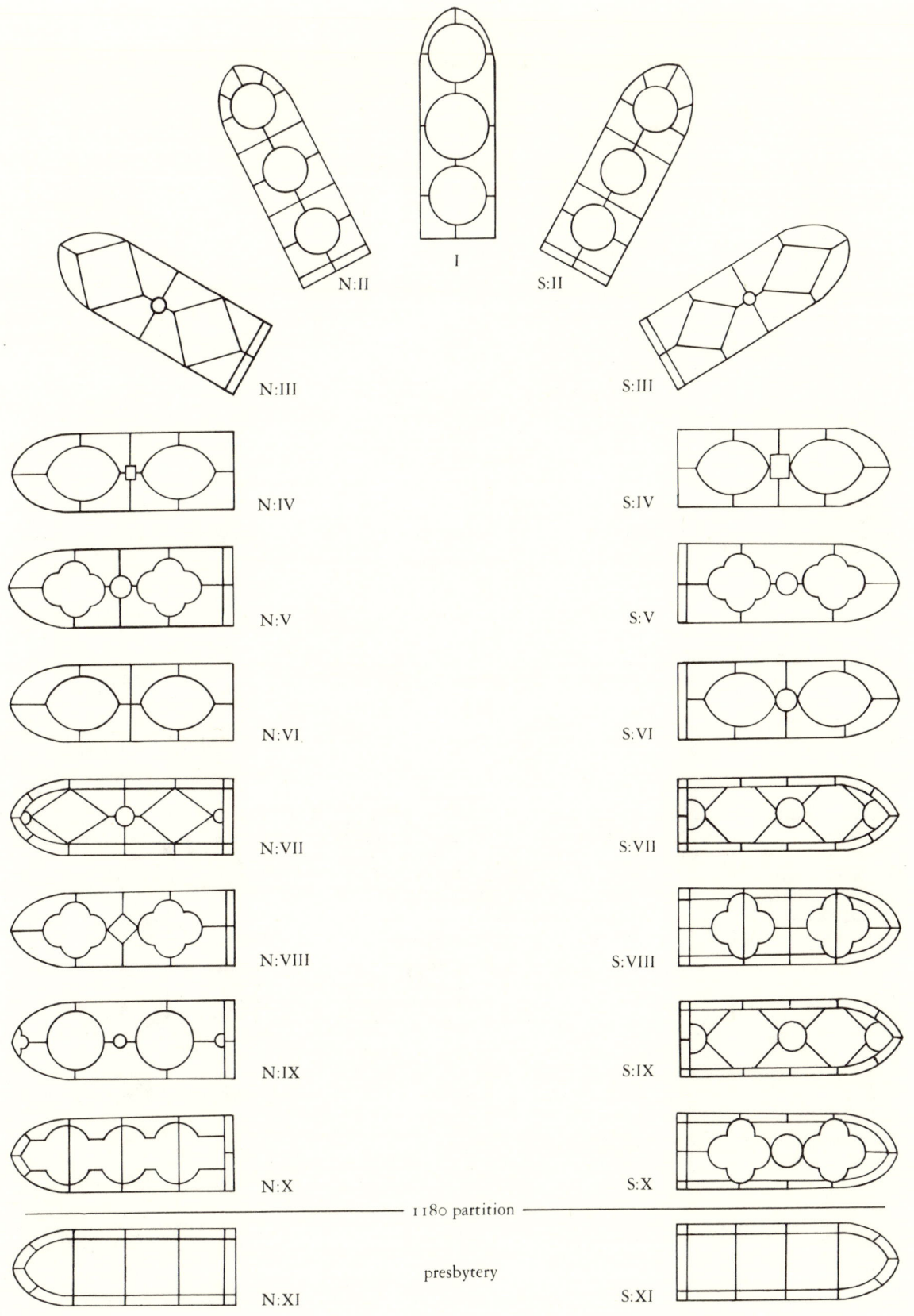

Appendix fig. 5. Compositions of Trinity Chapel clerestory windows.

APPENDIX FIGURE 6. THE CONTENTS OF THE TRINITY CHAPEL WINDOWS

Window & Panel nos.	Original no. of scenes	Textual Source	Name of Person Cured	Approx. Age	Affliction
n VII–10, 14	2	B IV, 77	Not given	Youth	Disadvantage in judicial combat
n VII–15 (from s VI?)	1+	—	—	Child	Crippled
n V–4	1+	B I, 13	Stephen of Hoyland	—	Visited by demons
n V–8	1+	B I, 14?	William Patrick	—	Toothache
n V–9	1+	B I, 12	William, priest of London	—	Paralysis
n IV–1	1	—	—	—	—
n IV–2	1+	B II, 9 or W IV, 26	Edmund of Canterbury or Robert of Lilford	Youth Youth	Blind & internal obstruction Attacked by ruffians
n IV–3, 4	2–3	W II, 6	Petronella of Polesworth (nun)	—	Epilepsy
n IV–9, 10	2	B II, 52?	Prior of St. Frideswide's, Oxford	Bearded Man	Crippled
n IV–11, 12	2	B II, 45?	Juliana Puintel	Woman	Stomach pains
n IV–13, 14	2	B II, 13	Henry of Fordwich	Youth	Madness
n IV–15, 16	2	B I, 22	Ethelreda of Canterbury	Young Woman	Quartan fever
n III–1	1	B I, 1? or W 1?	Benedict (monk) or William (monk)	Mature Man	Vision of St. Thomas
n III–2, 3?	1–2	B II, 28? or W VI, 159?	Ralph of Tongue or Roger of Valognes	Youth/ Boy Youth	Crippled Crippled
n III–4 (from n V?)	1+	W IV, 24	Godwin of Boxgrove	Youth	Giving alms (later cured of leprosy)

Window & Panel nos.	Original no. of scenes	Textual Source	Name of Person Cured	Approx. Age	Affliction
n III–5, 6	2	W III, 8	Oda & Matilda of Artois	Women	Dropsy
n III–10–12	3–4	B III, 77	Daughters of Godbold of Boxley	Girls?	Lameness
n III–13	1+	—	—	—	Leprosy
n III–14–18	5–6	W II, 3 (B IV, 2)	Eilward of Westoning	Mature Man	Unjust punishment
n III–19–21	3–4	B III, 60	Hugh of Jervaulx cellerer	Mature Man	Grave illness
n III–1–3	3	B IV, 30	Juliana of Rochester	Girl/ Young Woman	Blind
n II–4–9	6	B IV, 76	Richard Sunieve servant	Youth	Leprosy
n II–13–15	3–6	B IV, 62 or B IV, 66	Rodbertulus of Rochester or Philip Scot of Warwickshire	Child 8 years	Nearly drowned Nearly drowned
n II–19–21	3	B IV, 37	Matilda of Cologne	Mature Woman	Madness
n II–25–33	9	B IV, 64 (W II, 5)	Jordan Fitz-Eisulf & Sons	Children	Plague
s II–9–12	4	W III, 15	William of Kellett carpenter	Mature Man	Injury to leg
s II–13–14	2–3	W IV, 28	Adam, forester	Mature Man	Injured by arrow
s II–15	1+	—	—	—	—
s II–16	1+	—	—	—	Crippled
s VI–1–4	4	B VI, 3 (W III, 41)	John, servant of Sweyn of Roxburgh	—	Nearly drowned
s VI–8	1+	W IV, 32?	Warin	3 years	Dead
s VI–11	1+	—	—	Mature Man	Dead
s VI–12	1+	—	—	Youth	—

APPENDIX FIGURE 6, CONTINUED

Window & Panel Nos.	Original no. of scenes	Textual Source	Name of Person Cured	Approx. Age	Affliction
s VI–13	1+	B IV, 65 W II, 35	Cecily	Girl	Dead
		or			
		B III, 58	Constance, nun of Stixwold	Young Woman	Sick
		or			
		B I, 21	Daughter of Ralph of Bourne	Girl	Sick
s VI–14, 15	2	B IV, 95	Gilbert, son of William le Brun	Boy	Dead
s VI–16	1+	W IV, 32?	Warin (same as s VI–8?)	3 yrs.	Dead
s VII–1–6	6	W II, 45 B IV, 88	Geoffrey of Winchester	16 mos. & Child	Fever & buried in house
s VII–7–8	2–4/6	W II, 68 B IV, 94	James, son of Earl of Clare	Infant Child	Hernia Dead
s VII–10	1+	B III, 8?	Eilwin of Berkhamstead	Mature Man	Crippled
s VII–12	1+	B IV, 72 (W VI, 8)	Elias, monk of Reading	Mature Man	Leprosy
s VII–13–16	7	W III, 1 (B VI, 1)	William of Gloucester	Mature Man	Buried by fallen earth
s VII–22	1+	—	—	Woman	—

Appendix Figure 7. Chronology and Authorship of Canterbury Windows

	Choir aisle & clerestory	Sts. Dunstan & Alphage series	N.E. transept lower	N. oculus	Clerestory: Transepts & Presbytery	Clerestory: Trinity Chapel	Trinity Chapel ambulatory	Corona
	1174 fire in east end of cathedral							
1175	Rebuilding from west end of choir by William of Sens							
	Methuselah Master	Fogg Master & M. of Parable of Sower	nXIII Public Life nXI Sower	M. of Parable of Sower & Jesse Master	Joanna & Fogg Masters et al 1178 William of Sens fell, replaced by English William 1179			
1180	Entry into the choir at Easter — construction closed off by a partition						Becket windows planned	
1185						first two bays, north side: Petronella Master (N X) Jesse Master (N IX)	1184 building essentially complete	
1190							Fogg Medallion Master (n V, VI)	Master of Redemption (I) and others including Fitz-Eisulf Master
1195							Petronella Master (n IV)	
1200						others designed by Fogg Medallion Master Last Judgment for axial window (I)	designs by ? Master of Parable of Sower (s VI, VII)	Jesse Master
1205								
1207 Exile of Monks								
1210		Interdict						
1213 return								
1215						Petronella Master (N V) Fitz-Eisulf Master (N IV) & others	Petronella M. & Fitz-E. M (n III) Fitz-E. (n II, s II)	
1220							vaults painted	
1221 funds diverted to "new work"							translation of Becket July 7th	

NOTE ON APPENDIX FIGURES 8–19.

THE reconstructions of the "twelve" Canterbury typological windows are based on a re-examination of the medieval records, and consideration of the original window armatures. James's numbering has been used for the subjects, although they are not numbered in the texts. Some modifications to his suggested lay-out have been necessary, as in the case of subjects which were erroneously included in Window Eight in the fourteenth century roll, and which he removed to IX, 22–30; these have been found to fit in the Tenth Window. Problems concerning the contents of the Ninth Window have been discussed in Chapter VII. In the Twelfth Window only twelve couplets were supplied for the types, and some of the subjects separated by James are linked together by the fourteenth century scribe; hence I envisage 8 & 9, 10 & 11, 16 & 17, and 18 & 19 paired within a single frame.

Throughout the following charts subjects in CAPITALS are extant, whether *in situ* or not; subjects in italics have been lost, but had been identified in the records.

The reconstruction drawings in figs. 8–21 were generously made by B. C. Doughty, from measured charts of the armatures.

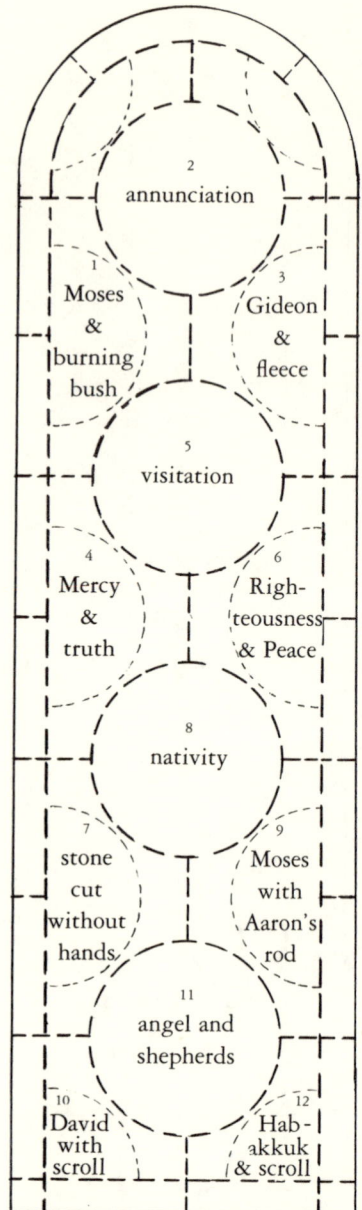

Appendix fig. 8. Conjectural reconstruction of First Typological Window (n: XVI, blocked).

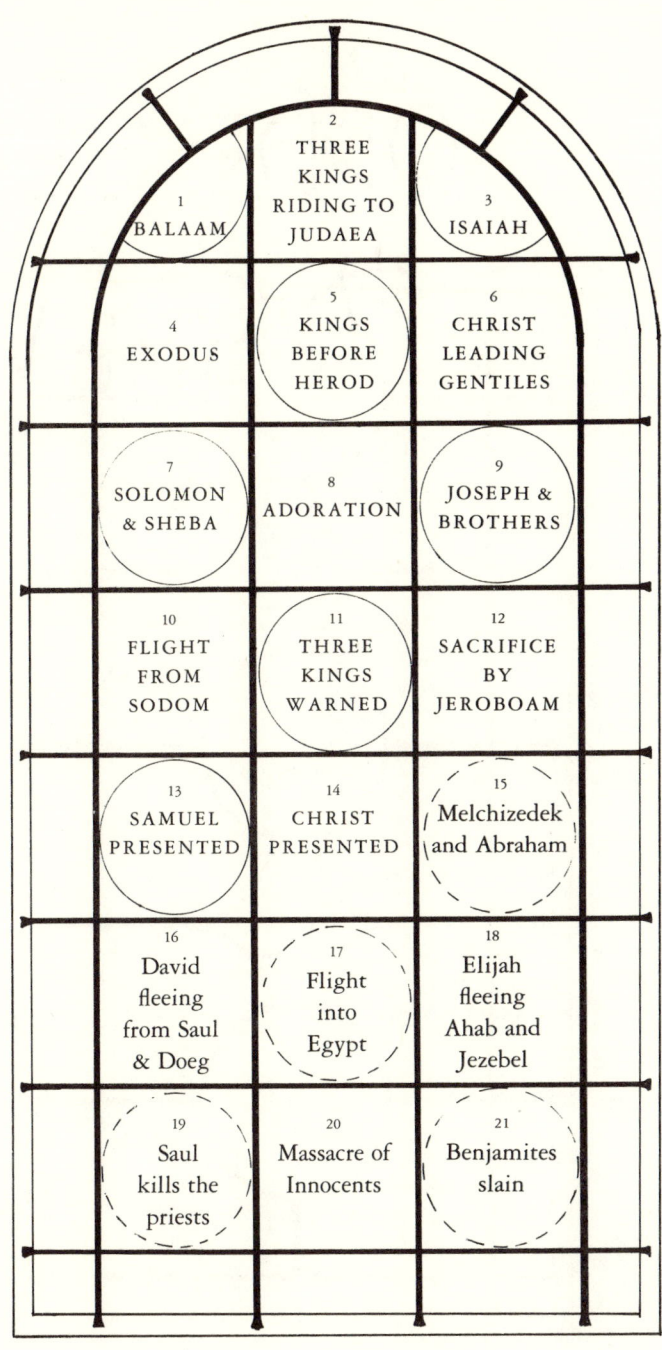

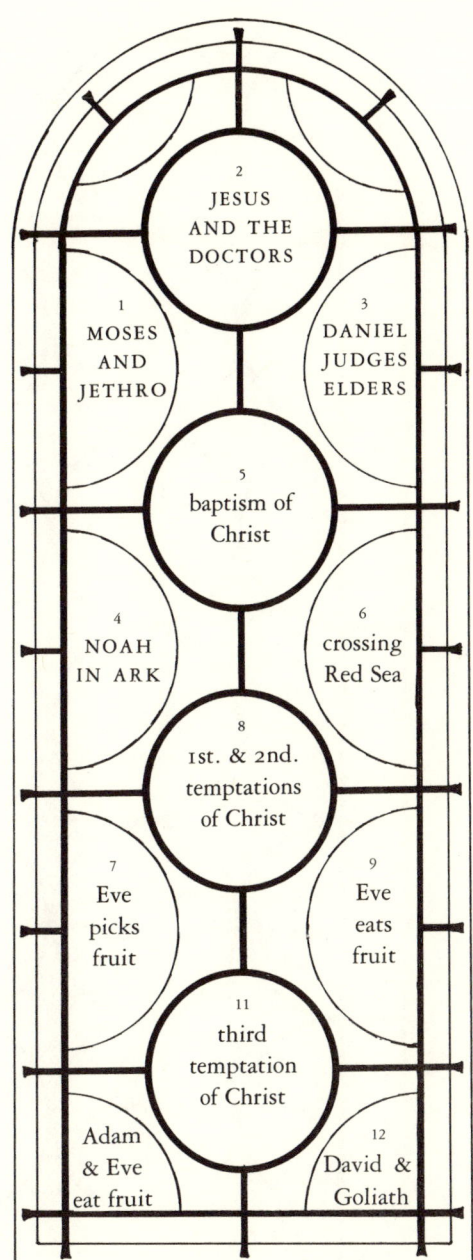

Appendix fig. 9. Reconstruction of
Second Typological Window (n:XV).

Appendix fig. 10. Reconstruction of
Third Typological Window (n:XIV)

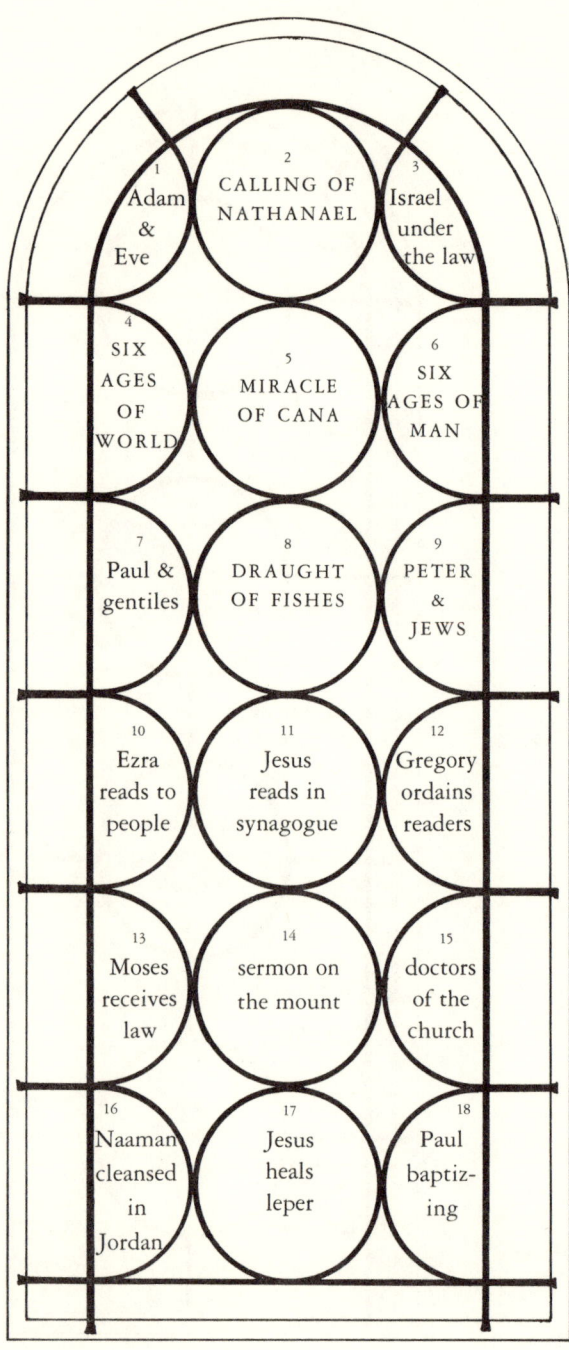

Appendix fig. 11. Reconstruction of Fourth Typological Window (n: XIII).

Fourth Typological Window (n: XIII) circle labels:

1. Adam & Eve
2. CALLING OF NATHANAEL
3. Israel under the law
4. SIX AGES OF WORLD
5. MIRACLE OF CANA
6. SIX AGES OF MAN
7. Paul & gentiles
8. DRAUGHT OF FISHES
9. PETER & JEWS
10. Ezra reads to people
11. Jesus reads in synagogue
12. Gregory ordains readers
13. Moses receives law
14. sermon on the mount
15. doctors of the church
16. Naaman cleansed in Jordan
17. Jesus heals leper
18. Paul baptizing

Appendix fig. 12. Reconstruction of Fifth Typological Window (n: XII).

Fifth Typological Window (n: XII) circle labels:

2a. Jesus casts out devil
1. Angel casts . . .
2b. Magdalene washes feet of Jesus
1b. . . . out devil
3. Drusiana feeds the poor
3. Drusiana clothes the poor
5. Jesus with Mary and Martha
6. Jacob with Leah & Rachel
8. Jesus & apostles gather corn
4. Peter fishing, John reading
9. Peter & Paul with the people
11. Jesus & woman of Samaria
7. apostles making bread
13. Synagogue & Moses
14. Samaritans brought to Jesus
10. Jacob & Rachel at the well
15. Gentile church comes to Christ
12. Rebekah & Eliezer

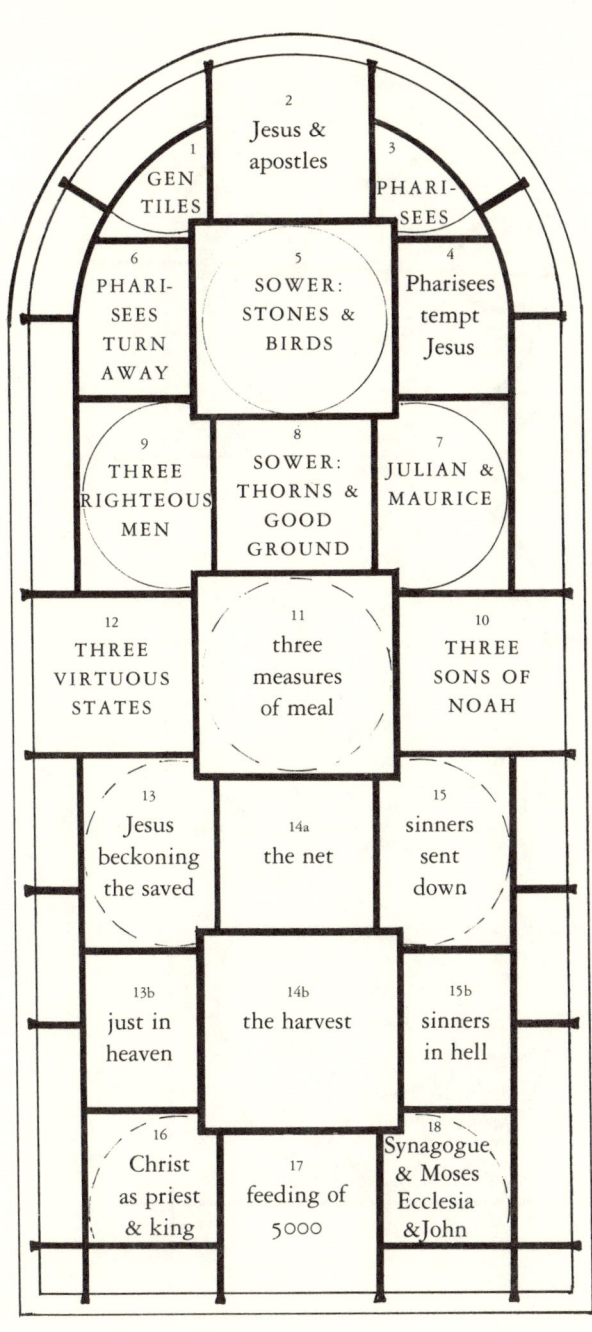

Appendix fig. 13. Reconstruction of
Sixth Typological Window (n: XI).

Appendix fig. 14. Reconstruction of
Seventh Typological Window (n: VIII).

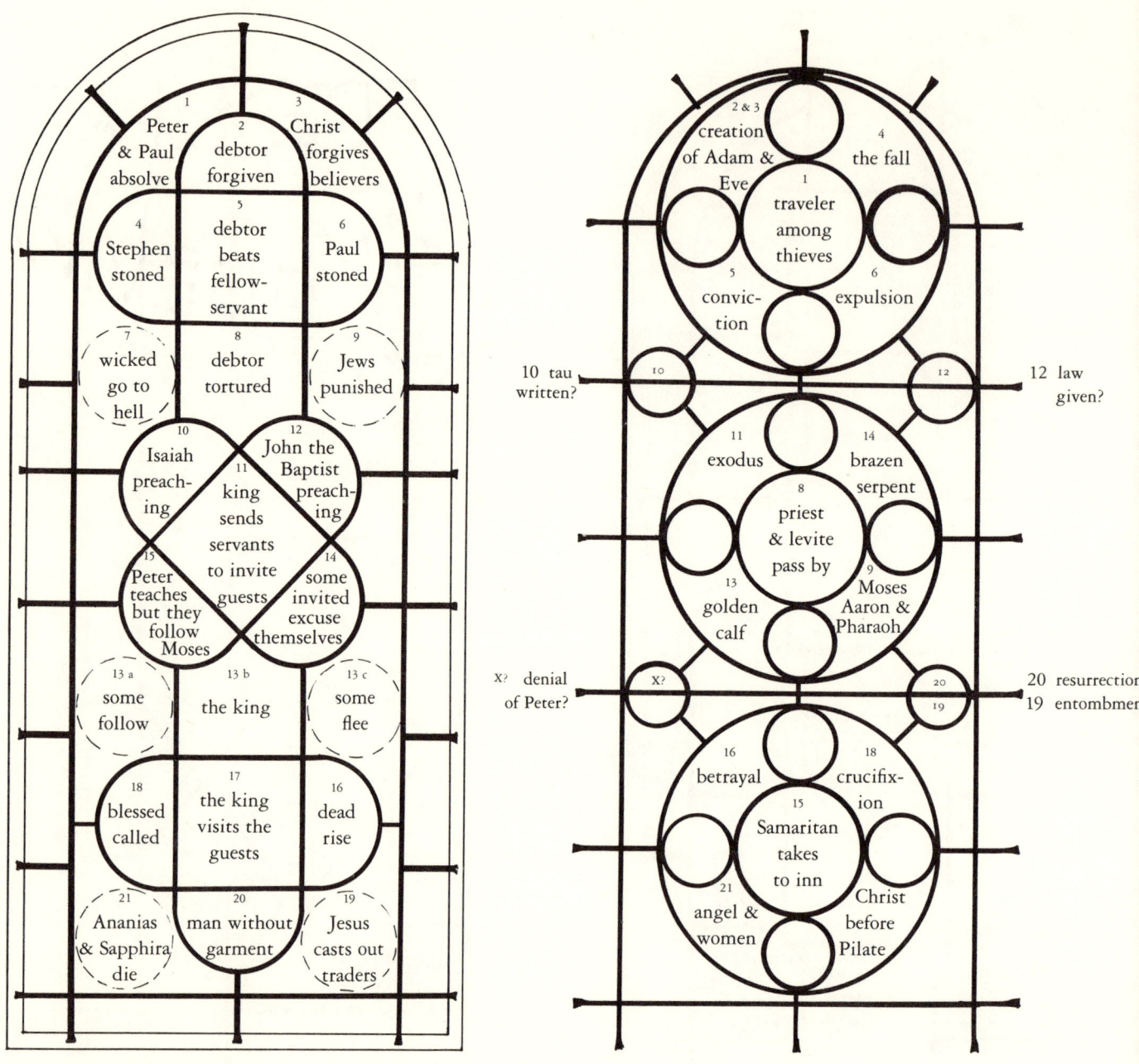

Appendix fig. 15. Reconstruction of
Eighth Typological Window (s: VIII).

Appendix fig. 16. Reconstruction of
Ninth Typological Window (s: XI).

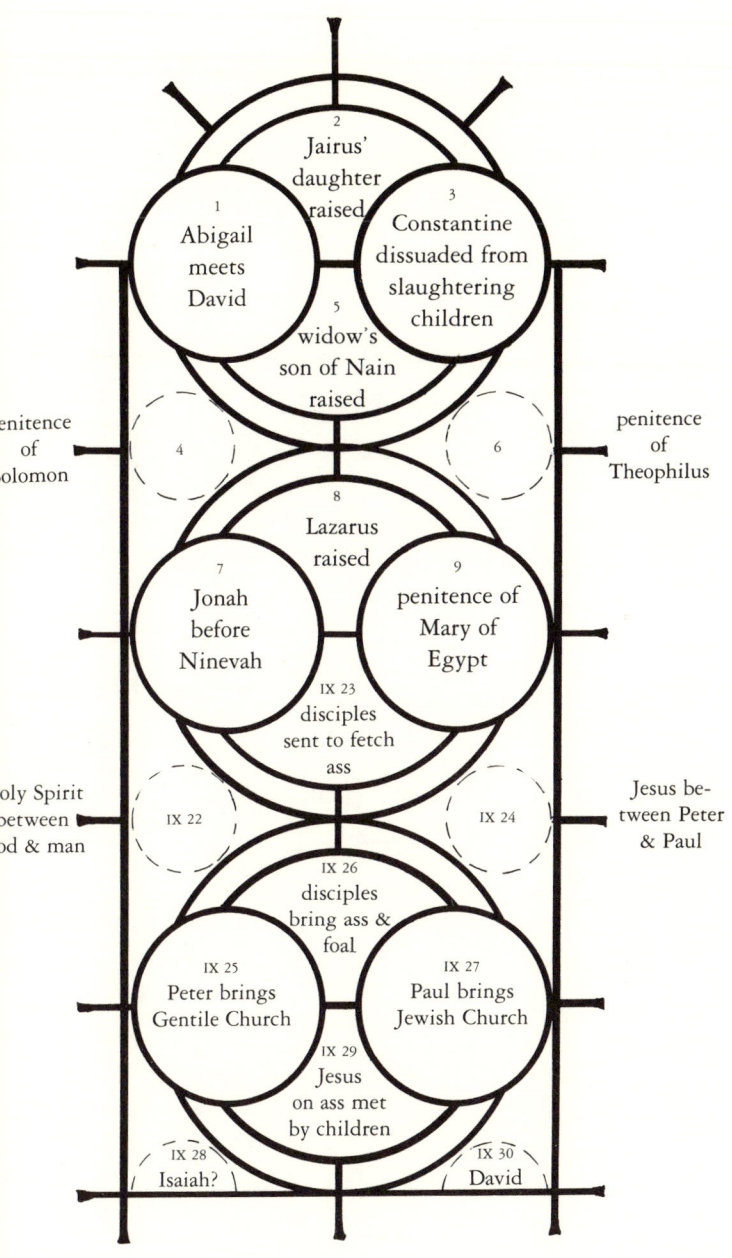

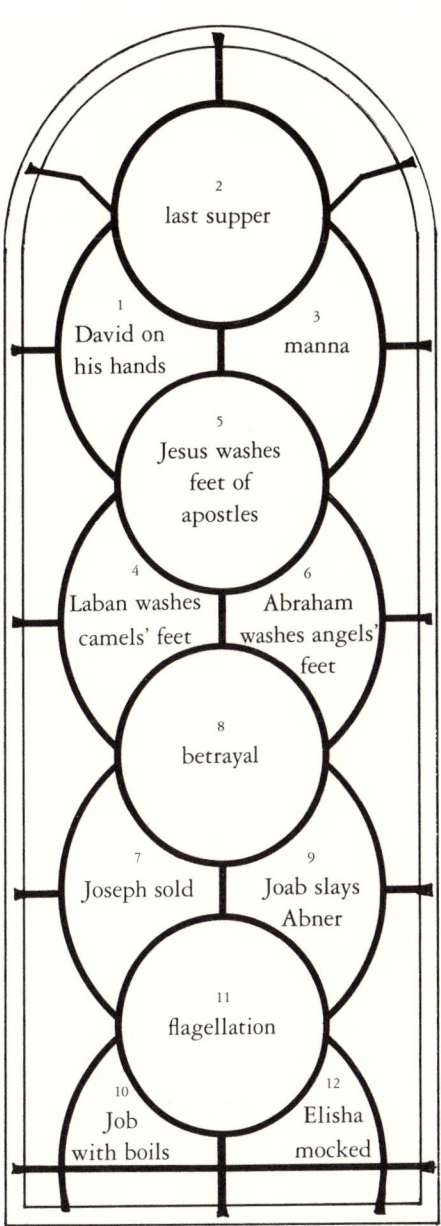

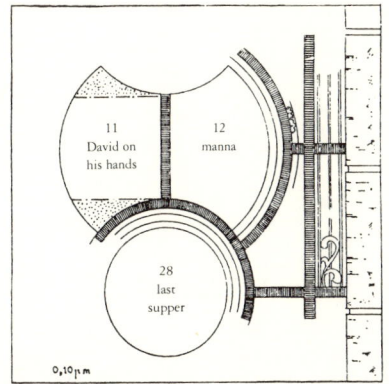

Within fig. 17 (left window):

2 Jairus' daughter raised

1 Abigail meets David

3 Constantine dissuaded from slaughtering children

5 widow's son of Nain raised

penitence of Solomon

4

6

penitence of Theophilus

8 Lazarus raised

7 Jonah before Ninevah

9 penitence of Mary of Egypt

IX 23 disciples sent to fetch ass

Holy Spirit between God & man

IX 22

IX 24

Jesus between Peter & Paul

IX 26 disciples bring ass & foal

IX 25 Peter brings Gentile Church

IX 27 Paul brings Jewish Church

IX 29 Jesus on ass met by children

IX 28 Isaiah?

IX 30 David

Appendix fig. 17. Reconstruction of Tenth Typological Window, with part of the Ninth (s: XII).

Within fig. 18a (right window):

2 last supper

1 David on his hands

3 manna

5 Jesus washes feet of apostles

4 Laban washes camels' feet

6 Abraham washes angels' feet

8 betrayal

7 Joseph sold

9 Joab slays Abner

11 flagellation

10 Job with boils

12 Elisha mocked

Appendix fig. 18a. Reconstruction of Eleventh Typological Window (s: XIV).

Within fig. 18b:

11 David on his hands

12 manna

28 last supper

0,10 m

Appendix fig. 18b. Lincoln Cathedral: Tentative Reconstruction of one of the Typological Windows (after Lafond).

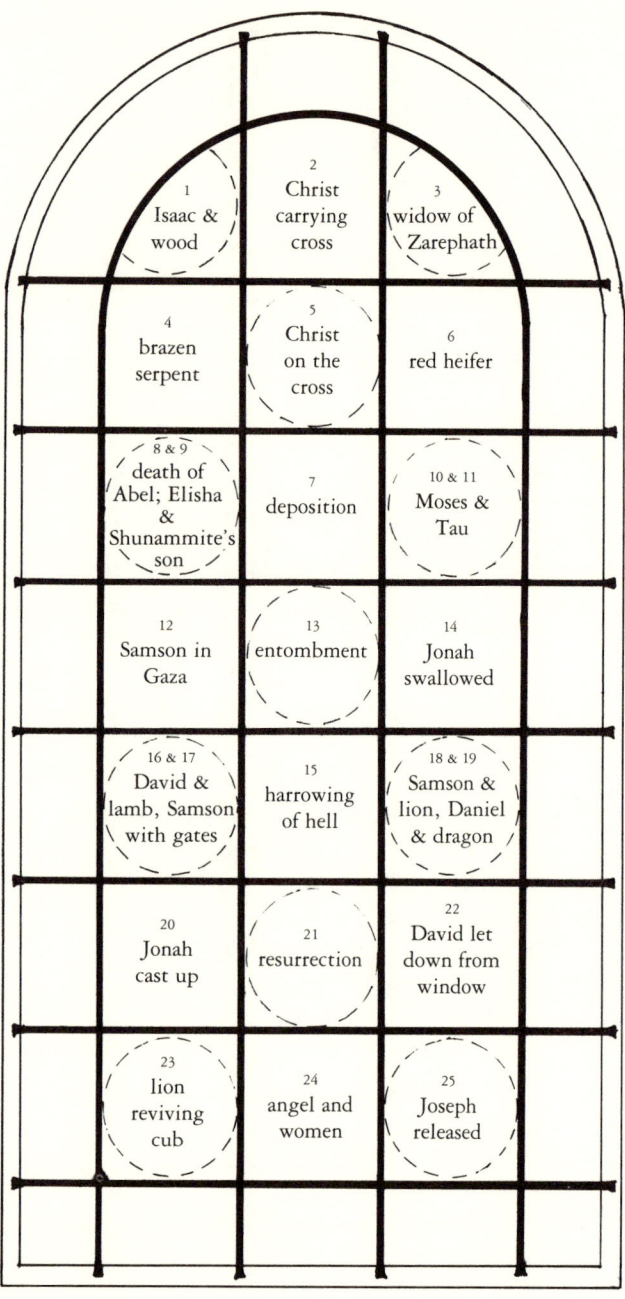

Appendix fig. 19. Reconstruction of Twelfth Typological Window (s: XV).

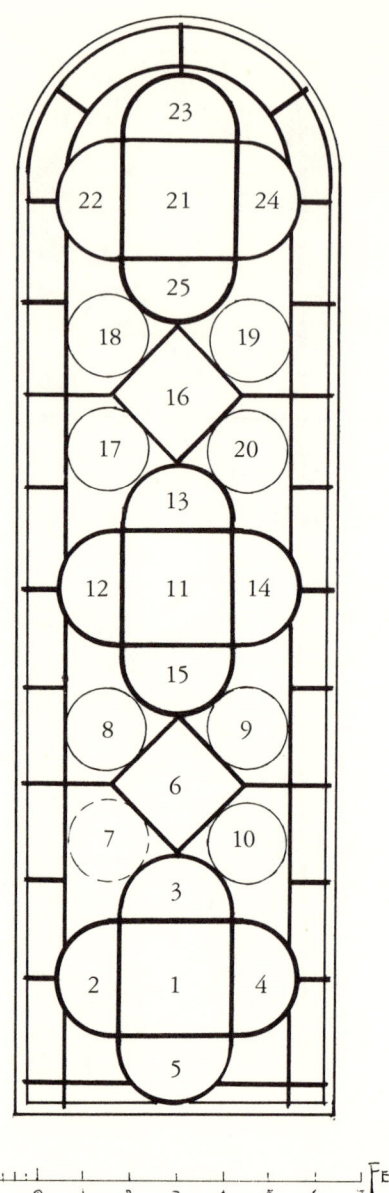

Appendix fig. 20. "Thirteenth" Typological Window, (corona east window, I).

23 MAJESTY
22 CONSECRATION OF AARON
     & HIS SONS
21 PENTECOST
24 MOSES AND JETHRO
25 MOSES RECEIVING THE LAW

18 ASCENSION OF ELIJAH
19 SUNDIAL OF HEZEKIAH
16 ASCENSION
17 HIGH PRIEST ENTERING
     HOLY OF HOLIES
20 ASCENT OF ENOCH

13 JONAH CAST UP
12 NOAH IN ARK
11 resurrection
14 ?Michal and David
15 MOSES & THE BURNING BUSH

8 SAMSON & DELILAH
9 JONAH SWALLOWED
6 ENTOMBMENT
7 Joseph in the pit
10 DANIEL IN BABYLON

3 SACRIFICE OF ISAAC
2 MOSES STRIKING THE ROCK
1 crucifixion
5 GRAPES OF ESHCOL
4 SIGNUM TAU

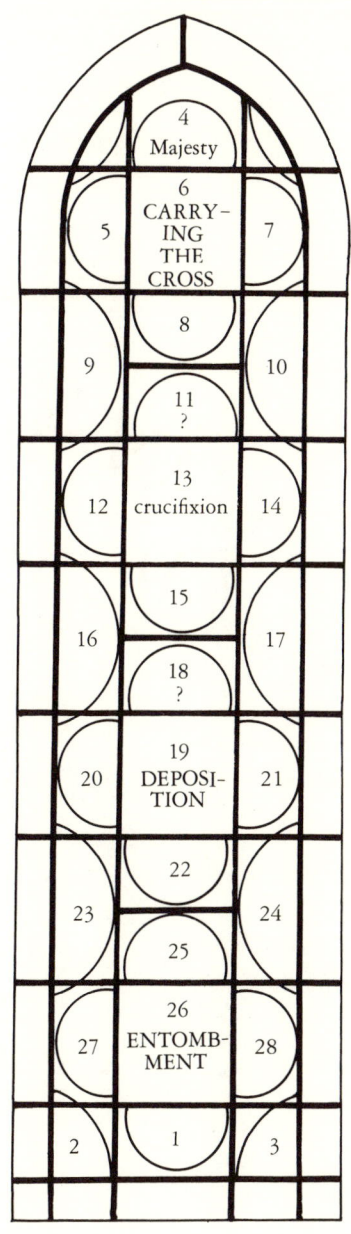

4 Majesty

5, 6, 7 CARRYING THE CROSS

8 grapes of Eshcol
9 CROWNING WITH THORNS
10 SCOURGING
11 ?

12 ECCLESIA
13 crucifixion
14 SYNAGOGUE

15 blood (of Christ) caught in a chalice
16 BRAZEN SERPENT
17 SIGNUM TAU
18 ?

19 DEPOSITION
20 ISAAC CARRYING WOOD
21 SACRIFICE OF ISAAC

22 PELICAN IN HER PIETY
23 ELISHA AND THE SHUNAMMITE'S
     SON
24 WIDOW OF ZAREPHATH
25 BENEDICTION OF JACOB

26 ENTOMBMENT
27 SAMSON AND THE GATES OF
     GAZA
28 DAVID AND THE LION

1-3 DONORS

Appendix fig. 21. Chartres Typological
Redemption Window (LIX).

The following table gives the number previously assigned to each window, when this was customary, and the new number assigned in accordance with the usage for the *Corpus Vitrearum Medii Aevi*.

APPENDIX FIGURE 22. CONCORDANCE OF
WINDOW NUMBERS

CLERESTORY		36	S:XII
Gostling	CVMA	37	S:XIII
1	N:XXV	38	S:XIV
2	N:XXIV	39	S:XV
3	N:XXIII	40	S:XVI
4	N:XXII	41	S:XVII
5	N:XXI	42	S:XVIII
6	N:XX	43	S:XIX
7	N:XIX	44	S:XX
8	N:XVIII	45	S:XXI
9	N:XVII	46	S:XXII
10	N:XVI	47	S:XXIII
11	N:XV	48	S:XXIV
12	N:XIV	49	S:XXV
13	N:XIII		
14	N:XII	LOWER WINDOWS	
15	N:XI	*North choir aisle*	
16	N:X	Rackham	CVMA
17	N:IX	I	n:XVI
18	N:VIII	II	n:XV
19	N:VII	III	n:XIV
20	N:VI		
21	N:V		
22	N:IV	*Trinity Chapel*	
23	N:III	Rackham	CVMA
24	N:II	I	n:VII
25	I	II	n:VI
26	S:II	III	n:V
27	S:III	IV	n:IV
28	S:IV	V	n:III
29	S:V	VI	n:II
30	S:VI	VII	s:II
31	S:VII	VIII	s:III
32	S:VIII	IX	s:IV
33	S:IX	X	s:V
34	S:X	XI	s:VI
35	S:XI	XII	s:VII

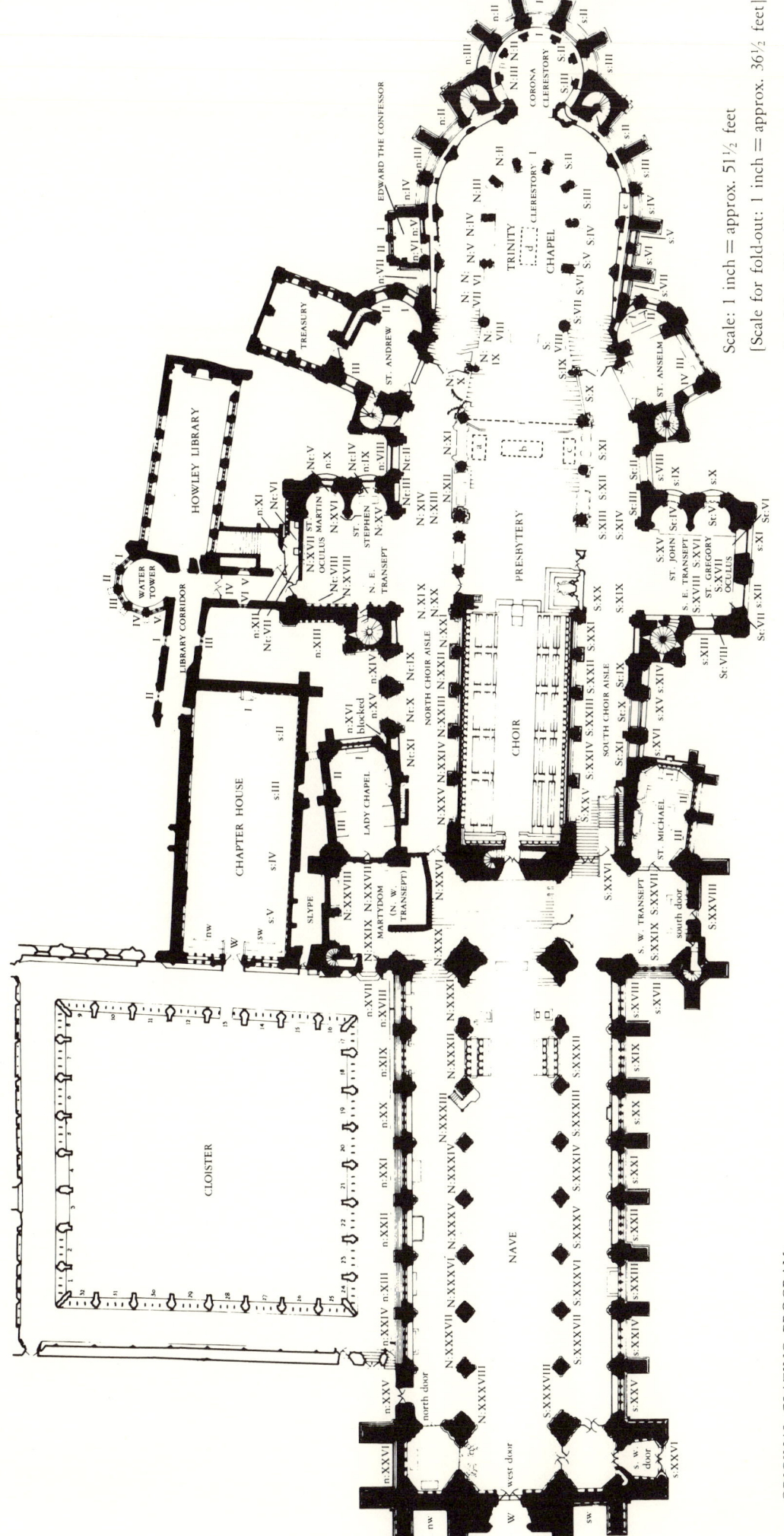

ORIGINAL GLAZING PROGRAM:

Genealogical windows — Clerestory choir N:XXV through Trinity Chapel N:III,
and S:III through S:XXV, except N: & S:XVII and
possibly S:XVIII

Typological windows — n:XVI through n:XI, n:VIII, s:VIII, s:XI, s:XII,
s:XIV, s:XV

Becket windows — Trinity Chapel n:VII through n:II, s:II through s:VII

Scale: 1 inch = approx. 51½ feet

[Scale for fold-out: 1 inch = approx. 36½ feet]

a   site of altar of St. Alphage
b   former site of high altar
c   site of altar of St. Dunstan
d   site of Becket's shrine after 1220
e   tomb of Hubert Walter
f   position of temporary partition put up in 1180

Plan of Canterbury Cathedral

Bibliography

ABBREVIATED TITLES USED IN REFERENCES

C.C.C. Canterbury Cathedral Chronicle, published by the Friends of Canterbury Cathedral.

Corpus, France I. *Corpus Vitrearum Medii Aevi, France* I. Marcel Aubert, Louis Grodecki, Jean Lafond, and Jean Verrier, *Les Vitraux de Notre-Dame et de la Sainte Chapelle de Paris.* Paris, 1959.

Corpus, France IV. *Corpus Vitrearum Medii Aevi, France* IV-2/I. Jean Lafond, *Les Vitraux de l'église Saint-Ouen de Rouen.* Paris, 1970.

Corpus, Scandinavia I. *Corpus Vitrearum Medii Aevi, Scandinavia* I. Aaron Anderson, Sigrid Christie, Carl Axel Nordman, and Aage Roussell, *Die Glasmalereien des Mittelalters in Skandinavien.* Stockholm, 1964.

Corpus, Switzerland I. *Corpus Vitrearum Medii Aevi, Schweitz* I. Ellen J. Beer, *Die Glasmalereien der Schweitz vom 12. bis zum Begin des 14. Jahrhunderts.* Basel, 1956.

Golden Legend. Granger Ryan and Helmut Ripperger, *The Golden Legend of Jacobus de Voragine Translated and Adapted from the Latin.* 2 vols., London, 1941.

Medieval Art. The Metropolitan Museum of Art, *Medieval Art from Private Collections—A Special Exhibition at the Cloisters October 30, 1968 through March 5, 1969.* New York, 1968. Introduction and catalogue by Carmen Gomez-Moreno.

P.L. J. P. Migne, ed. *Patrologiae cursus completus* [Latin]. Paris, 1844–64.

Psautier. Bibliothèque Nationale, Paris, Département des Manuscrits, *Psautier illustré (XIII siècle), Reproduction des 107 miniatures du manuscrit latin 8846.* Paris [1906]. Preface by H[enri] O[mont].

Vitrail. Musée des Arts Décoratifs de Paris, *Le Vitrail français.* Paris, 1958. Text by Marcel Aubert, André Chastel, Louis Grodecki, Jean-Jacques Gruber, Jean Lafond, François Mathey, Jean Taralon, and Jean Verrier.

Williams Coll. Canterbury Cathedral Library, Emily Williams Collection. Tracings and drawings made for Emily Williams before 1897.

The Year 1200 I. The Metropolitan Museum of Art, *The Year 1200: A Centennial Exhibition at the Metropolitan Museum of Art, I, Catalogue* (The Cloisters Studies in Medieval Art I). New York, 1970. Catalogue by Konrad Hoffmann.

The Year 1200 II. The Metropolitan Museum of Art, *The Year 1200: Background Survey* (The Cloisters Studies in Medieval Art II). New York, 1970. Edited by Florens Deuchler.

The Year 1200 III. The Metropolitan Museum of Art, *The Year 1200: A Symposium*, texts by François Avril, Rüdiger Becksmann et al., New York, 1975.

WORKS CITED

Ahnne, Paul, and Beyer, Victor, 1960. *Les Vitraux de la cathédrale de Strasbourg*. Strasbourg.

Arnold, Hugh, and Saint, Lawrence B., 1939. *Stained Glass of the Middle Ages in England and France*. London, (1st ed. 1913).

Austin, George, Sr., 1849. Obituary in *The Gentleman's Magazine* 185, N.S. 31 (June 1849), 659–60.

Ayres, L. M., 1969. "A Tanner Manuscript in the Bodleian Library and Some Notes on English Painting of the Late Twelfth Century," *Journal of the Warburg and Courtauld Institutes*, 31, 41–54.

———, 1970. "Studies in the Winchester Bible." Ph.D. dissertation, Harvard University.

———, 1974. "The Work of the Morgan Master at Winchester and English Painting of the Early Gothic Period," *Art Bulletin* 56, 201–23.

Baker, John, and Lammer, Alfred, 1960. *English Stained Glass*. New York.

Barnes, Patricia M., and Powell, Raymond, eds., 1960. *Interdict Documents* (Pipe Roll Society N.S. 34). London.

Beer, Ellen J., 1952. *Die Rose der Kathedrale von Lausanne und der kosmologische Bilderkreis des Mittelalters* (Berner Schriften zur Kunst). Edited by Hans Hahnloser. Berne.

Benedict of Peterborough, 1876. "Miracula Sancti Thomae Cantuariensis, auctore Benedicto, Abbate Petriburgensi," in James Craigie Robertson, ed., *Materials for the History of Thomas Becket* (Rolls Series No. 67). London, II, 21–298.

Boase, T.S.R., 1953. *English Art 1100–1216*. Oxford.

Bony, Jean, 1949. "French Influence on the Origins of English Gothic Architecture," *Journal of the Warburg and Courtauld Institutes* 12, 1–15.

———, 1957–1958. "The Resistance to Chartres in Early Thirteenth Century Architecture," *Journal of the British Archaeological Association*, 3rd ser. 20–21, 35–52.

Borenius, Tancred, 1932. *St. Thomas Becket in Art*. London.

Brieger, Peter, 1957. *English Art 1216–1307*. Oxford.

Britton, John, 1836. *Historical and Descriptive Account of the Metropolitan Cathedrals of Canterbury and York* (*The Cathedral Antiquities*, I). London.

Cahier and Martin, les Pères, 1841. *Monographie de la Cathédrale de Bourges*. 2 vols., Paris.

Caldwell, Samuel, Jr., 1951. "Memories of a Craftsman," *24th Annual Report of the Friends of Canterbury Cathedral*, pp. 22–23.

Cave, C.J.P., 1934. "The Roof-bosses in Canterbury Cathedral," *Archaeologia* 84, 41–61.

Caviness, Madeline Harrison, 1965. "A Panel of Thirteenth Century Stained Glass from Canterbury in America," *Antiquaries Journal* 45, 192–99.

———, 1967. *Catalogue of the Stained Glass of the Trinity Chapel, Corona and North Choir Aisle Triforium Windows of Canterbury Cathedral* (Transcripts in the Victoria and Albert Museum, Dept. of Ceramics and in Canterbury Cathedral Library).

———, 1970. "The Stained Glass of the Trinity Chapel Ambulatory of Canterbury Cathedral." Ph.D. dissertation, Harvard University.

———, 1973. "Canterbury Stained Glass," *Arts in Virginia* 13, 4–15.

———, 1974. "A Lost Cycle of Canterbury Paintings of 1220," *Antiquaries Journal* 54:1, 66–74.

———, 1975. "The Canterbury Jesse Window," *The Year 1200* III, 373–98.

Clayton and Bell, 1895. *Album of Water-colours* II, in the Victoria and Albert Museum, London, Dept. of Prints, 94. J. 34.

Cox, Lady Trenchard [Mary Désirée Anderson], 1959. "The Twelfth-Century Design Sources of the Worcester Cathedral Misericords," *Archaeologia* 79, 165–78.

Culmer, Richard, ca. 1643. "Cathedral Newes from Canterbury" reprinted by G. S[mith], *Chronological History of Canterbury Cathedral*. Canterbury, 1883, pp. 310–11.

Day, Lewis F., 1913. *Stained Glass* (Victoria and Albert Museum Handbooks). London.

Delaporte, Yves, and Houvet, Emile, 1926. *Les Vitraux de la cathédrale de Chartres*. 4 vols., Chartres.

Demus, Otto, 1949. *The Mosaics of Norman Sicily*. London.

Demus, Otto, and Hirmer, Max, 1970. *Romanesque Mural Painting*. New York.

Deuchler, Florens, 1967. *Der Ingeborgpsalter*. Berlin.

Dodwell, Christopher R., 1954. *The Canterbury School of Illumination*. Cambridge.

Dudley, Colin, 1969. "Sacred Geometry," *Canterbury Cathedral Chronicle* 64, 17–32.

Evelyn, John, 1955–1959. *The Diary of John Evelyn*. Edited by E. S. de Beer. 6 vols., London.

Evetts, L. C., 1941. "Genealogical Windows at Canterbury Cathedral," *Burlington Magazine* 78, 95–98, 112–18.

Fleury, Edouard, 1882. *Antiquités et monuments du département de l'Aisne*. Vol. IV, Paris.

Foreville, Raymonde, 1958. *Le Jubilé de saint Thomas Becket du XIIIᵉ au XVᵉ siècle (1220–1470): Etude et documents*. Paris.

Frankl, Paul, 1963. "The Chronology of the Stained Glass in Chartres Cathedral," *Art Bulletin* 45, 301–22.

Frodl-Kraft, Eva, 1970. *Die Glasmalerei: Entwicklung, Technik, Eigenart*. Vienna and Munich.

Gervase (Gervasius), 1879. *Tractatus de Combustione et Reparatione Cantuariensis Ecclesiae*, ed. in full, *Gervasii Cantuariensis Opera Historica* (Rolls Series 73). Edited by W. Stubbs. I, London, pp. 3–29; English translations in R. Willis. *Architectural History of Canterbury Cathedral*. London, 1845, pp. 36–62; and in Charles Cotton. *Of the Burning and Repair of the Church of Canterbury in the Year 1174*. Canterbury, 1930, pp. 6–24 (incomplete).

———, 1880. *Actus Pontificum*, in *Gervasii Cantuariensis Opera Historica* (Rolls Series 73). Edited by W. Stubbs. II, London.

Gilbert, Sir John, 1842. *Fragments towards the History of Stained Glass and the Sister Arts of the Middle Ages*. London.

Giles, John Allen, ed., 1845. *Vita Sancti Thomae*. II, London.

Glunz, H. H., 1933. *The History of the Vulgate in England from Alcuin to Roger Bacon*. Cambridge.

Goldschmidt, Adolph, 1926. *Die Elfenbeinskulpturen aus der Romanischen Zeit, XI–XIII. Jahrhundert*. IV, Berlin.

Gostling, William, 1744. *A Walk in and about the City of Canterbury*. Canterbury; 2nd ed., 1777.

Gough Nichols, John, 1875. *Desiderius Erasmus: Pilgrimages to Saint Mary of Walsingham and Saint Thomas of Canterbury*. 2nd ed., Westminster.

Grabar, André, and Nordenfalk, Carl, 1958. *The Great Centuries of Painting: Romanesque Painting from the Eleventh to the Thirteenth Century*. Geneva.

Gransden, Antonia, 1972. "Realistic Observation in Twelfth Century England," *Speculum* 47, 29–51.

Grodecki, Louis, 1948. "A Stained Glass Atelier of the Thirteenth Century," *Journal of the Warburg and Courtauld Institutes* 11, pp. 87–110.

———, 1950. "The Ancient Glass of Canterbury Cathedral," *Burlington Magazine* 92, 294–97.

———, 1951. "The Ancient Glass of Canterbury Cathedral," *Burlington Magazine* 93, 94.

———, 1955. "Les Problèmes de la peinture gothique," *Critique* 98 (July 1955), 610–24.

———, 1961a. "Les Vitraux allégoriques de Saint-Denis," *Art de France* 1, 19–46.

———, 1961b. "Les Vitraux de Saint-Denis: L'Enfance du Christ," *De Artibus Opuscula* (XL *Essays in Honor of Erwin Panofsky*). Edited by Millard Meiss. New York, pp. 170–86.

———, 1963. "Problèmes de la peinture en Champagne pendant la seconde moitié du douzième siècle," in *Romanesque and Gothic Art; Studies in Western Art* (Acts of the Twentieth International Congress of the History of Art, 1). Princeton, pp. 129–41.

———, 1965. "Le Maître de Saint Eustache de la cathédrale de Chartres," in *Gedenkschrift Ernst Gall*. Edited by Margarete Kuhn and Louis Grodecki. Munich, pp. 171–94.

———, 1973. "Nouvelles découvertes sur les vitraux de la cathédrale de Troyes," in *Intuition und Kunstwissenschaft: Festschrift für Hanns Swarzenski*. Edited by Peter Bloch, Tilmann Buddensieg, Alfred Hentzen, and Theodor Müller. Berlin, pp. 191–203.

———, 1975. "Les Plus Anciens Vitraux de Saint-Remi de Reims," *Beiträge zur Kunst des Mittelalters: Festschrift für Hans Wentzel*, Berlin, pp. 65–77.

———, 1976. *Les vitraux de Saint-Denis: Etude sur le vitrail au XIIᵉ siècle*. I, Paris.

Haskins, C. H., 1927. *The Renaissance of the Twelfth Century*. Cambridge, Mass.

Hasted, Edward, 1797–1801. *The History and Topographical Survey of the County of Kent*. 2nd ed., 12 vols., Canterbury.

Hayward, Jane, and Grodecki, Louis, 1966. "Les Vitraux de la cathédrale d'Angers," *Bulletin Monumental* 124 (1966), 7–67.

Heaton, Clement, 1907. "The Origin of the Early Stained Glass in Canterbury Cathedral," *Burlington Magazine* 11, 172–76.

Heimann, Adelheid, 1965. "A Twelfth-Century Manuscript from Winchcombe and Its Illustrations: Dublin, Trinity College, MS 53," *Journal of the Warburg and Courtauld Institutes* 28, 86–109.

Henderson, G., 1963. "The Sources of the Genesis Cycle at Saint-Savin-sur-Gartrempe [sic]," *Journal of the British Archaeological Association* 26, 11–26.

Hollaender, A., 1942–1944. "The Sarum Illuminator and His School," *Wiltshire Archaeological and Natural History Magazine* I, 230–62.

Homburger, Otto, 1958. "Zur Stilbestimmung der Figurlichen Kunst Deutschlands und des Westlichen Europas in Zeitraum zwischen 1190 und 1250," in *Formositas Romanica*. Edited by J. Gantner. Frauenfeldt, pp. 31–45.

Hudson, O., 1848. Water-color Tracings in the Victoria and Albert Museum, Dept. of Prints, Nos. 4154. 1–17.

James, Montague Rhodes, 1897. "On the Paintings Formerly in the Choir at Peterborough," *Proceedings of the Cambridge Antiquarian Society* 9, 178–94.

———, 1901. *The Verses Formerly Inscribed on Twelve Windows in the Choir of Canterbury Cathedral* (Cambridge Antiquarian Society Octavo Publication No. 38). Cambridge.

———, 1903. *The Ancient Libraries of Canterbury and Dover: the Catalogue of the Libraries of Christ Church Priory and St. Augustine's Abbey at Canterbury and of St. Martin's Priory at Dover.* Cambridge.

———, 1936–1937. "Four Leaves of an English Twelfth Century Psalter," *Walpole Society* 25, 1–23, pls. i–viii.

———, 1951, "Pictor in Carmine," *Archaeologia* 94, 141–66.

Johnson, James Rosser, 1965. *The Radiance of Chartres.* New York.

Joyce, J. G., 1841. *Specimens of the Ancient Stained Glass in Canterbury Cathedral Drawn for Thomas Willement.* Victoria and Albert Museum, London, Dept. of Prints, 93.H.29.

Katzenellenbogen, Adolf, 1964. *The Sculptural Programs of Chartres Cathedral: Christ-Mary-Ecclesia.* New York; first ed., Baltimore, 1959.

Kitzinger, Ernst, 1960. *The Mosaics of Monreale.* Palermo.

———, 1966a. "The Byzantine Contribution to Western Art of the Twelfth and Thirteenth Centuries," *Dumbarton Oaks Papers* 20, 25–47.

———, 1966b. "Norman Sicily as a Source of Byzantine Influence on Western Art in the Twelfth Century," *Byzantine Art—An European Art.* Edited by Department of Antiquities and Archaeological Restoration, Office of the Minister to the Prime Minister, Athens, pp. 121–46.

Knowles, David, 1951. *The Episcopal Colleagues of Archbishop Thomas Becket.* Cambridge.

Knowles, David; Brooke, C.N.L.; and London, Vera, 1972. *The Heads of Religious Houses: England and Wales 940–1216.* Cambridge.

Lafond, Jean, 1946. "The Stained Glass of Lincoln Cathedral in the Thirteenth Century," *Archaeological Journal* 103, 119–56.

———, 1955. "Les Vitraux de la cathédrale Saint-Pierre de Troyes," *Congrès archéologique de France* 113, 29–48.

Loftie, W. J., 1876. "Early Glass in Canterbury Cathedral," *Archaeological Journal* 33, 1–14.

Mâle, Emile, 1953. *L'Art religieux du XIIe siècle en France.* 6th ed., Paris.

———, 1958. *L'Art religieux du XIIIe siècle en France.* 9th ed., Paris.

Martène, Edmond, and Durand, Ursin, eds., 1717. *Thesaurus Novus Anecdotorum* III. Paris.

Mason, A. J., 1925. *Guide to the Ancient Glass of Canterbury Cathedral.* Canterbury.

———, 1920. *What Became of the Bones of St. Thomas?* Cambridge.

Matthaei Parisiensis Monachi Sancti Albani, 1866. *Historia Anglorum sive Historia Minor.* Edited by Frederic Madden. Vol. 2, London.

Nelson, Philip, 1913. *Ancient Painted Glass in England, 1170–1500.* London.

Oakeshott, Walter, 1945. *The Artists of the Winchester Bible.* London.

———, 1951. "*The Ancient Glass of Canterbury* by Bernard Rackham," review in *The Antiquaries Journal* 31, 86–89.

[Omont, H.], 1908. *Evangiles avec peintures byzantines du 11e siècle.* Paris.

Omont, H., 1929. *Miniatures des plus anciens MSs grecs de la Bibliothèque Nationale.* Paris.

Pächt, Otto, 1961. "A Cycle of English Frescoes in Spain," *Burlington Magazine* 103, 166–75.

———, 1962. *The Rise of Pictorial Narrative in Twelfth Century England.* Oxford.

Pächt, Otto; Dodwell, C. R.; and Wormald, Francis, 1960. *The St. Albans Psalter (Albani Psalter).* London.

Parker, Elizabeth, 1969. "A Twelfth-Century Cycle of New Testament Drawings from Bury St. Edmunds Abbey," *The Proceedings of the Suffolk Institute of Archaeology* 31, 263–302.

Plummer, John H., 1953. "The Lothian Morgan Bible: A Study in English Illumination of the Early Thirteenth Century." Ph.D. dissertation, Columbia University.

Poole, Austin Lane, 1955. *From Domesday Book to Magna Carta, 1087–1216.* 2nd ed., Oxford.

Powicke, F. M., 1929. *Stephen Langton* (Ford Lecures, Oxford, 1927). Oxford.

Rackham, Bernard, 1928. "The Early Stained Glass of Canterbury Cathedral," *Burlington Magazine* 52, 33–41 and 106.

———, 1936. *Victoria and Albert Museum, Department of Ceramics: A Guide to the Collections of Stained Glass*. London.

———, 1949. *The Ancient Glass of Canterbury Cathedral*. Canterbury.

———, 1950. "The Ancient Glass of Canterbury Cathedral," *Burlington Magazine* 92, 357.

———, 1951. "The Ancient Glass of Canterbury Cathedral," *Burlington Magazine* 93, 94–95.

———, 1957. *The Stained Glass Windows of Canterbury Cathedral*. Canterbury.

Read, Herbert, 1926. *English Stained Glass*. London.

Rickert, Margaret, 1965. *Painting in Britain: The Middle Ages*. 2nd ed., London and Baltimore.

Ritter, G., 1926. *Les Vitraux de la cathédrale de Rouen*. Cognac.

Robertson, James Craigie, ed., 1875–1885. *Materials for the History of Thomas Becket* (Roll Series No. 67). 7 vols., London.

Röhrig, Floridus, 1955. *Der Verduner Altar*. Vienna and Munich.

Sauerländer, Willibald, 1966. *Von Sens bis Strassburg: Ein Beitrag zur Kunstgeschichtlichen Stellung der Strassburger Querhausskulpturen*. Berlin.

———, 1970. *Gotische Skulptur in Frankreich*. Edited by Max Hirmer. Munich.

———, 1971. "Exhibition Review, 'The Year 1200,' A Centennial Exhibition at the Metropolitan Museum of Art," *Art Bulletin* 53, 506–16.

Saunders, O. E., 1932. *A History of English Art in the Middle Ages*. Oxford.

Saxl, Fritz, 1954. *English Sculptures of the Twelfth Century*. Edited by H. Swarzenski. Boston and London.

Smith, R.A.L., 1940. "The Central Financial System of Christ Church, Canterbury, 1186–1512," *English Historical Review* 55, 353–69.

———, 1943. *Canterbury Cathedral Priory: A Study in Monastic Administration*. Cambridge.

Sommer Johannes, 1966. *Das Deckenbild der Michaeliskirche zu Hildesheim*. Hildesheim.

Somner, William, 1640. *The Antiquities of Canterbury*. London.

Southern, R. W., 1953. *The Making of the Middle Ages*. New Haven and London.

———, 1963. *St. Anselm and His Biographer: A Study of Monastic Life and Thought, 1059–c.1130*. Cambridge.

[Sparke, Joseph, ed.], 1723. *Historiae Anglicanae Scriptores varii*. II, London.

Stanley, Arthur P., 1904. *Historical Memorials of Canterbury*. 10th ed., London.

Stettiner, Richard, 1895–1905. *Die Illustrierten Prudentius-handschriften*. Berlin.

Strzygowski, Joseph, 1899. *Der Bilderkreis des griechischen Physiologus*. Leipzig.

Stubbs, William, ed., 1865. *Chronicles and Memorials of the Reign of Richard I*. Vol. II, *Epistolae Cantaurienses, the Letters of the Prior and Convent of Christ Church, Canterbury, from A.D. 1187 to A.D. 1199*. London.

———, 1874. *Memorials of St. Dunstan, Archbishop of Canterbury* (*Rerum Britannicarum Medii Aevi Scriptores*, 63). London.

Sulkis, Ellen L., 1964. "The Four Stained Glass Windows of the North Ambulatory of Saint Etienne of Sens: Dating Dispute." Master's thesis, Columbia University.

Swarzenski, Hanns, 1936. *Die lateinischen illuminierten Handschriften des 13. Jahrhunderts in den Ländern am Rhein, Main und an der Donau*. Berlin.

———, 1943. *The Berthold Missal, Pierpont Morgan Library MS 710 and the Scriptorium of Weingarten Abbey*. New York.

———, 1967. *Monuments of Romanesque Art, the Art of Church Treasures in North-Western Europe*. 2nd ed., London.

Tolhurst, J.B.L., ed., 1937. *Breviary of Hyde Abbey, Winchester* III (Henry Bradshaw Society 76). London.

Tristram, E. W., 1944. *English Medieval Wall Painting: The Twelfth Century*. Oxford.

Urry, William, 1967. *Canterbury under the Angevin Kings* (University of London Historical Studies XIX). London.

van den Gheyn, J., 1906. *Le Psautier de Peterborough*. Haarlem.

van der Boom, A., 1960. *De Kunst der Glazniers in Europa 1100–1600*. Amsterdam.

Volbach, Wolfgang F., 1961. *Early Christian Art*. New York.

Walberg, E., 1929. *La Tradition hagiographique de Saint Thomas Becket avant la fin du XIIe siècle*. Paris.

Warner, G., 1928. *The Guthlac Roll* (Roxburghe Club). Oxford.

Watson, Arthur, 1934. *The Early Iconography of the Tree of Jesse*. Oxford and London.

Webb, Clement C. J., 1932. *John of Salisbury*. London.

Wentzel, Hans, 1954. *Meisterwerke der Glasmalerei.* Berlin.

Westlake, N.H.J., 1881–1894. *A History of Design in Painted Glass.* 4 vols., London.

William of Canterbury, 1875. "Miraculorum Gloriosi Martyris Thomae, Cantuariensis Archiepiscopi," in *Materials for the History of Thomas Becket* (Rolls Series No. 67). Edited by James Craigie Robertson. 1, London, 137–546.

William of Malmesbury, 1870. *De Gestis Pontificum Anglorum.* Edited by N.E.S.A. Hamilton. London.

[Williams, Emily], 1897. *Notes on the Painted Glass in Canterbury Cathedral.* Aberdeen.

Willis, Robert, 1972. *Architectural History of Canterbury Cathedral.* London, 1845. Reprinted as *Architectural History of Some English Cathedrals.* 1, Chicheley.

Wilson, Canon, 1913. "On Some Twelfth Century Paintings on the Vaulted Roof of the Chapter House of Worcester Cathedral," *Associated Architectural Societies' Reports and Papers* 32, 132–48.

[Winston, Charles], 1847. *An Inquiry into the Difference of Style Observable in Ancient Glass Paintings, especially in England, with Hints on Glass Painting.* 2 vols., Oxford.

Woodruff, C. Eveleigh, 1925. "The Chronicle of William Glastynbury, Monk of the Priory of Christ Church, Canterbury, 1419–1448," *Archaeologia Cantiana* 37, 121–51.

———, 1932. "The Financial Aspect of the Cult of St. Thomas of Canterbury," *Archaeologia Cantiana* 44, 13–32.

———, 1936. "The Sacrist's Rolls of Christ Church, Canterbury," *Archaeologia Cantiana* 48, 38–80.

Woodruff, Helen, 1929. "The Illustrated Manuscripts of Prudentius," *Art Studies* 7, 33–79.

Wormald, Francis, 1939. *English Benedictine Kalendars after 1100* (Henry Bradshaw Society 77). 2 vols., London.

———, 1943. "The Development of English Illumination in the Twelfth Century," *Journal of the British Archaeological Association* 3rd ser. 8, 31–49.

———, 1952–1953. "Some Illustrated Manuscripts of the Lives of the Saints," *Bulletin of the John Rylands Library, Manchester* 35, 248–66.

———, 1954. *The Miniatures in the Gospels of St. Augustine.* Cambridge.

Index

Plates

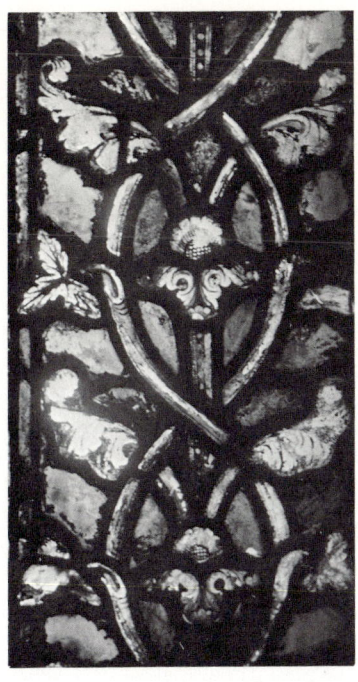

1. North choir aisle n:XV, border

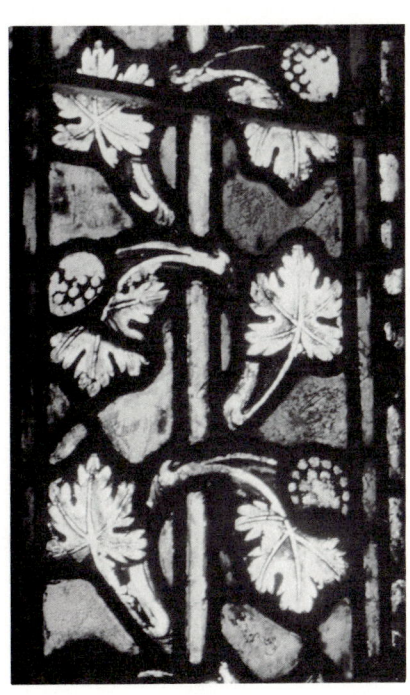

2. North choir aisle n:XIV, border

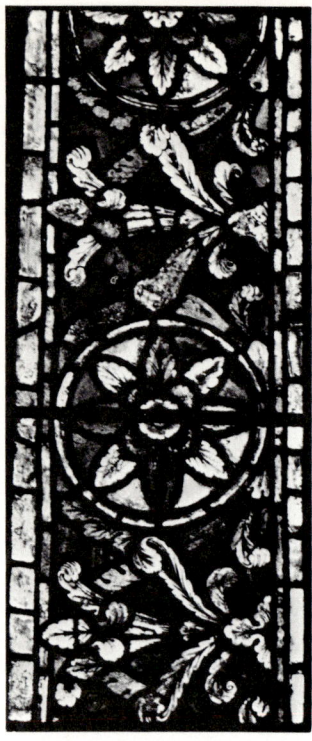

3

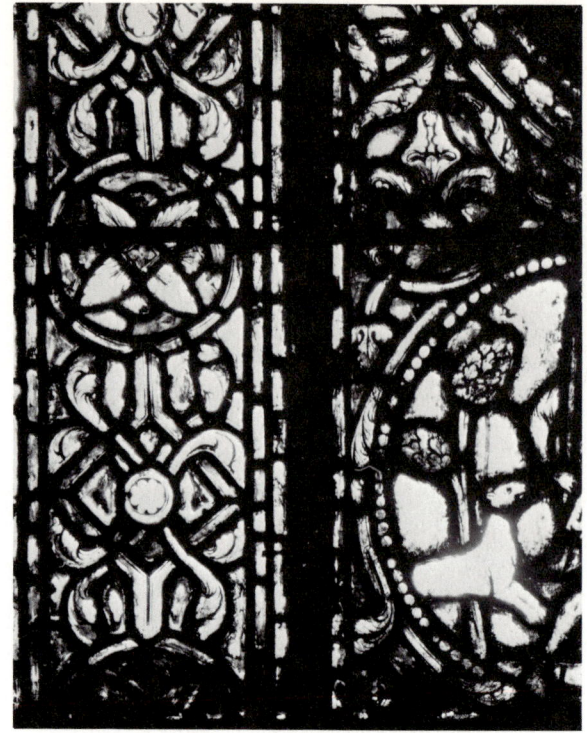

4

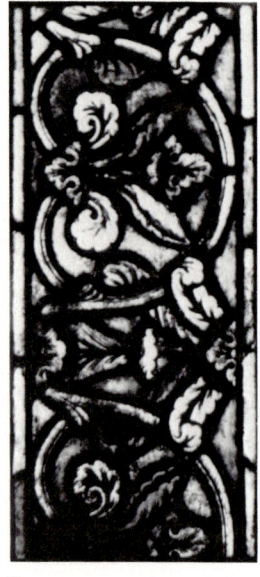

5

3. Crypt, east window, border

4. Chartres, St. Eustace window,
   border and *rinceaux*

5. Rheims, St.-Remi, clerestory border

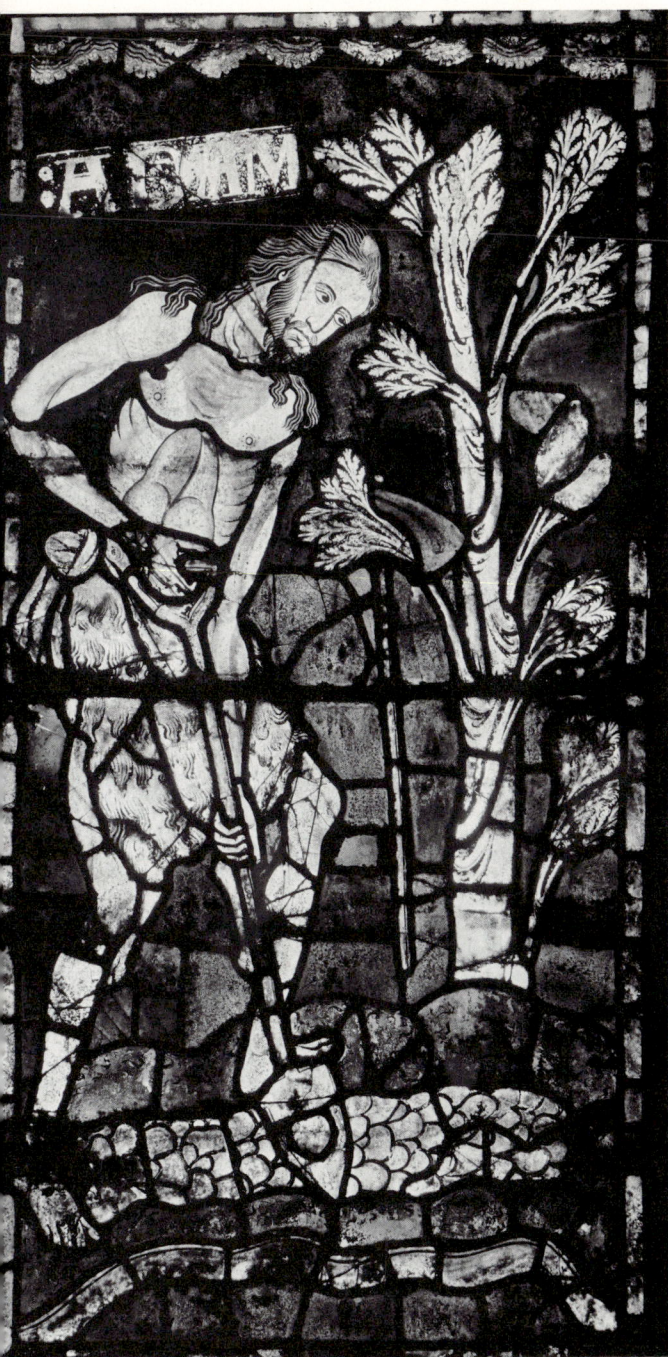

Adam, from clerestory N:XXV

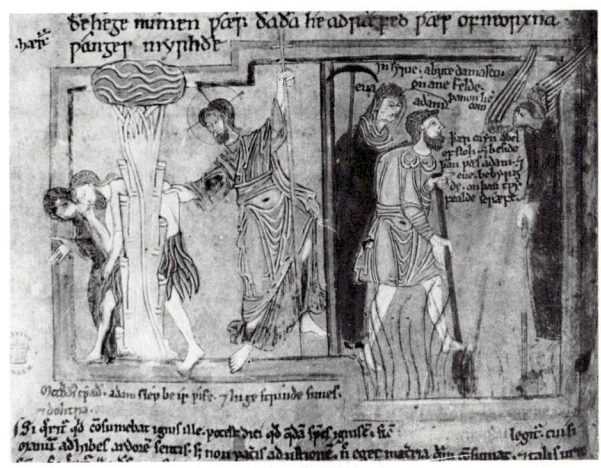

7. Aelfric, Pentateuch, British Museum, Cotton Claudius MS B.IV, f.7v, detail of Adam

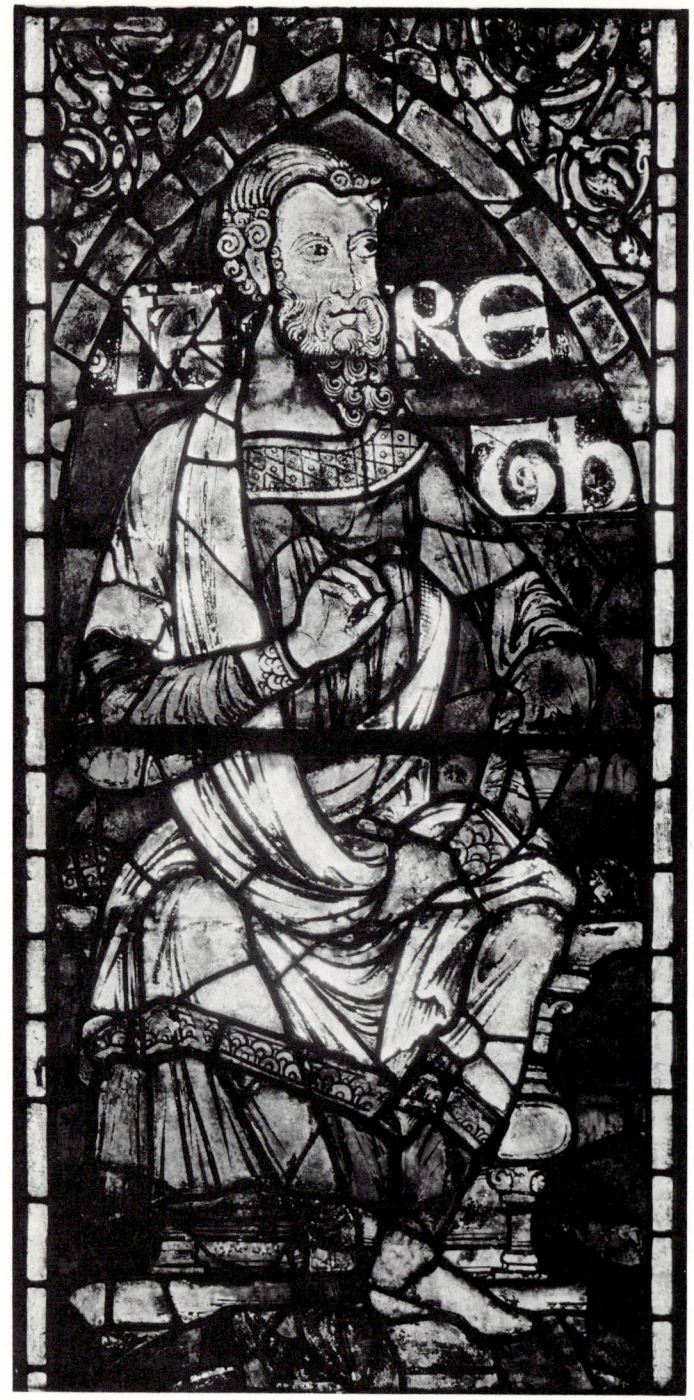

8. Jared, from clerestory N:XXII

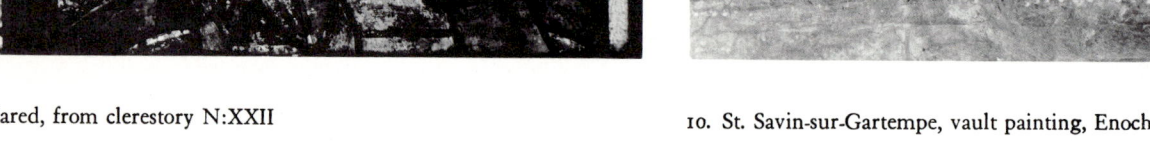

10. St. Savin-sur-Gartempe, vault painting, Enoch

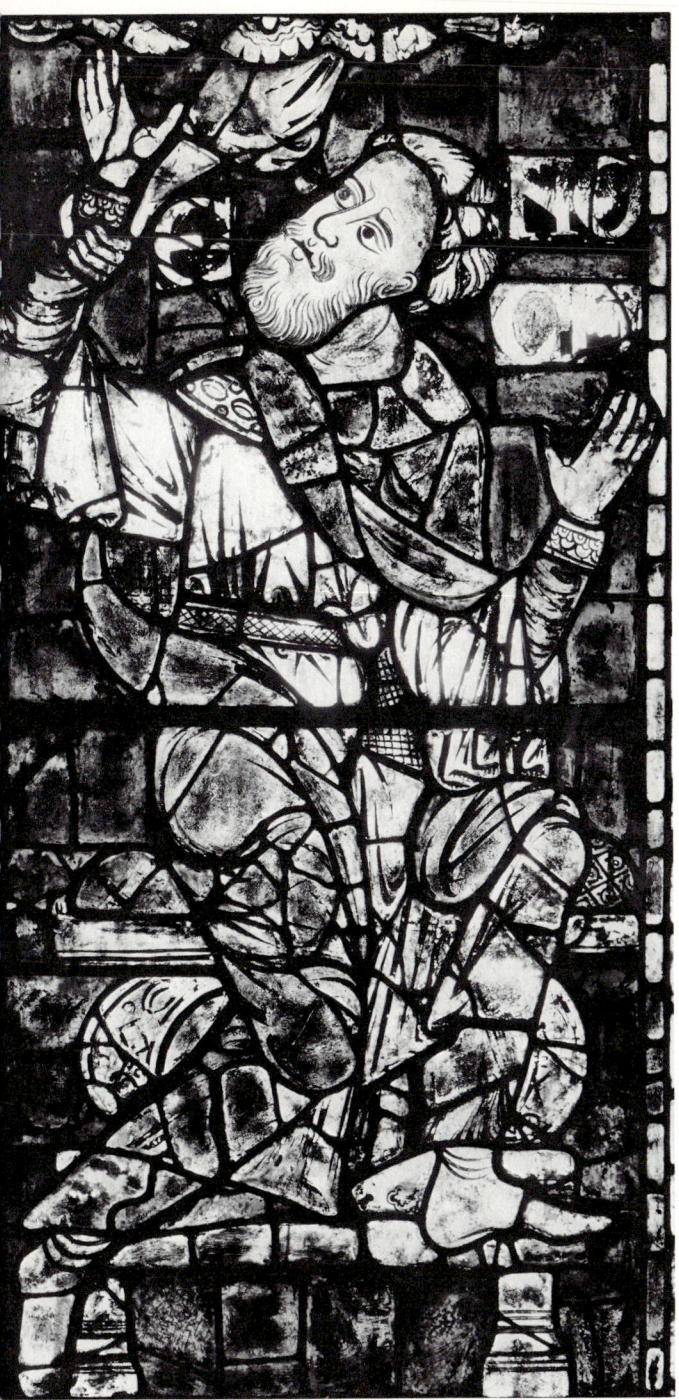

Enoch, from clerestory N:XXII

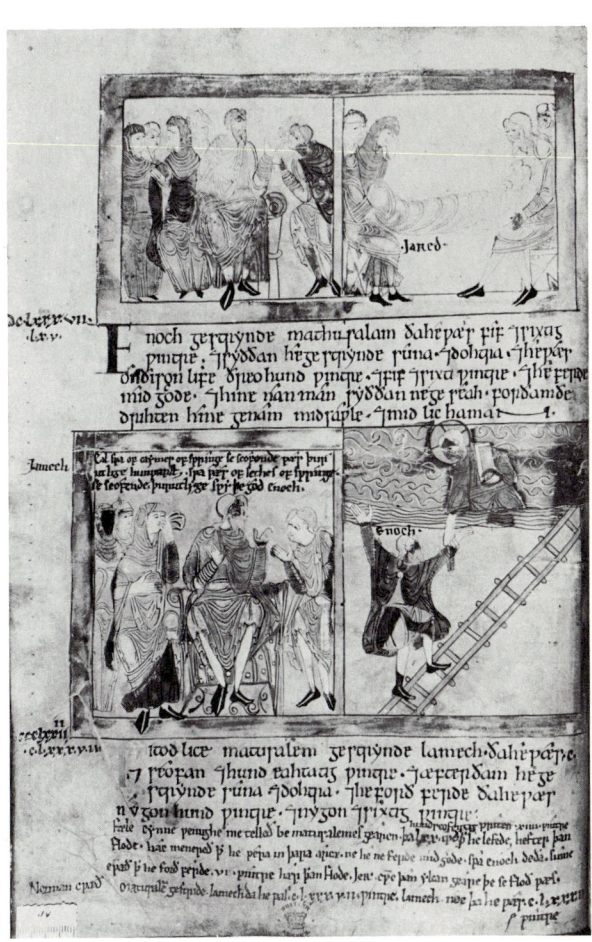

11. Aelfric, Pentateuch, British Museum,
Cotton Claudius MS B.IV, f.11v,
Jared and Enoch

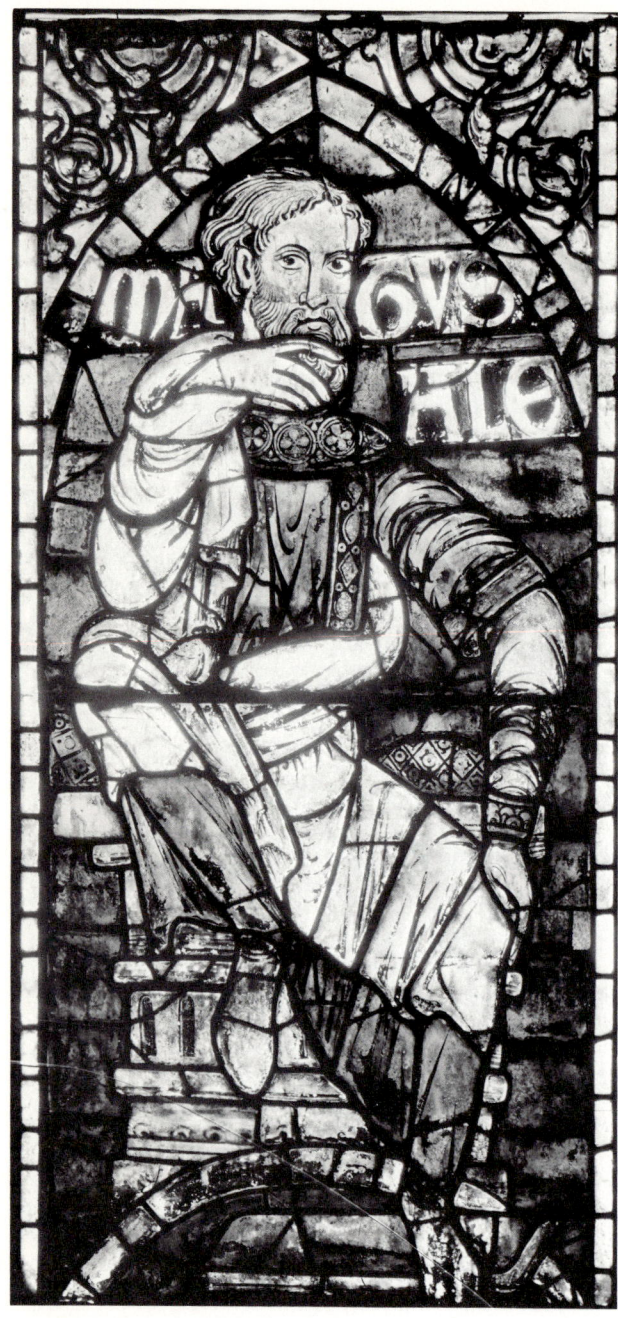

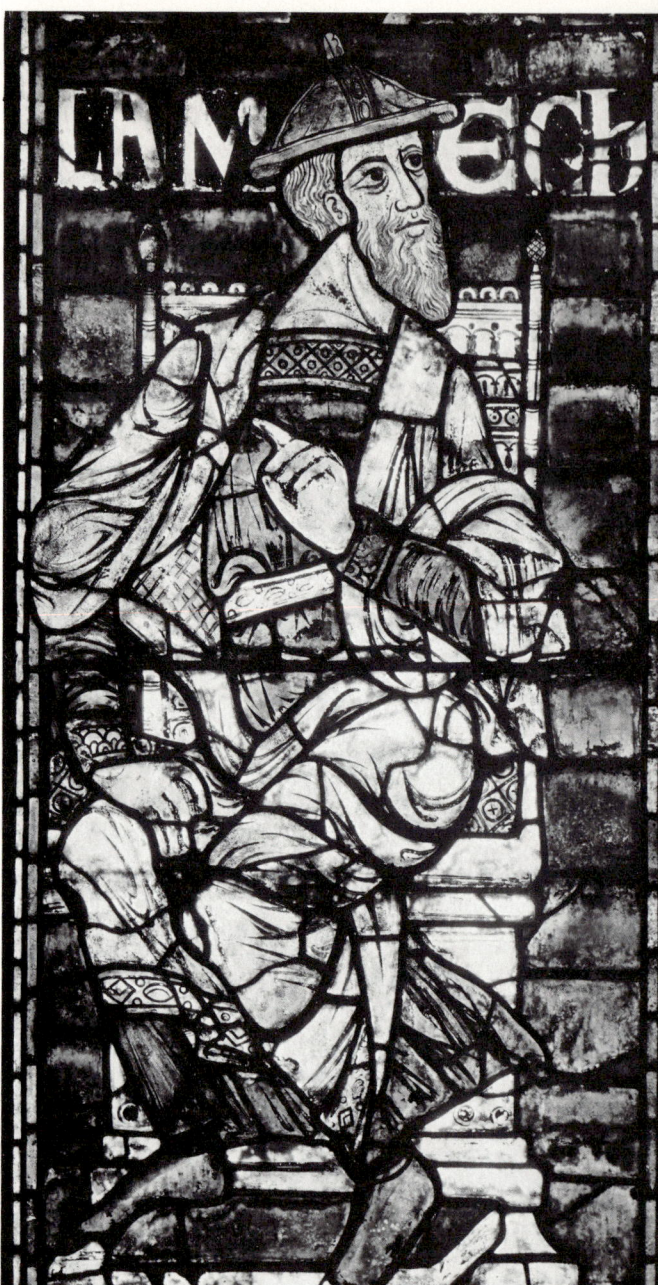

12. Methuselah, from clerestory N:XXI

13. Lamech, from clerestory N:XXI

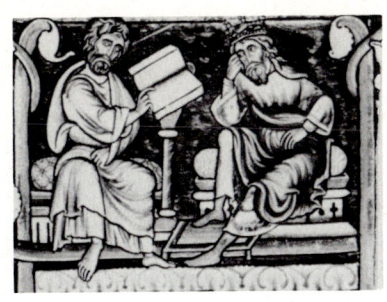
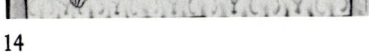

14

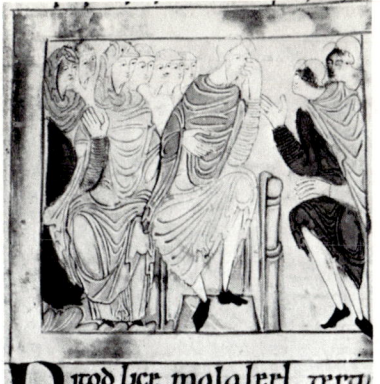

15

14. Winchester Bible, f.169, initial to Baruch

15. Aelfric, Pentateuch, British Museum, Cotton Claudius MS B.IV, f.11, detail of Cainan

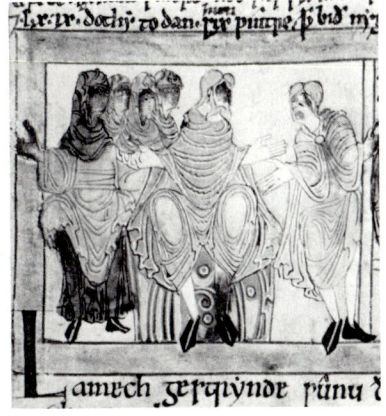
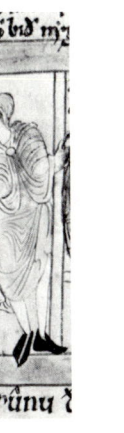

16

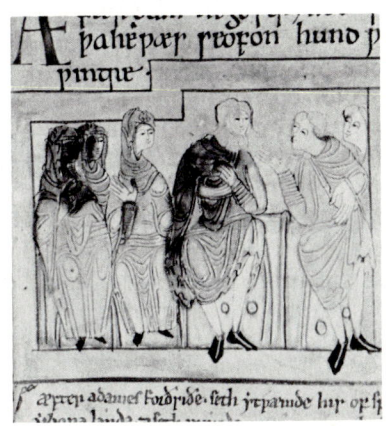

17

16. Aelfric, Pentateuch, British Museum, Cotton Claudius MS B.IV, f.12, detail of Methuselah

17. The same, detail of Lamech

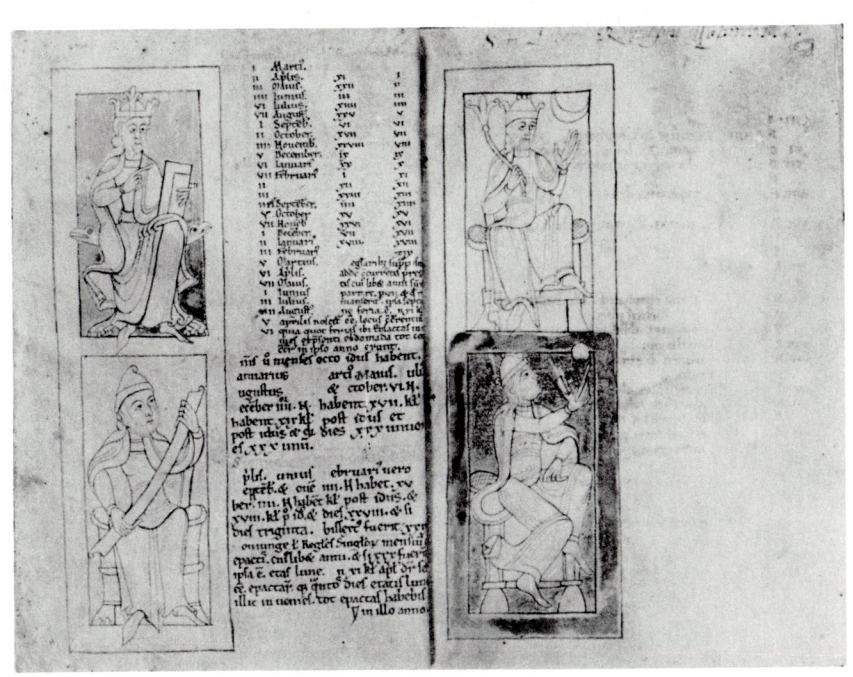

18. Astrological treatise, etc., Oxford, Bodleian Library, MS Bodl. 614, ff.1v-2

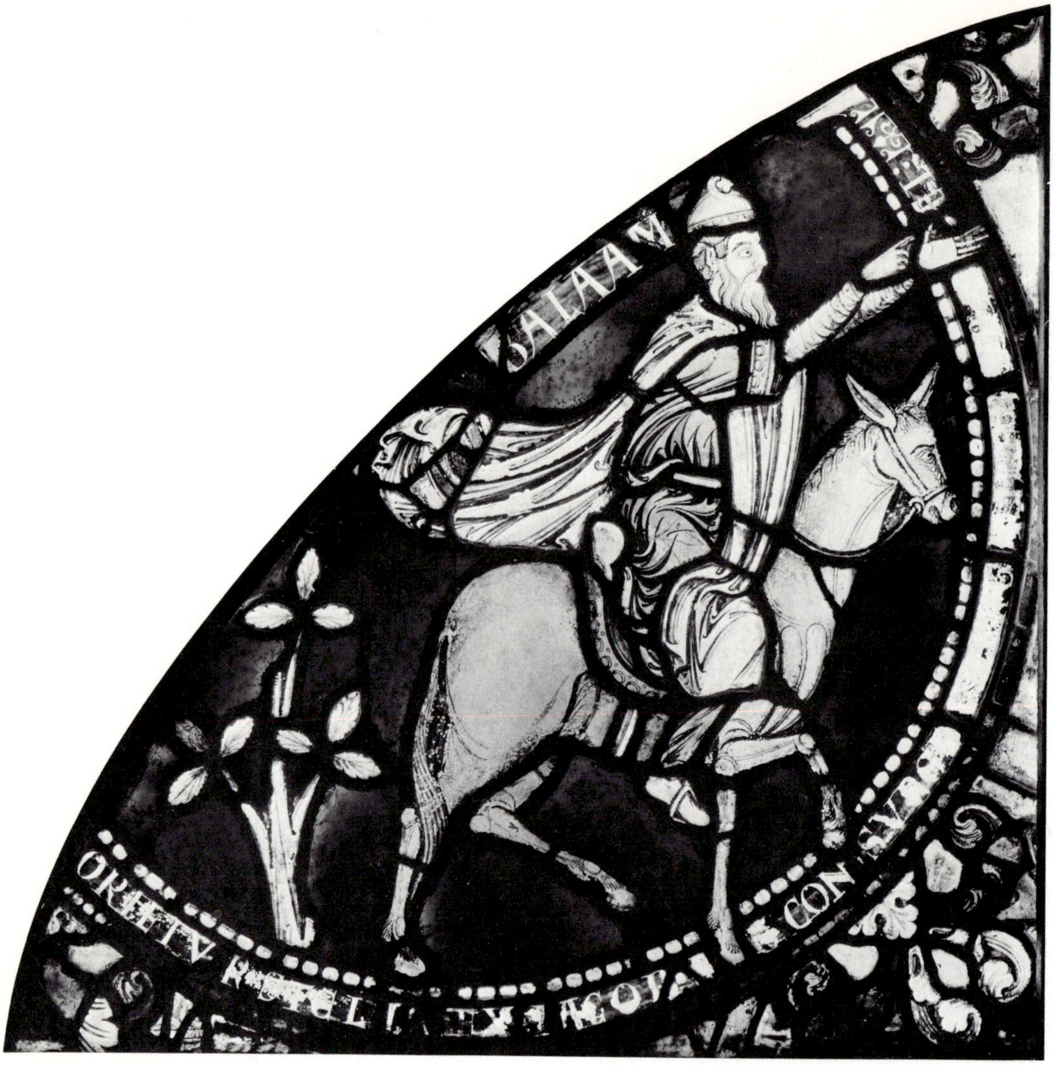

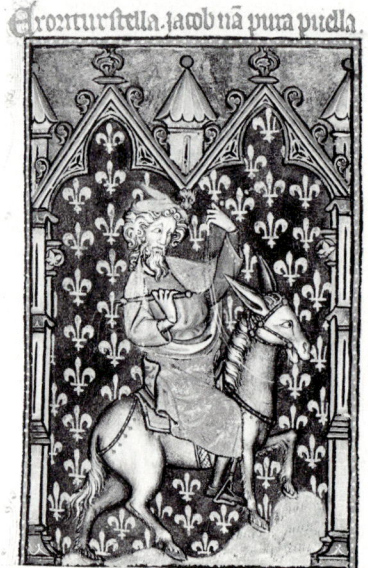

19. North choir aisle N:XV (1), Balaam

20. Peterborough Psalter, Brussels,
    Bibliothèque Royale, MS 9961–62,
    f.11, detail of Balaam

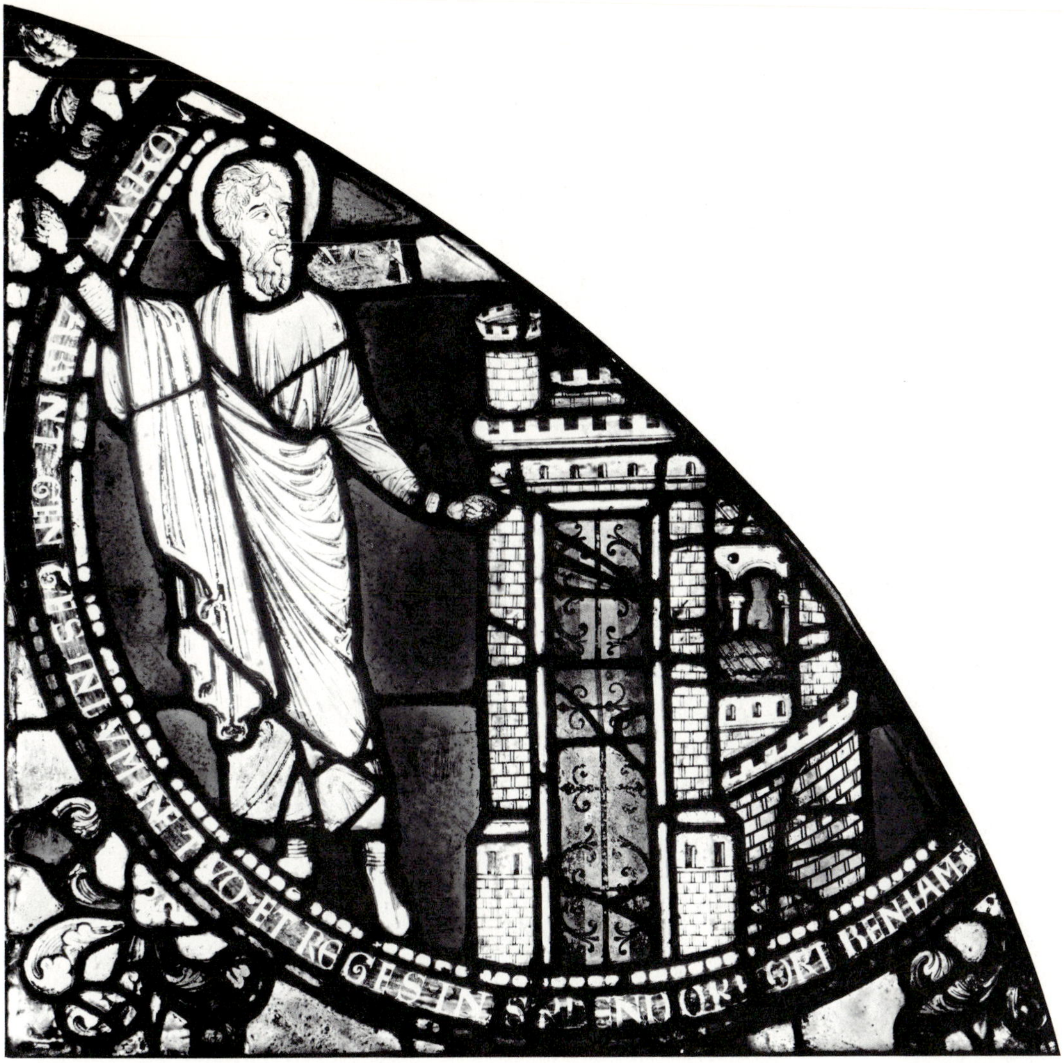

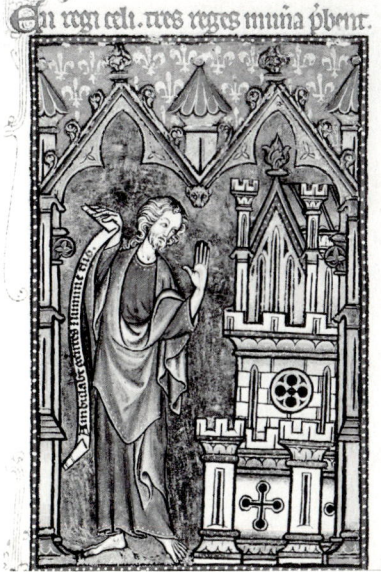

21. North choir aisle n:XV (3), Isaiah

22. Peterborough Psalter, Brussels,
Bibliothèque Royale, MS 9961–62, f.11,
detail of Isaiah

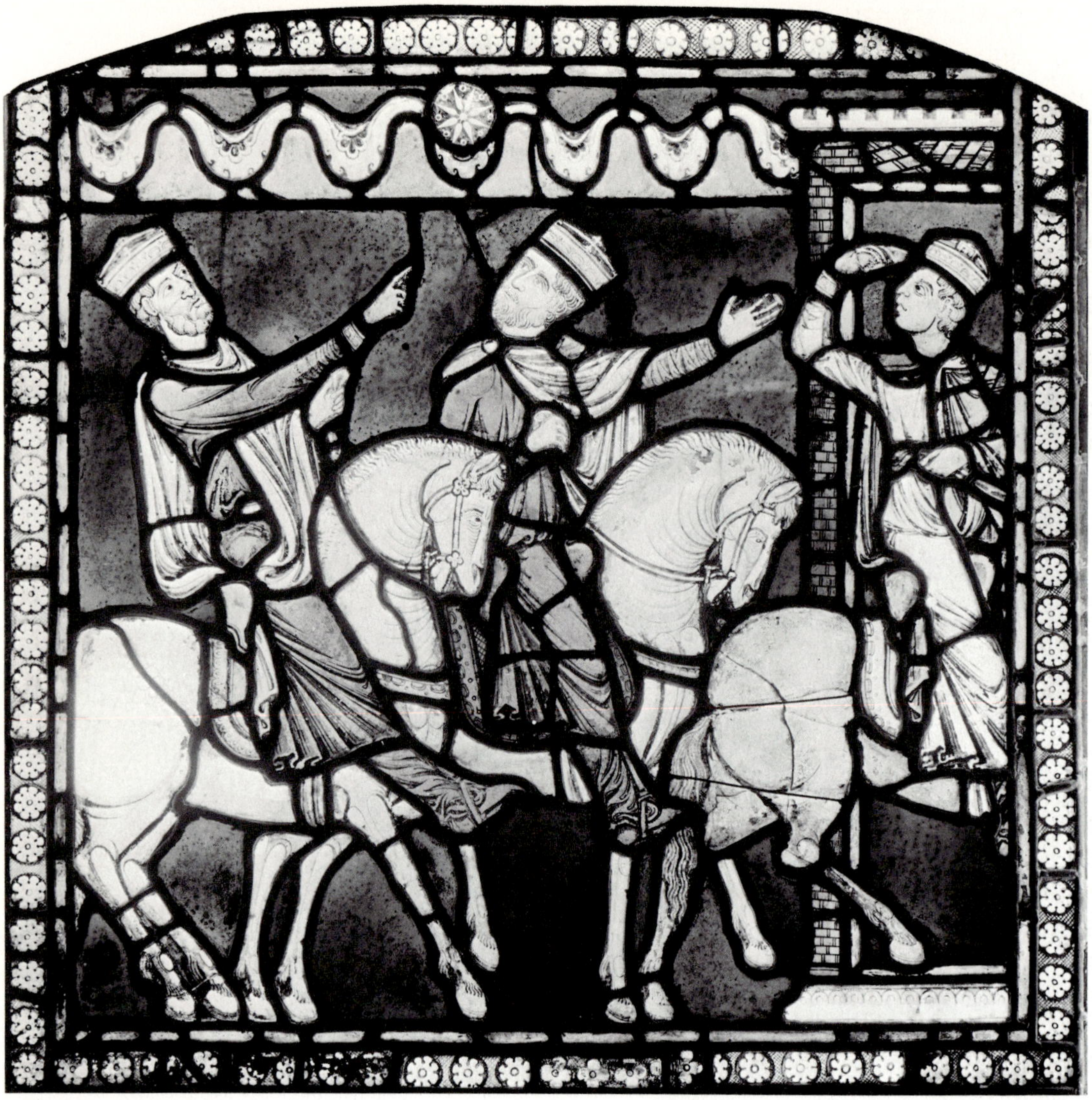

23. North choir aisle n:XV (2), Magi Riding
    to Bethlehem

24. "Psalter of Henry of Blois," British
    Library, Cotton Nero MS C.IV, f.12,
    magi riding and adoration

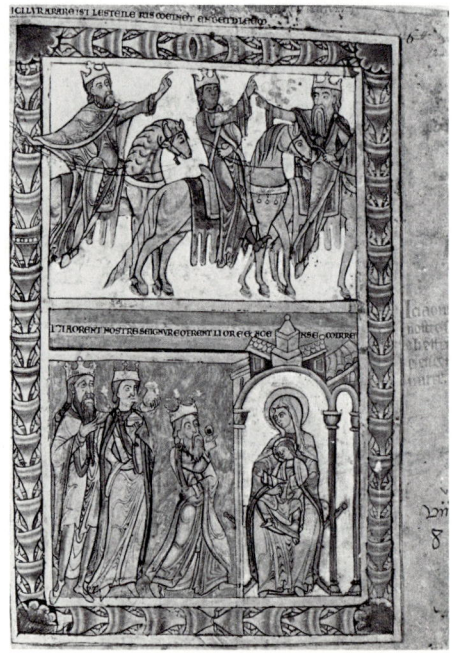

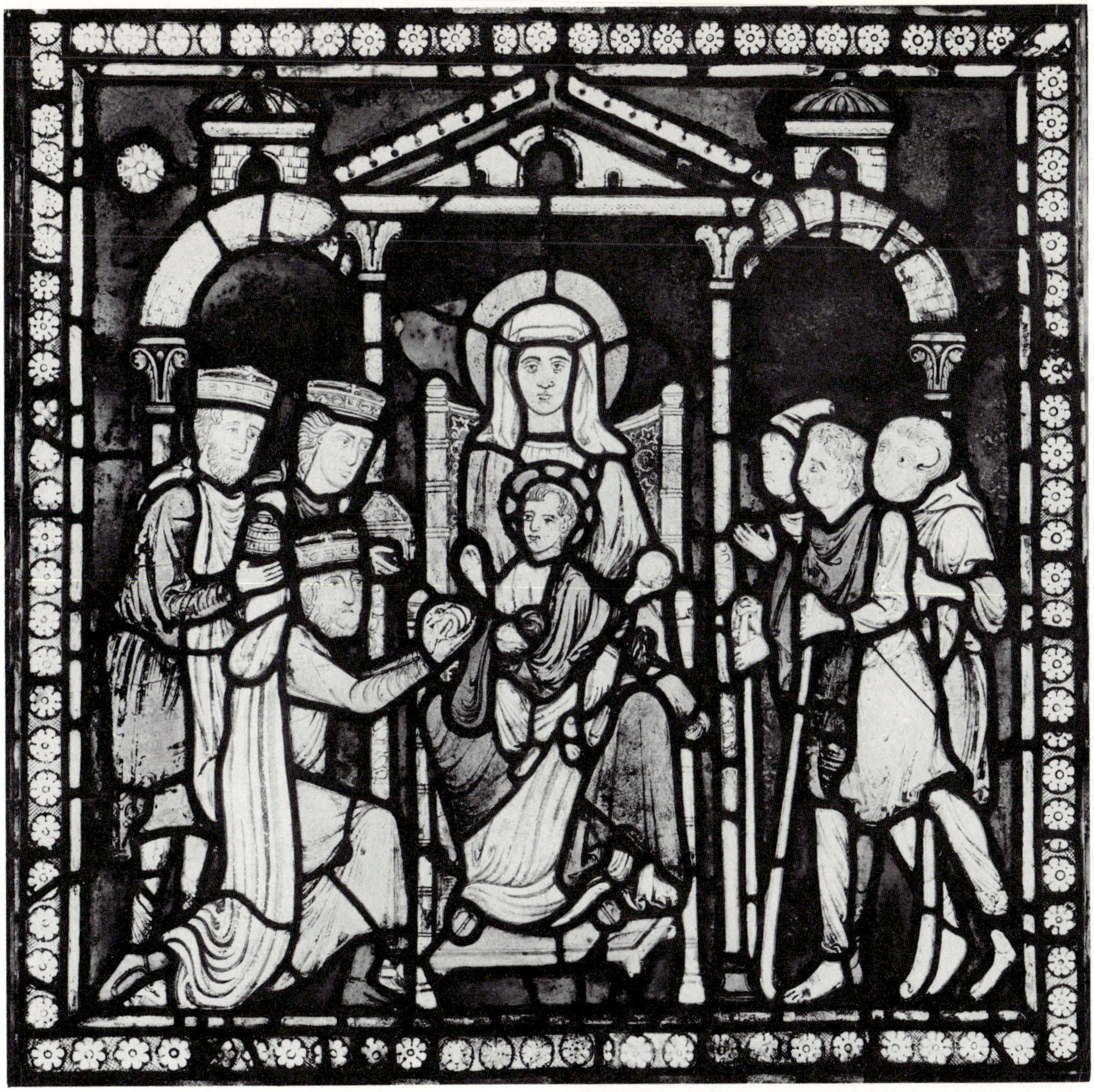

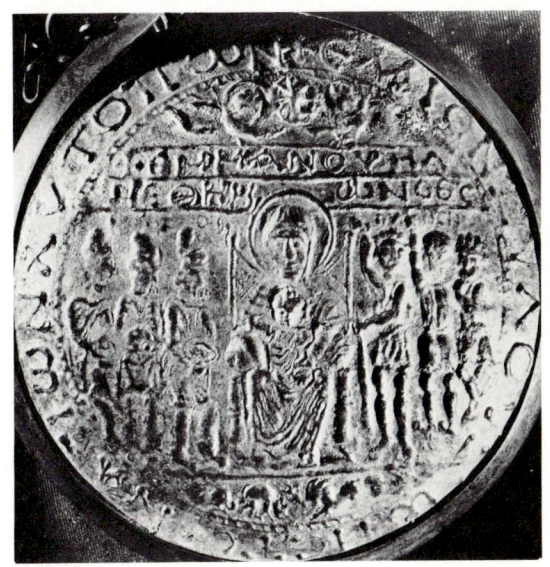

25. North choir aisle n:XV (8), Adoration

26. Monza ampulla of the sixth century,
    Adoration

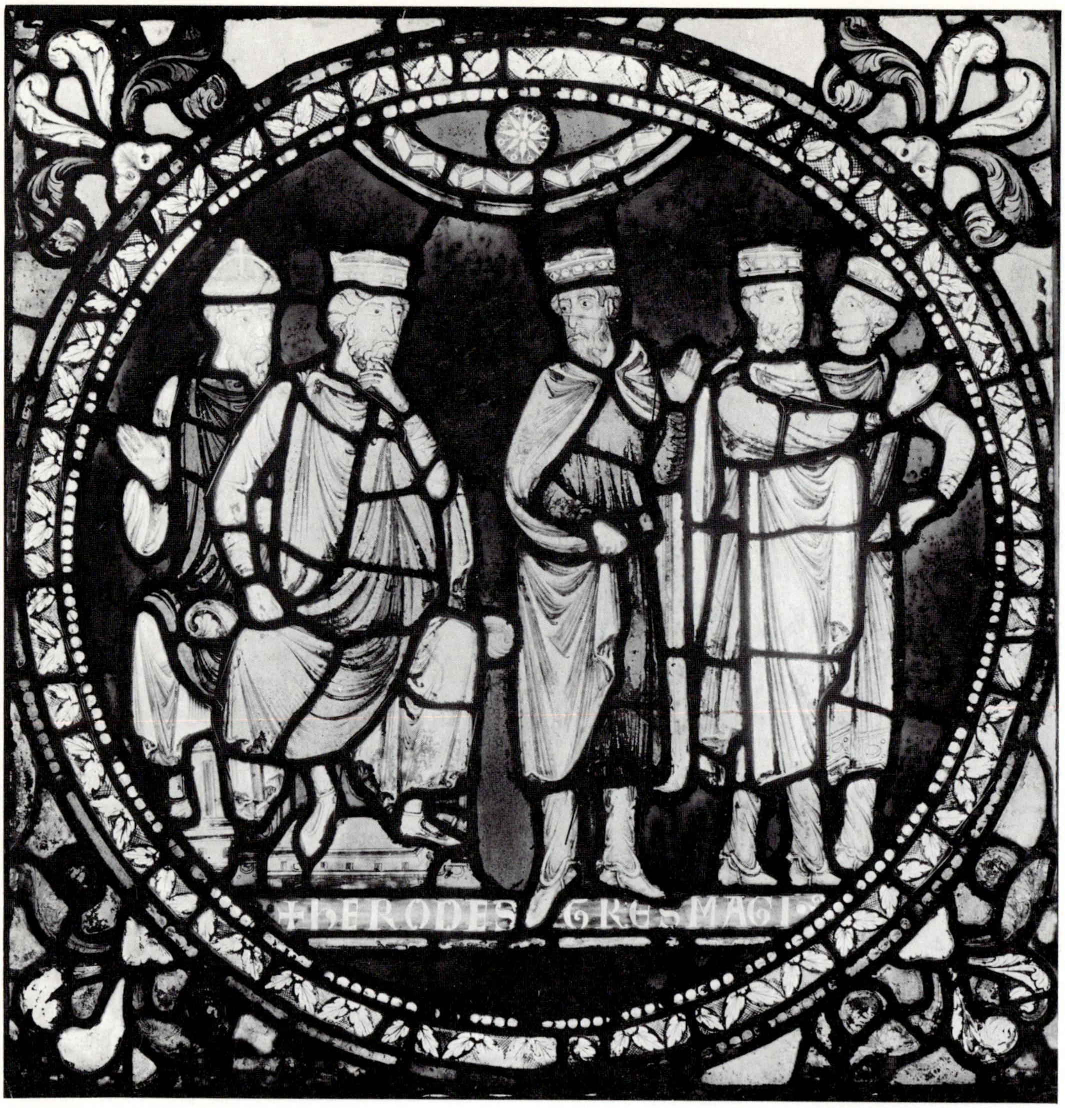

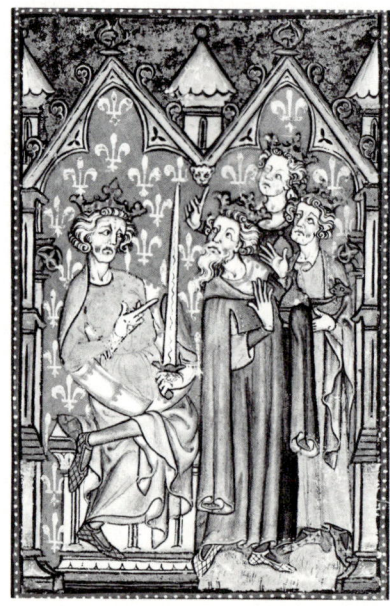

27. North choir aisle n:XV (5), Magi before Herod

28. Peterborough Psalter, Brussels,
    Bibliothèque Royale, MS 9961–62, f.11v,
    detail of Magi before Herod

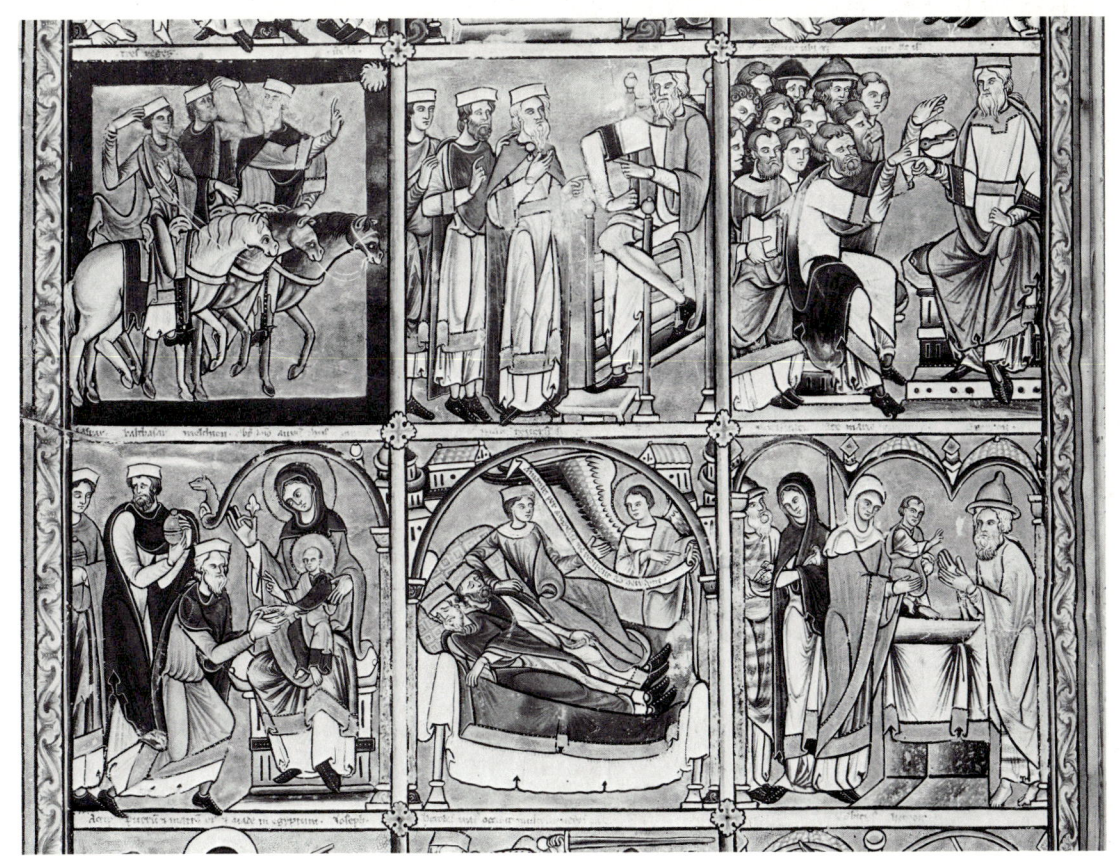

29. Great Canterbury Psalter, Paris, Bibliothèque Nationale,
    MS Lat. 8846, f.4v,
    detail, magi cycle and presentation

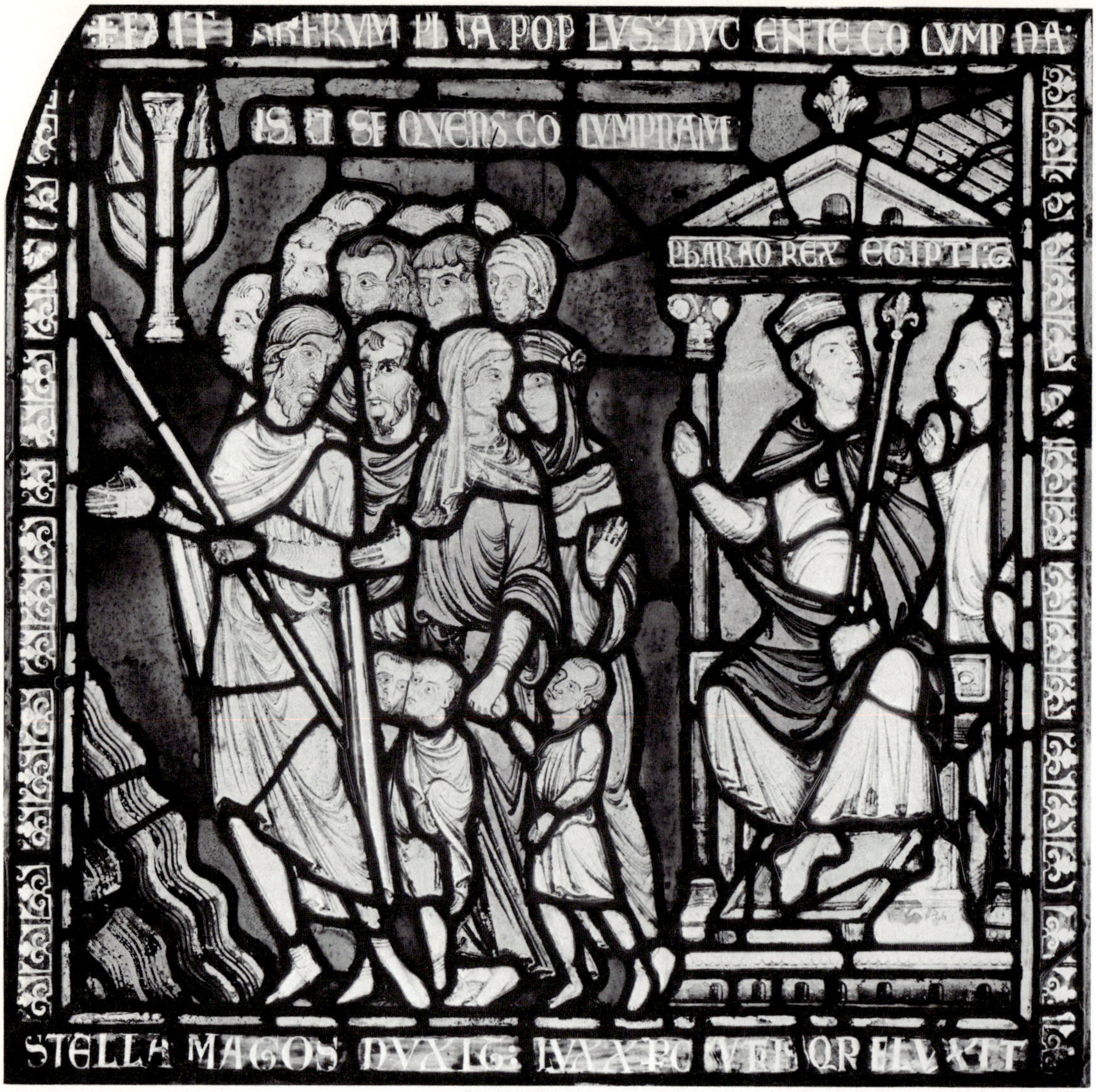

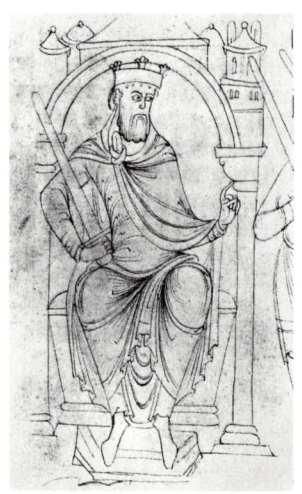

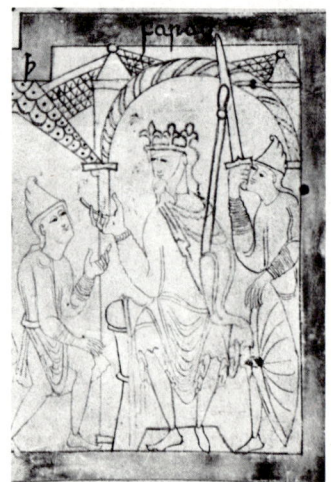

30. North choir aisle n:XV 4,
Exodus

31. Winchester Bible, f.350v,
detail of King Antiochus

32. Aelfric, Pentateuch,
British Museum, Cotton
Claudius MS B.IV, f.22,
detail of Pharaoh

31   32

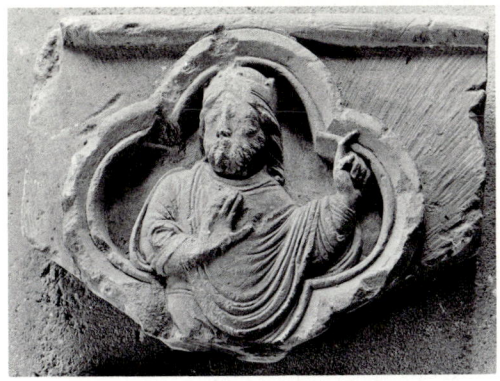

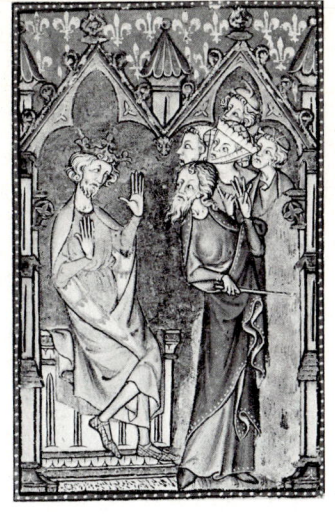

33. Canterbury Cathedral,
sculpture fragment from the
choir enclosure of 1180 (?)

34. Peterborough Psalter,
Brussels, Bibliothèque Royale,
MS 9961–62, f.11, detail of
the Exodus

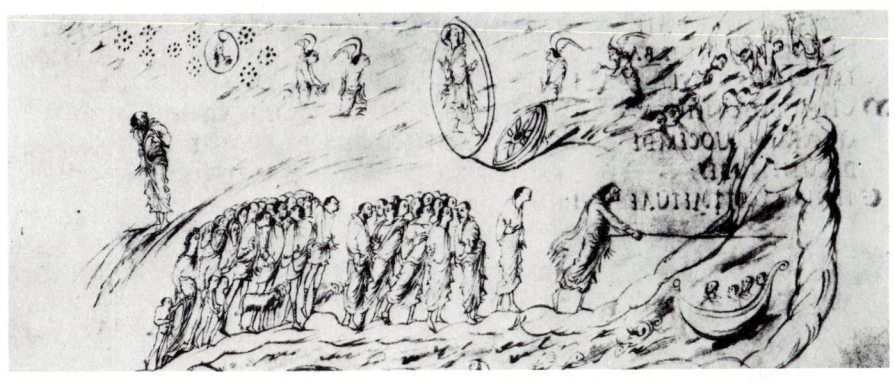

35. Utrecht Psalter, University
Library. MS 32,
f.44, Psalm 76, detail of
the Exodus

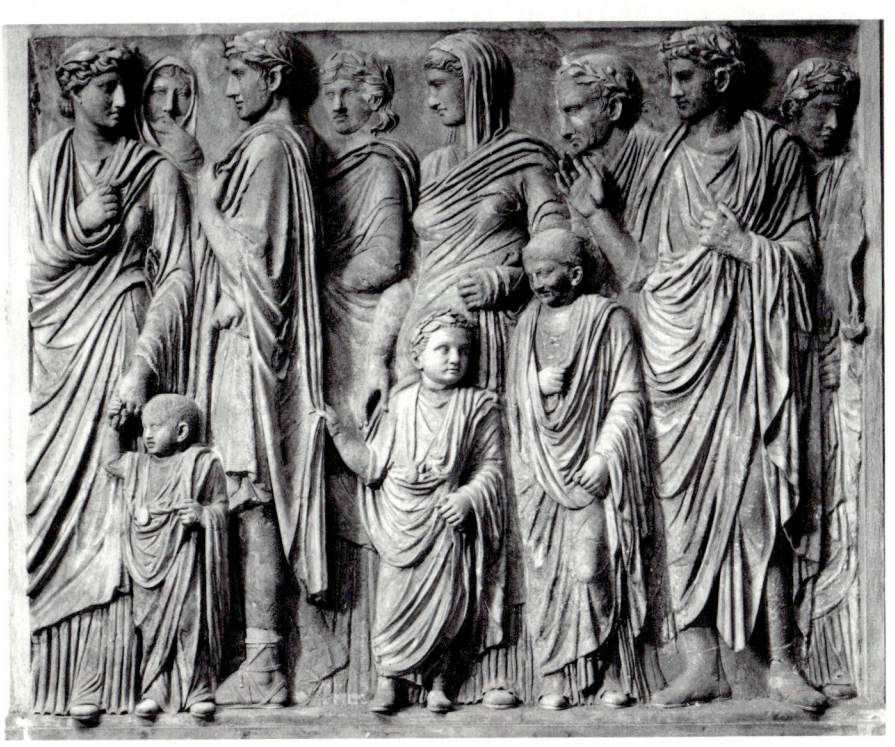

36. Ara Pacis Augustae, Rome,
detail of relief sculpture,
procession

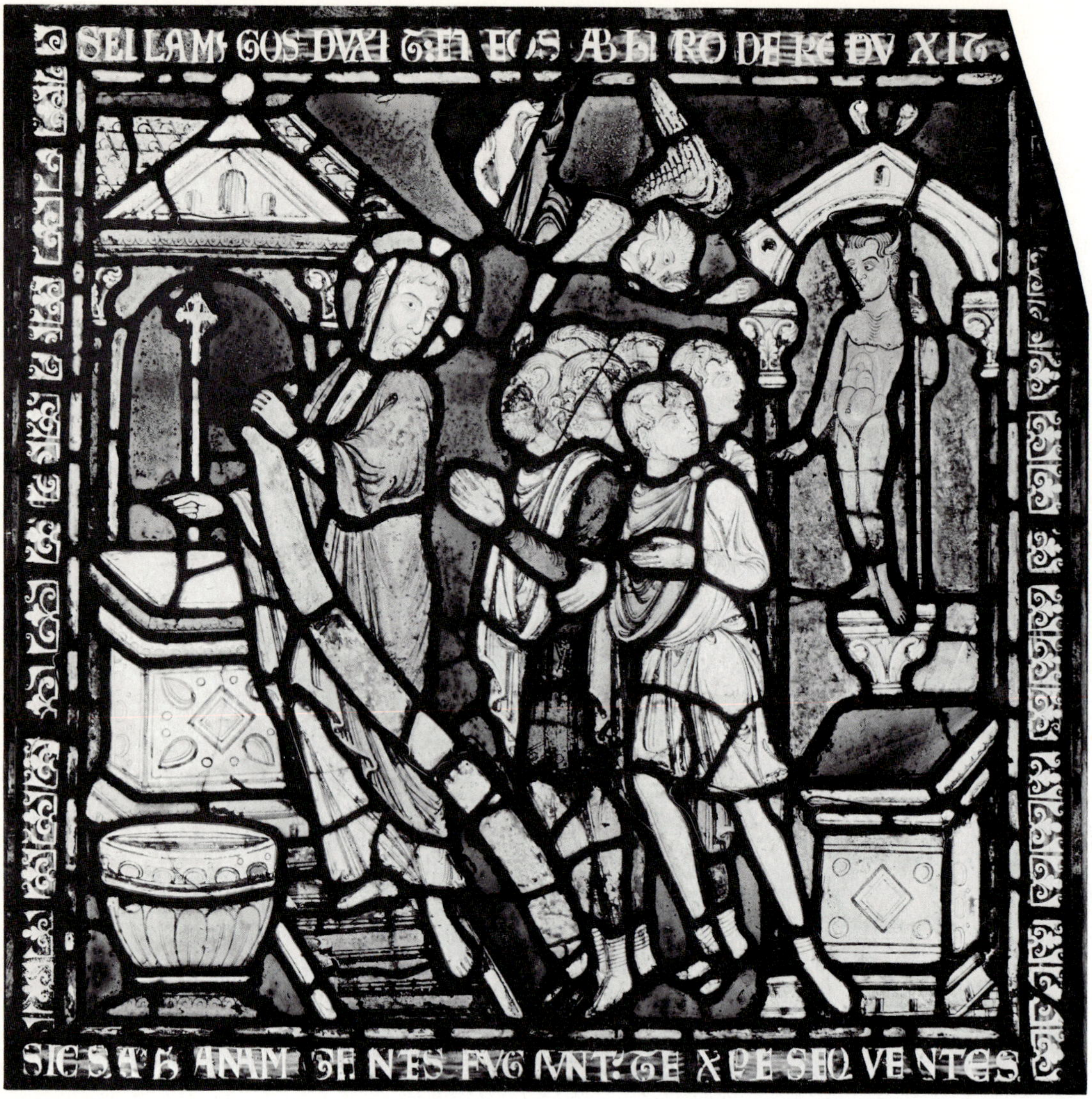

SELLAM GOS DVXIT: EOS AB IRO DE RE DVXIT.

SIC ST B ANIM GENTES FVG RVNT: CE XPE SEO VENTES

37. North Choir Aisle N:XV (6), Christ leading
the Gentiles away from pagan gods

38. Winchester Bible, f.350v, detail
Mattathias preventing idolatry

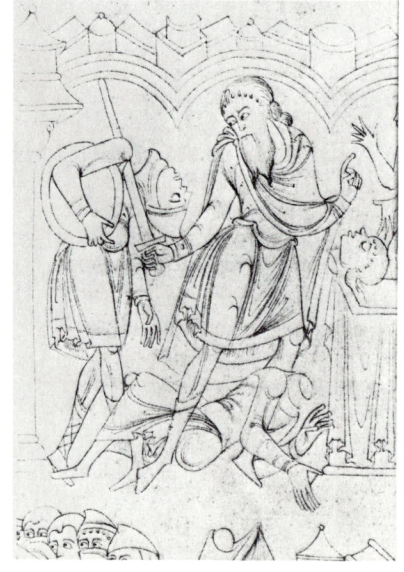

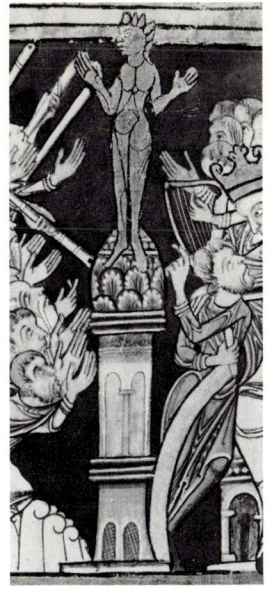
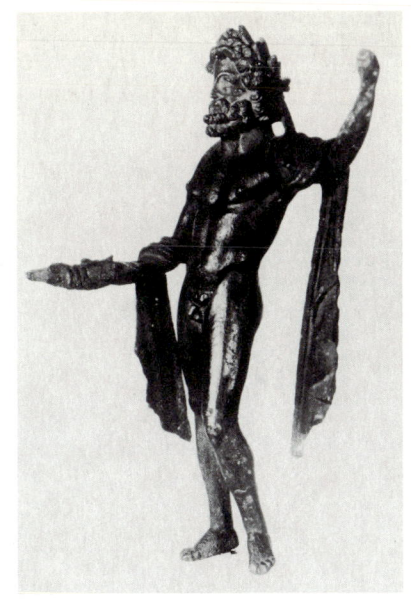

39. Lambeth Bible, London, Lambeth Palace
    Library, MS 3, f.285v, detail of idol

40. Bronze statuette of Jupiter,
    2nd–3rd century, Utrecht, Provincial
    Oudheidkundig Museum

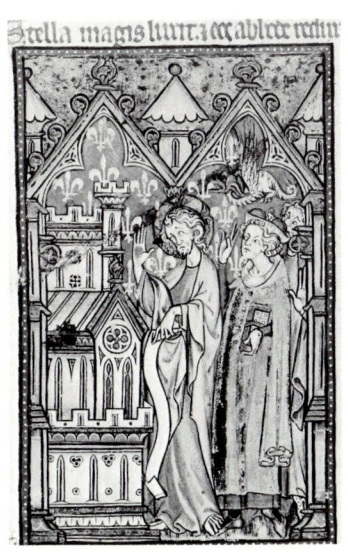
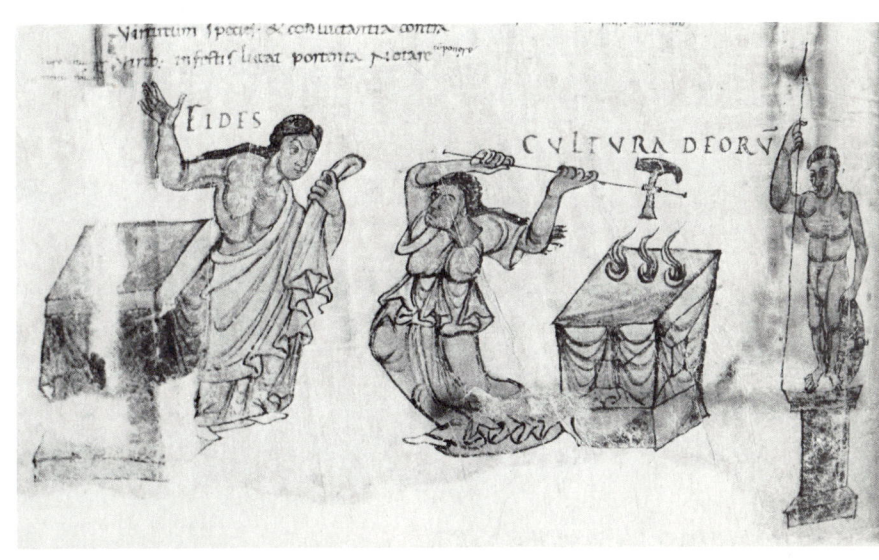

41

42

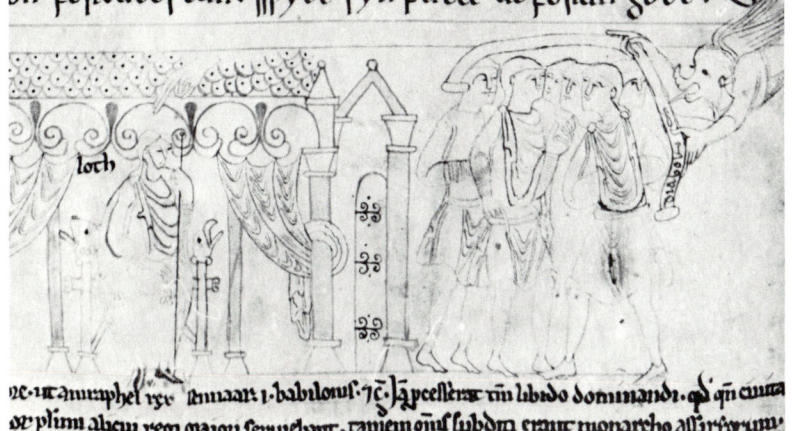

43

41. Peterborough Psalter, Brussels,
    Bibliothèque Royale,
    MS 9961–62, f.11v, detail of Christ
    leading the Gentiles

42. Psychomachia of Prudentius, Bern,
    Burgerbibliothek, MS 264 p. 68,
    combat between faith and the
    cult of the gods

43. Aelfric, Pentateuch, British Museum,
    Cotton Claudius MS B.IV, f.23v.
    detail of the men of Sodom
    ensnared by the Devil

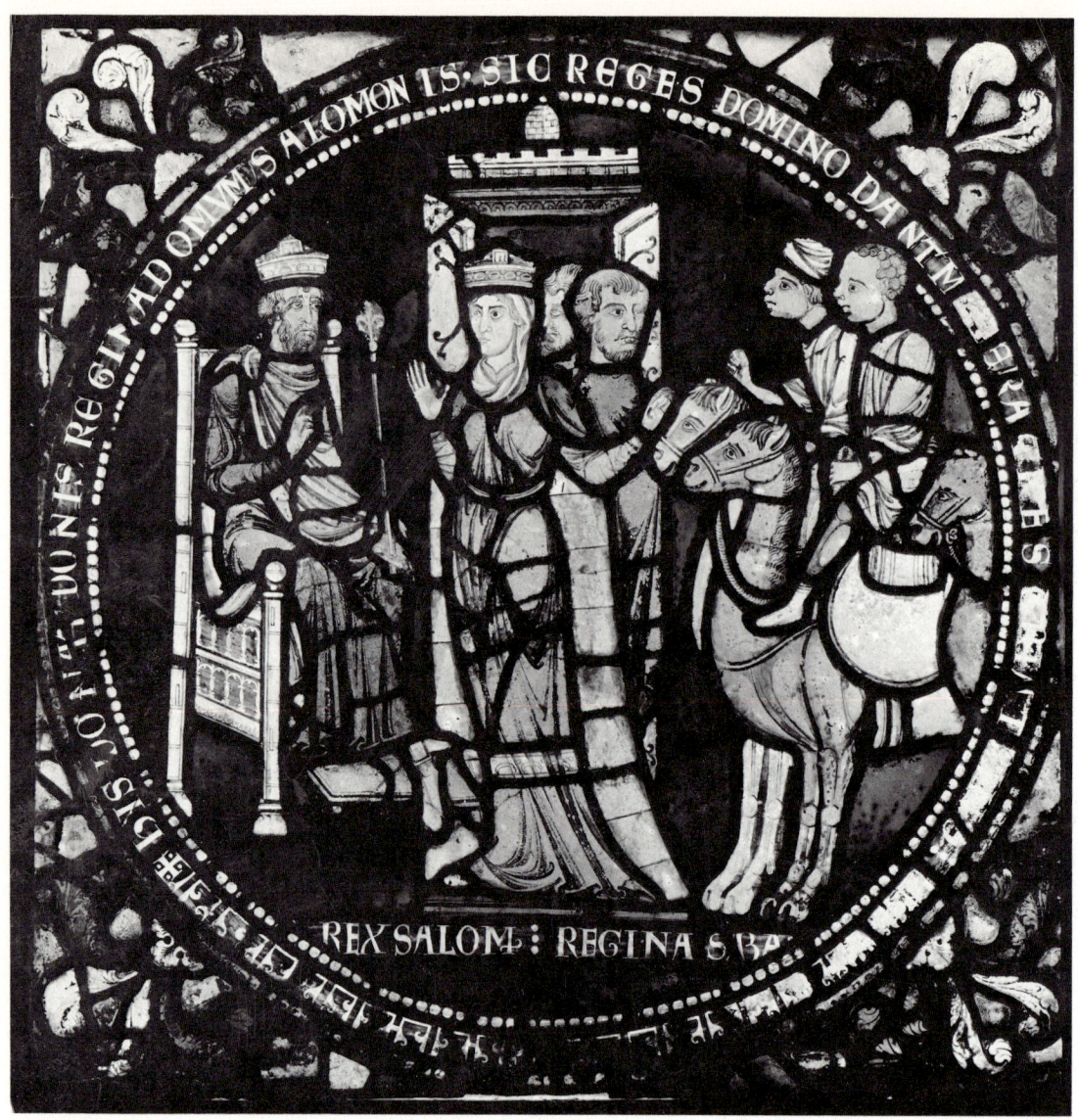

44. North choir aisle n:XV (7), Solomon and Sheba

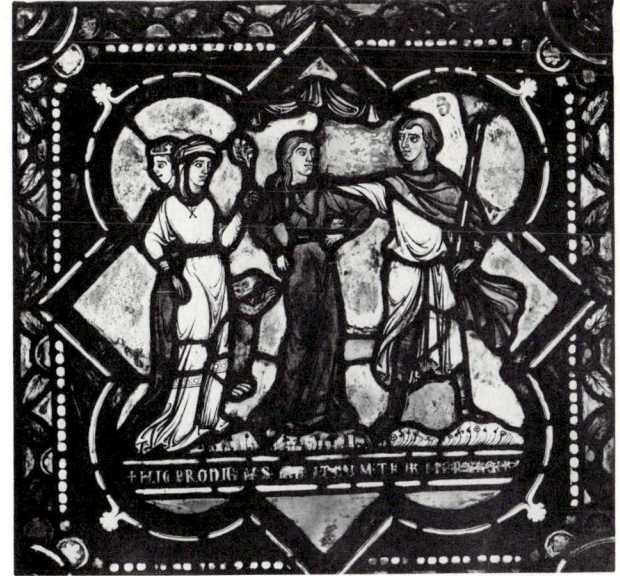

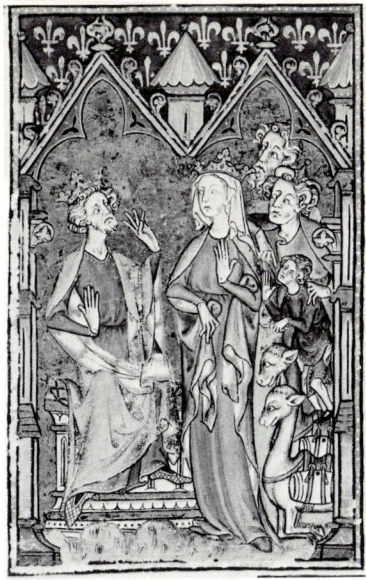

45

46

45. Sens, Prodigal Son window,
    harlots

46. Peterborough Psalter, Brussels,
    Bibliothèque Royale, MS 9961–62,
    f.11v, detail of Solomon
    and Sheba

47. St.-Quentin, Collegiate Church,
    Lady Chapel window, Solomon
    and Sheba

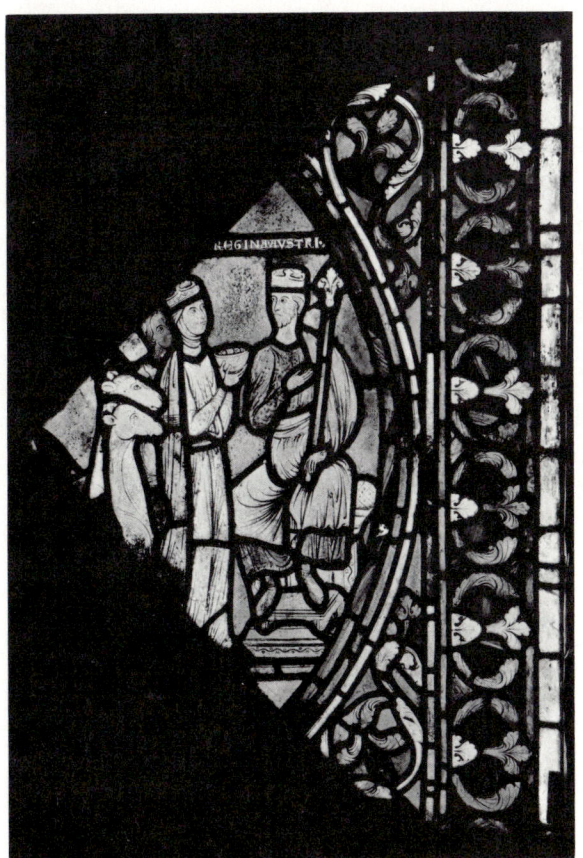

47

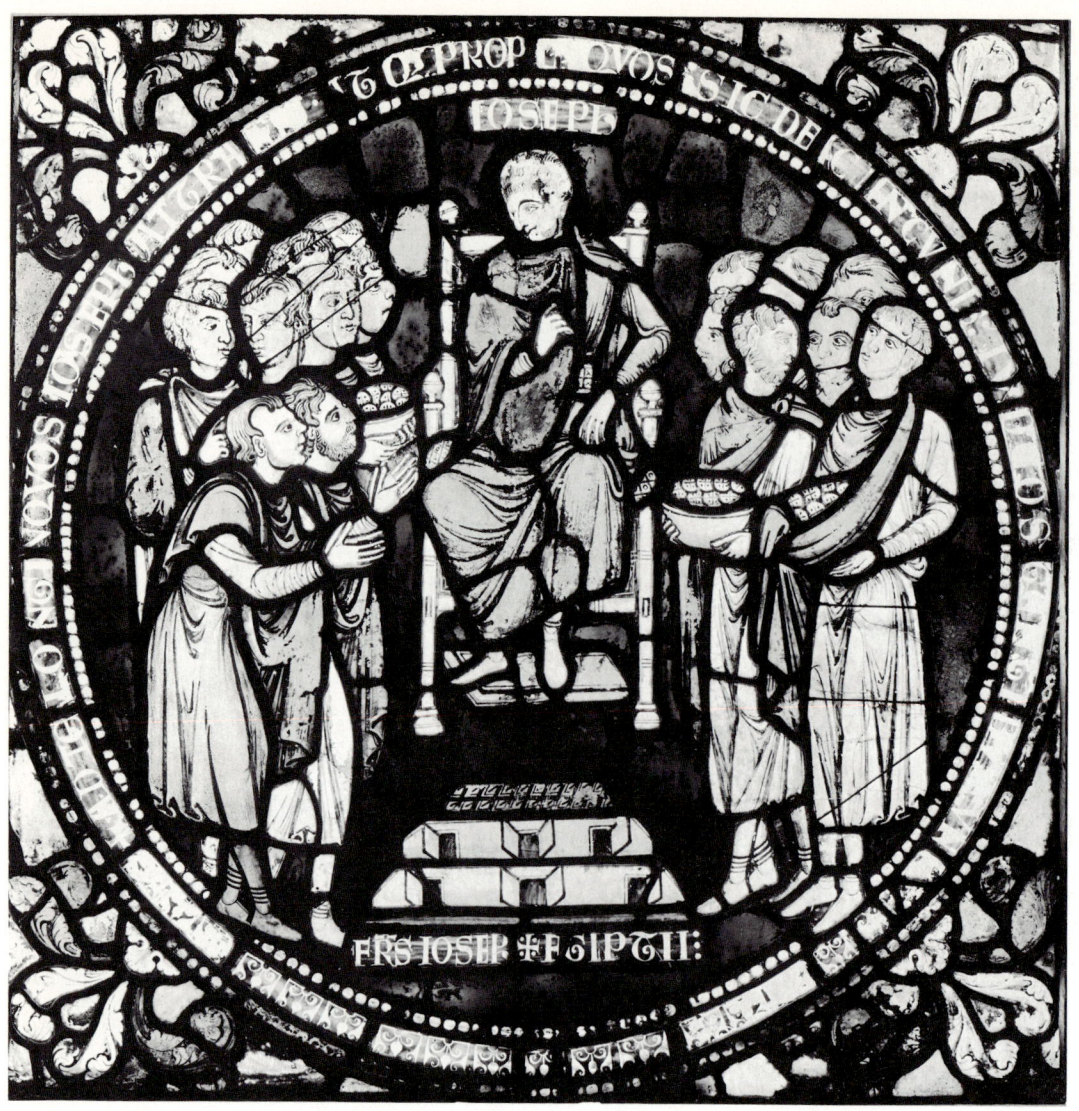

48. North choir aisle n:XV (9), Joseph and his brethren

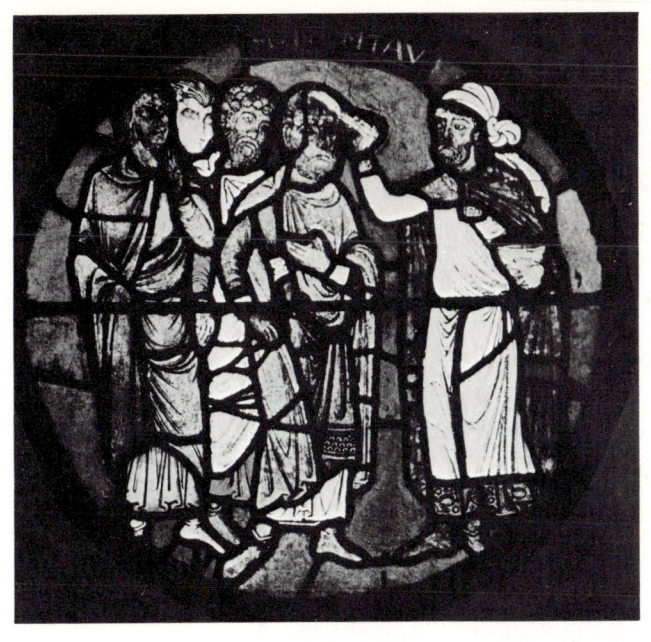

49. St.-Denis, *Signum Tau*

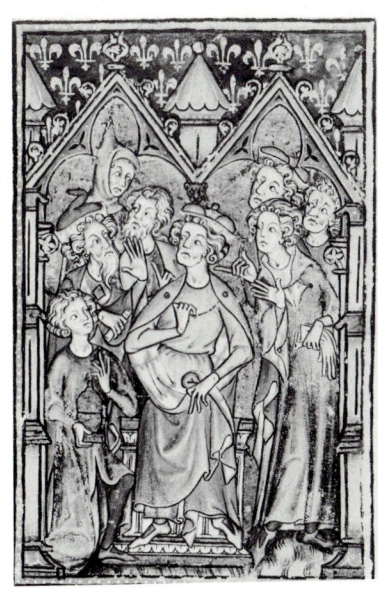

50. Peterborough Psalter, Brussels,
Bibliothèque Royale, MS 9961–62, f.11v,
detail of Joseph and his brethren

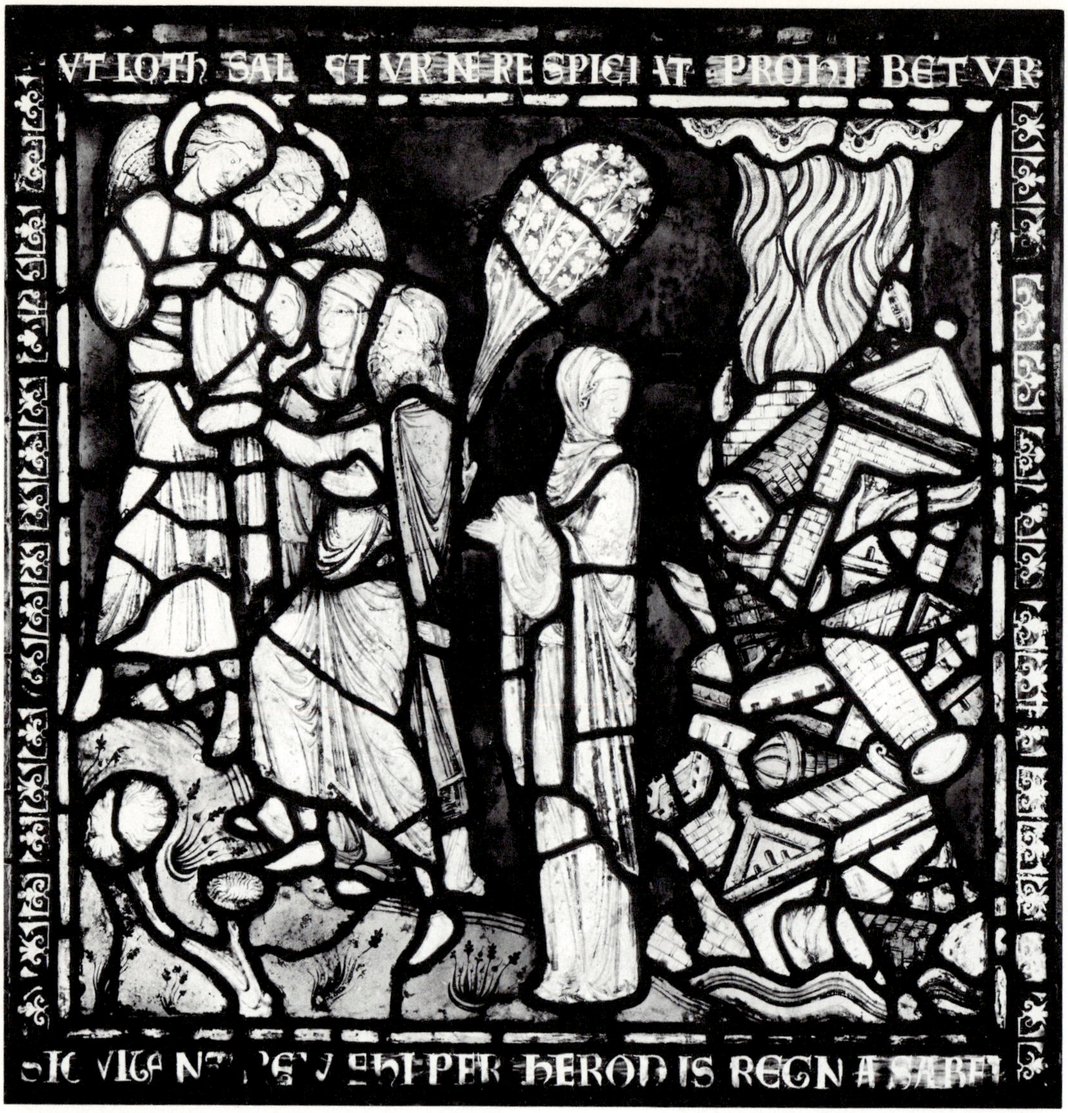

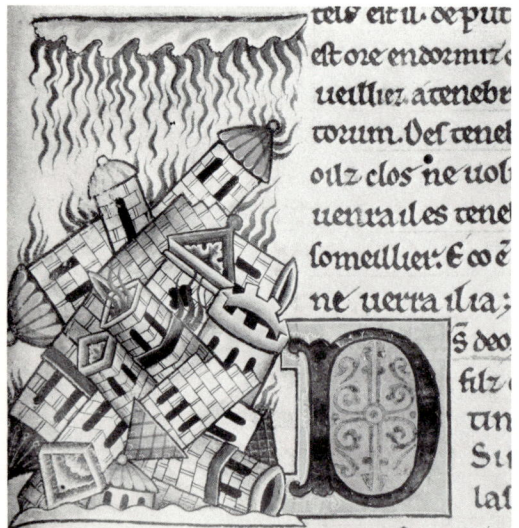

VT LOTH SAL ET VR NE RESPICIAT PROIBETVR

IC VIGANT PGV QHI PER HEROD IS REGN A SABET

51. North choir aisle n:XV (10), destruction of Sodom

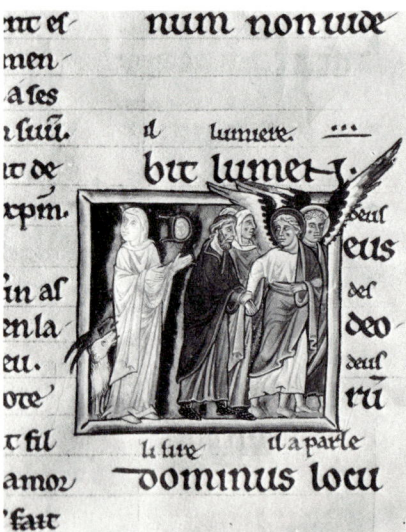

52. North French Psalter, New York, Morgan Library, MS 338, f.196v details with
    destruction of Sodom

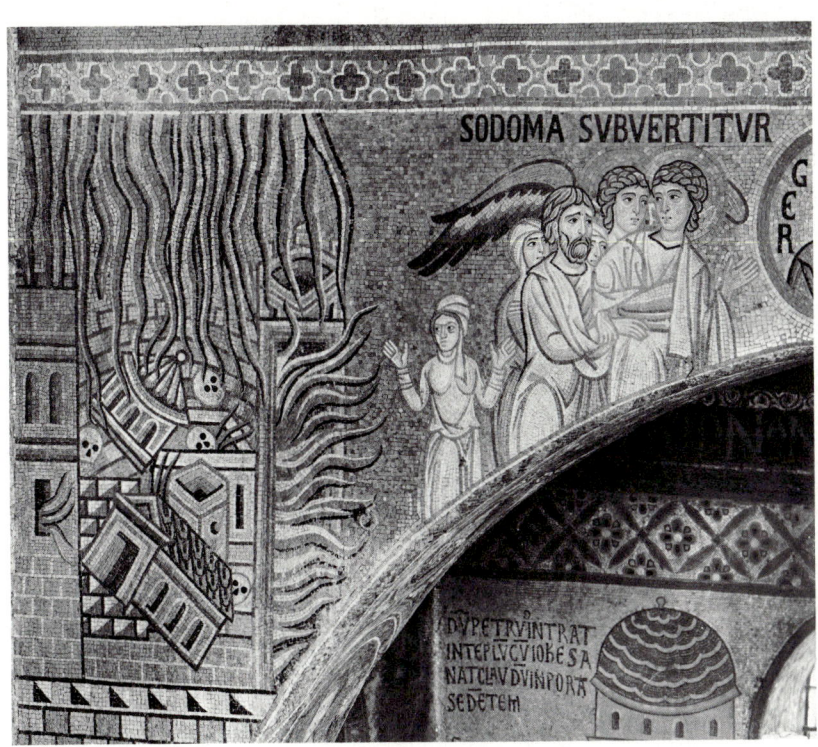

53

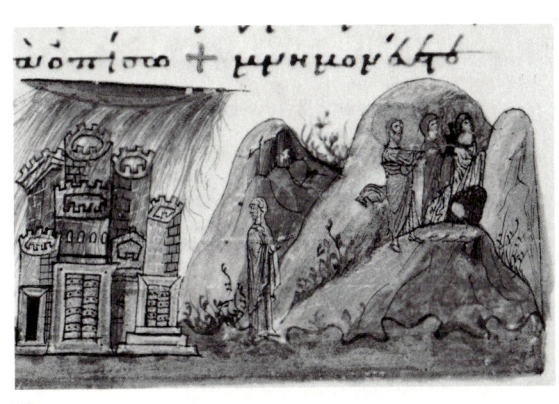

54

53. Palermo, Capella Palatina, mosaic of
   destruction of Sodom

54. Byzantine Gospels, eleventh century, Paris,
   Bibliothèque Nationale, MS grec. 74, p. 147,
   detail of destruction of Sodom

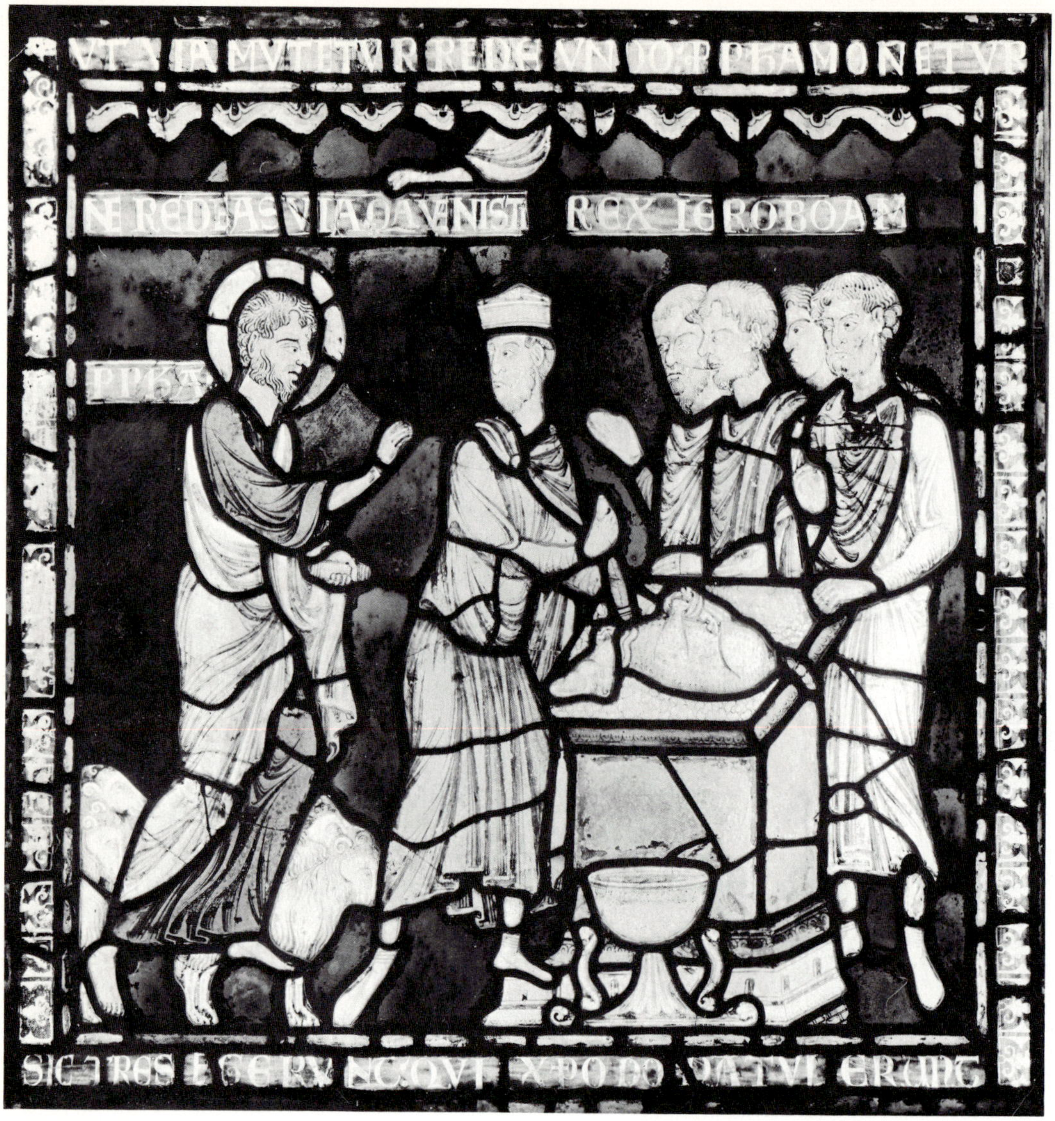

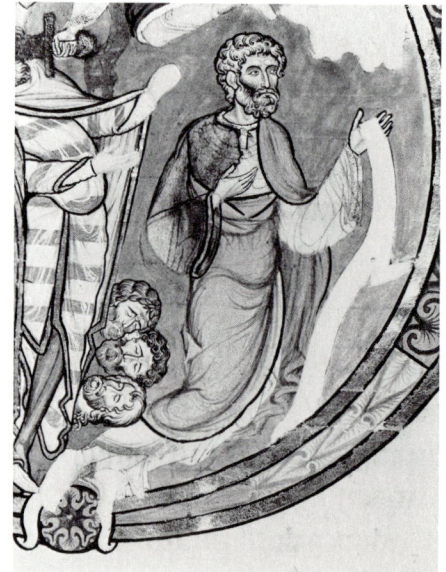

55. North choir aisle n:XV (12),
    sacrifice of Jeroboam

56. Winchester Bible, f.246,
    detail of Abraham

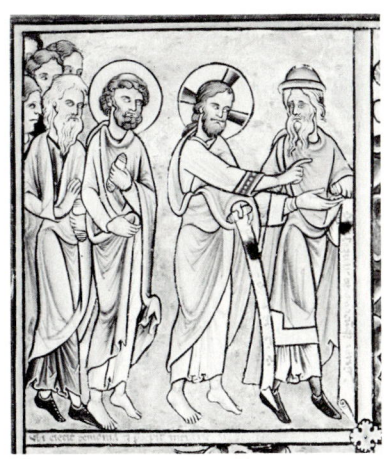

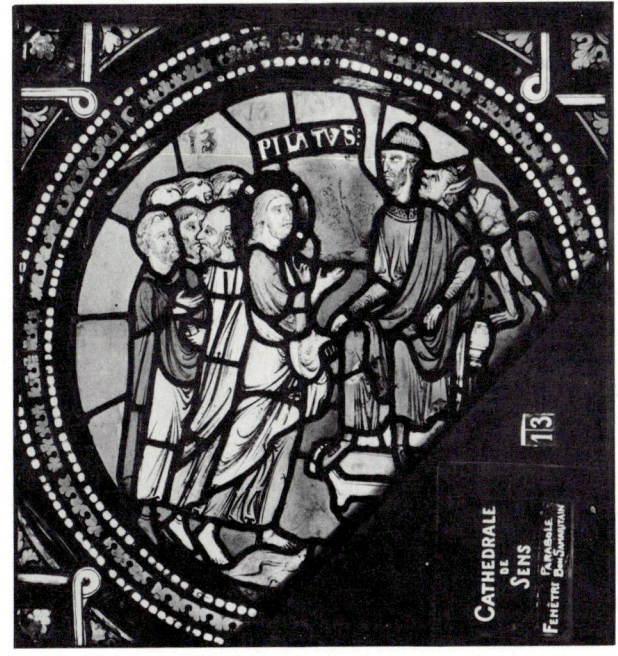

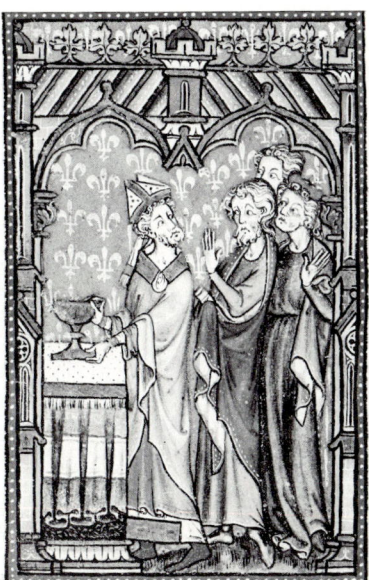

57. Great Canterbury Psalter,
Paris, Bibliothèque Nationale,
MS Lat. 8846, f.3v, detail of
Christ teaching

58. Sens, Good Samaritan window,
Christ before Pilate

59. Peterborough Psalter,
Brussels, Bibliothèque Royale,
MS 9961–62, f.12v, detail,
sacrifice of Jeroboam

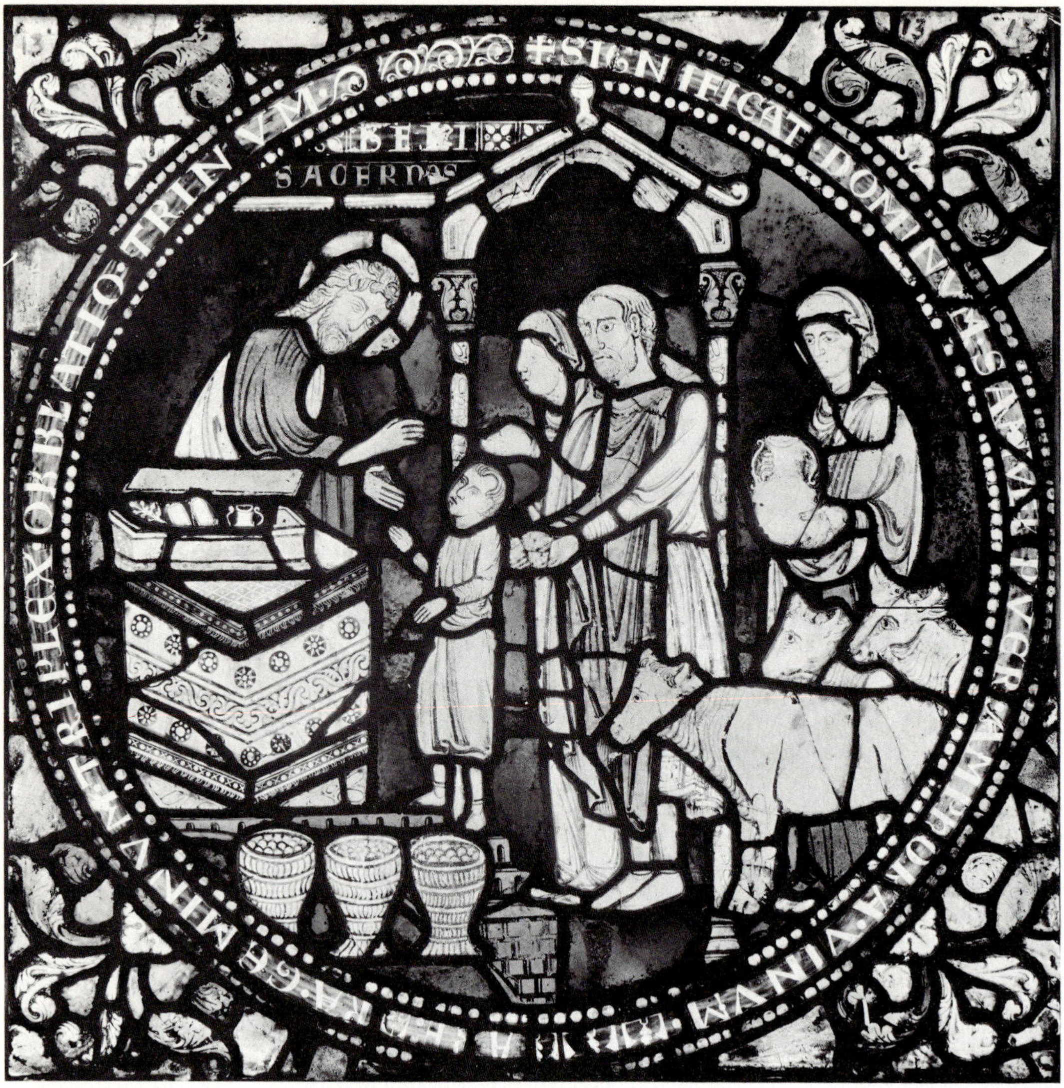

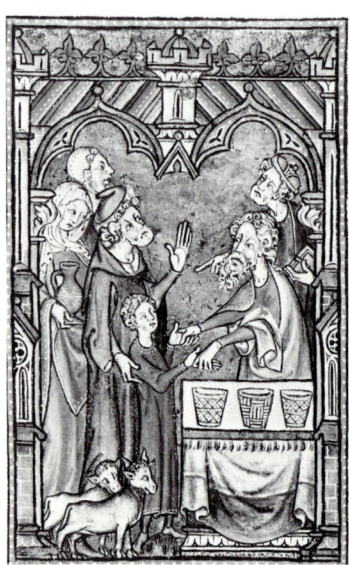

60. North choir aisle
n:XV (13),
presentation of
Samuel

61. Peterborough Psalter,
Brussels, Bibliothèque
Royale, MS 9961–62, f.12v,
detail, presentation
of Samuel

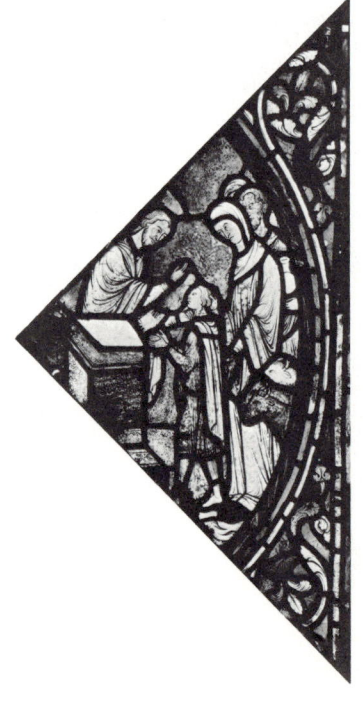

62. St.-Quentin,
Collegiate Church,
Lady Chapel window,
presentation of
Samuel

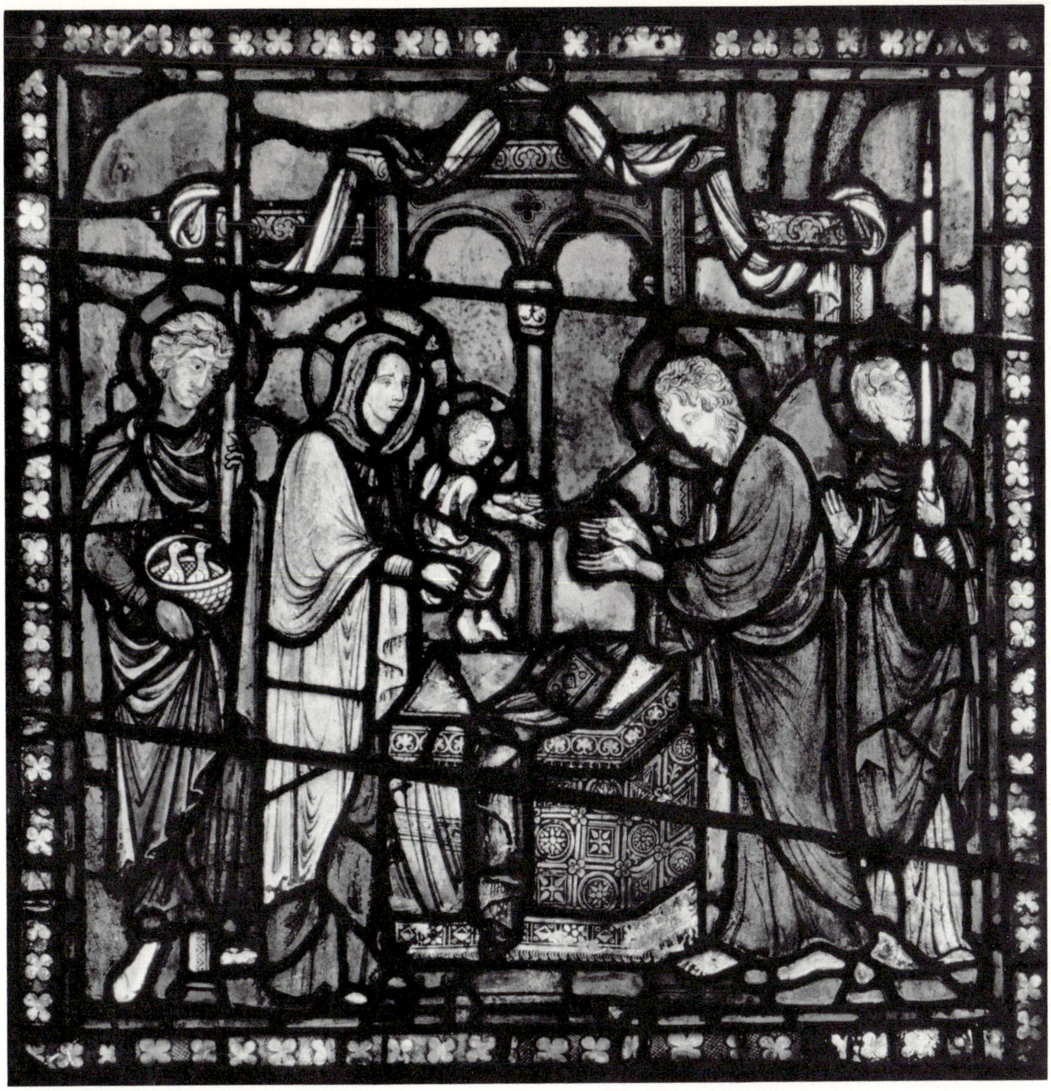

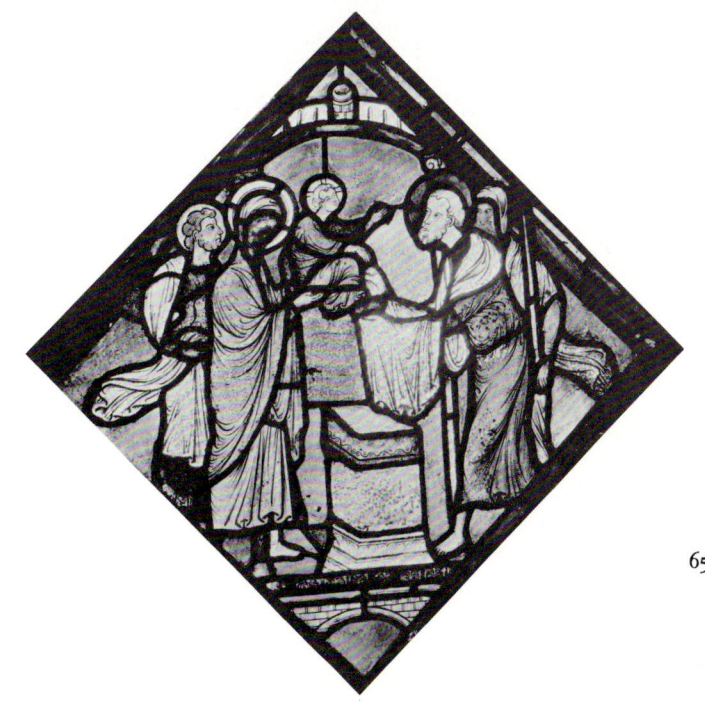

63. North choir aisle
n:XV (14),
presentation of
Christ

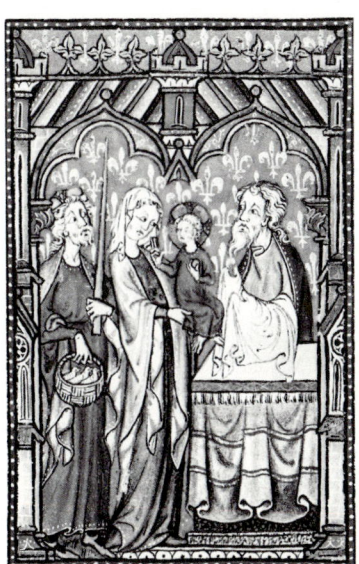

64. Peterborough Psalter,
Brussels, Bibliothèque
Royale, MS 9961–62, f.12v,
detail of presentation
of Christ

65. St.-Quentin,
Collegiate Church,
Lady Chapel window,
presentation
of Christ

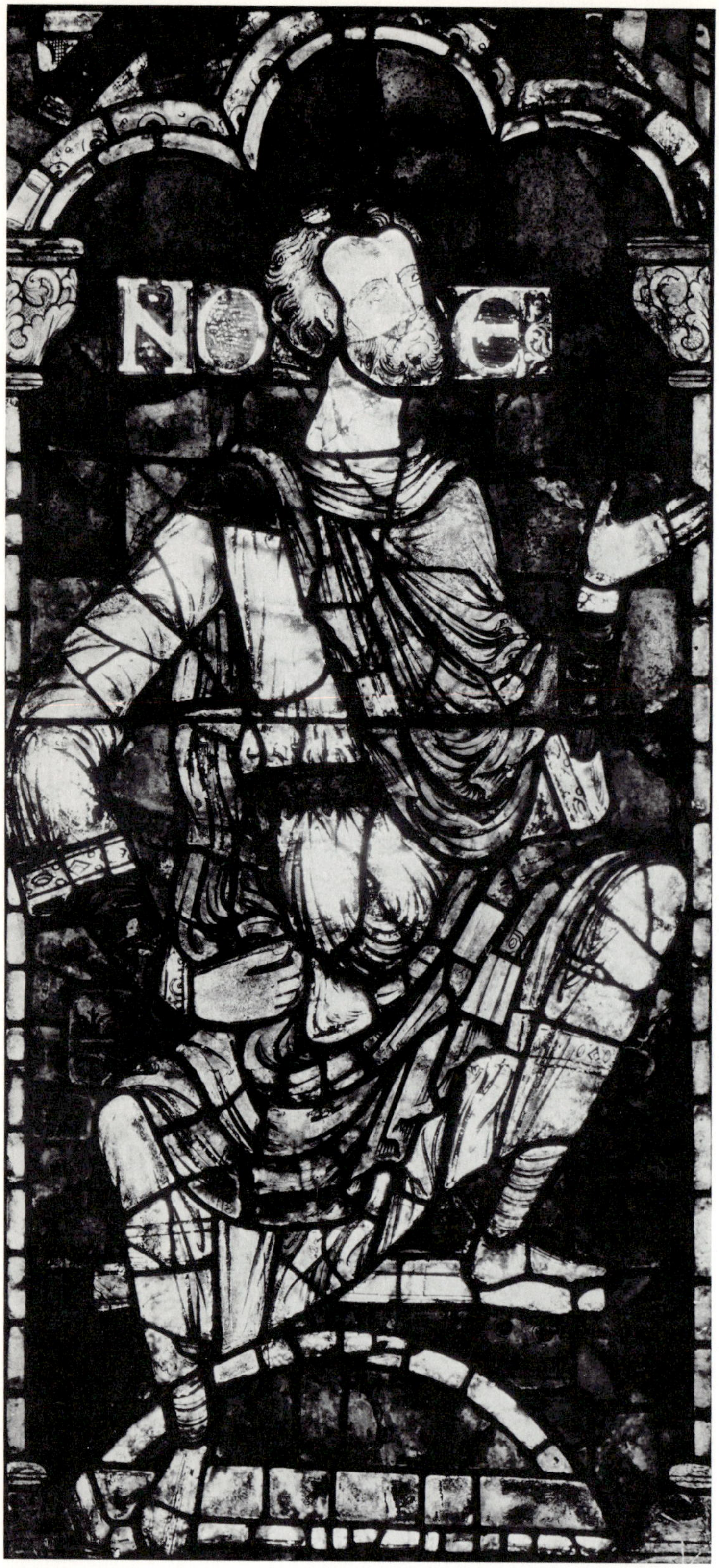

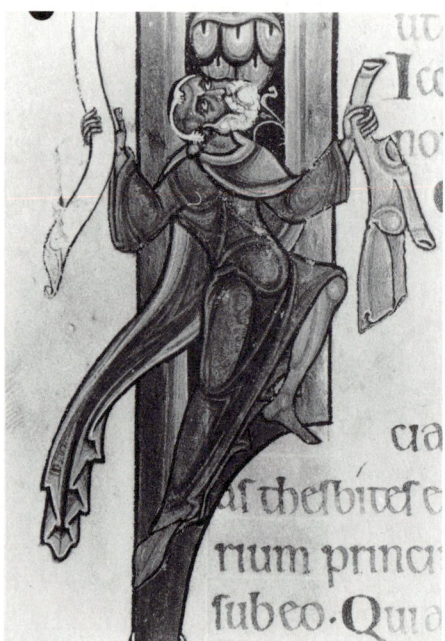

66. Noah, from clerestory N:XX

67. Shem, from clerestory N:XX

68. Winchester Bible, f.120v,
    detail of Elisha

69. Aelfric, Pentateuch, British Museum,
    Cotton Claudius MS B.IV, f.15v,
    detail of Noah

68

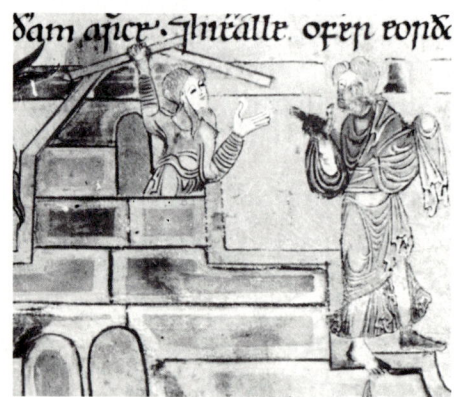

66

69

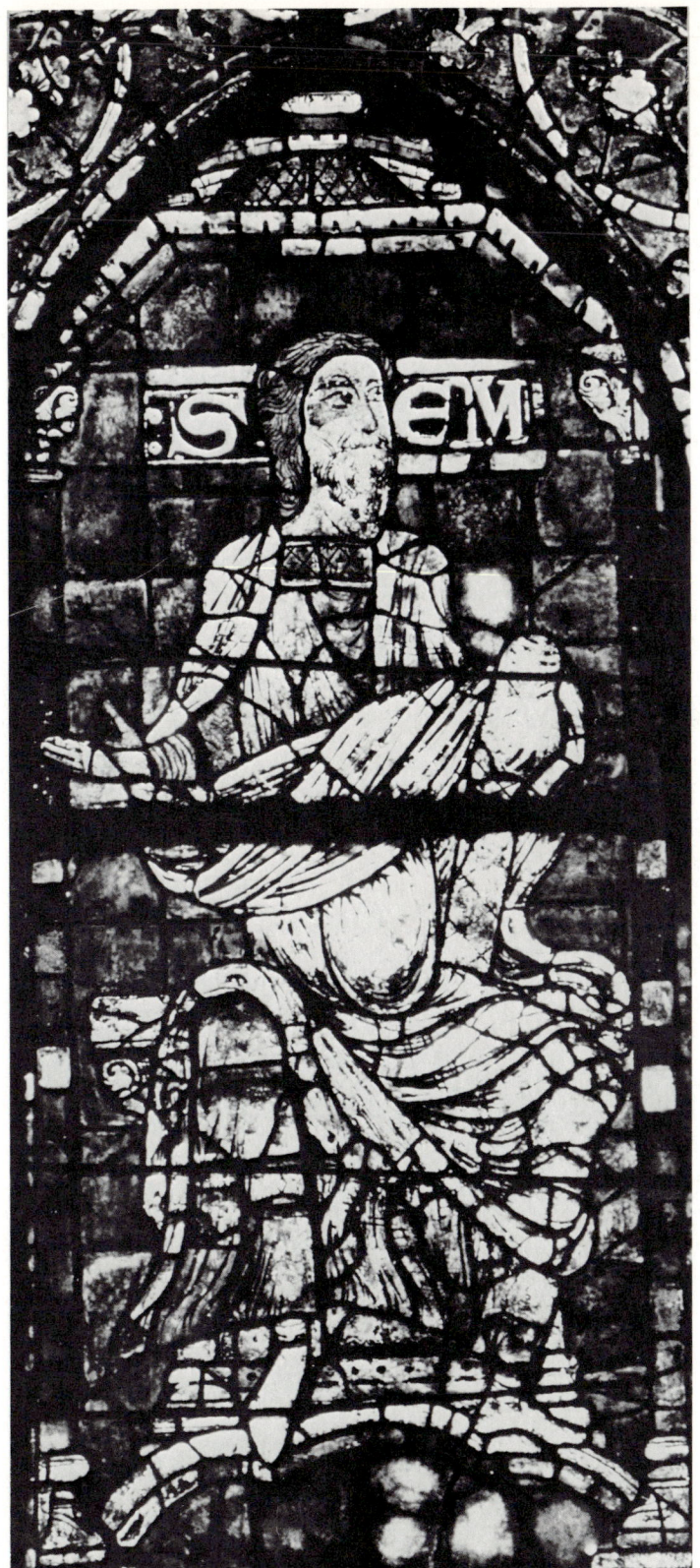

67

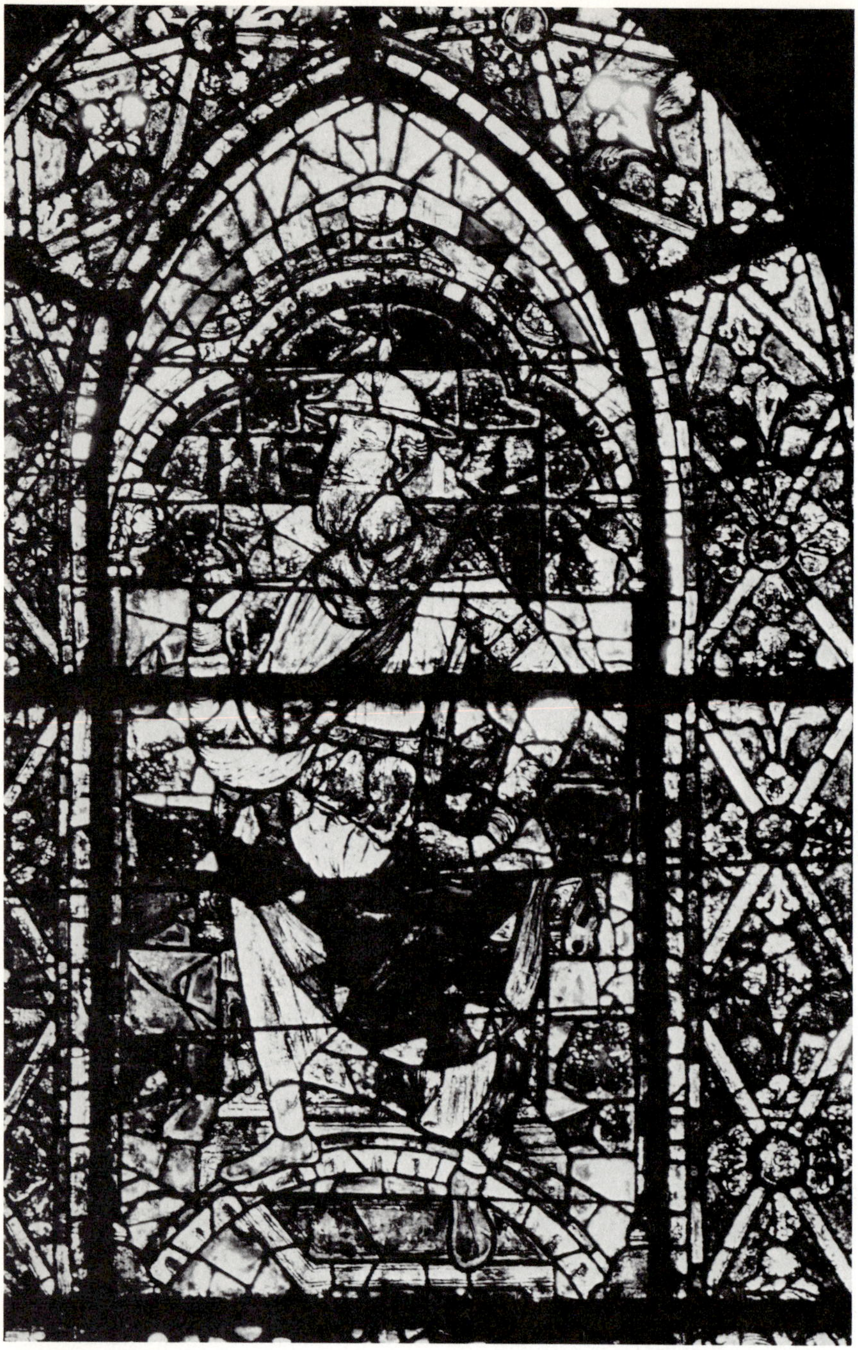

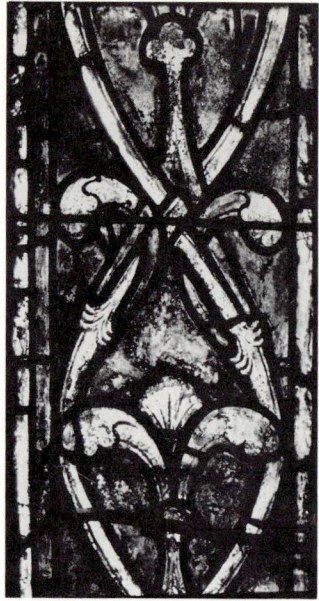

71

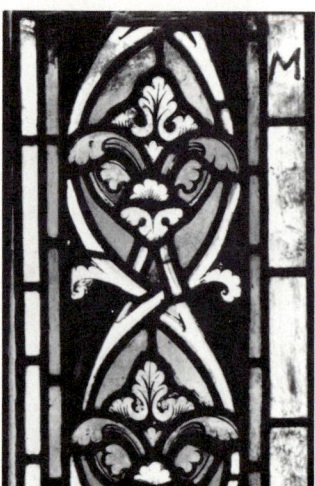

73

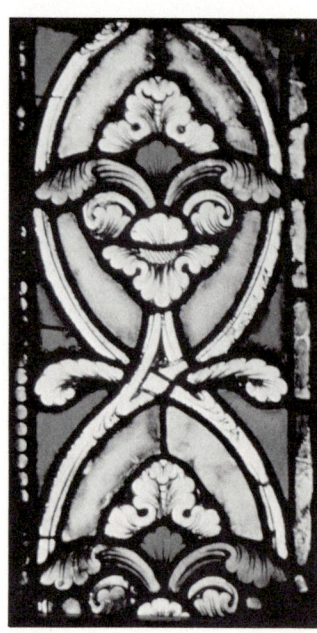

74

70. Neri, from clerestory S:XII

72

71. Clerestory N:XIV, border

72. Bury Bible, Cambridge, Corpus Christi
College, MS 2, f.147, detail of border

73. Sens, Good Samaritan window, border

74. Corona, Jesse window by Austin,
1861, border

75. Clerestory S:XIV, border

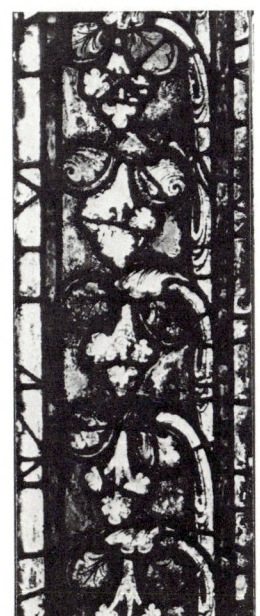

75

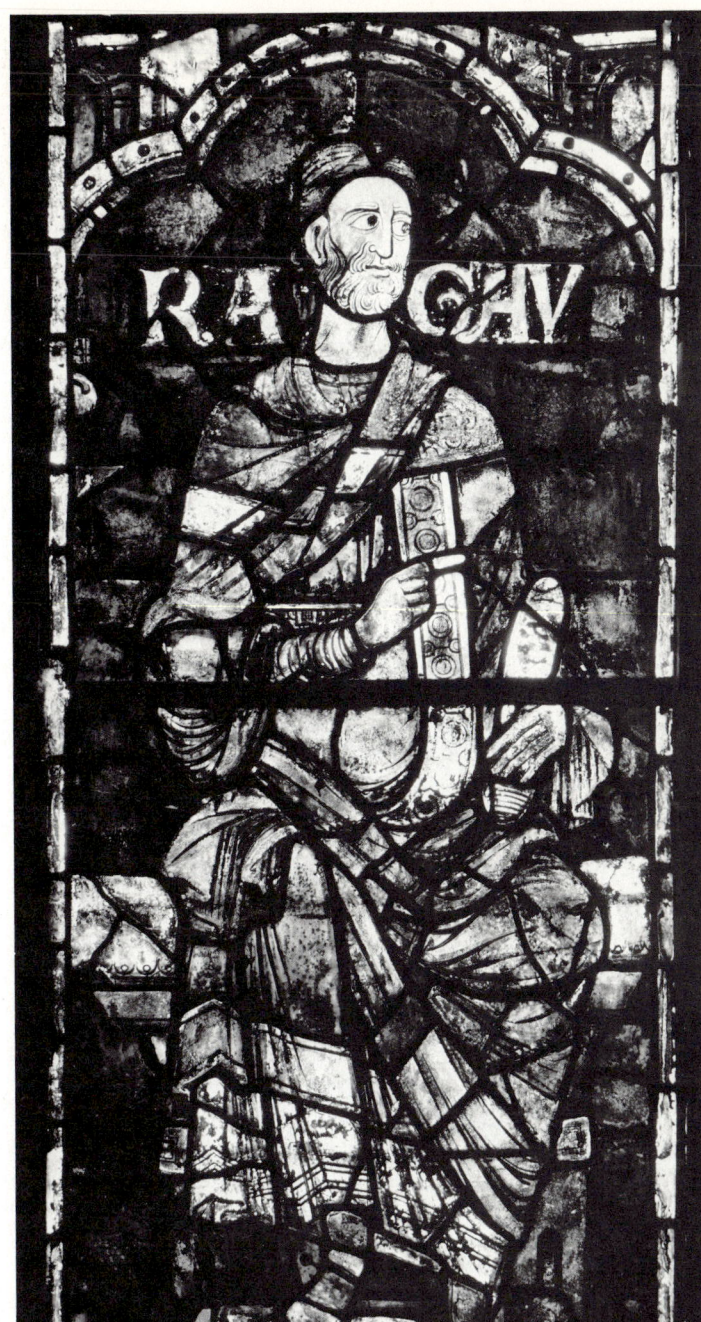

76. Reu, from clerestory N:XVI

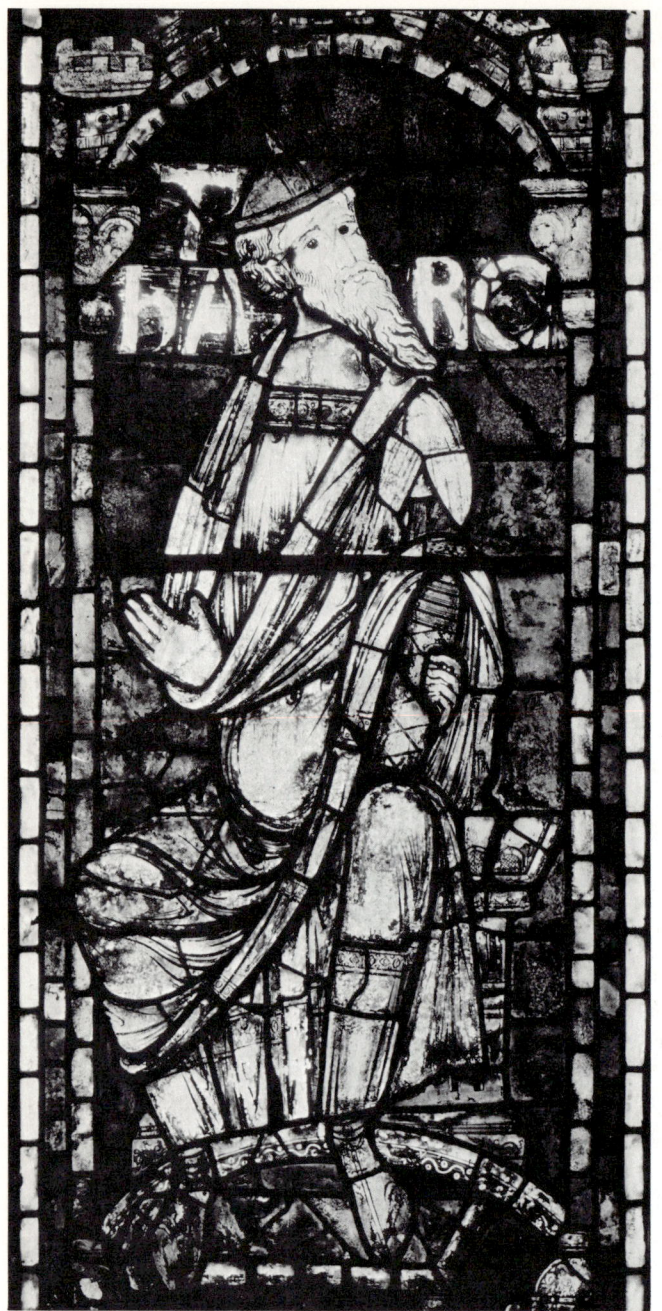

77. Terah, from clerestory N:XIV

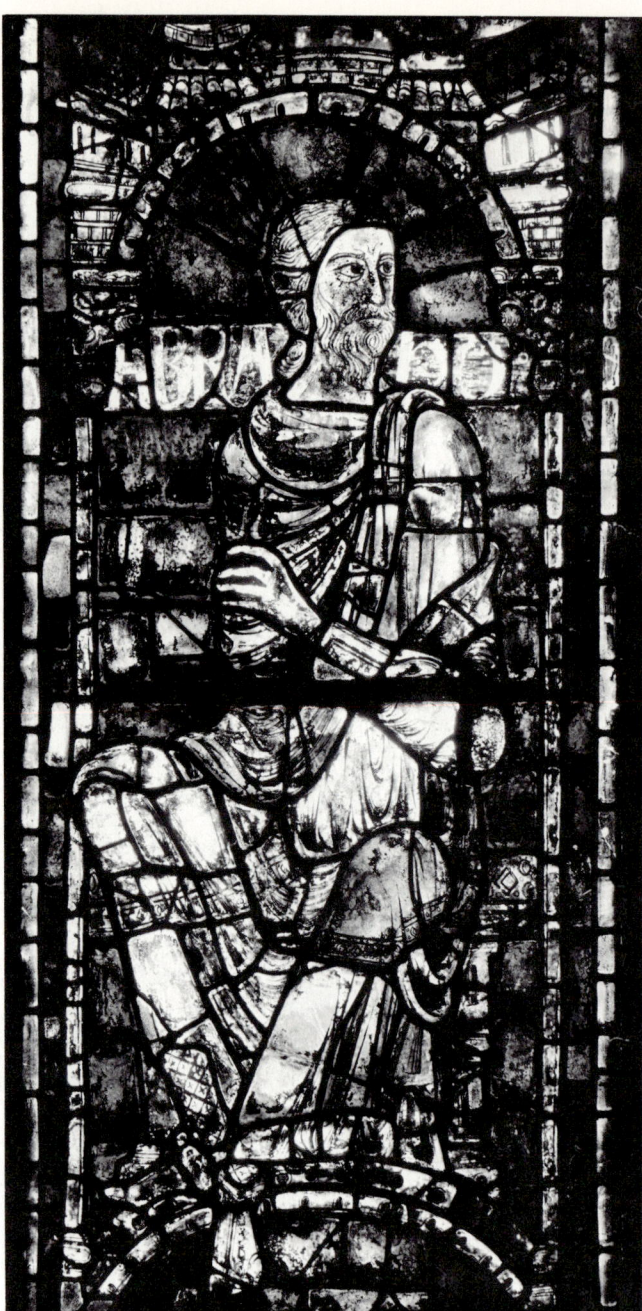

78. Abraham, from clerestory N:XIV

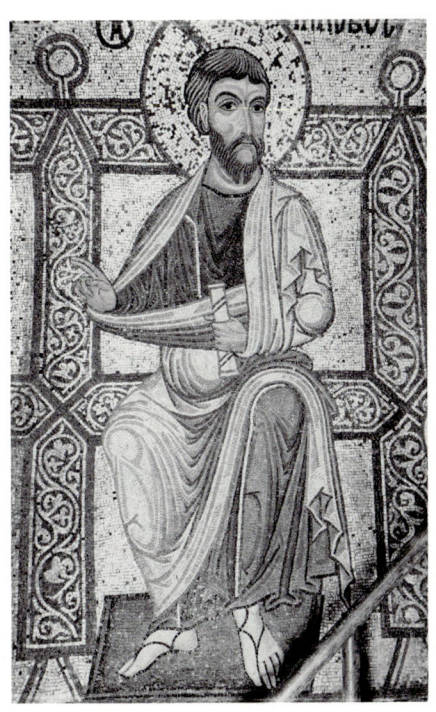

79

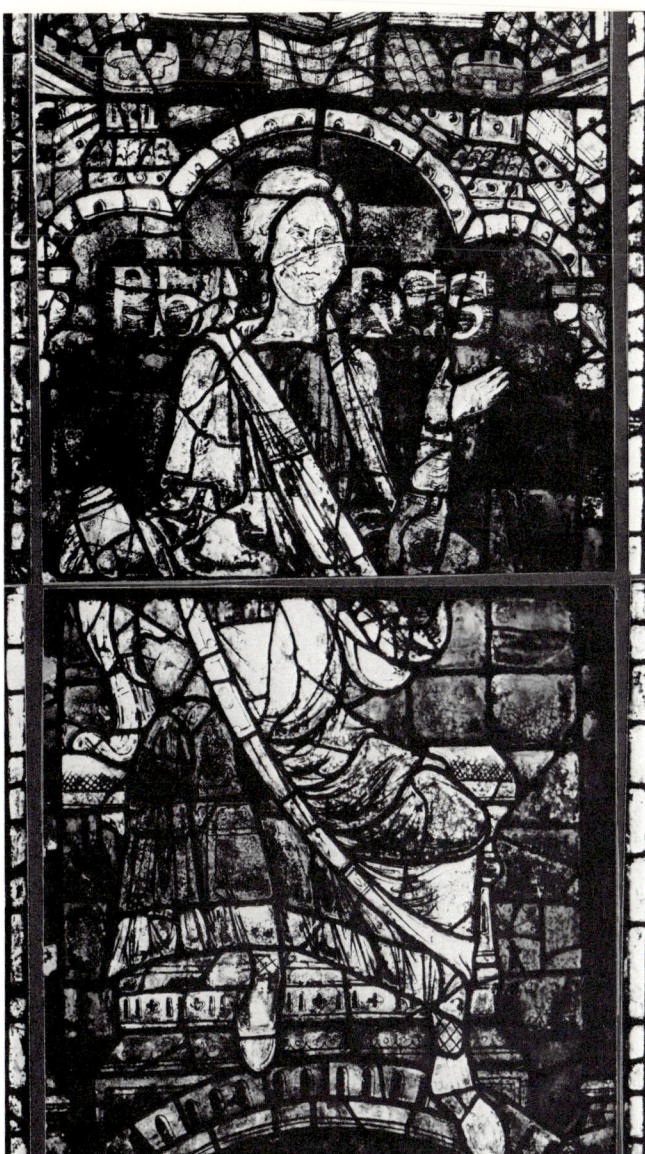

80

79. Palermo, Capella Palatina,
    mosaic, detail of St. James
    from Pentecost

80. Phares, from clerestory N:XII

81. Ingebourg Psalter, Chantilly, Musée Condé,
    MS 1695, f.18v, detail of Herod

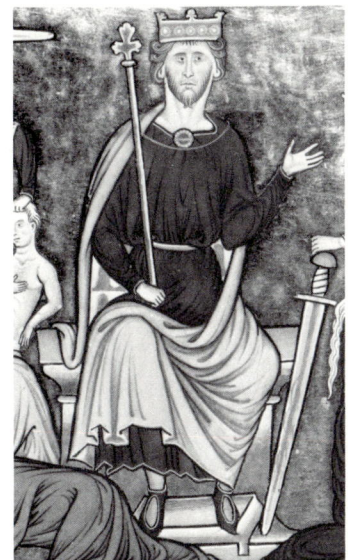

81

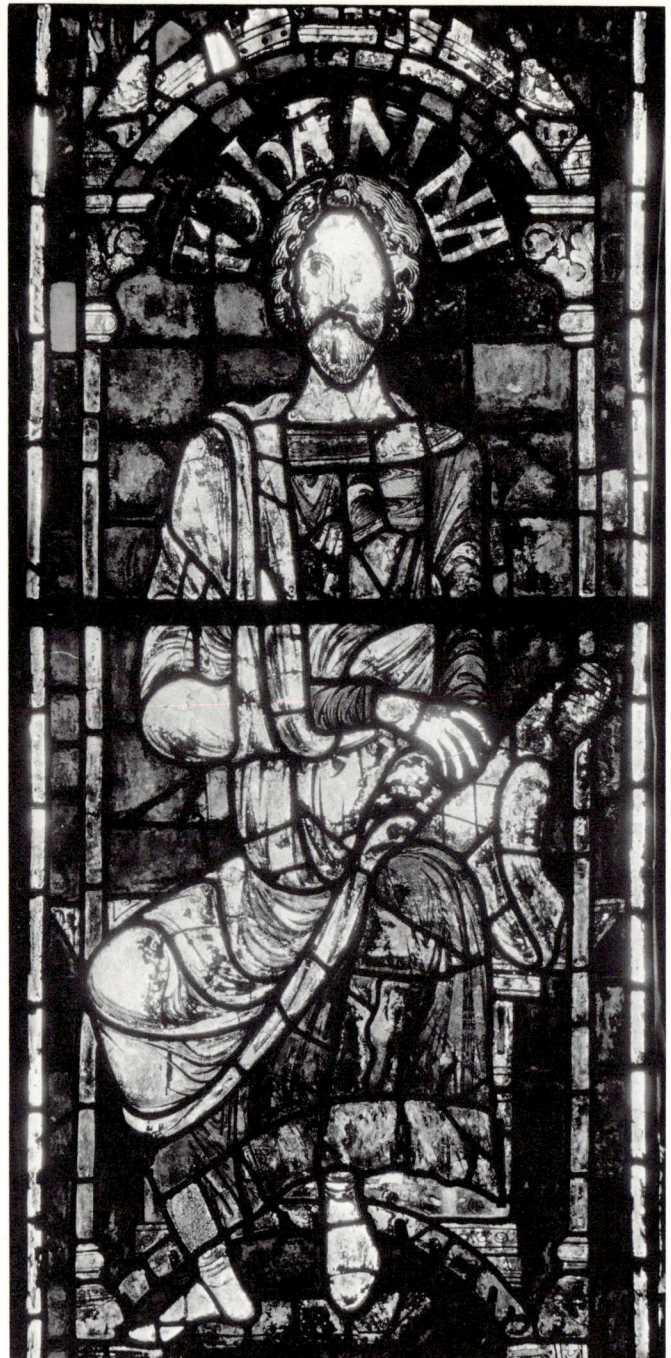

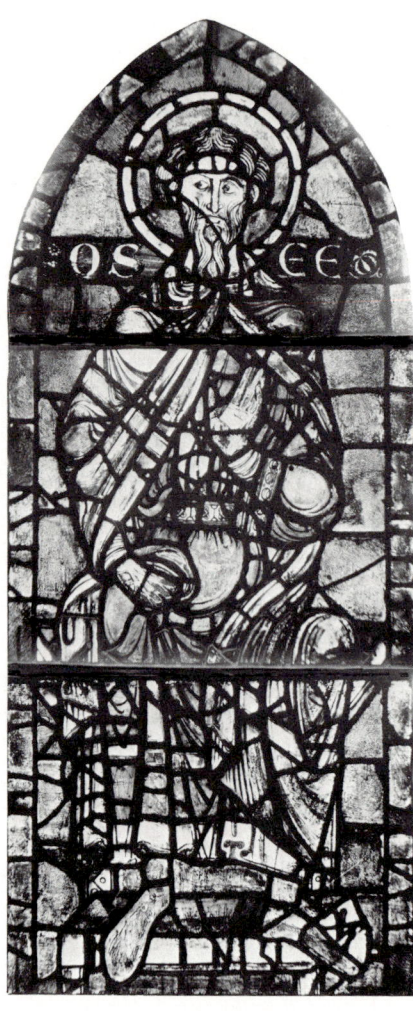

82. Joanna, from clerestory
S:XIV

83. Rheims, St.-Remi,
clerestory, Hosea

84. Winchester Bible, f.250,
initials to Psalm 110

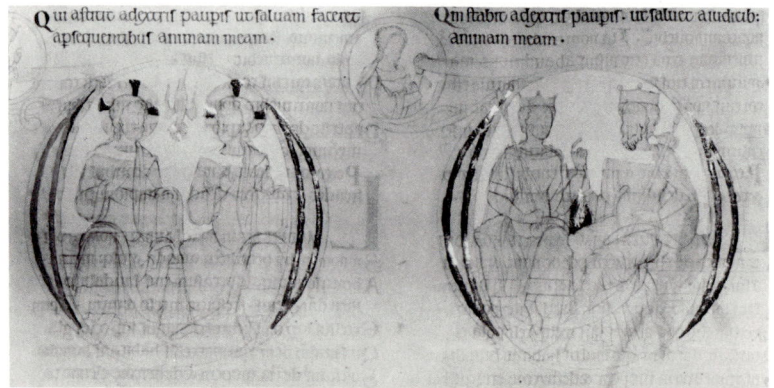

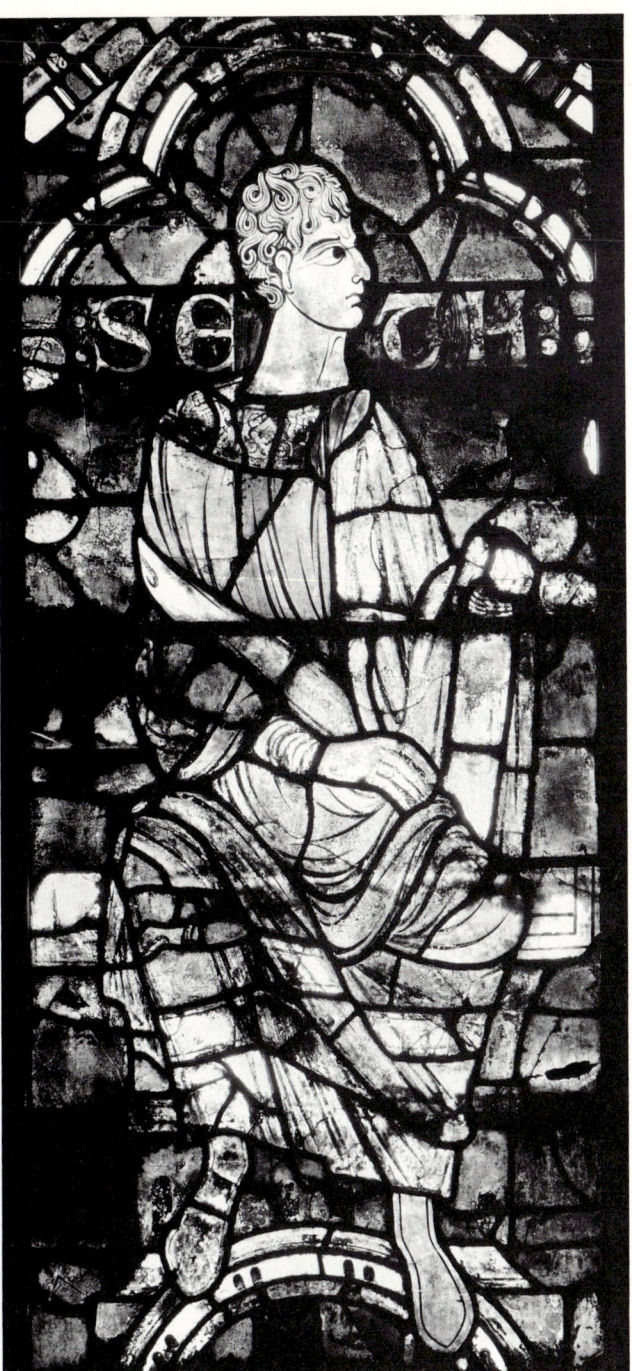

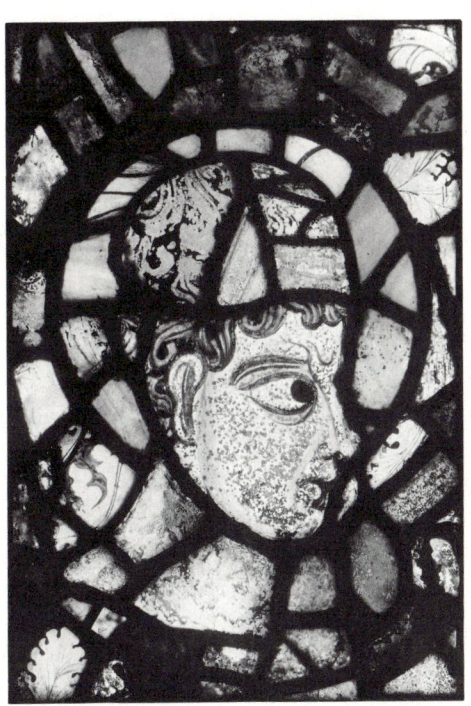

85. Semei, from clerestory S:XV

86. Victoria and Albert Museum,
    original head of Semei

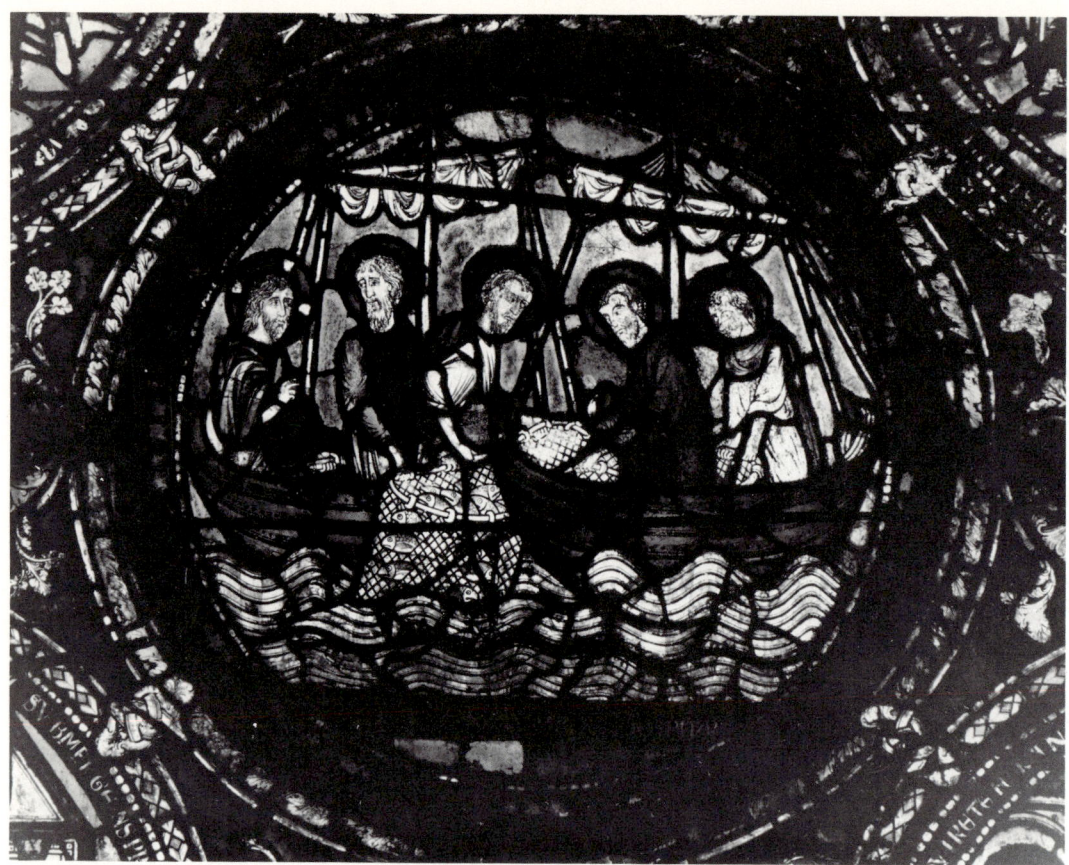

87. Miraculous draught of fishes, from the fourth typological window

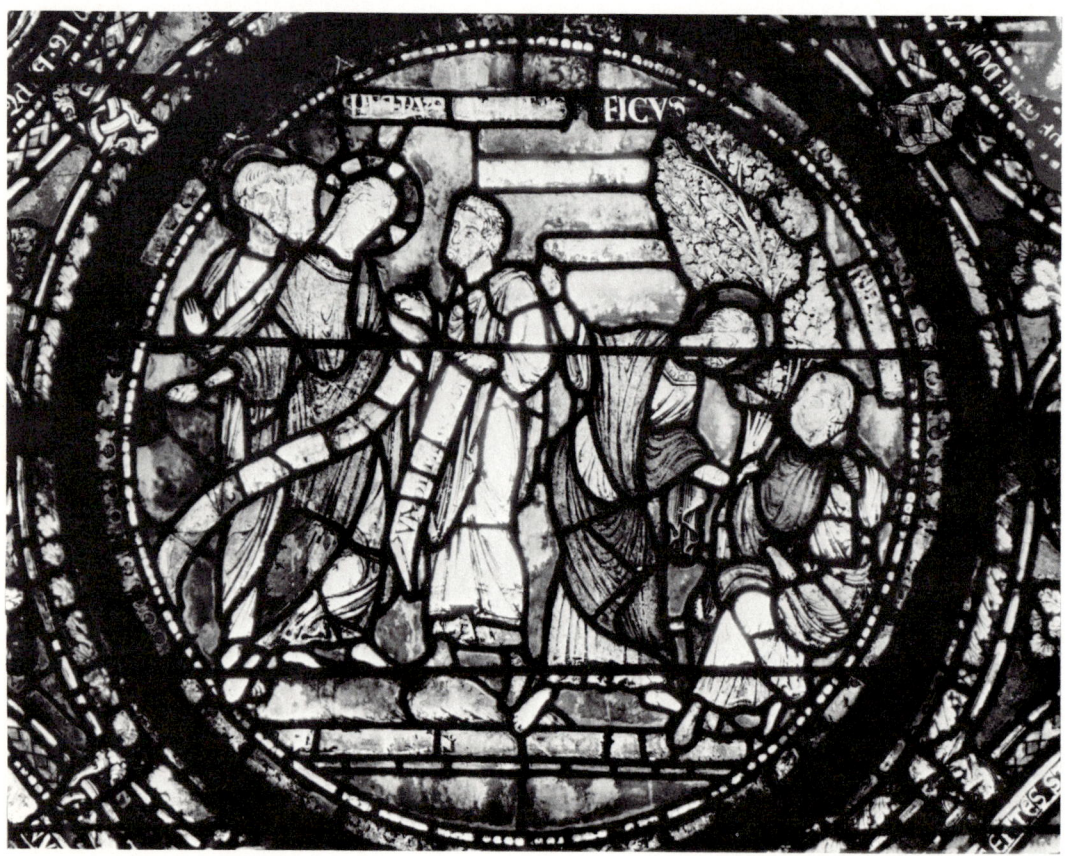

88. Calling of Nathanael, from the fourth typological window

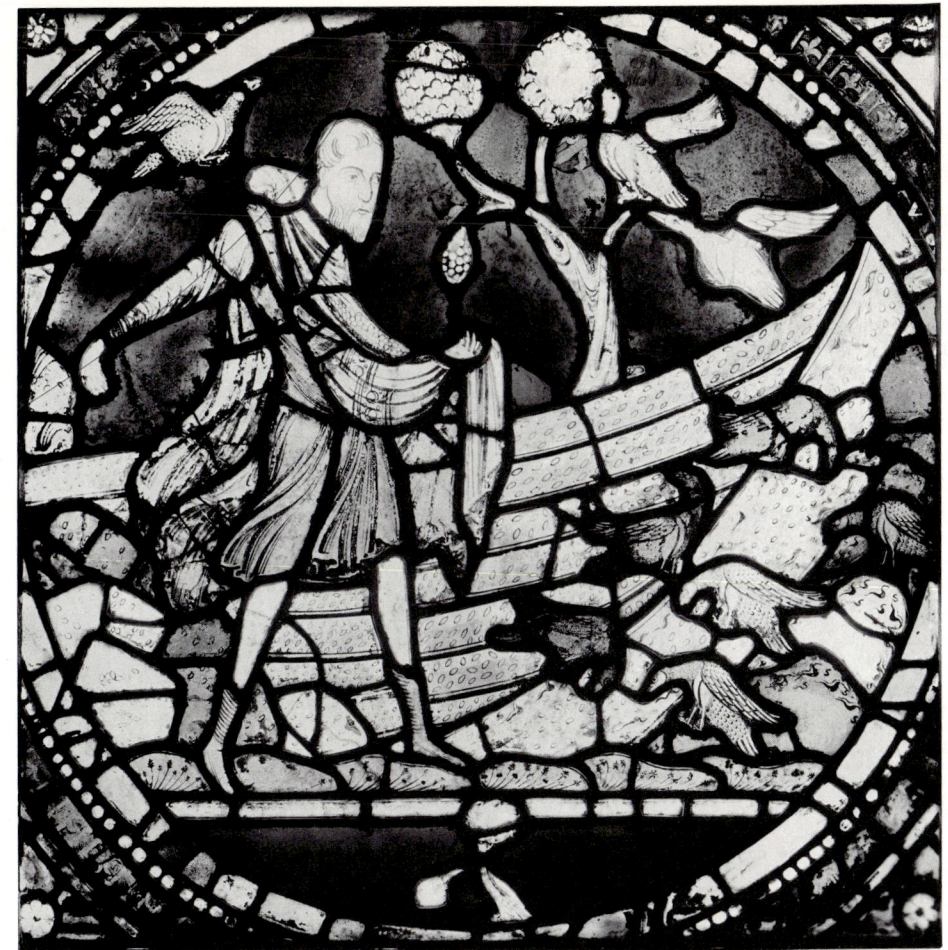

89

89. The sower on stony ground,
    from the sixth typological
    window

90. Utrecht Psalter copy,
    British Museum,
    Harl. MS 603, f.21,
    detail, Psalm 37

91. Hortus Deliciarum,
    the parable of the sower
    (copy, f.108v)

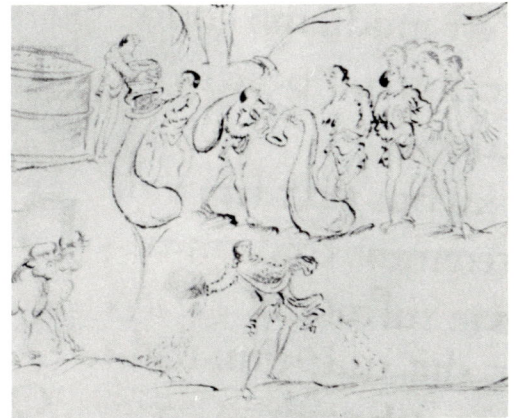

90

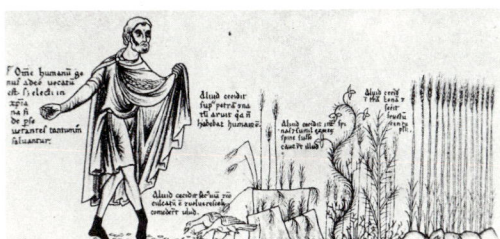

91

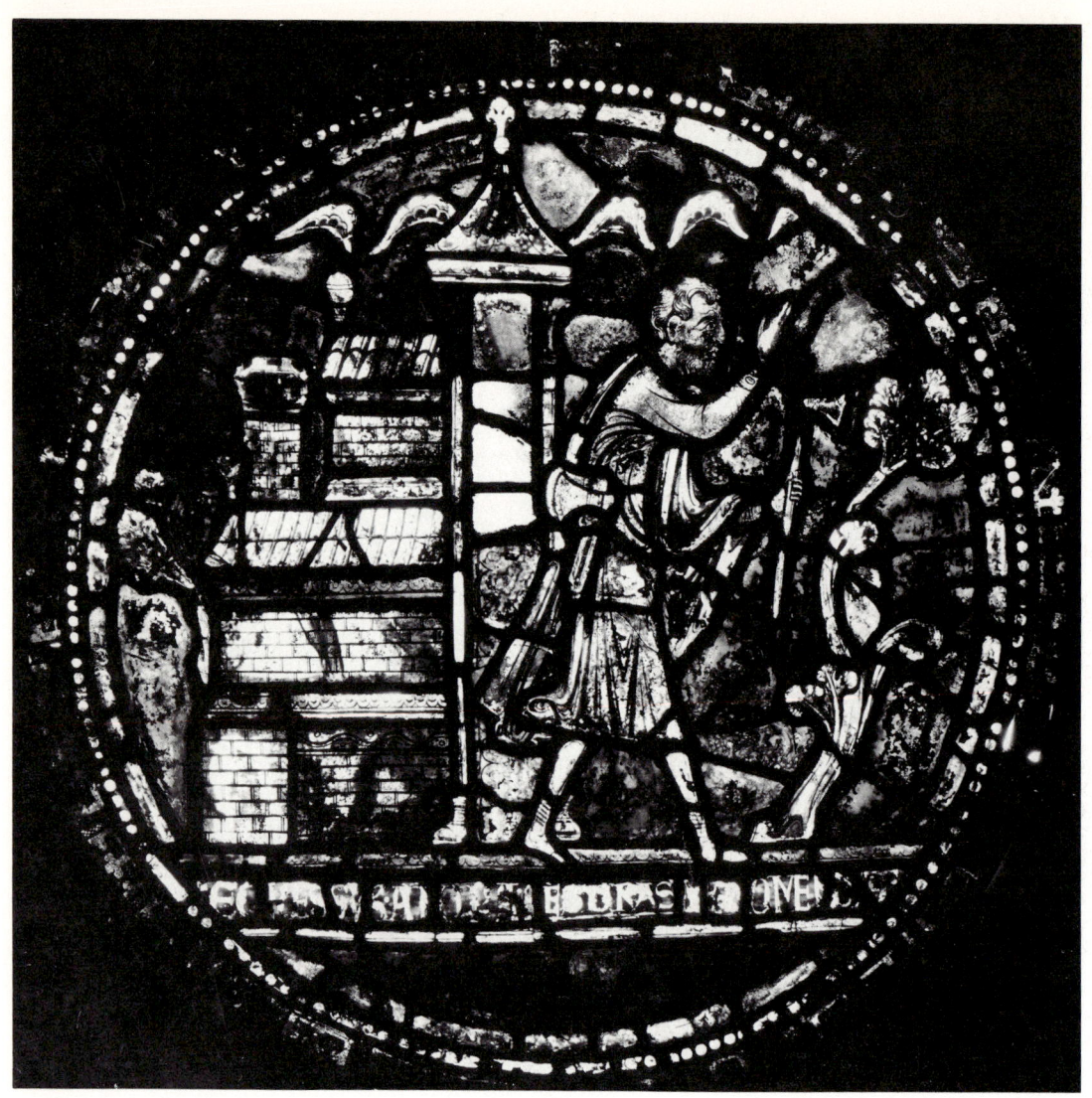

92. Trinity Chapel s:II (12), William of Kellett returning to work

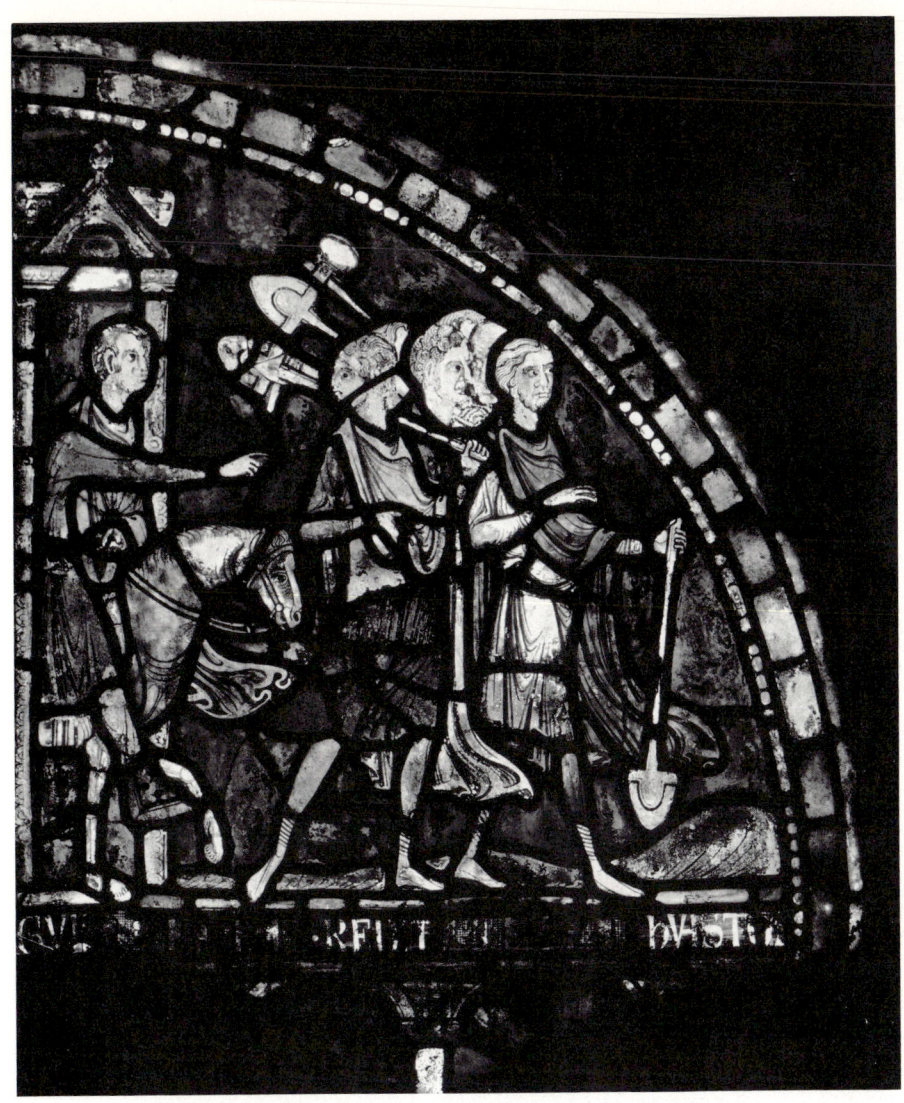

93. Trinity Chapel s:VII (19), the search party for William of Gloucester

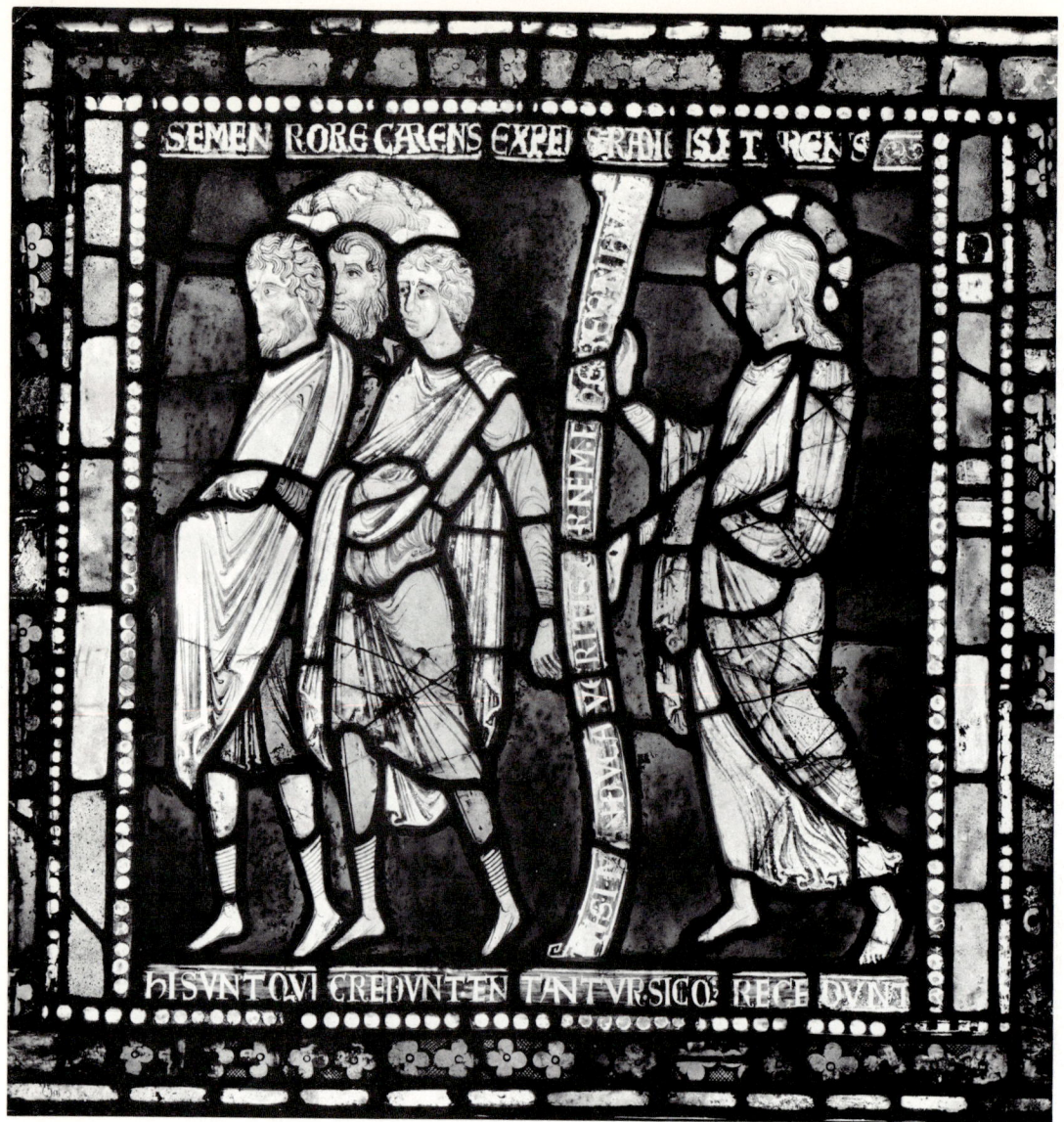

94. Pharisees turn from Christ, from the sixth typological window

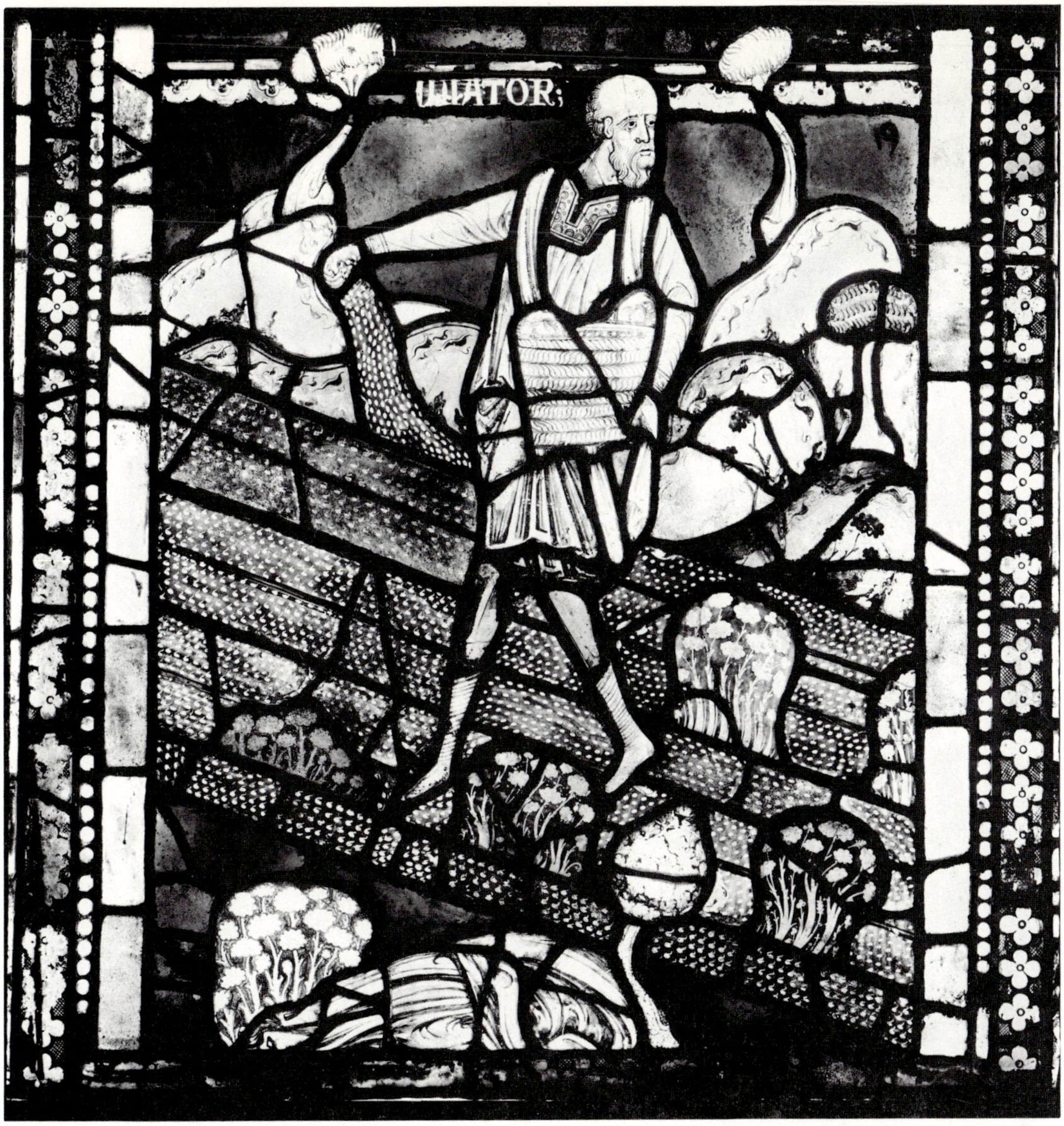

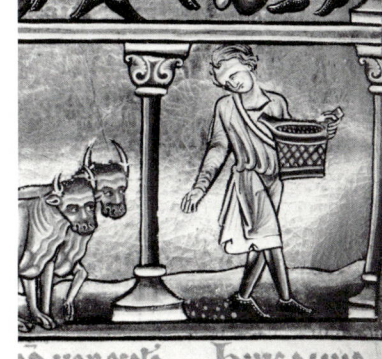

95. The sower in good ground and among thorns,
    from the sixth typological window

96. Great Canterbury Psalter, Paris,
    Bibliothèque Nationale, MS Lat. 8846, f.62v,
    detail, Psalm 37

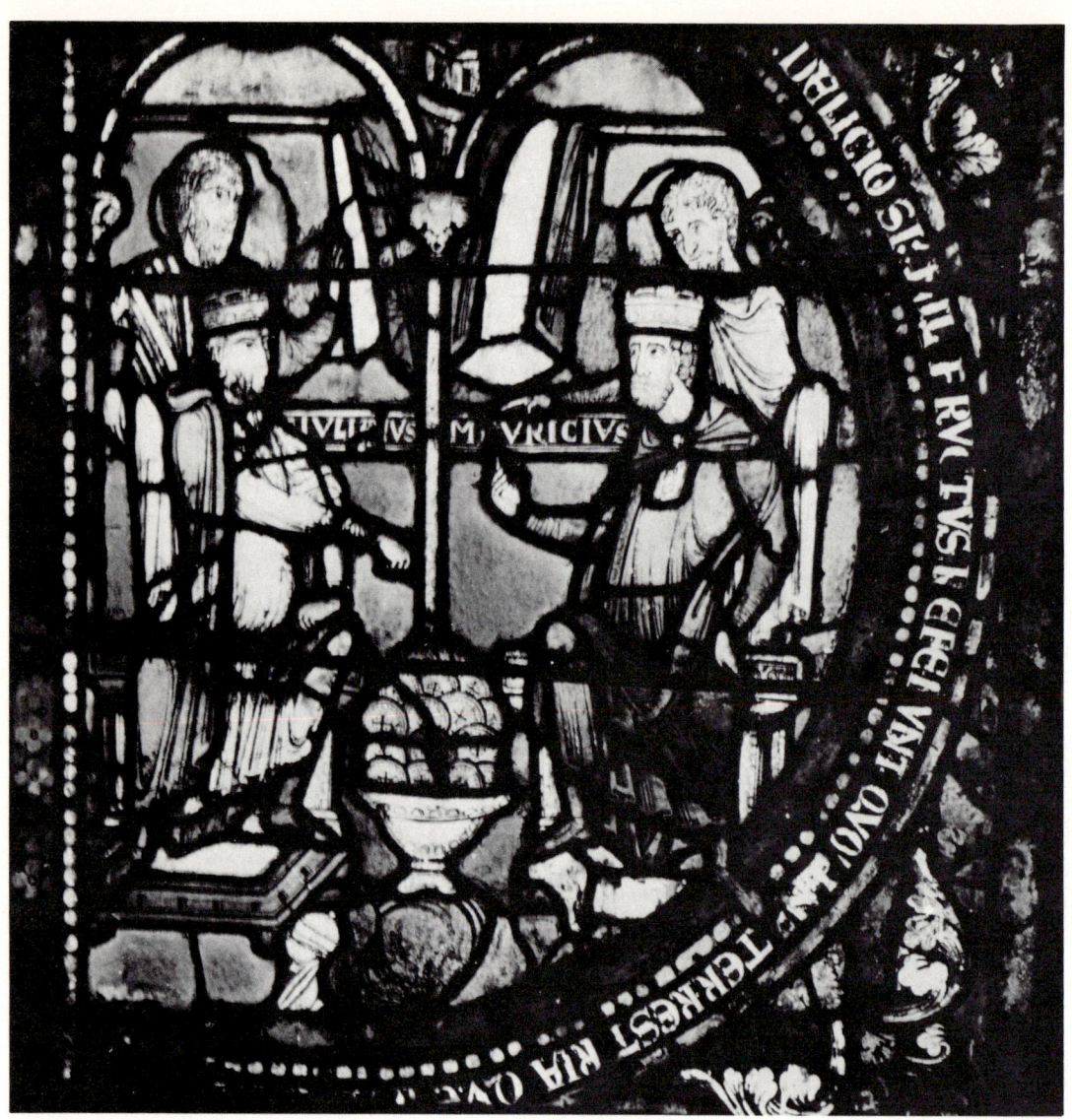

97. The Emperors Julian the Apostate and Maurice (the thorny ones),
    from the sixth typological window

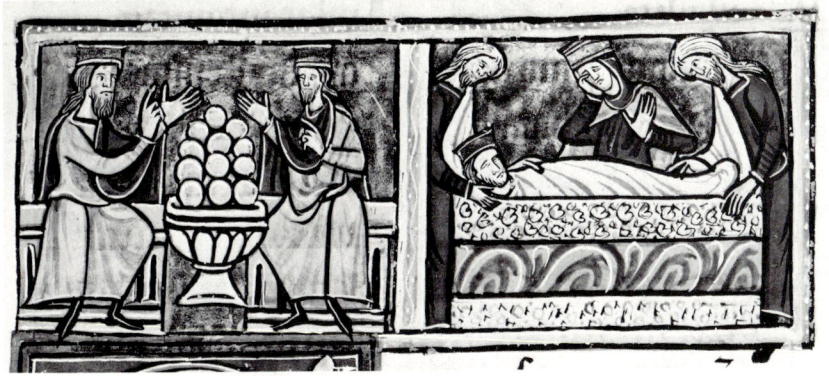

98. Little Canterbury Psalter,
Paris, Bibliothèque Nationale,
MS Lat. 770, f.124, Psalm 97,
Julian and Maurice (?)

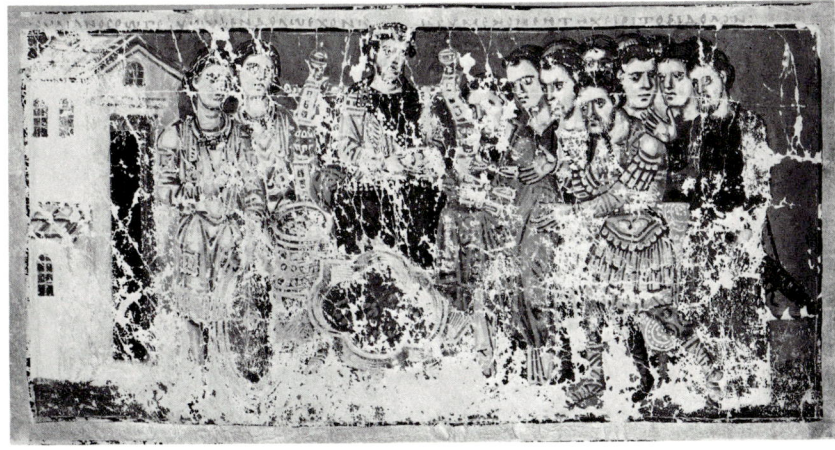

99. Homilies of Gregory Nazianzus,
Paris, Bibliothèque Nationale,
MS grec. 510, f.374v, detail,
Julian the Apostate paying
his soldiers

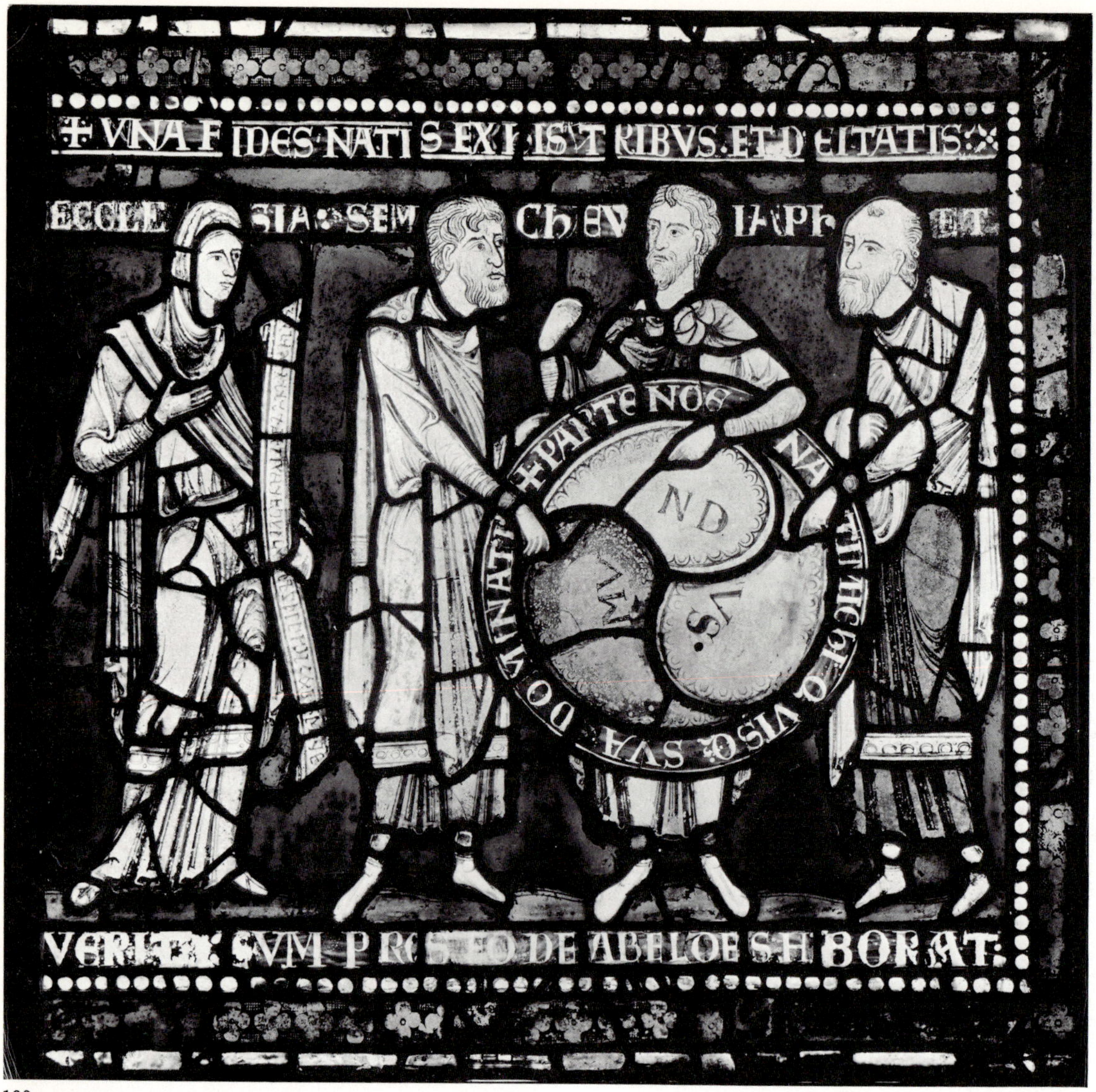

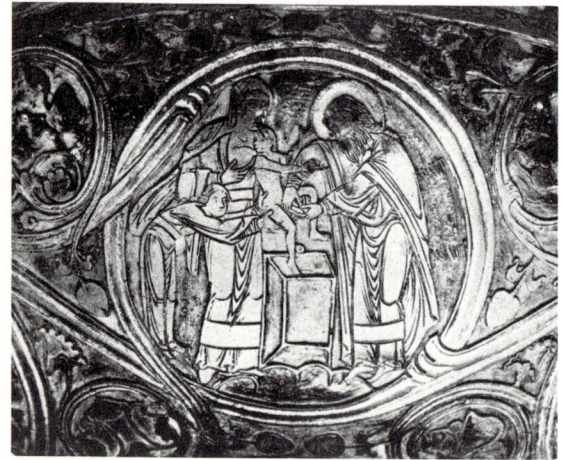

100

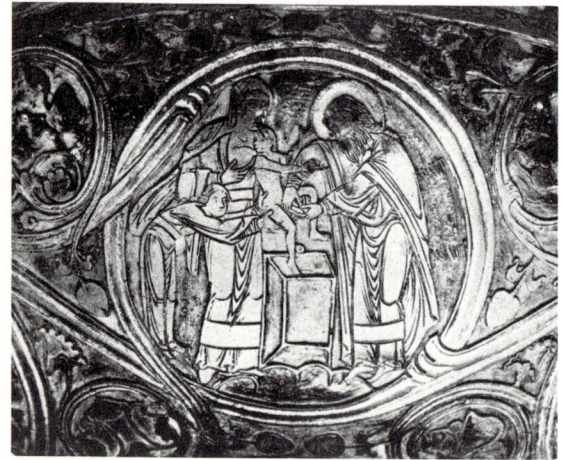

101

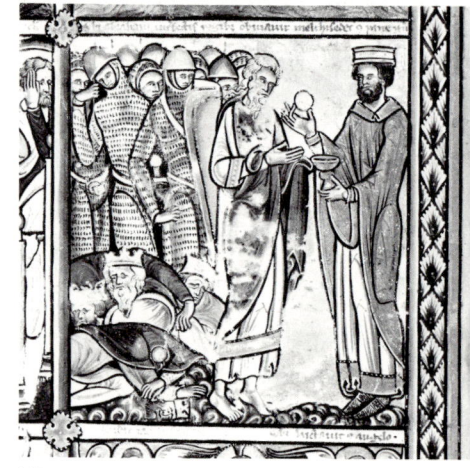

102

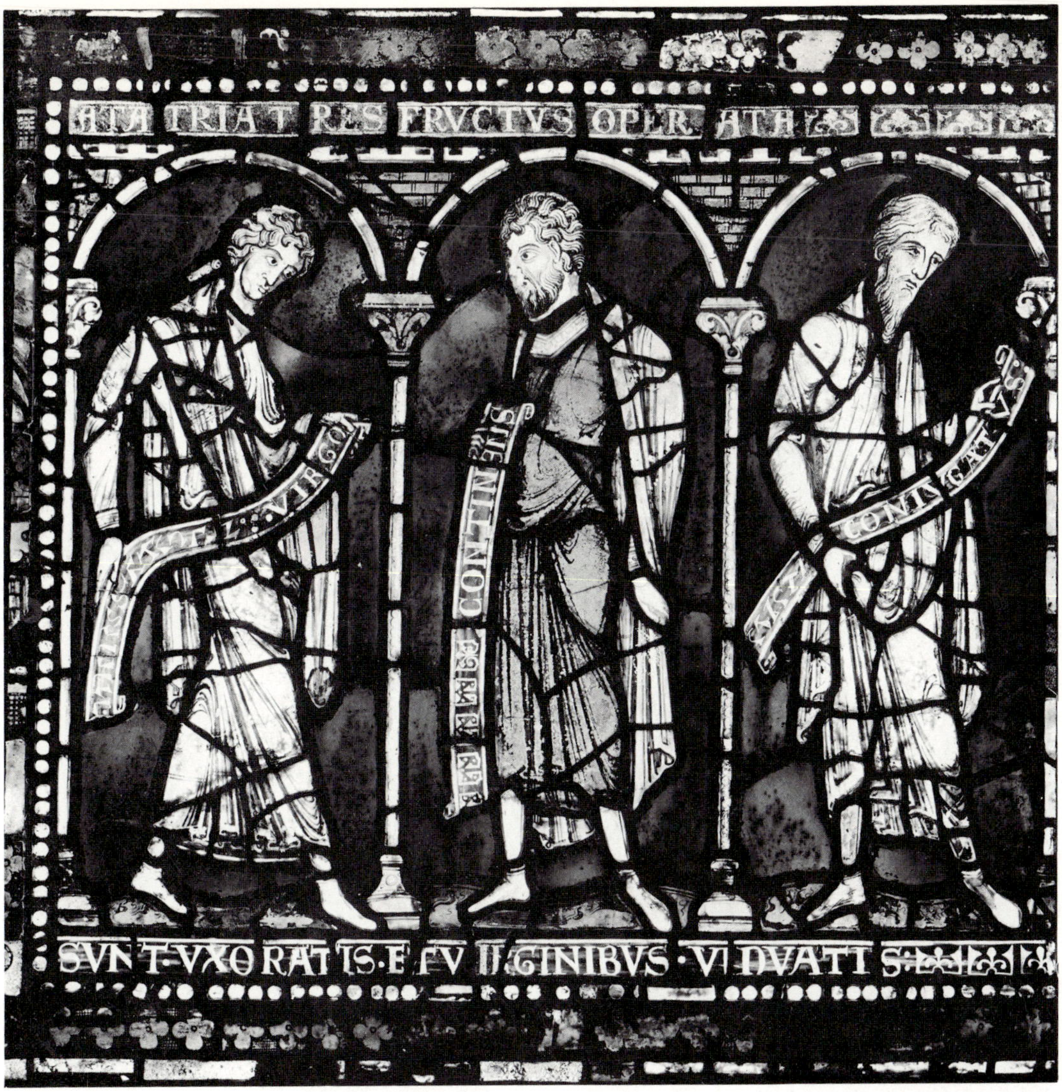

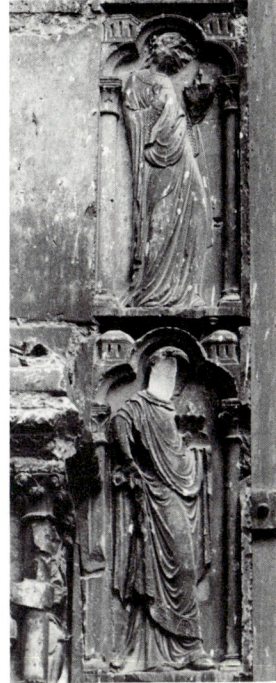

ATI TRIAT RES FRVCTVS OPER ATH

SVN T VXO RAT IS E LV IL CINIBVS VI DVATI S

103

100. Ecclesia and the three sons of Noah, from the sixth
typological window

101. Kennet Ciborium, detail of the circumcision of Isaac

102. Great Canterbury Psalter, Paris, Bibliothèque Nationale,
MS Lat. 8846, f.IV, detail, Abraham and Melchizadek

103. Three virtuous states, from the sixth
typological window

104. Sens, central west portal, jamb figures,
wise virgins

104

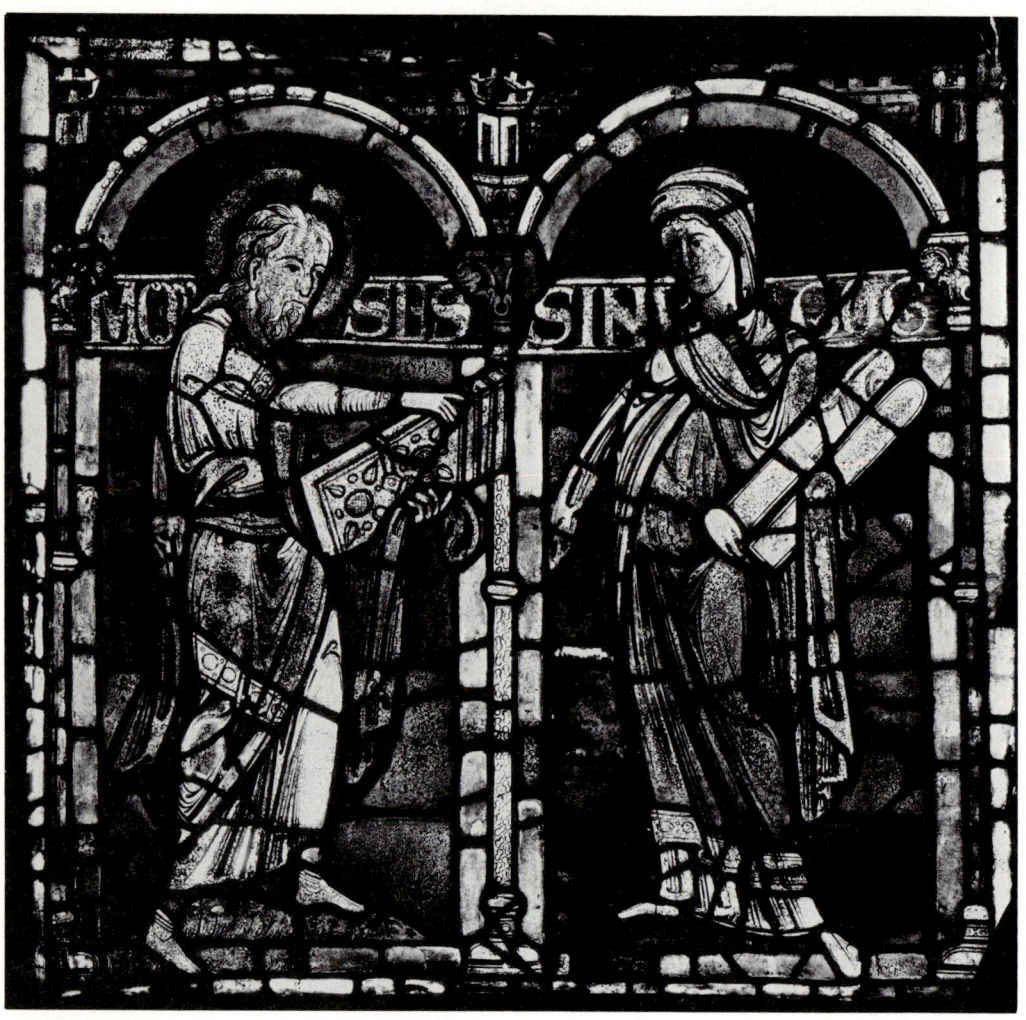

105. North oculus, Moses and Synagogue

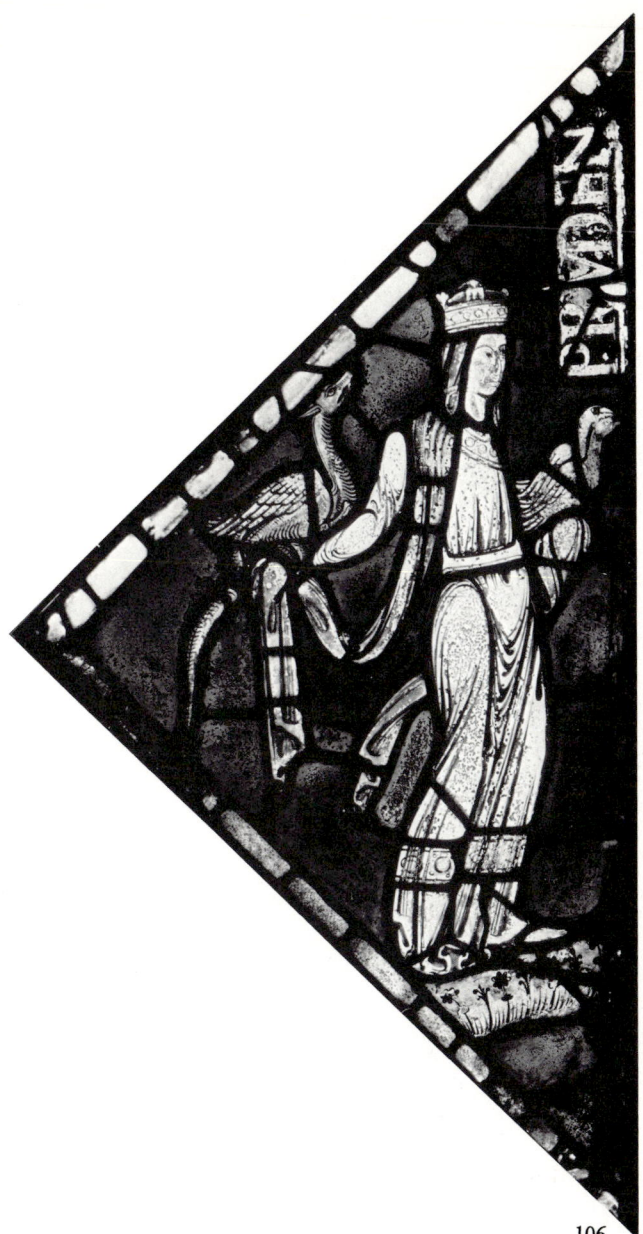

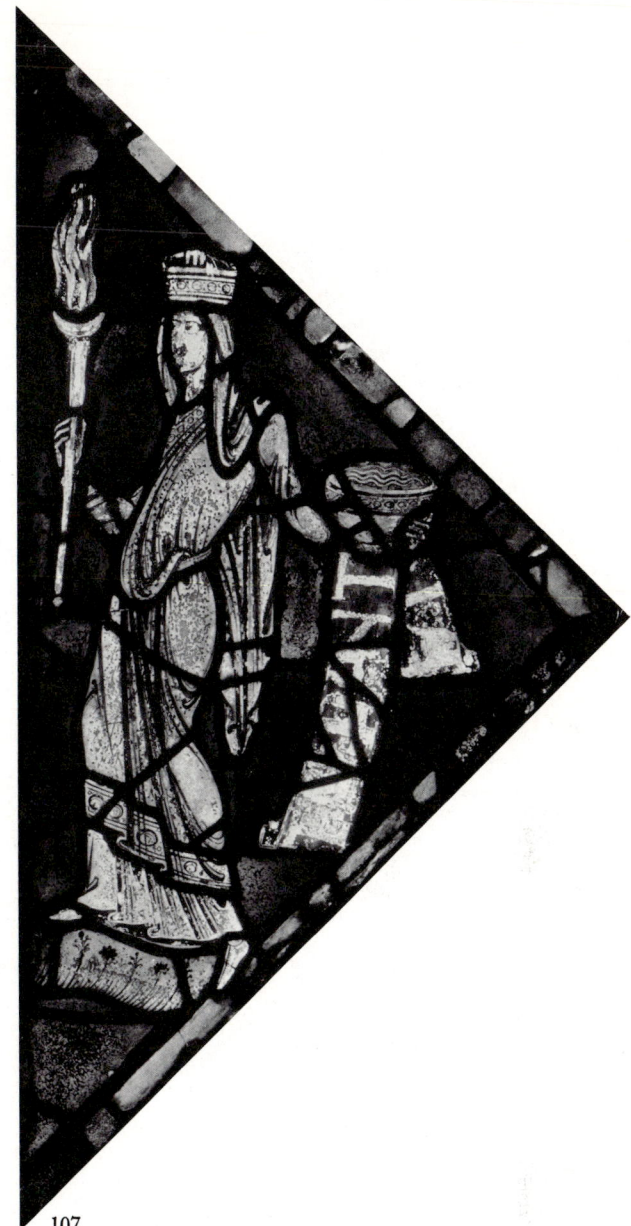

106

107

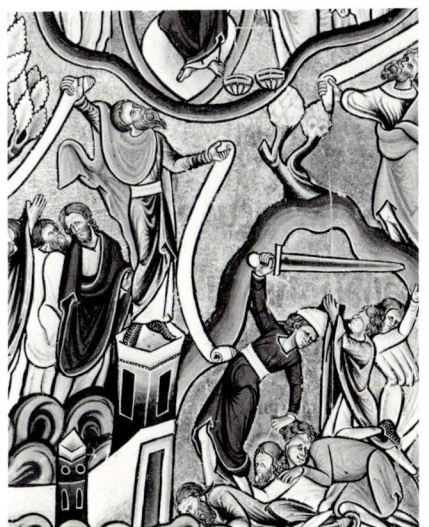

106. North oculus, Prudence

107. North oculus, Temperance

108. Great Canterbury Psalter, Paris,
     Bibliothèque Nationale,
     MS Lat. 8846, f.15v,
     Psalm 9, detail

108

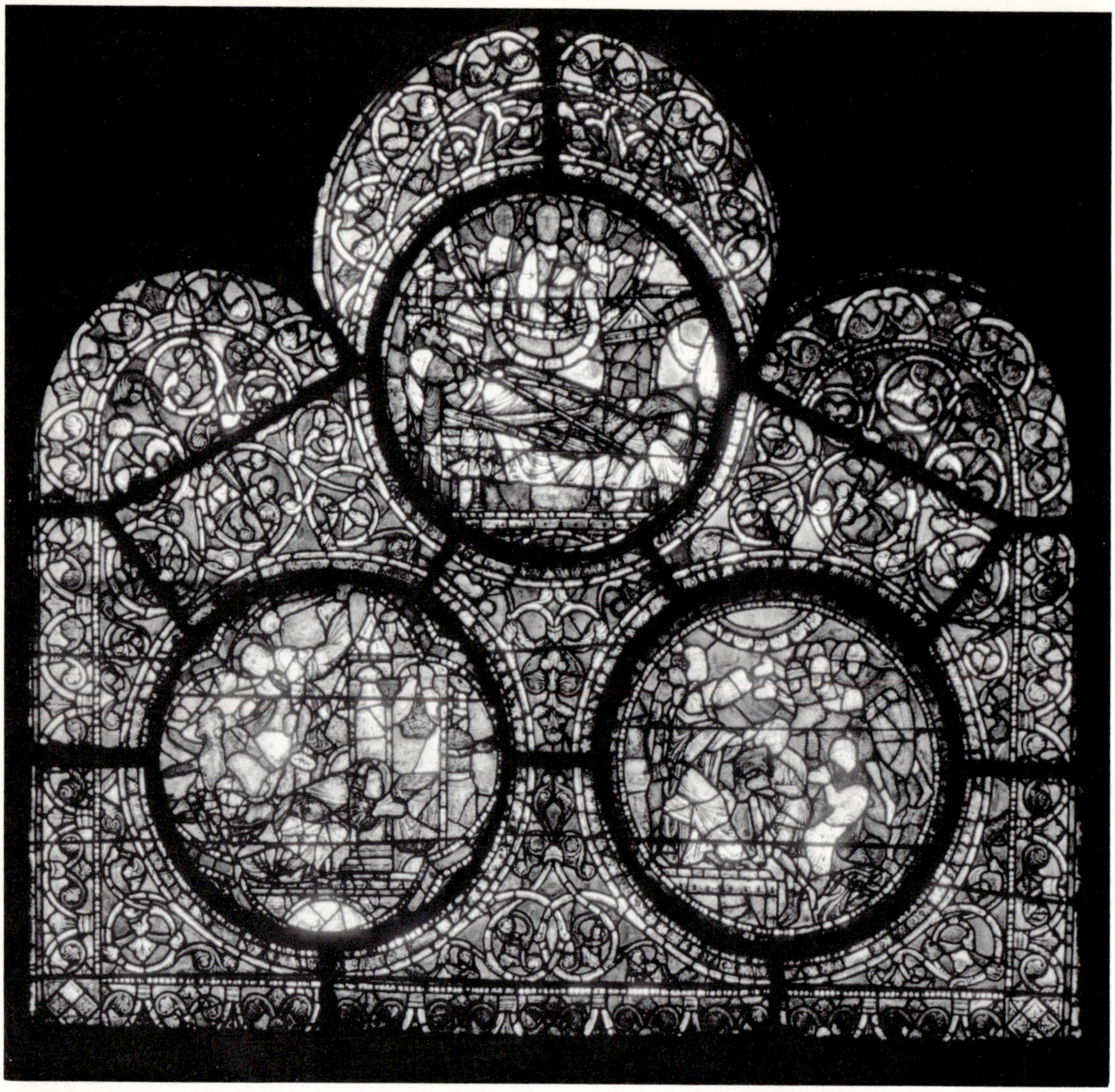

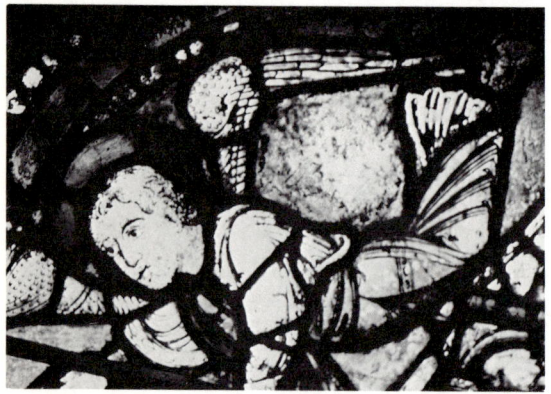

109

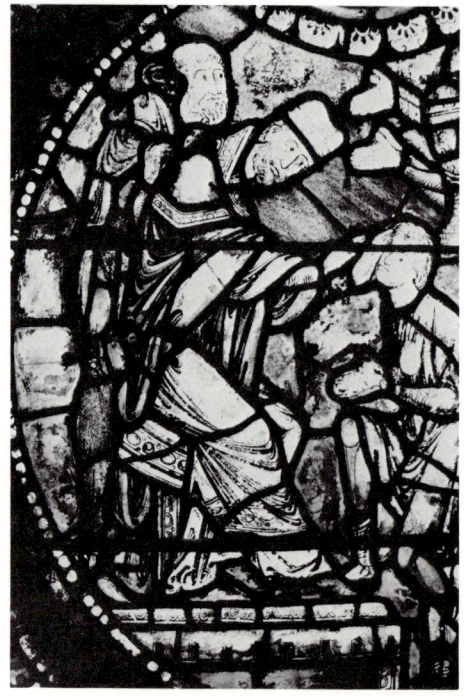

110

109. North choir aisle "triforium" Nt:X, scenes from the life of St. Dunstan

110. Detail of fig. 109, angel in the miracle at Glastonbury

111. Detail of fig. 109, St. Dunstan at Calne

111

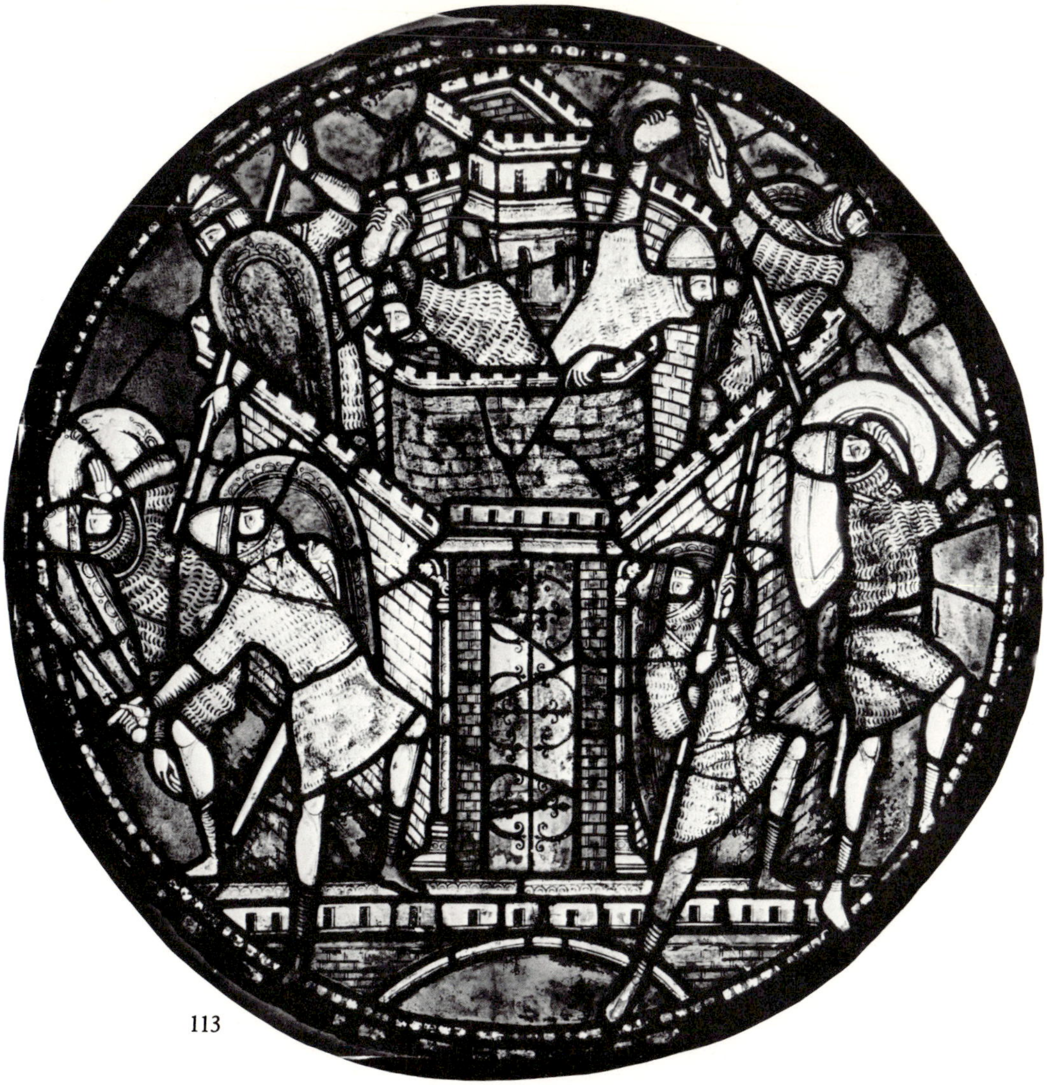

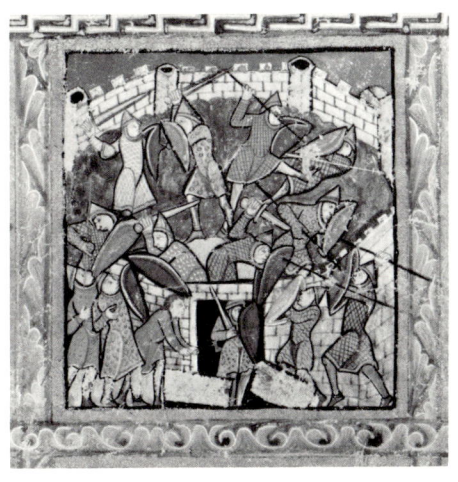

113

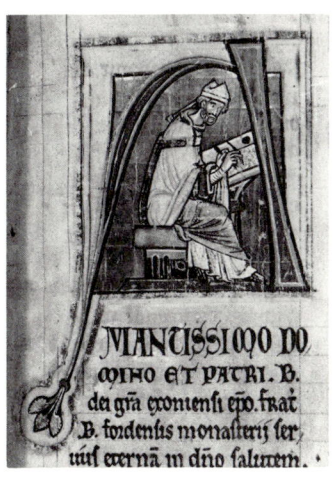

112

114

112. Baldwin, Cambridge,
Corpus Christi College,
MS 200, f.1, author
portrait

113. North choir aisle
"triforium" Nt:IX, seige of
Canterbury by the Danes

114. Prefatory page from a
Psalter (?), New York,
Morgan Library, MS 724,
detail

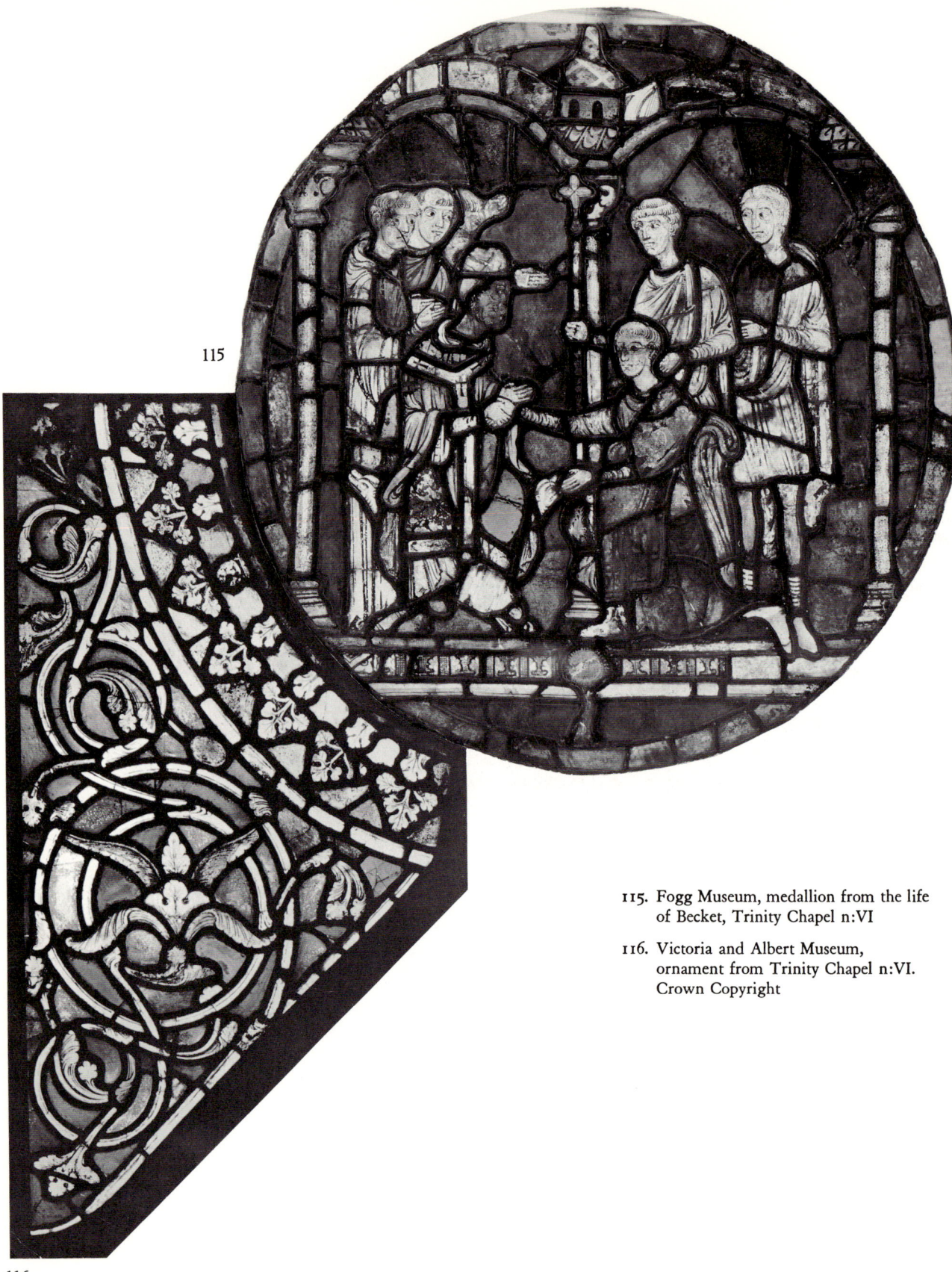

115

116

115. Fogg Museum, medallion from the life of Becket, Trinity Chapel n:VI

116. Victoria and Albert Museum, ornament from Trinity Chapel n:VI. Crown Copyright

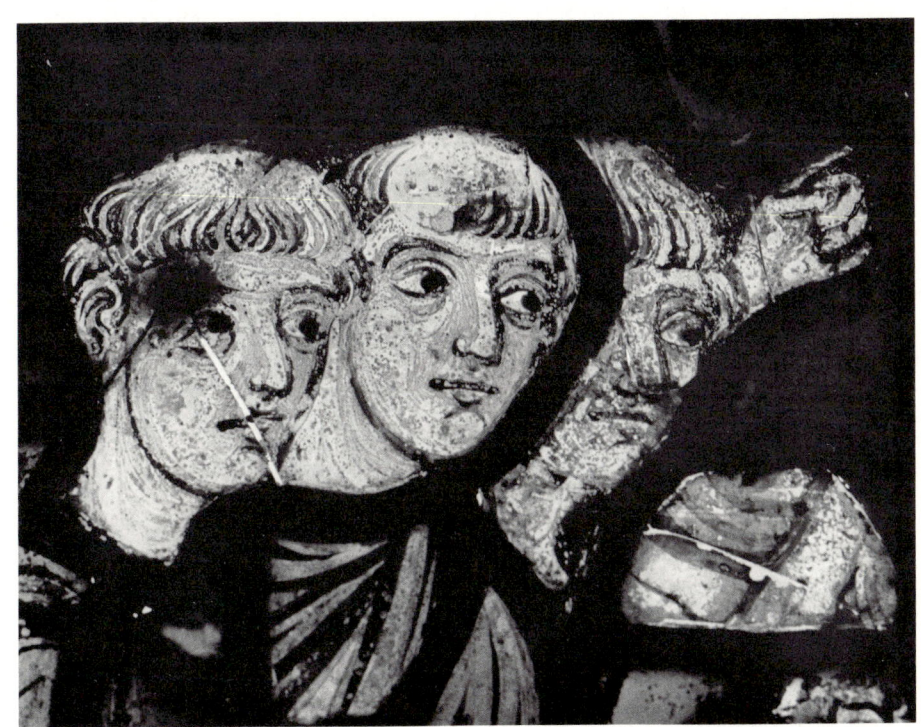

118

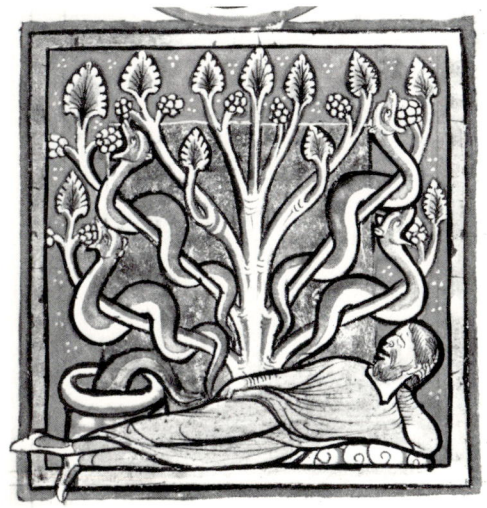

117

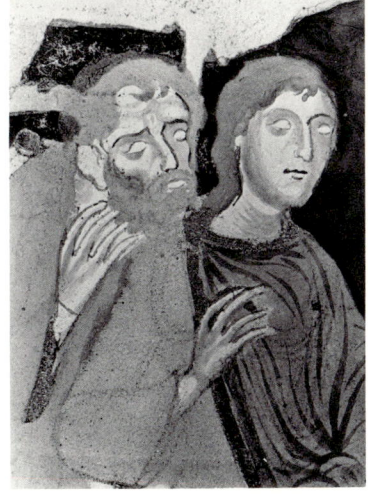

119

117. Workshop bestiary,
New York, Morgan Library,
MS 81, f.84v, detail

118. Fogg medallion, detail

119. Winchester Bible, f.246,
detail of unfinished
figures, partially painted
by the Morgan Master

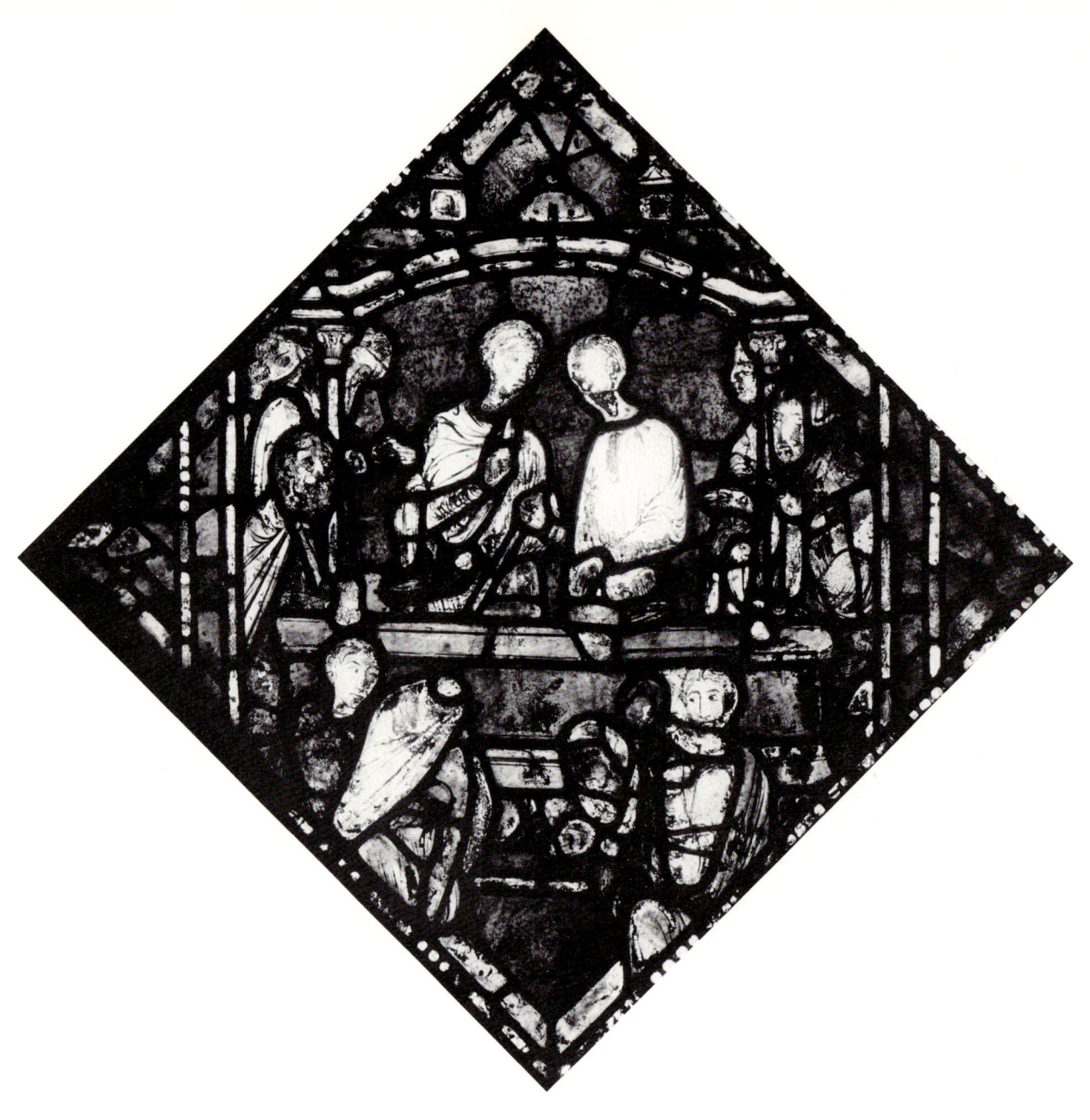

120. Trinity Chapel n:V (7), pilgrims at the
tomb of Becket

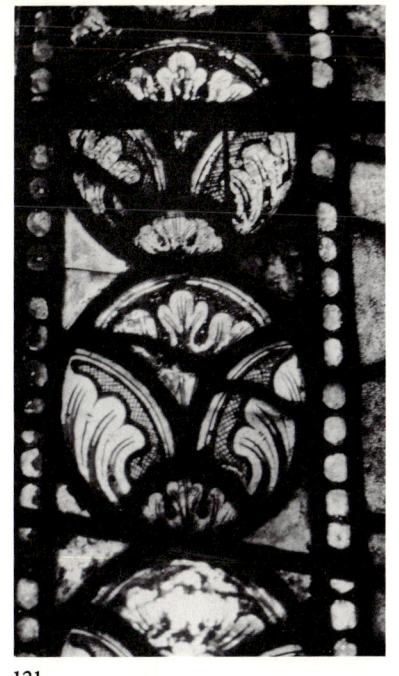

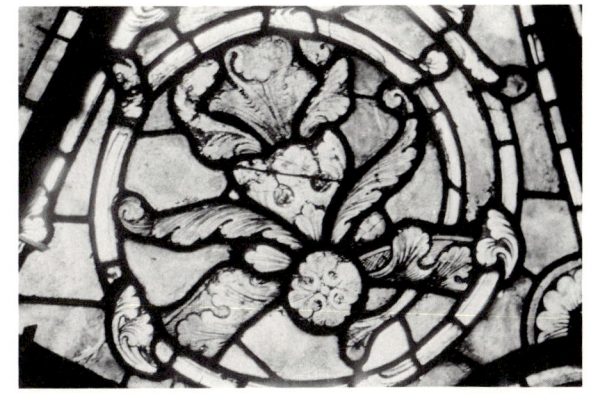

121

122

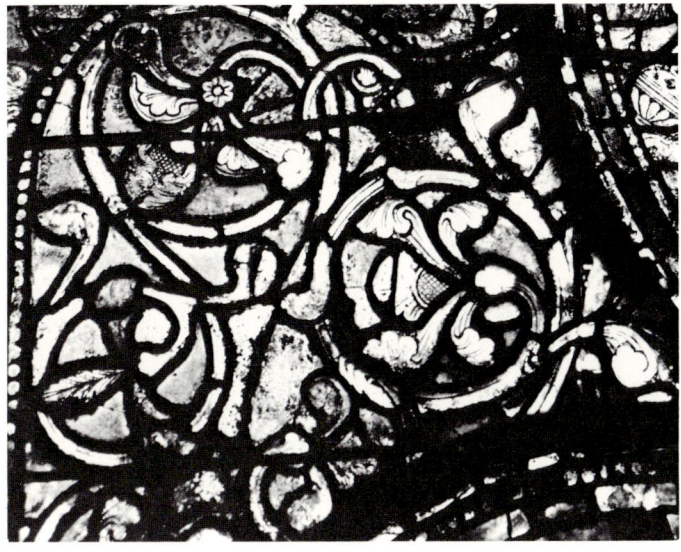

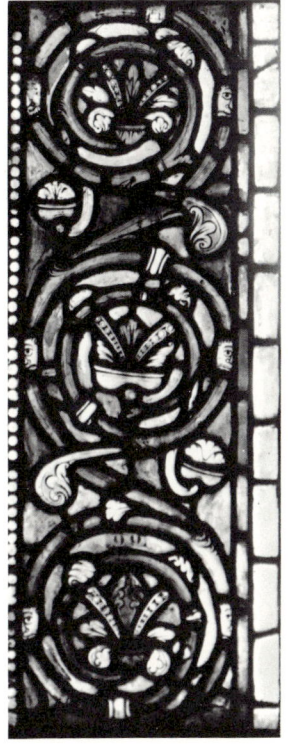

123

121. North choir aisle "triforium" St:XI, border

122. Clerestory N:VII, *rinceaux*

123. South choir aisle "triforium" St:IX, *rinceaux*

124. Châlons-sur-Marne, Cathedral Treasury, border

124

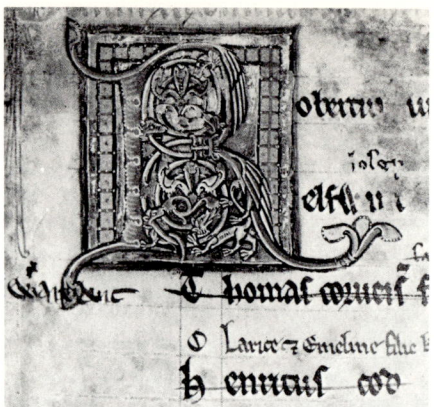

125. Christ Church Register K,
     Canterbury Cathedral Library,
     f.23, initial

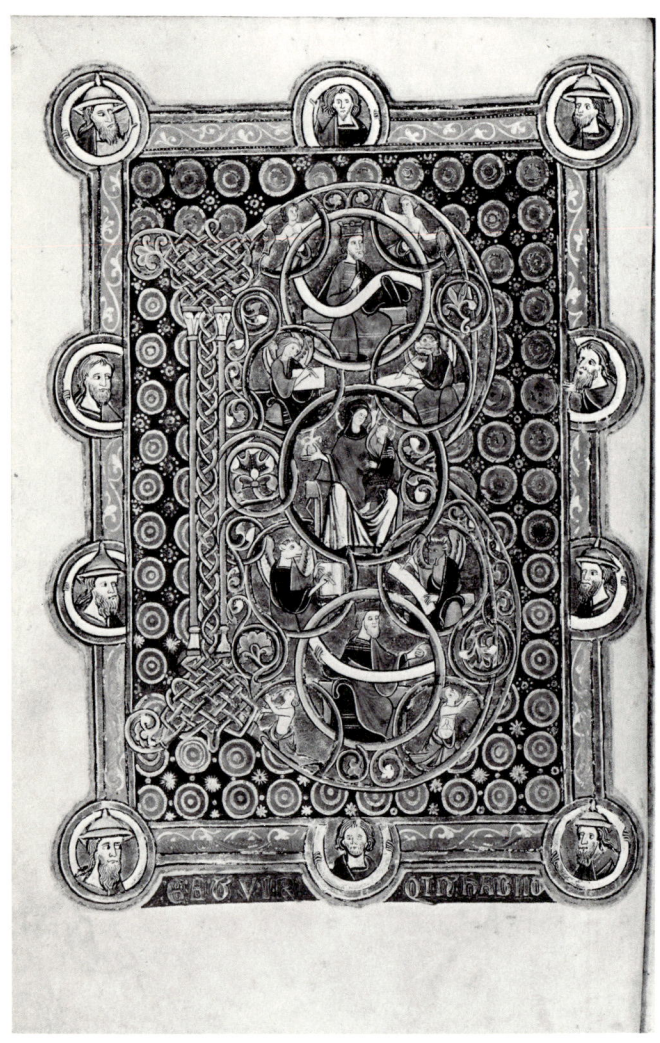

126. Little Canterbury Psalter,
     Paris, Bibliothèque Nationale,
     MS Lat. 770, f.11v,
     Beatus initial

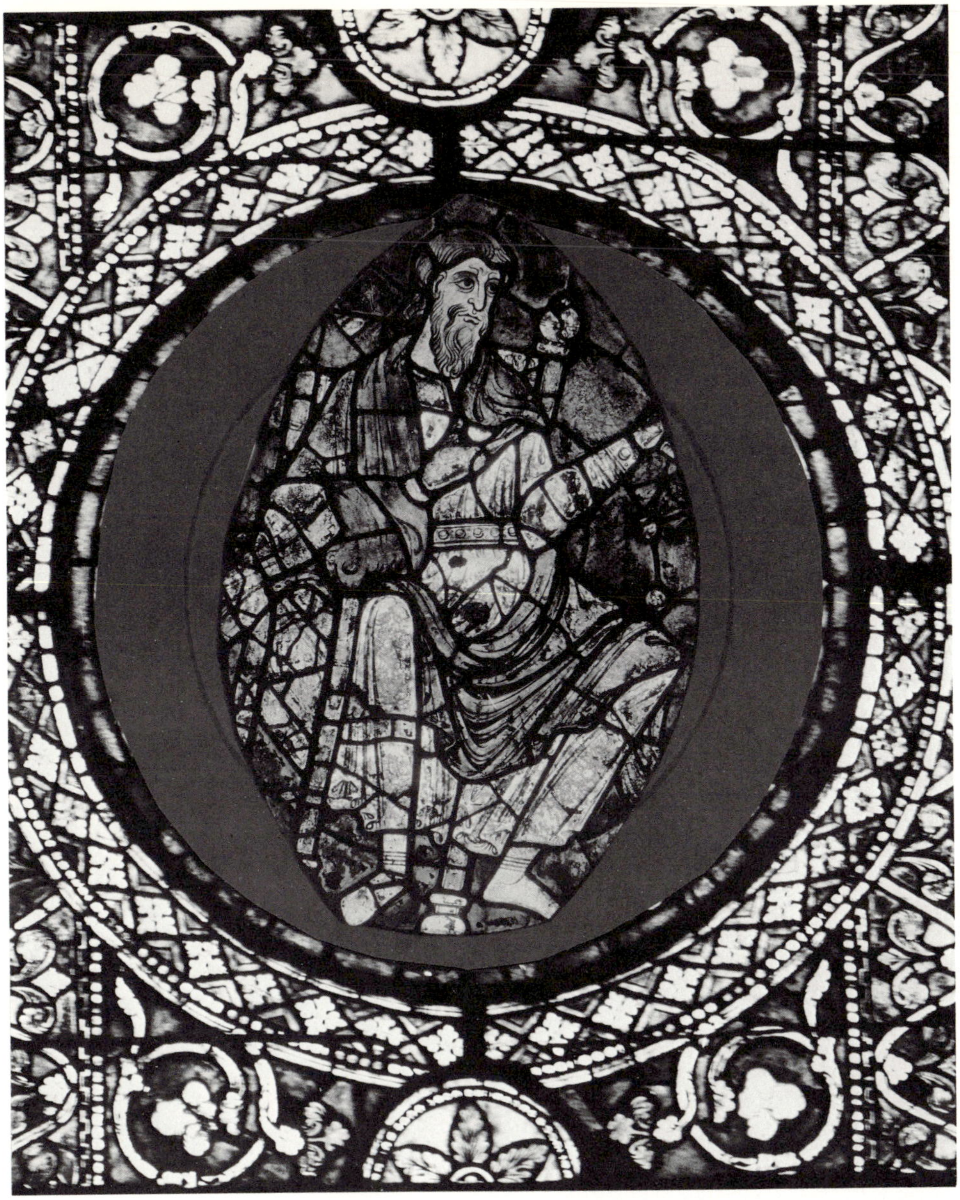

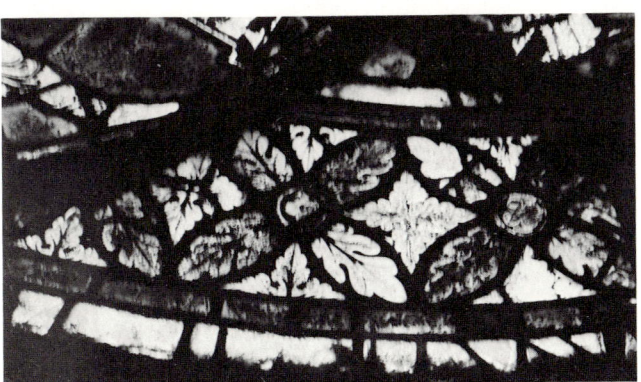

127. Salmon (?), from
clerestory N:IX, with
ornament *in situ*
(montage)

128. North oculus, border

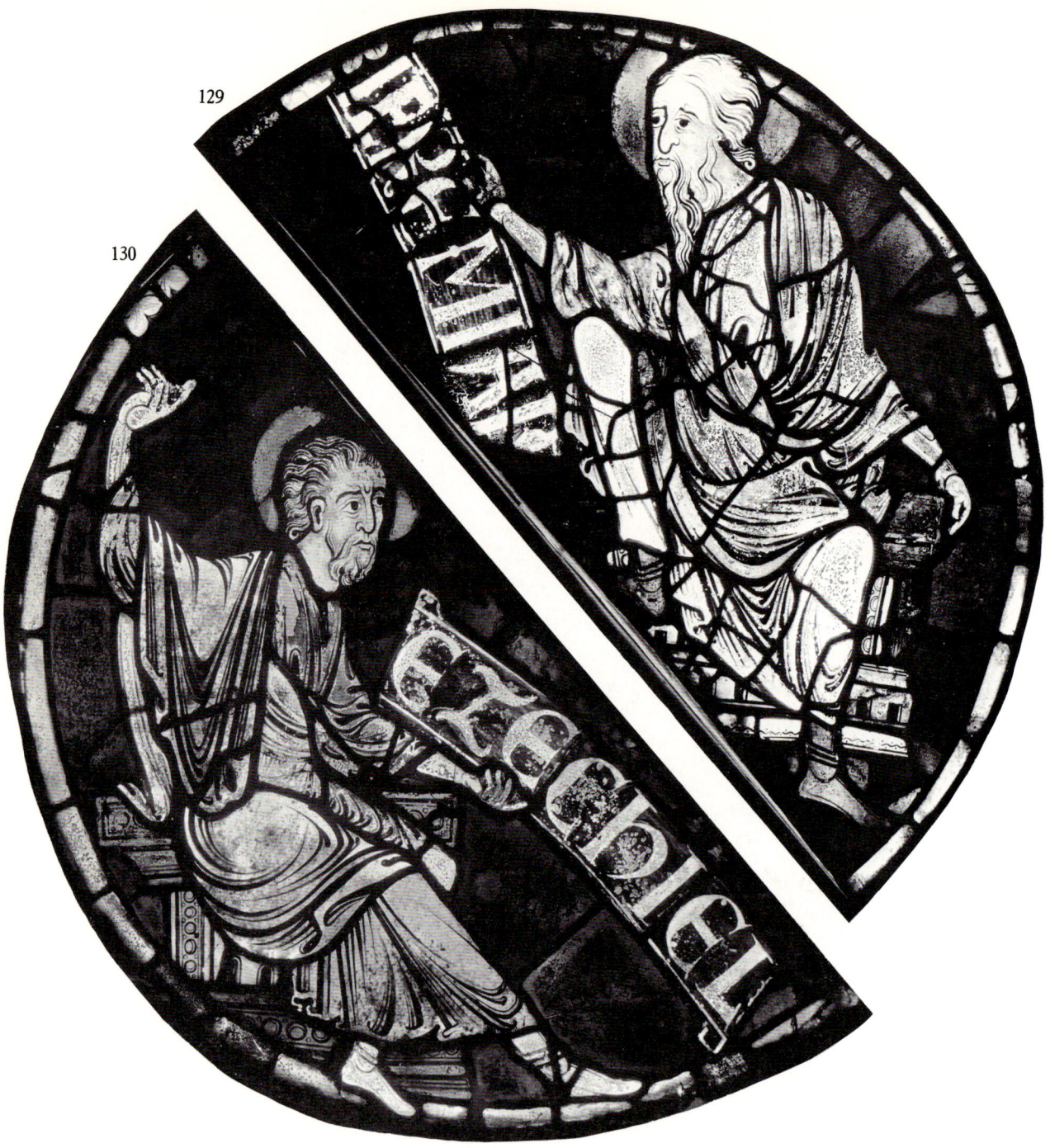

129. North oculus, Jeremiah
130. North oculus, Ezechiel

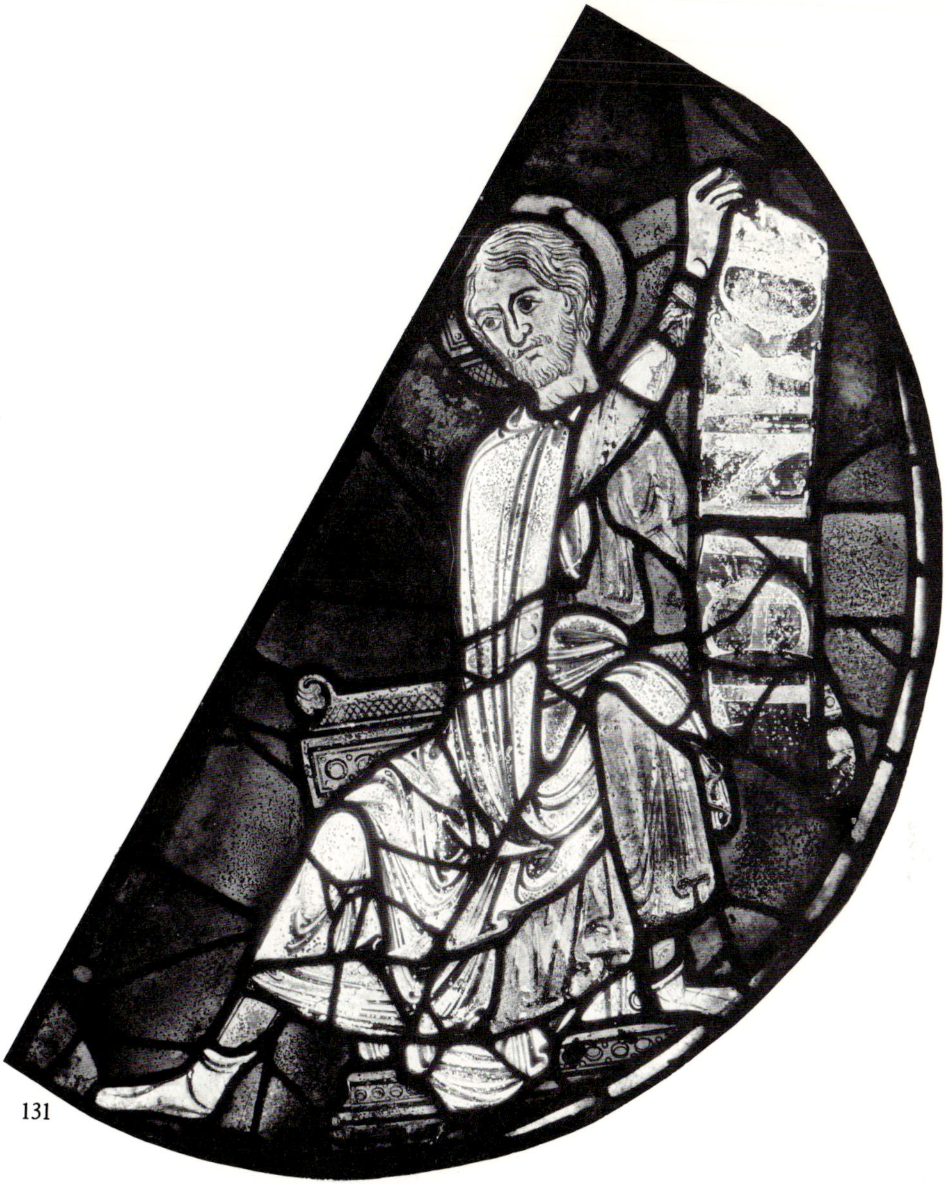

131

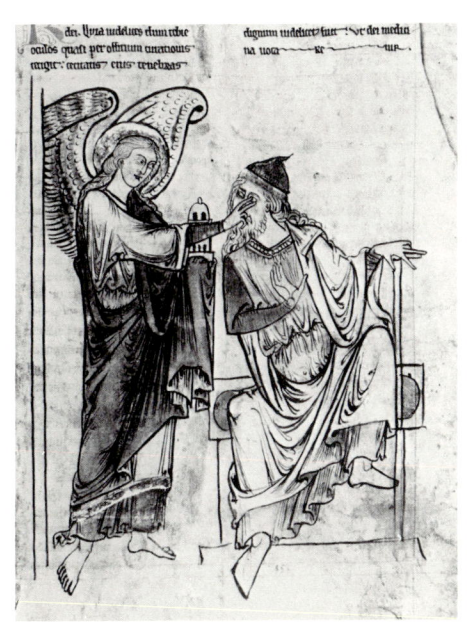

132

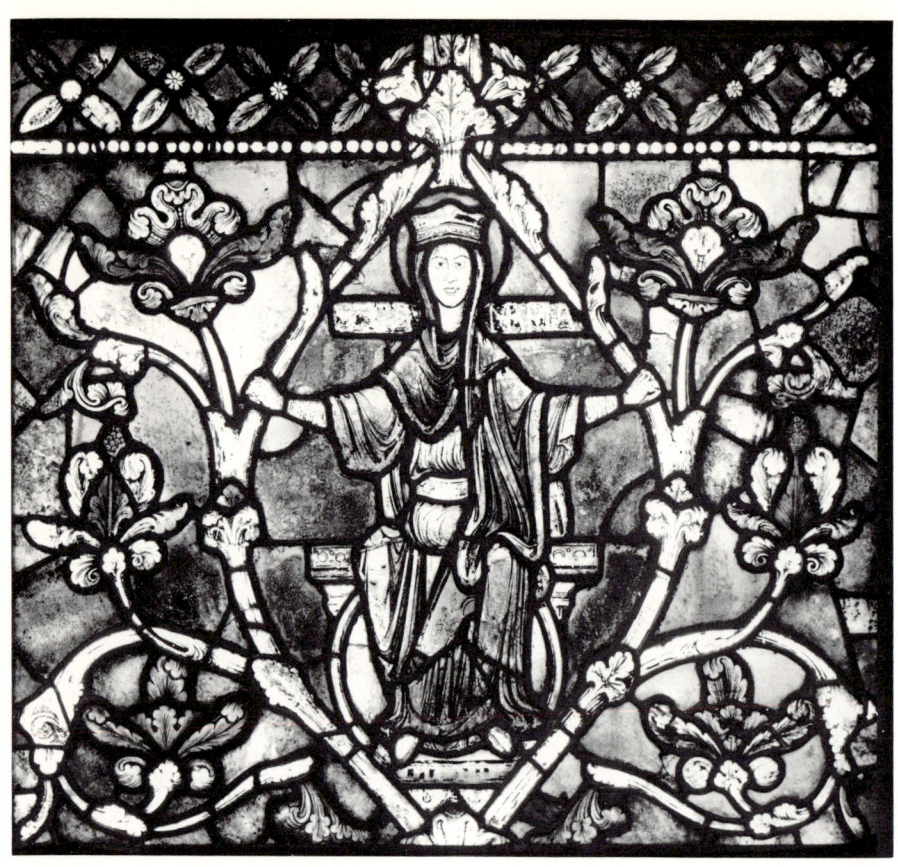

133. Corona, Jesse tree, Virgin

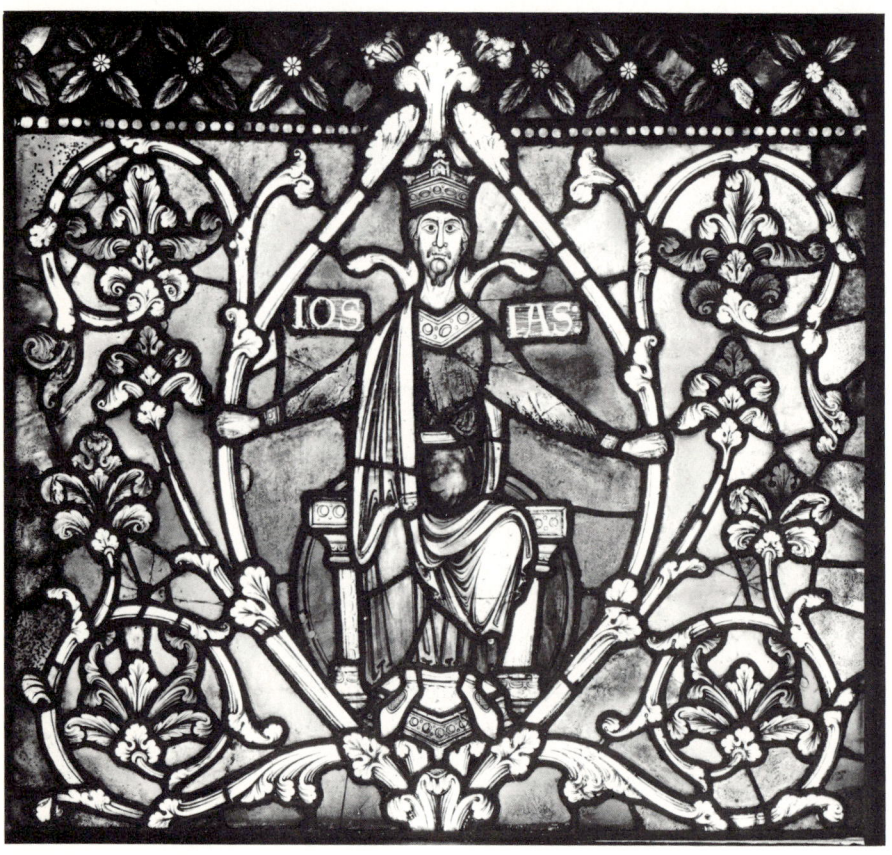

134. Corona, Jesse tree, Josiah

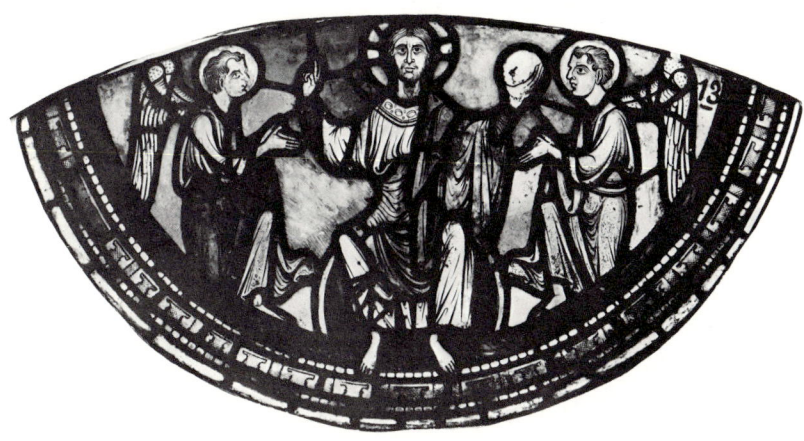

135. Sens, Becket window, Christ in majesty

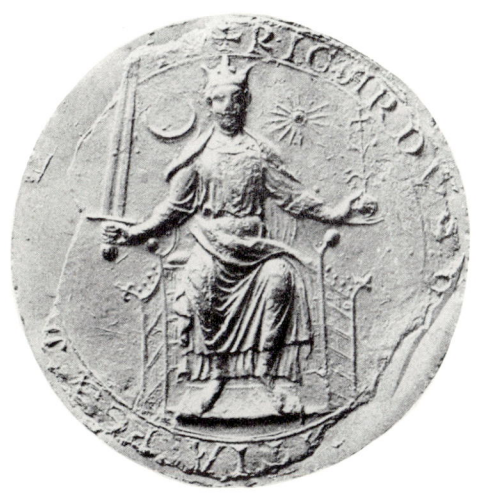

136. Second great seal of Richard I,
    before 1198

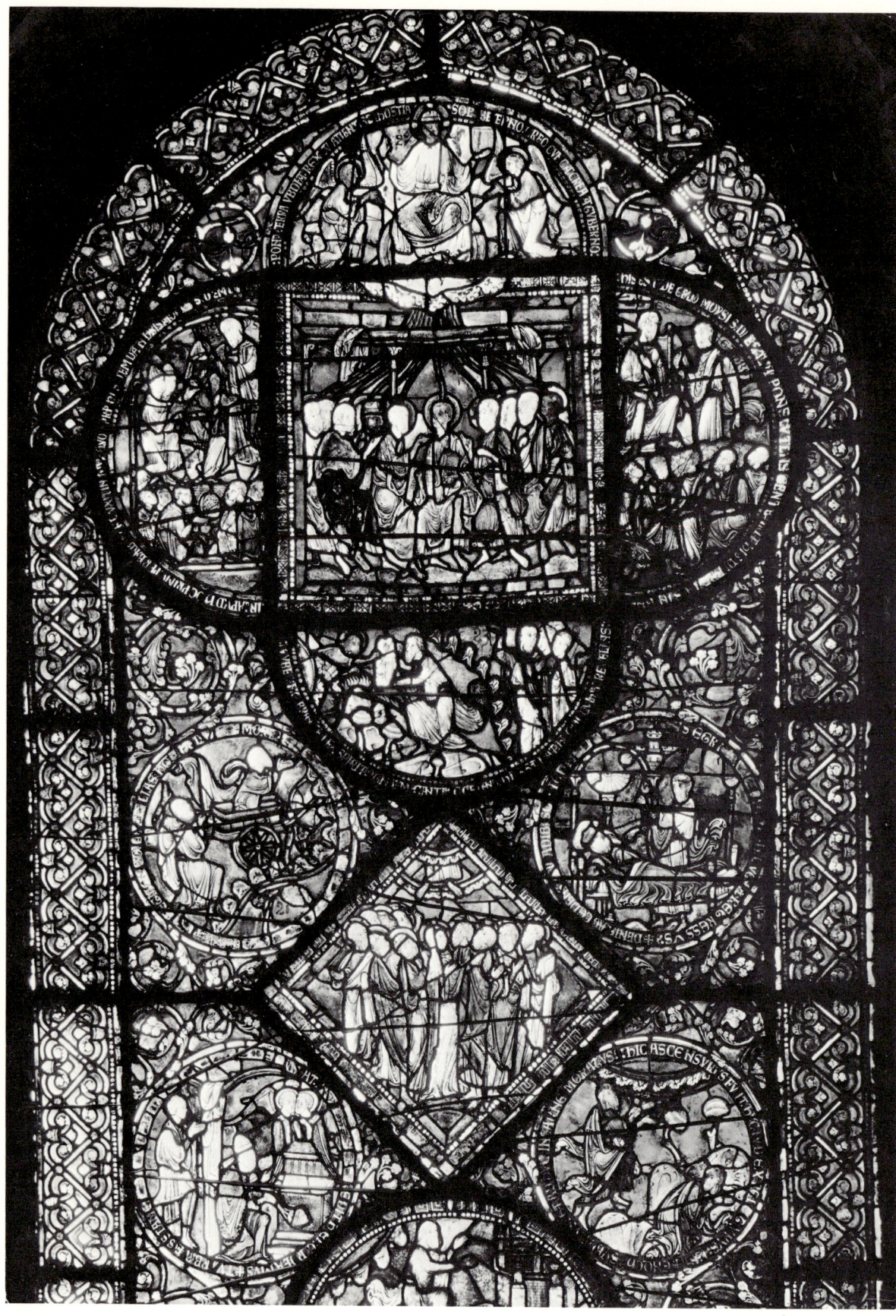

137. Corona, redemption window, upper part

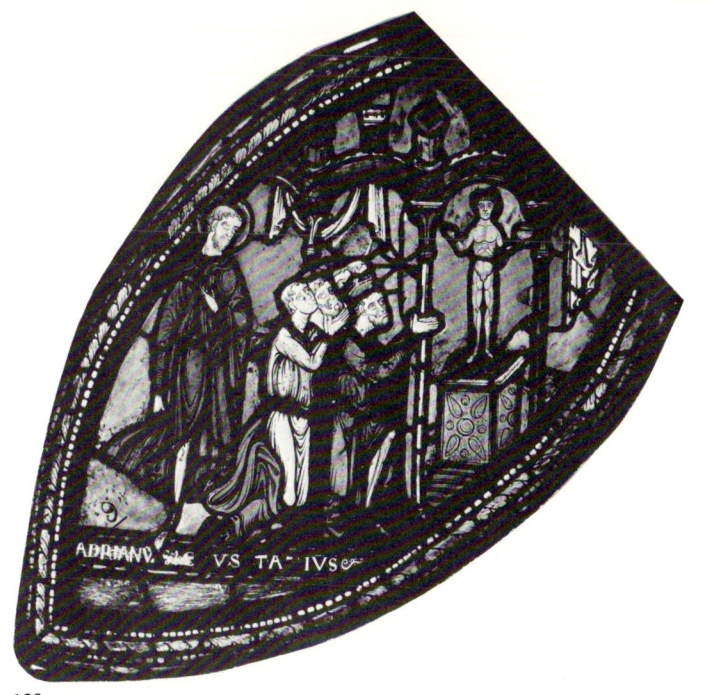

138

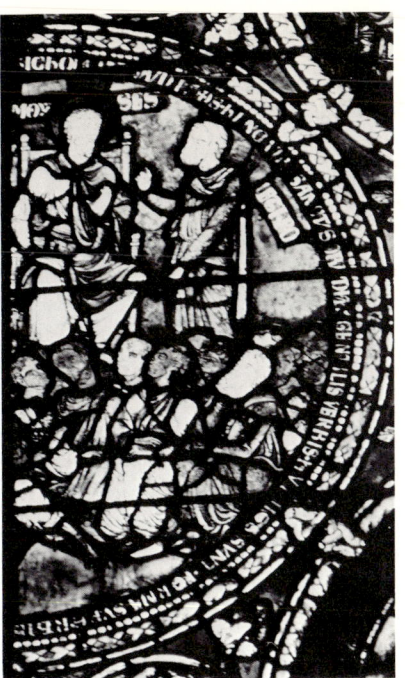

139

138. Sens, St. Eustace window, the saint refusing
to worship idols

139. North choir aisle n:XIV (2), Moses and Jethro

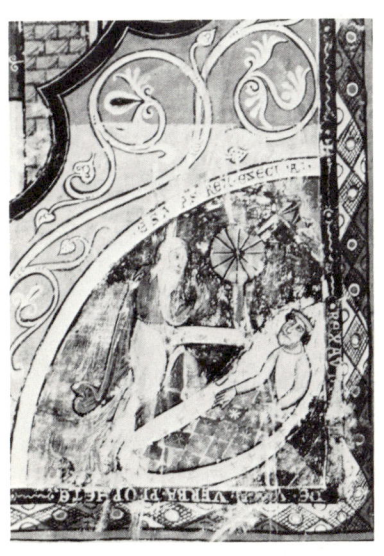

140

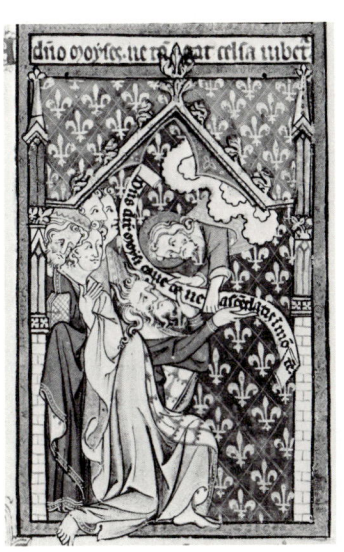

141

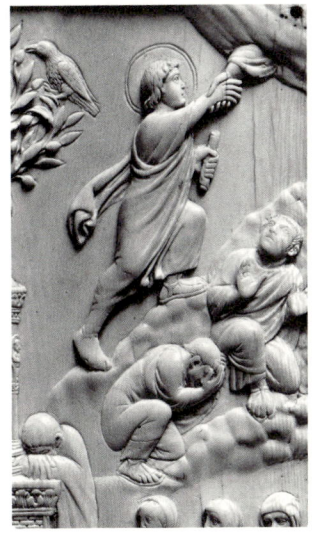

142

140. Gumbertus Bible, Erlangen,
Universitätsbibliothek, MS 121, f.171v,
detail, Hezekiah

141. Peterborough Psalter, Brussels,
Bibliothèque Royale, MS 9961–62, f.72v,
detail, God instructing Moses

142. Von Reider ivory plaque, Munich Bayerisches
Nationalmuseum, detail of Ascension

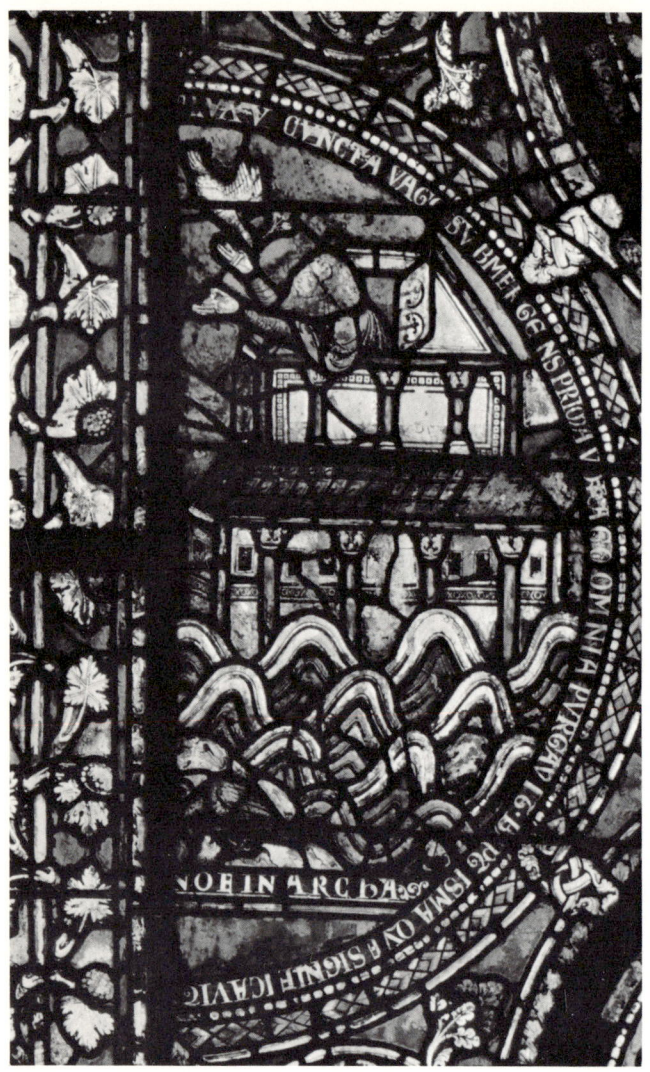

143

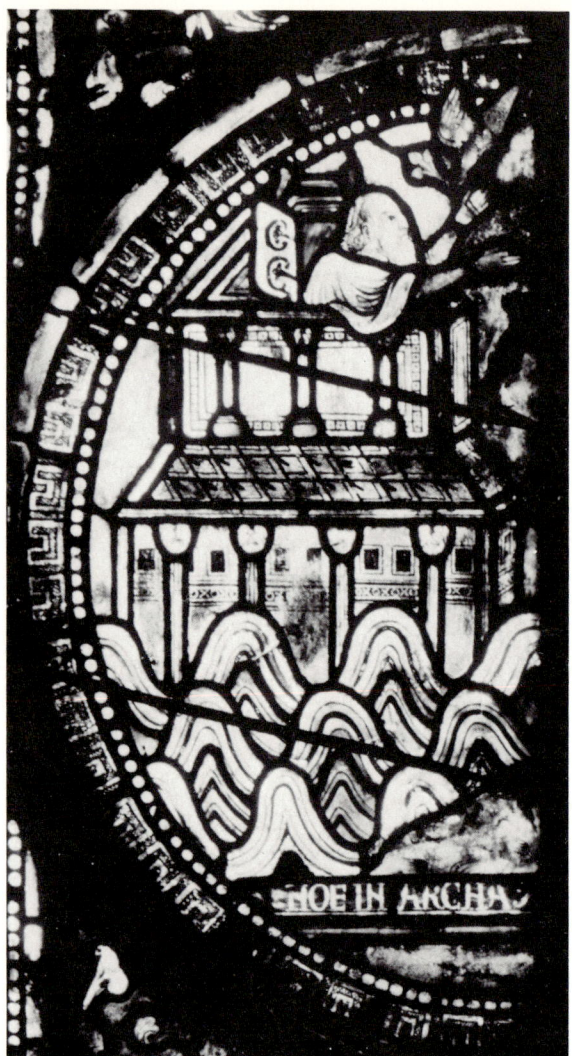

144

143. North choir aisle n:XIV (8), Noah's Ark

144. Corona, redemption window, 12, Noah's Ark

145. Homilies of Gregory Nazianzus, Paris, Bibliothèque Nationale, MS grec. 510, f.360, detail of Noah's ark

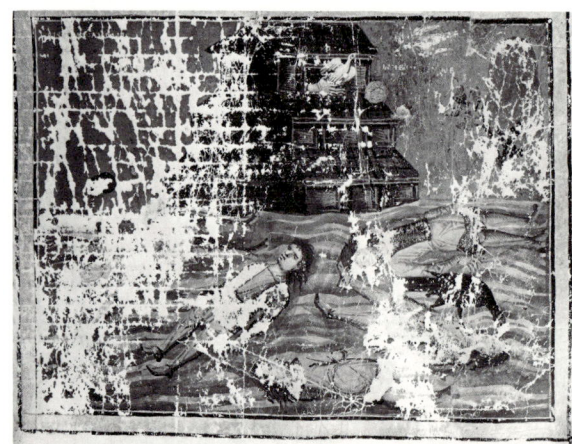

145

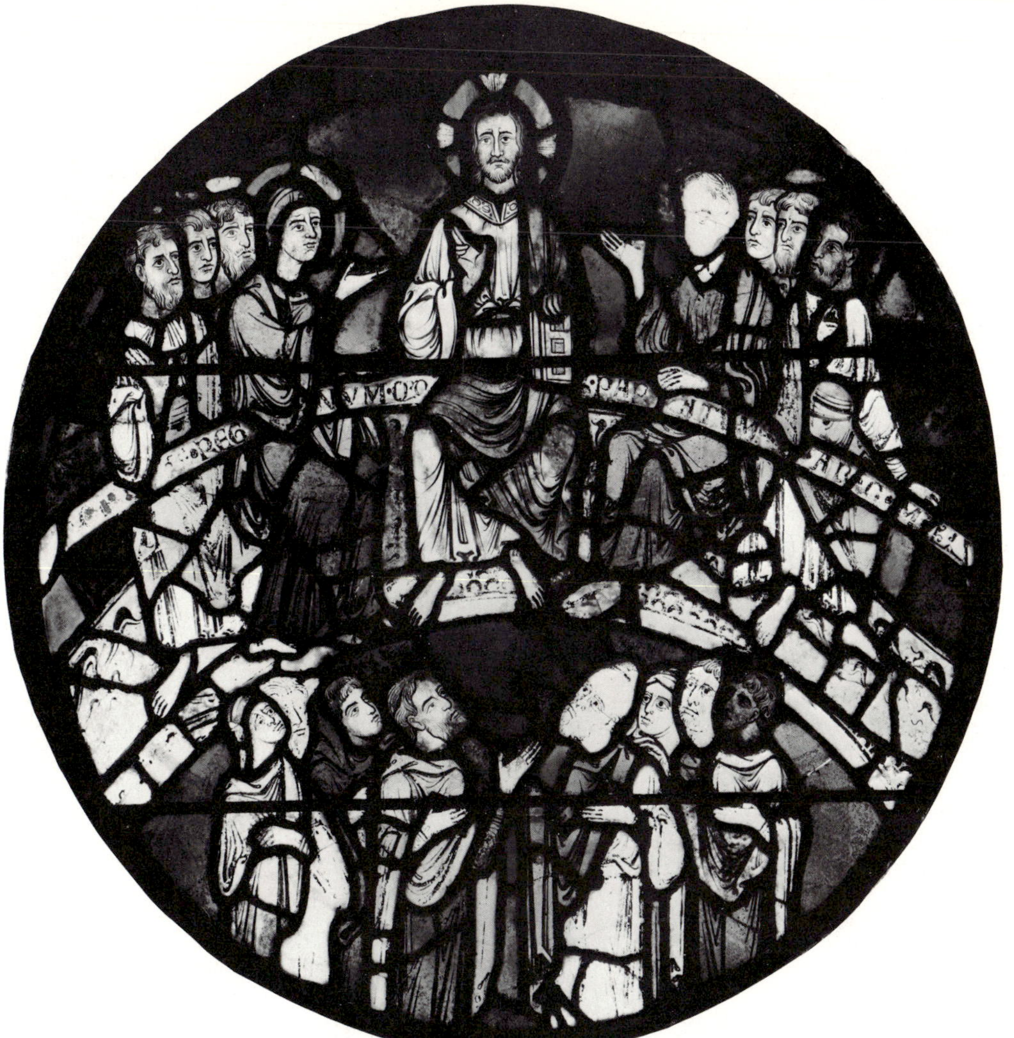

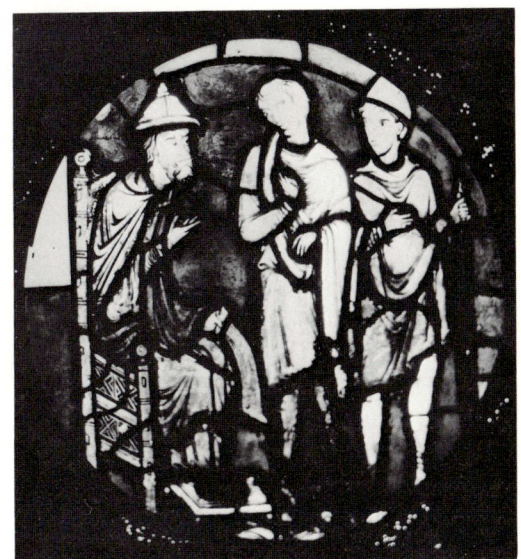

146

146. Virginia Museum of Fine Arts,
Last Judgment, from Trinity Chapel
clerestory I

147. Paris, Notre-Dame, south rose,
reused twelfth-century panel

147

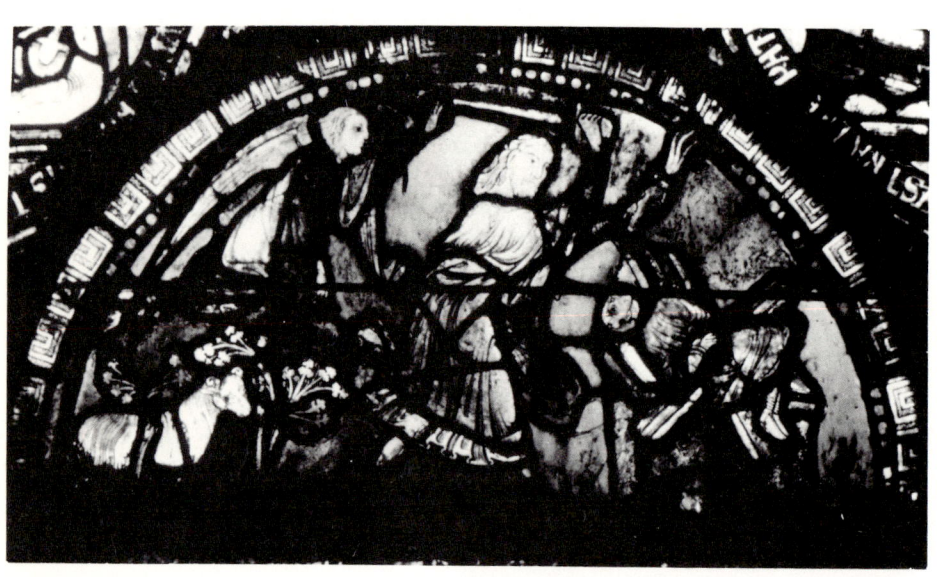

148. Corona, redemption window, 3,
sacrifice of Isaac

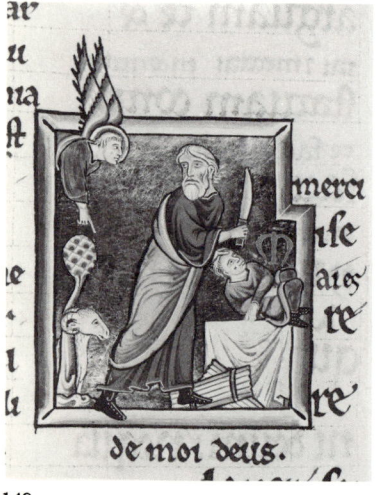

149

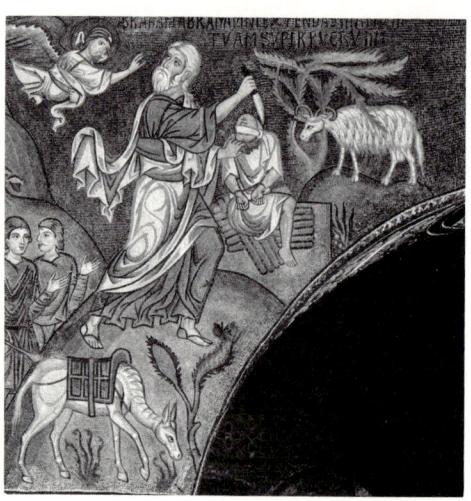

150

149. North French Psalter,
New York, Morgan Library
MS 338, f.220v,
sacrifice of Isaac

150. Palermo, Capella Palatina,
Mosaic, sacrifice of
Isaac

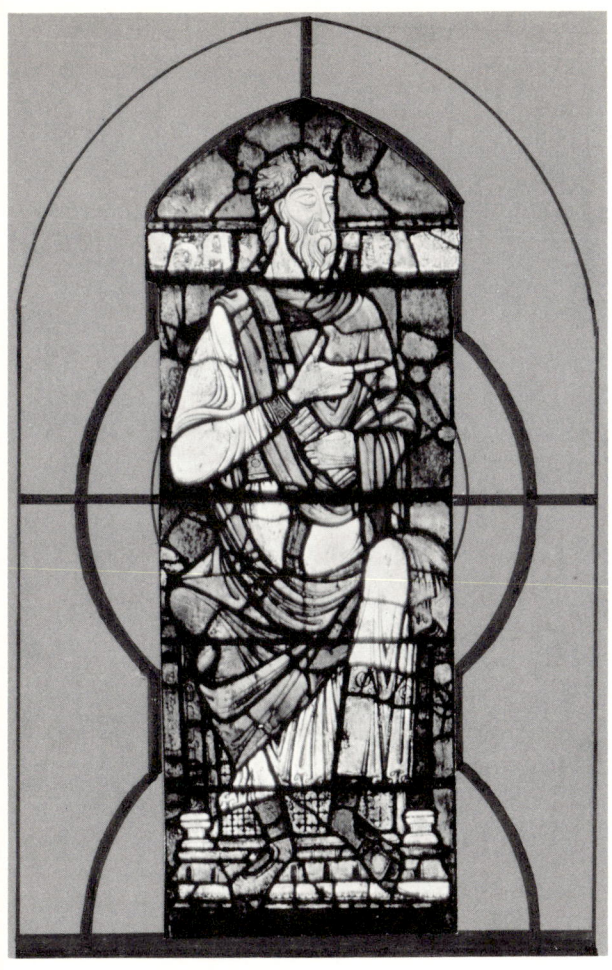

151

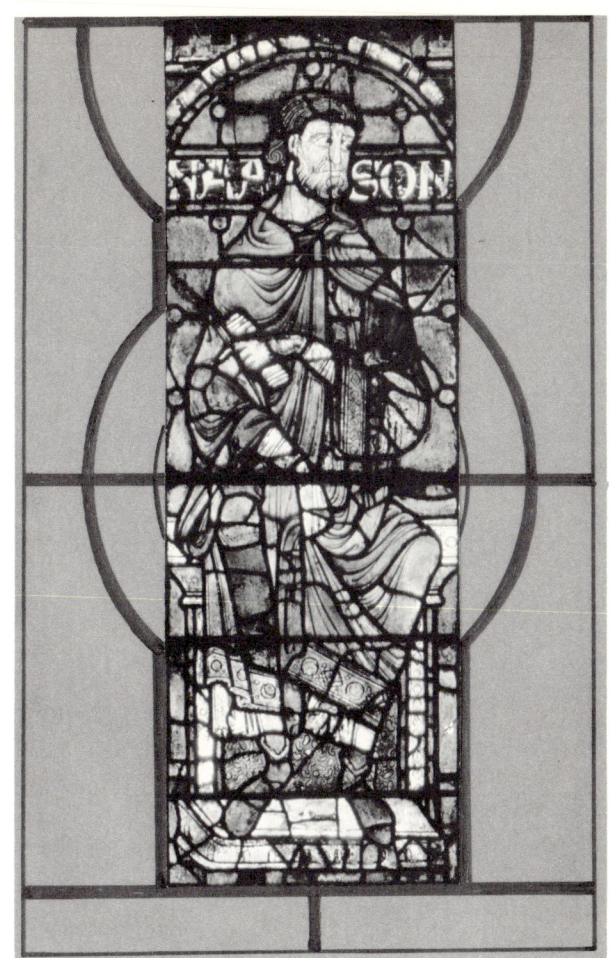

152

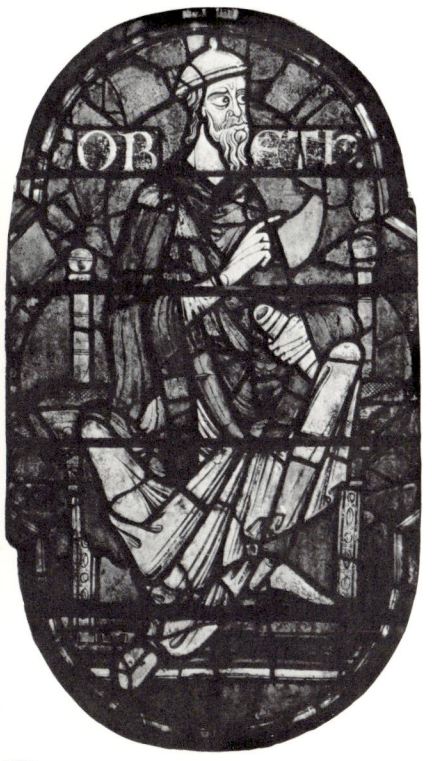

153

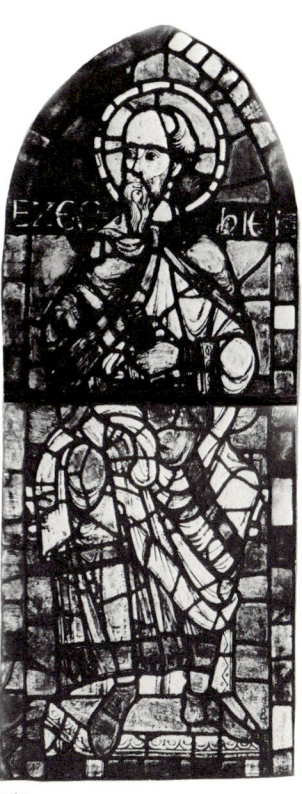

154

151. Amminadab, from clerestory N:X

152. Nahshon, from clerestory N:X

153. Obed, from clerestory N:VIII

154. Rheims, St.-Remi, clerestory,
Ezechiel

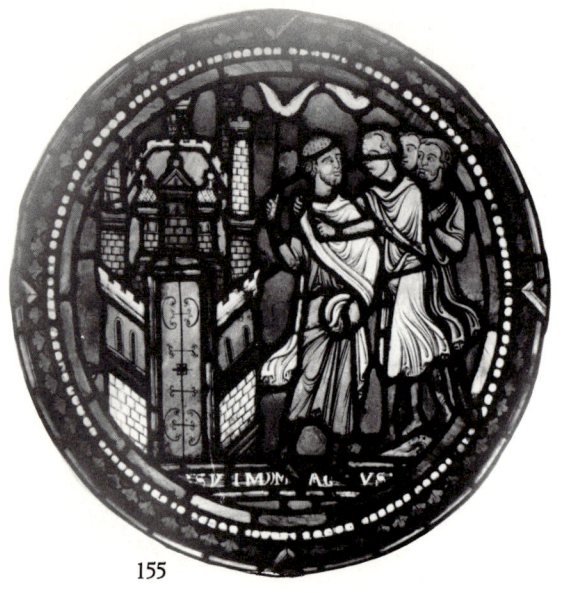

155

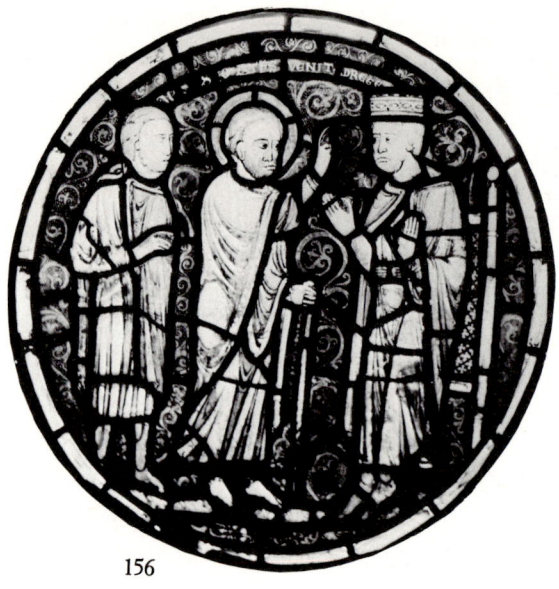

156

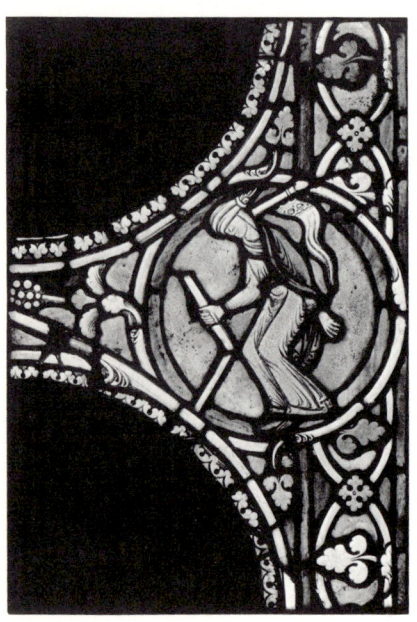

157

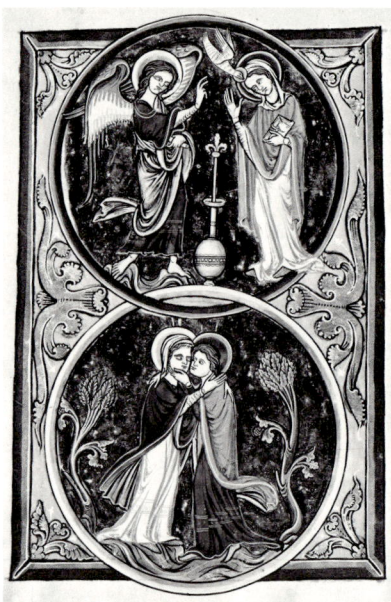

158

155. Troyes, St. Peter window, Simon Magnus

156. Paris, Notre-Dame, south rose, reused twelfth-century panel

157. Private collection, synagogue, from St.-Remi of Rheims (?)

158. "Psalter of Blanche of Castille," Paris, Bibliothèque de l'Arsenal, MS 1186, f.16, annunciation and visitation

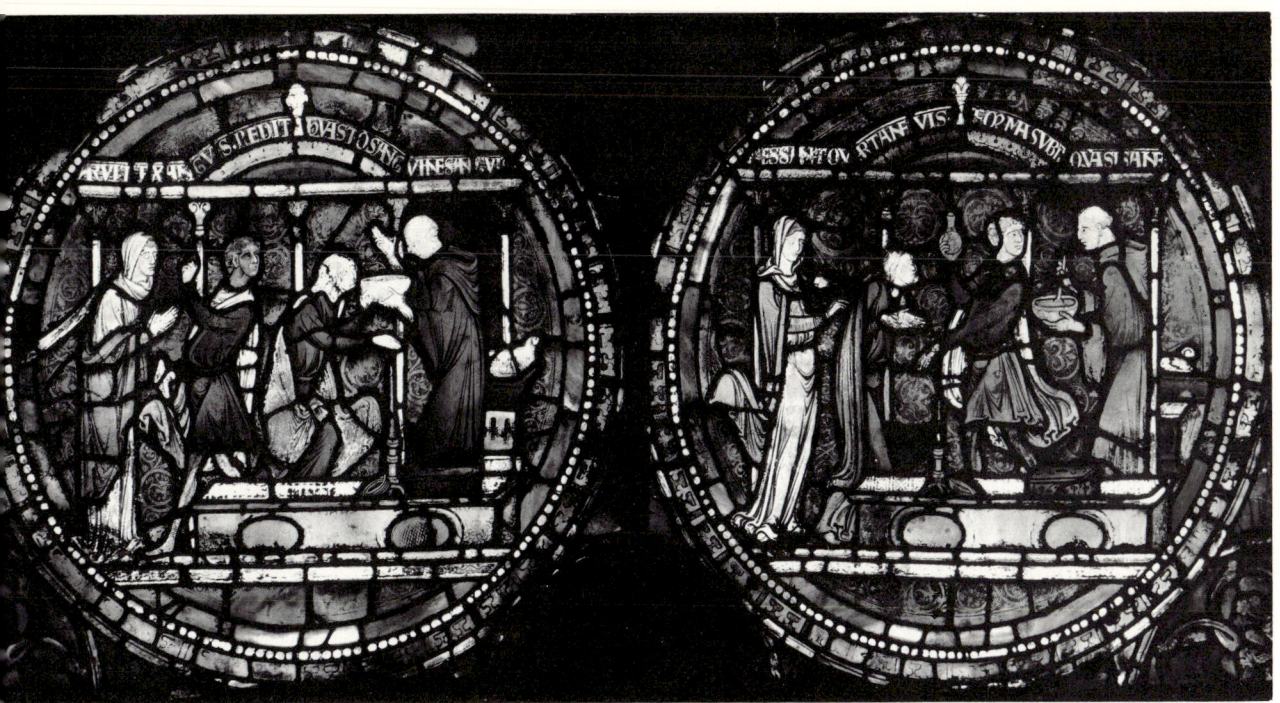

159. Trinity Chapel n:IV (15 & 16),
     Ethelreda of Canterbury at
     the tomb of Becket

160. Sens, Becket window, burial
     of Becket

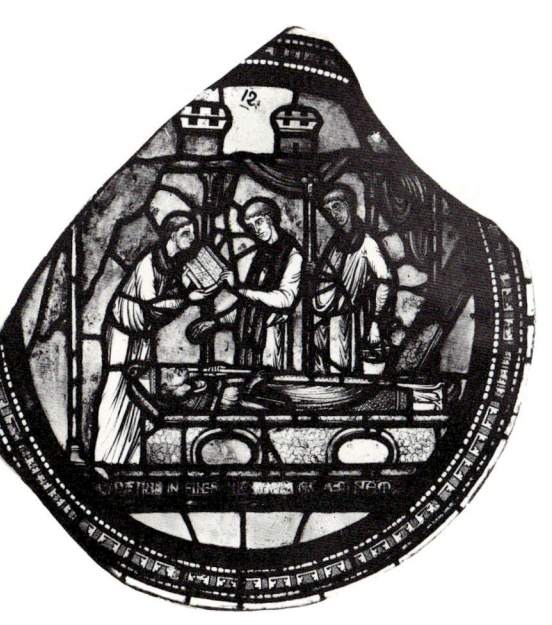

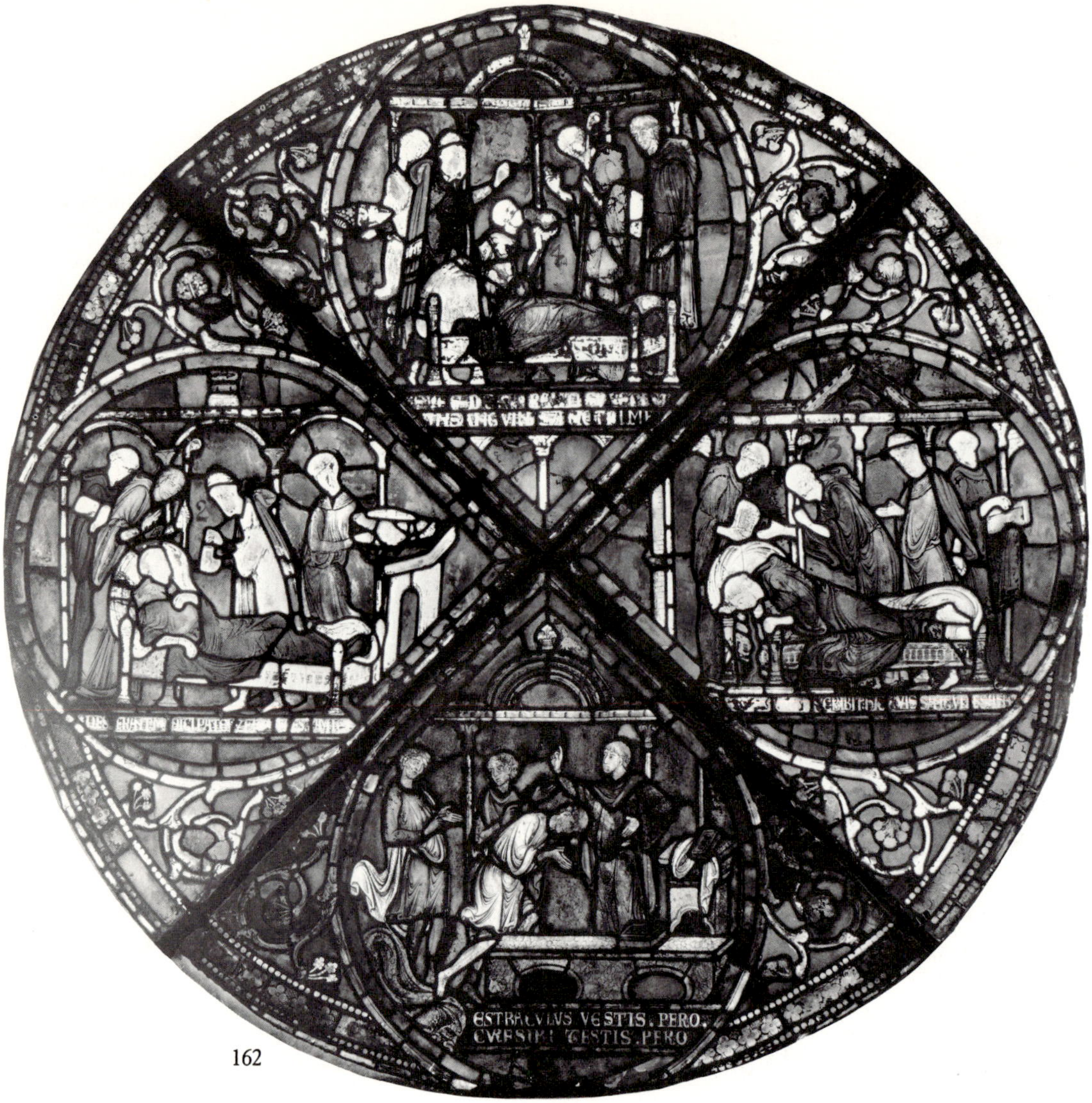

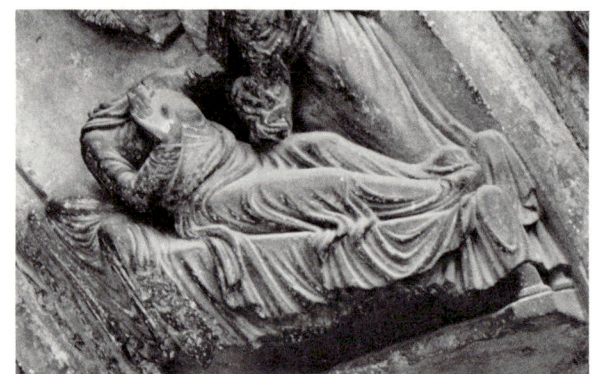

162

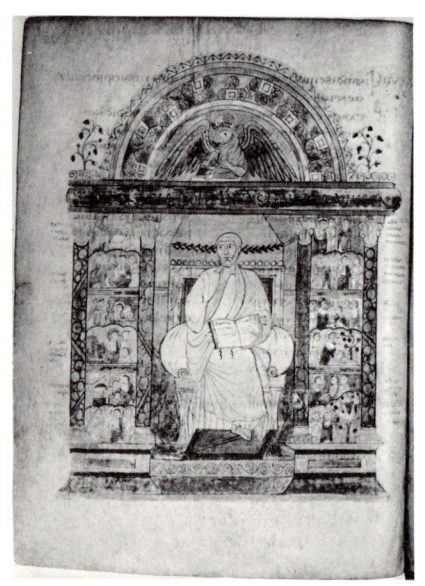

161

163

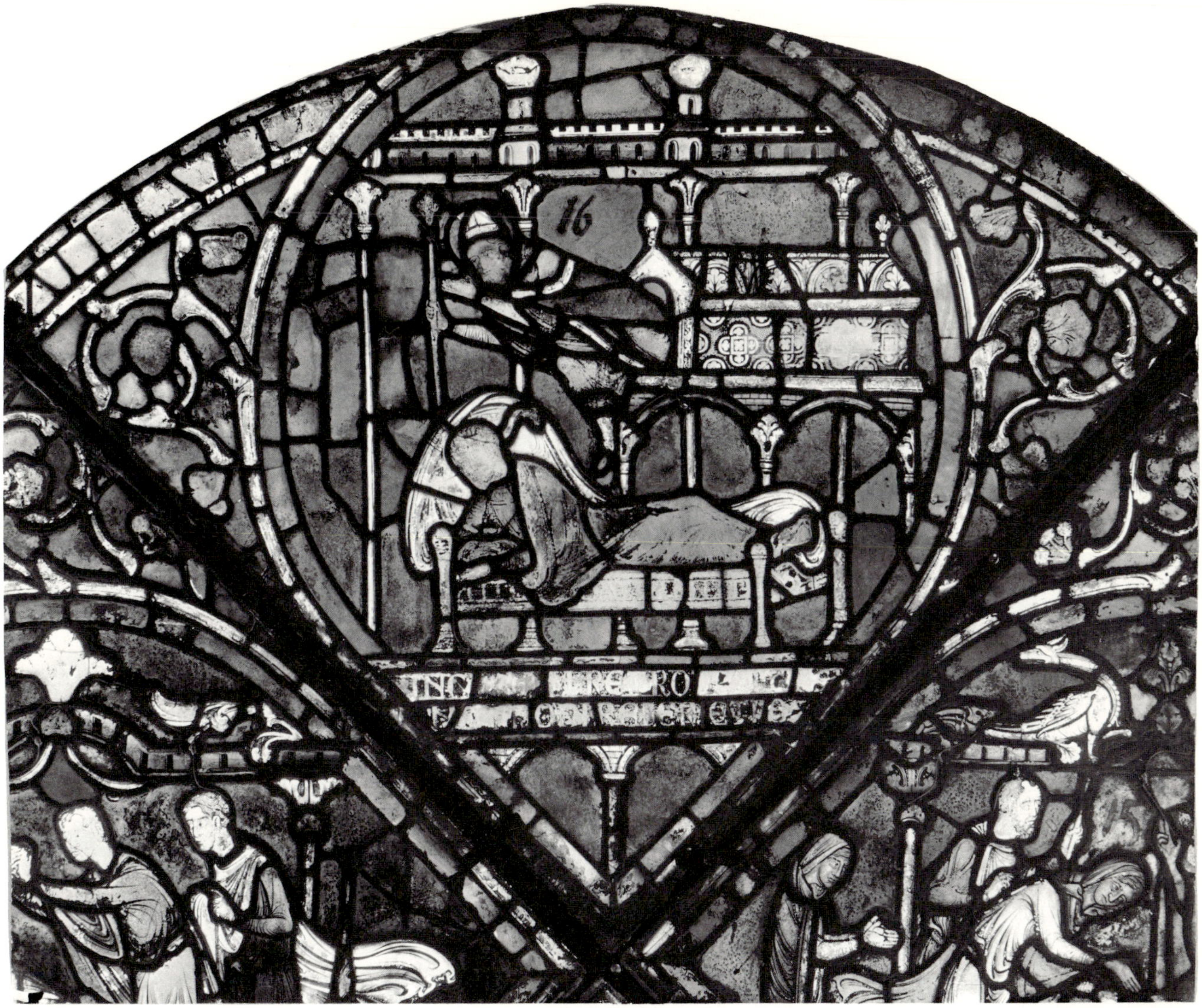

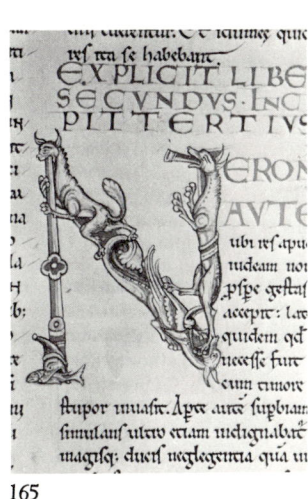

164

161. St. Augustine's gospels, Cambridge.
Corpus Christi College, MS 286, f.129v,
St. Luke

162. Trinity Chapel, n:III (19–22), Hugh,
Abbot of Jervaulx Cured

163. Sens, left west portal, voussoir,
birth of St. John

164. Trinity Chapel N:III (1), vision
of Becket

165. Josephus, Cambridge, St. Johns'
College, MS A.8, f.64, initial

166. Sens, Becket window, *rinceaux*

165

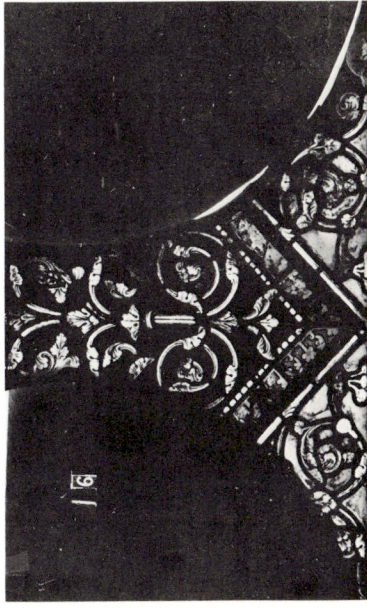

166

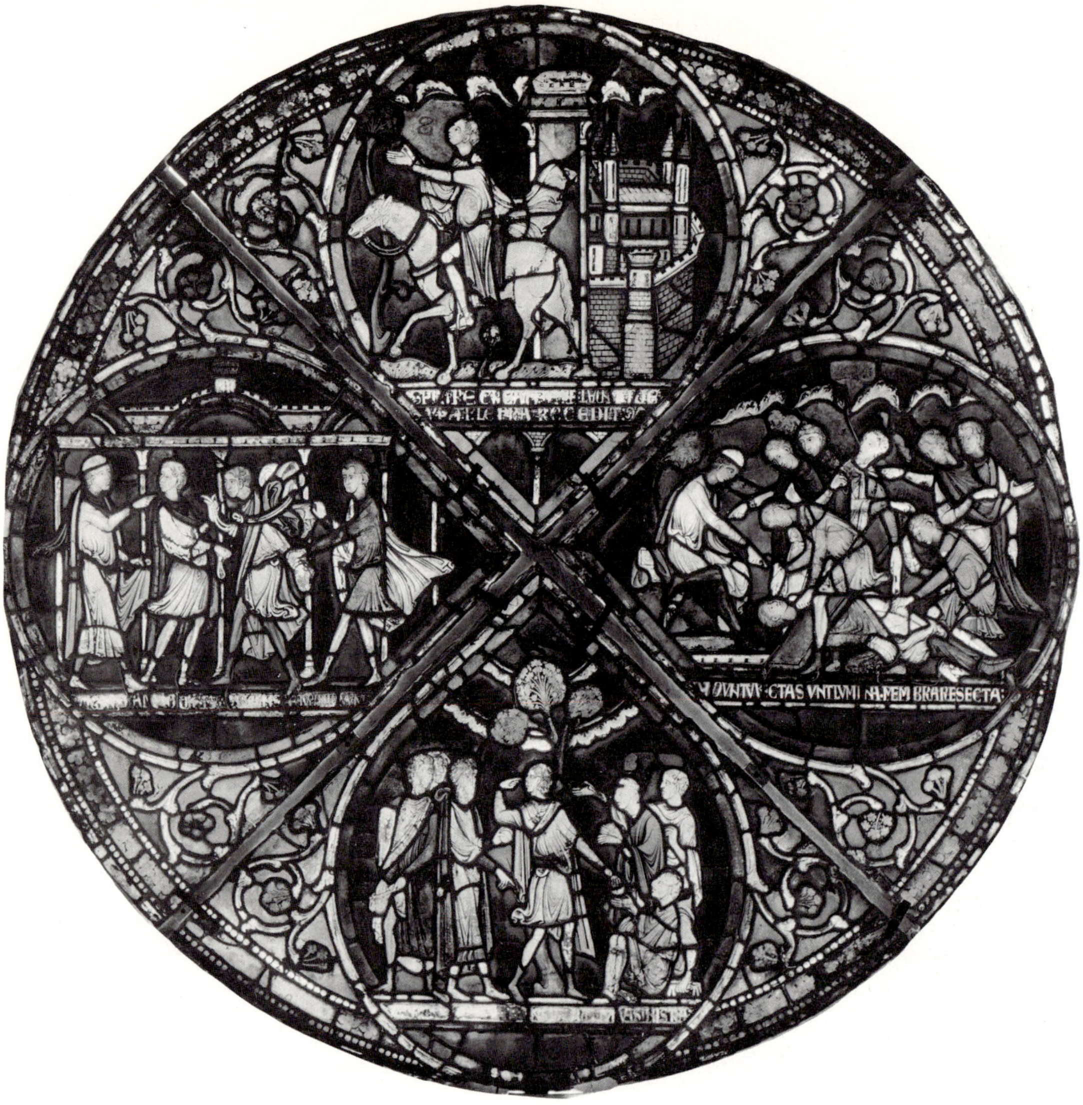

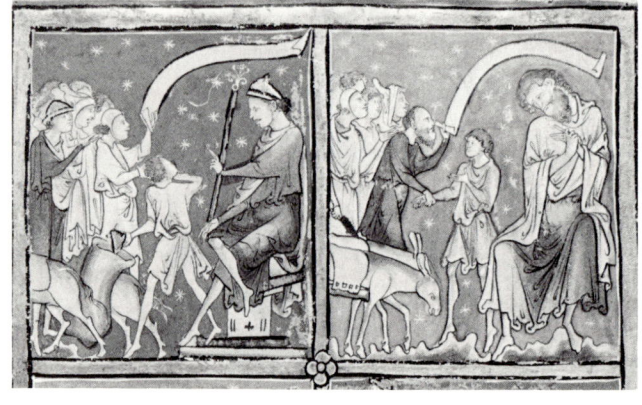

167. Trinity Chapel N:III (13),
a knight (14–16), Eilward of
Westoning unjustly punished

168. Psalter, Cambridge, Trinity
College, MS B.11.4, f.7v,
detail from Joseph cycle

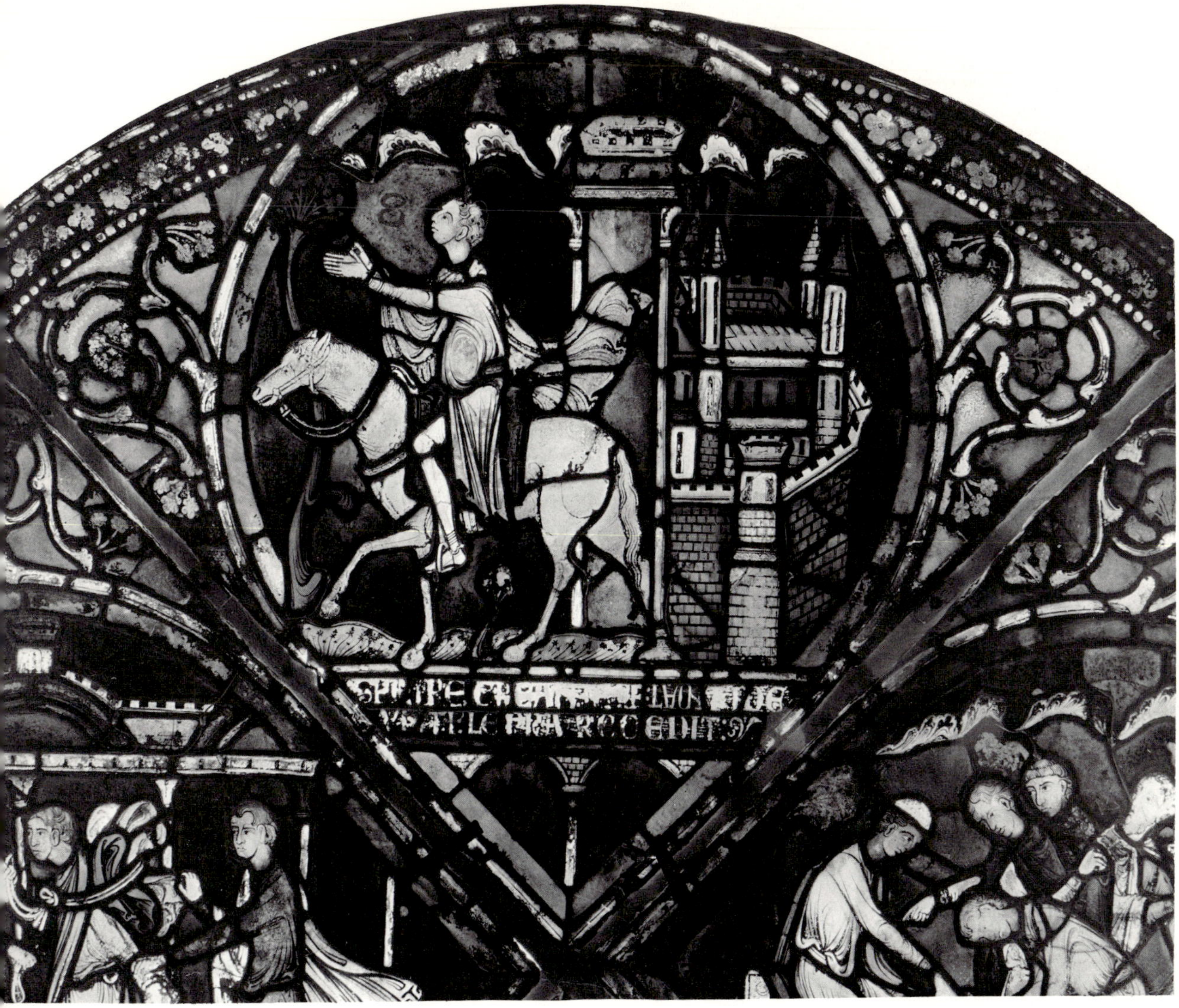

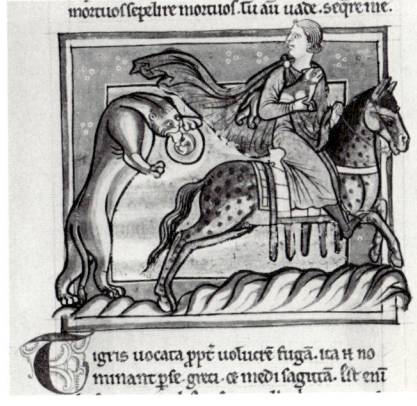

69. Trinity Chapel N:III (13), a knight leaving
    Canterbury

70. Workshop bestiary, New York, Morgan Library
    MS 81, f.35, detail

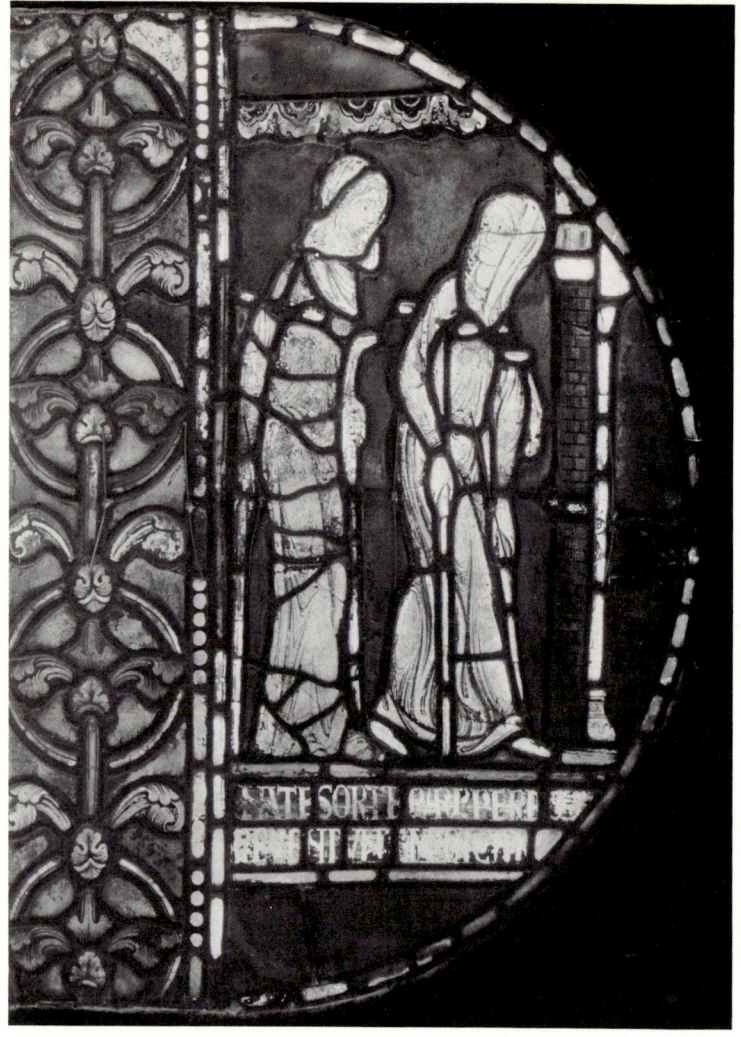

171

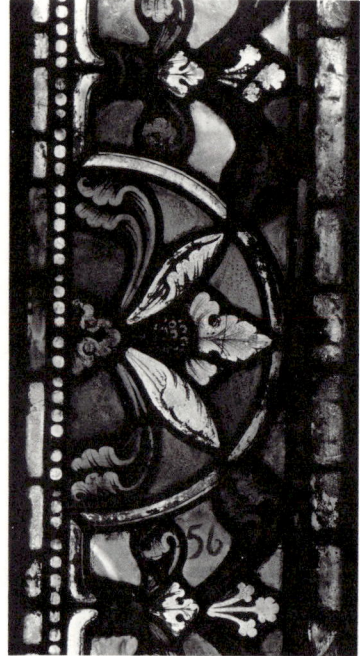

172

171. Trinity Chapel n:III (11), daughters of Godbold of Boxley

172. Trinity Chapel n:IV, border

173. Trinity Chapel s:VII, border

174. Trinity Chapel s:II, border

175. Trinity Chapel n:II, border

176. Sens, Becket window, border

177. South choir aisle "triforium" ST:IX, border fragment

178. Sens, St. Eustace window, border

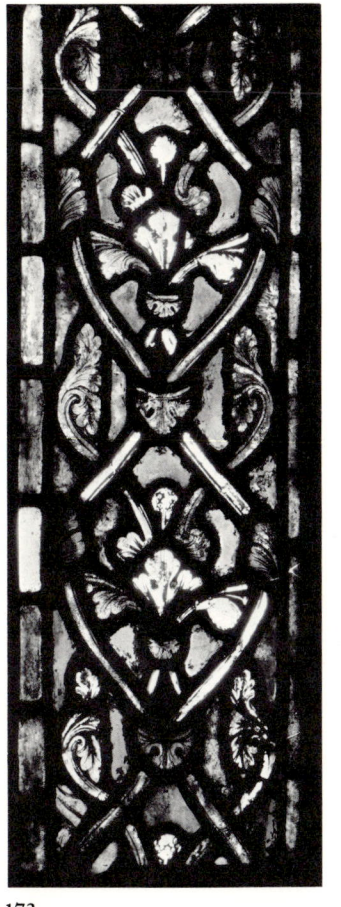

173

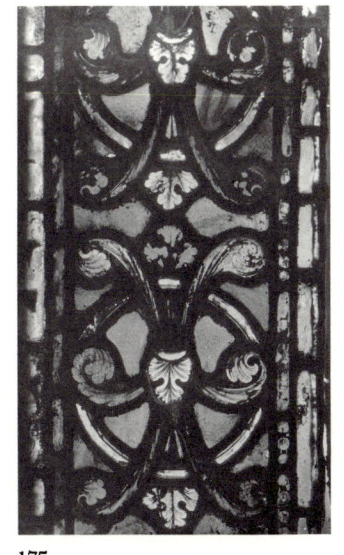

175

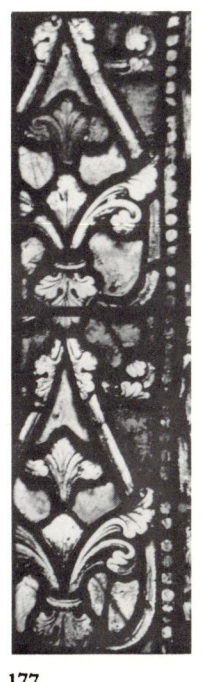

177

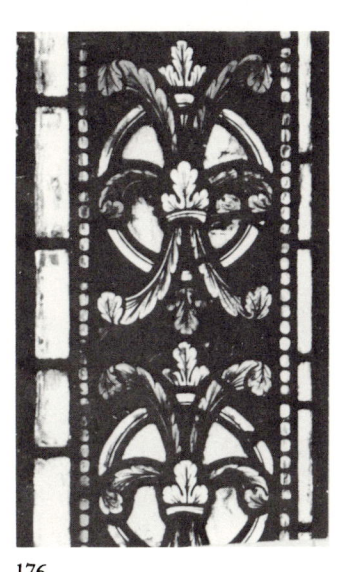

176

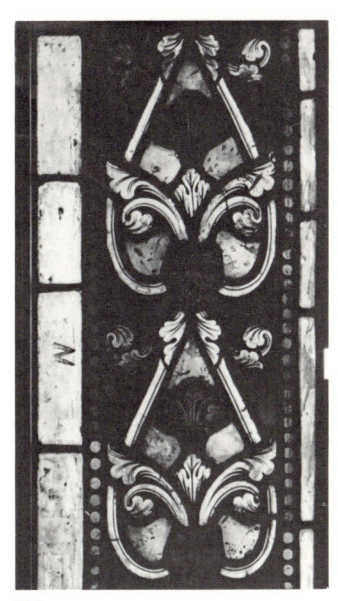

178

174

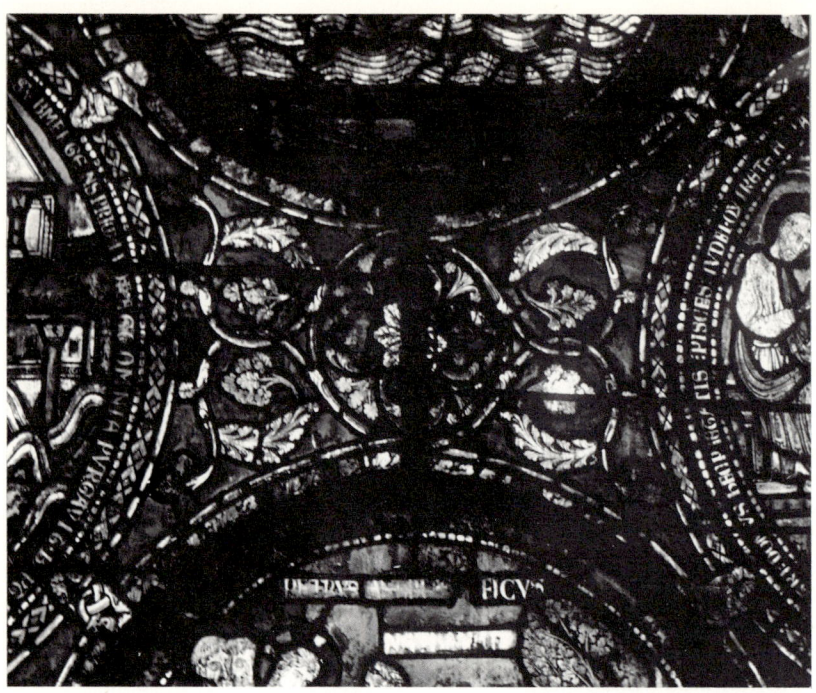

179. North choir aisle n:XIV, *rinceaux*

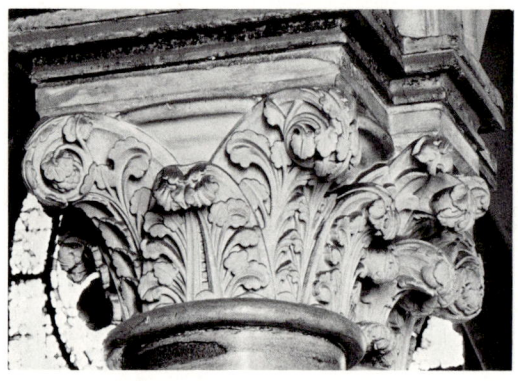

180. Trinity Chapel, double capital

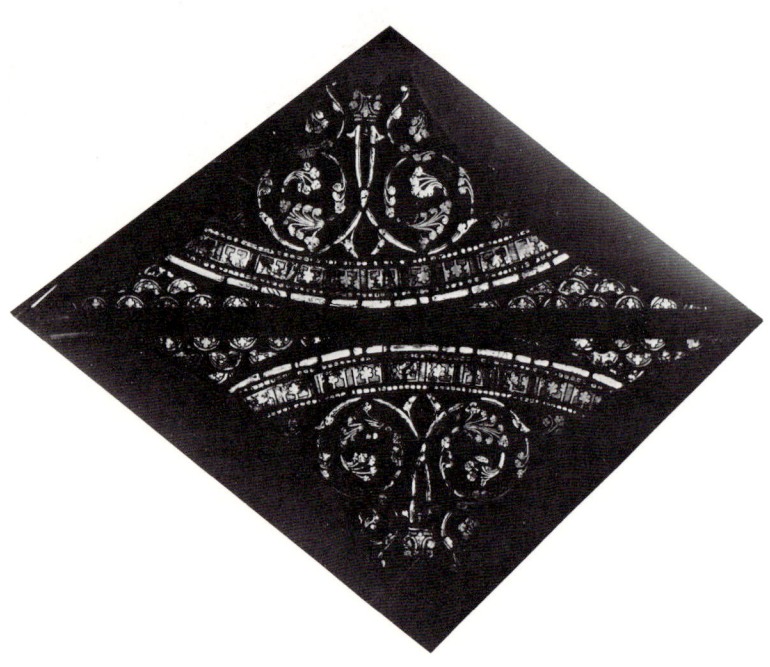

181. Sens, St. Eustace window, ornament

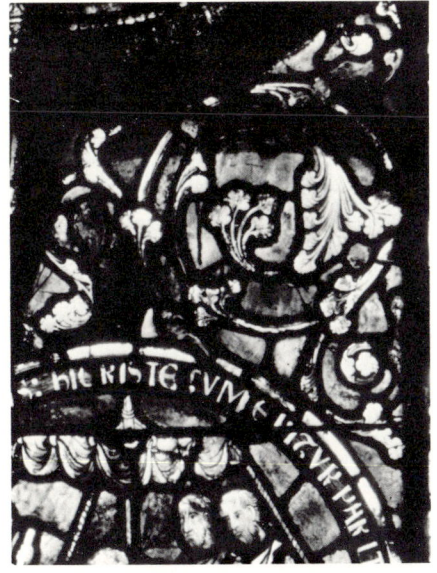

182

182. Corona, redemption window, *rinceaux*

183. Trinity Chapel s:II, ornament

184. Sens, Becket window, ornament

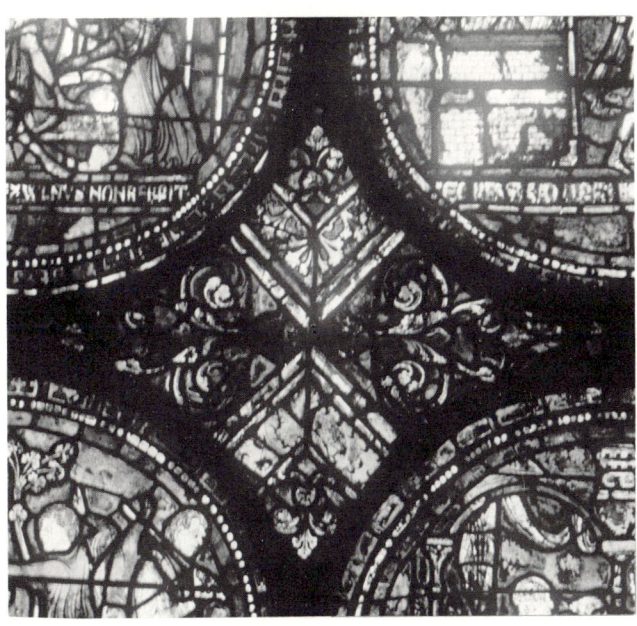

183

184

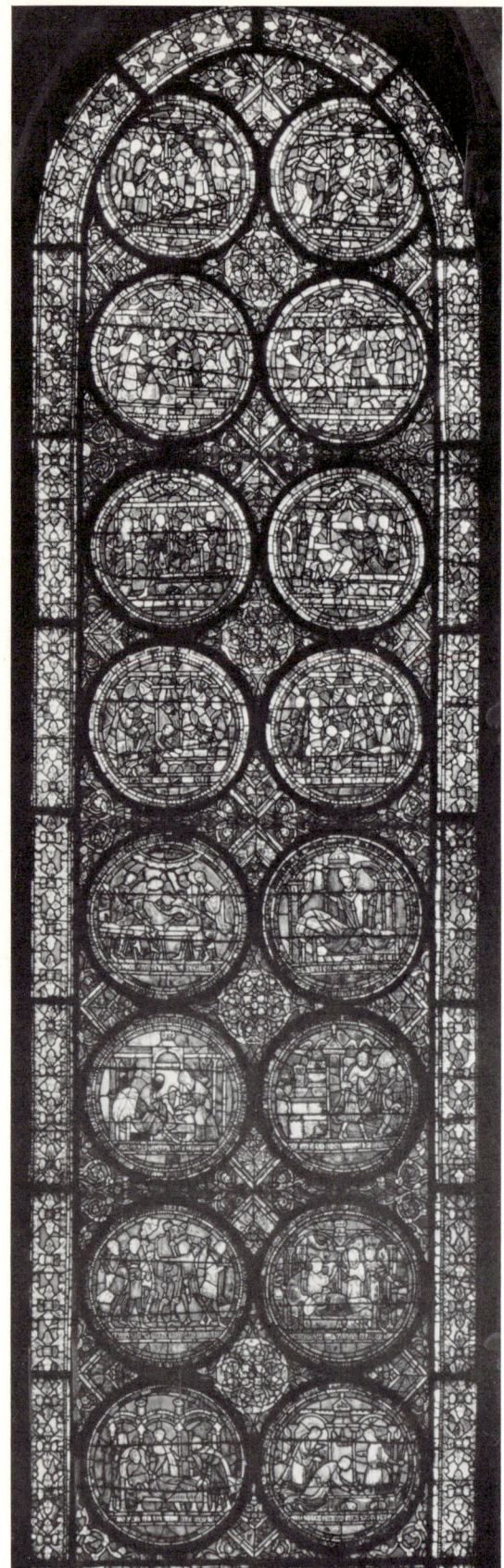

185. Trinity Chapel s:II

186. Sens, Becket window

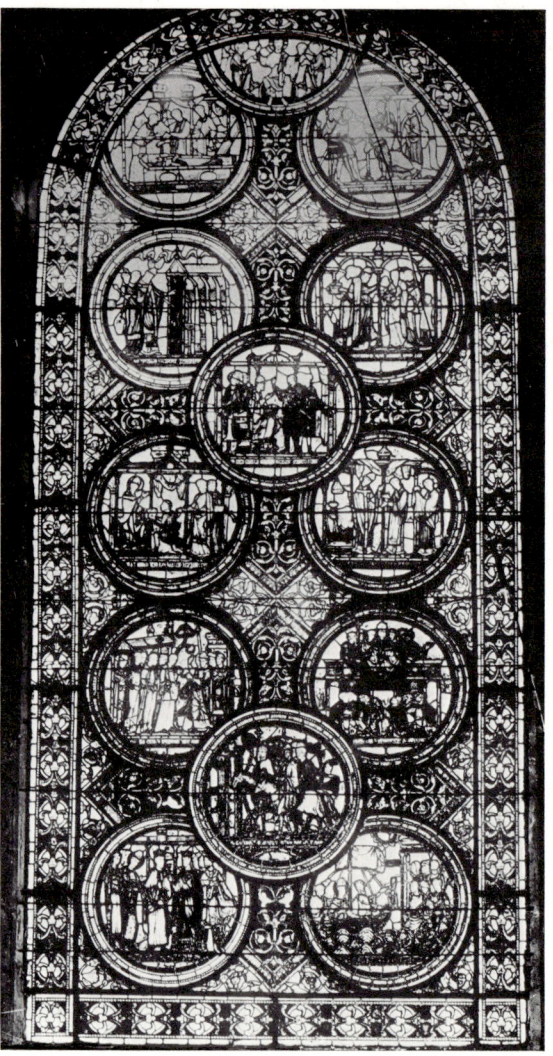

185

186

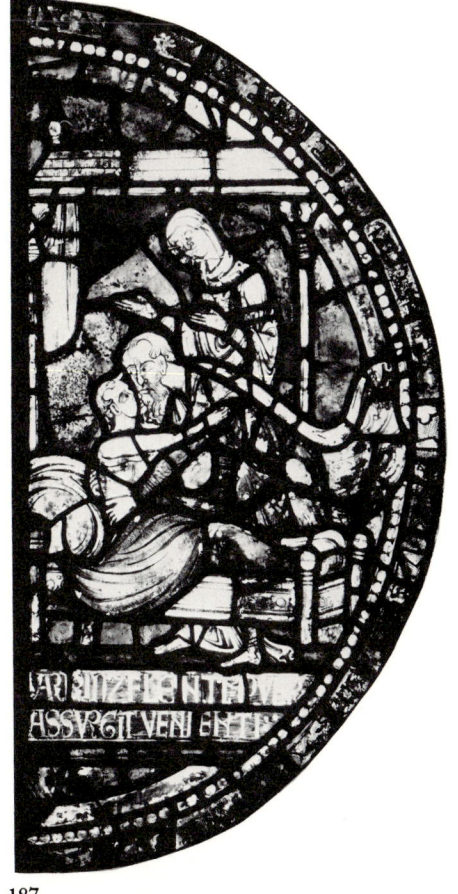

187

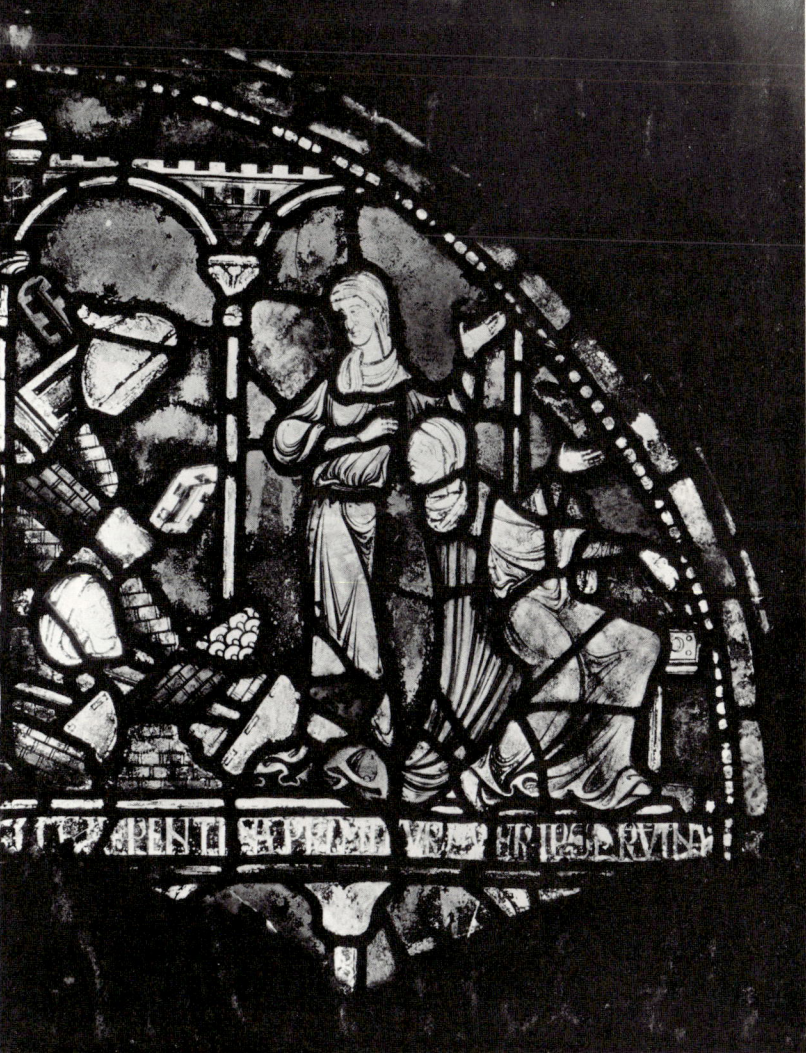

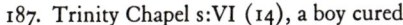

188

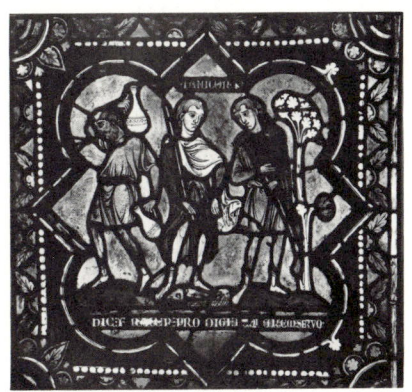

189

187. Trinity Chapel s:VI (14), a boy cured

188. Sens, Prodigal Son window, the prodigal returning home

189. Trinity Chapel s:VII (3), Geoffrey of Winchester
buried by a collapsed wall

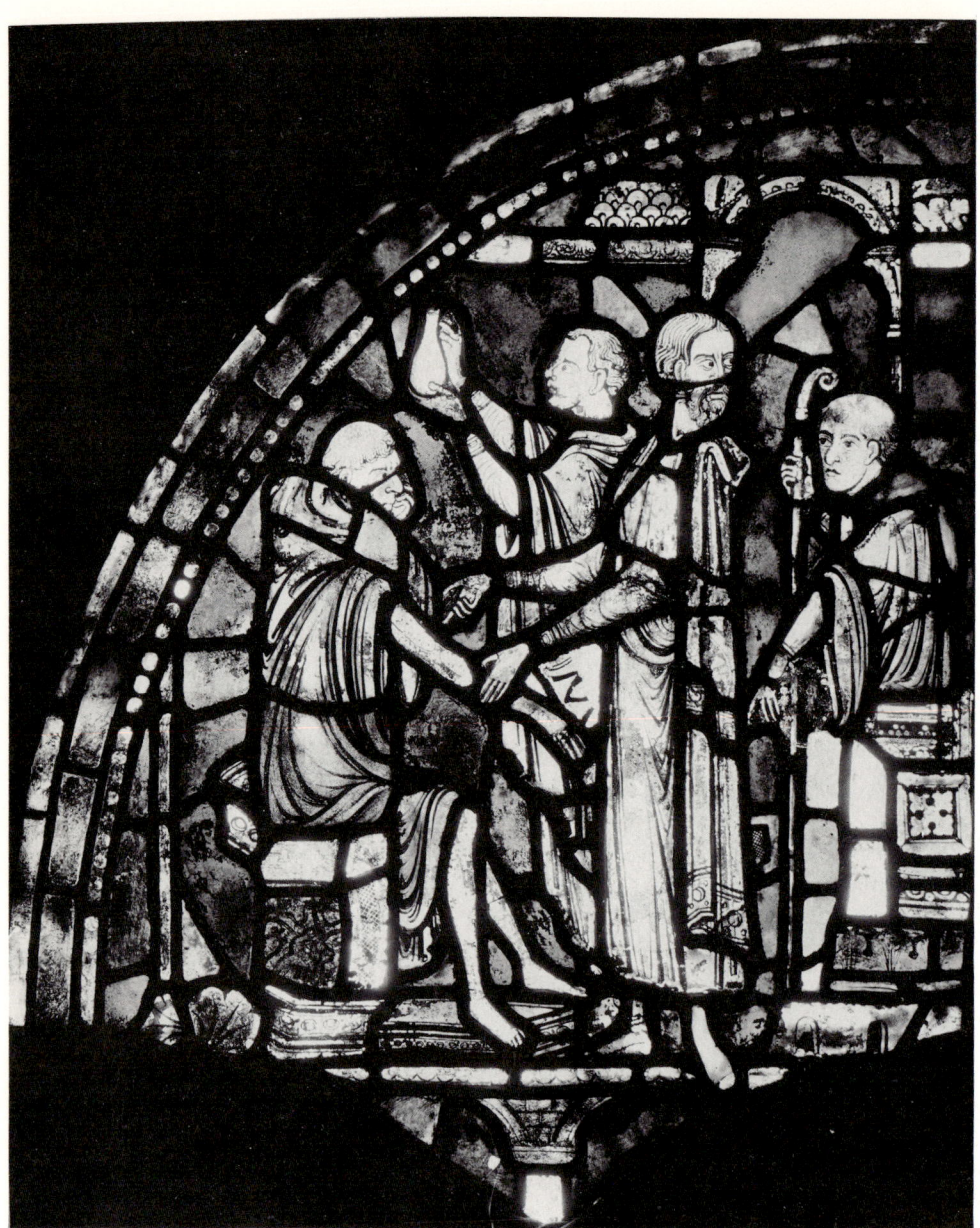

190. Trinity Chapel s:VII (12), uroscopic examination for leprosy

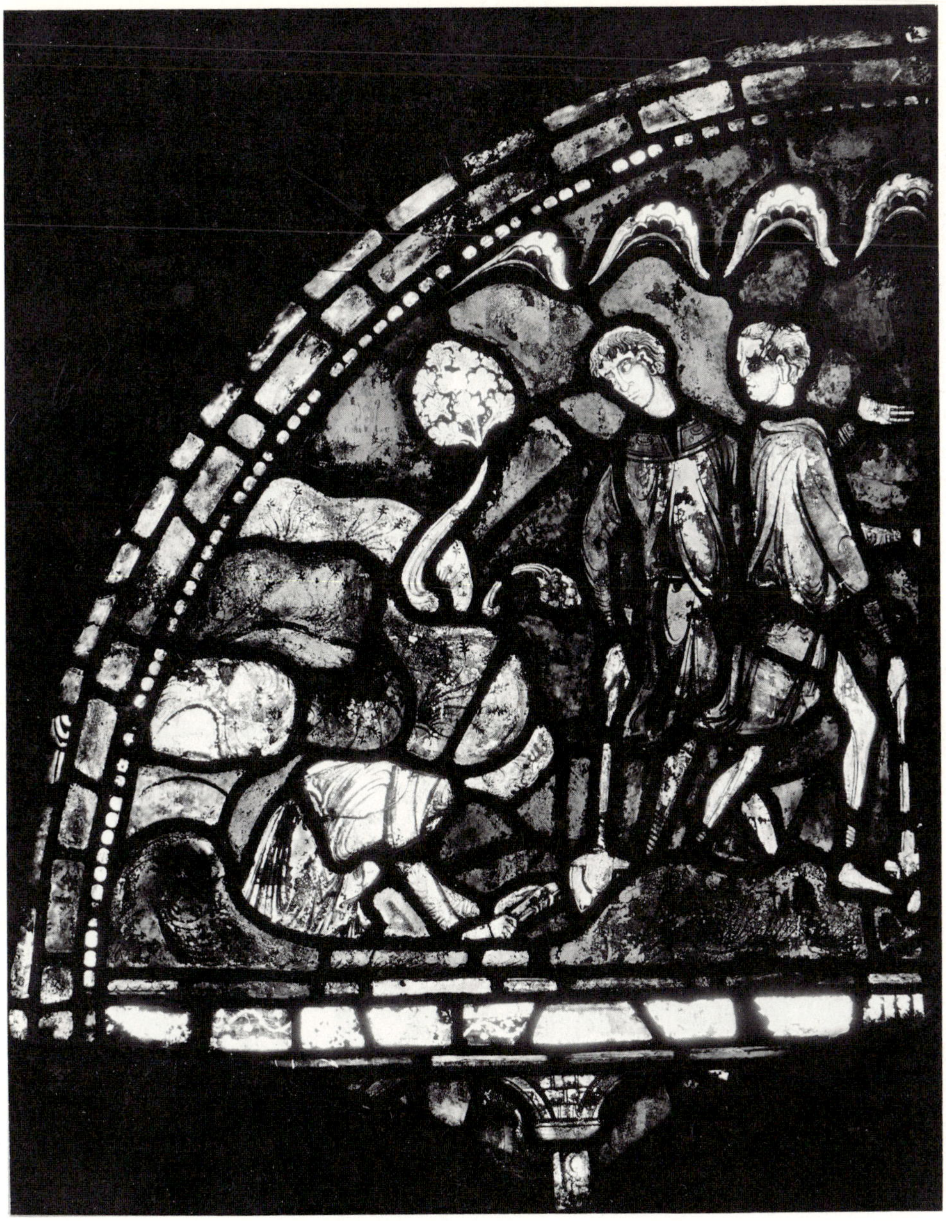

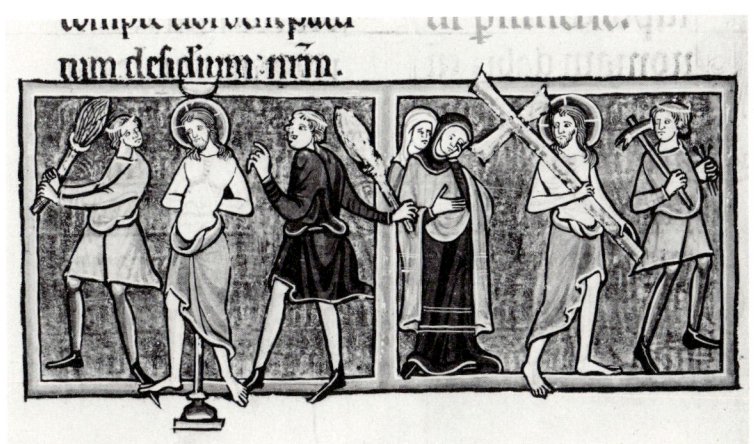

191. Trinity Chapel s:VII (13),
William of Gloucester
buried by a fall of earth

192. Little Canterbury Psalter,
Paris, Bibliothèque
Nationale, MS Lat. 770,
f.32v, Psalm 21,
flagellation and carrying
the cross

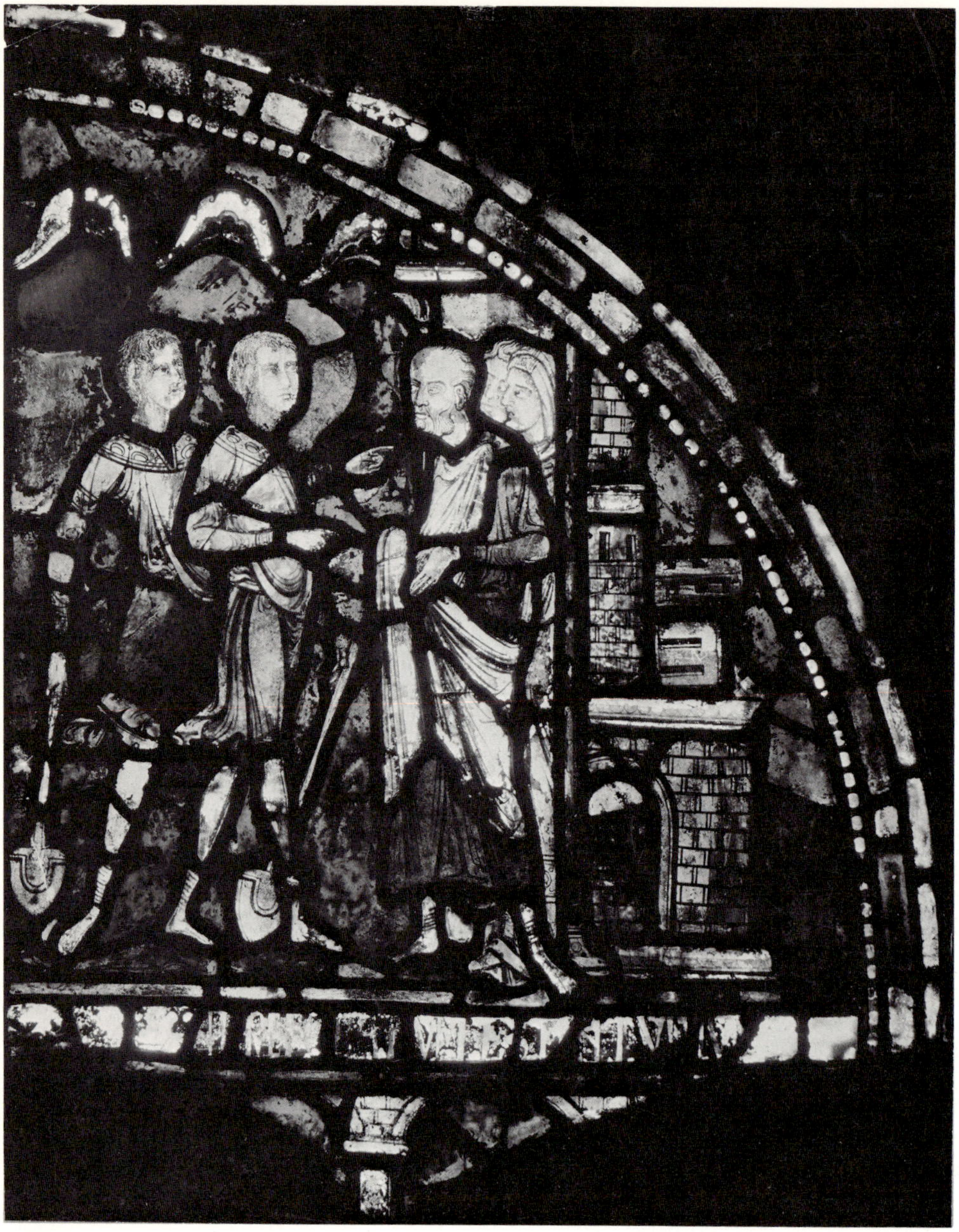

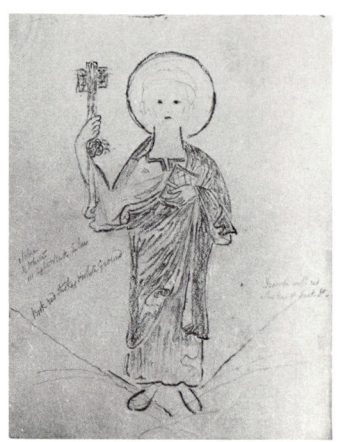

194. Trinity Chapel s:VII (14), William of Gloucester's accident reported

193. Austin Sketchbook, Canterbury Cathedral Library, Add. MS 1, drawing from Trinity Chapel vault painting of St. Peter

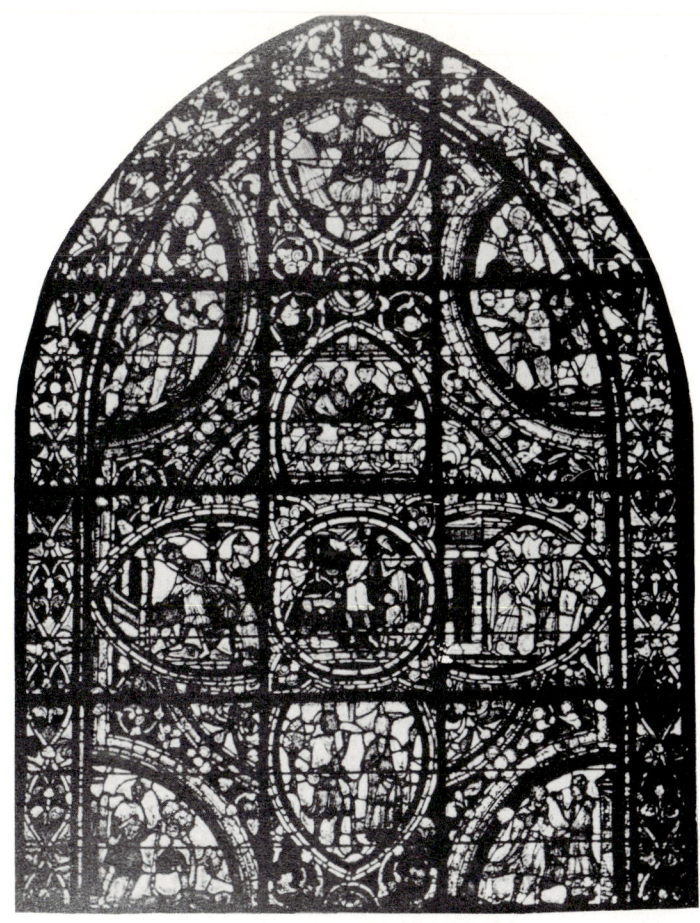

195. Chartres, Prodigal Son window,
upper part

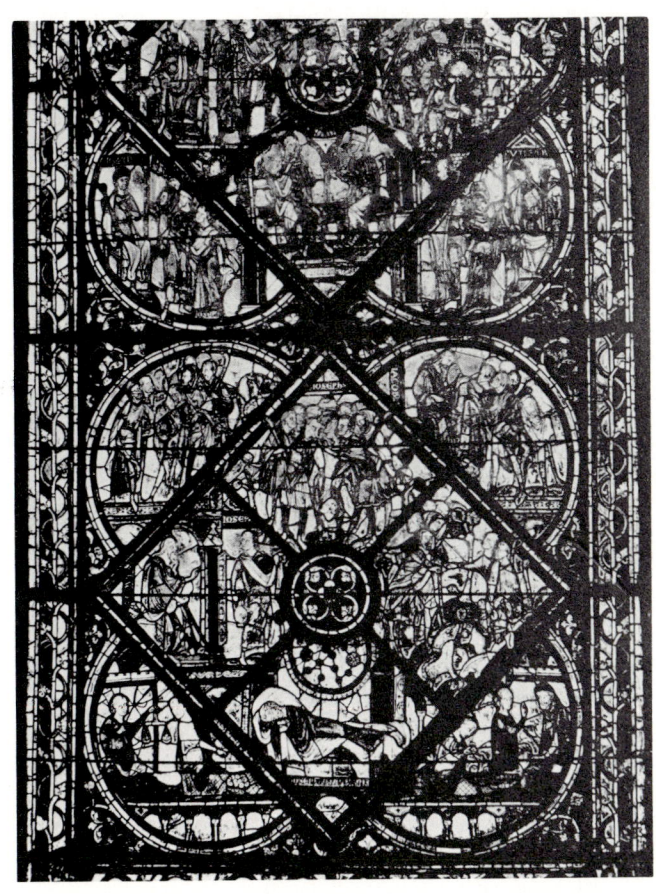

196. Chartres, Joseph window,
lower part

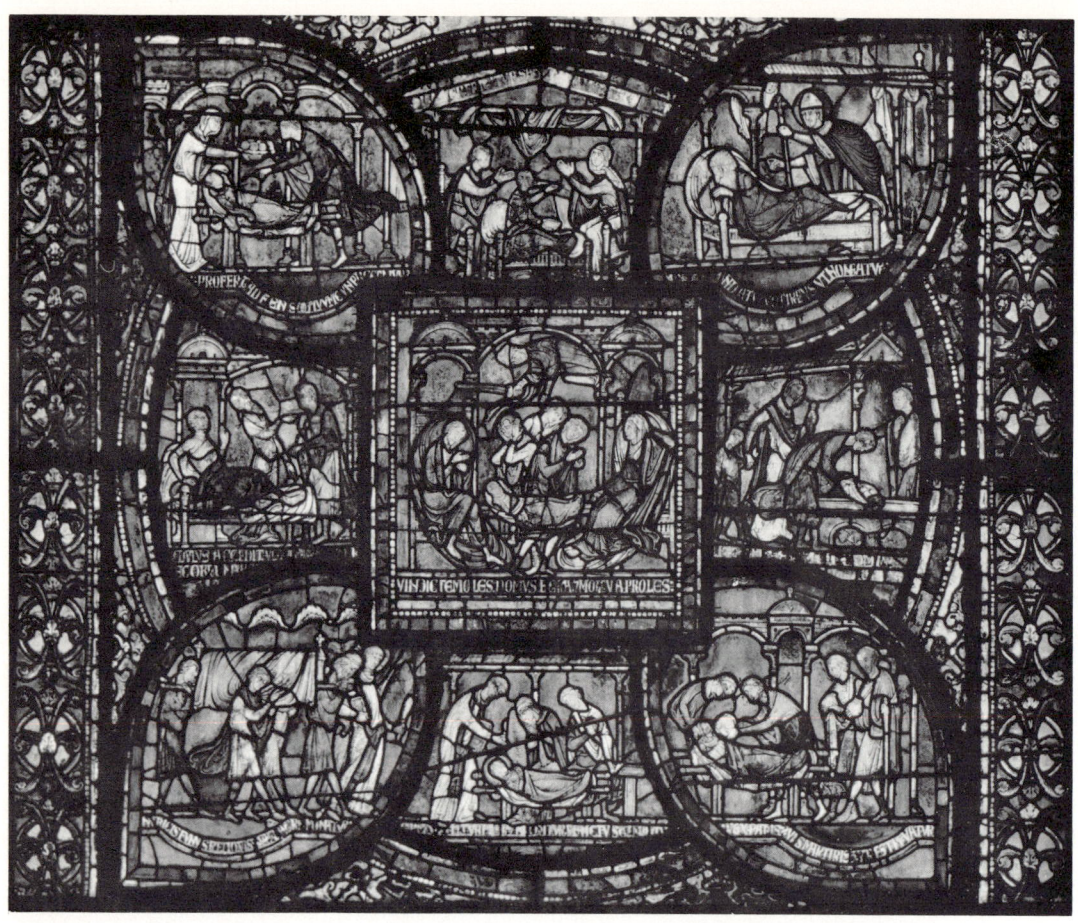

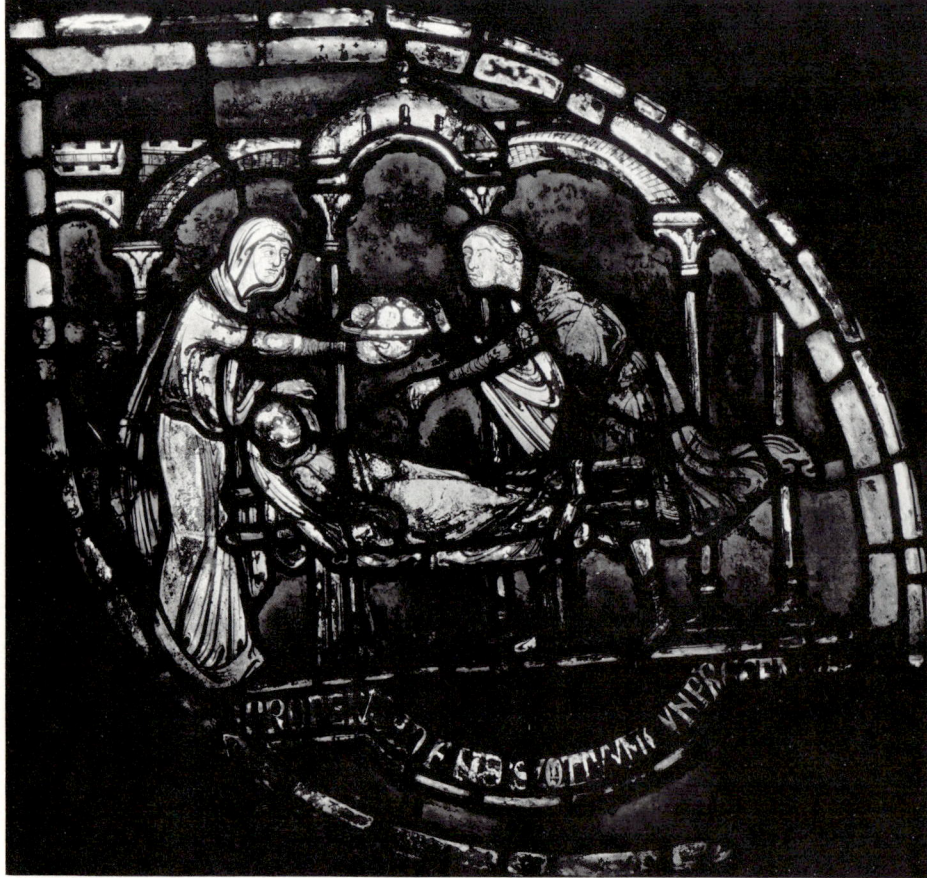

197. Trinity Chapel n:II (25-33), plague in the household of Jordan Fritz Eisulf

197a. Detail, 25

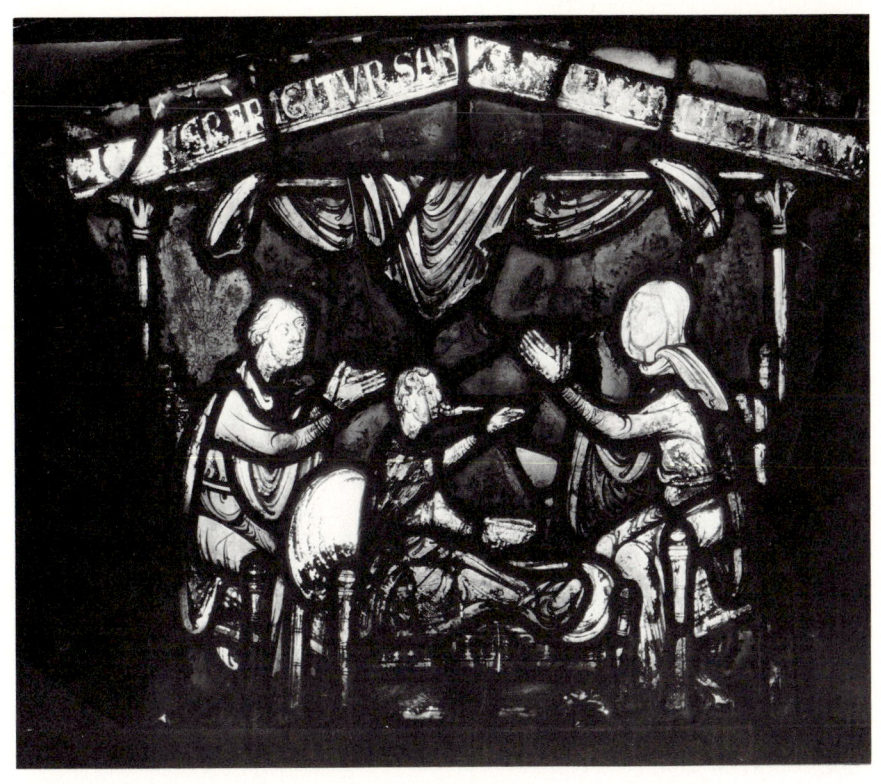

197b. Detail, 26

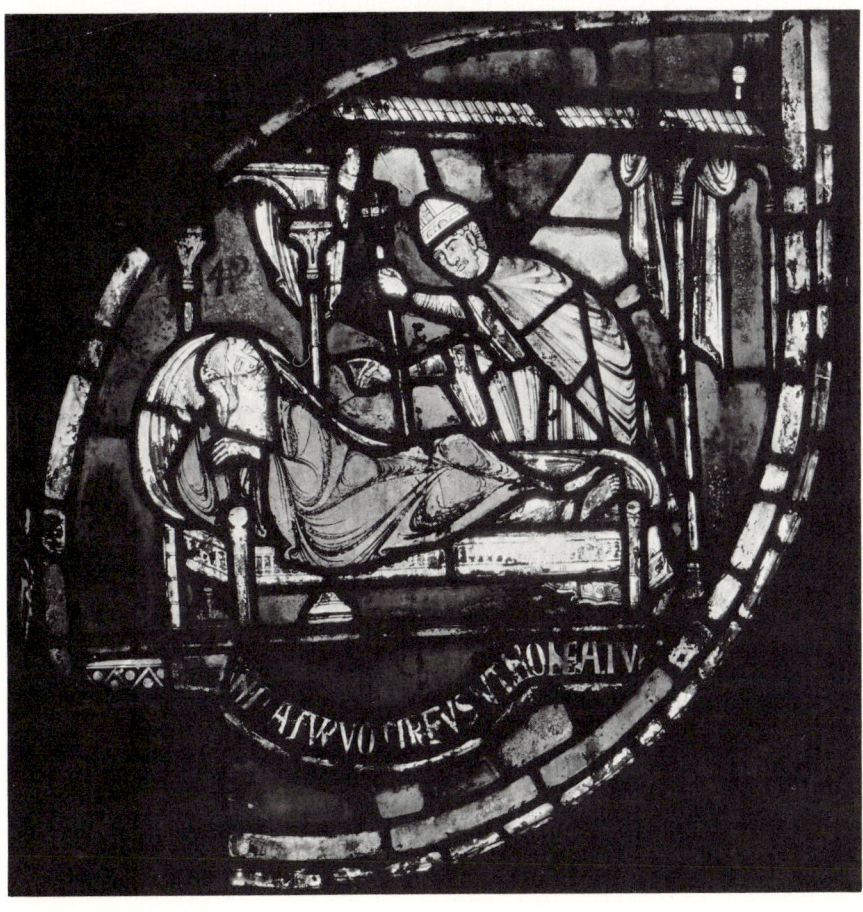

197c. Detail, 27

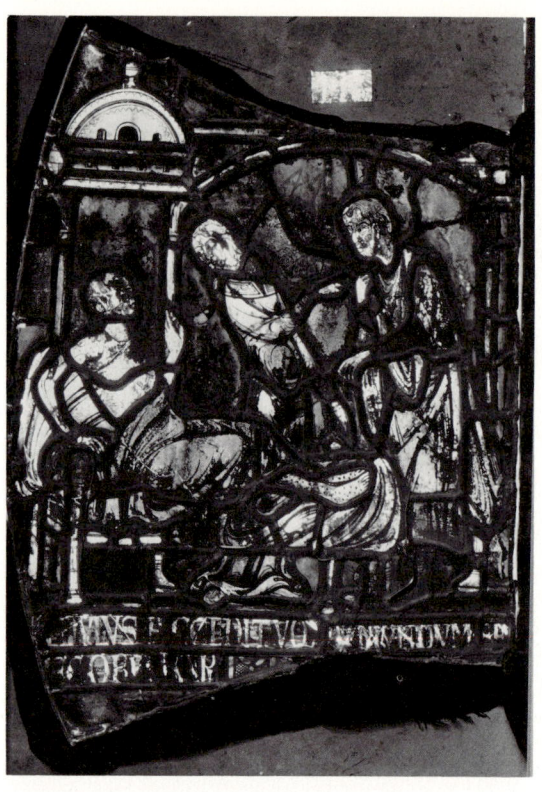

197d. Detail, 28

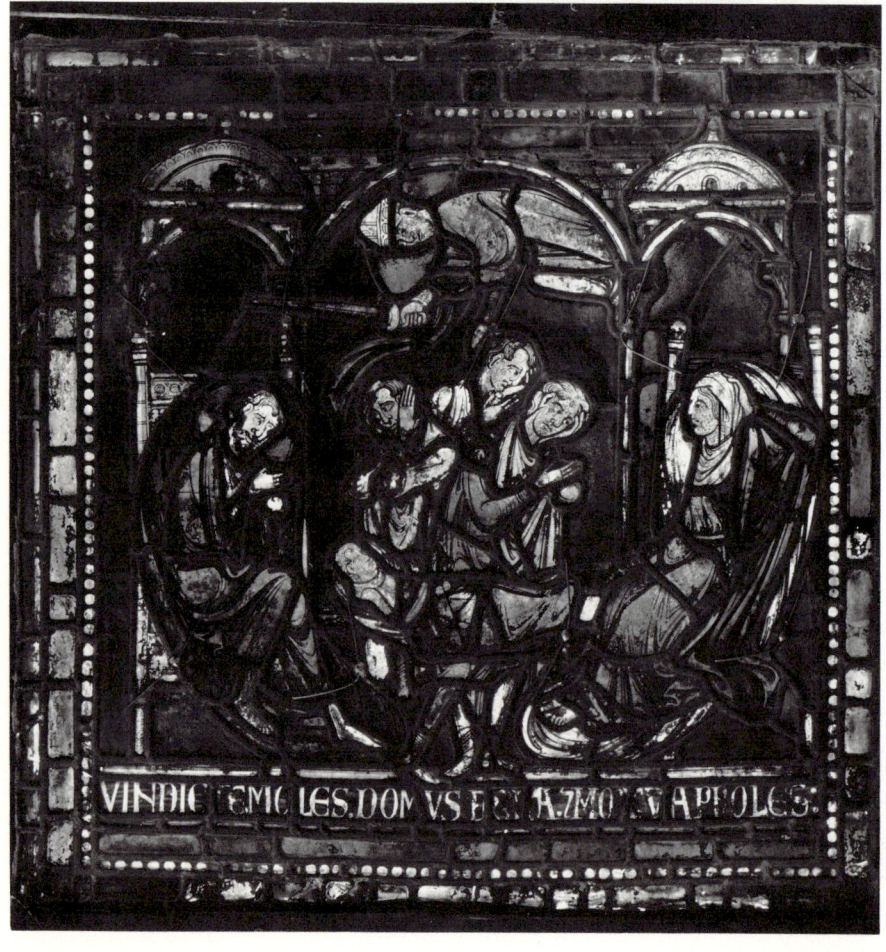

197e. Detail, 29

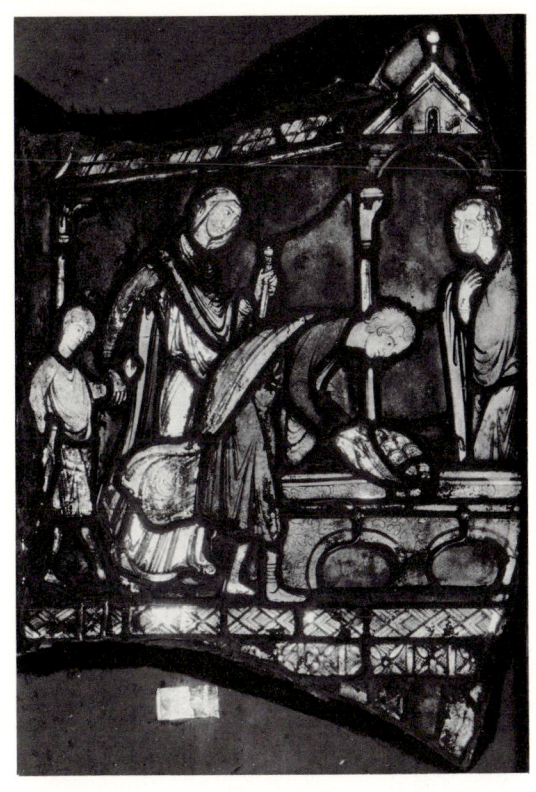

197f. Detail, 30

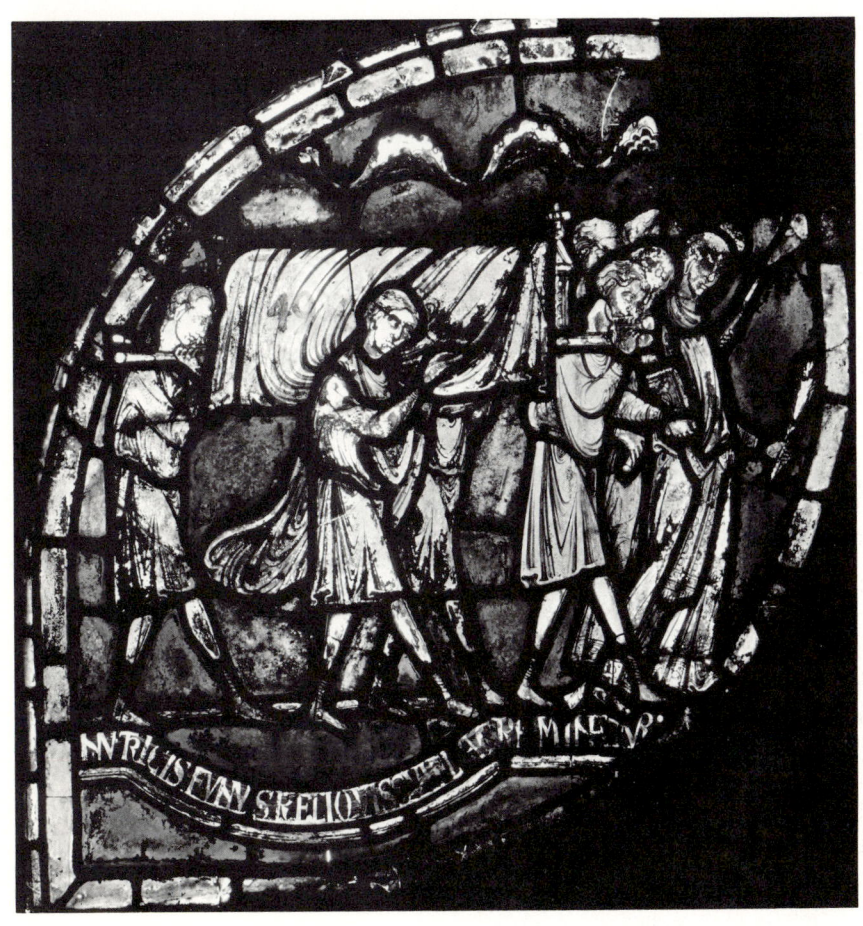

197g. Detail, 31

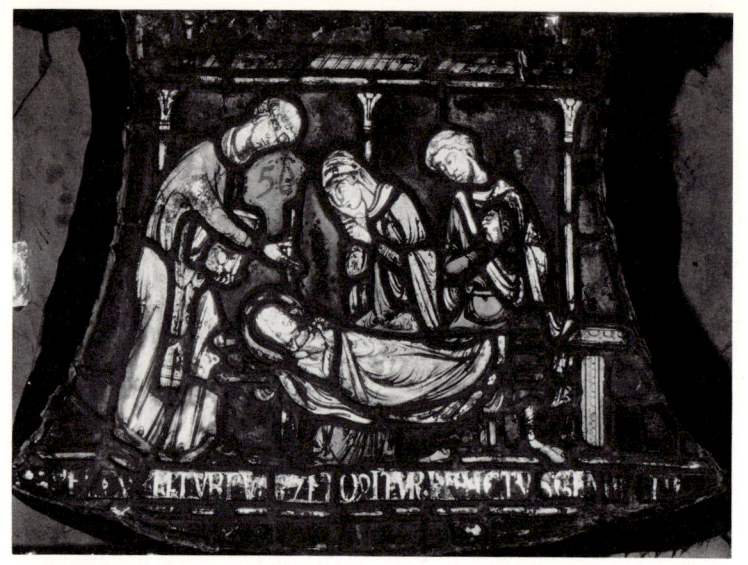

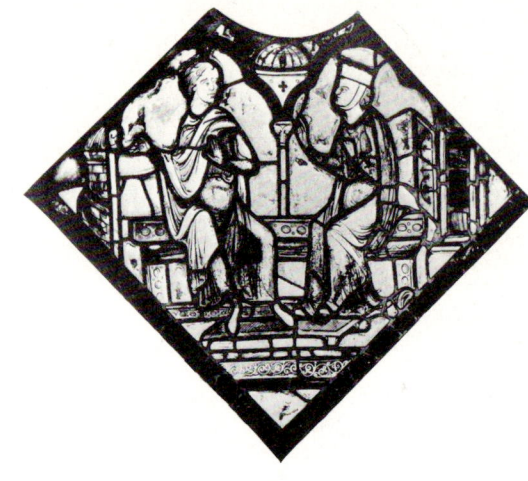

197h. Detail, 32

198. Chartres, Joseph window, Joseph and Potiphar's wife

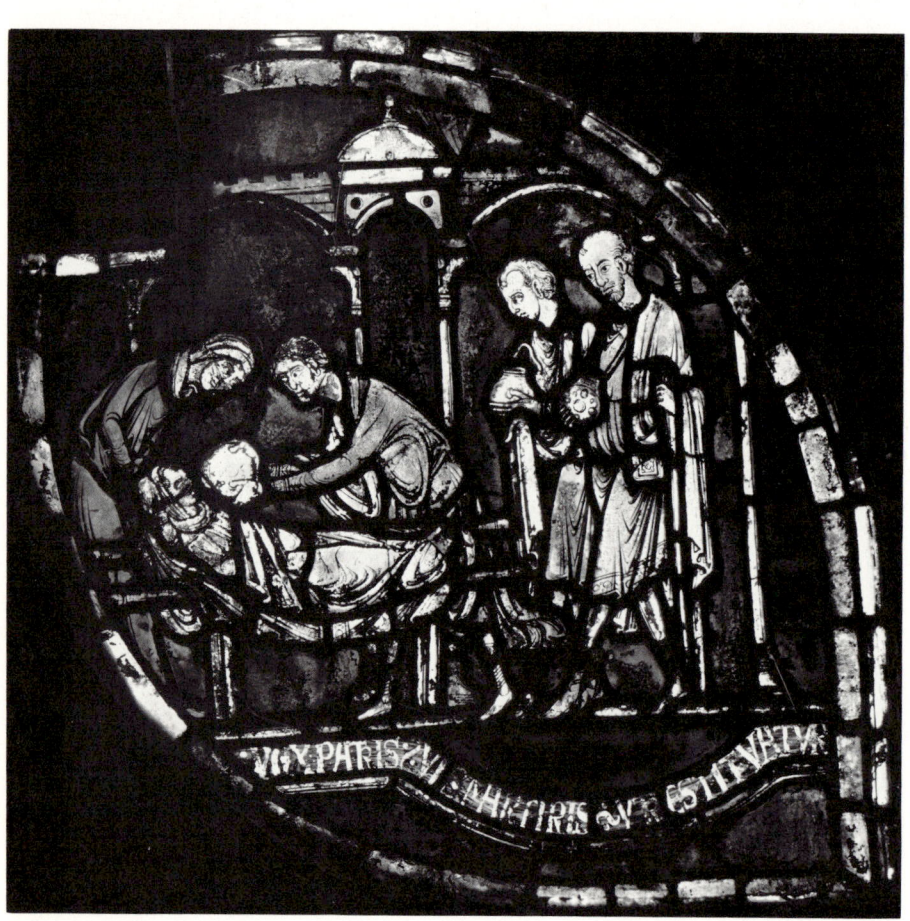

197i. Detail, 33

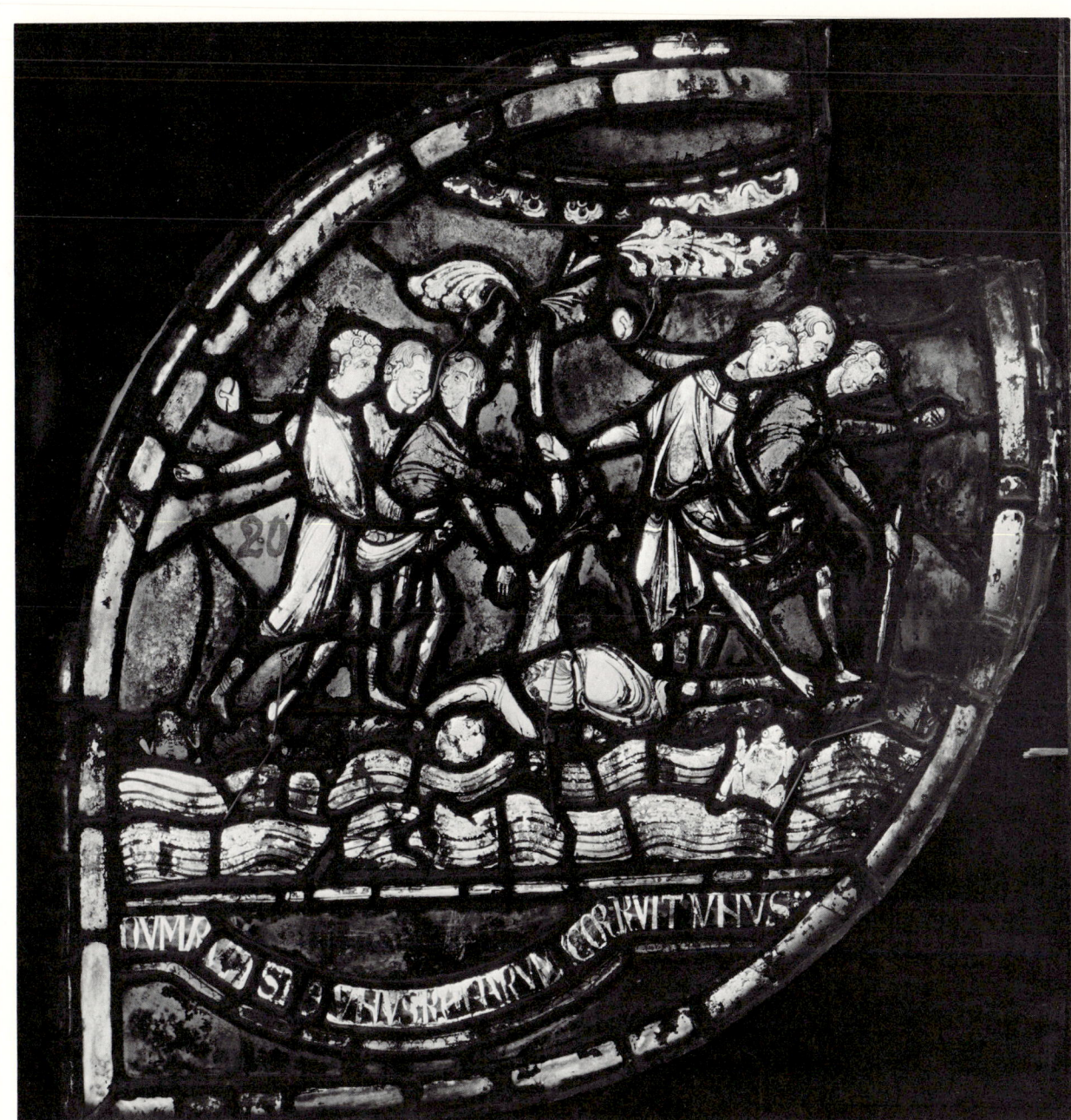

199. Trinity Chapel n:II (13), stoning frogs

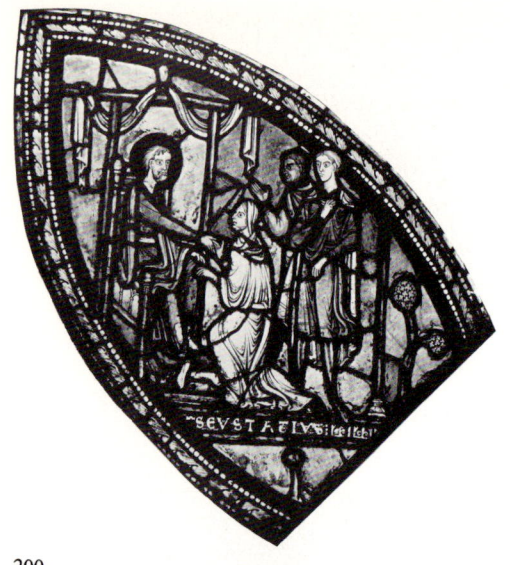

200

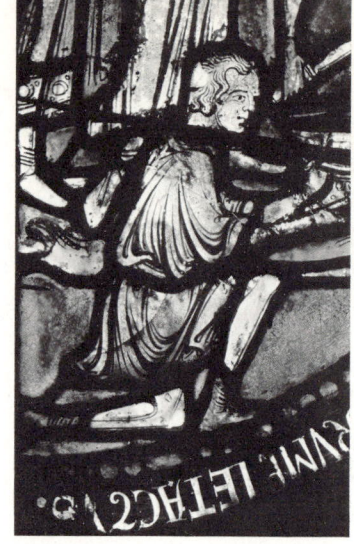

201

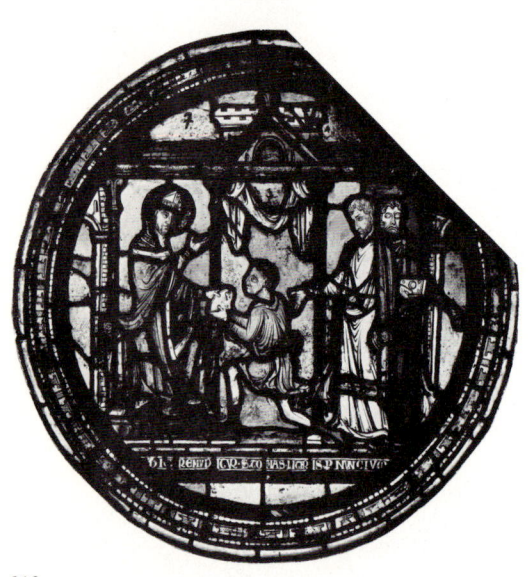

202

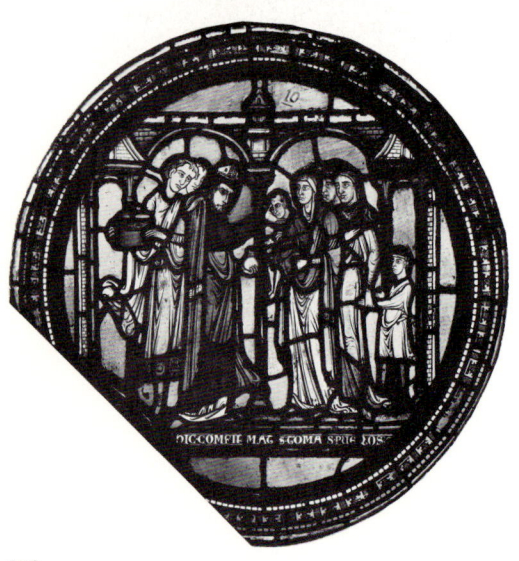

203

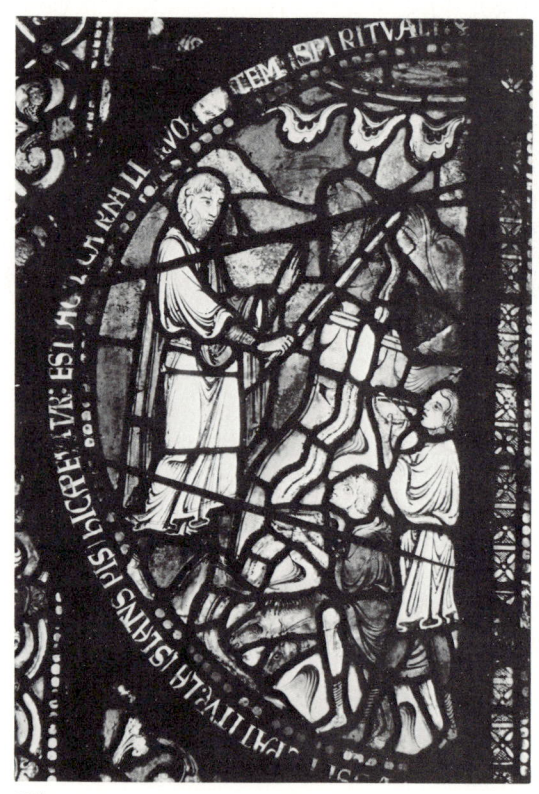

204

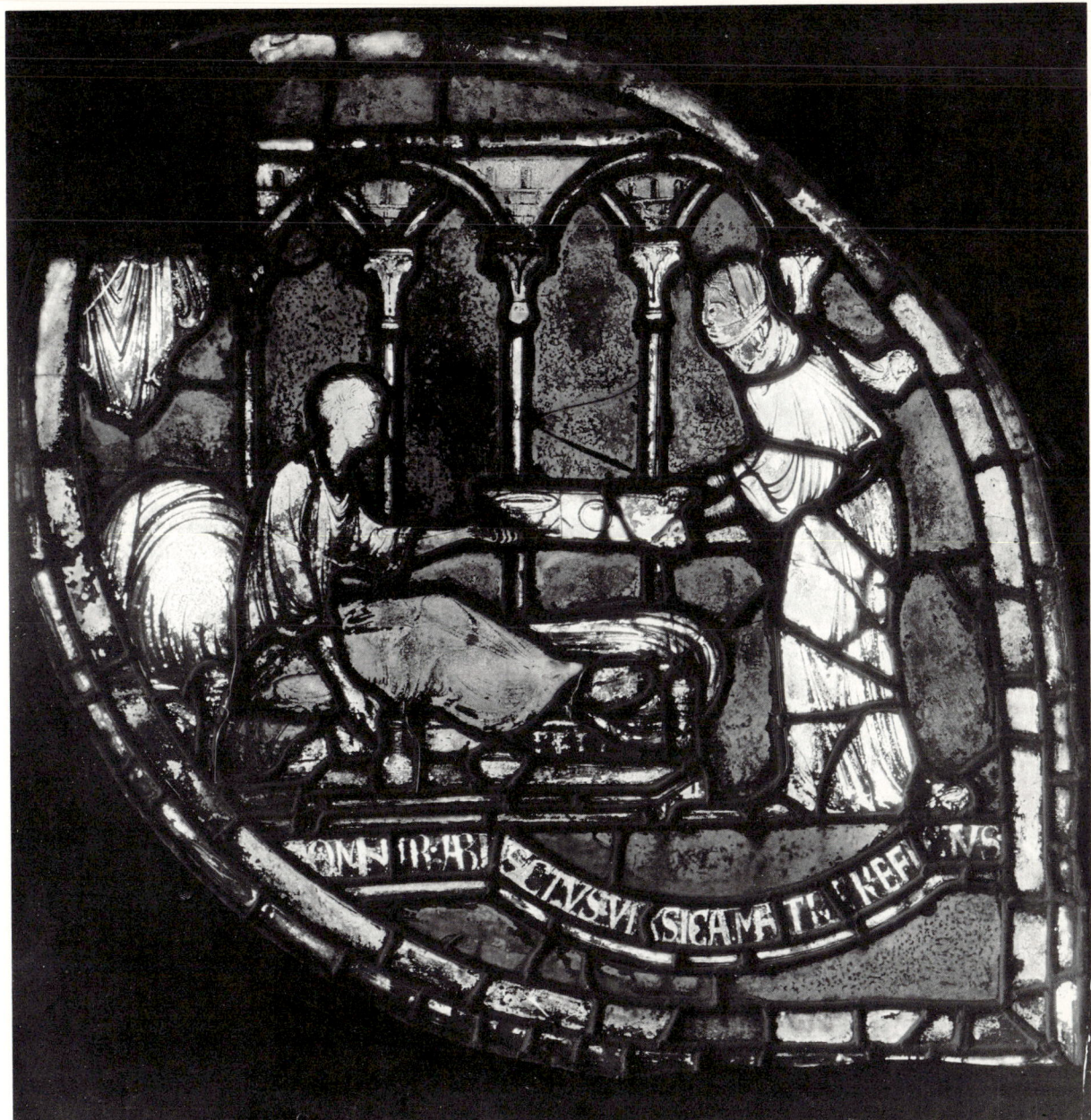

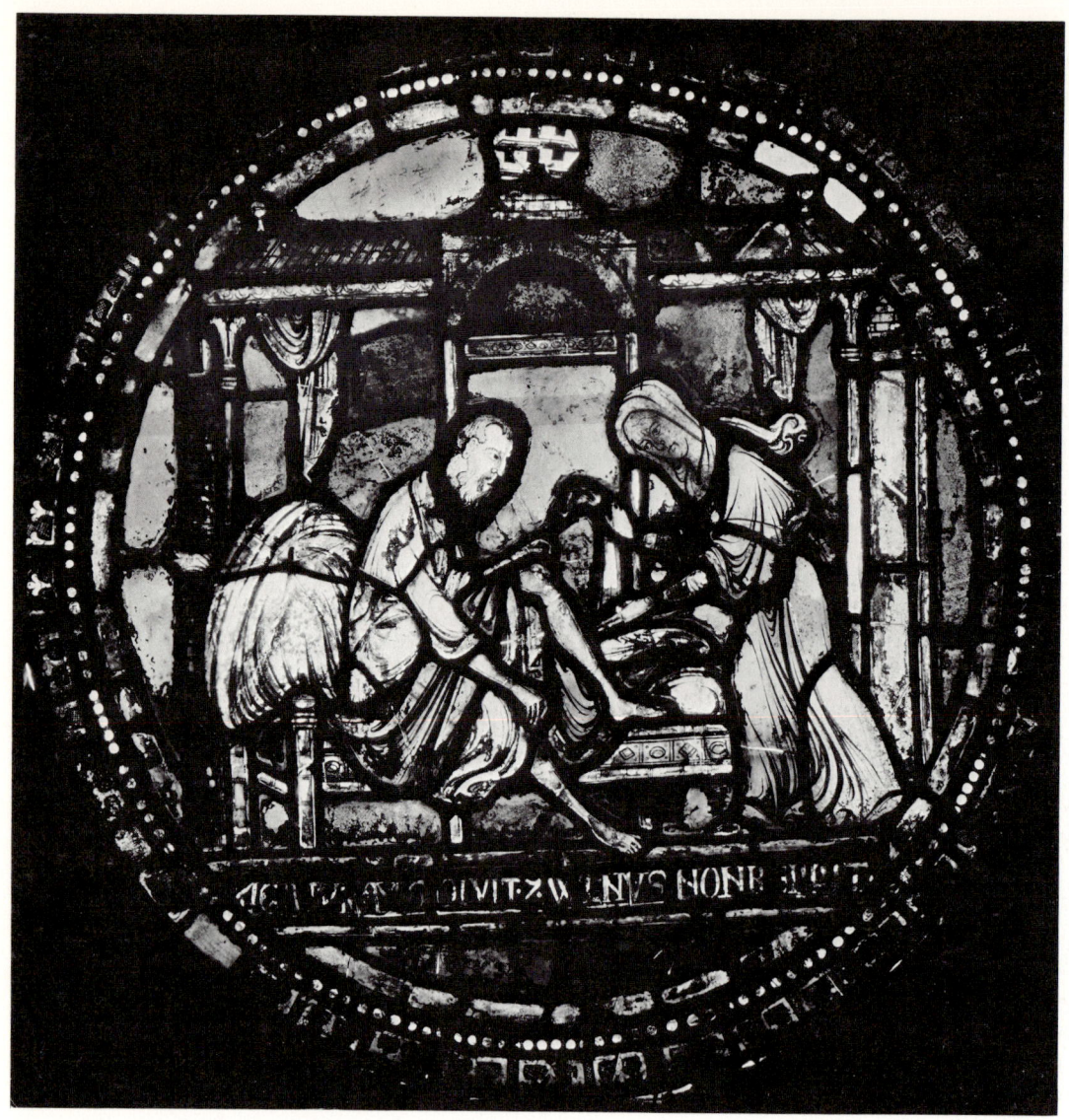

206. Trinity Chapel s:II (11), William of Kellett healed

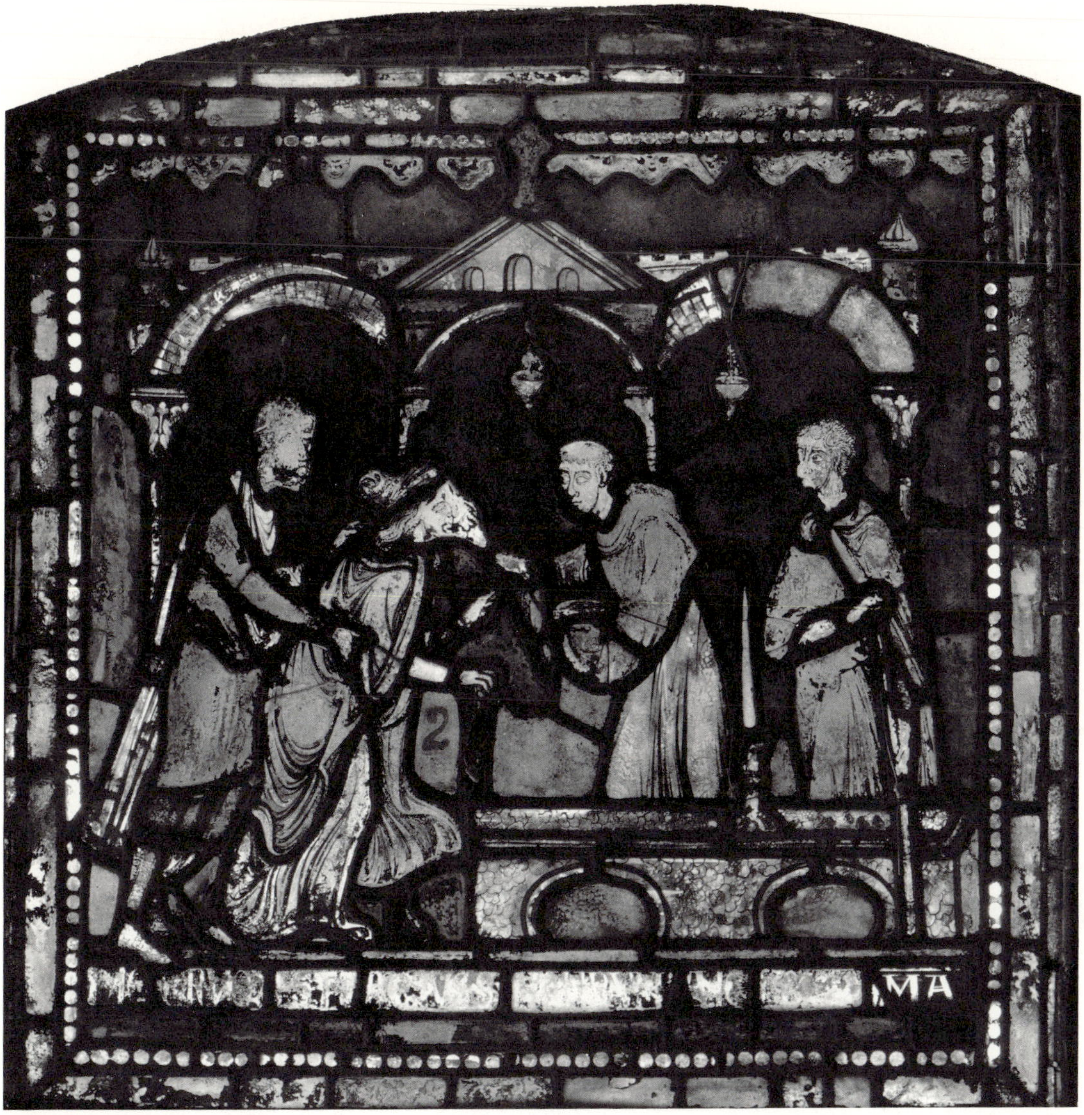

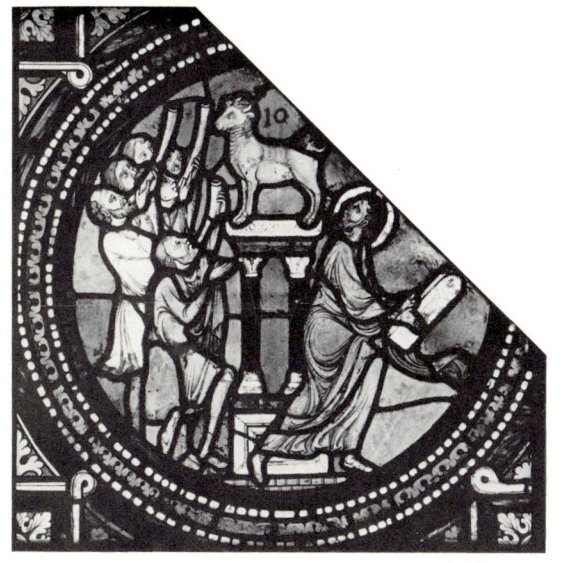

207

207. Sens, Good Samaritan window,
the golden calf

208. Trinity Chapel n:II (2), Juliana of
Rochester at the tomb

208

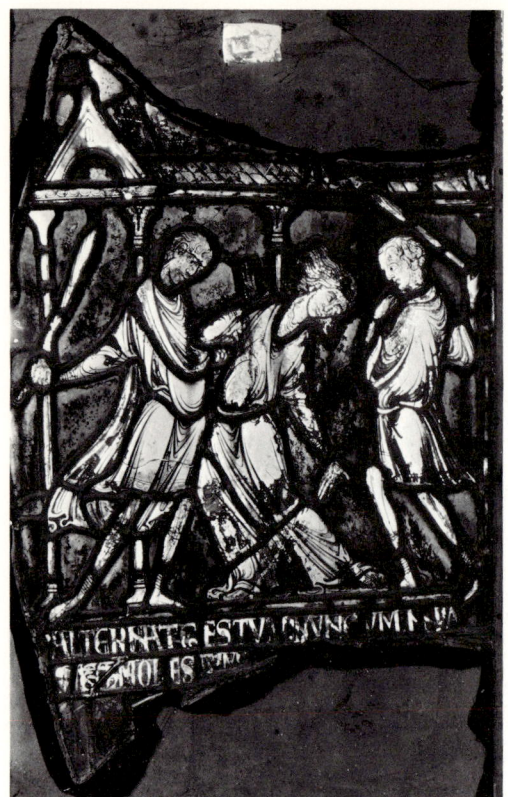

209

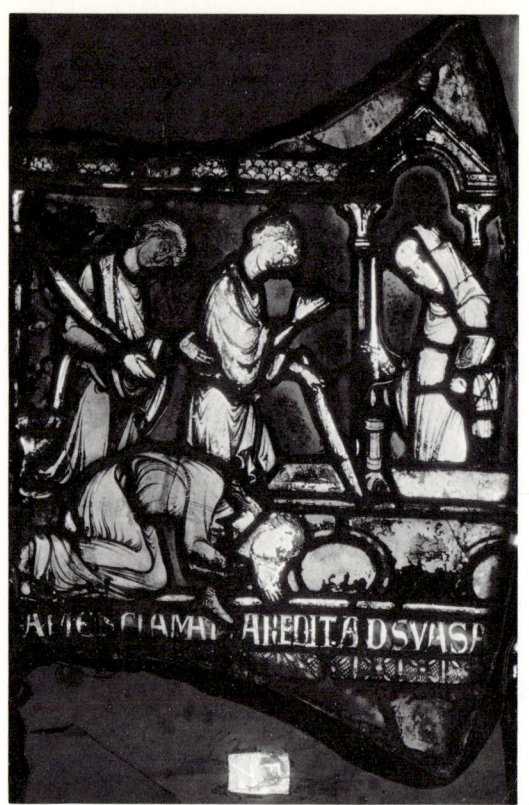

211

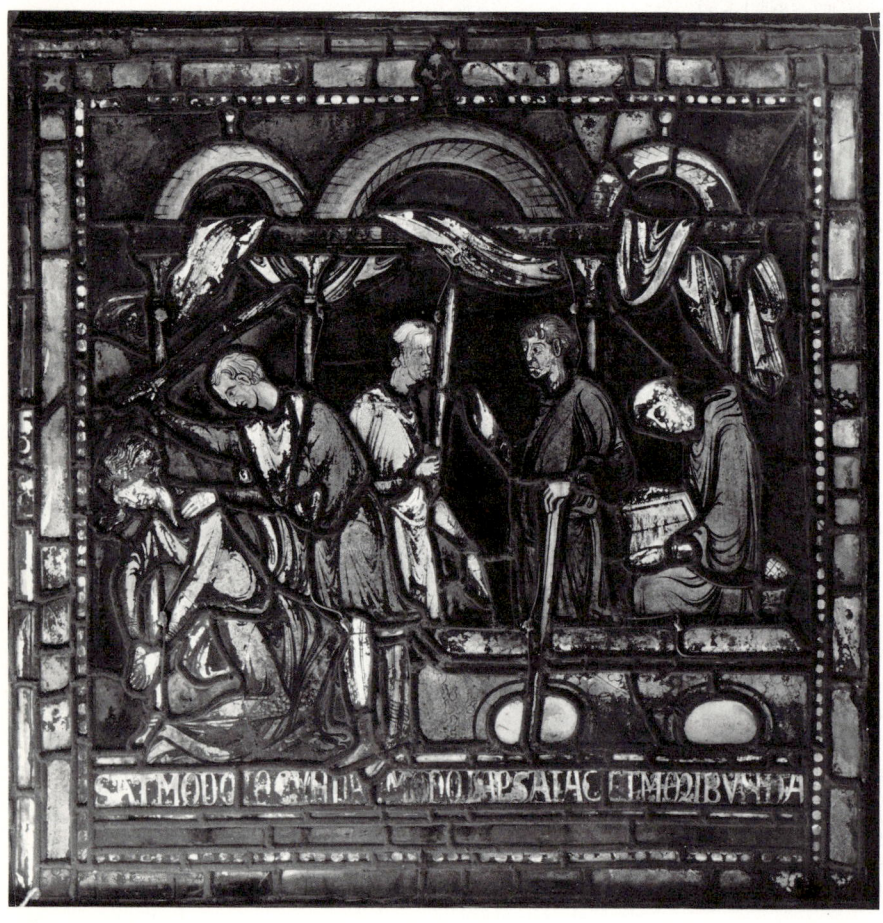

210

209. Trinity Chapel n:II (19),
Matilda of Cologne, a maniac,
beaten

210. Trinity Chapel n:II (20),
Matilda at the tomb

211. Trinity Chapel n:II (21),
Matilda cured

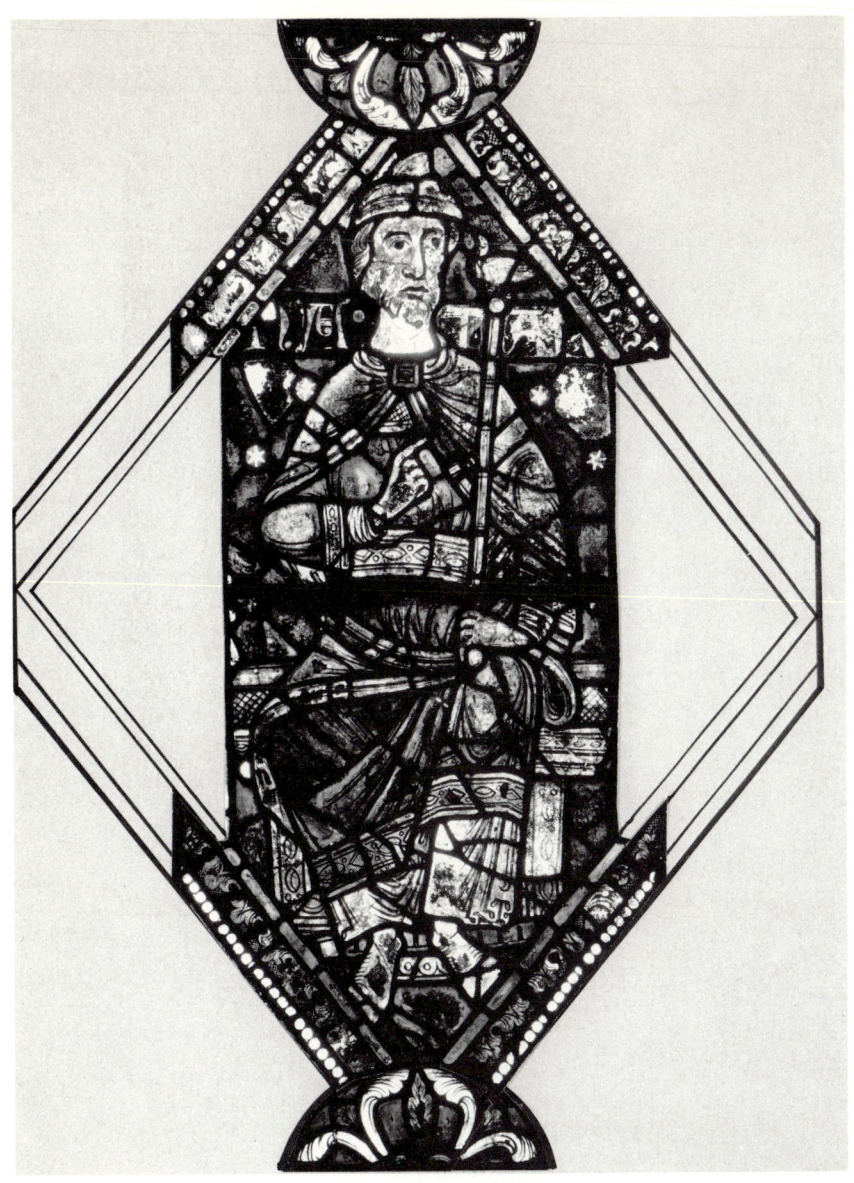

213. Nathan, from clerestory n:VII

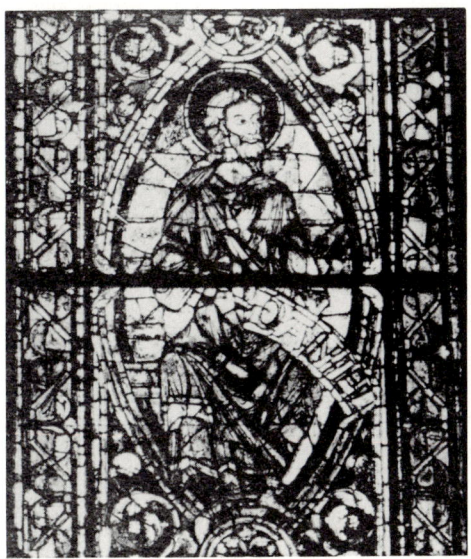

212. Chartres clerestory, Daniel

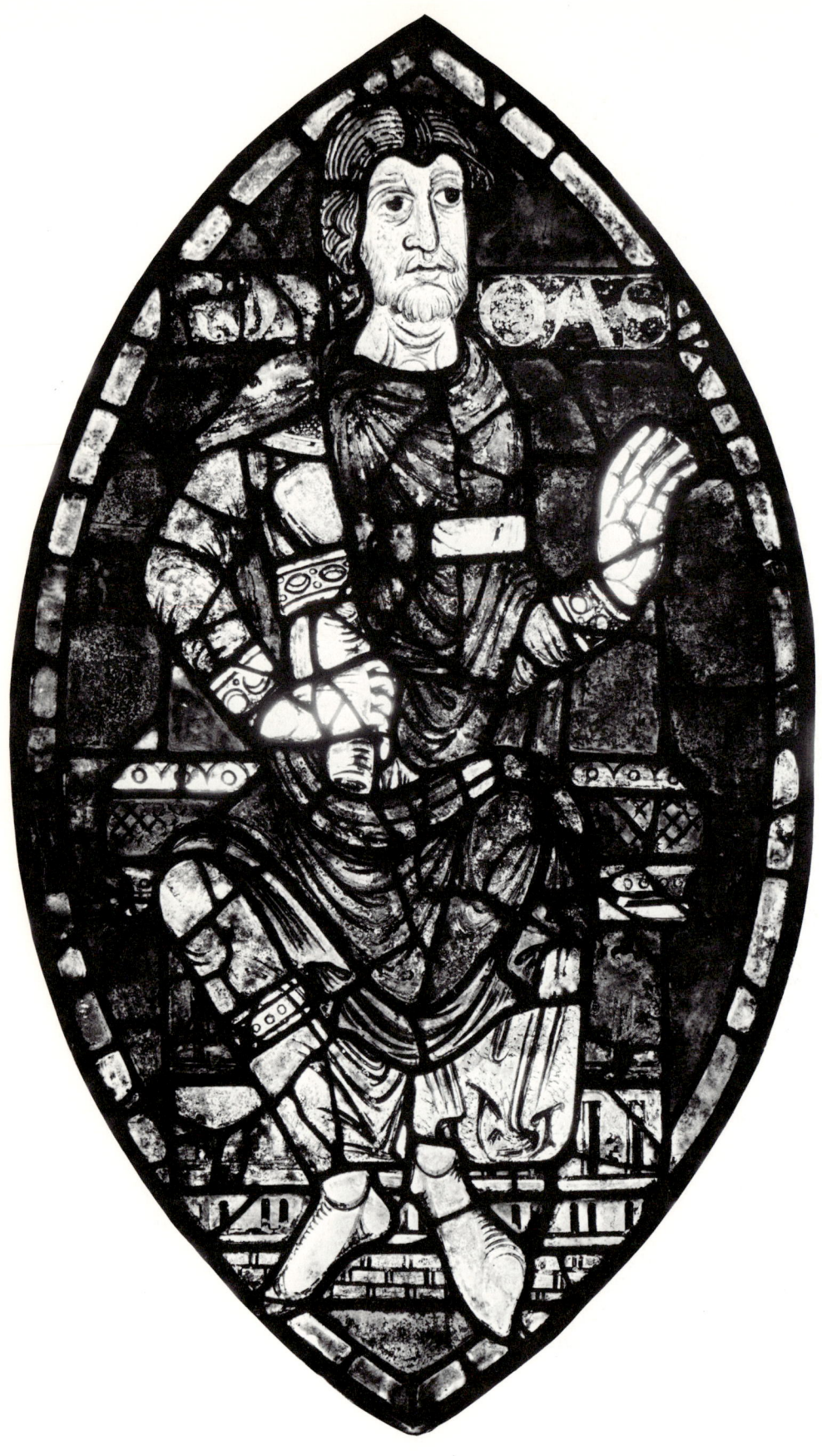

214. Rehoboam, from clerestory N:VI

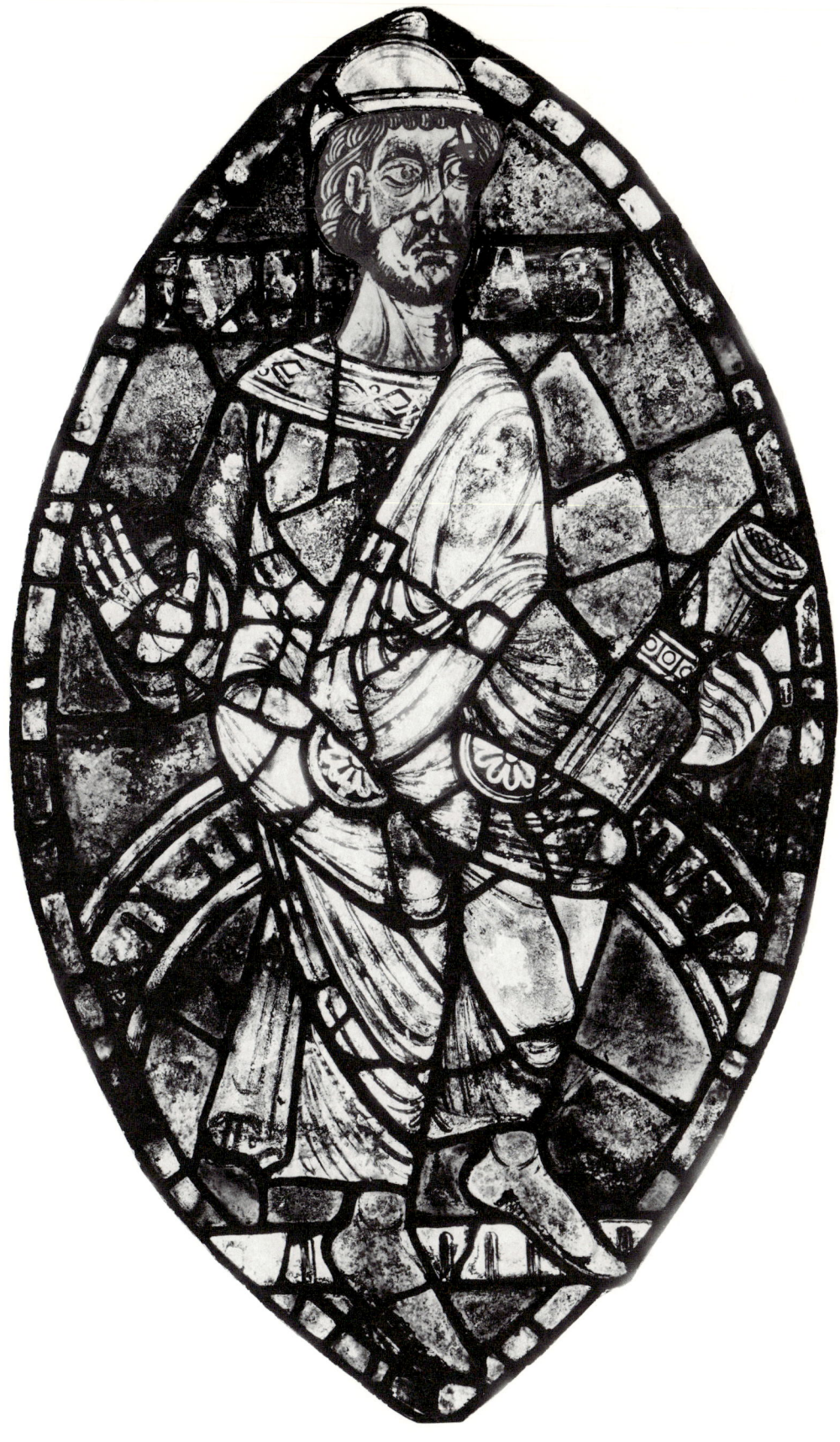

215. Abijah, from clerestory N:VI (original head montaged)

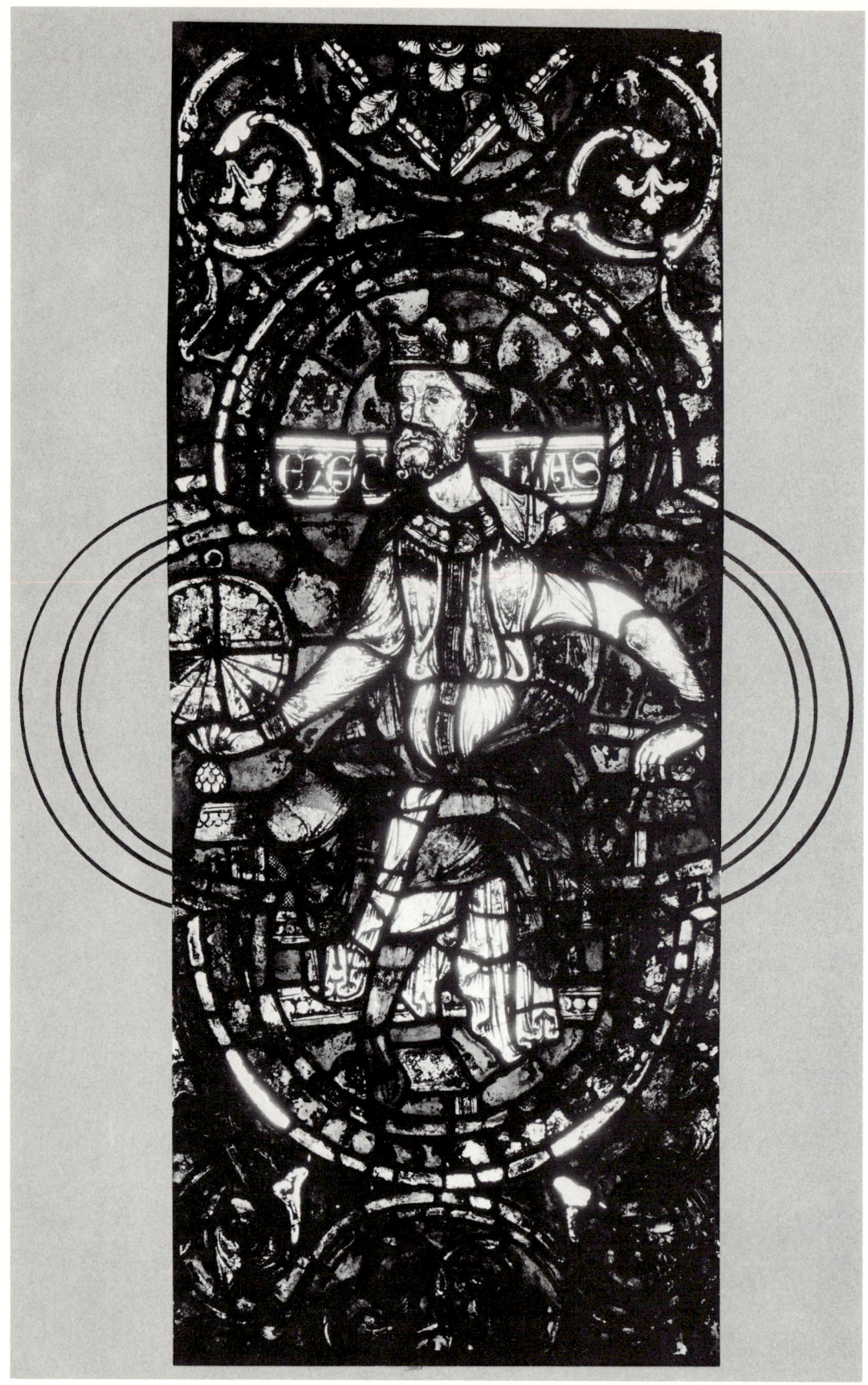

216. Hezekiah, from clerestory N:V

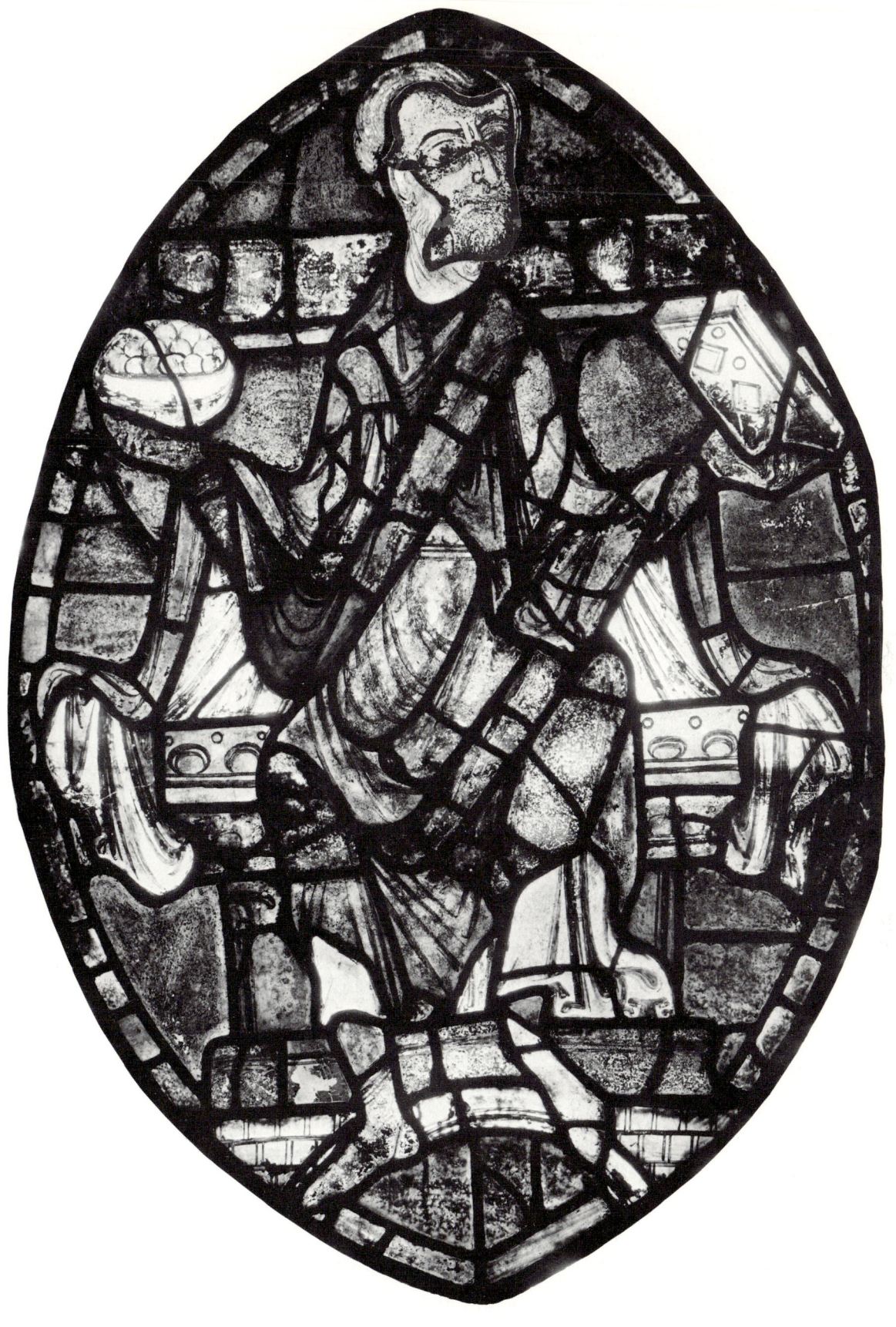

217. Jeconiah (?), from clerestory N:IV (original head now in clerestory
N:XXV, montage)

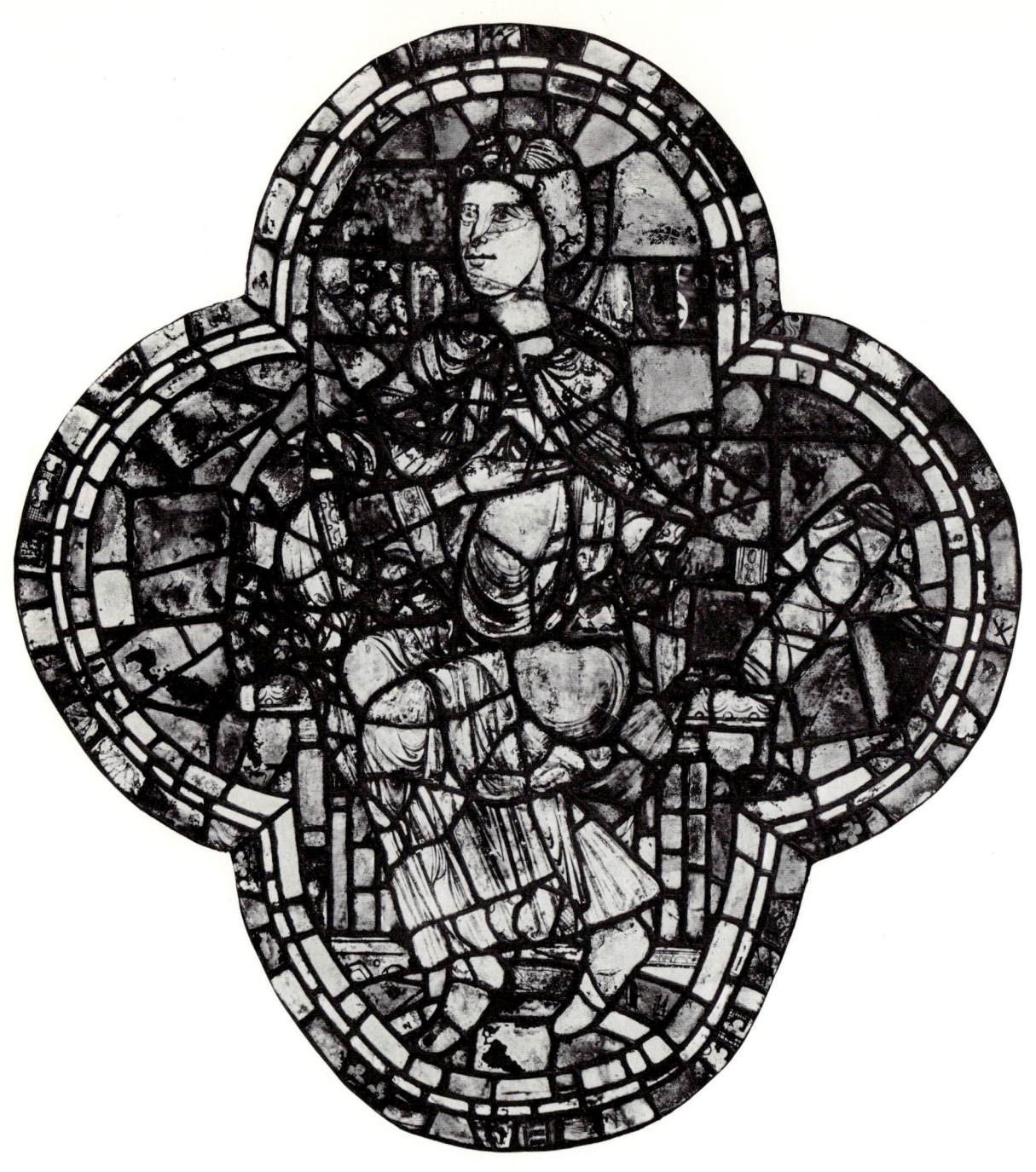

218. Cosam (?), from clerestory S:X